AT WAR AT SEA

At **WAR**
at **SEA**

Sailors and

Naval Combat

in the

Twentieth Century

RONALD H. SPECTOR

Viking

To my wife, Dianne F. Spector

VIKING
Published by the Penguin Group
Penguin Putnam Inc., 375 Hudson Street,
New York, New York 10014, U.S.A.
Penguin Books Ltd, 27 Wrights Lane,
London W8 5TZ, England
Penguin Books Australia Ltd, Ringwood,
Victoria, Australia
Penguin Books Canada Ltd, 10 Alcorn Avenue,
Toronto, Ontario, Canada M4V 3B2
Penguin Books (N.Z.) Ltd, 182–190 Wairau Road,
Auckland 10, New Zealand

Penguin Books Ltd, Registered Offices:
Harmondsworth, Middlesex, England

First published in 2001 by Viking Penguin,
a member of Penguin Putnam Inc.

10   9   8   7   6   5   4   3   2   1

LIBRARY OF CONGRESS CATALOGING-IN-PUBLICATION DATA

Spector, Ronald H., 1943–
    At war at sea : sailors and naval combat in the twentieth century / Ronald H. Spector.
        p.   cm.
    ISBN 0-670-86085-9
    1. Naval art and science—History—20th century.   2. Naval history, Modern—20th century.
  3. Sailors—History—20th century.   I. Title

    V53 .S66   2001
    359'.009'04—dc21   2001017551

This book is printed on acid-free paper. ∞

Printed in the United States of America
Set in Goudy
Designed by Patrice Sheridan

PREFACE

ince the first recorded naval battles between the Egyptians and their enemies 3,200 years ago, war at sea has been marked by some of the most fearsome and dramatic contests in military history. Naval warfare seemed to decide the fate of nations, as in the defeat of the Persians by the Greeks at Salamis in 480 B.C., the defeat of the Spanish Armada in 1588, and the failure of the British at the Virginia Capes in 1781. In the twentieth century, Japan's victory at Tsushima in 1905 established her as the dominant power in East Asia and propelled Russia farther down the road to revolution. The defeat of the German U-boats in two world wars ensured victory for the Allies. Conversely, the successes of American submarines in the Pacific, along with more conventional naval victories at Midway and in the South Pacific, were decisive in the defeat of Japan. During the four decades of the Cold War, the Americans, the Russians, and their allies spent billions to develop and deploy awesome new weapons including nuclear-tipped torpedoes, rocket-propelled depth charges, and nuclear-armed cruise missiles to prepare for an Armageddon on, over, and beneath the sea that, fortunately, never took place.

This book is an interpretive history of war at sea in the twentieth century. The start of the twenty-first century seems an appropriate time to take a look back at the extraordinary developments in naval warfare over the course of the last hundred years. For the first half of the century, navies devoted most of their plans, preparations, and resources to warfare on the high seas against warships and shipping. During the second half of the century, this type of war continued to dominate much of the attention and imagination of naval leaders, however, operations in support of land campaigns and attacks on land targets came to constitute the largest sphere of naval activity.

In both periods most observers have seen the most striking and important trend to be the continuing series of technological innovations that transformed naval warfare into a three-dimensional activity on, above, and under the sea, introduced dramatic changes in communications and sensors, and drastically increased the range, speed, and lethality of naval weapons and platforms. Looking back on this century of relentless and often revolutionary technological change, it is little wonder that most naval historians have chosen to emphasize technology and the performance of various weapons systems as the determining element in war at sea. Almost one hundred years before generals and military analysts announced the advent of a "military-technical revolution," the world's navies were already deep in the midst of one.

It is not surprising then that navies themselves have been obsessed with technology, sometimes to the exclusion of much concern with strategy or operations. Nevertheless, this book suggests that technological determinism is an inadequate method of explaining the evolution of war at sea in the twentieth century. Technological determinism fails to explain why navies with similar weapons systems chose to employ them in dramatically different ways, as the British and Americans did with naval aviation in the 1920s and 1930s. Nor does it explain how, when two opposing navies employ similar technologies in the same manner, one can be more successful than the other, as the Japanese were against the Russians in 1904–5. Or why a navy with inferior technology can sometimes be successful against one with superior technology.

Obviously these questions can be answered only by reference to people, their training, ability, political and cultural background, experience, knowledge, and expectations, and a host of other social and psychological factors that cannot be accounted for by reference to the state of technological development. Since the era of Clausewitz, thoughtful writers on military affairs have understood the importance of social and psychological elements in combat on land, but little if any attention has been paid to the influence of these matters on war at sea. To do so is the aim of this book.

Readers accustomed to conventional histories of naval warfare may find this book odd, even eccentric. I have made no attempt to present a comprehensive account of all major navies, campaigns, and battles of the twentieth century and still less of naval policy, strategy, and technology. Rather I have attempted to examine, in some detail, certain campaigns, battles, and tactical and technological developments that I believe illustrate important stages in the development of naval warfare.

My principal aim has been to examine not only battles fought and weapons employed but to attempt to answer some important questions about the complex relationship between naval technology, operations, and human factors. How well did navies as institutions understand and adapt to the human requirements of war at sea? What kind of people did twentieth-century navies want, and how successful were they at getting them? How were they recruited and trained? What was expected of seamen in the age of the machine? Did their jobs become easier or harder as new equipment and gadgets assumed some of the tasks previously assigned to men? How effective were they as fighters, and how successfully did they adapt to the stresses of combat? How good were the leaders in each era? Was leadership in twentieth-century navies mainly a matter of knowledge and expertise, or did it require particular personal qualities? At the highest levels, how did commanders direct their forces, communicate with subordinates, and receive information in fleets that were far more powerful, faster, and widely dispersed than those in the age of sail? Finally, why did seamen of all ranks choose to enter and remain in a way of life that was at best uncomfortable, demanding, isolated, and monotonous, and at worst arduous, unforgiving, and dangerous?

Whenever possible, the events discussed are described from the point of view of those who experienced them. To do this it has been necessary to utilize certain sources and methods that some may consider problematic. First, there are various types of aggregate records. These most often relate to recruitment and training, promotion, legal matters and punishments, desertions, and medical issues. Until well into the second half of the twentieth century navies did not purposely and systematically collect data about the morale and opinions of their sailors. Consequently, information on these subjects is far less complete and far more subjective than, say, the number of promotions in a year. Because seamen and junior officers seldom submitted official reports, it is necessary to examine contemporary letters, diaries, and personal journals. These must necessarily tell only a part of the story, because the narrator is seldom in a position to see the "big picture," let alone see it in perspective. His account will also reflect his own background, education, experience and expertise, opinions, and prejudices.

The second group of sources are memoirs and reminiscences in written form or as oral histories, composed a considerable time after the events they describe. These benefit from better perspective and sometimes greater maturity on the part of the informant but also raise problems and issues concerning the nature of memory. Memories may be incomplete, selective, or influenced by the memories of others. Scientists have also called our attention to the existence of "false memory," that is, "memories" of things that never occurred. In the case of oral histories, the informant may also be influenced by the personality, skill, and expertise of the interviewer, the organization of the interview, and the nature of the questions.

To make sense of these varied sources, the historian must examine not only what is said but also the structure of the narrative itself. What has the narrator chosen to emphasize, and in what order? What do his words mean to him, and do they have the same meaning to others? Above all, is there a "convergence of narratives," a kind of common story in which most of the informants appear to believe? If this story generally fits with what can be checked against official records and other primary sources, its credibility is strengthened. If it does not, it is necessary to explain the differences. With these issues in mind, I have attempted to present a balanced account of the extremely complex, often ambiguous developments and events which comprise the history of war at sea.

In presenting this narrative I have attempted to take into account the new approaches and scholarship of writers such as Thomas C. Hohn, Nicholas Lambert, Marc Milner, Mark Peattie and David Evans, Norman Polmar, John Sumida, and Peter Swartz, to name only a few. Consequently, those acquainted with conventional accounts of such familiar subjects as the introduction of the Dreadnought battleship, the development of naval aviation, and the Battle of the Atlantic will find somewhat different and, I hope, convincing interpretations here.

For the first half of the twentieth century this book attempts to examine questions about the relationship between men and naval warfare within the framework of a comparative analysis of the British, Japanese, and U.S. navies. For the period of the Cold War it focuses on the human challenges and problems of the U.S. Navy, including the unique issues raised by nuclear submarine operations. I begin with an account of the Battle of Tsushima, probably the most decisive naval battle of the last two hundred years.

ACKNOWLEDGMENTS

I n the preface to his well-known biography of Stonewall Jackson, G.F.R. Henderson observed that for a colonel to write a book about a general was to be guilty of "something worse than presumption." The same might be said about a marine who presumed to write about sailors. In the task of trying to save myself from at least the most obvious displays of ignorance I have been fortunate to have had the comments and advice of the following real sailors who agreed to read parts of the manuscript: Elizabeth Coombs, Commander J.A.J. Dennis RN (Ret.), Vice Admiral Robert F. Dunn USN (Ret.), Captain R.F.C. Ellsworth RN (Ret.), Adrian Holloway, Lieutenant Commander Ian Johnston RN (Ret.), Alvin Kernan, John Knight, Vice Admiral Sir Louis LeBailly RN (Ret.), Commander Fraser McKee RCN (Ret.), Captain J.A.F. Somerville RN (Ret.), John Speakman, Captain Peter Swartz USN (Ret.), and Major General Sir Julian Thompson, RM (Ret.). In addition a number of friends and colleagues read parts of the manuscript in various stages of completion and gave me the advantage of their expertise. They include Aizawa Jun, Akagi Kanji, Asada Sadao, Alexis Castor, Leslie Clark, Lynn Eden, Michael Hadley, Thomas Hone, Marc Milner, Mark Peattie, Norman Polmar, and Jon Sumida. Sarandis Papadopoulis and John Sherwood generously shared with me some of their extensive research on submarines and on fighter pilots, respectively. I alone am responsible for errors and defects that persist.

Research for this project in its early stages was supported by a fellowship at the Rutgers University Center for Historical Research. I am also

IX

grateful to Ritsumeikan University, Kyoto, for providing me with research support during my period as APSIA Visiting Professor in 1998. During that time my longtime friend and colleague Professor Asada Sadao of Doshisha University spent many hours of his valuable time doing spot translations for me of key parts of Japanese books and articles. I am also grateful to Professor Hosoya Masahiro, Professor Iguchi Haruo, and the other members of the Doshisha American Studies Center as well as to Rear Admiral Yoichi Hirama and the staff of the Japan Defense Academy. Dr. Murata Kanji of Hiroshima University arranged for me to visit Etajima and kindly came along as translator. In the U.K. I am especially grateful to Mr. Roderic Suddaby and the staff of the Department of Documents of the Imperial War Museum as well as to the wonderfully helpful people in the Department of Sound Recordings. I also thank Dr. Peter Liddle, Keeper of the Liddle Collection, Leeds University, David Brown of the Historical Division Royal Navy, Bridget Squires of the Whitehall Library, Ministry of Defense, and Carolyn Lye of the Churchhill Archive, Churchill College, Cambridge. Chris Howard Bailey and Valery Billings of the Royal Naval Museum were most considerate and helpful during my two visits there.

Like most students of the history of the U.S. Navy I owe a large debt to Mr. Cavalcante, Mrs. Kathy Lloyd, and the staff of the Operational Archives at the Naval Historical Center as well as to the expert staff of the Navy Department Library. I also thank the library of the Center for Naval Analysis and of the National Archives. I am also grateful to Kurt Piehler and Sandra Stewart Holyoake of the Rutgers Oral History Archives of World War II and Jan Herman of the Office of the Navy Surgeon General. The Institute for Defense Analysis, the Rutgers Center for Historical Research, and the Rand Corporation generously allowed me to try out some ideas from this book at their periodic seminars. I am most grateful for the interest and insights of those colleagues who attended.

During the six years this work was in preparation I was fortunate to have the help of some talented research assistants in the United States and Japan. They include Jim Alverson, Yanna Ginburg, Kobayashi Miyuki, and Sakurai Junri. Another group of students with keen eyesight and nerves of steel typed various parts of the manuscript. I thank Gillian Frazier, Jeannette Chapman Kurtz, and Michelle Lee. Special thanks to Hannah Thrush who, in addition to typing the final chapters, expertly converted the pile of discs, manuscript, and scribble to a single set of discs. Sherry Dowdy ably prepared the maps. My agent, Gerard McCauley, was a continual source of encouragement. My editor at Viking Penguin, Jane von Mehren, was with the project from its very beginning, patiently read through several drafts, and still managed to keep her sense of humor. I also thank her assistant, Jessica Kipp. Finally I thank my wife Dianne and my sons Daniel and Jonathan for their encouragement and support.

CONTENTS

AT WAR AT SEA

ONE

In the heavy rolling seas off Korea, as the afternoon sun gradually burned away the cold mist and rain, two great fleets of ironclads came together to fight a battle that would capture the imagination of the world and influence ideas about naval warfare for the next four decades. It was May 25, 1905, almost exactly one hundred years after the Battle of Trafalgar, and the contest known to the world as the Battle of Tsushima would be widely regarded as the twentieth-century repetition of Nelson's historic victory.

The two unlikely protagonists in this great drama at sea were Russia and Japan. One had long been regarded as the largest land empire of modern times, the other was a small island nation which had not been regarded as a modern state even as recently as 1890. Yet here they were on that afternoon in May 1905, two fleets comprising almost thirty ironclads, some of which were among the most advanced in design, bearing down on each other at a combined speed of more than thirty miles per hour, while the representatives of the traditional sea powers, Britain and France, and the ambitious newcomers, Germany and the United States, could only watch from the sidelines.

Tsushima was the final act of the Russo-Japanese War, a conflict that stemmed from intense rivalry for influence and advantages in Manchuria and Korea. The quarrel concerned railway concessions, leaseholds, and special privileges, the kinds of issues that absorbed the attentions of all the Great Powers during the last decade of the nineteenth century as they maneuvered for power and economic advantage in the increasingly

1

weak and moribund Chinese Empire. The immediate cause of the war was Japanese unhappiness with a concession by China allowing a Russian timber company to log on the south bank of the Yalu River in Korea. Japan considered Korea and Manchuria a vital area of influence. After six months of fruitless negotiations between Russia and Japan, the Japanese presented a final peace proposal in January 1904. By early February, having received no reply, the Japanese broke diplomatic relations.

On the night of February 8, 1904, Japanese destroyers made a surprise attack on the Russian Pacific Squadron at its base at Port Arthur, on Liaotung Peninsula at the tip of southern Manchuria. Decades later, Americans would view this assault as a kind of rehearsal for the Japanese surprise attack on Pearl Harbor. Yet unlike the Pearl Harbor attack, the Japanese strike at Port Arthur failed to cripple the Russian battle fleet, despite completely surprising the Russians. The Japanese destroyers only damaged two of the seven Russian battleships and a cruiser. That was enough, however, to give the Japanese, led by Admiral Togo Heihachiro, a slight edge at sea and to demoralize the Russian fleet so that the Russians made no move to interfere with Japanese troop landings in Korea.[1]

Nevertheless, the Port Arthur fleet remained a threat, and Togo knew he had to deal with it. A second Japanese torpedo attack and attempts to seal the harbor by sinking old ships at the entrance proved unsuccessful. Long-range bombardments by his battleships inflicted minor damage, but were eventually frustrated by fire from Russian coastal defense guns around the port. To add to Togo's worries, in early March the Russian fleet received a new commander, Vice Admiral Stephan Ossipovich Makaroff, the foremost tactician in the Russian navy, a hero of the Russo-Turkish War of 1877, and a bold and aggressive leader. Makaroff refused to wait passively in Port Arthur while the Japanese roamed the seas. He pushed repairs on the damaged battleships and trained naval gunfire spotters to direct the fire of the battleships and harbor batteries from the hills around Port Arthur. Under Makaroff, every patrol or bombardment attempted by the Japanese met with an aggressive countermeasure by the Russians.

In one such action on April 13, Makaroff led his five serviceable battleships out in support of some Russian destroyers that were engaging a larger Japanese force. When Togo's battleships appeared, Makaroff retired to within range of the Russian coastal defense guns. In clear view of the harbor, Makaroff's flagship, *Petropavlosk*, struck a mine and blew up. Makaroff and almost six hundred others were lost with her. Half an hour later, the battleship *Pobieda* also struck a mine and had to limp back to the harbor.

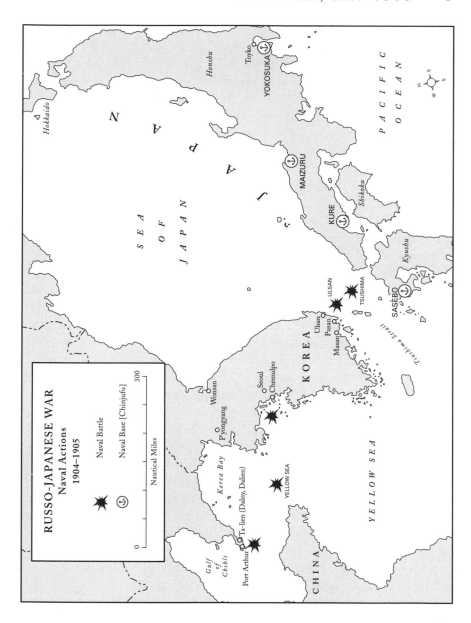

Makaroff's death seemed to destroy any remaining initiative or determination in the Russian fleet. Less than a month later, at the beginning of May, the Japanese army defeated the Russians at the Battle of the Yalu, securing their hold on Korea and a bridgehead into Manchuria. The Japanese then landed on the Liaotung Peninsula less than sixty miles from Port Arthur. The Russian navy made no effort to interfere with the landings, and the troops came ashore unopposed. Even when two Japanese battleships struck mines in mid-May within clear sight of Port Arthur, the Russian fleet, which now outnumbered the Japanese in battleships, failed to challenge Togo's fleet. Meanwhile, the Japanese army continued its advance down the Liaotung Peninsula, capturing the important port of Dalny. By early June 1904, the Japanese had laid siege to Port Arthur.

Things did not go all the Japanese way, however. A squadron of Russian cruisers based at Vladivostok, more active and enterprising than the Port Arthur squadron, succeeded in evading Japanese ships blockading the port. They raided the Sea of Japan and sank Japanese merchantmen, including the transport carrying special heavy mortars intended for the siege of Port Arthur.

On June 23, the Russian squadron at Port Arthur, now under Rear Admiral Witheft, finally attempted a sortie from the port. Togo steamed to meet them with his entire fleet, expecting a decisive battle. The odds were about even, but Witheft was unnerved at the prospect of being cut off from his base by what he later claimed was a "far superior" force.[2] He turned away and led his fleet back toward Port Arthur. Togo sent his destroyers and torpedo boats to attack the retiring Russians, but they scored no hits; only the battleship *Sevastopol* was damaged by a mine as she reentered the harbor.

At sea, Togo received the news of the failure of his torpedo attack with growing frustration. The Port Arthur squadron, timid and unaggressive as it might be, was still intact. Moreover, there was now reliable information that the Russians were preparing to send an entirely new fleet to East Asia. This was the so-called Second Pacific Squadron, under Rear Admiral Zinovy Petrovich Rozhestvensky, consisting of warships that had been in the Baltic at the outbreak of the war as well as new ships nearing completion in Russian yards.

Ashore, the Japanese redoubled their efforts to break through the defenses of Port Arthur. Yet by late July, the Japanese army troops under General Nogi Maresuke had still failed to pierce the fortifications of the city proper. They had, despite appalling casualties, including Nogi's three sons, advanced to a point within artillery range of the harbor and begun shelling the Russian squadron. It took several days of Japanese bombardment and damage to two battleships before Admiral Witheft finally was persuaded to take the fleet out of the harbor. By that time the admiral himself had been slightly wounded by a shell splinter that had hit his flagship, *Ratzvizan*.

Despite Witheft's less than Nelsonian leadership, the Russian sortie on August 10, 1904, was nearly successful. Togo, mindful that he had but four battleships to face both Witheft's fleet and the much-heralded Baltic reinforcements, kept his battleship squadron at long range and did little damage to the Russians, whose gunnery, though poor, proved no worse than that of the Japanese. Togo's cruisers, closing to shorter ranges, suffered damage without slowing down the Russian line.

By 5:45, with only thirty minutes of daylight remaining, it looked as if the Russians would succeed in escaping to Vladivostok. Then a lucky hit by two 12-inch shells on Witheft's flagship killed the admiral and most of his staff, throwing the Russian fleet into confusion. Rear Admiral Prince Pavel Ukhtomski assumed command and led the battleships back to Port Arthur, from which they would not emerge again. A few of the faster Russian cruisers managed to reach neutral ports, where they were interned. Following the engagement, known as the Battle of the Yellow Sea, the Japanese caught up with the Vladivostok cruiser squadron on its way to help the Port Arthur fleet. Finally, they were able to do some damage to this enterprising force; they sank one Russian cruiser and badly damaged another.

Despite the bad news from East Asia, the Russians continued their preparations for the dispatch of the Second Pacific Squadron. On October 9, the new fleet assembled at Reval for a final inspection by Tsar Nicholas II. Aboard the new battleship *Orel*, naval constructor V. P. Kostenko described the tsar as he "passed along the line of officers giving his hand to each. The insignificance of the Tsar's very ordinary and already very worn face, as well as the dull expression of his pewter like eyes could not be concealed, not even under the contrived mask of the good natured smile, once and for all frozen on his everyday visage. There was something un-naval about the way he wore his captain's uniform and the way he walked showed his unfamiliarity with the deck of a ship . . . Nickolai climbed to the central communication bridge and addressed the crew . . . then turning to the officers he added 'I wish you all gentlemen officers, a victorious voyage and a safe return, whole and undamaged, to the mother land.' With these words he ran his eyes along the line as though trying to guess who, contrary to his wishes, was fated to die soon."[3]

The seven-and-a-half-month voyage of the Second Pacific Squadron under Rear Admiral Zinovy Petrovich Rozhestvensky was both an epic and a nightmare. The squadron of worn-out old ships and hastily completed new ones suffered recurrent breakdowns and other mechanical problems that delayed Rozhestvensky's progress and added to his headaches. On the night of October 22 during their voyage through the North Sea, the Russian sailors, obsessed by persistent fears and rumors of Japanese torpedo boats operating from secret bases in Europe, opened fire on a fleet of British fishing trawlers that they imagined to be Japanese warships. One fishing trawler was sunk and others damaged, and two fishermen were killed. In the confusion, Rozhestvensky's cruisers and battleships also fired on each other. Fortunately for the Russians, their shooting was so poor that they did not inflict serious damage to their warships, but aboard the cruiser *Aurora* one sailor was wounded and the chaplain killed. This paranoia-induced mishap, now known as the "Dogger Bank Incident," almost led to war with Britain. In the end, tempers cooled and the Russians agreed to pay an indemnity and submit the incident to the judgment of an international tribunal.

Meanwhile, Rozhestvensky had sailed on down the west coast of Africa and around the Cape of Good Hope. His ships were supplied with coal by colliers of the Hamburg-Amerika Line, which met his fleet in neutral harbors or sometimes on the open sea. Worried about his coal supply and expecting to be attacked en route, Rozhestvensky insisted on taking on extra coal at each rendezvous. "The bunkers were overflowing," recalled the commander of the *Aurora*. "Some passages and two compartments of the forward living quarters were filled. In the remaining living quarters there was a hellish temperature because all of the ventilating passages had been closed against dust. . . ."[4] The frequent coaling in tropical waters drained energy and morale and left little time or inclination for battle drills and maneuvers.

Arriving at Madagascar in late December 1904, Rozhestvensky rendezvoused with his cruisers and destroyers, which had made the shorter voyage through the Suez Canal. He also received the news that Port Arthur had fallen and that a "Third Pacific Squadron," composed mainly of old coast defense ships, was being sent out to join him. Rozhestvensky was instructed to wait at Madagascar for these reinforcements, then to make for Vladivostok, if necessary engaging the Japanese fleet on the way.

At the beginning of February 1905, the fleet was joined by the *Oleg* and *Izumrud*, modern fast cruisers that had not been ready to leave with the fleet in October. One month later, Rozhestvensky, disdaining to wait for the antiques of the Third Pacific Squadron, led his ships to sea and disappeared into the Indian Ocean. Japanese scouts searched the East Indies and South China Sea in vain while newspapers speculated that the Russians might be planning to circumnavigate Australia. Then on April 8, at 2:30 in the afternoon, excited crowds on the promenade along the shore of Singapore sighted four long columns of ships, their bright yellow funnels belching great clouds of black smoke as the Russians sailed majestically past the city at a speed of eight knots.

Four days later the Russians anchored in the broad waters of Cam Ranh Bay off French Indo-China. Here direct orders from St. Petersburg obliged Rozhestvensky to await the arrival of his reinforcements. The fleet remained off Indo-China for a month, shifting its position a few miles from time to time to avoid the appearance of violating French neutrality. On May 8, the Third Pacific Squadron, consisting of the old battleship *Nikolai I* with the cruiser *Vladimir Monomakh,* both dating from the 1880s, and three small coast defense ships, *General Admiral Apraksin, Admiral Ushakov,* and *Admiral Seniavin,* steamed into Cam Ranh Bay. The squadron under Rear Admiral Nebogatov had made a surprisingly rapid voyage from Libau to the Mediterranean and through the Red Sea, arriving off Singapore only three weeks after Rozhestvensky.

Scarcely more than two weeks after his arrival at Cam Ranh Bay, Nebogatov became Rozhestvensky's de facto second in command. Rear Admiral Dimitri von Felkerzam, who commanded the second division of older battleships and was next in seniority to Rozhestvensky, died aboard his flagship on May 11, after a long illness. Nebogatov was senior to the only other flag officer in the fleet, Rear Admiral Oscar Enkvist, who commanded the cruiser division. Felkerzam's death was kept secret from the fleet, perhaps to avoid hurting morale; but for reasons never fully explained, Rozhestvensky also kept the secret from Nebogatov, who sailed into battle unaware that he was now second in command. As the Russian fleet left Indo-China in mid-May on the final leg of its voyage, tension in Japan increased.

Journalists and naval experts began to speculate about the outcome of a confrontation between the Japanese and Russian fleets. Few doubted that there would be a fight to the finish, not simply a running battle like Witheft's ill-fated thrust toward Vladivostok the previous August, but the first full-scale battle between fleets since the introduction of the modern battleship.

On paper the two fleets seemed fairly evenly matched. The Japanese battle fleet included only four battleships, *Fuji, Shikishima, Asahi,* and *Mikasa,* each mounting four 12-inch guns. Togo, however, planned to use his eight modern armored cruisers in the battle line as he had done earlier against Witheft. Most of these ships were armed with four 8-inch guns.

The Russian battle fleet included a division of four new battleships, the *Borodino, Alexander III, Orel,* and *Kniaz Suvorov,* with the same general armament as their Japanese counterparts. In addition, there was a less homogeneous second division comprising the modern battleship *Oslyabya* armed with four 10-inch guns and two obsolescent battleships, *Sisoi Veliky* and *Naravin*, mounting four 10-inch guns each. Attached to the second division was the old armored cruiser *Admiral Nakhimov*, mounting eight old 8-inch guns and ten new 6-inch "quick-firing" guns. With a top speed of sixteen knots, she was slower than many of the newer battleships.

Admiral Nebogatov's squadron, which had joined Rozhestvensky off Indo-China, comprised the old battleship *Nikolai I*, smaller and slower than the more modern ships and armed with two 12-inch and four 9-inch guns. Nebogatov's three coast defense ships were less than half the size of the most recent battleships and carried 9- or 10-inch guns in their main batteries. There was also an old cruiser, *Vladimir Monomakh*, a contemporary of the *Admiral Nakhimov* but smaller and less heavily armed.

Overloaded by extra coal and supplies, their metal hulls fouled by marine growths acquired during the long voyage through tropical waters, even the newest Russian battleships could not hope to match the speed of their Japanese opponents. Rozhestvensky's fastest ships, the nine modern destroyers, were grossly outnumbered by Togo's fifty-eight destroyers and large torpedo boats.

In addition to decreasing their speed, the overloading of the Russian battleships also made them less stable and more likely to capsize. It also gave them a much deeper draft, which placed the important belt of armor, intended to protect the ship's waterline, *beneath* the water, leaving the unarmored portion of the hull exposed to hits at the waterline. In addition, many of the smaller antitorpedo guns, which fired through ports or sponsons in the hull, were now much lower in the water and thus unworkable in heavy seas.

Russian shells had a higher muzzle velocity and thus greater penetrating power, but they were somewhat smaller than equivalent Japanese shells. In addition, the Japanese had begun to employ a new explosive called shimose that was more powerful than guncotton. A Japanese shimose shell exploded on impact, blowing the shell case into dozens of deadly metal fragments and producing clouds of smoke that often incapacitated those not killed by the blast.[5]

Yet the greatest disparities between the Russian and Japanese fleets were the least quantifiable: the disparities in personnel. Togo's ships and squadrons were commanded by officers who had long experience at sea and had served in the campaign against the Port Arthur fleet. Five of his vice admirals and seven of the rear admirals had previously served under his command.[6] Rear Admiral Shimamura, who commanded one of the cruiser divisions, had been Togo's chief of staff at the Battle of the Yellow Sea, nine months before.[7] Neither Rozhestvensky nor his two rear admirals had been in action against the Japanese before, and many of his officers were inexperienced or overage. Russian officers were on average about five to eight years older than their Japanese counterparts. The *oldest* rear admiral in the Japanese navy was *younger* than almost every rear admiral in the Russian.[8]

Compared to the Russian navy, which traced its lineage back to Peter the Great, the Japanese navy was a comparatively recent creation. The modernizing oligarchy that planned and directed Japan's great "leap across time" during the Meiji era, 1868–1912, was particularly interested in acquiring an effective modern navy at the earliest possible date. The Japanese were convinced that only with a strong Western-style navy could they confront the Great Powers in East Asia on an equal basis.

As Japan began placing orders for modern warships with European yards and developing her own shipbuilding industry, the Meiji government turned to the task of developing an appropriately trained force of sailors. In 1871, a naval academy for the training of officers was established near Tokyo. Many of its first students were young samurai who were veterans of the civil wars that had led to the Meiji restoration in the late 1860s. These high-spirited young men, whose primary loyalty was still to their clan or province, were in no state of mind to welcome a regimen of book learning under instructors who were primarily academic and technical experts.[9] When Admiral Nakamuta Kuranosuki, who served as superintendent in the 1870s, arrived at the academy he found that "a mood of bloodthirstiness" prevailed among many of the unhappy samurai-turned-students. "They had earlier received their baptism of fire and were too proud to receive instruction from those who had had no experience of battle."[10] He recalled two young students in particular who, when angry with certain professors, would "get a crowd together and break into their offices. They would fight hand to hand . . . break chairs and tables."[11] Discipline improved markedly with the appointment of Nakamuta and the arrival in 1873 of a British Royal Navy training mission under Commander Archibald L. Douglas. Douglas, a man of "great dignity and short temper," quickly moved to introduce British styles of discipline, ceremonies, uniforms, and customs. Douglas even introduced Sunday sermons delivered by Christian members of the Japanese staff, a proceeding the students soon dubbed "the amen lectures."[12]

At the end of the 1880s the Naval Academy moved from Tokyo to the beautiful but isolated island of Etajima, near Hiroshima. By that time the influence of the clans on naval officers' appointments had considerably declined, and by the turn of the century, entrance to the Naval Academy was based entirely on merit.[13] Between 1900 and 1904, an average of eighteen hundred young men a year took the entrance examinations, which consisted of a rigorous medical examination followed by academic tests. In 1904, 1,175 men out of an initial 2,326 survived the physical exam to sit for the competitive examinations in English, algebra, trigonometry, and Chinese. Only 349 passed, of whom 183 were finally admitted to the academy.[14] Having cleared this last hurdle, the successful candidate was enrolled in a four-year course at the Naval Academy, an institution so isolated and austere that an American naval attaché who visited in 1907 wondered whether American youth would be able to stand it.[15]

Cadets were divided into *buntai* or companies under the supervision of upperclassmen and were mercilessly hazed. One foreign observer described the physical training as "undoubtedly the most strenuous of any institution of learning in the world." Each cadet was required to complete a ten-mile swim from the nearby island of Miyajima to the Naval Academy.[16] A favorite team sport was *botaoshi*, which literally means "knock over the pole," a kind of "capture the flag," in which two teams competed to pull down the opponent's pole while protecting one's own "with nothing in the shape of personal assault barred."[17]

After four years of this regimen, the cadets received their appointments as midshipmen in a solemn ceremony in the presence of the emperor. The top three graduates received a dirk as an imperial gift. The three honoraries "march on to the stage one at a time while the band plays 'See the Conquering Hero Comes,' bow very low before his Highness, who slightly inclines his head, bow to an Aide de Camp who gives them the dirks which they hold high with both hands." Bowing again, the cadets backed stiffly off the stage, dirks held high, and remained motionless until the departure of the imperial party.[18]

At the conclusion of graduation, the newly commissioned midshipman, who had entered the academy from the land gate four years before, now departed from the sea gate to be rowed out to a warship that would carry him on a training cruise to Europe or America. As the band played "Auld Lang Syne," the ship steamed slowly down the bay between a long line of cutters manned by cadets and into the Inland Sea.[19]

Japanese enlisted sailors, both conscripts and volunteers, received their training at the naval bases at Yokuska, Kure, or Saseba. The recruits were lodged in plain, unheated barracks, and during the summer months the hours of training ran from 5:30 A.M. to 9:30 at night.[20] Foreign observers were universally impressed by the physical strength and endurance of Japanese sailors. An American naval officer described Japanese enlisted men as "splendidly developed physically and little affected by cold or bad weather conditions."[21] British journalist and naval expert Hector C. Bywater described how in a torpedo boat attack on the Chinese base of Wei Hai Wei during the Sino-Japanese War of 1894–95, "in weather conditions that might have daunted the boldest," some men aboard the "attacking boats were frozen to death but the survivors carried on."[22] A German naval officer observed that "Japanese bluejackets compare well in intelligence, physique, and courage with any Navy in the world."[23]

Russian naval cadets attended the far more pleasantly located Naval School at St. Petersburg. Competition for entry was limited to sons of officers and of some government officials. Unlike Etajima, which provided free room, board, and tuition, the Naval School required parents to pay for a good portion of their sons' education.[24]

Most Russian sailors were conscripts who served for a period of seven years. Because the best-trained, most experienced sailors were already serving in the Far East, Rozhestvensky's fleet had a high proportion of new recruits as well as chronic troublemakers, suspected revolutionaries, anarchists, and other undesirables whom the authorities in St. Petersburg sought to rid themselves of by sending them on a long voyage halfway around the world.

Russian sailors normally worked from 5:00 A.M. to 5:00 P.M. and were subject to corporal punishment for a wide variety of offenses. Engineer Lieutenant Alexi Pleshkov was "dumbfounded by the convict-like appearance of the crew. Their clothing is almost always terribly dirty. Their faces are pale and puffed."[25]

Relations between officers and men in the Russian fleet ranged from resentful and suspicious in many ships to near mutinous in some. Pleshkov noted the almost constant verbal abuse and curses to which enlisted sailors were subjected by officers and midshipmen. The officers' disdain for their sailors was warmly reciprocated. "Those noblemen's sons, well cared for and fragile, were capable only of decking themselves out in tunics and epaulettes," recalled one sailor in the battleship *Oslyabya*. "They didn't even know our names."[26] A captured Russian sailor was "astonished by . . . the informality which existed between the officers and men of the Japanese crew. With what respect and trust the Japanese sailors regarded their officers . . . our sailors . . . in their thoughts and conversations naturally began to compare the Russian with the Japanese officers, and the result of this comparison was, of course, not to the advantage of the former."[27]

With better-trained and better-led seamen, it is not surprising the Japanese battleships and cruisers could maintain a rate of fire almost twice as high as their Russian counterparts.[28] British naval attachés with the Japanese fleet in the months prior to Tsushima reported that firing practices were so frequent and lengthy that "a year's peacetime allowance [of ammunition] was consumed each week and that in aiming practice the general average of hits for the fleet had increased from forty to sixty percent."[29] By contrast, Rozhestvensky's fleet had held only one long-range firing practice during its long voyage. This took place off Madagascar, and "not a single hit was scored by the whole fleet."[30] Many of the Russian gunners had also had insufficient time to train with and become accustomed to their new telescopic sights. A midshipman aboard the *Vladimir Monomakh* claimed that he had to teach his sailors how to count up to one hundred before they could use the sights at all.[31]

As the day of battle neared, Captain W. C. Pakenhem, the British naval attaché in Japan who had been present during the Battle of the Yellow Sea, speculated that the desperate but determined Russians might attempt to ram the Japanese. "If one fleet has been headed by another the position of the inner fleet calls for bold remedy and it may be questioned whether that which promises extraction soonest is not by a prompt attack by the ram."[32]

Most naval observers and journalists, noting the great disparity in torpedo boats and destroyers between the two fleets, predicted that the battle would probably begin with a desperate mass torpedo attack by the Japanese.[33] Admiral A. T. Mahan, the American naval prophet, compared Togo's situation to Nelson's just before Trafalgar. Both were about to fight a decisive action. Yet, unlike Nelson, "behind whose inferior numbers stood other numerous unconquered fleets of Britain," Togo could not afford heavy losses. "Nelson expected to throw away his squadron if need be, confident that by so doing he would also sweep off the chess board a hostile piece of far greater value and so leave the situation decidedly bettered." Japan, however, "now has not the reserve Britain had then and her methods must conform to her means."[34]

Mahan expected the battle to begin with a night torpedo attack.[35] He hoped that "the tactical precautions and steadiness of the defense may equal the preparations and heroism of the offense for so only can an instructive military lesson be afforded."[36]

Lacking Admiral Mahan's enthusiasm for providing "an instructive military lesson," the sailors of Rozhestvensky's fleet could only hope that the heavy mist and intermittent rain would continue to obscure their ships as they began the final stage of their voyage through the Korea

Strait between the island of Tsushima and the west coast of Japan on the night of May 13. The route through the Korea Strait was the shortest and most direct route to Vladivostok, but it would also bring the Russian fleet close to the Japanese bases in southern Korea and southwestern Japan. Had Rozhestvensky chosen to avoid the Korea Strait entirely, sailing up the east coast of Japan and then taking the Tsugaru Strait between Hokkaido and Honshu, or the more northerly La Pérouse Strait between Hokkaido and Sakhalin, he might have led Togo, who had concentrated all his ships near the Korea Strait, on a merry chase. Yet there were navigational problems in transiting the two northern straits, and Rozhestvensky's confidence in the seamanship of his sailors was justifiably low. In addition, the long voyage around the east coast of Japan would have involved coaling in the open seas and the unpredictable weather of the North Pacific. So Rozhestvensky led his squadron into the Korea Strait on the night of May 26.

Togo was waiting with his battleships and armored cruisers at Masan on the south coast of Korea, opposite the island of Tsushima. His smaller cruisers and armed merchantmen patrolled the southern end of the Korea Strait. Togo's staff had divided the waters of the strait into numbered squares, each representing 10 minutes of latitude and longitude. At about 3:00 A.M., the merchant cruiser *Shinano Maru* sighted the large Russian hospital ship *Orel*. Drawing closer to the Russian vessel, the *Shinano Maru*'s lookouts could see the darkened shapes of Russian warships. As she steamed away into the mist, *Shinano Maru* radioed, "The enemy sighted in number 203 section. He seems to be steering for the eastern channel."[37]

At 5:00 A.M., Togo's battleships sailed from Masan. Aboard the battleship *Asahi*, officers gathered around the tobacco tray near the after turret, smoking cigars and listening to a phonograph. "Togo seems determined to lead again and all his chief officers will doubtless expose themselves as before," wrote Captain Pakenham. "It may be too much to hope they will suffer as little by this as they did in the last action. If Togo can get a good lead before closing, the punishment which fell so heavily on the *Mikasa* in the previous occasion this time will be more evenly distributed. This will be all the more important because if anything happens to Togo the next Admiral is in the sixth ship!"[38]

As the weather cleared around 7:00 A.M., Rozhestvensky's sailors could see the light cruiser *Izumi* about 8,000 yards off the fleet's starboard bow. As the morning went on, more cruisers joined the *Izumi* in shadowing the Russian fleet. Togo later wrote that the reports continually received from the cruisers "enabled me to clearly visualize the position of the enemy despite the fact that I was ten miles away. In this way, still not seeing the enemy with my own eyes, I already knew that its fighting strength consisted of the entire Second and Third squadrons and that he was accompanied by seven auxiliary ships, that he was deployed in two columns . . . and so on. Thanks to this information I was able to decide that I would meet the enemy with my main forces off Okinoshima at about 2:00 P.M. and attack the head of his port column."[39]

When Togo's battlefleet appeared at 1:30 in the afternoon to the north and starboard of the Russians, Rozhestvensky's fleet was still in its two-column formation, with the four battleships of the first division starboard and slightly ahead of the line of other ships, which were led by the *Oslyabya*. The Japanese enjoyed an advantage in speed of at least four knots over the slower Russian squadron, and Togo intended to exploit his advantage. Despite the Japanese admiral's later statement that his scouting reports enabled him to "clearly visualize the position of the enemy," Togo was surprised to discover the Russian fleet much closer and farther east than expected. "Without quite realizing it we had approached to within 10,000 meters," recalled Commander Matsumura, executive officer of Togo's flagship.[40]

Togo's original plan seems to have been to cut across the Russian formation and engage the weaker port column first, crippling it before the ships of the starboard column could come into action. The Japanese, however, now found themselves on the starboard rather than the port side of the Russian line. Moreover, Rozhestvensky had already begun to redeploy into a single-line formation. Togo ordered speed increased to fifteen knots and signaled to the fleet, "The fate of the empire rests upon this one battle, let every man do his utmost." He ordered a turn west, then southwest toward the Russians.

The two fleets were now converging in such a way that when they drew close enough to open fire they would be passing each other in opposite directions. This would mean a brief gunnery exchange after which Togo would find himself behind and to the south of the Russians. To prevent this, the Japanese admiral ordered his fleet to turn 180 degrees to bring it into a parallel course with the enemy. The quickest way to achieve this was for the ships to turn simultaneously onto the new course, but this would have placed Togo's weakest ships, his armored cruisers, at the head of his line and his flagship at the tail. To avoid this, Togo ordered his ships to turn in succession, in follow-the-leader fashion. This was potentially a very dangerous maneuver. Each Japanese ship, already within range of the Russians, would have to turn through approximately the same spot of ocean, an easy aiming point for the Russians. Also, while the maneuver was being carried out, the ships that had completed the turn would "mask" the guns of those that had not, preventing the latter from firing.

The Russians opened fire a few minutes after the Japanese began their turn, and as each ship passed through the axis of the turn, it received a hot fire from the Russians. Yet all came through with only minor damage. As the battleship *Asahi* followed the *Mikasa* and *Shikishima* through the U-turn, Captain Pakenham noted that "it was then possible to see down the length of the Russian lines. In the right column, the four biggest battleships loomed enormous, dwarfing all others into insignificance."[41] Russian fire, though rapid, was not very accurate. The range was still relatively long—about 7,000 meters—and Nebogatov's ships, at the rear of the Russian line, found their old guns out of range.

As the last ships of Togo's fleet completed their U-turn, the Japanese steadied onto a parallel and slightly converging course with the Russians. Togo's object was to use his superior speed to cross in front of Rozhestvensky and rake his ships with gunfire, a maneuver contemporaries called "crossing the T." The only way for the Russians to avoid this disastrous situation was to continue turning to the right, keeping their broadsides to the enemy as he attempted to cross to the front. This action, however, would take the Russians farther east, away from their goal of reaching Vladivostok. A cooler-headed or more experienced admiral than Rozhestvensky might in fact have ordered a turn to port, slipping behind the Japanese fleet that was racing ahead to cut him off. But Rozhestvensky appears to have given no further orders, and the Russian fleet simply followed the lead of the flagship.

When the range had fallen to 5,500 meters, Togo straightened his line and ordered "rapid firing." At this point, the Russian ships of the port column, still attempting to obey Rozhestvensky's order to form a single column, found themselves having to squeeze into line between the ships of the starboard column, while the latter had to stop their engines to avoid collision. "At this time our formation properly speaking was nothing but a mob," Admiral Nebogatov would later recall.[42]

Both sides now thundered away at each other as the range gradually dropped to less than three miles. Captains of both navies commanded their ships from inside small pillbox-shaped "conning towers" protected by heavy armor. Crowded inside with the captain were the wheel and compass, the quartermaster, the gunnery officer, the navigator, and one or more messengers. The Japanese admirals with a few members of their staff generally stationed themselves farther above, on the roof of the chart house, from which they enjoyed an unobstructed view but were

protected only by sandbags.[43] Aboard the *Suvurov*, Rozhestvensky commanded from inside a larger conning tower, which was crowded with
some fifteen officers and seamen.[44] From the conning towers, the captains passed orders to the engine room by telegraph and voice tube while
the navigator assisted with keeping the ship on station. High above the
conning tower on an exposed platform on the main mast was the range
finder, a horizontal tube-shaped apparatus mounted on a tripod, from
which ranges were transmitted by voice hose and tube to the conning
tower. From the conning tower, the range was transmitted to the guns by
electrical transmitters and indicators or by hand-worked range dials. Yet
while the range finder could provide the enemy's range, each of the
ship's guns had to be aimed and fired individually, depending on individual gunlayers and trainers to keep it on target. Consequently, the firing by both sides was generally inaccurate, and in the first ten minutes of
the battle the Russians shot as well as or better than the Japanese.

The armored cruiser *Yakumo* was hit by three heavy shells, which crippled her forward turret, and the armored cruiser *Asama* was forced out of
the line by a series of hits that crippled her steering gear. The *Mikasa* was
hit by at least a dozen enemy shells, one of which ripped into the hammock wrapping around the ship's compass a few inches from where Admiral Togo stood looking through his telescope.

Aboard the *Asahi*, a shell hit caused an explosion near the after
bridge, filling the air with fragments. "Of these one fell under foot. It
was the right half of a man's lower jaw with the teeth missing. Everything and everybody for twenty yards around were bespattered with tiny
drops of blood and minute particles of flesh that adhered to whatever
they struck."[45] Another shell exploded against the 12-pounder gun
commanded by Ensign Morishita, who had survived the mining of the
destroyer *Hayatori* the previous year. Earlier he had told Captain Pakenham of his premonition that he "had only escaped the mine to be
killed by a shell." Morishita and most of the men near the 12-pounder
were killed by the explosion of the 6-inch shell.[46]

Climbing onto the upper deck just after the explosion, the executive
officer, Togo Kichitaro, saw "armor plates twisted and bloody hands and
feet and mutilated corpses lying on the deck." Noticing Morishita's subordinate officer carrying his body below, Togo snapped, "Whose duty is it
to control the fire when the group commander is wounded?" and sent
him back to his post.[47]

Despite the hail of Russian shells, no Japanese ship other than the
Asama was seriously incapacitated by enemy fire. More than a third of

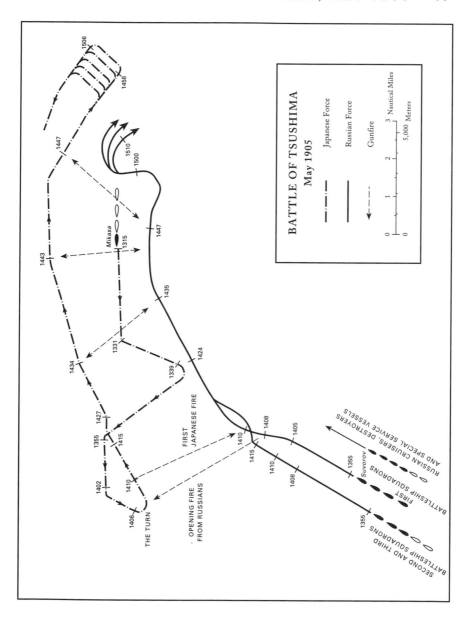

BATTLE OF TSUSHIMA
May 1905

Japanese Force
Russian Force
Gunfire

the Russian projectiles that struck the Japanese ships were duds, and others were ricochets, and the well-trained and battle-tested Japanese crews continued to perform coolly even in the face of such gory events as those in the *Asahi*.

As the ranges closed and the superior Japanese secondary batteries came into play, the Russians began to suffer severely. Japanese high-capacity shells—designed to burst on impact rather than penetrate armor—had four times the explosive power of Russian shells, and while the Japanese made no greater percentage of hits than the Russians, their rate and volume of fire was much greater.[48]

A Japanese heavy shell striking an unarmored portion of the side or deck immediately exploded, opening a hole seven feet high and six feet wide, and disintegrated into minute metal "particles which filled the air like driving mist." One sailor in the *Orel* was reportedly struck by at least thirty fragments from a single hit.[49] "I had not only never seen such a bombardment before," wrote Captain Vladimir Semeonov, who had been present at the Battle of the Yellow Sea, "but could never have imagined it. Shells rained down continuously one after another. . . . Plates and super structures on the upper deck were torn to pieces and the splinters caused many casualties. Iron ladders were crumpled up into rings and guns were literally hurled from their mountings. . . . In addition to this there was the unusually high temperature and liquid flame of the explosion which seemed to spread over everything. Of course the steel did not burn but the paint on it did. . . . Hammocks and rows of boxes drenched with water flared up in a moment."[50]

The entire engaged side of the *Alexander III* caught fire. "It was the war paint burning and the blaze was not extinguished till the greater part of it was burnt off. The red lead beneath the war paint did not burn, however, and she came out of the fire as red as if she had been repainted."[51] The rapid and devastating Japanese fire distracted and demoralized Russian gun crews, and their firing became progressively more erratic. After the first half hour of the battle, few Russian hits were made on Japanese ships.

The Japanese concentrated their fire on the flagships of the two leading Russian divisions, *Suvorov* and *Oslyabya*. The *Oslyabya*, whose high sloping sides and bright yellow funnels made her an excellent target, was hit by a large-caliber shell at the waterline near the bow, which caused serious but controllable flooding and cut the main electrical cable powering the forward 10-inch turret. Two more shells hit the turret, jammed it in place, and blew off the port gun barrel. Yet the high explosive shells could not penetrate the thick armor of the turret itself; only one man was killed inside and two others wounded. "There was some groaning and then gunner Bobkov was carried out. His foot had been torn off. As they were carrying him off on a stretcher he was cursing the officers and shouting furiously, "Monsters! Bloodsuckers! You see what you've started! May you be swept off God's Earth!"[52]

Additional hits disabled the *Oslyabya*'s remaining heavy guns, put all but three of the 6-inch guns on the engaged side of the ship out of action, and cut off all electric power. Three 12-inch shells from the *Asahi* shattered the armor plate and opened an enormous hole in the side of the *Oslyabya*, which began listing heavily to port, steaming helplessly in circles. By this time the crew had panicked. "Not waiting for orders everyone rushed along shouting frantically. The fitter sailors trampled [the injured] under foot mercilessly stamping on them as they struggled to get out. Men in the stokeholds and engine rooms hammered on the armored hatches, which could only be opened from above, shouting for people to come and release them. But who was cool enough for that? Everyone was too busy saving his own life."[53]

At 3:30 P.M. the *Oslyabya* turned over on her side and sank bow first beneath the sea, the first modern battleship to be sunk entirely by gunfire. By that time, Rozhestvensky's flagship, *Suvorov*, the other principal target of the Japanese fleet, had been badly damaged. The forward 12-inch turrets had been blown up, sending the armored roof high into the air. "Men fell faster and faster," recalled Captain Semeonov. "The dead were of course left to lie where they had fallen, yet there were not enough men to look after the wounded. . . . Signaling and distance judging stations, gun directing positions, all were destroyed. And astern of us, the *Alexander* and *Borodino* were also enveloped in smoke."[54] The officer commanding the *Suvurov*'s forward turrret was hit in the neck by a shell fragment that almost severed his head. As he was being carried out he was struck by a second fragment that nearly cut his body in two.[55] As the carnage aboard the Russian ships continued, surgeons and medical men attempted to care for the wounded. The most common injuries were "gashes of highly irregular shape and size with edges usually bruised and burned," caused by shell fragments or pieces of ship metal blown into deadly small pieces. "Internal injuries were barbaric," wrote the cruiser *Aurora*'s surgeon. "Splinters are not like smooth bullets, they made big holes with very jagged edges. There were many exposed splintered fractures of the skull and other bones."[56]

At 2:30 P.M., the splinters from a shell that had landed on the *Suvorov*'s bridge entered the conning tower, wounding Rozhestvensky. The *Suvorov*, her helm temporarily jammed, swung 180 degrees out of the line. Regaining steering control, she turned onto course to follow the rest of the fleet. By this time she appeared to the Japanese "so battered that scarcely anyone could have taken her for a ship, and yet even in this pitiful condition . . . she never ceased to fire as much as possible with such of her guns as were serviceable."[57]

The *Alexander III* and *Borodino*, also heavily damaged, were rescued by a thickening fog and decreasing visibility because of the smoke of heavy gunfire and burning ships. Contact was lost several times, and the Russians took advantage of this opportunity to transfer the wounded to a destroyer. Nebogatov, seeing the *Suvorov* knocked out, decided to take action and signaled the fleet to take a course northeast 23 degrees to Vladivostok. Temporarily free from Japanese fire, Nebogatov managed to roughly reform the Russian battle line and head north toward Vladivostok. The battleship *Borodino* was now in the lead, followed by her sister ship *Orel*, Nebogatov's older ships, and the *Alexander*.

Around 6:00, the Japanese battleships regained contact and used their superior speed to once again head off the Russian line. "So far as the general picture was concerned it was, one could see, just a crush," wrote Nebogatov. "In the inner-circle were we, in the outer circle were the Japanese. . . . They came nearer and we turned away. In this way something like two concentric circles were formed."[58] The *Alexander*, listing and on fire, capsized and sank at 6:50, taking her entire crew with her. The *Suvorov*, left behind in the running battle, fought on alone against Japanese cruisers and destroyers until she sank finally at 7:00 P.M. with all hands. A few minutes later, the *Borodino* was hit by a shell or torpedo and blew up. There was only one survivor.

The gathering darkness saved the *Orel* and Nebogatov's squadron from a similar fate. Togo withdrew his heavy ships and turned the battle over to his destroyers and torpedo boats. The Fourth Destroyer Flotilla, under Commander Suzuki Kantaro, who in 1945 would become Imperial Japan's last prime minister, sank the old battleships *Sisoi Veliky* and *Navarin* during the night.

The following morning, Togo's cruisers found Nebogatov's surviving ships, the *Orel*, the old *Imperator Pavel I*, two coast defense ships, and a cruiser. By 9:00 A.M. the Japanese cruisers had been joined by warships that took station at different points on the horizon encircling the Russians. Togo's ships opened fire out of range of all the guns aboard Nebogatov's old ships. Only the modern 12-inch guns in the *Orel* could reply, and only two of these were workable. The after magazine that supplied one of these guns had only four rounds remaining. In this hopeless situation, Nebogatov opted to surrender his small squadron rather than sacrifice an additional 2,000 men in a one-sided battle. A few of the remaining Russian ships, mainly cruisers, managed to escape to neutral ports, where they were interned. Only the cruiser *Almaz* and two destroyers were able to escape to Vladivostok. Togo had captured or destroyed thirty-one of the thirty-eight Russian ships in Rozhestvensky's squadron, including all of the battleships and coast defense vessels. Japanese casualties were 117 dead and about 600 wounded. The Russian losses were almost 5,000 dead, 6,000 captured, and an unknown number of wounded. It was, declared the eminent British naval historian Sir Julien Corbett, "the most decisive and complete naval victory in history."[59] What had begun as a contest in the distant regions of northeast Asia had ended as a stark and dramatic presentation of the unforgiving and lethal nature of war at sea between machine-age navies. In the first years of the twentieth century, statesmen and strategists were obliged to face the complex economic, social, and political—as well as technological—issues involved in planning and preparing navies for future Tsushimas. Among the most fundamental issues was the nature of the human requirements of the new war at sea.

TWO

"THE SUPREME INFLUENCE OF
THE HUMAN FACTOR"

Tsushima amply fulfilled Mahan's expectations for "an instructive military lesson." In the forty years since the armored steam-propelled warship firing explosive shells had first appeared, there had been few large-scale naval battles. The battle between the *Monitor* and the *Merrimack* and the other sea fights of the American Civil War and the battle between the Austrians and Italians at Lissa in 1866 had all come too early in the evolution of the new technologies to provide any lasting lessons. The battles between the Chinese and Japanese in 1894 and the Spanish and U.S. navies in 1898 were studied with interest, but they had not pitted the strongest and most modern warships against each other.

The ships that fought at Tsushima were as different from the ships that had fought at Hampton Roads, New Orleans, Charleston, and Lissa as the latter were from the ships of the Spanish Armada. They were the products of a half-century of confusing, often disorganized, but always rapid progress in all aspects of naval architecture, ordnance, and engineering. Iron and then steel replaced wood as the basic material of ship construction, allowing for the building of very large vessels that could be extensively subdivided into watertight compartments. From the time of the battle between the *Monitor* and the *Merrimack* until the 1890s, guns increased steadily in size, range, and penetrating power. Breechloaders replaced muzzleloaders during the 1880s. Steel armor-piercing projectiles were introduced around the same time, and by the 1890s a new type of "quick-firing" gun capable of firing up to fourteen rounds a minute had made its appearance.

Progress in the development of armor kept pace with developments in big guns and projectiles. The earliest French and British ironclads had been protected by wrought-iron armor about four inches thick. By 1866, this increased to nine inches, then to fourteen inches in the 1870s and finally to twenty-four inches in the British battleship *Inflexible*, launched in 1876. Advances in metallurgy that had produced the new naval ordnance also made possible new types of armor far stronger and lighter than simple wrought iron. By the late 1890s, the latest type of Krupp all-steel armor had almost three times the strength ton for ton as the armor in the *Inflexible*.

While guns and armor were growing in power and cost, a new family of underwater weapons, the mine and the self-propelled torpedo, were added to the naval arsenal. Carried by small, very fast ships called torpedo boats, the torpedo was capable of causing a powerful underwater explosion directly against the hull of a ship, posing a threat to even the largest naval vessel. At first slow and unreliable, the torpedo improved steadily in range, speed, and accuracy. By 1904, torpedoes, equipped with gyroscopes which provided an automatic means of steering, were effective at up to 2,000 yards.[1]

The Russo-Japanese War provided the first opportunity to discover how this array of complicated and powerful machines of war, developed over the previous forty years, would perform in actual combat. After the battle of Tsushima, there was a long and vigorous argument over exactly what had been learned. Some naval experts, impressed by the advantages conferred on the Japanese by the superior speed of Togo's fleet, called for an increase in the speed of the entire battle line. Noting the relatively long range at which the battle had begun, some argued for a battleship with an armament of only the largest guns, while others pointed out that most of the serious damage to the Russian fleet had been done by the fast-firing Japanese 6-inch guns at fairly close ranges.

Torpedo attacks, as Mahan predicted, had not proved very important in the Japanese victory. In fact, experts estimated that throughout the war only 2 percent of torpedoes fired at moving ships ever scored a hit.[2] Only one Japanese warship was definitely known to have been damaged by a torpedo.[3] On the other hand, fear of torpedo attacks had greatly influenced the decisions and tactics of both sides during the conflict and made them reluctant to operate at night. The serious losses caused by mines, which sank two Japanese battleships, a Russian battleship, five cruisers, and ten other warships, were largely ignored. To naval minds, Tsushima confirmed above all that the present would be like the past; that naval wars would be decided by twentieth-century Trafalgars. In these great contests, the gun would predominate, aided or hindered but never eclipsed by the torpedo.

While the debate over Tsushima raged, the future of the battleship had, in fact, been settled months before in Great Britain. In October 1904, Admiral Sir John Fisher, a maverick and a reformer, was appointed First Sea Lord. At that time, he was already planning the design of a radically new type of warship. When Fisher took office, the balance of world naval power had become very complex. Prior to the 1880s, the French and the British had been the only two navies that mattered. Throughout most of the nineteenth century, the British had easily, almost unconsciously, ruled the seas. Occasionally the French would appear to be about to challenge that rule and introduce some technical advance, which would lead to a short-lived "naval scare" in England. Beginning in the late 1880s, however, more and more countries with rapidly maturing industrial economies and rapidly growing geopolitical ambitions began to enter the competition for sea power.

The Victorian age refined and rechanneled violence and aggression while at the same time retaining, even accentuating, the old feudal ideals of bravery, honor, and duty.[4] These ideas were enthusiastically embraced by a middle class that also strongly believed in education, science, technology, and social progress. Naval warfare appealed to both inclinations. Navies were seen as embodying national pride and prestige, and warships represented late-nineteenth-century technology at its most complex and powerful. They were the finest products of chemistry, metallurgy, optics, and engineering. Kaiser Wilhelm II described the modern warship in 1901 as "a consummate expression of human purpose and national character."[5]

The romance of war at sea remained strong as well. In Britain, battleships, upon commissioning, were still issued four hundred cutlasses, and in Germany, engineering officers bickered with the naval hierarchy about the type of swords and sashes they would be allowed to wear. Naval warfare was viewed as clean and professional, without the complications of civilians, refugees, partisans, looting, or pillage. One-on-one ship duels such as that between the *Kearsarge* and the *Alabama* in the American Civil War and the *Huascar* and *Esmeralda* in the war between Chile and Peru in 1879 still seemed possible. The newer warship types, torpedo boats and destroyers, were viewed romantically as a kind of cavalry that would launch close-range torpedo attacks against heavily armed battleships and cruisers with the same dash and heroism—and the same chance of survival—as the light brigade charging the guns at Balaclava.

As the naval races quickened throughout the 1880s and 1890s, the French were still very much in it. During these decades they were building a swarm of fast torpedo boats that were intended to overwhelm the British ironclads and a class of fast, heavily gunned armored cruisers that threatened to sweep British shipping from the seas. French armored cruisers could run away from any battleship strong enough to sink them and run down and destroy any smaller cruiser. As raiders, they posed a threat to Britain's worldwide seaborne trade. The only answer seemed to be more British armored cruisers to counter the French ones, and ton for ton, armored cruisers cost even more than battleships.

Meanwhile the Italians, afraid of the French, began building monster battleships with the biggest guns in the world.[6] Russian naval expenditures increased 64 percent between 1889 and 1893, and in 1892, the Russians began constructing the fastest, most heavily armed cruiser in the world.[7] The Japanese navy that would fight at Tsushima was already under construction by the mid-1890s. By 1893, the first American battleships had been completed, and eight more were under construction by 1900.

Like the Americans and Russians, the Germans had had no real navy before the 1890s, but they were making up for lost time by building the second-largest fleet in the world. By 1901, the German Navy League had 600,000 members, forty times as many as its British counterpart. In 1898, on the urging of Navy Minister Admiral Alfred von Tirpitz, a brilliant propagandist and political insider, the Reichstag passed a bill providing for a fleet of nineteen battleships. In 1900, that number was increased to thirty-eight battleships and forty-eight cruisers.

Through it all, the world-famous prophet of seapower retired American admiral Alfred Thayer Mahan kept up a steady flow of books and articles demonstrating that big navies were historically inevitable, a geopolitical necessity. The German maritime magazine *Nauticus* declared that "a defense capability at sea is a condition of life for any state that wants to thrive and not fritter away its paltry existence."[8]

The British were as enthusiastic as any in their admiration for Mahan—after all, he was writing mainly about them. Yet the job of being the leading naval power was becoming increasingly trickier and more expensive now that so many other powers were entering the competition. When Fisher took office, British naval expenditures had increased more than 33 percent in the four previous years.[9] The taxpayers were growing restive, and even *The Times* referred to the "grievous and growing burden of naval spending."[10] The Chancellor of the Exchequer predicted that the continuing growth in naval expenditure would lead "straight to financial ruin," and the previous First Lord of the Admiralty, Lord Selborne, had reported to the prime minister that he was "in despair about the financial outlook."[11]

Fisher understood that he was expected to save money. At the same time he was determined to increase the fighting efficiency of the fleet. As Americans would phrase it fifty years later, he wanted "more bang for the buck." Fisher's first step was to ruthlessly eliminate the dozens of obsolete, weak, and slow ships stationed throughout the British Empire. Old ironclads of the 1870s and 1880s went to the scrap heap, along with large numbers of gunboats, sloops, and small, slow cruisers that had been employed in isolated parts of the world "showing the flag." In all, 154 vessels were decommissioned, of which ninety were scrapped. Their sailors went to the more modern reserve ships, where they served as "nucleus crews," permanent cadre of about two-fifths the numbers of the warships' total personnel. In wartime, reservists would be called to bring the ships to full strength within a matter of days; and the nucleus crew, which included all the key specialists already familiar with and experienced in operating the vessels, would bring the newcomers up to the mark in a short time. Thus Fisher, while saving money by scrapping old ships, actually increased the readiness of the fleet. Having disposed of most of the obsolete ships stationed abroad, Fisher brought many of the modern ones home to join the battle fleets in the Atlantic and Mediterranean. (By 1912 even the Mediterranean battleships had been called home.) All this to meet the increasing threat of the rapidly growing German navy.

By 1904, Britain could not hope for a commanding quantitative lead over her old rivals, France and Russia, as well as her new enemy, Germany—not without bankruptcy. But what about a qualitative lead, a lead that would at a stroke put Britain far ahead? Was there a way to cut back on the enormous expenditures for battleships and armored cruisers, perhaps by merging the two types?

Fisher had an additional plan in mind to reassert Britain's traditional superiority on the high seas. At the end of 1904, Fisher appointed a special admiralty "Committee on Designs" composed of senior naval officers as well as civilian scientific and technical experts. They were to consider a new type of battleship that Fisher proposed would be armed with a uniform battery of ten to twelve big guns with only a few additional light guns for defense against torpedo boats. The new vessel would have a new type of engine, called a turbine, which would give it a speed of twenty-one knots, more than 30 percent faster than the battleships at Tsushima. At the same time, Fisher advocated upgrading the armored cruiser to a ship similar in size and armament to the new battleship, but with lighter protection and a speed of more than twenty-five knots.

Built in record time and in great secrecy, Fisher's new battleship, HMS *Dreadnought,* was commissioned in September 1906. The *Dreadnought,* which was to give her name to an entire generation of super-battleships, displaced almost 18,000 tons, slightly more than contemporary battleships, and had a main battery of ten 12-inch guns with twenty-four 3-inch anti-torpedo-boat guns. Her turbine engines gave her a top speed of more than twenty-one knots and she could steam for days at seventeen knots. In addition, three new-style armored cruisers, the *Invincible,* *Inflexible* and *Indomitable,* were completed in 1908. Soon renamed "battle cruisers," they were as large as the *Dreadnought,* had an armament of eight 12-inch guns, and could steam at twenty-five knots. Their armor protection, however, was only six inches thick, less than that of the Japanese and Russian armored cruisers at Tsushima.

The *Dreadnought* amply fulfilled Fisher's aims. Though the price of the *Dreadnought* was slightly higher than that of conventional battleships, the inclusion of only big guns in her armament made her equal to two or three of the older battleships in long-range hitting power. And since she needed ammunition, spare parts, and fittings for only one type of big gun instead of two or three as in conventional battleships, additional savings were realized.

Yet Fisher intended his battleships and battle cruisers to be war winners as well as money savers. With their superior speed, they could keep out of range of an enemy warship's old-style 6-, 8-, or 9.2-inch guns and blow them to pieces with their larger number of 12-inch guns. Such a scenario, of course, presupposed that the big guns of the dreadnoughts could in fact hit their targets at very long range. By 1906, almost everyone expected that this would be the case. They pointed to the unprecedented range at which Togo had fought Admiral Witheft's squadron in the running fight in the Yellow Sea in August 1904. It was also understood that naval gunnery was improving rapidly under the leadership of Sir Percy Scott in the Royal Navy and Captain William S. Sims in the U.S. Navy. These two reformers had introduced new methods of gunnery training, telescopic sights, and new mechanisms to rapidly elevate and train the gun. The results were dramatic. After training in Scott's method, the British cruiser *Scylla* made fifty-six hits out of seventy shots, six times better than the previous year.[12]

There was no doubt about it, battle ranges in all navies were increasing. By 1913, the British battle practice range was 14,000 yards.[13] Yet the problem remained. At ranges over 4,000 or 5,000 yards, big guns were still unlikely to hit their target. Togo had fought Witheft at long range in the Battle of the Yellow Sea, and after a two-and-a-half-hour gunnery duel the Russian squadron almost escaped and did return more or less intact to Port Arthur. At Tsushima, Togo fought from relatively short range and the Russians were annihilated. The new methods of gunnery introduced by Scott and Sims were effective only at about 3,000 yards and worked best with the 6- and 7-inch medium-caliber guns which had been eliminated in the dreadnoughts.[14]

Long-range gunnery required sophisticated range finding, fire control instruments, and organization, which were still largely lacking by 1914.[15] At the Battle of the Falklands in December 1914, for example, the British, with perfect visibility and out of range of their opponents, scored only 7 percent hits.[16] That was a good score compared with those in the World War I battles in the North Sea, in which the British and Germans managed to achieve 0.33 to 4.0 percent hits.[17] As defense analyst Charles Fairbanks observes, "Long range gunnery under First World War conditions was like strategic bombing in the Second World War: a very capable weapons system had a potential largely negated by the lack of adequate equipment for ensuring that the explosive was delivered on target."[18]

Why then did navies after 1900 prefer to fight at longer ranges? Undoubtedly, one major consideration was the increasing threat of long-range torpedo attack. At the turn of the century, the effective range of torpedoes was generally believed to be less than 2,000 yards. By 1906, the British Admiralty predicted that torpedoes would soon be effective at 5,000 yards.[19] Many naval experts also expected that the introduction of new methods and devices for range finding and spotting would soon make long-range gunnery more accurate. Perhaps given the increased size, cost, and importance of battleships, it appeared that long ranges might provide victory at lower risk to the fleet with the bigger gun.

In any case, other navies soon decided in favor of dreadnoughts for their own fleets. The Germans, forced to start from scratch anyway, rethought their entire approach to warship design and by 1909 were building ships that were in many respects superior to their British counterparts. Fisher had hoped his new dreadnought and battle cruiser might lead on to a new type of capital ship that would combine the capabilities of the battleship, the cruiser, and the armored cruiser in a single man-of-war. In addition, he hoped and expected that the submarine, which was improving rapidly in seakeeping qualities, would soon be able to replace battleships and cruisers for purposes of local defense in the Channel and the North Sea. In this scenario, Fisher planned to deploy the new "fusion"-type battleship-cruisers for the protection of trade and to engage in battle in the more distant seas.[20]

Very few naval experts in Britain or elsewhere were willing to follow Fisher's lead, and the fusion-type superships were never built. Instead, the dreadnought type was embraced as the new standard for battleships. Less than three years later, the British and Germans were engaged in the largest and most expensive naval arms race ever seen. Between 1907 and 1908, the Germans began construction of seven dreadnoughts and one battle cruiser.[21] The British attempted to stay ahead in the race by laying down "two keels for one" in battleships and battle cruisers. They also attempted to maintain qualitative superiority by increasing the main armament of their battleships first to 13.5-inch guns and then to 15-inch guns in 1912. The size of battleships increased proportionately. By 1914, the newest British and German capital ships displaced more than 25,000 tons, making them almost 50 percent larger than the original *Dreadnought*. Between 1906 and 1914, the British built some thirty-two dreadnought battleships and battle cruisers and the Germans twenty-three.

All this was, of course, enormously expensive. The new 13.5-inch-gun battleships cost 14 percent more than their predecessors. A 13.5-inch-gun battle cruiser cost 24 percent more than the *Invincible*, the first battle cruiser. In 1912, the 15-inch gun battleships cost 60 percent more than the first-generation dreadnoughts. In Britain, the costs were met by new income and inheritance taxes on the wealthy and contributions from the Dominion governments. And after 1906 the Liberal government introduced steeply progressive tax policies, which meant that middle- and working-class citizens paid very little in taxes, helping to sustain popular support for a big navy.

Less frequently discussed than battleships and big guns was the impact of the modern style of naval warfare on the personnel of the new navies, or as the British press liked to call them, "the men behind the guns." Even with their preoccupation with technology, observers of naval affairs realized that these new machines of war demanded trained and effective manpower. The British seamen's magazine *The Fleet* declared that "in the annihilation of the Russian fleet [at Tsushima], the way had been paved by the man behind the gun, he was the dominant factor toward success."[22] An American naval officer agreed. In a prizewinning analysis of Tsushima, Captain Seaton Schroeder observed that "after all is said and done nothing remains so steadily confirmed as the supreme influence of the human factor. . . . More important than the production of the finest weapon is the production of the finest skill and nerve and endurance in using them; and this can exist only hand in hand with the familiarity born of constant practice by all from the Admiral and Captain to the gunpointer and mechanic."[23]

One fact demonstrated by Tsushima was that unless they were protected by heavy armor, the "men behind the guns" of an ironclad had a far greater chance of death or injury than their predecessors in the age of sail. "There are ships in the Imperial Russian Navy with a great number of guns quite unprotected," wrote the British naval expert Fred T. Jane a few years before Tsushima. "And in action the carnage around these guns is sure to be frightful."[24] The battle had amply fulfilled this expectation. Crews of the small- and medium-caliber guns in open or lightly protected positions had suffered gruesome casualties. Yet even men behind the steel bulkheads often enjoyed little more safety. A shell crashing through layers of metal spread hundreds of deadly metal splinters and shell fragments in all directions and filled the interior spaces with noxious gases. Other men, uninjured by fragments, were killed by concussion. Aboard the battleship *Orel* at Tsushima only three of sixteen line officers were uninjured at the close of the first day's fighting.[25]

Wooden warships of the eighteenth century were hard to sink, and when they did, they often sank very slowly, allowing time for the crew to abandon ship. Steel warships struck by heavy shells or torpedoes could sink very quickly, or capsize, as the *Oslyabya, Alexander III,* and *Borodino* had done. Men in the stokeholds and engine rooms had almost no chance of escape. One survivor of Tsushima described what must have taken place in those spaces aboard the sinking ships. "When the ship turned over with her keel in the air the sailors would have been flung down head first and after them, killing and maiming, would have dropped all those iron fittings not firmly fastened. There would have been banging, crashing and roaring. The electric lights would have failed at once. . . . Into these sealed compartments, water would have entered only slowly so those not killed would have lived for some time."[26] Men stationed on the upper decks had a better chance of survival, but even if they were able to abandon ship all wooden boats and rafts would invariably be shot to pieces. Men who escaped a sinking ironclad might be burned or wounded, unable to swim very long, and swimmers who were not well clear of the ship when it sank would be sucked down with it.

Surrender had been an accepted way to terminate an unsuccessful naval engagement in the age of sail, but by the end of the nineteenth century, surrenders were becoming rarer. Not a single Chinese ship surrendered at the Battle of the Yalu in 1894 despite a 23 percent casualty rate. Nebogatov's surrender of his handful of surviving ships on the second day of Tsushima was bitterly criticized, despite the fact that his ships were completely outranged and outgunned by the Japanese; he was sentenced to death by a court-martial.[27]

Given the changed circumstances of war at sea, it was no surprise that the percentage of casualties in the machine age rose sharply. During the entire war with Napoleon, the Royal Navy had suffered only 3 to 4 percent killed in battle and less than 12 percent wounded.[28] During the War of 1812, the U.S. Navy had about 2 percent killed in action.[29] By contrast, the Russian fleet at Tsushima suffered as many as 60 percent casualties, given that two of the five largest battleships sank with all hands, and two others had only a handful of survivors.

Even more striking was the disparity between the casualties on the winning side and those on the losing side. In the large sea battles of Nelson's day, the losing side had generally suffered two and a half to three times as many casualties as the winner.[30] By contrast, the ratio of Russian to Japanese casualties at Tsushima had been 48:1. Americans in the war with Spain in 1898 had annihilated two Spanish fleets at the cost of one American killed. Clearly, the new technology, properly applied by men qualified to exploit it, promised results of a decisiveness and one-sidedness never before imagined.

The widespread navalism and jingoism of the 1890s encouraged the view that the sailor was not only a skilled mariner and mechanic but a special type of man, one who embodied the best qualities of the nation. "What is more characteristically English than the Navy?" asked one popular writer in 1885.[31] Commenting on the differences between the "conglomeration of merchant seamen, prisoners, landsmen and genuine sailors" who manned the Royal Navy in the Napoleonic Wars and the seamen of the 1890s, the British naval expert H.W. Wilson described the latter as "picked men—they may be said to be the flower of the nation. They are taken in youth, taught and trained to instinctive obedience and high courage. . . . They are animated by the national spirit bred in men who know what England really is and who day by day behold her power and the splendor of her empire." Similarly the contemporary French sailor was also "a picked man; he does not want courage, discipline or training and he has a burning desire to revenge the defeats of the past."[32] A. Trystan Edwards, a former British sailor, explained that the bluejacket's uniform "symbolized a culture, a group of spiritual qualities, a manner of life. . . . Routine has given the blue jacket steadiness of nerve, health and cleanliness. It has made him energetic and alert. Moreover, it has imbued him with a consciousness that he is not an end in himself but an instrument."[33] Edwards's countryman, the naval historian John Knox Laughton, said that "sailors differ from their countrymen mainly in being finer specimens of the race."[34]

In Britain by the 1890s, the bluejacket, invariably portrayed as cheerful, courageous, handy, and resourceful, had become a potent selling symbol on advertisements, cigarette cards, tobacco, and soap.[35] The famous "Players Navy Cut" cigarette package was introduced in 1891. The design, which featured a bearded sailor framed by a lifeboat and two distant ships, "carried a special message to the Victorian public."[36] A popular music hall song written for the 1897 Diamond Jubilee described the Royal Navy's ratings as:

> Boys of the bulldog breed
> Who made old England's name.[37]

A new magazine, the *Navy and Army Illustrated*, which featured photographs of senior officers in full dress and of navy life, became a best-selling periodical, and the youth-oriented *Boy's Own Paper* featured so many stories of nautical adventure and heroism that one historian has called it "one of the navy's most enthusiastic not to say relentless recruiting agencies."[38]

However brave, patriotic, and dedicated the sailor of the new steam-and-steel navies, however admirable his character was imagined to be, there was virtually unanimous agreement among naval authorities that this would not be enough. The modern sailor had to be educated. "I believe the time will shortly come when we will permit no man to serve in the Navy who has not had some little experience as a chauffeur or as a machinist or as a mechanic or as an electrician or has not begun to learn some of the trades and vocational occupations needed in the Navy," U.S. Secretary of the Navy Josephus Daniels told Congress in 1916.[39]

Few were willing to go as far as Daniels, but all agreed that a far higher level of formal education and technical training would be necessary for sailors to fight and win future Tsushimas. By 1904, "boy seamen" joining the Royal Navy received five weeks of basic "mechanical work" and three months of gunning training before they went to sea for the first time. When they were rated "ordinary seaman" at age eighteen, they were then "instructed in the use of mechanical tools, in the working of water-tight doors, sluices, valves, fire mains, etc. and in stokehold work."[40]

At the end of the nineteenth century, at least one third of the crew of the newest cruisers had to be composed of sailors with some specialized skill or training. In the dreadnought-type battleships this requirement had grown to three quarters of the total crew.[41] At the turn of the century, even in the Russian navy, recruits experienced in factory work, skilled trades, or clerical occupations composed about 60 percent of new inductees, compared to about 2 percent in the Russian army.[42] "It is only the popular imagination that pictures a blue jacket as always heaving a rope or tossing an oar," wrote a British journalist serving in a battle cruiser. "A pair of pliers is more use to him than an oar; he has much oftener a piece of paper than a rope in his grasp."[43]

The roles and status of industrial-age sailors had altered considerably from the days of sail. In Nelson's time, close to the entire crew worked together as a single team in the sails and rigging or on the gundeck under the eye of their officers. By the 1890s, the crews of the new steel warships often worked in small parties in many different parts of the ship, and often away from their officers and under the direct supervision of other enlisted men. Sailors in machine-age navies were also far more specialized and carried a greater weight of individual responsibility than sailors in the age of sail. In Captain Scott's reforms in gunnery, for example, a key player was the gunlayer, an enlisted sailor, often fairly junior in rank, who controlled the elevation and depression of the barrel. "The gunlayer was the man in those days," recalled one former sailor. He "had to make all his own corrections to hit the target."[44] Recruits entering the Royal Navy were carefully screened for indications that they might possess special skills and aptitude for gunnery and torpedo assignments. Skilled gunners could expect extra pay and more rapid advancement.[45] In the German navy the captain of each ship personally selected the ratings to be turret captains as well as their key assistants. Men who had been trained in the use of smaller guns had to requalify to operate the guns of the main armament of battleship.[46]

Sailors in twentieth-century navies consequently required extensive specialized training beyond that which could be provided during an apprenticeship aboard a man-of-war or a training ship, although these remained a basic part of seamen's education. One solution, as Daniels suggested, was to recruit as many trained specialists as possible directly into the navy. Most navies adopted such a program in one form or another, but skilled men still young enough to join the navy and willing to forgo higher pay ashore were always hard to find. To provide crews for the rapidly expanding fleets of the 1900s, navies would have to create

their own technicians and specialists. By the first decade of the twentieth century, all great navies had specialized schools ashore offering
courses up to a year in length for blacksmiths, engine room technicians,
gunners, torpedomen, cooks, armorers, electricians, paymasters, hospi-
talmen, and many other specialties. In 1906, the U.S. Navy had more
than two dozen different specialties or "ratings" and nine specialized
schools.[47]

No navy faced these personnel problems in more acute form than did
the British Royal Navy, and few navies were more unready psychologi-
cally and socially to resolve them. While ships had changed dramatically
and seamen had come to resemble mechanics more than jolly tars, the
leadership of the Royal Navy had serenely avoided confronting most of
the major issues of the new sea warfare. They were the heirs of almost
one hundred years of success and unchallenged supremacy at sea. The
admirals of the 1890s had seen plenty of action and danger, and not a
few had won medals for bravery, yet most of these were in connection
with warfare *on land*.

Indeed, the navy had so often participated in land campaigns and
punitive expeditions that the Admiralty prepared a booklet called *Instructions for Naval Landing Parties*. In operations against "savages," for
example, a commander was advised to allow about 150 sailors and marines
for every 1,000 enemy warriors. In villages, houses with thatched roofs
were "easily fired by rockets," although the canny natives "sometimes removed the thatching on the approach of an expedition." Along with
this advice on tactics, officers were admonished to ensure that "on arrival in camp at night or daylight in the morning the men should be able
to cook their tea or cocoa without delay."[48]

While the Admiralty had thus mastered the problems of land warfare
to its own satisfaction, little thought was given to the strategy and tactics of a fleet action on the high seas. That was understandable. There
had in fact been few great naval battles within the lifetime of the British
admirals of the 1890s and none involving the Royal Navy. By 1880, only
one admiral on active duty "had ever fought another warship on the
open sea. . . . In the world in which they had grown up preparing for
a general war was not a subject to which sensible and decent people
devoted much time."[49] And, given the continuing involvement of the
Victorian navy in policing, punitive expeditions, bombardments, and
coercive diplomacy—the "low intensity warfare" of its day—the Admiralty had little time or incentive to devote to issues of war at sea. "I don't
think we thought very much about War with a capital 'w,'" recalled one
officer of that era. "We looked upon the navy more as a world police

force than as a warlike institution. Our job was to safeguard law and order, put out fires on shore and act as guide, philosopher and friend to
merchant ships of all nations."[50]

The Royal Navy's officers, who considered themselves the heirs of Nelson, were the products of a system that would probably have ensured that
Nelson never received a commission. Many British naval officers were superb seamen, brave and resourceful leaders, but as a whole they were a
narrow, reactionary, class-conscious, and inward-looking social group.

Before World War I, entry into the commissioned ranks of the Royal
Navy was available only to those whose parents could afford the high
fees to pay their tuition as naval cadets in HMS *Britannia,* the officer
training ship, or at the Royal Navy's colleges at Dartmouth and Osborne,
established in 1905. The tuition at Osborne and Dartmouth was equal to
that at many of the best public schools, and unlike the public schools,
the naval colleges offered no scholarships. Admiral Fisher estimated that
there were about 1,500,000 people in the United Kingdom with incomes
sufficient to pay the cost of officer training. Of the remaining 41,500,000,
"no single one can hope to become an officer in the navy."[51] "You cannot in a democratic state go on drawing 99% at least of your officers from
the 'upper 10,'" he went on to say.[52] Winston Churchill, as First Lord of
the Admiralty in 1912, introduced a plan for promotion of a handful of
enlisted sailors and marines to commissioned rank. Yet even this modest
program met with great opposition, and few sailors ever achieved officer
rank. As late as 1930, only fifty-five former seamen had received commissions in the navy during the previous decade.

Cadets entered the navy at the age of twelve or thirteen following a
physical examination, an interview, and a written examination. For
Cadet William Butler, who entered in 1912, the medical test consisted
of walking barefoot across a wet floor (to identify possible flat feet) and
looking at different pieces of colored glass to detect color blindness.[53]
The test and interview proved a more formidable experience, at least for
a boy of thirteen. "You were ushered into a room with a long table and I
believe there were several headmasters. There was an Admiral or so and
some Naval Captains."[54] Prior to the interview, candidates were required
to write an essay on a subject prescribed by the board. Robert Hale was
given the subject "Do you think war is necessary?" "I thought for about
eight and a half minutes and then I wrote, 'Yes, war is necessary because
if there were no war there would be no need of a Navy and I want to join
the Navy. So war is necessary.'"[55] William Sheppard was assigned the
topic "Imagine yourself as the Commanding Officer of a submarine. Relate your experiences." "I've got a very vivid imagination," Sheppard re-

called, "and that was right up my street and I took my submarine down to the Pacific and was still writing frantically when the time came to stop. And I was in the grip of an enormous jellyfish and I heard tones of laughter from the boardroom before I went in!"[56] As the Admiralty itself admitted, the written test was "in no sense of the word competitive and is only meant to ensure that the cadet is reasonably well advanced for his age and shows the capacity to go further."[57]

While the high tuition and personal interview ensured that only "gentlemen" of the upper-middle class, the gentry, and the aristocracy could become officers, the navy was by no means the most popular calling among the well-to-do. Many parents found the idea of committing their sons to a lifetime career at sea at the age of twelve unappealing. Moreover, as Admiral Fisher himself observed, "although the Navy is the senior service, the Army is considered by most people the most attractive, as more prestige socially is attached to it."[58] Young scions of the aristocracy tended to gravitate toward the elite guard regiments. The majority of entrants into the officer ranks of the navy were not dukes and earls, but the sons of upper-middle-class professional families and rural gentry. In a country in which there was a strong tendency for sons to follow their father's occupation whether it was clergyman or coal miner, it was not surprising that boys entering the navy most commonly came from naval or military families.[59] "My father was CinC of the home fleet at the time I went to Osborne," recalled Admiral Sir Charles Madden, "and it was just assumed that if you were the son of a naval family that's where you went. . . . So it was very much a closed shop, if not by intention, by practice."[60] Nevertheless, as one naval writer observed, though "the ranks of its officers all are largely drawn from the middle and professional classes . . . the ideas and traditions of the navy are of the old upper class."[61]

Few officers who entered the Navy at thirteen could recall, years later, why they had chosen the service, or had it chosen for them. One who could was Commander H. L. Jenkins, who remembered receiving a postcard from an uncle in the Royal Navy that pictured sailors scrubbing the decks. "They had bare feet. Water was washing all over the place and I said to myself, 'My golly, that's the way I can get my feet wet without being ticked off by Nanny when I walk through all the puddles,' which was my chief sport at the time."[62] Probably a far more common experience was that of Commander A.F.C. Layard, whose parents "decided the little man was going into the Navy. . . . I don't know that anything very much enthused me [about it] except that in those days the Navy was a great service and it was quite natural to want to belong to it."[63]

With the relatively small pool of potential officers to draw upon, it was hardly surprising that some naval cadets were at best marginal. Captain the Honorable Horace Hood, reporting on the cadets at Osborne in 1912, "was emphatic in his evidence that some of the boys were deficient in intelligence and unfit to become naval officers."[64] An Admiralty committee agreed with Hood's assessment but believed that the poor quality of naval cadets was due not to any failure of the system of selection but to an insufficient number of suitable candidates.[65]

Often, the first news that the successful candidate received of his appointment to Osborne was a letter from Gieves, the London and Portsmouth tailoring firm that supplied generations of officers with their uniforms and equipment. James Gieves, the proprietor, personally saw off every train from London carrying the new cadets to Osborne and Dartmouth.[66] At Portsmouth, a Gieves representative collected the incoming cadets at the station on Portsmouth Hard, distributed their outfits, gave them lunch, and walked them down to the railroad jetty to board the tug for Osborne on the Isle of Wight. All around them they could see the naval might of Britain. A pair of battleships or cruisers might be tied up to the railroad jetty. Nelson's flagship *Victory* was on display a few hundred yards away. Other ships were anchored in the harbor or in nearby Gosport. Much of the time a stiff cold wind, sometimes mixed with rain or sleet, would be blowing from the ocean.

Assembled near the jetty, the little cadets might appear to passersby to have no hands and no feet. "We were all dressed in uniforms about five sizes too big for us. . . . When people complained, Gieves said, 'Well they're going to grow so everything looks a bit long.' . . . The sleeves of [our mackintoshes] . . . jutted out over our hands and they were also down to our feet and were resting on the ground."[67] "The Admiralty seemed to think we should have as many clothes on as possible," recalled Commander W. O. Bradbury. "You had your new uniform cap which, of course, was very uncomfortable . . . a very thick monkey jacket under which was an equally thick waistcoat with brass buttons, trousers, thick flannel shirt, stiff collar, black tie, and a thick long sleeved vest and black boots on top of which you put your warm overcoat and Macintosh oilskins."[68]

At Osborne, cadets found a straggly conglomerate of temporary building joined by very long drafty corridors, each named after an admiral.[69] The three corridors each housed a class or "term." Classes entered the school at three different times during the year. At Osborne, which cadets entered first, and at Dartmouth, where they received more advanced education, the courses lasted two years each. Fisher insisted that at the new colleges "the education of all our officers without distinction must be re-modeled to cope with machinery instead of sails."[70] The naval colleges provided courses in subjects such as English, geography, history, modern languages, mechanical drawing, mathematics, science and practical engineering, navigation, and seamanship.

At Dartmouth the cadets' day began at 6:00 in the morning when the ring of a firebell "sent us naked down the dormitory through an icy over-chlorinated plunge bath and out again before the ringing stopped. Be-towelled but still wet, we stood at attention in front of our basins awaiting the order *wash necks* followed by *wash teeth*. As 0610 approached the order came to *get dressed* followed five minutes later by *say prayers*. After early morning studies life was conducted at the double. We doubled to breakfast and rushed it so that we could get a chance to secure a cubi-cle containing rough squares of paper known as "admiralty brown."[71]

Cadets "had to double past every senior term gunroom and when you were first term you were right at the end of the corridor so you had a long run."[72] During evening inspections "your toothbrush had to be on top of your tooth mug, and if the bristles were pointing to the left when they had to be pointed to the right, you got a tick."[73]

Most graduates who have recorded their memories of these institu-tions stress the colleges' preoccupation with discipline, obedience, re-spect for rank, and zealous suppression of any sign of independent thinking. "The Navy of that day was a very hard school for very young officers," recalled a midshipman who served in World War I. "Strict dis-cipline is necessary especially in wartime, but I cannot help thinking it was over done . . . and in a good many cases more apt to strangle initia-tive."[74] Captain S. W. Roskill, the distinguished naval historian, ob-served that in his days at Dartmouth, "the principal and prime aim of training was to inculcate absolute, instant and unquestioning obedience, [and] second to teach that wisdom increased with rank."[75] Vice Admiral K.G.B. Dewar wrote, "The system caught little boys before they learned to think and chilled them into a state of passive obedience."[76] "Of all the causes of the long tale of error and misjudgment that mar the Royal Navy's record in the early 20th century and World War I, I am sure it was this determination to stamp out any attempt by officers to think for themselves that was the greatest," concluded Captain Roskill.[77]

Whatever the academic shortcomings in the education of cadets at the Royal Navy colleges, they were still likely to be better educated than senior officers in the Edwardian-era Royal Navy. These older men were graduates of the *Britannia* and other old ships of the line moored to the dock as training vessels. Their education had been "haphazard and concerned almost exclusively with mathematics and various branches of what we would now call physics."[78] Their practical training had been almost entirely oriented to seamanship under sail and to the mastery of naval routine. They were, as one eminent naval historian observed, "highly trained and wholly uneducated."[79]

Both the *Britannia* and the naval colleges stressed physical training, discipline, and practical seamanship. In addition, the naval colleges emphasized athletics. Cadets "learnt all sports, rugger, tennis, hockey, squash, and also to referee."[80] "Life was undoubtedly easier for those who were good at rugger," recalled one former cadet. "The majority of the officers were appointed as much for their ability to play games as for any other reason."[81] None of this was surprising in a country which looked on sports not so much as a form of exercise as a mechanism for molding character and instilling ideals of honor and chivalry.[82] So pervasive was this belief that one historian has suggested that the Navy may "have confused warfare with ritualized games."[83]

Strict and instant obedience was expected. And at the naval colleges, as in the public schools of the time, there were frequent beatings with ropes and canes. "You got four cuts on the backside for almost anything." In a society in which children in institutions ranging from Poor Law homes to upper-class boarding schools were routinely disciplined by corporal punishment, this practice elicited little comment or concern. As one officer who attended Dartmouth in the early 1930s observed, "beatings . . . were common, salutary, and toughening. . . . Sailors and prospective officers . . . were brought up in the same tough mold. . . ."[84]

Though the naval colleges hardly encouraged independent thinking, they successfully served other purposes. A Dartmouth graduate was almost indifferent to personal hardship, close to unflappable, steady and reliable under any conditions, tough physically and mentally. An often repeated story told of a lieutenant commander who had survived four years of brutal treatment in a Japanese prison camp and inspired other prisoners by his fearless conduct. "How did you stand it?" he was asked. "Well," replied the officer, "four years at Dartmouth helped."[85]

Those who survived the naval colleges went to sea for further training in a man-of-war. Aboard ship the cadets continued their studies in gunnery, navigation, torpedoes, and engineering, stood watches on the bridge, carried cocoa to the officers on duty, and observed the specialist ratings at their work. They also began their practical education in leadership at sea by commanding one of the ship's steam-powered picket boats. When the bosun would pipe "Away picket boat's crew," the midshipman would run fearlessly along the narrow boom twenty feet above the picket boat and slide down the jackstay into the boat. "We learned . . . the knack of driving a picket boat through half a gale when full of cheerful senior officers returning late at night and in no mood to accept a wave in the sternsheets."[86]

The midshipmen took their meals in the gunroom, usually located near the wardroom or officers' dining room, and slept in hammocks in an area immediately below the gunroom. Two sublieutenants, the senior of whom served as mess president, presided over the gunroom with its senior midshipmen, "snotties," and junior midshipmen, "warts." Life in the gunroom resembled a Victorian tea party superimposed on a raucous fraternity initiation. There were formal etiquette and ceremony ("On guest night every officer in the gunroom will drink his majesty's health in wine.")[87] But there were also "gunroom evolutions," imaginative games to torment the midshipmen. When the mess president shouted "Breadcrumbs!" during meals aboard the battleship *Superb*, the warts were all to put their fingers in their ears so as not to overhear the conversation of their seniors. "If the sublieutenant then said 'okay, cancel breadcrumbs' and you took your fingers out of your ears you got a dozen with a dirk scabbard across the backside for listening. Fingers must be kept in the ears until a senior 'snottie' came and removed them."[88] A favorite after-dinner entertainment was "Angostura trail," in which a wart was blindfolded and an irregular line of Angostura bitters was spilled onto the deck. At the end of the trail was a piece of bread. The wart followed the trail on hands and knees by smell, encouraged in his efforts by the mess president, who would thrash him each time he lost the trail or hesitated too long. The game ended when the blindfolded wart found and ate the bread.[89] In the battleship *Neptune*, a popular game was to tie a wart's hands behind his back and place him facedown on a twenty-foot polished table. He was then "propelled from one end to the other like a human torpedo." Between his lips the victim held a match which he attempted to ignite on the surface of the table. Those who were successful received a drink, the unsuccessful a beating.[90]

By the time they reached the grade of lieutenant, around the age of twenty-two, the young officers had already spent more than nine years in the navy. "It was a very close club," observed a journalist who served with the Royal Navy in World War I. "To take a little boy of thirteen away from his home and isolate him from all the thought and development of his generation . . . was probably the most wasteful method that could be employed." It bred "a narrowness of point of view and . . . a preference for submitting to the faulty rule of an absolute authority rather than for opposing it in an organized effort towards self-improvement."[91]

Among many older officers, sails remained the preferred mode of power, and were used whenever possible well into the 1880s. Expertise in seamanship and ship-handling had been skills with the highest prestige, and ships had been judged by the smartness and alacrity with which their crews performed various evolutions under sail. "Sail drill was *the* thing of that period," recalled former seaman Lionel Yexley, "and every nerve was strained to make plain sail or send up and down top gallant mast and upper yards in the shortest possible time."[92] The elite of the crew were the upper yardmen, specially selected sailors who worked in the topgallant and royal yards and performed their acrobatic feats in the maze of canvas, wood, and rope 130 feet or more above the deck.

Officers of the Royal Navy displayed an extreme reluctance to part with their beloved masts and sails, despite the fact that they had no military value. After two sail training ships had been lost with all hands in the 1880s, the Second Sea Lord was asked whether he "considered absolutely necessary that these young men should be sent [to sea] in a vessel without any auxiliary steam power." He answered in the affirmative, insisting that "in a steam training ship you lose many of the advantages to be obtained by having a sailing ship. You would rarely go in and out of harbor or any difficult place without the captain getting steam up and thus lose the experience of working under sail."[93]

Sails for men-of-war were not finally done away with until 1901, when the sloop *Condor* went down in a gale. In 1903, an Admiralty circular directed that "physical and mechanical training is to be largely substituted for mast and sail drill."[94] Nevertheless a significant part of the naval cadet or apprentice seaman's training was still devoted to climbing the masts and working in the yards. Students in the Royal Navy's recruit training school at Shotley "had to go over the masthead before every meal."[95] As late as 1931, the Admiralty considered reviving the sail training squadron as a way of improving leadership and morale.

The affection lavished on sail did not extend to the guns or engines. Royal Navy line or "executive" officers stayed well clear of the engine room spaces. The image of the engineer as a kind of mechanic or tradesman, socially and professionally inferior to officers and gentlemen, was widespread. A program known as "the Selborne scheme" for common training of executives and engineers in the naval colleges as midshipmen, adopted in 1902, met with strident opposition from many officers and their families. "An executive [officer] is appointed to carry out the important work the ship was designed for," wrote Admiral Sir Richard Vesey Hamilton. "There never was a period in the history of the Navy when greater skill, nerve, judgment and the rare gift of intuitive power of instant decision were so much required as they are now by our captains and officers of the deck watch. . . . On their skill and judgment depend the safe conduct of over a million's worth of property and the lives of all on board. The engineer has no such responsibility as the executive; and powers of intuitive decision are rarely, if ever, required. As far as nerve trial goes, his post is an easy one; he is never in darkness, fogs, or thick weather, never has rain, snow, sleet or hail beating on his face; his duty is to obey promptly the orders he may receive from the bridge."[96] Sir Richard's casual assumption that standing a deck watch in bad weather was far more of a challenge than any problems that might occur in the ship's engineering spaces was neither unusual nor particularly controversial among officers of his rank and experience. "In twenty years time naval officers will wonder how the steam navy could possibly have been run and been administered by an executive who knew nothing whatever about steam or mechanical appliances," wrote Rear Admiral Lord Charles Beresford, a naval reformer and member of Parliament, in 1903.[97]

Until 1903–4 when Scott's improvements in the speed and accuracy of naval gunfire and the example of the Russo-Japanese War began to arouse serious interest in gunnery, the subject had been even more neglected than engineering. Officers disliked gunnery practice because it invariably spread soot and dirt throughout the ship, ruining the paint and smart appearance so important in the Royal Navy. "It was not unusual for flag officers to go ashore to get out of the firing and if the gunnery lieutenant worried himself it was looked upon as part of the eccentric behavior of a man cranky on guns."[98] Enlisted men shared this dislike of gunnery practice because heavy guns were believed to be prone to accidental explosions. Such accidents were in fact rare, but sailors believed otherwise, "and it was not unknown for the Petty Officer who was supposed to pull the lanyard to faint with fear and for ratings to report sick to avoid being present."[99] Lionel Yexley observed that "the idea of taking the target, when one was laid out, as representing the enemy's ship and teaching men how to lay a gun with the object of hitting it was the last thing that entered anyone's head."[100]

Engineering remained an underrated activity in the Royal Navy until well after World War I, but gunnery was a different matter. Scott's revolutionary reforms in gunnery and the resulting stunning improvements in accuracy came to the attention of the public soon after the turn of the century. Author and poet laureate Rudyard Kipling helped publicize the advances in naval gunfire, which he called "squirting death through a hose." The Germans soon became interested, and in the United States

Navy, Scott's disciple Captain William S. Sims was named Inspector of Target Practice and then Naval Aide to the President.

"Gunnery became the vogue," wrote naval expert Fred T. Jane, "and every blue jacket who managed to hit the target a time or two had his photograph in the newspapers." Ambitious younger officers soon came to look at specialization in gunnery as the path to advancement and prestige. The ever inventive Captain Scott meanwhile continued to devise new methods for even better shooting through centralized control of aiming, firing, and spotting by a single officer. Yet interest in the new gunnery could not by itself prepare an officer for command in modern war. The new preoccupation with naval ordnance tended to encourage overspecialization and "a system whereby officers were kept more interested in the functions of the nut-retaining breech screw or the testing of circuits than in those gunnery and torpedo problems which could be tackled only after long contemplation of war as a whole."[101]

Nor was the Royal Navy as an institution able to cope with the complex scientific challenges of truly long-range gunnery. Centralized fire control would succeed only if there was a way for the fire control personnel to accurately determine ranges while the ship and its target were converging and diverging rapidly and irregularly over long distances. Few senior officers, trained in the traditional seamen's arts, understood the mathematical and technical issues involved.

Arthur Pollen, businessman and inventor, had designed a system for predicting ranges based on the use of an early analog computer, with data supplied by visual spotters. This system produced remarkable results and remained the basis for the fire control systems in the U.S. Iowa-class battleships that participated in the Gulf War more than eighty years later. However, the Admiralty rejected Pollen's system in favor of an inferior but cheaper fire control system devised by gunnery officer Captain Frederick Dreyer. This system had a chance of working effectively only if a ship and its target were steaming on steady courses along parallel lines. Otherwise, it could prove even worse than the old system of individual sighting and firing of the guns.[102]

For the first but not the last time, the devices of naval warfare were becoming too complex to be left to the navy. Struggling with this bewildering array of organizational and technical problems, the Royal Navy's officers turned to the unfamiliar task of developing a modern enlisted force.

THREE

"THE CAT'S WHISKERS"

Fifty years ago we had 200,000 seamen in our mercantile marine, we scarcely have half at the present time," lamented a British naval expert in 1901.[1] Those merchant seamen had furnished a large pool of skilled manpower to man the warships of the Royal Navy in times of war. The turn of the century was a time of peace, and yet the number of seamen on active duty and in the reserve of the British navy exceeded the peak strength of the navy in the Napoleonic Wars.[2] The large number of new warships added to the fleet as well as the increasing size of the new vessels—the super-dreadnoughts of 1912 were more than 30 percent larger than the battleships that had fought at Tsushima and more than 20 percent larger than the original *Dreadnought*—resulted in manning requirements far exceeding those of the Victorian era. By 1897, the number of active-duty naval personnel had risen to 100,000 from only 65,000 in 1889–90. Between 1897 and 1904, the total increased to 130,000.[3]

Even had the large numbers of merchant seamen still been available, however, they would not have been qualified to perform all the varied tasks required in a modern warship. When centralized fire control was introduced in 1904, for example, battleships acquired fire control teams consisting of twenty to fifty men. Their role was to receive, record, and calculate range, course, and speed information and convert the data into information for the big guns. Musicians were believed to have special aptitude for this role of human computer, and between 1904 and 1912, the number of Royal Marine bandsmen tripled. At the lower end of the skill

44

spectrum, the superfast cruisers and battle cruisers of the 1900s, with their huge power plants, required greater numbers of stokers to satisfy their voracious appetite for coal.[4]

Not only did the Royal Navy have to find recruits to meet its expanded manning requirements but it was obliged to replace almost 10 percent of its personnel every year to fill the places of men whose enlistments had expired. Moreover, while a battleship could often be built in three years or less, it took six years to qualify an ordinary seaman as a specialist in torpedoes or gunnery.[5] Shortages of sailors meant the Navy could keep only a portion of its ships in commission and the readiness of reserve ships would depend on the number and type of ratings allocated to them from the active fleet.[6] Manpower considerations influenced many British naval policy decisions including the distribution of the fleet, the choice of ship types, and the number of ships in commission.

Beginning in the 1890s, the Royal Navy was involved in an active recruiting program. The training ships made regular visits to coastal cities and towns picking up recruits as they went; officers, petty officers, and coast guard stations were also encouraged to enlist boys from their districts. A majority of new recruits were enlisted by the Royal Marine Recruiting Staff. It had offices headed by recruiting officers in larger cities such as London, Birmingham, Glasgow, Bristol, and Southampton. These officers also supervised a network of recruiting sergeants in smaller towns and country districts.[7]

The sergeants usually set up shop in a public house where the publican provided a room free of charge on the understanding that the presence of a recruiter would result in an increased number of young men visiting the pub. Lionel Yexley described one of the best-known of these sergeant recruiters: "He was a well set up man with a black, neatly trimmed beard and piercing black eyes which seemed to fascinate the boys to whom he used to spin sea yarns in the little back parlor of the pub. Those yarns will never be surpassed if they are equaled, for Sergeant Blank had cultivated the art of descriptive lying to an extent which would have put Baron Munchhausen to shame."[8]

Only about a quarter of the recruits were the sons of navy fathers, and many saw the ocean for the first time when they arrived at the training ships or schools.[9] Most of the recruits were self-selected and joined the navy with only the grudging acquiescence of their parents, and often against their active opposition. To many adolescent boys, parental disapproval seemed only to make their choice more desirable. Charlie White and Stan Smith wanted to enlist at age fifteen, but were required to have their parents' consent. "Charlie's parents were unlikely to sign his enlistment papers, while I, with a doting grandmother and five maiden aunts to contend with, hadn't a ghost of a chance. Rising to the occasion, with the best of intentions, we signed each other's papers."[10]

To Lionel Yexley and other navalists, a desire to join the navy seemed almost a necessary hereditary characteristic of young Englishmen. "British mothers have wept over British sons who have chosen the sea life ever since British peoples cut the water that lave our shores. . . . They will do it as long as there is a British boy to obey the call. And that call when it comes will harden each young heart to a mother's pleadings, to a mother's tears; it will induce him to leave the home circle and home comforts to lead a life of hardships and danger from the tropics to the Poles. . . . He cannot help it, it is in his blood—and when these things cease to be, the British Empire will be tottering to its fall."[11] Elliott Mills's *The Decline and Fall of the British Empire*, which became a best-seller following its publication in 1905, warned that among the most important signs of British "decline" would be the "growing tendency of the English . . . to forsake the sea except as a health resort."[12]

More than a few young men did join because they accepted the romanticized view of the navy popular in the late Victorian and Edwardian years. Alexander Grant was given a booklet about the navy by a family friend who was a former sailor. On the back cover was a picture of a chief boatswain in dress uniform with a sword. "There and then I decided to join," recalled Grant, "and told the old sailor that one day I would wear a sword like that on the back page."[13]

Victor Hayward, who served in HMS *Tiger*, met an old school friend home on leave from the navy. "And there he stood . . . cap stock at a rakish angle and bearing the name of HMS *Orion*, one of our dreadnought battleships. He was surrounded by an admiring bevy of young girls, eyes sparkling with excitement . . . enough said. When I was old enough, I answered the call of the sea."[14] Leading seaman gunner Arthur W. Ford, who joined around the same time as Hayward, emphatically agreed. "When you got that uniform on you sort of felt you were somebody, you know? And when these girls came along and touched your collar for luck and all this business you know . . . you thought 'I'm the goods.'"[15] Signalman William Sweet recalled that "people used to think the navy was better. You were the senior service . . . you were the cat's whiskers."[16]

Since the great majority of new recruits came from what contemporaries called "the laboring classes," it is not surprising that many joined because of lack of opportunity in civilian life or even to escape outright destitution. In Edwardian Britain, where 28 percent of the population were too poor to maintain minimum nutritional standards in their diets, life expectancy in working-class neighborhoods was under thirty-five years, and half the families in Scotland lived in one- or two-room houses, service in the navy appeared to many a heaven-sent opportunity.[17]

"I joined the Navy because I was hungry," recalled Petty Officer William Prayl. "I used to pick up orange peels in the street and eat that—good old days they call them! They were terrible."[18] Royal Marine sergeant John Dunkinson declared that "starvation made me join the Marines."[19] As late as the 1930s, poverty and hunger remained an important spur to recruitment. One man who enlisted in 1938 said that he "joined for three square meals a day and a pair of boots."[20] While not many recruits were in danger of starvation, most came from large families in towns and regions where wages were low, unemployment high, and education opportunities rare and beyond reach.

Some men's motives combined the practical and the romantic. William Bruty, who enlisted in 1913, recalled that he couldn't "see any prospects of continuing my education beyond the age of sixteen," and welcomed the chance to enter the navy as a boy artificer. However, he also recalled the impression made on him by "these naval reviews down in Southsea which used to [have] the most magnificent ships which ever was on review."[21]

It took very little time for many of the newly caught fifteen- and sixteen-year-olds to develop second thoughts. An Admiralty report described the refusal of many boys to sign their enlistment papers once they had arrived at the training depot. "In some cases, this is due to false stories told to them by disaffected youngsters, in others they have witnessed boys being caned or birched; in others again they have found no comfortable provision being made for them and have slipped away unseen."[22]

One of those who attempted to "slip away unseen" was a Yorkshire boy named John Chessman, who had left school at thirteen, worked as a miner and a shoemaker's assistant, and joined the navy at the youngest possible age. Shortly after enlisting at the recruiting center, Chessman began to suffer strong doubts. "Just then I felt the urge to go out and start on the long walk home. . . . I moved toward the door. About to open it, I felt a steely grip on my shoulder and the [recruiting] sergeant spun me round. 'Nah then,' he said, 'you ain't thinking of leaving us. . . .' He turned the key in the lock and put the key in his pocket."[23]

Chessman and other youths who entered the navy at fifteen and a half or sixteen were enlisted as boys and so served until around their eigh-

teenth birthday, when they were promoted to ordinary seaman and began their twelve years of active service. New recruits received their initial training aboard one of the training ships at Portsmouth, Devonport,
Falmouth, Portland, and Queensferry. Often the new recruits' first experience of the navy would be the sight of an old three-decker training ship
rolling and creaking in a windswept, lonely harbor. The ships were the
old hulks of line-of-battle ships moored to the shore. Cold, wet, and un-
sanitary, they were gradually replaced by barracks. The first of these
opened in 1905 at Shotley near the town of Harwich, where one of the
hulks, HMS *Ganges,* was moored in the creek opposite the training
school for seamanship training.[24]

At the training establishments, boys were taught to swim, clean ship,
wear and care for their uniforms, and acquire basic seamen skills.[25] As at
the naval colleges, life aboard the training ships and at Shotley was austere and demanding, sometimes brutal. Training went on in all weather.
In winter, boys' hands soon began to crack and bleed from prolonged exposure to damp, freezing weather. Army and marine recruits were issued
overcoats, but enlisted sailors had only their T-shirts and blouses. "All
the while I was there the food was poor, punishment severe and stoppage
of pay rife," recalled one sailor who had trained aboard HMS *Ganges.*[26]
"Discipline in those days was very strict," recalled a Royal Navy chaplain. "One might use a stronger word than strict. The cane and the birch
were administered for what would now be considered trivial offenses."[27]
William Halter, a trainee aboard HMS *Impregnable* in 1907, recalled a
typical instance:

> So they get this poor boy and . . . they pull his shirt out . . . and he'd be
> laid flat across the gymnastic horse and the webbing would be put round
> each wrist and each ankle threaded through this grating. And there be
> two police corporals there pulling that taut. . . . The cane was about three
> feet long and quite thick, as thick as your thumb, and bang! The first one
> would go down. And of course it usually brought a yell from the poor
> devil.[28]

As late as the 1930s, a former boy seaman could write of HMS *Ganges*
that "it seemed to be staffed by some of the most sadistic and bloody
minded chiefs and petty officers in the Royal Navy."[29] According to one
account, the Home Secretary had proposed "to use the daily training
routine of the *Ganges* boys as a model for instituting a system of short,
sharp sentences for young offenders." However, he planned to omit the

5:00-A.M. reveille and daily boat pulling and mast climbing as "too hard for young criminals."[30] In an effort to escape life at Shotley, boys would develop "a sudden loss of memory or hearing. Grave enough, but not sufficiently so to fool the medical officer." Other boys talked of going out hidden in milk churns.[31] Successful escapes were few, however.

Despite the persistence of archaic elements and a disciplinary system better suited to the age of Captain Bligh, the Royal Navy's training system did change. After 1903, increasing attention was paid to instruction in gunnery, electricity, and torpedoes. In addition, all boy seamen were trained in the use of simple tools and served a tour in the stokehold or the coal bunkers in preparation for roles they would actually have to fill if their ships were required to steam at high speed in some emergency.

While the majority of new recruits entered the navy through the Boys Training System, men with special skills, such as armorers, blacksmiths, shipwrights, and plumbers, were enlisted directly into the service as petty officers. The highest rank and pay went to the skilled engineering technicians called engine room artificers, who formed a special privileged class among the enlisted sailors.

The great majority of engine room personnel, who fueled and operated the ship's propulsion plant, were called stokers and were paid at a somewhat higher rate than seamen. Stokers were enlisted between the ages of eighteen and twenty-five. Being considerably older than the boys, they were more independent and less easily intimidated. Stokers tended to provide more than their share of disciplinary problems, and in 1906 a group of young stokers at Portsmouth, angry at what they saw as arrogant and unjust treatment by an officer, precipitated one of the largest peacetime riots in the Royal Navy's history.

Like the stokers, marines were recruited separately. Unlike seamen, who signed a continuous service contract, marines were required to swear an oath of allegiance and were particularly conscious of their separate legal status vis-à-vis the sailors. Although they spent much of their time at sea, they were trained as infantry and referred to their mess as a "barracks." About one quarter of a warship's manpower was provided by marines. They traditionally messed and slept between the officers' quarters and the mess deck, a reminder of their original function of policing the unruly sailors of Nelson's day.

Twentieth-century Royal Marines were organized into regiments of the Royal Marine Light Infantry and the Royal Marine Artillery. The infantrymen wore the traditional red coats and were referred to as "red marines," while the artillerymen with their blue coats were called "blue marines." The Royal Marine Light Infantry was organized into three divisions, each located near one of the principal naval bases at Chatham, Portsmouth, and Plymouth. These divisions provided a manpower pool for shipboard marine detachments and for expeditionary forces in time of war or emergency. The Royal Marine Artillery had a single division located at Eastney near Portsmouth. Aboard the largest ships, marine detachments were about half red and half blue marines. Light cruisers, however, had only red marines. The detachment commander, called the Officer Commanding Royal Marines, could be either of the artillery or light infantry.

Marines traditionally manned a portion of the ship's guns. In battleships, battle cruisers, and cruisers, the Royal Marine Artillery usually manned the main armament while the Royal Marine Light Infantry manned the secondary armament.[32] Other duties of marines included providing guards and sentries and serving as officers' valets. Their most distinctive role was to serve as the backbone and spearhead of naval landing parties, a mission unchanged since the nineteenth century.

Although navies of the late nineteenth century were becoming far more militarized than their Napoleonic predecessors with regulation uniforms, hand salutes, and rifle drill, Royal Navy sailors still drew a sharp distinction between themselves and soldiers of the British army. While sons of the nobility and landed gentry generally considered the army more stylish than the navy, the working-class youths of the mess decks still saw the army as less glamorous, more rigid and impersonal, and more addicted to pointless "stomping and square bashing."[33] "To the sailorman this pomp and display of a military review was distasteful; it is foreign to his mental makeup."[34] Asked whether he would have as soon joined the army as the navy, Stoker James Leary replied, "Oh, definitely no. No. . . . And if I'd gone to join the Army I daren't show my face at home again. In them days people used to look down on the Army and upwards more to the Navy. . . . You couldn't just get into the Navy if you had a bad character or anything like that."[35]

All in all, the various recruiting schemes—early recruitment of seamen, later enlistment of stokers and marines, and lateral entry for artificers and other skilled technicians—proved sufficient to provide the increased manpower needed for the rapidly growing fleets of the Edwardian era.

Life aboard the new twentieth-century warships appeared at first sight to have changed relatively little from the days of sail. After visiting HMS *Warrior*, an 1864 armored frigate preserved at Portsmouth, a World War II veteran of the Royal Navy "realized that our 1940 accommodation was identical to that provided for the 1864 crew of that ship."[36]

A man-of-war was a clearly demarcated class society in which the classes were dramatically unequal. In the battleship *Royal Oak,* laid down shortly before the start of World War I, the captain received about a quarter of the available living space, the other officers about a third, and the seven hundred ratings shared the remainder.[37] A Russian naval officer was particularly impressed by the captain's quarters aboard the dreadnought *Hercules.* They included a day cabin, a sleeping cabin, a bathroom, and a dining room. "I must admit that in the Russian Fleet I have never come across admiral's quarters of such spaciousness, to say nothing of the captain's. . . . The day cabin had a large fireplace. . . . The bathroom . . . was always ready for use as the water was kept constantly heated by steam from the ship's boilers."[38] A sailor, in contrast, had a kit bag and kept personal belongings in a small ditty box stored in an overhead rack. John Chessman believed that "everything utilitarian [aboard ship] was meant to deliberately mark a sharp line between the officer class and the enlisted man."[39]

Seamen ate and slept in large crowded compartments divided into "messes" of twenty to thirty men. Each mess had its meals at a table approximately twenty feet long by four feet wide arranged in rows at right angles to the side of the ship and suspended from the ceiling bulkhead by a metal bar. The sailors sat on long planks or stools, so close together that the men in one mess could easily lean against the backs of the men in the next.[40]

Above the tables in this combined bedroom–dining room were hooks from which hammocks were suspended for sleeping. Each hammock was nine inches from its neighbor, which made many berthing compartments intolerably crowded. Some men opted to sleep on the tables, others slept "under the tables. They're outside in the gangway, [some slept] in the shipwrights shop . . . and some of the more hearty ones slept in the open air on the upper deck. . . . You were packed like sardines. Well that's alright in harbor where you can open up the ports and hatches. But when you're at sea, and sometimes you're at sea for a week or two, the stench is terrible."[41]

Larger ships had bathrooms with cold-water troughs for washing. Buckets sufficed for bathing. In destroyers, which lacked bathrooms, ablutions were performed with a bucket while standing in the break of the forecastle on the upper deck. "You might cadge some hot water from the cook if he was in a good mood. If you had a stern wind blowing you would be frozen to death."[42]

Just as in the era of sailing ships, the possibility of death at sea through drowning, falls, and other accidents was never far away. The presence of large and complicated machinery created a new class of hazards. Boy First Class Victor Hayward estimated that there were about one hundred fatal accidents in HMS *Tiger* during the six and one half years he served in her between 1914 and 1920.[43]

In the Royal Navy, seamen's rations remained basically unchanged from the 1860s until 1907. Breakfast aboard a British man-of-war was served at 5:00 A.M., dinner was at noon, and supper was at 4:15. Although seamen often worked far into the night, no additional food was available until the following morning.[44] The preserved beef customarily provided was "often mistaken by the uninitiated for a piece of wood and it is sometimes hard to convince visitors to the contrary." Warmed for eating, the beef emerged from the pot "in the form of a conglomerate of strings . . . so much so that it has earned for itself the cognomen 'clues [hammock cord] and lashings.'"[45] Before 1897, sailors were expected to consume these delicacies with only their hands and a spoon, since the Admiralty considered knives and forks "prejudicial to discipline and manliness."[46]

Life at sea was uncomfortable and demanding, even without the crowded conditions and poor food. Men were called at all hours of the day and night to deal with the contingencies that frequently arose in operating a large, technically complex man-of-war. Among the most onerous and distasteful duties was "coaling ship," the laborious, often repeated exercise of transferring and storing thousands of tons of coal from colliers or lighters into the ship's bunkers. Parties of sailors with shovels boarded a collier and began shoveling coal into canvas bags. The two-hundred-pound bags were hoisted aboard ship by derricks and dumped into wheelbarrows. Men rushed the wheelbarrows to manholes and tipped the coal down chutes into the bunkers. "Within minutes the ship was enveloped in a fog of coal dust. A thick layer formed around the eyelids which became very troublesome. . . . All food from the galley carried a fine film of it and it penetrated everywhere."[47]

The normal strict uniform regulations were put aside and everyone worked in whatever seemed most suitable. "Rugger and soccer shirts, long shorts, short shorts, hard hats, felt hats and Knickerbockers . . ."[48] In the coal bunkers where the heat was greatest, stokers "usually worked completely naked except for wooden clogs which were a necessity on the hot metal decks. Occasionally boiling water dripped down on them from the pipes above."[49]

A battleship or battle cruiser might take on as much as 2,500 tons of coal, and coaling could continue many hours. "I spent my first Christmas day in the Navy coaling ship, starting at 5:30 A.M. and finishing at 6:00

P.M.," recalled a former midshipman. "Anyone who was not on duty, and it didn't matter if you were a schoolmaster or the padre, had to take part. . . . We usually got a corned beef sandwich at mid-day and when it was over you had to scrub the ship clean. When we'd finished we'd have to get the bath ready for the senior midshipmen."[50]

Much time and energy were devoted to satisfying the obsession with brilliant paintwork, spotless decks, and gleaming brass which so preoc-cupied naval officers in the late Victorian and Edwardian years. One sailor claimed that two dozen sheets of emery board and two dozen tins of polishing paste were consumed each week to smarten the appearance of a single turret aboard a battleship.[51] In many ships, clips designed to lock watertight doors firmly in place had been filed and polished so in-tensely that their doors could no longer be considered watertight. In the battleship *Furious* an ornate brass medallion had been fitted in place by drilling holes directly through a watertight bulkhead.[52]

What in later years would be called environmental health hazards were plentiful. Even the newest warships were poorly ventilated and un-healthy. Tuberculosis remained common in the Royal Navy well into World War II. In summer, or in tropical climates, the heat and humidity on the mess decks were almost unbearable. Since many sailors were sta-tioned at or near the guns, partial deafness and damage to eardrums were widespread.

The most extreme conditions could be found in the stokeholds and engine room spaces. A nineteenth-century journalist left this vivid de-scription of the stokehold of a battleship around the turn of the century:

The door of the farthest fire is thrown open and a splendid glare sweeps the black iron walls, showing up the . . . grim faces of the blackened men sweating in the dust. And then the stoker of that fire, standing a little back, sends shovel after shovel of coal flying cleanly through the little opening. . . . Nothing drops in the middle, nothing hits the side of the lit-tle oval door but with splendid straight strokes he drives each helping into its place with absolute certainty. Stopping an instant, he peers his black devil face into the flaming six foot horror of the fire, then wraps a rag round hand and shovel, clears the blazing ashes and clangs the door shut again.[53]

Loss of salt and body fluids from the intense heat and exertion tended to cause dizziness, nausea, and vomiting. The heat was even more in-tense in the coal bunkers, which had to be cleared by hand. "If it was part of the general scheme of things to render a stoker efficient for his job by baking him . . . nothing could be better than to set him to work in the reserve bunker," recalled former stoker Charles Vincent. "The place was like an oven. It was immediately over the engine room and the great steam pipes ran just under the floor. Moreover it was long and narrow and almost devoid of breathable air. I do not think it was possible for a man to work for more than a quarter of an hour at a time in that hole. The heat was something awful and the thick cloud of coal dust that arose each time the baskets were tipped made the atmosphere almost unbearable."[54]

Boilers, of which even an older battleship could have eighteen or more, needed to be cleaned frequently. During this operation the engine room crews "lived in a fog of asbestos dust, soot, and boiler brick dust." Under ordinary conditions one fourth or more of the ship's boilers were being cleaned at any given time.[55]

As in Nelson's day, British men-of-war were amply supplied with rats and cockroaches. Aboard the battleship *Iron Duke*, cockroaches were so numerous that sailors held "races with them on the tables, and they painted stripes on them and they used to have bets on them."[56] G. M. Clarkson recalled an incident in which one of his messmates "suddenly put his hand behind him. This rat had run up his trousers . . . he couldn't do anything. He was speechless. We got hold of him and carefully turned his trousers back and there was the rat's tail. We seized hold of his tail, pulled him out, and bashed him down." On another occasion Clarkson found a rat in his hammock just as his mess was preparing for an admiral's inspection. "I hit it and there was a corpse and blood all over." While Clarkson disposed of the corpse his messmates hurriedly scrubbed down the deck and bulkhead.[57]

Flogging disappeared from the Royal Navy by 1881 and corporal punishment was confined to midshipmen and boy seamen, but until 1912 sailors were still subject to strict discipline and dozens of complicated, often incomprehensible regulations. *King's Regulations and Admiralty Instructions* totaled more than nine hundred pages. Not content with that, commanders proceeded to devise more rules of their own. A popular compilation was *A Battleship Commander's Orderbook*, an additional three hundred pages of regulations on such vital subjects as the disposition of towels and soap, the placement of the cap ribbon on sailors' caps, and improper leaning on the forecastle rails.[58] "Full grown men are treated like children and without necessity," declared member of Parliament and naval authority Arnold White. "When they ought to be learning gunnery or engineering they are harassed over idiotic matters of irrelevant detail. I have heard of an instance of an officer who insisted on lifting the lower part of the trousers of liberty men about to go ashore with the object of seeing that their socks were uniform."[59] With so many rules and regulations, it was not surprising that many sailors would run afoul of some of them. Between 1902 and 1911, the number of official punishments awarded in the British navy exceeded the actual number of enlisted men.[60] "Your biggest job in life is keeping clear of trouble," recalled one sailor. "You were being chased all the time. You had a certain time to everything. To get yourself washed, get breakfast, fall in. . . . You had to do so much that was not in the book and use your wit and cunning."[61]

The most common punishment in the Royal Navy was "10 A," which could be imposed for up to two weeks for minor offenses. The offender's grog was stopped and he was not allowed smoking privileges. He took his meals on an exposed part of the upper deck under the eyes of a sentry. In addition to extra work he was required, during certain hours of the day, to stand facing the bulkhead on the upper deck, an activity sailors referred to as "keeping the flies off the paintwork."[62] A battle cruiser captain explained that this practice was similar to making a child stand in a corner. "Sailors were simply childish men and must be treated as children."[63] Some captains devised more imaginative versions of this punishment for those caught smoking at unauthorized times and places. "There were wooden cups for cigarette ends and for spitting. They were called 'spid kits.' They would sling it around the chap's neck and he would have to walk up and down the upper deck all through the dinner hour carrying this spid kit with chaps spitting in it."[64]

For more serious offenses there was "punishment in cells." John Chessman described the cells in the dreadnought HMS *Warspite:* "They were below the anchor chains. When the chains were dropped, the whole forepart of the ship trembled. And when those chains, with lengths as thick as a man's arm thundered over the steel bed plates into the decks below, the people in the cells must have thought all hell was let loose round them."[65]

Prisoners slept on bare boards on the decks of the unheated, unventilated cells and were fed only hard biscuit and water for the first and last three days of their confinement. In between they were allowed a pint of cocoa, two potatoes at lunch, and a pint of tea at dinner. They were required to pick two pounds of oakum per day. "Oakum, before it is picked, is made up of short lengths of tarry rope and the poor oakum picker suffers severely by losing the skins from his finger ends."[66] If the oakum was not picked fine enough the prisoner had to repeat the process along with his additional two pounds for the next day. "Each night we carefully notched our bed boards to keep a record and mentally reckon up the time we still had to serve," recalled one Royal Navy stoker. "The commander inspected us as we stood at the cell doors when he made his 9 o'clock rounds. 'Any complaints?' he would ask in the traditional naval manner. 'No sir,' we always replied, giving him to understand that we were having a glorious time."[67]

Given these conditions, it is not surprising that navies of the early twentieth century suffered from what would now be called a "severe retention problem." Over one third of sailors in the Royal Navy left the navy as soon as their initial enlistment was up.[68] Others were unwilling to wait so long. Around one thousand men a year purchased an early discharge from the navy by making a lump-sum payment to the Admiralty, supposed to compensate for the expense of supporting and training them. Journalist James Woods, a former Royal Navy petty officer who wrote under the pen name Lionel Yexley, claimed that his magazine, *The Fleet*, received almost five hundred letters a month from men inquiring about how to "buy themselves out" of the navy.[69] Desertion provided another way out. In 1901–2, almost four thousand seamen and stokers were listed as having "run." When Rear Admiral Prince Louis of Battenberg, a relative of the royal family and future First Sea Lord, visited the United States and Canada on a goodwill tour, sixty-eight men from his flagship took the opportunity to jump ship.[70]

Throughout the Edwardian years there was a steady increase in collective acts of sabotage or insubordination by groups of sailors, usually intended as protests against what they saw as intolerable conditions or injustices in their ship. There was a full-scale mutiny in the battleship *Zealandia* shortly before the outbreak of World War I and rumors of near mutiny in many others. The Admiralty's response was to quietly court-martial the culprits and attempt to keep the incidents out of the press.

Even greater anxiety was caused by what some newspapers and politicians saw as creeping trade unionism among the sailors. Groups of seamen such as artificers, telegraphists, and stokers had begun forming societies to provide death benefits and some rudimentary savings and insurance plans to their members. These associations also published "loyal appeals" to the Admiralty calling for improvements in service conditions, such as better pay and opportunities for promotion.

The lower deck societies were essentially cautious and narrow in their aims. Most represented the interests of the petty officers, and their membership never amounted to more than 10 percent of the enlisted force.[71] They were nevertheless viewed by many officers and civilians as a kind of naval branch of the militant labor unions and socialists.[72] In 1912, Vice Admiral Sir Francis Bridgeman, the Second Sea Lord, saw evidence of "a deep laid scheme—resulting from the mischievous socialist literature that our men are now flooded with."[73] "Socialism is becoming a tremendous factor in the Navy," declared a lieutenant in the cruiser *Hermes* in 1913, "particularly among the engineers. They of course have their unions and that is the commencement of all evil in my opinion."[74]

While some continued to prattle about "socialistic influences," a few more insightful individuals recognized that far-reaching reforms would be required to solve the Royal Navy's morale and retention problems as well as deal with the growing threat of "indiscipline" and "regrettable incidents." "The Admiralty has demanded intelligence, a steadier brainier type and in the main has got it. But the Admiralty has not paid for it," said one naval critic in 1911.[75] Yexley's magazine, *The Fleet*, played a key role in publicizing conditions and problems of the lower deck as well as providing an outlet for the more articulate or more incautious sailors to express their views. Most officers saw Yexley and his magazine as a subversive influence, but Admiral John Fisher consulted him frequently on personnel matters and acted on some of his suggestions. *The Fleet*, in turn, enthusiastically applauded Fisher's reforms in battleship design, fleet deployments, and modernization and supported him against his critics.

Among Fisher's first measures in personnel reform was a program to improve the deplorable messing arrangements in Royal Navy ships. Beginning in 1907, sailors received a standard ration that included the basic necessities of diet, supplemented by a cash messing allowance of fourpence a day, for purchase of additional food and staples from the ship's canteen. Because few sailors spent as much as fourpence a day on canteen purchases, the new messing allowance actually represented a modest salary increase, a very welcome development in a service where pay had not changed since 1853.

Along with improvements in the food allowance came refrigerators, bakeries, and trained cooks in some of the larger ships and a full set of cutlery issued free to the men. Characteristically, the captains of many ships used this development to institute an additional inspection. In the battleship *Dreadnought*, the knives and forks, all cleaned and shiny, had to be set out for Sunday inspection, arranged around the salt and pepper shakers "handles toward the port and one inch away, knives and forks in rotation."

A second improvement in the sailors' financial situation resulted from changes in the uniform regulations. Unlike soldiers, British sailors were required to pay for their own uniforms. This was no simple matter, for by the turn of the century, the set of clothing items which constituted the sailor's "uniform" had become elaborate and costly. Frequent clothing inspections were held and sailors were obliged to replace worn-out or missing items at their own expense. Even the sailor's sewing kit was subject to inspection to ensure that it had the proper number of threads and needles. The Admiralty could never countenance anything so radical as the issuance of a free uniform. Beginning in 1906, however, uniform requirements became less elaborate and some of the more absurd clothing regulations were done away with, resulting in another small savings to the sailors. In a final burst of generosity, shortly before the outbreak of World War I, the cabinet approved a substantial marriage or "separation" allowance for married sailors and an increase in basic pay of about 15 percent for sailors who had served more than six years.

Both Fisher and Winston Churchill, who became First Lord in 1911, chipped away at the navy's archaic and arbitrary system of naval justice and punishment. Corporal punishment with the birch was abolished and caning could be administered only on the captain's orders. Cell punishments were limited. The most ludicrous aspects of the 10A punishments were abolished in 1912. An extra working drill was substituted for the older practice of "keeping the flies off the paintwork." For more serious offenses, petty officers could opt for court-martial rather than summary punishment.

While the reforms of the Fisher-Churchill era made the sailor's life marginally more attractive, neither pay nor regulations played a major role in enabling the sailor to live and work effectively in the uncomfortable and demanding world of a steam-and-steel man-of-war. Like people in other authoritarian institutions, sailors developed an effective parallel society with its own values, rules, customs, and leaders. "A ship, although technically a unit, is humanly an aggregate of small communities or states, each with its own laws, its separate customs, its particular duties," observed a journalist in the battle cruiser *Lion*.[76] Sailors developed and enforced their own rules of civility and tolerance in the crowded conditions of the mess deck. "On the mess deck," wrote one former sailor, "the blue jackets are crowded so close together that taciturnity and churlishness are at a discount."[77] "You had long spells together at sea," recalled able seaman Richard Rose. "You talked about home affairs, girlfriends, things like that, just confiding in each other. I've said things to other chaps and other chaps said things to me, I'd never have dreamed of saying normally."[78]

Many sailors compared mess deck life to that of a large and noisy family. As in a family, each member's abilities, habits, weaknesses, and in-terests were well understood. Seamen obeyed and enforced their own rules and customs, which might only incidentally resemble the official navy regulations. Lionel Yexley observed, "A man might offend against every clause of the King's regulations . . . and no one would think a scratch less of him, provided he was a good seaman and ready to do his work. . . . But let him be guilty of a mean action toward a ship-mate or violate the code of honor and no mercy was his."[79]

Newcomers were encouraged, if need be coerced, into learning these rules and customs of behavior on the mess deck. "There was a great em-phasis on behaving yourself," recalled Engine Room Artificer William George Bruty. "People like you. You put yourself out to be liked. You didn't kick over the traces, didn't disobey."[80] While officers had enor-mous power and responsibility, these distant figures played little part in the day-to-day life of most sailors. Real authority rested with the leading seamen and petty officers.

At the top of the hierarchy were the regulating chief petty officer or "master at arms," known as "the jaunty"; the sergeant major of marines, "stripy"; and the regulating chief stoker, the "steam jaunty." These men were backed by considerable formal authority but preferred to rule through force of personality, experience and, if need be, physical coer-cion. "Their method could be summarized thus: 'I am the great chief of this dhow. I won't run you in, I'll knock a hole into yer. Come, hop it. Get a hustle on.'"[81]

Artificer William George Bruty experienced the system firsthand:

Under the influence of my tot of rum . . . I was clumsy enough to drop the spanner that I'd been using. It went clattering down into the bilges. . . . [The chief engine room artificer] says to me, "Have you dropped a bit of that spanner Bruty?" I said, "Yes, chief." . . . So he said, "Well you'd better go down and pick it up then." And I, under the influence of my tot of rum, said "Well if you want that spanner chief, you'd better come down and get it yourself," which was the most disastrous thing I could have said because two hairy arms came down beneath the floor plates, picked me up by the scruff of the neck, handed me up. . . . And he sure gave me the biggest hiding I'd had for a long time. And he said, "That'll teach you the proper marks of respect to be given to the chief." . . . Unbeknown to me he went up and told the senior engineer, "If he comes up and complains give him some more punishment. Stop his leave and [give him] extra work. But if he doesn't complain, give him a recommend."[82]

Though petty officers exercised considerable power, sailors had ways of dealing with those whose abuse of authority went too far. "Sometimes mysterious accidents happened. A dark night, a fall into the harbor, a fracas ashore, the tyrant being discovered with serious injuries, the clip of a hatch tampered with and the hated victim removed to hospital."[83]

It was this system of voluntary and enforced cooperation and conviviality on the mess deck that made life at sea bearable and encouraged the friendships, teamwork, mutual confidence, and support that psychologists would later label "cohesion." Contributing to this cohesion was the fact that the Royal Navy was fundamentally a volunteer service. For most sailors, life at sea, with all its demands and discomforts, was the life they had chosen. For men from the mines and factories of Edwardian England, it was seldom a complete change for the worse. And, above all, they were constantly reminded, by their distinctive uniforms, by frequent ceremonies, fleet reviews, and royal visits, that they were different, special, the object of deep, if ill-informed, admiration by most of their countrymen. As Signalman William Sweet had accurately observed, the navy was "the cat's whiskers."

Yet if the British bluejacket, by 1914, was better educated, more technically sophisticated, and more self-reliant than his predecessors of thirty years before, the same could not be said of British officers. Indeed, it seemed that the higher the rank, the more doubtful the qualifications of the commander. Churchill found a "frightful dearth of first class men in the vice admirals and rear admirals lists."[84] "The fact is that in 1914 the Royal Navy was almost totally unprepared for war and remained in that condition for most of the period 1914 to 1918," wrote Commander Stephen King-Hall. "There were a number of shockingly bad admirals afloat in 1914. They were pleasant, bluff old sea dogs with no scientific training; endowed with a certain amount of common sense, they had no conception of practice and theory, of strategy and tactics."[85]

It was fortunate for the Royal Navy that its strongest potential enemy, the German navy, was led by men whose outlook was even more parochial, narrow, and reactionary than their own. This was surprising, for Germany was, in most respects, the most modern country in Europe. German steel production was equal to that of Britain, France, and Russia combined. Her chemical and electrical industries led the world. Her population was the best-educated on the continent, and German universities set the standard for scholarship throughout the world. The excellence of German technology, science, and medicine was acknowledged everywhere. Germans were proud of their well-earned reputation for efficiency and scientific management.[86]

All of these qualities were reflected in German warships. By 1908, German designers, making the best of the crisis caused by the dreadnought revolution, were planning ships that in some respects were superior to their British counterparts. German warships had wider beams, heavier armor, and an extensive network of watertight compartments to protect against shellfire and underwater damage. The wide beam also made them very steady gun platforms. The Germans' leadership in optics gave their ships excellent range finders and night fighting equipment.

To a greater degree even than the Victorians, the Germans of the Wilhelmian era believed they could do anything. The German navy was a symbol of that confidence. "Our fleet embodied the sense of power resulting from the unification of the empire," wrote Admiral Reinhard Scheer, who commanded the German High Seas Fleet in World War I.[87] Unlike the German army, whose recent ancestor was the Prussian army, the German navy was a genuinely national institution. As such it was widely popular with upper-middle-class professionals, businessmen, civil servants, and academics, who imagined it to be a more inclusive, more progressive, more truly "German" organization than the army.

Yet just as the archaic superstructure of the Kaiser court and feudal nobility remained awkwardly atop the modern, rationally organized society of Wilhelmian Germany, so an exclusive and backward-looking officer corps presided over the technological marvels of the German navy. Indeed, there was a close connection between the two, for the Kaiser took an active, sometimes obsessive interest in his navy and its officers. Much of the social prestige of the navy was derived from this royal patronage. Kaiser Wilhelm II frequently appeared in naval uniform, attended naval reviews and maneuvers, even dabbled in ship design. One German seaman even claimed that the navy's uniform regulations, which specified that the blue-lined edges of the woolen jerseys were to reach to the collarbone, was due to "the very particular desire of Her Most Serene Highness, the Empress Augusta Victoria, who could not abide hairy male chests."[88] The naval officers basked in the reflected glory of the imperial connection and aspired to equal social status with the elite guards officers of the army.[89]

In fact, less than 14 percent of German naval officers came from noble families. Instead, sons of industrialists, academics, military officers, and higher civil servants flocked to fill the vacancies for officer cadets. Ministers, generals, and admirals worried that these parvenus might lack the proper "domestic upbringing." After all, as the Prussian admiral Ludwig Schroder observed, "the military leader does not need intelligence but character."[90]

Yet if there were relatively few members of the aristocracy among the naval officers, the new aristocrats of wealth and education did their best to adopt the lifestyle and values of the old. Aspiring officers were expected to acquire proficiency at such pasttimes as riding, dancing, and fencing. Officers were frequently in debt and frequently drunk. Dueling was not uncommon, and courts of honor judged all matters of personal conduct and morality concerning line officers.

The three officer branches of the German navy were actively hostile toward and suspicious of one another. The engineer officers were outranked by even the most junior line officers and lacked most of the prestige and social prerogatives of "the line." Both they and the deck officers engaged in continual wheedling and agitation to share in more of the perquisites of the line. In 1906, the chief of the naval cabinet, Admiral Georg von Müller, proposed that in the future, engineer officers be recruited exclusively from the lower middle class so as to ensure "that a certain social gulf was permitted to exist between the executive officer corps and the naval engineer officer corps." Admiral Tirpitz declared British and American attempts to develop a single officer corps with common engineer training a "huge mistake."[91] Given the low prestige but demanding educational qualifications for the engineer corps, it is not surprising that the German navy suffered from a chronic shortage of highly qualified technical personnel throughout World War I.

Like their British counterparts, German sailors were relatively well-educated and technically adept. About half of the navy's enlisted force filled technical billets of one kind or another as compared to one eighth in the German army.[92] By the turn of the century the Germans, like other navies, had been obliged to abandon the practice of recruiting exclusively in coastal areas and ports and to call on the more highly skilled and better-educated young men of the industrial towns and cities.

German sailors were proud of the navy's prestige and of their ships. Seaman Richard Stumpf recalled that "whenever a squadron or formation executed a maneuver very quickly and precisely it would receive a sign of approval. . . . The crews of the various ships used to compete with one another for this praise. . . . Each of us would be very proud if our ships finished three seconds earlier than the others. Later on the matter would be discussed in the taverns where other sailors were taunted at their defeat."[93]

Unlike the long service ratings in the Royal Navy, who were signed on for a minimum of twelve years, German sailors served only three-year enlistments. "A continuously high standard in battle practice was not to be attained under our system," Admiral Scheer recalled. "Because every year a portion of each crew went to the reserve and had to be replaced by recruits, who for the most part came to the sea as utter novices."[94] German sailors also spent less time at sea than their British counterparts and new ships tended to get brand-new crews, thus ensuring the most advanced battleships would have the least experienced sailors. In a navy in which commands tended to be filtered through three layers of officers and petty officers, the line officers' remoteness from the seamen was probably even greater than in Britain. Certainly punishments were even more savage. Flogging continued to be ordinary punishment aboard ship until 1918, and seaman boys were routinely tied to the mast for minor infractions.[95]

Technically excellent, the German navy possessed only very fragile cohesion and lacked a strong sense of identity and tradition. Despite their highly advanced weapons, they, like the British, had been preparing for a kind of war that was already outmoded. Yet even had the British and German officers been a collection of geniuses and visionaries, they would still have faced formidable difficulties in the looming world conflict. They were going to war with a primary weapon system, the dreadnought, that had been in existence less than ten years and with which they had, at most, a half-dozen years of practical experience. Other weapons, the wireless, the submarine, the airship, and the airplane, were even newer and less well understood. While most naval leaders and their admiring public firmly believed that navies would continue in the grand old way, all signs pointed to a future war of a kind never seen before.

FOUR

"THE BIGGEST SEA BATTLE THAT HAS EVER BEEN"

I t was a little after 2:00 P.M. on May 31, 1916. The normally fog-shrouded and misty North Sea was, on this day, sunny and brilliant. The light cruiser *Galatea* and her sister ships of the First Light Cruiser Squadron were completing a sweep of the area to the east of the coast of Denmark. The *Galatea*'s wireless officer was taking advantage of the rare good weather to sun himself on the quarterdeck when the bugle suddenly sounded action stations. Later, he wrote, "I had heard that we were going to action stations for drill purposes sometime during the afternoon. So I strolled forward to my station. . . . But as I went up the ladder onto the foc's'le I was deafened by the report of the foc's'le six inch gun firing and was almost blown down the ladder again by its blast. I nipped into my little W/T hutch . . . and as I entered there rattled down the communications tube from the upper bridge, in a small brass case, the first enemy report of the Battle of Jutland: 'enemy in sight consisting of one destroyer.'"[1] The main fighting fleets of Britain and Germany, comprising more than 250 warships including almost 60 dreadnoughts and over 100,000 men, were approaching at a combined speed of almost fifty miles an hour to fight their first and only naval battle of World War I.

After almost eighteen months of false alarms and fruitless sorties and patrols, few could believe that the day had finally come. "I remember feeling distinctly skeptical about it," wrote one British officer, "recalling the many previous false alarms we had experienced."[2] In the battleship *Malaya*, the sailors "only realized we were in for proper action when we heard . . . firing ahead."[3] In the German battleship *Helgoland*, sailors "felt immeasurably relieved, at the word 'enemy has commenced firing.'"[4]

Two years earlier, in August 1914, the mood and expectations had been quite different. "We expected immediate action," recalled Chief Steward Ernest G. Fox of the battleship *Marlborough*. "Most men, most officers expected to meet the German fleet almost within a day or two."[5] As war began, the armies of the Great Powers all took the offensive. Germany attacked France, Russia attacked Germany, Austria attacked Serbia, and France attacked Germany. Their navies were expected to do the same. "The real tone was of high expectation that at any moment the enemy might come out and the long anticipated fight might take place," wrote an officer in HMS *Lion*.[6] "We all thought it was going to be one glorious bang and that was it," observed Signalman George Haigh.[7] Aboard the battleship *Dreadnought*, officers even began surreptitiously sharpening their swords.[8]

In Germany, anticipation ran just as high. "There was only one opinion among us from Commander in Chief down to the latest recruit about the attitude of the English fleet," wrote a German admiral. "We were convinced that it would seek out and attack our fleet the minute it showed itself and wherever it was. This could be accepted as certain from all of the lessons of English naval history."[9] Seaman Richard Stumpf assumed it to be "almost inevitable . . . that the English, having started the war, would also have to attack. And if they did not come we would go and seek them out."[10] All German naval training and maneuvers had been based on the belief that a battle would be fought early in the war. The scene of the battle was expected to be in the area between the North Sea islands of Borkum and Heligoland, called the Heligoland Bight, close to the German coast where the Elbe and Weser rivers flow into the sea.

Yet the first weeks and months of war passed without the twentieth-century Trafalgar anticipated by all. There was a British raid into Heligoland Bight at the end of August that resulted in the sinking of three German light cruisers and a destroyer. But this action, called the Battle of Heligoland Bight, was not followed by any similar British moves or any German counteroffensives. The Germans stayed close to their North Sea bases in the estuaries of the Elbe and Weser. (The Kaiser had, in any case, ordered that the battleships were not to be risked without his permission.)

Meanwhile, the British battle fleet, now called the Grand Fleet, moved to its war base at Scapa Flow, far to the north in the Orkney Islands. Here it remained while the German armies drove deep into

France and Belgium, and while the French and British checked the Germans just short of Paris, then drove the Germans back at the cost of more than 300,000 casualties. Here it remained while, in Poland, a small German army under Hindenburg and Ludendorff destroyed two Russian armies and inflicted enormous casualties; and while the war in the west settled into murderous positional warfare along a continuous line of trenches from the English Channel to the Swiss frontier. "Here is the finest war the world has ever seen and I am out of it," lamented one young naval officer.[11] The apocalyptic visions of the most bellicose military writers and strategists had been amply fulfilled on the battlefields of France, Belgium, and Poland. But what about the titanic clashes at sea envisioned by navalists like Mahan, Tirpitz, Fisher, and a host of other experts and popular writers?

In the last years of peace, both British and German strategists had concluded that modern mines, long-range coastal guns, and the threat of torpedo boat and submarine attacks had made an offensive into Heligoland Bight or a close blockade of the German coast extremely hazardous, if not impossible. The same consideration also made a German operation in the English Channel extremely dangerous. The British therefore abandoned their plans for a close blockade of the Heligoland Bight and its German bases. Instead, from their bases at Scapa Flow and northern Scotland the British controlled the waters between southern Norway and the northern tip of Scotland, cutting off all shipping to and from Germany. The British didn't need to worry a great deal about the North Sea's exit into the Channel, since it was as hazardous for the Germans as the bight was for the British. In essence, the Royal Navy instituted a distant blockade, effectively closing the exits from the North Sea to the German fleet. The distant blockade lacked the drama and excitement of a seek out and destroy mission against the German fleet, but it was effective. By the winter of 1915, there were already serious shortages of food and raw materials in Germany.

If the distant blockade was disappointing to the British, it caused positive consternation to the Germans. All German naval policy, even the design of warships, had been based on the assumption that in the event of war the British fleet would attack the Germans near their bases in the Heligoland Bight. Even when German maneuvers in the spring of 1914 had demonstrated that this was extremely unlikely, the admirals had refused to face the implications of their strategy.[12] "What will you do if they do not come?" Tirpitz reportedly asked his fellow admirals a few months before the outbreak of war. Now the Germans were forced to confront precisely that question. The German battle fleet, called the High Seas Fleet, was more than twice as powerful as the combined French and Russian battle fleets. Its thirteen dreadnought battleships and five battle cruisers were all less than six years old. Yet it was still inferior in numbers to the Grand Fleet, which had twenty-one dreadnoughts and four battle cruisers in the North Sea. That disparity in numbers made the German admirals disinclined to risk a battle until the British fleet had been whittled down considerably.

How the whittling down was to be accomplished remained unclear. German torpedo boats lacked the range to carry out a night torpedo attack on Scapa Flow in the way that Togo's torpedo boats had done at Port Arthur. Underwater weapons—mines and submarines—appeared more promising. Mines were laid in waters adjacent to British bases and submarines were stationed outside these bases and in other areas likely to be frequented by British warships. The British submarines did the same in areas adjacent to German bases. By the end of the first month of August, both sides had lost smaller ships to submarines and mines.

The war began to settle into a pattern of patrols, raids, feints, and ambushes by destroyers, minelayers, submarines, and minesweepers. These small ships, hardly noticed in the bombastic navalist literature of prewar years, now bore most of the burden of the actual fighting. The Germans scored a spectacular success when submarine U-9 sank the old British armored cruisers *Cressy*, *Hogue*, and *Aboukir* in late September 1914. More than 1,400 men, most of them middle-aged reservists and young naval cadets, were lost. This incident, together with the sinking of the old cruiser *Hawke* a month later, convinced both British and Germans that the submarine was a potent weapon.

Admiral Sir John Rushworth Jellicoe, commander in chief of the Grand Fleet, needed no convincing. A hero of earlier colonial wars and one of the most respected officers in the navy, he was a walking collection of contradictions. Brave and absolutely unflappable in battle and with a brain as fast as a computer, he was also a hypochondriac and a chronic worrier. An outstanding organizer, he could never bear to delegate authority. A technical expert and a specialist in gunnery, he lacked confidence in the technical qualities of his own ships and admired the better armor and underwater protection of the Germans. It was "highly dangerous," he warned Churchill, "to consider that our ships as a whole are superior or even equal fighting machines."[13]

Jellicoe's immediate subordinates, the commanders of the Grand Fleet's battleship squadrons and divisions, were an uninspiring lot. "My vice-admirals are always a little shaky," Jellicoe told the First Sea Lord. "[Sir George] Warrender gets awfully deaf at times and is inclined to be absent minded. [Sir Cecil] Burney is first rate when in good health which unfortunately is not always the case. . . . He suffers from bad rheumatism. . . . His depression is inclined to make him pessimistic and over cautious. [Sir Lewis] Bayly is, I fear, occasionally a little mad. [Sir Frederick Doveton] Sturdee is full of fads."[14]

Vice Admiral Sir David Beatty, who commanded the Grand Fleet battle cruisers, a semi-independent force, was an exception to this pattern of mediocrity. Like Jellicoe a hero of colonial wars, Beatty, at age thirty-nine, had been the youngest man to become an admiral in the Royal Navy since the eighteenth century. He was a dashing and glamorous figure, married to an American heiress, fond of polo, and a favorite of the press. In contrast to his commander in chief, he was an aggressive fighter and an optimist, perhaps because he lacked both Jellicoe's imagination and his depth of technical knowledge. Beatty needed to concern himself less about his subordinate commanders since he had most of the handful of flag officers whose brains had not gone to sleep. They included Rear Admiral William Pakenham, of Tsushima fame, and Rear Admiral Sir Horace Hood.

The situation at the outbreak of war offered Jellicoe plenty to worry about. The Grand Fleet's main anchorage at Scapa Flow was almost completely unprotected against submarines or even surface attack, and other bases in the north of Scotland were little better. As a result, the Grand Fleet spent the first four months of the war constantly on the move, fleeing from real and imaginary threats by submarines and mines. On one occasion, a seal, mistaken for a submarine, caused twelve battleships to get underway and spend the night at sea. A real submarine sank the light cruiser *Pathfinder* a few days later. Jellicoe shifted the fleet to the west coast of Scotland, then took it entirely out of the North Sea to Lough Swilly on the north coast of Ireland. Scapa's defenses were gradually improved with searchlights, booms, antisubmarine nets, and minefields so that by the close of 1914 the base was pronounced fairly secure.[15]

As autumn gave way to winter, with still no prospect of a meeting with the German fleet, British impatience and frustration grew. The only truly decisive fleet actions occurred far away, off the coasts of South America. Vice Admiral Count Maximilian von Spee, commanding the German Asiatic Squadron, had successfully crossed the Pacific, eluding the dozens of Australian, British, French, and Japanese ships searching for him. Arriving off the west coast of South America, he defeated a British cruiser squadron under Rear Admiral Christopher Craddock in a battle off the Chilean coast near the town of Coronel. The armored cruisers *Goodhope* and *Monmouth* were sunk with all hands in Britain's first naval defeat in more than one hundred years.

In England the initial shock and incredulity over Coronel soon turned to anger at the Admiralty, which was widely blamed for pitting Craddock's old cruisers against the more modern, more heavily armed, and faster German squadron. "Craddock's death and the loss of the ships and gallant lives in them can be laid at the door of the incompetency of the Admiralty," wrote Admiral Beatty to his wife. "They have as much idea of strategy as a board school boy."[16]   •

As First Lord of the Admiralty, the irrepressible Winston Churchill had always been a controversial figure. Only thirty-nine years old, he was the embodiment of energy and boldness, but his understanding of naval operations was limited. He received little help from the Admiralty, which was not an effective organization for planning and directing a worldwide naval war. The First Sea Lord was Prince Lewis of Battenberg, a relative of the royal family and one of the most respected officers in the navy. Like many other senior officers, he was in poor health, and he had also been the target of a campaign of slander and rumor about his supposed "German sympathies." The chief of the war staff, Vice Admiral Frederick Charles Doveton Sturdee, though a fine seaman and tactician, was a poor manager and a doubtful strategist. His ill-considered decisions had nearly turned the Heligoland Bight operation into a disaster and had contributed to the loss of the Cressy, Hogue, and Aboukir as well as to the Coronel debacle. Sturdee could not delegate authority and did not understand the functions of a war staff. Many of the other senior flag officers were also micromanagers. Junior officers were afraid to stand up to their bosses and were seldom consulted by them.

A few days before Coronel, Prince Lewis finally resigned. To replace him, Churchill called upon Admiral Fisher, now seventy-three years old but still full of fire and energy. Only hours after receiving word of Craddock's defeat, Fisher and Churchill were planning countermeasures. In a bold gamble, Fisher persuaded Churchill to detach three battle cruisers from the Grand Fleet and send them secretly to the West Indies and South Atlantic to deal with von Spee. The new Princess Royal was sent to the West Indies and the Invincible and Inflexible were ordered to the South Atlantic. To command the striking force, which also included three cruisers and two light cruisers already in the South Atlantic, Fisher selected Sturdee, whom he was eager to be rid of.

In early December, Sturdee's fleet annihilated von Spee's squadron in the Battle of the Falklands. Only one German ship escaped. British losses were trivial. The battle cruisers lived up to Fisher's expectations, outrunning the enemy and choosing the range to allow their larger 12-inch guns to be used to maximum effect. British fire had not been particularly accurate, however, despite weather that had been unusually clear and bright, conditions unlikely to be encountered in the North Sea.

News of the victory of the Falkland Islands caused considerable elation in Britain but could not obscure the fact that while the British army had suffered more than 200,000 casualties in its retreat from Mons and at Ypres the Grand Fleet had done little beyond maintain the blockade. "When is the navy going into action Jack?" a Royal Navy stoker recalled being asked frequently by civilians. "'Right now' some fed up sailor would reply, suiting action to the word and whaling into his tormentors. Many sailors were very touchy on the question, which more often than not, was asked in all sincerity. It was not our fault that the High Seas Fleet refused to fight. . . ."[17]

If the relative inactivity of the battle fleets was a disappointment and source of embarrassment to the Royal Navy, it was a devastating psychological blow to the German navy. As early as August, Seaman Richard Stumpf complained that "everything is the same as it used to be. The monotony has a depressing effect. Expressions of disgust at our inactivity are heard everywhere."[18] The endless round of "patrols" and cautious, fruitless sorties a few hundred miles into the North Sea simply added to the frustration and impatience. "Only the army was praised. It was supposed to have done everything," recalled Chief Petty Officer Karl Melms of the battle cruiser *Von der Tann.* "We were very annoyed with our regime. When we went to sea, we went only 30 or 40 miles past Heligoland and back. We were furious."[19]

After one of these false starts, Stumpf wrote: "By noon we gave up all hope of action. . . . I no longer care if we get to fight or not. Once again our principal interest is food, recreation and shore leave. . . . It is extremely difficult to be kept waiting all the time in the knowledge that our tremendous power is being wasted. The atmosphere is strained and embittered. One senses it among the officers and men. . . . No wonder all of us wish to leave the ship. Whenever there is a call for volunteers for the submarines or for the [naval infantry brigade in] Belgium, everyone steps forward."[20]

Admiral von Tirpitz, ever conscious of domestic politics, warned, "If we come to the end of a war so terrible as that of 1914 without the Fleet having bled and worked, we shall get nothing more and all scanty money there may be will be spent on the army."[21] Tirpitz, as Navy Minister, was powerless to direct operations, however.

Though German sailors took pride in the victory of Coronel and the success of the U-boats, many held the same sort of doubts about the superiority of their equipment that Jellicoe had raised about British ships. These misgivings were reinforced by the performance of German cruisers and destroyers early in the war. German light cruisers, almost all armed with 4.1-inch guns, had proved unequal to their British equivalents armed with 6-inch guns. This had led to the loss of the famous German raider *Emden* and contributed to the disasters at Heligoland Bight and the Falklands. "If *Leipzig, Nuremburg,* and *Dresden* and *Koenigsburg* had even come close to their opponents in artillery, they would never have stood by helplessly while they were being sunk," observed Seaman Stumpf.[22]

The German destroyers, called torpedo boats, were even more of a disappointment. The torpedo branch had always enjoyed great prestige in the German Navy, similar to that accorded to fighter pilots in later decades. When in civilian clothes, German torpedo boat officers often wore straw hats with a red "Stander-Z," the naval signal for "attack," embroidered on their hatbands.[23] Yet, with their limited range and scant gun armament, the torpedo boats had been generally ineffective. "On August 28 [the Battle of Heligoland Bight] our 'black ones' had an opportunity to show what they could do in battle. But they achieved nothing," wrote Stumpf. "The English destroyers ran right over them, sank the lead ship (V-187) and damaged several others severely. They came limping back to port with their tails between their legs and were no longer confident they were unbeatable."[24]

German sailors in more responsible positions than Stumpf and his shipmates shared his concern about German equipment. Rear Admiral Franz von Hipper, who commanded the German battle cruisers, worried about the fact that British battle cruisers were not only faster but were also armed with 12- and even 13.5-inch heavy guns as opposed to the 11-inch guns used in most German battle cruisers.[25]

The Germans continued to avoid action until the Grand Fleet and High Seas Fleet could meet on more equal terms. In fact, such a condition was already at hand in October and November 1914. Only one British capital ship, the *Audacious,* had been lost to the German attrition war of mining and submarine attacks, but Sturdee's operations in the South Atlantic had led to the absence of three battle cruisers, and four other ships were in dock. The distinguished naval historian Paul G. Halpern estimated that by October 1914, the actual ratio between the British and German fleets, in terms of combat-ready battleships and battlecruisers, was 22:19, a situation that continued into December.[26]

The Germans lacked precise information about the readiness and strength of the Grand Fleet, but they were aware of the loss of the *Audacious* and, after the Falklands battle, must have known that two and possibly more battle cruisers had been detached from the Grand Fleet. Yet the Germans did nothing. In contrast to the German army's Great General Staff, renowned for its effective planning and rapid assessment of changing operational situations, the German Naval Command, divided between the ineffective and vacillating Kaiser, the fleet commanders, and the Naval Staff, still had not effectively come to terms with a war situation so different from what it had anticipated. In addition, neither the Kaiser nor the High Seas Fleet commander, Admiral von Ingenohl, was inclined to take great risks for victory. The most that von Ingenohl was willing to undertake was a series of raids on the east coast of England by the battle cruisers to bombard coastal towns and provide cover for minelaying.

On November 3, Hipper's battle cruisers bombarded Yarmouth and one of his light cruisers laid mines in the area. Hipper's shells missed the town entirely, and he failed to sink the handful of antiquated British ships in the harbor. Von Ingenohl brought the German battle fleet to the edge of Heligoland Bight but no farther. In any event, his warships were not needed, since the British Admiralty's response to the raid was too slow and bumbling to interfere with Hipper's escape. As the German High Seas Fleet returned from the bight, however, the armored cruiser *Yorck* strayed into one of the Germans' own defensive minefields and was sunk.[27]

While the Germans prepared for another raid, one of the most important naval successes of the war had been achieved by a British fishing trawler in the North Sea. In late November, the ship's nets unexpectedly brought up a heavy object, a chest from a sunken German torpedo boat. The chest contained code and cipher books including the principal German code used between Berlin and its embassies, consulates, and ships on foreign station. The British had already acquired a copy of the principal High Seas Fleet code from the Russians, who had seized it from the wreck of the German light cruiser *Magdeburg* in the Baltic. They also possessed a copy of the German merchant ship and U-boat codes, captured by the Australians from a German merchantman. In the hands of talented cryptographers, whom the Royal Navy had recruited from Oxford and Cambridge, these finds were sufficient to enable the British to decipher and read German naval messages throughout the remainder of the war.

On December 16, Hipper's force sortied for another raid on the east coast of England. This time, von Ingenohl brought the High Seas Fleet as far as the Dogger Bank, the sandbanks in the middle of the North Sea, in support. British codebreakers deduced from intercepted messages that another raid was being planned but not that the High Seas Fleet was coming out. The Admiralty ordered Beatty's battle cruisers and a battle squadron of six dreadnoughts under Vice Admiral Sir George Warrender to intercept Hipper. Jellicoe protested strongly against dividing the fleet.

He was proved right: Warrender and Beatty's squadron, cruising near Dogger Bank to cut off Hipper's retreat, ran head on into the path of the German High Seas Fleet. In the early-morning hours, in high seas and bad weather, Warrender's destroyers exchanged fire with cruisers and torpedo boats of von Ingenohl's battle fleet. "Here at last," commented a British Naval Staff study, "were the conditions the Germans had been striving for since the beginning of the war. . . . The destruction of War-render's squadron could, at one blow, have completed the process of at-trition and placed the British and German fleets on a precisely even footing."[28]

Ingenohl, however, feared that he might have run into the advance elements of the entire Grand Fleet. He ordered a turn to the southeast back toward Germany. Had von Ingenohl held on for another ten min-utes, he might have earned a far larger place in the history books along-side DeRuyter, Nelson, Teggethoff, and Togo. As it was, Warrender and Beatty were spared a nasty surprise and were left free to try to ambush Hipper, who had gone on to bombard the towns of Scarborogh, Hartle-pool, and Whitby. In squally weather in the late morning, the *South-hampton*, flagship of Commodore William Goodenough, who commanded Beatty's light cruisers, sighted the German light cruiser *Stralsund* and re-ported this contact to Beatty. As he exchanged fire at long range with the *Stralsund*, Goodenough was joined by the light cruiser *Birmingham*. Goodenough could see the *Stralsund* being joined by two more light cruisers and additional torpedo boats. These were the screen of Hipper's battle cruisers and Beatty's squadron was just to the east, between the Germans and their base.

Goodenough failed to report the appearance of the additional Ger-man cruisers, however. And consequently, Beatty ordered the light cruis-ers *Nottingham* and *Falmouth*, which were headed for Goodenough's reported contact, to resume their position five miles ahead of the British battle cruisers and continue to look for the rest of Hipper's squadron. *Southampton* and *Birmingham* were left to deal with what they still be-lieved to be a single enemy cruiser.

That was bad enough, but worse error was to follow. Beatty's flag lieu-tenant was Lieutenant Commander Ralph Seymour, who, throughout the war, was to demonstrate an impressive talent for choosing exactly the right signals to completely baffle Beatty's subordinates. In this case, Seymour neglected to word the signal specifically to *Falmouth* and *Not-tingham* but addressed it to all four of Goodenough's light cruisers. Be-lieving that the signal applied to him, Goodenough obediently broke off his engagement with the German cruisers and turned to the north-northeast toward Beatty and away from Hipper.

Hipper evaded Beatty only to run into Warrender's battleships a few minutes later. The battleship *Orion,* of the second battle division, had a clear view of the Germans, and their captain begged the division commander, Rear Admiral Robert Arbuthnot, for permission to open fire. Arbuthnot's reply was "No, not until the Vice Admiral signals 'open fire.'" While they dickered, the German ships drew farther away and disappeared into a squall.[29]

In late January 1915, radio intercepts again warned the British of another German raid aimed at the British fishing grounds around the Dogger Bank. This time Beatty caught up with Hipper early on the morning of January 24. With visibility over twenty miles and the Germans more than two hundred miles from safe waters, it seemed that Beatty's five faster and more heavily gunned battle cruisers would easily annihilate Hipper's four, one of which, the *Blücher,* was actually only a large armored cruiser.

Trouble began for the British almost immediately when one of the battle cruiser captains misinterpreted Beatty's signal and fired at the wrong ship, leaving two German battle cruisers to fire unopposed at Beatty's flagship, *Lion.* In the first phase of the action, the *Blücher* was crippled and the battle cruiser *Seydlitz* had half of her main armament knocked out. The *Lion* was hit by several shells and had to fall behind the pursuit. The other battle cruiser commanders were having trouble reading Beatty's flag signals, which even when they could be read were very confused and confusing.

Rear Admiral Sir Archibald Moore, who was now in tactical command, interpreted one of *Lion's* ambiguous signals to "attack the rear of the enemy" to mean "attack the *Blücher.*" That ship was already damaged and straggling behind the German battle cruisers. Moore's division, the *Indomitable* and *New Zealand,* abruptly turned hard left to attack the hapless *Blücher.* Seeing this, the battlecruiser *Tiger* also turned toward the *Blücher.* Captain Brock of the battle cruiser *Princess Royal* was certain a blunder had been made but had no choice but to follow the *Tiger* or take on Hipper single-handed. While Brock and Beatty watched in rage and frustration, the British ships finished off the *Blücher,* which put up an unexpectedly tough fight, and allowed the German battle cruisers to escape in this encounter, which became known as the Battle of Dogger Bank.

Beatty berated his captains and admirals for failure to use their common sense and take the initiative in the two encounters with Hipper. "Had he the slightest Nelsonic temperament in him, he ought to have gone on regardless of signals," wrote Fisher concerning the captain of the *Tiger*. "In war the first principle is to disobey orders; any fool can obey orders!"[30]

What Beatty and Fisher had in mind would, by the end of the century, be recognized as a fundamental principle of success in war: that in battle an officer should seek to carry out the *intention* rather than the literal orders of the commander. Yet to expect this sort of understanding of British naval officers in 1915 was unreasonable, even fantastic. Those officers had made their career in a service in which initiative was seldom tolerated, much less encouraged. "Nelsonic temperament" was unlikely to be found in a system that rewarded those who carried out orders smartly and meticulously.

Arbuthnot, Goodenough, and Moore, whose lack of initiative had been so strikingly displayed in the North Sea operations, were not atypical weak links in the chain. In fact, the former two were known for their unusually aggressive attitudes. No officer in the Royal Navy before 1914 had been encouraged to pay much attention to problems of command, tactics, or operational art. Promotion and advancement went to junior officers who excelled in ship handling, navigation, and knowledge of new technologies, especially gunnery. How the new weapons were to be used received far less attention. As for senior officers, they often understood neither the new technology nor how to use it.

Beyond these human and institutional weaknesses in the Royal Navy, there were other problems in communicating with and directing the complicated new fighting machines of the Grand Fleet. These problems, in what would now be called "command and control," arose, first, from the sheer size of the forces involved. Even disregarding Beatty's battle cruisers, Jellicoe had more than 150 ships under his command when the Grand Fleet was at sea. In addition, the North Sea environment made it hard to control ships through visual signaling, as Beatty had so painfully discovered.

By 1914, wireless telegraphy or radio had become widely available, with ranges and capabilities far exceeding anything in the Russo-Japanese War. Jellicoe, with his interest in technology, was well aware of the potential of wireless. However, he saw it as a danger as well as an opportunity. Messages sent by wireless could be received by enemies as well as friends. Even without the type of enormous code-breaking successes achieved by the Admiralty, it was still possible to gain valuable information from studying the origin, frequency, quantity, and other characteristics of wireless messages. Jellicoe, therefore saw as his principal challenge not the exploitation of wireless communication but the limitation and control of messages so as not to disclose information to the enemy.

With barely adequate means of command and control, with flag officers and captains unaccustomed to acting on their own initiative, Jellicoe believed he had no choice but to prepare a detailed written guide to his subordinates governing operation under every possible contingency. Called the *Grand Fleet Battle Instructions*, these guidelines filled some seventy closely printed pages. This was micromanagement on a breathtaking scale, and Jellicoe has been roundly criticized for adopting this method of command and control. Far better to have developed a commonly understood game plan or "doctrine" through frequent personnel meetings and discussions between the admiral and his subordinates. Yet given the mind-set and professional experiences of most of his commanders, it seems unlikely this would have proved a fruitful approach. Men in their forties and fifties who had been conditioned from boyhood to avoid any sort of analytical and critical thinking were unlikely to be transformed into bold and independent leaders simply by being required to attend meetings.

That left the *Grand Fleet Battle Instructions*. As Jellicoe's critics have emphasized, these were far more concerned with avoiding a defeat than winning a victory. Jellicoe's preoccupation with German mines and submarines was as strong as ever. He believed that a principal German aim in any encounter would be to lead the Grand Fleet into some sort of ambush by submarines or into a newly planted minefield. This meant, in effect, that even if the Grand Fleet should be lucky enough to catch the German Fleet outside the protection of the Heligoland Bight, the British would be unable to pursue aggressively for fear of torpedo attacks by German destroyers and submarines. In addition, German warships were believed to carry mines to be dropped overboard into the path of a pursuing enemy.

About the only way the British were likely to win a decisive victory under these circumstances was if the German fleet obligingly remained within range to slug it out with the Grand Fleet in a prolonged gunnery duel. Jellicoe knew that was unlikely, but he also knew that as long as the Grand Fleet continued to exist as a superior force it could carry out its essential war-winning mission of maintaining the blockade of Germany and safeguarding Britain's worldwide lines of communications. The destruction of the German battle fleet would not necessarily ensure defeat of Germany, but the loss of the Grand Fleet would almost certainly lead to a British defeat. Jellicoe, observed Churchill in an oft-quoted remark, "was the only commander who could lose the war in an afternoon."

The Battle of Dogger Bank with the loss of the *Blücher* and heavy casualties in the battle cruiser *Seydlitz* served to further lower the morale in the High Seas Fleet. Many sailors saw the departure of the other ships leaving the *Blücher* at Dogger Bank as a betrayal. Von Ingenhol was sacked and replaced by Admiral Hugo von Pohl, a hero of the Boxer Rebellion. Von Pohl continued von Ingenhol's practice of sweeps into the North Sea not far from Heligoland. By this time, most of the naval high command were lobbying for a campaign of commerce warfare by submarines to counter the increasingly damaging British blockade.

In February 1915, the Germans announced that all the waters around Great Britain and Ireland constituted a war zone in which all Allied shipping would be sunk without warning. Germany had only a few dozen submarines, but they proved highly effective, sinking more than 2,500,000 tons of shipping by May of that year. The sinking of neutrals and passenger ships, however, brought the Germans close to war with the United States. Against the protests of most of the admirals, the German government ordered the cessation of the unrestricted submarine campaign in April 1916.

Given the extreme reluctance of the Germans to risk battle with the larger British fleet and the cautious attitude of Jellicoe, which was fully supported by the Admiralty, a major battle between the two main fleets seemed highly improbable. Nevertheless, on May 31, 1916, the improbable happened.

In May, Admiral Reinhard Scheer, who had succeeded von Pohl and was an advocate of a more aggressive strategy for the High Seas Fleet, received approval for a sortie by the entire High Seas Fleet into the North Sea in the direction of the Skagerrack, the strait between Norway and Denmark. Scheer had no intention of taking on the entire Grand Fleet, but hoped to pick off any detached elements that might come out in response to his advance. In any case, U-boats would be stationed off naval bases in England to ambush British ships as they came out.

British signals intelligence learned about the planned German sortie even before Scheer sailed, and the Admiralty ordered Jellicoe from Scapa Flow and Beatty from the Firth of Forth to take position near the area of the North Sea called the Long Forties, due west of Denmark, ready to meet or head off the Germans. In the late evening of May 30, Jellicoe's battle squadrons began to steam out of the bleak waters of Scapa Flow. At the same time, Beatty's battle cruisers began to glide down the Firth of Forth toward the open sea. Aboard the *Lion*, Chief Gunner Alexander Grant stood next to Major of Marines F.J.W. Harvey as the ship passed beneath the Forth Bridge. Major Harvey told Grant he felt uneasy because the ship's mascot, a lucky cat, had been left behind in the hasty departure.[31] By 1:00 A.M. on May 31, three hours before Scheer's departure, the entire Grand Fleet of thirty-seven battleships and battle cruisers was already at sea.

As dawn broke over the North Sea, British sailors could view the spectacle of the entire Grand Fleet under way. It was a sight few of them would ever forget. From the flagship, *Iron Duke*, "as far as you could see, looking over the bows, there would be ships going down over the horizon. And as far as you could see astern, more ships. And each side to port and starboard would be cruisers and destroyers, really a breathtaking sight."[32] Seen from a distance, the Grand Fleet appeared simply as huge columns of smoke on the horizon. "Then the cruisers spread ahead . . . would come into sight, and then, at last this huge armada of anything up to thirty battleships advancing in five or more columns surrounded by a close screen of destroyers. This was a spectacle the like of which will never be seen again."[33]

That morning, Hipper and Scheer were heading almost due north toward Norway. Meanwhile, Jellicoe steamed southeast to rendezvous with Beatty's battle cruisers between the Long Forties and the Skagerrack. Around 2:00 P.M., Beatty had just turned north toward his rendezvous point with Jellicoe when the *Galatea*, the easternmost ship in his screen, spotted a Danish merchant ship and closed in to investigate. As she approached the merchantman, the *Galatea* sighted two German destroyers.

The *Galatea*'s wireless report, "Urgent, two cruisers, probably hostile, in sight bearing ESE, course unknown," reached Admiral Beatty at 2:20 P.M. Beatty's battle cruiser force was steaming about sixty miles ahead of Jellicoe. With Beatty's flagship, the *Lion*, were five other battle cruisers, *Princess Royal*, *Queen Mary*, *Tiger*, *New Zealand*, and *Indefatigable*; four new Queen Elizabeth–class battleships under Vice Admiral Hugh Evan-Thomas; fourteen light cruisers, including the *Galatea*; and twenty-seven destroyers.

The two German cruisers—actually destroyers—reported by the *Galatea* were advanced elements of Hipper's scouting force of five battle cruisers, five light cruisers, and thirty destroyers. Hipper was about fifty miles from the rest of Admiral Scheer's High Seas Fleet, which comprised sixteen dreadnoughts and six older battleships with additional light cruisers and destroyers.

Both Beatty and Hipper altered course toward the position of the contact. To Lieutenant Heinrich Bassinge in the light cruiser *Elbing*, "the enemy cruisers seemed to increase like rabbits. Each time I looked they seemed to multiply, first two, then four, then six, eventually eight, but still no firing."[34] Once he had the British in sight, Hipper turned southeast to lead Beatty toward the High Seas Fleet. Beatty also turned south to cut off the German line of retreat. Evan-Thomas's battleships, steaming five miles from Beatty, had missed a critical signal to alter course and continued for about ten minutes in the wrong direction, putting them out of position to take part in the first phase of the action.

Watching from the cruiser *Southampton*, Lieutenant Stephen King-Hall "caught a faint distant glimpse of the silvery hulls of the German battle cruisers, though owing to the great range, only parts of their upper works were visible for short intervals. . . . As our battle cruisers came into line both sides opened fire."[35] Machinist Otto Frost, who was aboard a torpedo boat, recalled that "the air became misty with smoke, despite the sunshine, and the boiling sea took on a greenish hue."[36] Well before 4:00 P.M., heavy shells were falling all around the British as German battle cruisers fired at distances of more than nine miles. Blasts from their own turrets blew salt water and dust into the eyes of those on the weather decks.[37] Aboard the *New Zealand*, Petty Officer William Read had the plate of his false teeth cracked by the force of the turret blast, and Admiral Pakenham had the back of his mackintosh blown off.[38]

"With each salvo fired by the enemy I was able to see distinctly four or five shells coming through the air," wrote *Derfflinger*'s gunnery officer. "They looked like elongated black spots; gradually they grew bigger and then—crash they were here. They exploded on striking the water or ship with a terrific roar."[39] A midshipman described the flight time of a heavy shell as seeming "more like thirty minutes than the thirty or so seconds it actually is. A great ripping gush of flame breaks out from the enemy's guns and then follows a pause in which one can reflect that in that great no-man's land, two or three tons of metal and explosive are hurtling towards one."[40]

The explosion of a heavy shell on a ship usually caused numerous fires to break out everywhere in the area of impact.[41] One 12-inch shell hit caused "a sheet of golden flame along with strong stink and inpenetrable dust. Everything seemed to fall everywhere with an appalling noise."[42] Noxious gases emitted by the exploding shells filled the nearby compartments, incapacitating many who had managed to survive the explosion. Fire hoses that had not been wrecked by the explosion were turned on the rapidly expanding fires in the area. The result was "about four inches of water on all the mess decks from the firehoses and washing in it were odds and ends of clothing, boots and burnt articles," recalled marine private H. Willhons, who served in HMS *Lion*. Loss of power often accompanied fire, causing sailors to "stumble about through the water in the dark, striking matches or by the dim light of a candle."[43] Fire-fighting parties had to work their way gingerly around the sharp metal edges of decks and bulkheads torn up by an explosion. Molten lead dropping from lead-sheathed electrical cables on the ceiling bulkhead added to the hazards.

There was also the threat of additional fires. A capital ship's big guns were mounted on a turntable in a heavily armored gunhouse that sat atop a long vertical shaft several decks deep. Below the gunhouse were "handling rooms" with hoists and conveyor belts for shells and propellant; the magazine where the ammunition was stored was below the handling rooms. In battle a considerable amount of ammunition would often be out of the magazine, waiting to be loaded into the hoists or the guns. If a shell exploded in the vicinity of this ready ammunition, a conflagration could result, with flames traveling quickly down the turret from the gunhouse through the hoist and into the handling rooms and magazines, incinerating everyone in their path and setting off additional explosions.

The majority of sailors on both sides had no direct view of the fighting. Men stationed below the weather deck would have at best only a partial, indirect, and distorted knowledge of the general course of events or even what was happening to their own ship. "A modern ship in action is divided into two separate worlds," observed the medical officer of a battle cruiser. "The one, stationed in the conning tower, control positions and turrets . . . the other between decks in the engine rooms and stokeholds, in the shell rooms or magazines and here and there between decks working as fire parties, repair parties or first aid parties. The absence of news and the enforced idleness at the commencement of an action when one can simply hear the ship firing and neither know what enemy is being engaged nor what course the action is taking is undoubtably very trying. . . ."[44]

"This kind of fighting demands the purest form of courage," concluded stoker "Clinker Knocker" writing about the boiler room of a man-of-war in action. "If a shell put the forced draft fans out of action we would be charred to cinders by liquid flame in the back flash which would surely follow if the air pressure were cut off. And if a shell wrecked our boilers, we would be boiled. We must not let our imaginations run riot. . . . A man has to exercise perfect mastery over his emotions, carrying out his duties in a mechanical manner. I glance at my two companions. I know they are thinking the same things I am. We laugh! Each tries to convey to the other that we don't give a damn. But it is a pretense, and a poor one to boot."[45] Deep in the handling room of a German battleship waiting to open fire, Seaman Richard Stumpf found that "we had nothing to do so we yelled and carried on without restraint. Deep in our hearts we were all afraid and tried to still our fear by making noise."[46]

Approaching and diverging at the combined speed of a modern automobile on an expressway, the two fleets tore along in roughly parallel directions but at widely varying distances with frequent changes of course. During the first twenty-two minutes of the action, the distances between the opposing ships changed at an average rate of 350 yards each minute.[47] In an age before radar and computers, the task of hitting a distant enemy ship under these conditions was difficult indeed. It was no longer practical to have the big guns of a ship laid, trained, and fired independently as at the Battle of Tsushima. Instead, a gunnery officer controlled the entire process of aiming and firing the guns. From gun control positions on the foremast high above the deck, spotters observed the fall of shot and reported "overs" and "shorts." Range takers observed the changes in range using range finders equipped with powerful optical instruments. Utilizing all this information, the gunnery officer and his assistant determined the range and deflection and transmitted this information to the gun crews.

Both British and German gun control personnel had primitive slide rules and manual calculators to help process all the complex information flowing in from rate takers, spotters, and range finders. The British apparatus was far more sophisticated than the German, but the cumbersome and inflexible Deyer system of fire control that the Royal Navy had favored over the far more advanced Pollen system actually worked less well in coping with the frequent and rapid course and range changes of the first phase of the battle than even the more old-fashioned German system. In addition, differences in British and German training practices probably gave an edge to the Germans. The British had trained their gunnery personnel for steady fire at long ranges, as in a chase. This was understandable, since the British expected to be pursuing a weaker foe, as at the Falklands and Dogger Bank. The Germans, on the other hand, had to be constantly aware of the need to escape or evade the British fleet when necessary. Consequently they trained their gunnery personnel for constant changes in range and rapid alterations of course.[48] German stereoscopic range finders, manufactured by the famous Zeiss optical firm, were also superior to the British.[49]

During the first phase of the battle, the light and wind conditions also favored the Germans, and their shooting was far more accurate. The *Lion* was hit by three shells, which put her Q turret near the middle of the ship out of action. With the gunhouse on fire, the severely wounded turret commander, Major F.J.W. Harvey, managed to reach the voice pipe and order the men in the handling room below to close the magazine doors and flood the magazines. This action saved the ship, for fire soon spread from the gunhouse into the other parts of the turret, igniting shells that were being held ready in loading cages outside the magazines. A tremendous explosion rocked the *Lion*. "Flames shot as high as the masthead."[50] Yet the ship remained afloat, her speed unimpaired.

The *Indefatigable*, the last ship in the line, was not so fortunate. Around 4:15 P.M., two 11-inch shells from the German battle cruiser *Von der Tann* set off a magazine explosion below her forward turret. "There was an interval of about 30 seconds," recalled an officer in HMS *New Zealand*, the next ship ahead. "At the end of the interval . . . the ship completely blew up. . . . The main explosions started with sheets of flame followed immediately afterwards by a dense dark smoke. . . . All sorts of stuff was blown high in the air, a 50 foot steam picket boat, for example, being blown up about 200 feet, apparently intact though upside down."[51] In the *Lützow*, Admiral Hipper could hardly believe his good fortune. When one of his officers reported the sinking of the *Indefatigable*, he gave a sardonic reply: "It was only when he had seen for himself that there were only five instead of six ships that he . . . rewarded Commander Prentzel with a grateful glance and lit a fresh cigar."[52]

Less than half an hour later, the battle cruiser *Queen Mary* was hit by a salvo that penetrated her armor deck and started a fire in her magazines. In her midship Q turret, an explosion "broke off [her] left gun outside the turret and the rear end fell into the working chamber. . . . The turret was filled with flying metal and several men were killed. A lot of cordite caught fire below and blazed up and several people were incinerated."[53] Shortly thereafter, the *Queen Mary* also blew up, taking with her all but twenty of her 1,286 men.

Hipper's good fortune would not last. A quarter of an hour before the sinking of the *Queen Mary*, Evan-Thomas's fast battleships had caught up with the battle cruisers and now had the Germans in their sights. "There had been much talk in our fleet of these ships," recalled von Hase. "They were ships of the line with the colossal armament of eight 15 inch guns, 28,000 tons displacement and a speed of 25 knots. They fired a shell more than twice as heavy as ours."[54] And with their heavy guns, the most modern fire control equipment, and the best trained gunnery personnel in the British fleet, Evan-Thomas's battleships were soon scoring hits on the German battle cruisers at a distance of more than 19,000 yards. To relieve the pressure on his big ships, Hipper ordered a torpedo attack by his fifteen escorting destroyers led by the light cruiser *Regensburg*. They ran head-on into a flotilla of twelve British destroyers that Beatty had already ordered to attack the German battle cruisers.

Shaking violently as they tore along at over thirty-five miles an hour, the British destroyers opened fire and maneuvered to take position for a torpedo attack. "There then followed a glorious sort of disorganized melee in which destroyers of both sides were dashing about at 30 knots in all directions," recalled one British officer.[55] "The din was ghastly," wrote sublieutenant David Wainright of the destroyer HMS *Nomad*. "We were going all out, the ship shivering with speed. Our three 4 inch guns were all firing; the German destroyer shells were exploding around us, the projectiles from the big ships whistling overhead and the perpetual thunder of their guns."[56] As the destroyer *Nicator* opened fire, her second torpedo jammed leaving the torpedo tube. The warhead partially broke off from the body of the torpedo and hung by a few remaining screws precariously over the side. While the fully armed warhead bumped and scraped against the ship, sailors desperately struggled to detach it using a boat hook. After some tense moments, the warhead's remaining screws parted and it tumbled into the sea, barely missing the *Nicator*'s propellers.[57] As in earlier encounters, the Germans found themselves outgunned by the British. Two German destroyers were sunk, and the others fired their torpedos without scoring hits. The British scored only two hits, sinking the destroyer V-29 and causing minor damage to a battle cruiser.

While the destroyers were in the midst of their dogfights, Hipper was relieved to see thick clouds of black smoke to the south. Scheer's battleships were joining the battle. Around 4:30, Goodenough in the *Southampton*, two or three miles ahead of Beatty, also sighted the Germans and steamed toward the German fleet. After the communications error that had caused him to lose contact with Hipper's ships during the Scarborough raid, Goodenough reportedly vowed that "if ever he saw another German ship he would not lose sight of her until one or the other was sunk."[58] Now Goodenough closed to within 12,000 yards of the High Seas Fleet before radioing to both Beatty and Jellicoe, "Have sighted enemy battlefleet bearing approximately southeast, course of enemy north." Under fire from at least four German battleships, Goodenough's squadron kept contact with the German fleet and continued reporting to Jellicoe.

Having sighted the German fleet a few minutes after Goodenough, Beatty reversed course to lead the Germans toward the Grand Fleet. With the opposing fleets now steaming steadily north with relatively few changes of course or speed and with better light, British gunnery greatly improved. Although the Germans continued to score hits, their battle cruisers now came under a devastating rain of giant 15-inch shells from Evan-Thomas's fast battleships. The *Lützow* was hit by four 15-inch shells and a 13.5-inch shell from the *Princess Royal*, destroying her communications and causing flooding.[59] The *Derfflinger* was hit by three 15-inch shells, which started fires on the lower decks and filled the ship with smoke and gases from the exploding shells.[60] The *Seydlitz* was hit by no less than six 15-inch shells. One shell hit in the forward electrical engine room. Fumes from the burning wreckage were blown by the ventilating fans into the engine room spaces. The fans had to be stopped. Heat in the engine room spaces rose to more than 105 degrees. Shells also disabled the electrical lighting in the bunkers, but the stokers steadily continued filling their coal baskets by flashlight. Holes in the *Seydlitz*'s hull admitted tons of seawater, and after an hour her bow was only just above the waterline. "The water rose higher and higher round the fore turret," recalled Engineer Commander Otto Looks, "until it was up to our necks and we felt like men cut off by the tide in a sandbank."[61] Yet *Seydlitz* continued to steam and fight.

To add to Hipper's troubles, three more British battle cruisers now came on the scene. Jellicoe had sent the Third Battle Cruiser Squadron south to reinforce Beatty. Composed of the *Invincible, Inflexible,* and *Indomitable*, the squadron, commanded by Rear Admiral Sir Horace Hood, was fresh from gunnery training exercises at Scapa Flow. Hood was one of the few truly outstanding admirals in the Royal Navy, and under his direction the squadron quickly polished off Hipper's light cruiser screen, disabling the *Wiesbaden* and damaging the *Pillau* and *Elbing*.

Reports from his light cruisers that they were under fire from "many battleships" convinced Hipper and Scheer that they had run into the main British battle fleet.[62] The Germans turned south and east away from the supposed position of the enemy battle fleet, and Hipper ordered his destroyers to attack Hood's battle cruisers. The German destroyers were able to score hits on only one British destroyer, which later sank. Had the Germans continued on their previous course, they might have encountered Jellicoe much earlier, with the Grand Fleet still in cruising formation. As it was, Hood's intervention had the effect of masking the approach of the Grand Fleet, which, by that time, was less than thirty miles away.

Aboard his flagship, *Iron Duke*, Admiral Jellicoe could barely contain his impatience. For almost one hour, from 4:45 to 5:40, he had received no reports from Beatty about the location, course, and speed of the German fleet, even though the mission of the battle cruisers was to act as scouts for the battle fleet. That hour was the legacy of all the complacency, unrealistic training, lack of initiative, and mindless authoritarianism that had characterized the navy's leadership during the previous three decades. Not only did Beatty send no reports, but neither did Evan-Thomas or any of the light cruiser commanders except Goodenough's flagship, *Southampton*. After 5:40 P.M., as Jellicoe's own scouting cruisers began to come in sight of Beatty's forces, a few more reports came in, including additional information from Goodenough's squadron still shadowing the German battle fleet. Twice Jellicoe signaled to the *Lion*, which could now be seen from his flagship, "Where is the enemy battlefleet?" Fifteen minutes after the first signal, Beatty finally replied with information that indicated that the High Seas Fleet was less than seven miles away.

On receiving Beatty's reply, Jellicoe stepped quickly onto the compass platform. The wind whipped against his old Burberry raincoat and white muffler. It was now evident that the German fleet was much closer than Jellicoe had guessed from the few earlier reports and that it was south, on the starboard bow of the Grand Fleet, rather than directly ahead. In the distance he could see only haze and numerous gun flashes. The admiral looked at the magnetic compass card for about twenty seconds. "I watched his keen brown weather beaten face with tremendous interest wondering what he would do," recalled one of his officers. "I realized as I was watching him that he was as cool and unmoved as ever. Then he looked up and broke the silence with the order in his crisp, clear voice. . . . 'Hoist equal speed pendant south east.'"[63] Deployment by equal speed pendant was a new evolution only recently added to the signal book and had never actually been tried by the fleet. Moreover, Jellicoe was ordering a deployment to port, *away* from the direction of the German approach. Jellicoe's chief of staff, Sir Charles Madden, recalled that he wondered "for one ghastly minute if the chief had suddenly gone off his head. He had been waiting and working for nearly two years for this supreme moment. Now it had come, had it proved too much for him? Was he cracking up? And yet as I watched his calm, unruffled demeanor, I felt reassured and still more so when, before all ships had acknowledged the signal, the commander in chief turned to the flag captain and said, 'Start the deployment.'"[64]

The flag captain blew two short blasts on the siren and ordered the helmsman onto the new course. The Grand Fleet was cruising in six parallel columns. The battleship column farthest north continued on a steady course, while the leading ships of the other columns turned together to port, then to starboard as the columns moved into a single line. Madden wrote later that a few days after the battle, he and his staff spent hours reconstructing the battle situation and testing alternate deployments. After many hours of study, they concluded that "deployment by Equal Speed Pendant was not only the best, but virtually the only correct solution. It had taken the commander in chief only 30 seconds in the moment of crisis to arrive at the same conclusion."[65]

Completing its deployment just as the German battleships came into sight, the Grand Fleet was now steaming steadily in a slightly curved line across the head of the German column and blocking its escape route to the east. It was a brilliant maneuver and put the Germans in the position of being able to bring only a few guns to bear against the firepower of the entire British line. Moreover, visibility, such as it was, now favored the British; the leading German ships could see only occasional gun flashes to the north.

The British had still not exhausted their store of bad luck, however. As the Grand Fleet deployed, two armored cruisers, the *Defence* and *Warrior* in Jellicoe's scouting force, pursuing some German light cruisers, found themselves less than 8,000 yards from the German battle line. Unable to see the British battleships, the German concentrated all their fire on the two cruisers. "The ships were practically continuously hidden by splashes," observed a sailor watching from a British battleship. "The *Defence* was hit heavily and blew up in one fearful cloud of smoke and debris. The foretop fell with a sickening splash into the water and then the *Warrior*, herself damaged, listing to starboard and in places on fire, raced over the spot where the *Defence* had been."[66]

The *Warrior* was saved by the battleship *Warspite*. When the *Warspite* was taking her place with Evan-Thomas's fast division at the end of Jellicoe's line, her steering gear suddenly jammed and she steamed in circles within short range of the German fleet. The ship was hit by at least thirteen shells. One shell hit underneath the engineering spaces blowing the "oil tanks to pieces. Everything was in an awful state of dust, oil fuel and filth. A Marine passed the remark 'This will mean a drop of leave.'"[67] Protected by her heavy armor, the *Warspite* was still able to steam and fight after her steering gear was brought under control following a harrowing quarter hour. "I was in the most dreadful state of terror the whole time," wrote a turret officer. "Big gunfire is a beastly thing if you are the target."[68]

During the deployment, much of the damage to the German capital ships was done by Hood's Third Battlecruiser Squadron, which hit Hipper's flagship, *Lützow*, with at least eight heavy shells, leaving her fatally damaged. They also scored three hits on the *Derfflinger* and a minor hit on the *Seydlitz*. However, Hood's flagship, *Invincible*, was hit by a shell that pierced the roof of one of the turrets and ignited the ready shells outside the magazine. This caused the same gigantic explosion that had destroyed the *Indefatigable* and the *Queen Mary*. The *Invincible* blew up, splitting almost exactly in half so that the bow and stern rested vertically on the bottom of the ocean and could be seen protruding out of the water. All but six of the battle cruiser's 1,026 men were lost.

Despite these successes, Scheer was now in a desperate situation. The leading ships of his battle line now faced the six-mile line of British capital ships, which were pouring an uninterrupted rain of shells at the German vessels. His battle cruisers, already badly damaged in their earlier encounters with Evan-Thomas, Hood, and Beatty, were almost out of action. His battleships, outnumbered and silhouetted against the setting sun, were coming under heavy fire, and some had already been damaged.

After only few minutes, Scheer made his decision. Given his slower speed, he could not run for home, nor could he afford to change course and slug it out with the larger British battle line. Instead he ordered a "battle about turn," an emergency maneuver in which each ship beginning with the hindmost successively peeled off from the line, turning a complete 180 degrees into a new line headed in the opposite direction. As the German ships began to disappear into the mist, Scheer ordered a torpedo attack.

For a few minutes, Jellicoe remained unaware of what the Germans had done, and even when he became aware of what had happened he was far from eager to lead his fleet into the fog and mist in hot pursuit of the Germans. Like many other British admirals, Jellicoe believed that German capital ships carried mines and would drop them off their stern into the path of pursuing warships.[69] After turning to avoid the German torpedoes, Jellicoe led his fleet off to the southeast across the path of Scheer's retreat.

Less than half an hour later, Scheer, having reversed course for home, again blundered into the British battle line. Crossing the German T once again, the British scored thirty-five hits on the German battleships and battle cruisers. Seaman Stumpf, in the handling room of an 11-inch turret on the disengaged side of the battleship *Helgoland*, heard a strange sound. "Crash, crash, the sound reverberated. It was the death cry of an English shell. I fell down to the deck and listened. . . . Suddenly I got a terrific slap. All at once everything became still . . . the ship had been hit. 'Thank God,' someone called out, 'now we'll get leave to go home.' He was silenced at once. 'Shut up! Who knows how many got killed.'"[70]

Still unable to see the British line and under increasingly heavy fire, Scheer ordered his battle cruisers to "charge" the enemy battle line to cover another turnabout by the German fleet. The German ship *Lützow*, hit by five more British shells, was already sinking, but the other four battle cruisers complied as best they could and were joined by the German destroyers, which carried out an unsuccessful torpedo attack that again induced Jellicoe to turn away. That was enough to save Scheer, though all but one of his battle cruisers were now damaged and out of action as they steamed off with Scheer to find protection in the darkness of the coming night.

Jellicoe was not willing to fight a night action with the Germans even if he could find them again, but the British fleet still blocked the German line of retreat and Scheer would have to slip by somehow. As darkness fell, both fleets were steaming south "down the sides of a very long, very slender V." If they met at the point of the V, Scheer would be cut off and possibly destroyed. Scheer's ships were too slow to cut ahead of the British line, so he would have to pass by the rear of the British fleet. Jellicoe, anticipating such a move, had stationed most of his destroyer flotillas to his rear.

Neither side knew the exact whereabouts of the other, but Jellicoe arrived at the bottom of the V and passed through it only a few minutes before Scheer's battleships. "The V became an X—the courses of the fleets crossed, neither side was aware of what was happening—and from . . . the hour of midnight onward they began to draw apart."[71]

Crossing behind the British battle fleet, Scheer ran straight into Jellicoe's destroyers and light cruisers. Half a dozen confused firefights broke out between 10:00 P.M. and 2:30 A.M. Commander Stephen King-Hall described one of these encounters between the light cruisers, *Southampton* and *Dublin*, and more than a half-dozen German light cruisers.

At that moment, the Germans switched on their search lights and we switched on ours. Before I was blinded by the lights in my eyes, I caught sight of a line of light grey ships. Then the gun behind which I was standing answered my shout of "fire"! . . . It is impossible to give a connnected account of what happened. The range was amazingly close—no two

groups of ships ever fought at so close a range in the history of that war—
there could be no missing the target. A gun was fired and a hit obtained—
the gun was loaded, it flamed, it roared, it leaped to the rear, it slid to the
front—there was another hit. . . . The action lasted three and a half minutes. . . . In those three and a half minutes we had 89 casualties and 75%
of the personnel on the upper decks were killed or wounded.[72]

Both the Southampton and the Dublin were damaged in this brief but
deadly encounter, and the German light cruiser Frauenlob was sunk by a
torpedo fired by the Southampton.

As Scheer's battleships fought to get clear of Jellicoe's destroyers and
cruisers, the sights and sounds of the fighting were visible from the rear
of the British battle fleet. Jellicoe and his staff could see some of the gun
flashes and searchlights themselves but were certain that the fighting involved only the German destroyers and light cruisers that were scouting
for Scheer or attempting to carry out an attack on the British battle
fleet.[73] Because Jellicoe would never risk his battleships at night in waters full of enemy destroyers, he assumed Scheer would not either.

A number of British battleships actually sighted German battleships
and battle cruisers but refrained from opening fire without orders to do
so. In one case, the battleship Malaya sighted German battleships and
the gunnery officer asked permission to open fire. "The captain refused
on the ground that the admiral was only two ships ahead and therefore
able to see everything the Malaya could!"[74] Lack of alertness due to fatigue and the numbness that comes after a long period of mental and
physical strain could only have reinforced the normal lack of initiative
and reluctance to question authority of Jellicoe's commanders. None of
the British battleships and only a handful of the cruisers and destroyers
made any report to Jellicoe about what they had seen of the German
fleet. Jellicoe might still have cut off the Germans had he known of a signal that the British had intercepted from Scheer asking for zeppelin reconnaissance in the area of Horns Reef near the coast of Denmark. This
message, clearly indicating the German escape route, was not passed on
to Jellicoe.[75]

During the night, Telegraphist A. J. Bristoe, aboard the Iron Duke,
"thought of the changes that could come after a Glorious First of June [a
famous British naval victory over the French in 1794]. More help to our
troops in France and perhaps for us more liberty, an end to the prisonlike
existence at Scapa Flow."[76] Dawn comes at 3:00 A.M. in the summer in
the high northern latitudes. The morning of June 1, 1916, was cloudy

and the sea a choppy green. In the cruiser *Chester*, Engine Room Artificer Gordon Davis was off watch and climbed up to the afterdeck. In the
distance he could see a hovering German zeppelin. For Davis, the sight
of the zeppelin made him "realize immediately that a repetition of the
GLORIOUS FIRST OF JUNE would not materialize."[77] In the *Iron Duke's*
main wireless office, "we waited for the rush of sighting reports. Nothing
came."[78] At that moment the High Seas Fleet was steaming through a
heavy fog off Horns Reef about thirty-five miles east of the British fleet.
One hour later, Jellicoe learned from the Admiralty's signal intelligence
that the German fleet was too far away to be overtaken. "We had them
on toast! How could they possibly avoid us?" thought telegraphist Bristoe. "We had been cheated. Someone or something had blundered."[79]

As the Grand Fleet steamed back to its bases through waters strewn
with wreckage and debris, sailors experienced a range of emotions. Some
shared Bristoe's feelings of surprise and disappointment. Others felt ex-
hilarated and confident of having achieved a success. "We genuinely believed we had won the battle despite our losses," recalled Telegraphist
Frederick Arnold of the battleship *Malaya*. "We were still very much a
fighting force and the enemy had scattered to their bases."[80] Whatever
their views about the battle's outcome, all the survivors shared a common feeling of relief at having come through alive. "Well, I think I have
seen the biggest sea battle that has ever been and I don't want to see another," wrote Steward K. L. Philips of the light cruiser *Yarmouth* one
week later.[81]

Scheer's return to harbor was more eventful than Jellicoe's. The battleship *Ostfriesland* struck a mine and was heavily damaged. The already
damaged battleship *Koenig* had taken on so much water that she had difficulty crossing the harbor bar. The *Seydlitz*, with her decks awash, took
thirty-six hours to work her way back to the Jade River. "We were relieved to be back in harbor, but also very sad as we had the task of bury-
ing our dead," recalled Signalman Franz Motzler of the *Koenig*. "With
great enthusiasm everybody went to battle. . . . But after the battle all
looked different. There was no winner and all our losses seemed so senseless."[82] In the returning battle cruiser *Von der Tann*, the crew received
hot coffee and snacks. However, Chief Petty Officer Karl Melms and
many of his shipmates "did not take them. We lay down on deck in a corner of the ship, we did not care where, and went to sleep as we had not
slept for 48 hours."[83]

FIVE

"SOMETHING NOT QUITE RIGHT WITHIN"

The Battle of Jutland, the largest naval engagement of World War I and the greatest clash of battleships in history, was over. The British had lost three battle cruisers, *Queen Mary*, *Indefatigable*, and *Invincible*; three old armored cruisers, *Defence*, *Warrior*, and *Black Prince*; and eight destroyers. The Germans had lost the battle cruiser *Lützow*, four light cruisers, five destroyers, and the old battleship *Pommern*, torpedoed by a British destroyer in the last minutes of the confused night actions of June 1 and sunk with all hands. Outnumbered by almost 30 percent, the Germans had inflicted far greater losses on the British and quickly claimed a victory. The British, having twice lost the chance of inflicting crippling damage on the German battle line and then trapping the High Seas Fleet in the North Sea only to let it slip by in the dark, felt thoroughly frustrated.

Strategically little had changed. A British journalist observed soon after the battle, "The German fleet has assaulted its jailor but is still in jail."[1] Indeed, as far as the ratio of strength between the High Seas Fleet and the Grand Fleet was concerned, Scheer was far worse off than before the battle. Six of his surviving capital ships were out of action, while Jellicoe had been able to replace all but two of his six lost or seriously damaged capital ships with new ones just coming out of dock or joining the fleet. Had the High Seas Fleet renewed the battle in the next week or two, the ratio of undamaged ships would have been 24:10 as compared to 37:21 before Jutland.[2]

The outcome of the battle is often explained in terms of the characteristics and performance of British and German technology, with German technology receiving a far better rating. British battle cruisers were too lightly protected, making them vulnerable to fatal hits by only a few heavy shells. German ships sacrificed speed and gunpower for superb protection and watertight integrity. The *Lützow*, the only modern German capital ship sunk at Jutland, absorbed twenty-four heavy-caliber hits and still had to be sunk by German destroyers after her crew was taken off. The *Seydlitz* received twenty-two heavy hits and remained afloat, as did the *Derfflinger*, which received seventeen.[3] British ammunition and shells were more prone than German to explode if they caught fire, a primary factor in the loss of the three British battle cruisers. In addition, British shells in some cases tended to break up before penetrating very far into the armor of the target ship. In spotting the fall of shot, German optical instruments were clearly superior to the British. The result was that in most encounters, the Germans usually scored the first hits. On the basis of this type of analysis, one eminent historian has suggested that the result of the battle could be explained in a sentence: Jellicoe was "a sailor with a flawed cutlass."[4]

Yet a closer examination reveals that in fact the two technologies came close to canceling each other out. If the British had problems with their shells, the Germans had troubles with their big guns, as one model tended to jam. If Scheer's tougher ships made it easier for him to survive a gunnery duel, his inferior speed made it likely he would have to fight at a tactical disadvantage. Moreover, the British had some "unsinkable" ships too, in the case of the battleship *Warspite* and the battle cruiser *Tiger*, each of which survived fifteen heavy-shell hits. If the Germans' range finders were superior, their overall fire control system was more primitive than that of the British. In some German battleships, the big guns were still aimed and fired individually instead of being aimed and fired simultaneously from a central control point as in all British battleships.

Overall, the gunnery performance of the two sides was about equal. The British scored about a hundred heavy-caliber hits on German ships while the Germans scored about eighty-five, but the British fired more rounds. The German battle cruisers scored almost two and a half times as many hits as Beatty's battle cruisers, yet Hood's Third Battle Cruiser Squadron had the highest percentage of hits of any of the capital ships at Jutland. All in all, the Grand Fleet battleships scored one and one half times as many hits as Scheer's battle squadrons.[5] German destroyers had once again proved inferior to their British counterparts.[6]

Instead of saying that Jellicoe had a "flawed cutlass" it might be more accurate to say that his team was still learning to fence, but then so were the Germans. The critical components in the battle were all related to the human element. Leadership and command and control are the most obvious, and the conduct of Beatty, Jellicoe, and Scheer has been endlessly debated. With radar still in the future and no aerial reconnaissance, these admirals were still largely dependent on what they could see from their own ships, which, in the fog and mist of the North Sea, was often very little.

Most of the captains and flag officers in the Grand Fleet had come up the ladder of command in the days before the introduction of wireless. They had little understanding of electronic communications.[7] In almost all ships, the signals officer, who had general authority over the ship's wireless telegraphy department, was not himself a qualified wireless communicator but an officer or chief petty officer who had come from the ranks of flag signal experts.[8] It is not surprising, then, that many ships' wireless departments were undermanned and poorly organized or that captains tended to be overly dependent on visual signals. Some commanders did not even bother to repeat important messages by wireless, instead relying on flag signals, which were almost invariably hard to spot in the mist and smoke. During the battle "the din in W/T (wireless) headphones from the transmissions of two huge nearby fleets was such that many signals were hopelessly drowned out and stressed out operators had to be relieved every ten to fifteen minutes."[9] Often noted as well was the overcentralization and lack of initiative on the part of British commanders, who seldom took action on their own, no matter how compelling the circumstances, and failed to keep their commander in chief informed of the rapidly changing tactical situation.

Even in the matter of big guns, projectiles, and armor, the decisive considerations concerned human judgment, organization, and training. The reason that Beatty's flagship, *Lion*, could survive more than a dozen heavy shell hits and still steam and fight had less to do with the thickness of her armor or the quality of German shells than it did with the organization and leadership of her chief gunner, Alexander Grant. Grant recognized early on that there were inherent safety hazards in the common British method of handling charges and shells. He observed that "the magazine crews, full of enthusiasm and determined that the guns should not have to wait for cordite, had removed every lid from all the cases, piling up the handling room with shells," thus making the turret vulnerable to catastrophic explosion, especially from high-angle fire.[10] Against the opposition of every turret officer on the ship, Grant instituted new precautions and rules for turret crews, which limited the number of charges and shells that could be out of the magazines at any one time. These rules almost certainly prevented the kind of catastrophic ammunition fires and explosions that had destroyed the *Lion's* sister ship *Queen Mary* and two other battle cruisers.[11]

Other ships were not so fortunate. In the *Tiger,* overeager handling room and magazine crews had allowed common shells to be mixed with armor-piercing "to avoid delays."[12] The inevitable result was that shells fired in the same salvo fell in widely dispersed patterns, making effective spotting and fire direction difficult. The same desire to "avoid delays" had prompted the gun crews of the *Malaya's* 6-inch gun battery to bring up "large quantities of cordite charges . . . and shells from the magazine [to be] placed ready in both batteries."[13] A single shell bursting on the gun deck "opened cordite cases all along the battery, [which] soon was an inferno."[14]

These events and others like them demonstrate that even more than tactics and command, it was the state of organization and training in the Grand Fleet that made the critical difference. Jellicoe complained after the war that the Germans had more opportunities and better facilities for gunnery practice than did the British.[15] Beatty's battle cruisers, which did the worst shooting at Jutland, had had the least amount of gunnery practice. One officer recalled that during the eight months prior to the battle "[we] only fired our main armament four times and our armament once." In part, this was because the Firth of Forth area of Scotland was unsuitable for firing practice. Instead the battle cruiser fleet concentrated on training techniques of rapid firing through competitive gun drills. This practice actually encouraged the unsafe practices Grant had tried to suppress in the *Lion*. Hood's battle cruisers, which had the best record at Jutland, had just completed shooting exercises and training the week before.[16]

British destroyers lacked practice or training in offensive tactics, especially torpedo attacks. Vice Admiral Sir Robert Arbuthnot, whose boldness—or stupidity—had led to the loss of the *Defence, Black Prince,* and *Warrior* at Jutland, had been in charge of destroyer training before the war. A notorious martinet, Arbuthnot was interested almost exclusively in physical fitness and the faultless appearance of ships and men. Once the war began, the constant demands on destroyers to screen the fleet, escort convoys, and carry out patrols left little time for offensive training. "The net result was that some destroyers did no torpedo or gunnery practice for months at a time."[17] The Thirteenth Flotilla, attached to Beatty's battle cruiser fleet, had never even operated together as a single flotilla prior to the battle.[18] As a result, the numerous destroyer attacks on the German fleet as it broke through the rear of the British line, on the night of May 31, were largely ineffective. An officer on HMS *Moorson* described one torpedo attack delivered during daylight on the 31st as a "very confused affair." As destroyers tried to get the range for a shot at the enemy vessels, they found themselves constantly obliged to make sudden course changes to avoid collision with other friendly destroyers.[19]

There were many technicians, petty officers, and warrant officers besides Grant who were aware of problems in organization, training, or equipment in the fleet and understood the solutions. Yet the very nature of the Royal Navy precluded any effective action, except in rare cases such as Grant's. "In my mess were a few wise petty officers, experienced in the ways of the service," wrote Telegraphist A. J. Bristoe of HMS *Iron Duke*. "I remember them saying after Jutland that there must be something not quite right within the fleet that small mistakes happen; small mistakes that led to far reaching consequences. . . . They had a feeling that officers could . . . take some of the senior ratings, especially key men, into their confidence, ask them to submit suggestions on any small matters falling within their duties. . . ." Yet Bristoe "could not see it happening. The class distinctions between officers and lower deck were very wide and rigid."[20]

While the performance of weapons and equipment at Jutland may have been a source of disappointment, the performance of ordinary sailors on both sides proved all that might be desired. Naval theorists had feared that sailors might be unnerved by the sights and sounds of modern naval warfare. The sailors of Jutland proved as fatally steady and unshakable as the men of the Somme, however. Indeed, the relative lack of fear among the ship's company was frequently mentioned in recollections of men who survived the battle. "It struck me how unconcerned the men seemed during the scrap and oblivious to the dangers lurking," wrote Engine Room Artificer Arthur Crown, who served in HMS *Shannon*.[21] Torpedoman William A. Parsons "saw no one that was scared" aboard his destroyer,[22] while an officer in HMS *Tiger* reported, "The most marked feature of the action that came under my personal observation was the coolness and discipline of the engine room and artisan staff generally."[23]

An engineer officer aboard the battle cruiser *Seydlitz* described how a rare incidence of panic was handled: "A sudden thud and Leading Stoker Wessels reeled and fell, his cap flying off. Only a glancing blow. Wessels coolly rose, picked up his cap and, muttering something to himself, shoveled on. . . . A few timid youngsters who thought it was a hit through the armor, dropped their shovels in terror. But they were taught better 'Hamburg-fashion' by oldsters and soon pulled themselves together."[24]

Many men observed that they were so preoccupied with their immediate duties that they had little time to worry about anything else. A typical experience was that of Engine Room Artificer Gordon Davis aboard the light cruiser *Chester,* whose battle station was on a platform above the main engine room from which he controlled the port turbines. Immediately prior to the battle, Davis felt "that anal sensation one experiences when something dreadful is going to happen," but once the ship opened fire he "felt quite normal again and in any case had plenty to do to occupy [him] controlling the turbines to the revolutions ordered; reading gauges and temperatures and keeping the engine room register completed."[25] Midshipman R. M. Dick, of HMS *Barham,* recalled, "All of us worked incessantly like automatic machines . . . scarcely conscious of what we were doing. The first hit on the ship came as a tremendous shock, one I am not likely to forget for many a long day, [but] after the first experience we hardly seemed to notice."[26] Other sailors appeared to find combat little different from a drill. Signalman John E. Atrill concluded that "everyone seemed to think we were at ordinary maneuvers instead of engaged in the biggest naval fight during the war."[27] The *Warspite*'s executive officer, Commander Humphrey Walwyn, found "everybody very cheery and anxious for news. . . . The Marines of the port [disengaged] six inch supply room were playing cards on the deck quite happily."[28]

Some men found other preoccupations to take their minds off the immediate threat to their lives. Stoker Samuel Roberts of HMS *Warrior* worried about his younger brother in the battleship *Warspite.*[29] Signalman Reuben Poole "prayed a lot."[30] Electrical Artificer Frank Hall, belowdecks in the battleship *King George V,* was disturbed by the noise and "fearful thuds against the sides. . . . But, on the other hand, I was thinking how proud I shall be to be able to tell my wife and my parents of my experiences."[31] High in the mainmast of HMS *Lion,* Boy Telegraphist Arthur Lewis felt "scared" but also " important" because others were constantly asking him what was happening. "I thought, this is going to end as the greatest battle in history and I have taken part in it."[32]

Ambroise Baudry in his treatise on the naval battle of the future expected that sailors might be shaken by seeing friendly ships on fire or sinking, much as a soldier could be demoralized by heavy casualties in his unit. Yet the sight of three British battle cruisers and a cruiser blown up with obvious catastrophic loss of life appears to have had little negative impact on the men aboard their sister ships. "News of the outside began to trickle in about [the losses in] Beatty's cat squadron," recalled Engine Room Artificer C. B. Clarkson of HMS *Malaya*, "and the only thought then was vengeance and give the enemy some more."[33] Captain G. P. Bigg-Withers of the battleship *Benbow* told his wife that "we saw ships being hit and blowing up, even our own, without a tremor. One just thought 'bad luck' when we saw some 1,000 lives of our officers and men suddenly lost and carried on. It had no effect on us."[34]

Of course, only a small minority of the combatants had an opportunity to observe the battle as a whole, and even these observers often failed to accurately evaluate what they saw. Dozens of Jutland veterans have recalled how they "cheered when passing the wreckage of the *Invincible* assuming that it could only be a German ship."[35] Men out of sight of the action were encouraged by their leaders to interpret news and rumors in the most favorable light. "Cheers were heard every now and again as the good results of our shooting were being passed round the ship," recalled Signalman Atrill. "The first shout was 'we've just sunk a German dreadnought, Kaiser-class.' Followed by loud cheers. Then: 'we've just sunk a cruiser.' More cheers. It was quite good sport as we thought we must be sinking all the German navy. . . ."[36]

Casualties aboard one's own ship were another matter. "Some of the dead were so burned as to be unidentifiable," recalled Telegraphist Frederick Arnold of the battleship *Malaya*. "The living badly burned cases were almost [entirely] encased in wrappings of cotton wool and bandages with slits for the eyes. The few walking cases . . . presented a grim, weird and ghoulish spectacle."[37] Chaplain Thomas F. Bradley of HMS *Tiger* wrote that "the cries of the wounded and burned men were very terrible to listen to. They . . . were sometimes brought in with feet or hands hanging off. . . . A midshipman wounded in several places had his left eye lying on top of a mass of bruised flesh that filled up the cavity of the eye. He was taken to the Captain's cabin and died during the night."[38]

There can be no doubt that sailors found these sights unnerving, and many may later have suffered long-term mental and emotional reactions or post-traumatic stress syndrome. Most veterans reported becoming rapidly hardened to these scenes of horror, however. Signalman Franz Motzler of SMS *Koenig*, passing the kitchen on the way to deliver a message, saw "a dead cook with his head and both arms in the coffee kettle. Several seamen were so thirsty they were pouring coffee from the same kettle into their cups. Who worries about dead men at a time like this!"[39] Similarly, Acting Sublieutenant W. M. Phipps-Hornby "was regaled by the cook with an account of how, on the previous day, he had found his mate lying dead in the waste with the top of his head neatly sliced off, 'just as you might slice off the top of an egg sir' . . . by that time I had become so inured to death and wounds and blood that I was able to listen, unmoved, continuing with my meal [all] the while."[40]

Caring for the large number of casualties taxed medical facilities to the limit. Chaplain Bradley reported that aboard HMS *Tiger* the deck of the casualty clearing station "very soon became packed with wounded and dying men and when fresh cases were brought in, we had some difficulty in avoiding stepping on the others. . . . Morphine was given to a lot of the wounded. After a time . . . we were able to sort them out, putting the slightly wounded in one place and more serious in another."[41] In HMS *Warrior*, the surgeons used one of the bathrooms as an operating theater. They began performing surgery at 9:30 p.m. and went on until 5:00 the following morning, working mainly by candlelight.[42]

Sailors aboard ships that blew up or sank generally fared much worse. Those who escaped the ship were often burned or injured and could not survive long in the water. There were very few occasions during the long battle when ships could stop to pick up survivors. Most warships were forced to pass by at full speed engaging or pursuing the enemy. If survivors were too close to the passing ships they might be drowned by their wake or sucked into the propellers. Shells exploding in the water caused additional deaths among the hapless swimmers.

One of the few men to survive the catastrophic sinking of the *Queen Mary* later recounted the half hour he spent in the water.

> The swell of the battle cruiser squadron passing by washed me under again and I then got hold of a plank. About ten minutes after a division of our destroyers passed and appeared not to see us; in reality they did and signaled for help being unable to stop themselves. That was the worst part and a lot of people gave up hope and sank. I was again washed clear of my piece of wood by the swell of the destroyer but eventually got two pieces of wood under my arms.
>
> HMS *Laurel* then turned up and lowered a boat. . . . They picked a lot of us up [but then were] ordered to make off at full speed as enemy cruisers and destroyers were closing on her. . . . There were still about six left in the water, it was terrible to have to leave them. We only got away just in time, however.[43]

While men found it wrenching to have to leave survivors of their own ships, some British sailors professed to be indifferent to the fate of German survivors. "Had we slowed down to stop to pick them up, it would have been fatal," recalled Signalman J. J. Newman of the light cruiser *Yarmouth*. "Had they been honorable fighters like my own race my heart would have gone out to them but no, they did not deserve it."[44] Midshipman Royer M. Dick "could not help feeling thankfulness that there could be no possibility of our being sent out in boats—as we were in the Falklands—to pick up drowning Germans."[45]

Overall, British casualties at Jutland totaled more than 6,000 men killed. The Germans lost some 2,500 killed. At the Wilhelmshaven dockyard, working parties, picking their way through the burned-out turrets and flooded deck space of a battle cruiser, found a burned-out compartment in which the calcinated dead still stood at their posts. As the hatch was opened, the bodies instantly dissolved. "They heard a faint rustle and all that was left was dust; dust on their hands, their trousers, their boots, dust and fragments of white bone."[46] At Scapa Flow, the entire dockyard staff worked through the night making coffins.[47] In a single afternoon, the British had lost more seamen than were killed in action in the twenty years of war against Napoleon.

Compared to the hundreds of thousands who would be killed on the Somme one month later, 8,500 casualties seem almost trivial. Yet there was a special horror in the kind of instantaneous mass death that naval warfare was capable of producing. More than 1,000 men killed in a few minutes in the *Indefatigable*, *Queen Mary*, and *Invincible*. More than 800 in the German battleship *Pommern*. "The modern naval battle is different from everything else in the world," wrote one of Beatty's officers. "Nowhere else do men band together in such numbers and wielding such powers. . . . And a single stroke of a single weapon might wipe out a thousand lives."[48] Not for another three decades would any weapons of land warfare attain this level of destructiveness, and by then the targets were as likely to be civilians as combatants. Indeed, even while officers and men in the British and German battle fleets were carefully evaluating the experience of Jutland, repairing damage, and preparing for what almost all expected would be a second great battle, an altogether new, more destructive, more all-inclusive naval war was already beginning.

"Some folk will still believe that this war is a grand picnic for us," wrote Signalman John E. Atrill of the battleship *Marlborough* shortly after Jutland. "But let 'arm chair critics' come and have a go and spend a week with us [at Scapa Flow] about December, they would alter their tune, I'm thinking,"[49] By the time of Jutland the Grand Fleet had already spent two winters at Scapa Flow. Unlike the German fleet, which was based near large ports and cities, the British fleet was based at one of the most remote and inhospitable corners of the British Isles. "It was so bleak up in the Orkneys," recalled one sailor, "barren and bleak—just bloody heather everywhere and cold grey seas."[50] The Orkney Islands appeared to be covered mainly by soggy peat and were devoid of trees and most vegetation. "Only very occasionally could the sea be described as 'calm,' even less frequently did the sun shine. Fog and driving mists were often the order of the day. In that confined area strong winds raised short steep seas."[51] In winter, darkness fell around 3:00 P.M., and rain squalls, snow squalls, and howling wind were constant. The dissolute appearance of the terrain reinforced the sailor's sense of loneliness and isolation. "Of those who spent some time in that part of the world it has been said that they passed through three stages. First they talked to themselves, then they talked to the sheep, and lastly, they thought the sheep talked to them."[52]

For new sailors joining the Grand Fleet, the journey began with a twenty-eight-hour trip aboard a crowded troop train, "the Jellicoe Express," from London to Thurso in northern Scotland. From Scrabster, a small harbor near Thurso, men boarded ships for Scapa Flow. "The old boat left and as it passed Dunnet Head we received the full welcome of the Pentland Firth—not just ordinary waves but hills and valleys of deep green sea—the meeting through thousands of years of the Atlantic Ocean and the North Sea, creating a nine to ten knot current."[53] A veteran captain of a Pentland steamer is said to have observed of his passengers, "It was only the hope o' deein' that kept them alive."[54]

New sailors usually arrived to find their ships crowded with additional specialists, stokers, watch standers, and seamen required by war. Even officers found themselves deprived of many of their normal amenities. Aboard Beatty's flagship, *Lion*, the warrant officers' mess, built for twelve, had twenty-four members, some of whom slept in hammocks for lack of cabin space.[55] Officers were sometimes able to go ashore on the barren island of Flotta for a few hours, enlisted sailors almost never.

Confined in their steel boxes, most sailors never saw the sun during most of the winter months. Telegraphist A. J. Bristoe compared his state of mind to that of "long term prisoners."[56] The boredom was broken by only two events: coaling ship and going to sea. Ships were normally on "four hour notice" while in harbor at Scapa, which meant that they had to be constantly ready to get under way in less than four hours. Sailors coped with their enforced confinement in varying ways. "Gambling of any sort," recalled one sailor, "was strictly forbidden and therefore flourished."[57] The most popular game was "crown and anchor," a kind of combination of craps and roulette played on a canvas layout that could be quickly rolled up and concealed at the approach of authority. The proprietors of the game routinely posted scouts on all the approaches to the gaming space and usually had one or more of the ship's petty officers on their payroll. Even after paying these necessary business expenses, operators of crown and anchor games usually ended the month with ten to twenty times the amount they could expect to see in their pay.

Officially sanctioned efforts to combat boredom included concert parties and theatrical entertainments. An old merchant ship, the *Borodino*, which had been converted into a kind of floating PX, was also fitted with a full-size boxing ring and space for several hundred spectators. Those sailors who could not find seats aboard the *Borodino* watched the match from any available vantage point on their own ship's decks, masts, or funnels.[58] Another supply ship, the *Ghourko*, was converted into a floating theater with full-size stages, large seating space, dressing rooms, lighting, and concert pit. Any warship that desired to stage a play or revue could make use of the *Ghourko*'s facilities. Many of these could be very ambitious productions with costumes ordered from shops in the West End of London.

As 1916 gave way to 1917, sailors' frustration at the inaction of the big ships increased. Many believed that after Jutland "the authorities were not going to risk that again and consequently were going to keep us out of harm's way for the rest of the war. There were always plenty of people putting in for a draft to destroyers, submarines, etc."[59] Midshipmen after promotion to sublieutenant "took all possible steps to leave the fleet." The most sought-after posts were in the Royal Naval Air Service, minesweepers, coastal motorboats, and submarines.[60] As it happened, the preferences of sailors and midshipmen proved more prophetic than they knew, for the war was about to enter a new phase in which these small ships would determine the outcome of the conflict at sea.

SIX

"THE MOST FORMIDABLE THING"

There are two things which are going to win or lose this war and nothing else will affect it a damn," wrote Admiral Sir David Beatty in January 1917. "Our armies might advance a mile a day and slay the Hun in thousands, but the real crux lies in whether we blockade the enemy to his knees or whether he does the same to us."[1] Within a few weeks, the truth of Beatty's assertion would be put to the test.

Beatty had succeeded Jellicoe as commander in chief of the Grand Fleet when the latter had gone to the Admiralty as First Sea Lord in December 1916. Neither this development nor any German moves had produced much outward change in the naval war in the North Sea. Admiral Reinhard Scheer had come out on August 18, 1916, relying on the navy's zeppelins to give him plenty of warning of dangers or opportunities. He also had protection provided by U-boats stationed across the British fleet's probable approach routes. Warned by British signals intelligence, Jellicoe also put to sea that August day. It was a pointless exercise, however; a series of accidents and mistakes in reconnaissance by both sides meant that the fleets never met for a full engagement. Scheer's submarines sank the British light cruiser *Falmouth* and the British submarine E-23 damaged the German battleship *Westfalen*.

In early October 1916, Scheer sent out a screen of destroyers to capture prizes in the North Sea. These went as far as the Dogger Bank and were followed by the High Seas Fleet. British intelligence again warned of the raid and diverted shipping out of the path of the raiders. German signals intelligence, noting the large volume of messages, advised Scheer that the British knew he was out. Scheer reversed course and returned to Germany.[2]

In a report to the Kaiser in early July 1916, Scheer had already concluded that "even the most successful result from a high sea battle will not compel England to make peace. The disadvantage of our geographical situation as compared with that of the island empire itself, and the enemy's vast material superiority cannot be coped with to such a degree as to make us masters of the blockade inflicted on us. . . . A victorious end to the war at not too distant a date can only be looked for by the crushing of English economic life through U-boat action against English commerce."[3]

By October 1916, the German high command was already beginning to discuss this type of action at sea, and on January 9, 1917, they reached their fateful decision: they would oppose the British blockade with a new kind of blockade, one calculated to win the war in six months. Berlin announced the resumption of unrestricted submarine warfare beginning on February 1. The U-boats were expected to sink about 600,000 tons of shipping a month. Great Britain, totally dependent on imports, would be starved into surrender. In February, the first month of the new offensive, fewer than one hundred German submarines sank 540,000 tons of shipping. In March the total rose to 594,000 tons.

It is one of the enduring myths of World War I that the British ignored the potential of the submarine until the war revealed its real capabilities. It is certainly true that the first practical seagoing submarines, which began to appear at roughly the same time as the first dreadnoughts, received far less attention in picture magazines, navalist publications, and the popular press than the new battleships. In 1902, Admiral A. K. Wilson, who later succeeded Fisher as First Sea Lord, had pronounced the submarine to be "underhanded, unfair and damned un-English." He proposed that submarine crews should be treated as pirates. Wilson's fulminations not withstanding, other admirals had begun to show a marked interest in undersea warfare. The D-class submarines that had entered service with the Royal Navy in 1908 could remain at sea for a week and had the range to reach the coast of Germany.[4] The potential of such warships had not been lost on the admirals. "From 1908 onwards," recalled an early submarine commander, "submarines had enough success during maneuvers to open the eyes of all senior officers not willfully blind."[5]

Fisher had always favored employing large numbers of submarines in the North Sea to ambush German warships and patrol the German coast. After Churchill became First Lord in 1911, the Admiralty had begun to discuss employing long-range submarines to blockade German bases and developing high-speed submarines to act as a tactical arm of the battle fleet.[6] By the end of 1913, Churchill and the Board of Admiralty had actually started planning to secretly substitute twenty-two submarines for two of the four super-dreadnoughts budgeted for 1914–15.[7] Churchill's intention was to repeat what Britain had achieved in 1906 when the technological surprise of the dreadnought had confused and disrupted the naval plans of the other powers. As he later wrote, "I intended to let the Germans lay down and be thoroughly committed to their whole dreadnought program for the year so that we should be given the advantage."[8] Far from being neglected, the submarine was regarded by the British in 1914 as a kind of superweapon.

The superweapon worked only moderately well. British and German submarines patrolling off enemy bases and routes of approach managed to pick off a number of warships. In addition, they greatly multiplied the anxieties of fleet commanders and inhibited their actions, forcing them to take elaborate and costly precautions. They failed to sink a single dreadnought battleship or battle cruiser, however, making no fundamental difference in the balance of the war at sea. But what if the submarine should be directed against shipping rather than men-of-war? Fisher had raised this possibility on two occasions in 1912 and 1914 in papers prepared for the Admiralty and the cabinet, but neither Churchill nor any of his advisers could believe that "this would ever be done by a civilized power."[9]

The Germans had their own views of what was "civilized." Seven hundred eighty-five civilians, including fifty-nine children and thirty-five infants, were killed when the Cunard liner *Lusitania* was sunk without warning by U-20 in 1915, the first and most famous catastrophe of the U-boat war. And by the end of the war, more than 15,000 British civilians lost their lives in submarine-related attacks along with several thousand other noncombatants whose countries were not even at war with Germany.[10] On February 3, 1917, an American seaman was killed when a German submarine opened fire on lifeboats carrying survivors of the freighter *Eavestone*, sunk off the west coast of England. Three weeks later, on February 25, 1917, the Cunard liner *Laconia*, carrying civilians, including Americans, was torpedoed without warning by a U-boat. Although the ship was listing to starboard, the crew managed to lower a lifeboat down the projecting port side. Damaged in its slide down the ship's hull, the boat rapidly filled with water, but it remained afloat and, with its nineteen passengers, drifted off into the darkness. Near the center of the boat two ladies found it necessary to stand continuously on their feet, so deep had settled the water-logged boat. Even as they stood the icy water swirled about their waists. At half past one o'clock, gentle grey-haired Mrs. Hoy sank down and tucked her head back like a tired child and entered into the last sleep. After this, Miss Elizabeth Hoy's mind seemed unhinged. . . . She kept shaking the hands of the stiffening remains of her mother and pouring endearments into those deaf ears. . . . And one by one, throughout the night the cold fingers of death touched these innocent people until . . . at dawn . . . eleven survivors found themselves shipmates with eight staring corpses. . . . To free the laboring boat from all dispensable encumbrances . . . the sprawling bodies were one by one slid overboard and committed to the sea.[11]

Among the dead were Miss Elizabeth Hoy and Tom Coffey, a seaman. Both the Hoys and Coffey were Americans. By the end of March, at least five American merchant ships had been sunk by U-boats.[12] On April 6, 1917, the United States entered the war against Germany. The German superweapon had brought the most powerful industrial nation and the world's third-largest navy into the war on the side of their enemies. The immediate prospects for Britain remained grave, however, with one out of every four ships leaving the British Isles during the spring of 1917 never returning.[13] In April, 860,000 tons of shipping were lost.

As a man who excelled at imagining all the worst possibilities of new technologies, Jellicoe was neither surprised by nor unprepared for the U-boat onslaught. When Jellicoe arrived at the Admiralty at the end of 1916, he had established a new Anti-Submarine Division under Admiral A. L. Duff to direct the operations of ships and airplanes engaged in anti-submarine work and to coordinate research and development efforts in the area of anti-submarine warfare.

The Anti-Submarine Division's immediate response to the submarine emergency was to organize anti-submarine patrols of trawlers, patrol boats, destroyers, and sloops to hunt submarines in areas where they were most likely to be found. Intelligence reports on U-boats were utilized to try to route merchant ships away from suspected submarine positions.[14]

Although they were called "undersea boats," World War I submarines spent most of their time on the surface, submerging only to attack or escape. German submarines were powered by diesel engines on the surface, but had to use battery-powered electric motors when submerged. The electric motors could propel a submarine only at about one third to one half of her surface speed. In addition, the batteries required frequent recharging, which could only be done on the surface by the ship's diesel engines. Running the diesels submerged would have quickly burned up the air inside the hull.

Even while attacking, U-boat captains preferred to conserve their few torpedoes and sink unarmed merchant ships with the 4.5-inch deck gun. The British attempted to take advantage of this practice by fitting out heavily armed decoy ships, or "Q ships," disguised as defenseless merchantmen. Innocuous-looking Q ships were intended to lure U-boats on the surface within range of their guns and to destroy them. The Q ships enjoyed some successes, particularly early in the war, but by 1917, German U-boat commanders had become very good at spotting these decoys. The general British practice of defensively arming genuine merchant vessels was somewhat more successful, since it at least forced the submarine to dive and attack with one of its scarce torpedoes.

There was no reliable way in 1917 to detect a submerged submarine. Some primitive hydrophones were in use, but they could only be used aboard a ship that was barely moving, since the noise of engines or water against the hull could drown out the noise made by a U-boat. If the U-boat was also moving slowly or lying stationary on the bottom, it would be extremely hard to detect. Moreover, the early hydrophones could give no indication of the direction from which the sounds they picked up originated.[15]

Another method of detection was to moor long lines of wire nets to buoys that would indicate the presence of a submarine. Even if the submarine was not detected, it might become fouled in the net or destroyed by mines attached to the nets. By 1917, these net "barrages" or barriers had become a favorite method for attempting to detect or block the passage of U-boats through narrow channels or straits. German submarines returning to or leaving their bases by way of the English Channel had to pass through a series of nets and minefields stretching from Folkestone to Cape Gris Nez in the Strait of Dover. At night the area was patrolled by trawlers using searchlights and flares to detect any U-boats attempting to maneuver through on the surface.

If a submerged U-boat was detected, it could be attacked by depth charges, large canisters of explosives set to detonate at a certain depth below the water. Depth charges could be dropped or rolled overboard or fired from special depth-charge throwers introduced in August 1917. A single depth charge was powerful enough to destroy a U-boat, but only if it landed very close to the hull. A canister of 120 pounds of TNT had to explode within twenty-eight feet of the submarine to do serious damage.

In any case, relatively few depth charges were available until the fall of 1917. In July 1917, smaller anti-submarine vessels carried only four depth charges.[16]

Despite all British efforts, shipping losses continued to climb. At the end of March 1917, Sir Edward Carson, who had become First Lord of the Admiralty the previous December, wrote to Beatty that the submarine campaign was causing him "grave anxiety and I do not see any daylight in our efforts to combat this menace." Admiral Fisher raised the question "Can the Army win the war before the Navy loses it?"[17] Outlining the course of the submarine campaign for Admiral William S. Sims, the newly arrived American naval representative in London, Jellicoe observed that "it is impossible for us to go on with the war if losses like this continue."[18]

Both Sims and Beatty urged the Admiralty to reinstitute the old system of sailing merchant ships in groups under escort, called convoying, which had served well to protect shipping against raiders in the age of sail. A number of other naval officers and politicians had also urged that this system be tried. Yet to the Admiralty's experts, perched atop their mountain of statistics, reports, and technical studies, the suggestions about convoys appeared merely a product of the ill informed. The Admiralty's own analysis suggested that there were far too many ships sailing to far too many different destinations and too few escorts available to protect them. They doubted whether merchant ships of many different types and nationalities could station in a large convoy and execute the necessary maneuvers for zigzagging or changing course. From a military point of view, convoys were a passive, "defensive" measure that simply resulted in bunching the targets for the U-boats. "The larger the number of ships forming the convoy, the greater is the chance of a submarine being enabled to attack successfully," concluded an official Admiralty study. "A submarine could remain at a distance and fire her torpedo into the middle of the convoy with every chance of success."[19] Patrols and sweeps were "offensive" in nature and therefore to be preferred.

"Offensive patrols" sounded properly aggressive. In reality, it was, in the words of an experienced World War II sub hunter, "like a single rifleman trying to protect a caravan in the Sahara by strolling at random to and fro along the route."[20] Ignorant of naval history and with no real general staff for collecting and evaluating operational information, the Admiralty continued to resist the idea of convoy until the end of April 1917. By that time, losses had become so severe that the anti-submarine division decided that even an unsuccessful convoy could not make things much worse. The entry of the United States into the war meant that many more destroyers and other escort vessels would be available and that convoys could be assembled in American ports. In addition, the Admiralty had belatedly discovered that the number of ships to be protected was far fewer than it had believed. That was because the Ministry of Shipping and the Admiralty had been counting every vessel departing from a British port as an oceangoing ship requiring protection. In fact, only about 250 of the 5,000 weekly arrivals and departures were transoceanic steamers.

On May 10, the first experimental convoy sailed from Gibraltar, and reached British ports without any losses twelve days later. By July, transatlantic convoys were in operation from Hampton Roads, New York, and Halifax, and other convoys operated from Gibraltar, Sierra Leone, and Dakar. The convoy system resulted in an almost immediate reduction in shipping losses. Indeed, only a tiny fraction of the ships in any convoy were ever lost to submarines.

These remarkable results were primarily due to the fact that instead of making ships more vulnerable, as the Admiralty feared, convoys made them far more difficult to locate. As Winston Churchill observed, "The size of the sea is so vast that the difference between the size of the convoy and the size of a single ship shrinks in comparison almost to insignificance. There was in fact nearly as good a chance of a convoy of nearly forty slipping unperceived between patrolling U-boats as there was for a single ship. . . ."[21] Convoys could be warned by radio away from known U-boat locations. And if the convoy was attacked, U-boats exposed themselves to immediate counterattack by the escorting warships.

Yet not all ships sailed in convoys, and convoys were not available to all ports. Submarines continued to sink at least 300,000 tons of shipping per month until June 1918. It was not until May 1918 that British shipping gains through construction, purchase, and transfer of registry finally exceeded the number sunk by U-boats. Greater numbers of submarines were sunk in relation to shipping lost in 1918 as more escorts, and more anti-submarine vessels, and as greater numbers of improved mines and depth charges became available. Code breakers in the Admiralty also became more adept at acquiring and disseminating timely U-boat intelligence. Over the course of the war, the submarine threat was contained primarily by safeguarding the targets rather than destroying the U-boats.

By the end of 1917, war at sea had become almost unrecognizable to those who had thought of naval warfare in terms of big ships with big guns. The submarine, a vessel smaller than any of the ships in the Grand

Fleet, had become "the most formidable thing the war has produced," in the oft-quoted phrase of American ambassador Walter Hines Page.

The submarine was a small pointed cylinder enclosed within a ship-shaped outer hull. The interior space was almost completely occupied by weapons and machinery. At either end were the sub's six torpedo tubes. A large space toward the rear housed the diesel engines, and an adjoining space housed the electric motors for underwater propulsion. In the center of the boat just beneath the conning tower was the control room, a maze of pipes, wires, valves, and levers from which the chief engineer and his assistants monitored the engines, hydroplanes, and ballast tanks that enabled the submarine to surface or submerge.

Forward of the control room, the galley, wardroom, captain's cabin, and officers' sleeping quarters each occupied a space the size of a small railway compartment. The rest of the crew slung their hammocks among the torpedoes, supplies, and machinery. A Berlin newspaper reported in 1917, "One gunner claimed he could not sleep if he did not have two or three of the shells with him in bed."[22] The U-50 class long-range U-boats had eight bunks for their crew of thirty-five enlisted sailors.[23]

"The conditions of life on board of a submarine are in general not much more difficult than on board of other classes," U-boat skipper Kapitanleutnant Freiherr von Forstner told the Berlin newspaper.[24] Forstner's shipmates may have smiled at this breathtaking understatement, for it was in fact the utter dissimilarity between life in submarines and life in other warships that gave submarine duty its unique character.

Submariners in all navies were picked men, chosen for their technical expertise, steady nerves, reliability, and good judgment. In the German navy, candidates had to pass a battery of medical and educational tests before being assigned to the submarine school. Here students were trained aboard a school ship that was fitted with models or mock-ups of submarine controls and machinery. At the conclusion of their course, the successful candidates were detailed to older submarines for practice cruises.[25] The officers were usually young men in their twenties with a sense of self-confidence, fearlessness, and invulnerability ordinarily found only in race car drivers or mountain climbers. It was probably no coincidence that many early British submarine officers were enthusiastic gamblers and poker players.[26] "The submarine officer's job is more a one man job than any other in the navy," observed Lieutenant Stephen King-Hall.[27] A battleship's success in naval combat depended upon entire teams of fire control men, gunners, engineering personnel, torpedomen, and others, but the submarine's battle was controlled and directed by the captain, stationed at his periscope in the conning tower.

Success or failure depended almost entirely on the skill, nerve, and judgment of this single individual.

Submarine crews, usually composed of only a few dozen men, spent weeks in the half-light and stale air of their boat. Men slept and worked in the same set of clothes throughout the voyage. "Water and soap [were] very precious," and few bothered to bathe or shave.[28] "You ought to have seen the privy," declared one U-boat sailor. "You can pump the filth out down to sixty feet deep but deeper than that [the toilets are] shut. . . . But if you can't help yourself there are empty cans lying around." Sometimes the air became so foul that oxygen had to be supplied from bottles.[29] British submariner William Halter remembered that "when we came to the surface and the conning tower was opened at the top the rush of fresh air used to have the same effect as alcoholic drink."[30] Doctors reported that U-boat crews experienced increased incidence of respiratory ailments, digestive problems, and insomnia.[31]

Aboard the U-boats, food was frequently in short supply, and crews could experience nutritional problems unless they were lucky enough to find stores from captured vessels.[32] The American counsel at Queenstown reported that German submarine boarding crews carried "sacks and often plunder the ship systematically taking away tobacco and concentrated foods such as bacon, cocoa and sugar."[33] "Sacks of wonderful American meal, fresh butter, and loads of margarine . . . fine white English bread. English marmalade, ham and beef, bacon and beans, good soap. . . . All of these things were now completely strange to us," wrote a German U-boat sailor upon seeing supplies captured from a trawler during the last year of war.[34] By 1917, after three years of the Allied blockade and the disastrous harvests of 1916–17, hunger was widespread in Germany.

Despite such conditions and a casualty rate of almost 40 percent, the submarine service remained popular in all navies throughout the war. Until the last months of 1918, most U-boat sailors were volunteers. As late as February 1918 the American naval attaché in France reported that "the enlistment of crews of submarines presents no difficulty whatever and there are numerous volunteers."[35] A semiofficial British study of the submarine war concluded that "the discipline of the German submarine crews was never broken. . . . The submarine compliments remained steadfast to the last. Cases of insanity, though by no means unknown, were not so prevalent as one might expect. . . . No instance has yet come to light of a submarine's crew refusing en masse to put to sea no matter how dangerous an enterprise might be before them."[36]

German propagandists and popular writers attributed the steadfastness of the U-boat crews to their devotion to the fatherland. "These men never utter a murmur or a word of complaint at their hardships; indeed they have no time for that," wrote journalist and illustrator Claus Bergen. "At their post of peril on the ocean with death continually lying in wait, they think of nothing but the service of the fatherland like true German seamen and soldiers."[37] Writing after the war, the president of the German Navy League invoked the "will for victory, zest for action and patriotic optimism" of the U-boat crews as an inspiration for German youth.[38]

That U-boat sailors were highly susceptible to "patriotic optimism" was amply supported by their conduct in the 1930s when many became enthusiastic Nazis. Yet patriotism or a sense of duty was hardly sufficient to explain what enabled this determined handful of men, led by officers in their twenties, to persevere in the face of the terrifying hazards and everyday hardships.

It was in fact this shared experience of danger and hardship that gave submarine crews their special discipline and cohesion. "We were like a great family isolated on the wastes of the oceans," recalled one U-boat sailor. "I cannot conceive of a finer or more loyal community of life and labor than that of a U-boat."[39] Naval ceremony and red tape were summarily dispensed with. Officers and men shared the same rations and the same kitchen, although the officers often took their meals at a diminutive table separated by a curtain. "If the officers were dining and a rating needed to pass from one end of the boat to the other, the only barrier between them was the ratings' 'excuse me.'"[40]

"I had to exert myself to keep the aloof pose of a naval officer and not get too friendly because inwardly I regarded each man as a pal," wrote one former U-boat commander. "After all it could not have been otherwise. We were facing death together and a horrible death at that. Whenever I called the men together to speak to them I used to take an especial precaution to keep my dignity so I could go ahead with my remarks without any fear of getting too friendly for the moment with the men who were really the finest and best of friends."[41] It is possible that this officer might have overestimated his men's good feelings toward him. Nevertheless, it is hard to conceive of a commander of a battleship or cruiser referring to his men as "pals" and "best friends."

In Germany, the young U-boat commanders soon became popular heroes. Pictures of famous U-boat "aces" like Otto Hersing, the first U-boat skipper to sink a British warship, and Otto Weddigen, who sank the *Cressy*, *Hogue*, and *Aboukir*, and Lothar Arnauld de la Periere, Walter Forstmann, and Max Valentiner, each of whom sank more than 300,000 tons of shipping, appeared in popular newspapers and magazines and on commemorative postcards. An endless string of popular books and pamphlets celebrated the deeds of the "German David" against the "English Goliath."[42]

The senior officers of the German navy viewed the newfound celebrity of the submarine service with growing unease. If the submarine campaign, "the war of the ensigns and lieutenants," was the decisive element, where did the admirals fit in? The budget department of the Reichsmarineamt worried that emphasis on submarine warfare appeared to "offer prospects for positions only to younger people and not in sufficient numbers for persons in higher stations of life."[43] German admirals told the press in April 1917 that too much attention was being paid to the exploits of the U-boats at the expense of other elements of the navy.[44]

If the U-boat captain was the star, the entire cast played critically important roles. "The affinity between everyone in the boat was not based on close physical contact alone but upon a deep understanding of their dependence on one another for their safety," recalled a British submariner.[45] A mistake or a momentary failure to act on the part of any member of the crew could lead to disaster or death for all of his shipmates.

Submariners were an elite within an elite, the final step in the evolution of the "hands" of the sailing era into a select body of highly trained technician-fighters. Yet if submarine warfare was waged by a small elite, its ultimate impact was to widen the scope of naval warfare far beyond its traditional boundaries.

On the ground floor of Admiralty House in Whitehall on the west wall of a large drawing room overlooking Horse Guards Parade was a huge chart showing the position of all convoys in the waters surrounding the British Isles. A pneumatic tube connected this chart room with the signals intelligence offices on the floors above. As cylinders rattled into the wire basket showing U-boat positions, these too were plotted on the chart.[46] The chart room was the nerve center of the war against the U-boat, a war that involved an enormous number of individuals and organizations ashore as well as afloat. The battle against the U-boats involved not only the opposing fleets but the thousands of cargo ships and their crews along with hundreds of fishing trawlers, coasters, patrol boats, motor launches, and other auxiliary craft, all manned by reservists or civilian volunteers, which maintained the anti-submarine barriers, laid mines, patrolled inshore waters, and escorted convoys. Ashore, the

Admiralty, the Ministry of Shipping, the railroads, stevedores, dockyard workers, welders, blacksmiths, and electricians were all directly involved in the contest against the U-boats. How quickly and efficiently ships could be unloaded, repaired, and built had as great an impact on the campaign as the sinking of a U-boat.

In this way, the tendency toward "total war"—the total mobilization of a nation's manpower, industry, and resources for military victory—that had already engulfed the warring nations of Europe was now extended to naval warfare as well. Nor were the casualties of the new total war at sea only sailors.

In the spring of 1917 the Germans extended their attacks to clearly marked hospital ships under the rationale that these were simply disguised troop transports. In a portent of things to come, the British retaliated by bombing the town of Freiburg in the Black Forest, killing several civilians.

"The brotherhood of the sea was a fine manly free-masonry," wrote one British propagandist. "Not until the coming of the German submarine commander was the brotherhood of the sea destroyed."[47] That was a mild comment beside the rage and amazement expressed by many in the United States and Allied countries at the new style of war at sea. Winston Churchill referred to the submarines as "water rats." Wesley F. Frost, the American consul at Queenstown, a city where many survivors of sunken ships were first landed, ended his careful factual and legal analysis of the German submarine campaign in his book with the assertion that "it becomes indubitable that actual and virulent malice and murder were in the hearts of Prussians." The Germans even lacked "the mitigating excuses—the savage blood, the ignorance, the religious superstition—which have extenuated the crimes of Turk and Templar. The Prussians present the evil prodigy of men of enlightenment, progress and fine idealism, purposely violating their consciences and hardening their hearts into a fierce and cold repudiation of all the principles they had themselves helped to erect."[48] Frost returned to the United States in June 1917 and soon afterward embarked on a nationwide lecture tour. A British edition of his book was published under the title *Devils of the Deep* and a French edition under the title *Assassins of the Sea.*[49]

The Germans reacted to charges of being pirates and assassins with a barrage of self-righteous justifications. The British practice of arming their merchant ships and encouraging them to ram the U-boat if sighted and the even more underhanded practice of fitting out warships disguised as merchantmen gave submarine commanders no choice but to attack without warning. In any case it was the British, with their illegal blockade of Germany, a blockade that extended even to imports of food, who had forced Germany to reply in kind. Watching an unarmed full-rigged sailing ship sunk by gunfire from a U-boat, artist Claus Bergen wrote of "the sadness natural to every true seamen at the sight of the destruction of so splendid a vessel. But in this matter beauty and poetry count as nothing against our duty to the fatherland. If we were to starve like rats in a trap then surely it was our sacred right to cut off the enemies' supplies as well."[50]

At least a few U-boat commanders displayed a real enthusiasm for exercising their sacred right. Lieutenant Wilhelm Werner of the U-55 ordered the crew of the torpedoed merchantman *Torrington* to line up on the deck of his boat. Their life belts were taken from them and the U-55 submerged with the merchant crew still on deck. Lieutenant Helmut Patzig of U-86 sank the clearly marked hospital ship *Landovery Castle* in June 1918, rammed her lifeboats, and opened fire on the survivors in the water. Altogether, eighteen U-boat commanders were officially listed as war criminals by the British.[51]

Not all U-boat commanders behaved in this manner. Some took considerable risks to tow lifeboats to safety or to radio the position of sunken ships, and some U-boat sailors privately expressed reservations about this new style of warfare. Still the Germans ended the war not only unrepentant, but proud of their new "miracle weapon." "Like scarcely any other weapon U-boats have become the common property of all Germans," wrote a naval author.[52] After the war, U-boat sailors were extolled as models of German comradeship, bravery, and patriotism. "A small group of men, bound to each other by a common destiny and all intent upon a mighty purpose," as former U-boat commander Paul Neureuther put it. The U-boat campaign was described as "an heroic epic."[53]

For the British, the U-boat remained a grim threat to the very end. As late as October 1918, the Admiralty was in a near panic over intelligence that the Germans were about to embark on an accelerated program of submarine building that would give them more than three hundred new submarines by the end of 1919. Yet the war was about to end as it had begun, on land, in France and Flanders.

In the spring of 1918, the German army, reinforced by troops from the Eastern Front, where Russia had collapsed the year before, launched the first of five great offensives intended to bring about the collapse of the British and French armies. The German attacks made deep penetrations, in some places of forty miles or more, but they failed to break the Allied armies and the German army suffered heavy casualties. In July as the last massive German offensive ground to a halt, the British and French, reinforced by a large new American field army, attacked all along the Western Front. On August 8, the Germans suffered a crushing defeat in the vicinity of the French town of Amien. On this "Black Day of the German Army," Canadian and Australian troops drove the Germans back nine miles, destroying several divisions and capturing sixteen thousand prisoners. By September, the Germans were back where they had started their offensive in March.

That same month, the American First Army attacked and pinched off the St. Mihiel salient east of the Marne River and attacked the German defenses in the area of the Meuse River and the Argonne Forest. The Battle of the Meuse-Argonne continued to rage until late October as the French and Americans sought to dislodge the Germans from their positions in the rugged terrain, but elsewhere the German defenses were collapsing. In October, while the First Lord of the Admiralty was in Washington explaining the gravity of the new U-boat threat to the Navy Department, British and French armies broke through the main German defenses on the Hindenburg Line. Austrian defenses along the Piave River collapsed, and the Austrians indicated that they were willing to conclude a separate peace. The Germans had already requested an armistice on October 5, and on October 20 they agreed to end submarine attacks on passenger vessels.

"We have arrived at . . . the most likely psychological moment, if ever . . . for the High Seas Fleet to make some demonstration," wrote Admiral Beatty a few days after the German request for an armistice.[54] The German admirals emphatically agreed. The High Seas Fleet had come out only once since 1916. That was in April 1918, when Scheer had brought out his entire fleet to strike at the convoys carrying supplies from Scandinavia to Britain. Since these convoys were protected by an escort of four or five battleships, it had been an excellent opportunity for the Germans to realize their aim of picking off a portion of the British battle fleet. The Germans, observing radio silence, had put to sea without the British learning of their sortie. But the High Seas Fleet sailed on the wrong day to intercept a convoy. While the Germans searched the empty ocean, the battle cruiser *Moltke*'s engines had malfunctioned, crippling the ship. Wireless messages concerning the *Moltke* were intercepted by the British, and the entire Grand Fleet, now reinforced by five American battleships, had sailed from its new base at Rosyth, Scotland, to intercept the Germans near the Long Forties. But the Germans, still having found no convoy, had already begun to return to their bases.

With the beginning of the armistice negotiations in October, the German admirals became frantic to strike some blow that might justify the battle fleet's four years of relative inactivity.[55] Scheer, who had now become head of the navy high command, and Hipper, who had succeeded him as commander of the High Seas Fleet, both favored this course of action. Hipper's chief of staff, Rear Admiral Adolph von Trotha, declared that "a battle for the honor of the fleet in this war, even if it were a death battle, would be the foundation of a new German fleet of the future."[56]

In fact, Trotha and his staff were already at work on a plan for a final sortie of the High Seas Fleet. Destroyers would attack the Flanders coast and the mouth of the Thames in order to bring out the British Grand Fleet. Retiring German forces would lead the pursuing British fleet over submarines and minefields. The German battle fleet would then engage the Grand Fleet late in the day near the Dutch coast. Some German officers even discussed the idea that the Kaiser might be invited to come aboard the flagship to die a glorious death with his fleet.[57]

Whether or not they planned to issue an invitation to the Kaiser, Scheer and Hipper took pains to keep their plan from the German government, which was in the midst of complicated negotiations for an armistice. Rumors about preparations for a final suicide sortie quickly spread among sailors of the High Seas Fleet, who were increasingly uneasy at seeing their officers drinking drunken toasts to death or glory. The sailors had long since ceased to believe in glory and were unenthusiastic about dying for the prestige of the navy. The months and years of inactivity, boredom, and confinement had seriously demoralized the crews of the battleships and battle cruisers riding idly at anchor in Kiel and Wilhelmshaven.

The temporary "high" felt by many after the Battle of Jutland had long since dissipated. "What a miserable boring and stupid life we lead! I would rather carry rocks all day if it served some useful purpose," wrote Seaman Stumpf less than six months after the battle.[58] Relations between officers and men, never very good, had deteriorated even further. Stories and rumors concerning officers' mistreatment of and lack of consideration for their men were rife. One story concerned a sailor who received three telegrams notifying him that his wife was dying but was not granted leave until after she was dead. Another concerned a stoker's wife who applied for help to the navy's charitable fund and was told to knit stockings for the officers' ladies. A sailor who applied for an extension of his leave because his wife was about to give birth was refused.[59]

"On the battleships we had difficulty in finding a really capable officer

of middle rank who was still fit for U-boat service. Thus we were de-
nuded of the type of officer with just those qualities essential for good relations between officers and men. . . . The same conditions prevailed in
the NCO corps," Admiral von Trotha wrote.[60] The petty officers and engineer officers, who had poor relationships with their men and a jealous
rivalry with the line officers, often concealed cases of malingering or insubordination "because they wanted to keep the executive officers out of
their bailiwick."[61]

The sailors resented the officers' better food, more comfortable quarters, and generous opportunities for vacations and leaves. As food shortages became acute during the winter of 1916–17, resentment was
replaced by frustration and rage. In monetary terms the officers' food ration was almost twice that of the enlisted men, and their rations were
prepared in special kitchens. The mainstay of the sailors' diet was a stew
composed of 75 percent water with small quantities of sausage, potatoes,
and turnips, which the sailors dubbed *Drahtverhau* (chopped barbed
wire).[62] Seaman Joachim Ringelnatz claimed that the majority of sailors
in his ship were suffering from malnutrition and that the diet was ruining his teeth and gums.[63] "Damn the officers! Never again shall they be
allowed to drag us into a war! Let them either practice some honorable
profession or drop dead," was Stumpf's succinct observation.[64]

By the summer of 1917, there were hunger strikes and work stoppages
in the fleet. On August 2, there was an attempted mutiny by sailors of
the dreadnought *Prinzregent Luitpold,* which resulted in ten death sentences and scores of lesser punishments. Two of the death sentences were
carried out after Admiral Scheer personally sabotaged the accuseds' attempts to appeal to the Kaiser as was their right under the German code
of military justice.[65]

The navy blamed the whole episode on socialist agitators, instituted
food complaint committees, and made real efforts to improve the sailors'
rations. A program of nationalist indoctrination by spokesmen of extreme right-wing parties was instituted, which the sailors scornfully referred to as "two hours' love of the fatherland."

By the fall of 1918 there were few sailors in the High Seas Fleet ready
to plunge into a final death-and-glory mission—and few officers qualified
to lead one. Weary of privation and austerity, discouraged by stories of
the collapse of German defenses in Belgium, the sailors looked hopefully
toward an armistice and end to the long war. They reacted to stories of
preparations for a final sortie with anger and incredulity. "Could they
possibly believe that the attack would have a favorable effect on the out-

come of the war? Every German seamen knew the superiority of the British fleet and could reckon on the fingers of his hand that there would still be a Grand Fleet even if each German ship were to take an English vessel with it as it sunk. Did it not seem more likely that the officers were simply seeking that 'death with honor' which their code demanded?"[66] On October 28 and 29, there were disturbances at Wilhelmshaven aboard the light cruiser *Regensburg* and the battleships *Kronprinz Wilhelm, Koenig,* and *Markgraff.* Sailors refused to weigh anchor, barricaded themselves in various parts of the ships, refused to load coal, and disabled equipment. Hipper temporarily called off the sortie and dispersed the ships, some of which were now flying the red flag of revolution, to their home ports. In Kiel, rebellious sailors joined forces with dockyard workers, sailors in the shore installations, and local troops in the widening rebellion.

The German naval officer corps speedily collapsed in the face of this widespread revolt. Few were willing to risk their lives to restore order, and many were happy to blame the collapse of the fleet on Bolshevik agitators and the new government in Berlin. "The authority of the officers has vanished," wrote Stumpf on October 30. "They surrender in droves."[67] Ironically, it was only through the efforts of the much despised warrant officers and petty officers that the ships were kept in sufficient condition to be surrendered to the victorious Allies after Germany signed an armistice agreement on November 11.

Over the next decade the mistakes, lessons, and achievements of the naval war were minutely examined and discussed. Strategy, tactics, policies and personalities, ships and weapons were endlessly debated. About the human dimension, however, there was widespread agreement. The explanation could be found, it was said, in national character or heredity. The Germans, though brave, efficient, and technically adept were intimidated and "overawed by the prestige and intimidating strength of the Royal Navy."[68] They lacked the true maritime instinct. "The Germans have never been a sea nation," wrote Beatty's chief of staff many years after the war. "Efficient as they are they have not the real seamen spirit or character. Great as was the navy Kaiser Wilhelm and Tirpitz created . . . there was something lacking. Was it tradition, character or something different, their first action on contact was invariably to be to turn for home."[69] In contrast, the British navy had "sea instinct."[70] Admiral Sir Reginald Bacon declared that "nothing but heredity could have inspired the men of the merchant navy to sail continuously and calmly when at any moment an unseen mine or torpedo could have sealed their fate."[71]

Even the Germans seemed to accept this line of argument. "The German people did not understand the sea," Admiral Tirpitz concluded.[72] Karl Dönitz, a young U-boat officer who later became Hitler's top naval commander, believed that "the blame for the defeat lay in the continental mindedness of our government, our army leadership and the entire German people."[73]

Curiously, no one ventured to ask whether it was hereditary traits that kept the U-boat crews at sea in the most trying conditions and in the face of a 40 percent casualty rate. That might have turned the discussion from heredity and instinct to questions of leadership and organization, subjects both British and German admirals were unhappy about examining too closely. To the British, the heredity argument was comforting reassurance that despite all the disconcerting disasters, blunders, and missed opportunities of the naval war, England was still the natural ruler of the seas. For the German officers it served to absolve them of any personal or institutional responsibility for the meager achievements and humiliating collapse of the High Seas Fleet. It was certainly preferable to Seamen Stumpf's analysis of the causes of the naval mutiny. "It is sad, tragic that it could go as far as this. . . . My God why did we have to have such criminal conscienceless officers? It was they who deprived us of all our love for the fatherland, our joy in our German existence and our pride in our incomparable institutions. Even now my blood boils with anger whenever I think of the many injustices I suffered in the Navy."[74]

On November 21, 1918, as the morning sun burned away the fog, the Grand Fleet of 370 warships put to sea to meet nine battleships, five battle cruisers, seven light cruisers, and forty-nine destroyers of the High Seas Fleet led by the British light cruiser *Cardiff*. The British fleet, in two columns, steamed down opposite sides of the German line, then reversed course to escort the Germans to their place of surrender at Rosyth. In the Grand Fleet there was a feeling of disappointment as well as triumph, we "thought it dreadful at the time that the High Seas Fleet should have such a tame 'Der Tag' [the prewar German phrase for the decisive German-British naval battle]," wrote a midshipman, "and all of us resented it that Waterloo should precede Trafalgar and that Trafalgar should never have happened at all."[75]

Steaming with Beatty were six American battleships that had been a part of the Grand Fleet since the fall of 1917. The U.S. Navy's contribution to the war effort had been important, perhaps decisive, but it had essentially played a supporting role to the British navy. In the next war the roles would be reversed.

SEVEN

"LOOK UPWARD TO THE SKIES"

At dawn on July 19, 1918, the first of the Allied offensives that would finally end the war were getting under way. Seven Sopwith Camel biplanes took off from the flying-off deck of HMS *Furious*, a battle cruiser converted to a makeshift aircraft carrier. Each Camel carried two 50-pound bombs. As dawn broke over the North Sea, the seven planes, in two flights of three and four aircraft, set course for the German zeppelin base at Tondern. One plane was forced down by engine trouble, but the others flew on across the Heligoland Bight to Tondern. The flight leader, Captain W. D. Jackson, dived on the northernmost zeppelin shed and scored a direct hit in the middle of the roof. More bombs followed, and the shed erupted in flames that rose to a thousand feet, quickly reducing the two zeppelins inside to ashes. The next flight scored hits on a second, empty shed and set it on fire.[1]

One month later, six fast shallow-draft coastal motorboats on a raid across the Heligoland minefields were attacked by six German seaplanes. The seaplanes made repeated bombing passes over the small boats, which easily evaded their bombs and replied with their machine guns. "As one of the seaplanes flew to drop a bomb the engine was shut off and the bomb would usually drop ahead," wrote one British officer. "Through our peculiar design we could become almost stationary very quickly."[2]

After a time the Germans broke off their attack, but they returned a few minutes later accompanied by four single-seat fighters, which attacked the boats with their machine guns. "I could see the bullets splashing in the water," recalled Lieutenant Cedric Outhwaite, "then crack,

crack, crack as they hit the boats and then splashing in the water ahead as the attacker passed on. . . . I could see my shots as we used tracer bullets and I was working both guns full-out."[3] One plane was shot down by the motorboats, but the boats themselves ran short of ammunition and some of their guns jammed. Within a quarter of an hour all six boats had been sunk or disabled. One was so riddled that "one could almost see through the side in places."[4]

At the same time, Admiral Tyrwhitt's cruisers and destroyers were cruising near the Heligoland Bight, shadowed by a zeppelin. One destroyer towed a large lighter with a Camel aboard. As the destroyer worked up to full speed and turned into the wind, the pilot would rev his engine to full power, then roll down the length of the lighter and into the air. Or that was the theory. In practice, only two successful takeoffs had ever been made when Lieutenant S. D. Culley's plane rose from its lighter on the morning of August 10 and headed for the zeppelin. Both soon disappeared into the clouds. An hour later the sailors watching from below heard the sound of machine-gun fire and saw "a sheet of flame sweep across the white cloud bank and a shower of splintered metal."[5] "The airship buckled in the center," recalled Lieutenant Outhwaite. "It seemed to drop for ages before reaching the water, throwing it up in sheets as it struck."[6]

Admiral Tyrwhitt signaled his ships, "YOUR ATTENTION IS CALLED TO HYMN NUMBER 224, VERSE 7." The verse read:

> O happy band of pilgrims
> Look upward to the skies
> Where such a light affliction
> shall win so great a prize.[7]

These three little-noted naval actions, which occurred a few months before the surrender of the German fleet, provided a glimpse into the future of war at sea. All three incidents were dramatic examples of the ways in which air and sea power could work together to create an entirely new kind of warfare. And each provided its own lessons. The raid on Tondern highlighted the ability of fast land aircraft launched from the sea to penetrate a defended enemy base. It was not the first time the feat was accomplished; as early as 1915 two British seaplanes armed with torpedoes had successfully attacked and sunk three Turkish merchant ships in harbor in the Dardennelles.[8] And it solved a problem that had existed since Nelson's day: navies' relative ineffectiveness at attacking enemy bases and fortifications. Admiral Togo's repeated and unsuccessful attempt to get at the Russian fleet in Port Arthur had served to reinforce this point. Air power changed everything, and no naval base was safe from attack.

Imaginative naval leaders had not been slow to grasp the implications. Wheeled aircraft flown from a carrier could fly faster and higher and lift much heavier loads than a seaplane. As early as August 1917, Beatty had called for the construction of flying-off decks on large, fast merchant ships to enable them to launch torpedo planes. His plan was for the torpedo bombers, supported by large land-based seaplanes, to carry out a mass surprise attack on German naval bases at Cuxhaven and Shilling Roads.[9] Suitable aircraft and ships were unavailable in 1917, but by the fall of 1918 the *Argus*, a ship designed to land as well as launch aircraft, was in commission, other aircraft carriers were under construction, and the Royal Navy was planning large-scale air raids on German naval bases in 1919.[10]

Even without aircraft carriers the Grand Fleet embarked more than a hundred aircraft that could be flown off platforms mounted on the turrets of battleships and cruisers to be used for scouting and air defense against zeppelins. That was quite a change from Jutland, where the Grand Fleet's seaplane carrier had actually been left behind before the battle. By 1918 the Grand Fleet's fighters had made life so dangerous for the zeppelins that the German advantage derived from airship reconnaissance had largely disappeared.[11]

Less regarded was the battle between the motorboats and the German planes. Significantly, it was the fastest sea battle yet. The motorboats were moving at least thirty knots, the German planes at close to eighty. "One of the strangest actions ever fought at sea," the British official history concluded.[12] Yet, as Paul Halpern observed, it was also one of the most portentous. For the first time "an entire naval force had been eliminated by aircraft."[13]

Aircraft, to a greater extent even than submarines, promised to revolutionize naval warfare by drastically altering the scouting and screening functions of the fleet, by making all warships regardless of their location potentially vulnerable to attack, and by drastically changing the speed and range at which naval actions would be fought. It also introduced a new type of naval warrior who would be as different from the old as the engineers had been from the seamen.

At the end of the war, the Royal Navy appeared to be at the leading edge in the development of this new dimension in naval warfare. Its aircraft had proved their usefulness in gunfire spotting, anti-submarine warfare, and reconnaissance as well as in the more dramatic roles of fleet air defense and attack on enemy warships. The naval arm of the newly established Royal Air Force had almost 3,500 aircraft and 55,000 officers and men. Besides the *Argus*, three more aircraft carriers were under construction or conversion. Yet this commanding British lead would disappear in little over a decade.

Before the Great War ended, the British government, acting upon the recommendations of a high-level interdepartmental committee chaired by General Jan C. Smuts, decided to create a separate air force which would take over the air assets of the Royal Naval Air Service and the army's Royal Flying Corps. The Smuts committee's report declared that "an air fleet can conduct extensive operations far from, and independently of, both army and navy. . . . There is absolutely no limit to the scale of its future independent war use. And the day may not be far off when aerial operations with their devastation of enemy lands and destruction of industrial and populous centers on a vast scale may become the principal operations of war."[14]

The leaders of the newly established Royal Air Force could not have agreed more. General Sir Hugh Trenchard, the first Royal Air Force chief of staff, soon became an outspoken advocate of "airpower." He argued that far from being merely a support for armies and navies, airplanes could carry out a decisive and independent role in wartime by destroying the enemy's air force and then crippling his vital industries and cities.

This preoccupation with what would soon come to be called "strategic bombing" left little room for concern about naval aviation. The Royal Air Force, with sole responsibility for aircraft design, procurement, maintenance, and pilot training, was little inclined to devote much of its steadily shrinking budget to research and development of the specialized types of aircraft needed for carrier operations. In addition, there were no institutional arrangements whereby the Royal Navy's operational experience and tactical doctrines could be taken into account in the design and procurement process.[15]

The result was that the Royal Navy received only a limited number of generally low-performance aircraft. By the late 1930s they were completely outclassed by contemporary aircraft in the American and Japanese navies as well as by most land-based planes. The Royal Navy also began to lag in carrier development. Although the British had by far the largest number of carriers in their fleet in the 1920s, most of these ships were obsolescent. In 1939, the British had only one carrier under ten years old in commission, whereas the Japanese had three, as well as two recently modernized ships, and the Americans had four.[16] After years of bureaucratic infighting, the Royal Navy finally regained control of procurement, manpower, and training for its air arm in 1937. Although several highly effective new aircraft carriers were begun, the navy still lacked sufficient money and time to modernize its aircraft inventory before World War II began.

An even more serious consequence of the creation of the Royal Air Force was that all of the men of the Royal Naval Air Service were immediately transferred to the new organization. The result was "the loss to the Royal Navy of nearly all its officers who were experienced and enthusiastic advocates of naval aviation."[17] Even after 1926 when the Admiralty and the RAF agreed that 70 percent of the pilots in the Fleet Air Arm would be naval officers, the development of a cadre of experienced senior naval aviators was very slow. One sublieutenant who applied for flight training was summoned to appear before the ship's captain in full dress uniform. While standing rigidly at attention he was confronted with his application paper.

"What is this?" demanded the captain.

"My application to become a pilot, sir," replied the sublieutenant.

"What did you join the navy for?" asked the captain.

The young officer replied with the stock phrase "To serve at sea, sir." The captain nodded and tore up the paper.[18]

Naval officers "appointed to [British] carriers were not generally of the highest caliber," recalled S. W. Roskill.[19] In contrast, by 1926, the U.S. Navy already had one vice admiral, three rear admirals, two captains, and sixty-three commanders qualified as naval aviators or naval aviation observers.[20]

Development of the new air weapons consequently fell to the Americans and Japanese. By 1920, these two navies, which had figured only marginally in the calculation of the naval balance of power at the time the *Dreadnought* was launched, were far more powerful than any European fleet except the Royal Navy; the U.S. Navy was in many respects virtually equal even to the British. By the time the High Seas Fleet surrendered to the Grand Fleet, most of the battleships and battle cruisers of both the British and German navies were being eclipsed by new capital ships under construction at Newport News, New York, Sasebo, and Yokosuka. This "new order of sea power" was formally recognized in the Washington treaties signed in 1922.

World War I had left the Japanese and Americans with a number of contentious issues in the Far East. Japanese troops sent to Siberia at the invitation of the Allies to fight the Bolsheviks in the summer of 1918 were still there long after the Great War had ended. Tokyo and Washington had also clashed over Japanese demands for concessions and privileges in China. Finally, American leaders felt uneasy about Japan's acquisition of some of the former German island colonies in the Pacific. Complicating these problems was the fact that the Anglo-Japanese Alliance formed in 1902 as a safeguard against Imperial Russia was still in effect twenty years later.

The Washington treaties checked the rapid growth of Japanese-American antagonism over East Asia and the beginning of a new arms race. They replaced the increasingly awkward Anglo-Japanese Alliance with a series of multilateral agreements and declarations. Among them was an agreement that limited battle fleets both qualitatively and quantitatively and provided for a ten-year capital-ship-building "holiday," with limits on the construction of other types of warships as well.[21] The new preeminence of the United States and Japan was formally recognized by establishing "ratios" for the size of their battle fleets. The United States was accorded "parity" with Great Britain, an arrangement that would have seemed unthinkable only ten years before. The Japanese agreed to a ratio of 60 percent of the British and American tonnage.

While the British struggled with war debts, a large but aging fleet, and an economy seriously weakened by war and the loss of foreign markets, it was the two non-European navies, the American and Japanese, that were to take the lead in naval aviation during the next two decades.

Before the end of the nineteenth century the United States Navy not only lacked any ambition to compete with Britain but relied on the predominance of the Royal Navy to simplify its own security problems. Beginning in the 1890s, however, the United States began a program to construct a modern battle fleet. This policy gained impetus with the American victory in the war with Spain in 1898 and the two-term presidency of Theodore Roosevelt. Economic expansionism, a new style of truculent nationalism, Mahanian navalism, and the influence of various presidents, congressmen, and navy secretaries have all been offered as explanations for this unprecedented naval expansion.

Whatever the explanation, the growth of the navy was indeed rapid and impressive. By the time of the war with Spain, the United States had four battleships and two armored cruisers. Eight years later, Roosevelt ordered sixteen of the navy's battleships on a voyage around the world. By 1909, the United States ranked second only to Britain in number of battleships and a close third to Germany in tonnage. After that the Americans became reluctant to match the frantic Anglo-German dreadnought-building race and so fell behind somewhat by 1914. In 1916, however, Congress authorized an enormous capital-ship-building program that was halted only by the Washington treaties.

For the United States Navy, as for the British, the rapid growth in size and number of ships in commission had meant a critical need for additional manpower. In 1896, two years before the Spanish-American War, the total authorized strength of the U.S. Navy had been 10,000 men, only 1,800 more than ten years earlier. By the turn of the century, the total had doubled to 20,000 men, and by the time Roosevelt's "Great White Fleet" began its voyage around the world in 1907, the navy had about 37,000 men. In 1914 it had 51,000, and at the time of the Washington treaties 86,000.[22]

During the nineteenth century the U.S. Navy had recruited its sailors from among the traditional seafaring population of coastal cities in the United States and abroad. In 1890, only 58 percent of the navy's enlisted force were citizens and 47 percent native-born.[23] "What pride can an officer feel in his vain attempts to arouse some national spirit and esprit in such crews," lamented Commander William F. Fullam.[24]

It is less than surprising that given the rampant nativism and suspicion of immigrants held by many old-line Americans at the turn of the century, naval officers should conclude that only white American-born men would do. "We want boys who have never seen and do not know any other flag than the American, who have good American backgrounds, who have no old world allegiances or affiliations. We want the brawn of Montana, the fire of the South and the daring of the Pacific slope," declared Commander Francis H. Higginson, commandant of the Newport Naval Training Station, in 1890.[25] As late as 1919, the Navy Department explained to a congressman who wished to know why recruiters never advertised in foreign-language periodicals published in the United States that "the boy from the farm is considered by the naval recruiting service to be most desirable material." Foreign-language papers were most likely to be read by "men residing in the larger industrial cities."[26]

The navy's efforts were remarkably successful. In 1899, 20 percent of the enlisted force were noncitizens. In 1910, despite a 600 percent growth in the number of sailors, less than 2 percent were noncitizens and more than 88 percent were native-born Americans. By the early 1920s the navy had less than 3 percent naturalized citizens and less than one third of 1 percent foreigners in its ranks; this in a period in which almost 14 percent of Americans were foreign-born.[27]

The navy's program to eliminate African-Americans from the service was equally successful, though considerably less publicized. There is good evidence that blacks constituted about 10 percent of all navy enlistees in the 1880s and 1890s.[28] Yet by 1906 less than one in thirty sailors was African-American and by 1930 there were fewer than five hundred black sailors in a navy of eighty thousand men.[29] Long before this time the navy had adopted an informal policy of segregating blacks and assigning them only menial jobs. Navy Secretary Josephus Daniels explained to a senator in 1917, "There is no legal discrimination shown against colored men in the Navy. As a matter of policy, however, and to avoid friction between the two races, it has been customary to enlist colored men in the various ratings of the messman branch . . . and in the lower ratings of the fire room, thus permitting colored men to sleep and eat by themselves."[30] By the 1920s the navy had temporarily halted all first enlistments of black Americans, and it did not resume them until 1933.

The navy justified its de facto policy of segregation by pointing to the existence of strong animosities and prejudices that would make it impossible for white sailors to live aboard ship in close proximity to blacks, let alone take orders from black petty officers. The virtual disappearance of African-Americans from the navy, however, did little to efface racial hatreds among white sailors. Eugene E. Wilson, a former naval aviator and Annapolis graduate, described an incident that occurred while sailors on leave were attending a bullfight in Callao, Peru, during the 1920s. When a black matador entered the ring, "that aroused all the latent southern chivalry in our Navy, and there was a good deal of it, and they began to jeer the colored matador shouting 'C'mon you bull, get the black so and so.'"[31]

For several years in the late 1920s there were reports of bluejackets on leave assaulting African-Americans on the New York subway and forcing them off the trains. One New Yorker reported, "I personally have witnessed the annoyance to passengers by Navy men in trains . . . at late hours of the night and without provocation. These fellows intoxicated with bad rum, make themselves a general nuisance. . . . Passengers of color have no protection on the subways of the city."[32] After two African-Americans had to be hospitalized following a fight in the subway, the NAACP wrote the Secretary of the Navy urging that "sailors from United States battleships . . . be curbed in their lawlessness."[33] The commandant of the Third Naval District reported that prejudices existed on both sides and that he found "no evidence of preconceived or concerted actions by sailors to attack blacks, only isolated incidents." The three sailors from one battleship who had been involved in the incident were restricted to the ship and assigned extra clean-up duties "for participating in a fight ashore."[34]

The nativist, whites-only navy was expected to attract only "men from the best walks of life," in the words of Navy Secretary Daniels.[35] Like the Royal Navy, the U.S. Navy established an ambitious and comprehensive recruiting system, one geared to presenting the twentieth-century blue-jacket not as a rakish adventurer with a girl in every port but as a sort of well-traveled high-tech Boy Scout. "Only men of sound mind and clean life are acceptable," Daniels wrote. "The Navy is no place for shiftless, purposeless men. No liquor is allowed aboard ship, no gambling, and profanity is a violation of the regulations."[36] Daniels told Congress, "We have changed the style of our recruiting literature. We burned a bushel of literature which showed young men going into tropical climates and associating with women half-dressed [sic]. These posters promised if a man enlisted into the Navy or the Marine Corps he would have opportunities that appeal to the lowest. . . . Instead every piece of literature that now goes forth says that the young man who now comes into the Navy will have an opportunity to be educated."[37] Naval officers were especially annoyed at the practice of some judges who offered youthful offenders a choice between imprisonment and joining the navy. "The Navy is not a reformatory," complained Assistant Secretary Franklin Roosevelt to the press in 1915.[38] Yet, well into the 1930s judges continued to sentence young men to years of character building in the sea service.

Despite the continued presence of these few youthful felons, the navy was generally successful in finding the high-quality recruits it was seeking. Large numbers of young men were attracted by the possibility of foreign travel, the opportunity for technical training, or simply boredom with civilian life and desire for adventure.[39] Midshipman J. R. Haile, who enlisted in the 1920s, listed the reasons farm boys joined the navy in the 1920s as "a desire to see the world; distaste for the hard work and close confines of the farm or a strong indisposition for the educational atmosphere to be found about a school."[40]

One officer observed that enlistments tended to pick up "as soon as cold weather begins" because "many men who are employed in the open . . . have learned that a man in the Navy always gets three square meals a day and has a warm place to sleep."[41] The state of the economy also had a marked impact on the number of applicants for enlistment. Recessions or localized spells of unemployment were powerful inducements to try the relatively stable and secure jobs offered by the navy. From 1905 to 1914 the navy accepted only about one in four men who applied for enlistment.[42]

Unlike the Royal Navy, the U.S. Navy had no system of long-term enlistments. In 1910 more than 74 percent of the total enlisted force had served less than four years, the length of one enlistment. In 1921, the figure was 83 percent. "Instead of congratulating ourselves that 7,800 vacancies which occurred during the last year were made good by recruit enlistment, we should rather deplore the loss of 25% of the enlisted force in one year," declared Lieutenant Ridley McLean.[43] A substantial number of men proved unwilling to wait the required four years before leaving the service. In the years between 1900 and 1908, the U.S. Navy lost an average of slightly more than 15 percent of its enlisted force each year to desertion.[44]

Beginning in 1909, the navy took steps to cut desertions and increase the retention rate of its enlisted men. Shore leave was made more frequent and easier to obtain, and extra pay was offered for reenlistment. In 1907, for the first time, men were permitted to "purchase" an early discharge before the expiration of their first enlistments. Most important, the navy made a determined effort to improve the quality and variety of the sailors' food. "Kickers will kick on food quicker than anything else," an experienced sailor observed. "If a man gets good grub he can stand a lot of inconveniences, but as soon as he *thinks* he is not getting as good food as his ration ought to give him, he gets dissatisfied, loses interest in his job and the first thing he knows he is in trouble."[45]

Acting on such views, which were shared by many officers, the navy moved to centralize food preparation in the hands of trained cooks and to give officers direct responsibility for the performance of the commissary steward and mess staff. By 1905, electric ice cream machines had been installed in some of the larger warships. Paymaster George P. Dyer believed that this was appropriate food for the navy's "clear-eyed intelligent American youths . . . who know what clean living and good fun are and they have the usual American notion of the festive nature of ice cream."[46]

These innovations proved effective in reducing desertions. The rate fell from 15.5 percent in 1908 to 3.8 percent by 1916. The rate rose to around 8 percent in the early 1920s, then dropped to 3 percent after 1925 and declined to almost nothing during the depression of the 1930s.[47] The navy was less successful with reenlistments, which were influenced by general employment opportunities as well as conditions in the service. In the early 1920s one officer observed that "reenlistments are so few as to be negligible. . . . The shortage of men and the inefficiency of enlisted personnel keeps the greater number of battleships tied up at the yards."[48]

The situation changed drastically with the onset of the Great Depression. During the next decade, reenlistment rates averaged around 88 percent. Jarvis Cartwright, a farmer's son from North Carolina, remembered seeing "sailors from Norfolk, spending money and dancing with the honky-tonk queens. . . . I knew that a Petty Officer, Second Class earned seventy-two dollars a month. I remember one day working the fields and daydreaming about the time I could join the Navy and earn seventy-two dollars. When I did get in the Navy, May 8, 1939, they gave me five dollars every two weeks. I was really living. I could smoke those Ready-Rolls every day."[49] In 1935 only 11.7 percent of applicants for enlistment were accepted. Gerry Miller, a young recruit from California, had to wait a year and a half after being accepted to finally enter the navy in 1940.[50]

For those lucky few young men the navy represented a welcome refuge, or a desperate last resort from the bitter hardships of the 1930s. "In Union Station about a hundred men were assembled from all over the Rocky Mountains to take the oath," wrote Aviation Ordnanceman Alvin Kernan of his enlistment in early 1941. "Every one was young—17, 18, 19—for the most part kids who couldn't get jobs. Here and there were men in their twenties, jobless workers at the end of their rope, or incorrigible 'fuckups' who had gotten into some kind of trouble at home. . . . Most were from small towns, usually from broken families, notable for bad teeth and bad complexions, the marginal American young produced by more than ten years of the hardest of hard times."[51]

Like their British counterparts, young Americans who joined the navy to escape joblessness or trouble at home often found that they had escaped into a hard and unforgiving world. Their new homes were likely to be far more livable, however, than those of the Royal Navy. Until 1907, when Theodore Roosevelt sent the American fleet around the world, living conditions aboard an American warship differed little from those on similar ships in the Royal Navy. Yet, thereafter the two sharply diverged. The British bluejacket retained his indifferent food, his hammock, and his rum rations. Even in newer British warships, such as the Leander-class light cruisers completed in the early 1930s, the mess decks were small and cramped and there was an insufficient number of hooks to sling hammocks or overhead racks for storage. "The bathrooms were small, tiled apartments fitted with a few galvanized tip-up basins served by a single hot and cold tap."[52]

The U.S. Navy banned alcohol aboard ship, but introduced ice cream, Hollywood movies, and libraries, replaced hammocks and seabags with wooden bunks and metal lockers, and began to experiment with cafeteria-style messing. "No class of working man lives so well as the enlisted force of the Navy," boasted the Bureau of Navigation.[53] Whatever the truth of that claim, it was a fact that by the 1920s the U.S. Navy's food had become the envy of other navies—and of the U.S. Army and Marine Corps as well. British sailors who came in contact with the American navy were impressed by what they saw as the relative opulence of the facilities for sailors. Chief Stoker Frederick Wigby, who was housed at the Brooklyn Navy Yard while his ship was under repair, described the barracks as "very modern. We had bunks instead of hammocks. The food was plentiful and very good indeed and was served up in a lovely gleaming dining hall. The whole place was very efficiently run. It had shops, a gymnasium, theater and swimming pool—quite a change from our old barracks at Chatham."[54] Signalman Alistair Reid found American ships "more comfortable" than equivalent British ships. "There wasn't necessarily more room, but the men were more comfortable."[55]

Of course, comfort was relative. Sailors in the famous American "four-stacker" destroyers, completed toward the end of World War I and still in service during World War II, messed and slept just below the forecastle. "Being so far forward, they took a beating from the sea on both sides and overhead. . . ."[56] Those in the after crew quarters, located near the very rear of the ship over the propellers, had little headroom and received the full vibration of the engines.[57] The four-stackers did offer the convenience of metal lockers for the crew. These shared space with the pipe-framed, wire-sprung bunks, which had hammocks as mattresses. The crew's lavatory facilities were in the after deckhouse "so that from either of their quarters men had to pass over the open deck to reach them, those from forward, half the length of the ship."[58]

Between the wars, the U.S. Navy, like the British, had come to embrace athletics as an all-purpose solution for raising morale and pride in the ship, combating boredom, and distracting sailors from less wholesome pursuits. During a typical year in the 1920s, the battleship *Tennessee* was involved in eleven boat races, thirty-two track meets, three boxing and three wrestling matches, eleven basketball games, three swim meets, and twenty-two baseball games as well as several football games.[59] The football games were held in a 4,500-person stadium near the fleet base at San Pedro, California, and the stadium seats were always filled.[60] When the ships went to sea for exercises it was not unusual to leave the football or baseball team ashore so that their practice routine would be uninterrupted. In 1934 the Commander, Battle Force, Pacific Fleet, found it necessary to cut back on the fleet athletic schedule so that there would be time for gunnery practice.[61]

Because fuel was expensive, and ammunition even more so, the ships of the U.S. fleet spent relatively little time at sea, much to the disappointment of sailors who had believed they were enlisting "to see the world." The battleships of the Pacific Fleet, for example, made relatively few long cruises and went to Hawaii only twice a year for fleet maneuvers.[62] The rest of the year, the crews often worked a five-day week and were always back in port by Friday afternoon. Following the captain's Saturday-morning inspection, the crew had liberty until Sunday evening. [63]

In addition to the omnipresent athletic events, sailors frequently spent their liberty at concerts performed by ships' bands and at Saturday-night dances. San Pedro, Newport, Norfolk, and other Navy towns also offered a host of less wholesome activities. "The Pike" in Long Beach, California, where the fleet's battleships anchored, abounded in bars and brothels ready to welcome sailors on liberty. Because most "respectable girls" wanted nothing to do with sailors, men who desired female companions had little choice beyond the Pike. In large ships, each division might have its own brothel of choice. Not surprisingly, venereal disease and alcoholism were endemic problems, although the latter may have been more common among officers, who had both greater means and greater opportunity to indulge their fondness for booze.[64]

As in the Royal Navy, day-to-day management and leadership were in the hands of the senior petty officers, who had their own methods of maintaining discipline. Many petty officers remained in the ship for years at a time, and it was possible to advance from recruit to chief petty officer all in the same ship. Several senior petty officers in older battleships had been aboard for twenty years or more. These men, usually bachelors, provided a valuable element of continuity and local expertise that was highly valued in a service where officers changed jobs at two-to-three-year intervals.[65]

If the situation of petty officers in the navies was similar, the situation of officers was not. "The relationship between American officers and men was puzzling to the British," recalled Charles Blackford, a sailor in one of the American destroyers based at Queenstown in World War I. "With [the Royal Navy], not even a ship's boat could leave without a midshipman in it. Officers used enlisted men as personal servants. Occasionally I would be requested to carry a personal note to a British officer in the yard. . . . They would try to tip me. When I refused that it left them confused and ill at ease."[66] Alistair Reid found "less saluting, stiffening and stomping" in the U.S. Navy than in the Royal Navy.[67] Again the differences were of degree rather than kind. Few American sailors viewed their officers as laid-back, fatherly types. "If some state would only start a movement to compel Naval officers to treat the enlisted men like human beings and not like dogs . . . that state would earn the thanks and gratitude of over 60,000 enlisted men," wrote one sailor in 1914 to his hometown paper.[68] "I have heard officers speak to boys in tones that chilled me," wrote Petty Officer Felix Shay, "not harsh words—just impersonal sneers without purpose or reason. . . . I have known boys to go ashore on Saturday morning without money and stay until Monday morning without food or sleep just to escape the pleasant discipline of the U.S. Navy."[69]

These complaints were little different from those of British bluejackets of the same period. Where the American sailors—and the American public—emphatically differed was that they refused to tolerate the notion that officers were in any way superior to enlisted men, save in rank and responsibility. "Will the officers of the Navy abandon their poppycock assumption of social superiority?" demanded a high school principal asked to recommend enlistment to his students. "I am not going to send a single student of mine into the Navy until the Navy becomes a democratic institution. I do not mean that suitable obedience should not be rendered officers . . . [but] I will not tolerate the old feudal constitution of the Navy in which officers are lords and sailors villains."[70]

British seamen, products of a socially stratified society, generally accepted the social and intellectual, perhaps even moral, superiority of their officers and demanded only fair and considerate treatment. Americans held no such views. "The gap between enlisted men and officers in the American Navy during WWII was medieval," recalled Alvin Kernan. "The enlisted men accepted the division as a necessary part of military life, but so American were we that we never dreamed that it could affect our status as freeborn citizens, who because of a run of bad luck and some unfortunate circumstances like the Depression just happened to be down for a brief time."[71]

There was in fact some "social distance" between enlisted men and officers in the U.S. Navy, but only enough to make both sides uneasy. Until 1940 almost all officers were graduates of the U.S. Naval Academy at Annapolis. Cadets were appointed to the academy upon nomination of their senators or representatives from all states and territories according to their representation in Congress. Attendance was absolutely free of charge, and after 1933, graduates received a bachelor's degree.

Alongside the class-based, privately funded British and German officer selection systems, this seemed a true merit system. Yet, while poor boys were accepted to the academy and more than a few went on to become admirals, the great majority of those who entered Annapolis were from well-to-do families, by American, if not by British, standards. More than half of the young men enrolled at the Naval Academy between 1847 and 1900 were the sons of attorneys, bankers, diplomats, merchants, manufacturers, congressmen, and judges. Another 17 percent were sons of physicians, clergymen, engineers, and educators, and 10 percent were sons of army and navy officers.[72] Only 1 percent had fathers who were unskilled factory workers or farm laborers. Blacks were wholly excluded and Jews extremely rare. Episcopalianism was the religion of more than 40 percent of the naval officer corps, and before 1900 almost all shipboard services were conducted according to the Episcopal rite.[73]

Like Osborne and Dartmouth, Annapolis education was not designed with any concern for intellectual rigor. In fact, when one takes into account the very different societies in which they were situated, the similarities in educational philosophy among the three naval academies, Japanese, British, and American, are striking. Commenting on the academic examination of a group of recent Dartmouth graduates in 1934, a distinguished civilian professor concluded that the young officers "can memorize facts and they can write down these facts clearly and simply but they cannot think for themselves and the subject matter of their answers . . . is often childish and stereotyped. Several groups of essays might each have been written by the same person."[74] Similarly, Rear Admiral Draper Kauffman recalled that the emphasis in teaching at Annapolis was "to memorize not think." Admiral Gerald Miller remembered "a lot of learning by rote."[75]

In 1923 the Naval Academy's Board of Visitors had reported that "a sound symmetrical general education is lacking" at Annapolis. The curriculum did not provide "even the fundamental training in the physical sciences," while the humanities were thrown together in a single department the midshipmen eloquently labeled "bull."[76] Another Board of Visitors report called attention to the "unspoken willingness" of the academy faculty "to use subjects of instruction as a means of discipline."[77] Admiral Kauffman, later a superintendent of the academy, would probably have agreed. "It most certainly did not produce an educated man," he recalled. "The educated men who graduated from the Naval Academy got their education later."[78]

It seems unlikely that navy leaders would have been much concerned by this sort of criticism. "They weren't trying to educate us. They were trying to instill a certain set of standards of performance, an appreciation of the Navy and to build some habit patterns. . . ."[79] Above all, the goal was to build character. "Character is the big thing," declared Admiral Thomas C. Hart. "It is presence and personality and looks, it is qualities of mind but particularly . . . guts, all of that is in it."[80] Successful midshipmen were expected to develop qualities of reliability, leadership, integrity, good judgment, and loyalty to the service and to each other.[81] The last was especially stressed. Midshipmen left Annapolis with a lively regard for the reputation and standing of their service—and even more concern for their own reputation in the service.

Despite the emphasis on character, some midshipmen apparently found it hard to live up to the combination of leadership, judgment, and discretion expected of them. From the turn of the century onward, there were periodic hazing scandals, often precipitated by some particularly cruel or brutal practice by upperclassmen. "When practiced with a sense of humor . . . hazing could do a lot of good," observed Admiral Kauffman. But "occasionally sadistic First Classmen would carry it too far, much too far in some cases and controlling that element of the First Class was very difficult. Controlling them by commissioned officers was well nigh impossible because people didn't squeal. The only practical way to control it was by class organization and that was not effective."[82]

Whatever its shortcomings, the U.S. Navy was in many ways particularly well suited to take on the challenges posed by the new technologies of the interwar years. In 1899 the line and engineer corps had been merged (a step most European naval experts considered shocking and foolhardy). After 1899, all aspiring naval officers were required to study engineering and Annapolis graduates were considered qualified for both line and engineering duties. In addition, during the 1920s and 1930s the navy followed a policy of assigning some of its brightest line officers to civilian universities for graduate study in engineering. These policies gave the combat leaders of the U.S. Navy a breadth and depth of technical knowledge unmatched among line officers in other navies.

Until the 1930s, commissioned rank in the navy was virtually limited to Annapolis graduates. Although a Naval Reserve had been established in 1900 and large numbers of Naval Reserve officers had been required during World War I, the regular officers viewed them as a necessary evil and purged the service of most of them by 1921. Those who remained were not promoted. Reservists responded by forming their own lobby, the Naval Reserve Officer Association, and lobbying Congress for improved status and promotion. They scored an important victory in 1925 when Congress established the Naval Reserve as a permanent organization and provided for the creation of Naval Reserve Officer Training

Corps units at selected colleges and universities. Yet far more than the pressure of outsiders, it was the new challenges posed by the three-dimensional warfare made possible by aircraft and submarines that was fundamentally to transform the leadership of the U.S. Navy.

Aviation was the first of the elements that would create an important new class of naval officer and enlisted man. During World War I, the U.S. Navy had employed more than 500 aircraft in Europe. The navy squadrons, mainly composed of seaplane-bombers, patrolled shipping lanes, hunted submarines, and attacked U-boat bases on the German-occupied Belgian coast. U.S. Navy aviation expanded from nine officers and twenty-three men with seven aircraft in 1914 to approximately 40,000 men including 7,000 officers with 2,100 planes in 1918.[83]

This was an impressive performance. In 1919, after extensive hearings on aviation issues, the General Board of the Navy, a committee of admirals that advised the Secretary of the Navy on ship design and other aspects of naval policy, concluded that "fleet aviation must be developed to its fullest extent." The board predicted that in fleet engagements of the future "the advantage will lie with the fleet which wins in the air" and recommended the establishment of a naval air service "capable of accompanying and operating with the fleet in all waters of the globe."[84]

Significantly, a large number of World War I aviators and support personnel had been reservists. Almost from the beginning, outsiders, both reservists and civilians, were closely involved with the development of naval aviation. Lieutenant John H. Towers, the canny chief of the navy's Bureau of Aeronautics during the Great War, employed former "bankers, stockbrokers and corporation executives to look after his accounting and budgeting requirements," hired women clerks and secretaries and appointed Harvard graduate and banker Gordon Balch as a director of the "Naval Reserve Flying Corps."[85]

What Towers called "the backbone of our Naval Air Reserve during the war" was an odd organization of enthusiastic, wealthy and well-connected Ivy League graduates led by F. Trubee Davison, the son of a partner in the legendary banking firm of J. P. Morgan.[86] As a volunteer with the American Ambulance Service in France during the summer of 1915, Davison had become fascinated by aviation and impressed by the famous volunteer aviators of the Lafayette Escadrille.

Returning to the United States, Davison spent the next eighteen months organizing a volunteer aviation unit among the members of the Yale crew and other undergraduates. Members of what would eventually be known as the First Yale Unit learned to fly at private flight schools near their families' estates on Long Island and in Palm Beach, Florida. With money furnished by their parents and friends, the group were able to purchase their own aircraft.

The Navy Department, understandably impressed with an organization whose budget for airplanes equaled more than 50 percent of the entire 1916 congressional appropriation for naval aviation, had little hesitation in incorporating the First Yale Unit into the newly formed Naval Reserve Flying Corps.[87] "The great aircraft force, which was ultimately assembled in Europe," wrote Admiral Sims, "had its beginnings to a large extent in this youthful group from the Yale campus. They were used also as a nucleus for the training of an air force at home and were to be found as instructors, as commanders of stations or in other executive positions."[88] Members of the unit also served overseas with the Northern Bombing Group and with Sims's staff in London.

The surviving members of the First Yale Unit, together with other well-connected reservists drawn from elite colleges and from Wall Street, went on to form a powerful and knowledgeable lobby for naval aviation in the interwar years. F. Trubee Davison, badly crippled in a training accident, became the first Assistant Secretary of War for Air in 1926. Artemis Gates, another former member, served as Assistant Secretary and later Under Secretary of the Navy for Air during World War II. His opposite number in the War Department was Robert M. Lovett, one of the group's aces. Another ace, David Ingalls, became vice president and general manager of Pan American Airlines. James Forrestal, a veteran of one of the similar groups formed at Princeton and Harvard, served as Under Secretary and Secretary of the Navy during World War II. While the U.S. Navy had had civilian friends and supporters before 1914, including a very vocal Navy League of the United States, never before had it had to deal with a group with the degree of expertise and practical experience of the reserve aviators.

The role played by the civilian elites highlighted the fact that naval aviation was both too dynamic and too manpower-intensive to fit comfortably within the traditional framework of Annapolis-trained line officers. "No individual with the requisite mental or physical capacity exists who can meet the requirements of being a thoroughly experienced aviation officer and at the same time a thoroughly experienced battleship officer," declared Lieutenant F. W. Wead in 1926.[89] For the next two decades, questions about the procurement, roles, and status of aviation personnel were to be at the heart of debates and decision about airpower and naval warfare.

EIGHT

"ESSENTIALLY AND FUNDAMENTALLY A DIFFERENT PROFESSION"

A s the sun rose above the choppy Atlantic, the sailors could see the low volcanic cone of the Galapagos Islands. It was 1929. The aircraft carrier *Saratoga*, the largest warship in the world, accompanied by a single cruiser, steamed south at high speed just to the southeast of Isle Isabela, the largest of the islands in the archipelago. The *Saratoga* and her giant sister, *Lexington*, converted from two unfinished battle cruisers scheduled for scrapping under the Washington treaties, had been with the fleet since 1927, but this was the first occasion on which an aircraft carrier had operated far from the battle line. Flying his flag in *Saratoga* was Rear Admiral Joseph Mason Reeves, an 1894 gradu- ate of the Naval Academy.

For the 1929 Panama war games, Reeves had persuaded Admiral William V. Pratt, commanding the aggressor fleet, to allow him to take the *Saratoga* on a lone raid against the Panama Canal. The *Saratoga* headed south, well out of range of the cruisers defending the approaches to the canal. Rounding the Galapagos Islands, the carrier turned north for a thirty-three-knot run toward the canal. An "enemy" destroyer and a cruiser sighted the carrier, but neither got off a report before they were ruled sunk by the *Saratoga* and her escorting cruiser *Omaha*. Before dawn, *Saratoga* launched a full deckload of seventy planes against the canal. The attack achieved complete surprise. The planes were judged to have destroyed the canal locks and most of the surrounding airfields, and the *Saratoga*'s fighters successfully defended the carrier against the tardy air attacks of the canal's defenders. Although the *Saratoga* was later ruled sunk by enemy battleships, her raid was still a spectacular coup and came at the climax of a decade of technological and tactical advances for naval aviation.[1]

Behind this impressive aviation achievement was Admiral Reeves, who had become Commander, Air Craft Squadrons, Battle Fleet, in 1923. The first American aircraft carrier, the small converted collier *Langley*, had just been commissioned the year before as an experimental vessel. Reeves was interested in making *Langley* not simply an aviation laboratory but an effective tactical unit of the fleet. He insisted that the *Langley* carry the maximum number of aircraft and reorganized flight deck operations to enable the ship to land a plane every thirty seconds.[2] To increase the accuracy of his bombing planes, Reeves encouraged experiments with low-level bombing delivered by aircraft at the end of a steep dive. During fleet exercises in 1926, a squadron of Reeves's dive-bombers scored several hits on the fleet flagship *Pennsylvania* before her antiaircraft gun crews could train on them.[3]

The following year in the annual fleet exercises off Hawaii, the *Lexington* and *Saratoga*, remaining out of range of land-based bombers during the day, closed to within one hundred miles of Oahu during the night. In the morning they launched a large air strike against the main Pacific Fleet base at Pearl Harbor. Surprising the defenders on a Sunday morning, Reeves's bombers showered the ships in the harbor with dozens of flour-filled bags, simulating bombs. It was a vivid forecast of things to come.

Since the early 1920s the flamboyant and outspoken army aviator Brigadier General William Mitchell, an advocate of an independent air force, had kept public attention focused on military aviation. In a series of highly publicized bombing tests against the former German battleship *Ostfriesland* and the old American battleships *Alabama*, *Virginia*, and *New Jersey*, Mitchell's pilots demonstrated that bombing planes could sink even heavily armored men-of-war. While the navy criticized the "artificiality" of the tests, Mitchell declared that "the problem of the destruction of seacraft by air forces has been solved and is finished."[4]

Responding to Mitchell's publicity campaign and to pressures from Congress and within the service, the Secretary of the Navy created a new Bureau of Aeronautics in 1921. It had broad authority for aviation training and aircraft design, development, and procurement. Rear Admiral William Moffett became the bureau's chief and during his long tenure in the post proved himself more than a match for Mitchell as a publicist and political insider. "He was a master showman," recalled Commander Joy Bright Hancock, one of Moffett's aides. "I don't know who headed up the Barnum and Bailey thing. . . . But I would say Admiral Moffett could run them a close second any day. . . . He could go directly to people. Get them stirred up and thinking and agreeing. You always came away agreeing with him."[5] One of Moffett's aides gave this account of Moffett in action:

> I was sitting behind my desk in the engine section one morning . . . when the phone rang. "This is Moffett," came the Admiral's voice. . . . "You'll find me in Congressman Butler's office. . . . Bring that estimate on the cost of the Mustin plan. Get it, got it?"
>
> "Aye, Aye, sir."
>
> "Wait a minute, change that," came the staccato bark. . . . "You call up Marvin MacIntyre, tell him to come to the Bureau. Then you write up a news release for him—one like this: 'The greatest forward step in the history of aviation was taken today when Congressman Butler, Chairman of the House Naval Affairs Committee, announced approval of the Mustin Five Year Naval Aviation Building Program.'"
>
> "Did he really approve it, Admiral?" I interposed.
>
> "Of course not," came the reply. "He hasn't even seen it. But when he reads his name in the afternoon *Star*, and looks at the editorial Mac will get for us, he'll think he invented it himself."[6]

Moffett provided a strong impetus for the development of advanced aircraft and aviation tactics and was quick to exploit every technical breakthrough. He skillfully exploited tensions and controversies within the navy to further the cause of naval aviation. Moffett reassured conventional-minded admirals by his oft-repeated assertion that "naval aviation must go to sea on the backs of the fleet."[7] His argument that naval aviation was a supplement to, not a rival of, the surface fleet appealed to even the most battleship-oriented officers, most of whom had come to realize the importance of aviation in fleet scouting and gun fire spotting. The question of whether the aircraft carrier would eclipse the battleship as the capital ship of the future was one that Moffett adroitly avoided, though more outspoken airpower advocates like retired admiral William S. Sims had no hesitation in making this claim. At the same time, Moffett astutely exploited the threat that the navy might lose its aviation assets to General Billy Mitchell's proposed independent air force to persuade the navy hierarchy to enhance the status and career prospects of naval aviators, some of whom found Mitchell's arguments not unappealing.[8]

Moffett's cause received an unintended boost from Mitchell in 1925. The latter took the occasion of the crash of a navy dirigible to tell the press, "These accidents are the result of the incompetency, the criminal negligence and the treasonable administration of our national defense by the Navy and War Departments."[9] The army ordered a court-martial for Mitchell, but his remarks touched off a wave of public speculation and controversy over aviation. To dampen the public outcry, President Calvin Coolidge appointed his friend and college classmate the respected businessman Dwight Morrow to head a presidential commission on the state of military and naval aviation. Moffett used the commission hearings to make the case for retaining aviation within the navy, while working to strengthen the influence of the airmen within the service. Predictably, the Morrow commission rejected Mitchell's call for an independent air force, but did recommend measures that, when subsequently enacted into legislation, significantly strengthened naval aviation.

The legislation created a new post of Assistant Secretary of the Navy (Aeronautics). First occupied by engineering professor Herbert Warner, then by First Yale Unit veteran David Ingalls, the new office provided airmen with a civilian advocate at the highest levels of the navy. The same law also mandated that all commanding officers of aircraft carriers and naval air stations be qualified aviators. Because few airmen were yet senior enough to hold such commands, the law provided that senior officers who passed a shorter flying course could be designated "aviation observers" and thereby qualified for aviation commands. In this way, some of the most respected older officers, such as Reeves, Captain Harry E. Yarnell, and Commander Ernest J. King, as well as lower-ranking but talented officers such as Commander Frederick C. Sherman and Commander William F. Halsey, were co-opted into the ranks of naval aviation. Reeves and Yarnell qualified as "observers" while King, Sherman, and Halsey were designated "aviators." Their membership added much-needed clout for aviation in the higher ranks of the navy.[10]

Moffett pushed development of airships and seaplanes as well as aircraft carriers, but by the early 1930s it seemed clear that carrier aviation would predominate. The introduction of the air-cooled radial engine early in the 1920s made possible carrier-based aircraft that could fly farther, higher, and faster than previous airplanes equipped with the old, heavier water-cooled engines. The radial engine was also five to six times as reliable. Other innovations, including brakes on landing gear, arrester hooks for carrier landings, and more efficient flight deck procedures,

such as those encouraged by Reeves, and the introduction of radiotele-
phones between planes and ships, all served to make carrier operations
more effective and as formidable as Reeves had demonstrated during the
Panama war games.

Yet the sometimes grudging, sometimes enthusiastic acceptance of
aviation in the navy was due to more than technical progress or the efforts of innovators like Moffett and Reeves. It also had much to do with
the navy's strategic concerns. By the 1920s the U.S. Navy, which had
grown into the largest fleet in the world almost in a fit of absentminded-
ness, without a clear purpose or mission, finally found itself face to face
with a real threat and a clear mission. Planning and preparation for a war
with Japan dominated all the navy's thinking in the 1920s and 1930s.

The Washington treaties left the U.S. Navy unchallengeable in the
eastern half of the Pacific, but with no fleet base west of Hawaii the navy
would be hard pressed to defend the Philippines or U.S. interests in
China with its limited "treaty" fleet. Earlier planning for war with Japan,
embodied in the so-called Orange Plans, had envisioned a rapid voyage
across the Pacific from Hawaii by the American battle fleet, accompanied by transports carrying a relief army to the Philippines.[11] After
World War I, when Japan acquired the formerly German Marshalls, Carolines, and Marianas island chains in the Central Pacific, the possibility
of a rapid thrust across the Pacific appeared increasingly remote. Some
American strategists, however, saw Japan's acquisition of these territories as more of an opportunity than a setback. It was now possible to seize
bases along the route to the Philippines, something that would have
been impossible with the islands in the hands of a neutral country.
While some admirals continued to insist on a lightning thrust across the
Pacific, more and more came to see a future war with Japan as a relatively
lengthy series of operations to capture island stepping-stones in the Central Pacific.

It was here that the role of aircraft became vital. Navy and Marine
Corps planners, studying possible attacks on the islands, understood that
they would be defended by land-based planes that could be attacked only
by carrier aircraft. The attacking fleet would also have to deal with what
were expected to be strong fortifications on the islands. Navy planners
were unhappy at the prospect of pitting their valuable battleships against
well-concealed coast defense batteries. Instead, airplanes were to take on
this task. Moffett, seeing an opportunity, hastened to assure the Secretary of the Navy that "bombing aircraft, protected by fighting aircraft,
both necessarily operating from carriers, should be effective . . . in si-
lencing of enemy coastal defense guns."[12] In this way the more conserv-

ative admirals' faith in the battleship actually served to reinforce support for naval aviation.

While aviation had made great strides in capabilities and influence within the navy, the fundamental personnel problems remained unsolved. In 1924 there were only about 300 qualified naval aviators in the service, a decrease from 1922—this despite the fact that there were about 560 billets for aviation officers in the navy and the Lexington and Saratoga, then under construction, would require 175 additional pilots.[13] Between 1922 and 1928 the number of officers qualified as pilots increased by only 152, although Moffett had by now received congressional authorization to plan for a 1,000-plane naval air force.[14] In 1929 the commander in chief of the U.S. fleet observed that the hundred naval aviators embarked in one carrier, the Saratoga, represented more than 20 percent of the commissioned aviators in the navy and more than 60 percent of "officer pilots trained and experienced in carrier operations." This represented "a wealth of personnel . . . which the Navy could ill afford to concentrate in one vessel in time of war."[15] Naval aviation during the interwar years was in much the same situation as the Royal Navy during the Edwardian era. It was a rapidly expanding, technologically complex organization that lacked sufficient personnel to man the large numbers of sophisticated weapons platforms authorized by politicians who admired advanced weaponry but had little interest in manpower.

In part the personnel crisis was a product of the general contraction of the U.S. Navy in the 1920s and early 1930s when Congress was disinclined to authorize a navy of even "treaty size." The limited amount of new construction, mostly cruisers, that was undertaken in this period was not coupled with any increase in overall naval personnel. By 1929 the navy had fifteen hundred fewer men than it had had in 1921. At the same time almost 7,000 enlisted personnel had been assigned to aviation support, a net loss to the rest of the navy of 8,000 men.[16]

At another level the controversy over personnel was caused by differences between the surface navy and the aviation components over whether aviators were career practitioners of a new form of naval warfare or simply line officers with a particular specialty like submariners or ordnance experts. The Bureau of Navigation, which assigned officers to duty, took the view that aviators required frequent rotation to line duties at sea in order not to lose their seagoing skills. Of one hundred pilots trained during 1923, for example, so many were rotated back to the surface navy that the net gain in pilots was only twelve.[17] Moffett and the aviators argued that aviation required years of continuous professional development and experience at successively higher levels of responsibility. To assertions that aviation duty was simply a specialty like submarines or destroyers, they replied that "aviation is essentially and fundamentally a different profession, while submarines and destroyers have much in common with other naval surface craft. . . . Aviation material and methods form a profession in themselves, which in the case of naval aviation should be closely allied with the regular naval profession. At the same time the two are not the same and one cannot be an expert in both. . . . Practically every country in the world . . . has accepted the assignment of personnel to aviation as a permanent life work."[18]

At the most fundamental level, however, the chronic shortage of aviation personnel stemmed from the refusal of Moffett and other career officers to change the nature of the naval officer corps. Naval aviation might be "essential and fundamentally a different profession," but it should still be the exclusive province of the Annapolis-trained career officer. Given the fiscal and manpower realities of the 1920s and 1930s, this was an impossible goal. Although flight training was eventually offered to qualified midshipmen and a growing number chose to enter aviation upon graduation, they were still far too few to appreciably ease the personnel shortfall. The only alternative was to find additional pilots in the Naval Reserve or to provide aviation training to enlisted men. Both these expedients were adopted during the 1920s, but only against strong opposition from many senior officers.

Despite the fact that in the world war many of the most successful pilots—whether German, British, French, or American—were or had been enlisted men, the U.S. Navy had little enthusiasm for retaining any enlisted fliers. By the beginning of the 1920s, however, the shortage of naval aviators was so acute that the Bureau of Aeronautics recommended to the chief of the Bureau of Navigation that the Pacific Fleet be authorized to provide training to qualified enlisted men. Candidates were required to be first class or chief petty officers under thirty years of age with clean records and able to pass the physical examination for aviation. Those who successfully completed the training were designated "naval aviation pilots."[19]

The Bureau of Aeronautics regarded this program purely as an emergency measure and talked of phasing it out in only a few years.[20] Yet the aviator shortage made its continuance a necessity, and by July 1924 there were 124 naval aviation pilots on active duty. The congressional legislation that enacted Moffett's five-year, 1,000-plane program also contained a provision that "after July 1, 1928 the number of enlisted pilots in the Navy shall not be less than 30% of the total number of pilots employed. . . ."[21] By 1930 there were 230 naval aviation pilots on active duty.

Moffett and his successors viewed this provision for enlisted pilots with grave misgivings. They suspected, correctly, that the existence of enlisted pilots, trained in a nearly identical aviation course at Pensacola, Florida, tended to blur the distinction between officers and enlisted men. More seriously, it tended to undermine the line officers long-held contention that all responsible tasks in the navy could only be performed by Annapolis graduates. "The determining factor . . . appears to lie in the fact that an airplane pilot is in a very real sense, the commanding officer of the plane," wrote Rear Admiral Ernest J. King, Moffett's successor as chief of the Bureau of Aeronautics. "Flying an airplane therefore involves not only the mental caliber, but the training and indoctrination that is the normal sphere of officers rather than enlisted men."[22]

The Bureau of Aeronautics official position was that the naval aviation pilots were useful in ferrying aircraft, flying the mail, acting as copilots, and flying noncombat aircraft but that their utility as aviators was more limited than that of officers. The bureau pointed out that the attrition rate for enlisted trainees at Pensacola was significantly higher than that of officers. Even after enlisted men successfully completed the demanding flight training offered at Pensacola, Moffett argued, naval aviators "do not feel sufficiently confident of [their ability]."[23] The unique officerlike abilities required in a pilot were emphasized. Only an officer "fully trained and imbued with the traditions of the Navy [could] . . . properly assist and support the line officers on the bridge. . . ."[24] Rear Admiral Arthur B. Cook explained to the House Naval Affairs Committee that enlisted men lacked "ability to grasp strategical and tactical naval situations."[25]

The most influential proponents of enlisted aviation were the successive chiefs of the Bureau of Navigation. It is possible that they had a higher estimate of enlisted men than other flag officers, but they certainly had other strong motivations. Faced with meeting the manpower needs of an entire navy, they probably looked upon the assignment of enlisted men to aviation as a way of freeing officers for more important assignments. Navigation and Aeronautics also engaged in endemic feuding over a broad range of issues, which may have influenced the degree to which they supported or decried enlisted avation.

While Moffett lobbied for a change in legislation that would lower the quota on enlisted pilots from 30 to 20 percent (a change that occurred in 1932), Navigation pushed for the formation of an experimental fighter squadron composed mainly of naval aviation pilots. VF-2 or "Fighting 2" was established in 1927, with fourteen enlisted men and four officers. Flying from the *Lexington* and *Saratoga*, commanded by such future carrier admirals as J. J. Clark and Apollo Soucek, Fighting 2 soon established a reputation as an elite unit, famous for its gunnery and precision formation flying. In 1940, VF-2 became the first squadron in naval aviation history to have all eighteen planes awarded the navy "E" for excellence.[26] Even while pointing with pride to the success of VF-2, the Bureau of Aeronautics continued to insist as late as 1939 that enlisted pilots "should not be employed except in emergencies to take the place of regular line or reserve pilots."[27]

Yet the realities of war were soon to end speculation about the relative merits of enlisted versus commissioned pilots. As the Americans entered a stubborn conflict against a powerful navy whose pilots were predominantly enlisted aviators, attitudes changed. Squadron and group commanders soon discovered that most of their naval aviation pilots had far more experience and knowledge of aircraft types than their young commissioned aviators.[28] "Prior to World War II there was quite a difference between officers and enlisted pilots," recalled Naval Aviation Pilot Howell Sumrall. "However, once the war was on we all had the same objective. . . . The skipper informed everyone that they were to check their rank on the flight deck and that they would fly wing on anyone he assigned because we were far more experienced than they and he wanted to keep them alive. . . ."[29] Eventually, almost all of the naval aviation pilots received temporary or permanent commissions in the course of World War II.

Reserve aviators were viewed with less skepticism but were far from welcome. In 1921, reserve aviators who had fought in World War I wished to transfer to the regular navy were discouraged by subjecting them to a written examination so difficult and arbitrary that it later became the subject of a congressional inquiry. As late as 1928, "it was being said in high places within the Navy Department that it was preferable to accept the pilot shortage rather than take into service 'civilians who have not the basic naval training required for efficient naval aviation.'"[30] This stance, whatever its sentimental appeal to Annapolis types, could scarcely be maintained in the face of the severe pilot shortage. Moffett, a strong supporter of the reserves, encouraged former aviators to remain in the service, helped in the development of new reserve flying units, and lobbied successfully for money to pay reservists for their minimum of fifteen days of active duty a year.[31]

In 1934, Congress authorized another increase in the number of air-craft in the fleet. Over the next five years, the total number of planes would grow 100 percent to a total of 2,000. The navy recognized that it would require either still more enlisted pilots or reservists to fill the personnel gap in aviation. The Bureau of Aeronautics reluctantly proposed finding additional ensigns for flight training in the Naval Reserve. President Franklin Roosevelt and his budget director, eager to cut costs in the depths of the Great Depression, proposed instead a new category of flier, the "naval aviation cadet."[32]

Naval aviation cadets would be recruited directly from civilian life. Candidates were required to be twenty to twenty-eight years of age and unmarried. Men with at least some college education were strongly preferred. "They had to have most of their teeth except wisdom teeth and they had to be in good condition. They could not be overweight or underweight . . . and they had to present a good overall appearance," recalled one aviation cadet. "They had to be clean shaven. They had to have 20/20 vision and precise depth perception. Their hearing had to be acute and they had to be mentally alert. In fact, they had to be almost physically perfect and agree to remain unmarried for four years."[33] The navy apparently believed that "physically perfect" aviators were to be found almost exclusively among white males of northern European decent. Among the list of reserve aviators on active duty during the first year of the Pacific war there are almost no Hispanic or Slavic names, few Polish, Jewish, or Italian names, and no Asian ones.[34]

Despite the stringent requirements, there was never a shortage of applicants for flight training. Young men of the late 1930s had grown up in an era when aviation possessed a glamour and excitement equaled by almost no other activity in the United States. Well over half of the surviving naval aviation cadets contacted by former aviator Captain Joe Hill when he was writing Some Early Birds in the 1980s mentioned Charles Lindbergh's flights and the feats of other famous aviators as a prime reason for their interest in becoming pilots. Several had taken flying lessons at their own expense prior to joining the navy.[35]

These men would most likely have agreed enthusiastically with the navy recruiting slogan of the 1990s "It's not just a job, it's an adventure." Yet if thoughts of adventure were always present, thoughts of the job market could never be far from the mind of any young man in the 1930s. Though the aviation cadets belonged to the fairly privileged minority of the population who had been able to attend college, their economic prospects were far from secure. Cadet Walter Michaels had been unable to find a job as an engineer after graduation from NYU. Cadet Ed Kiem had been obliged to drop out of Worcester Polytechnic after two years for lack of money. Cadet Charles Herbert "was starving to death" as a ninety-seven-dollar-a-month schoolteacher in West Virginia, and his first paycheck bounced. Cadet Walter Hibbs had no money to pursue his ambition to attend medical school.[36] To these young men and hundreds of others the navy seemed an opportunity almost too good to be true.

Those who survived the basic elimination process at a Naval Reserve air base received a year of training at Pensacola, followed by three years of active duty with the fleet. Throughout this period they retained the rank of "cadet" (above warrant officer but below ensign) and were not finally promoted to ensign in the Naval Reserve until the completion of their four years. This saved considerable money but also engendered discontent among many aviation cadets, who resented their relatively low status and pay in the navy.

As the navy expanded still further in the shadow of the Munich crisis and Japanese expansionism in Asia, Congress passed the Naval Aviation Reserve Act of 1939. The act provided for a total of 6,000 reserve pilots. All aviation cadets who had completed their training prior to the passage of the act were immediately commissioned as ensigns in the Naval Reserve. Newer aviation cadets would receive their commission upon completion of their first seven months in the program and be required to serve seven years on active duty. Characteristically, the Bureau of Aeronautics took issue with the section of the act that provided for one reserve rear admiral and one reserve brigadier general in the Marine Corps. The bureau feared that "officers of these ranks would increase the difficulties of regular officers in dealing with the Naval Reserve."[37]

In the end it was the Naval Aviation Reserve Act of 1939 and expanded versions passed in 1940 and 1941 that "served as the chief vehicle for providing new pilots for the fleet." As early as 1941, almost half of the aviators in the navy, Marine Corps, and coast guard were reservists, and a significant proportion of the regulars were 1934–39 graduates of the naval air cadet program, who had been offered regular commissions in 1941. At the Battle of Midway in June 1942, 65 percent of the U.S. aviators had completed their training in 1941 or later.[38]

After the United States entered the war, the navy received approval for a program to train thirty thousand navy and marine aviators a year in seventeen newly established training centers stretching from Florida to Texas. As late as June 1940, only 16 percent of officers in the navy were aviators, but within two years, because of the newly authorized procurement programs, the number of naval aviators would exceed by more than two and a half times the number of officers in all other line specialties.[39] For the first time in twentieth-century naval history a major, potentially decisive mode of warfare had been entirely entrusted to a body of noncareer, short-service officers.

Through the end of 1941 all apprentice pilots, whether regular or reservist, aviation cadet or enlisted, trained at the naval air station at Pensacola, Florida. With its good weather, long gentle beaches, and almost landlocked waters, Pensacola was an ideal training base for aviation. At Pensacola student aviators spent twenty-six weeks and about two hundred flying hours (three hundred until the late 1930s) moving progressively from slow, sturdy biplane trainers to older combat aircraft and finally to night and instrument flying. In addition, there was classroom instruction in the dynamics of flight, aircraft engines, radio, navigation, and aerology. The attrition rate was high. Even in the 1920s, when the great majority of students were recent Annapolis graduates, between 30 and 50 percent failed to qualify because of physical defects, academic deficiencies, or inaptitude for flying.

An important step in the winnowing-out process was the "solo check," given after only a relatively few hours of airborne training. "This is a tense and difficult time for the class," recalled one aviator. "Rumor and speculation are rife and all kinds of confidential 'dope' are circulated. The chief instructors' supposed preferences concerning everything from steepness of turns to brands of cigarettes is considered vital information. . . . Only experienced pilots realize the problems and responsibilities confronting the two [instructors] who sit in the forward compartments of the two check planes. They never touch the controls except in an emergency. They merely give signals and see what happens. . . . The majority of checks are fairly clear cut one way or the other. It is the borderline cases that are difficult. If the verdict is yes, the student may go out and crack up. If it is no, a competent pilot may be lost to aviation."[40]

One of those who successfully passed the solo check was Lieutenant Spencer S. Warner. "You are so elated over your first successful flight that nothing [else] matters," he wrote. "You walk back to lunch differently than you ever did before. You feel that you really amount to something in the world now. There is a firmness and determination in your step and possibly you swagger just a bit. You walk this way until after your first crash."[41]

Before 1935, student aviators, following their graduation from Pensacola, received experience in flying all types of navy aircraft from giant four-engine seaplanes to single-seat fighters. With the increasing demand for aviators in the late 1930s, however, the training syllabus became shorter and more specialized. Pilots selected for carrier aviation went directly to Naval Air Station Miami for about seven months of training, then on to special carrier training groups for training in gunnery and aerial tactics and for qualifications in carrier takeoffs and landing.

Across the Pacific, the "Orange Navy" was also becoming increasingly interested in aviation. To many Japanese naval officers, the arms limitation agreements signed at Washington in 1922 were a catastrophic event. Well before World War I, Japanese strategists had determined, on the basis of abstruse mathematical and technical calculations, that the Japanese navy would have to be at least 70 percent as strong as the U.S. Navy to ensure an even chance of victory in war with America. The Washington treaties allowed only a 6:10 ratio between the two fleets, thus dooming Japan, in the eyes of many of its admirals, to inevitable defeat. "Unspeakable agony," wrote Vice Admiral Kato Kanji, chief naval technical adviser at the conference, in his diary. "How lamentable for Japan's future!"[42]

The Japanese Navy Minister, Admiral Kato Tomosaburo, took a different view. Togo's chief of staff at the Battle of Tsushima, Kato was a towering figure in both national politics and naval affairs.[43] He saw national security as comprising industrial, political, diplomatic, technological, and financial factors as well as naval power. For Kato Tomosaburo, "avoidance of war with America . . . constitutes the essence of national defense."[44] He pointed out that even were Japan to build every single capital ship called for by her naval planners, the yearly maintenance cost alone of such a fleet would be equivalent to one-third of the entire national budget. "To speak plainly," he declared, "we cannot fight a war without money. . . . The United States is the only country with which war is probable, but it is the only country where we can float a foreign loan, therefore we cannot fight a war with the United States."[45] From that point of view, the Washington treaties did not so much limit the Japanese navy as limit the United States.

Ratification of the Washington naval treaties touched off two decades of bitter factional rivalry within the Japanese navy's officer corps. Probably the most significant division was between the Navy Ministry and the Naval General Staff. The two organizations were entirely separate. The ministry was responsible for the naval budget, ship construction, weapons procurement, personnel, relations with the Diet and the cabinet, and broad matters of naval policy. The General Staff directed the operations of the fleet and the preparation of war plans. Until the 1920s the Navy Ministry, under the leadership of powerful ministers like Admiral Yamamoto Gonbei and Admiral Kato Tomosaburo, had played the predominant role in naval affairs, while the Naval General Staff occupied a distinctly secondary position.[46] Officers of the General Staff resented this inferior status; during the 1930s they made increasingly successful efforts to reverse the situation. The Washington treaties had accentuated and given focus to this endemic rivalry. Those admirals who favored continued cooperation with the Anglo-American powers and who supported the Washington disarmament agreements were to be found principally in the Navy Ministry; the opponents of the Washington treaties system were to be found principally in the Naval General Staff.[47]

While opponents of the treaties usually framed their arguments in terms of ships and tonnages, the impact of the treaties on the navy's officers and enlisted force was actually far more drastic. The smaller navy dictated by the Washington treaties and by the tight fiscal policies of the government led to immediate retrenchment in personnel. Characteristically the navy started its retrenchment by eliminating lower-ranking sailors and drastically reducing the intake of new officers and petty officers, all in an attempt to protect its existing corps of commissioned and petty officers.[48] The entering Naval Academy class of 1922 was more than 70 percent smaller than the previous year's class. In the end, however, seventeen hundred officers and twenty thousand petty officers and sailors had to be prematurely retired, including 90 percent of the vice admirals.[49] These drastic personnel measures added a potent mix of individual fears, resentments, career frustrations, and anxieties to the debates on naval strategy and arms policy. After Washington, officers at the Naval Academy "felt very mistreated and low in morale," recalled Admiral Takagi Sokichi. "Some became drunk; others absented themselves from duty."[50]

Despite their vociferous protests, however, most Japanese naval leaders were not wholly displeased with the Washington agreements. For one thing, they allowed Japan to construct unlimited numbers of cruisers, destroyers, and submarines; they also halted the fortification of American bases in the western Pacific, which the farsighted Admiral Kato Tomosaburo had all along regarded as more crucial than haggling over ratios.[51] Moreover, the United States displayed no inclination during the 1920s to bring its fleet up to treaty strength. Still, few naval leaders— outside of the handful of moderates in the Navy Ministry—were prepared to tolerate any further limitations. Yet that was precisely what the British and Americans demanded at the London Naval Conference of 1930.

At London, the United States insisted that the 6:10 ratio established for capital ships be extended to cruisers as well. The Japanese believed that they would need at least a 7:10 ratio in this class to safeguard their superiority in East Asian waters. In the end, the two countries reached a comprise called the Reed-Matsudaira formula whereby the 6:10 formula was accepted in principal but the United States agreed not to build beyond a 7:10 ratio until the next disarmament conference, scheduled for 1936.

Back in Japan, Kato Kanji and the Fleet Faction attacked the London disarmament agreements as dangerous to security, humiliating, and a violation of the Naval General Staff's right of supreme command. A major domestic political battle broke out over the ratification of the treaty. Moderate admirals of the "treaty faction" supported Prime Minister Hamaguchi Osachi, whose party won a smashing victory at the polls; in February 1930, the treaty was subsequently accepted by the Diet.[52]

In November 1930, Hamaguchi was shot by a fanatic from an ultranationalist patriotic society. Even before his death, the storm of criticism over the London agreements had obliged Hamaguchi's government to promise larger naval appropriations. Moving quickly to consolidate its position, the Fleet Faction prevailed upon Prince Fushimi Hiroyasu, a member of the royal family, to become chief of the Naval General Staff. During what historian Asada Sadao has characterized as "his long and undistinguished career," Fushimi amply served the purposes of the extremists in the Fleet Faction. This included helping Kato Kanji to incessantly prod the Navy Minister, Admiral Osumi Mineo, to purge the senior admirals associated with the disarmament treaty and force them into early retirement. Henceforth, the middle-grade officers of the Naval General Staff, younger disciples of Kato Kanji, were to play an increasingly powerful role in shaping naval policy.[53]

Obsessed with what they saw as their inferior position vis-à-vis the U.S. and British navies, the Japanese continually searched for weapons and tactics that would give them a decisive, qualitative superiority. They led the world in the development of torpedoes and by 1933 had perfected a twenty-four-inch oxygen-fueled torpedo with a maximum range of 12 miles at forty-nine knots, nearly twice the range of contemporary foreign torpedoes. Large long-range submarines were developed to intercept the American fleet soon after it began its passage across the Pacific from Hawaii. These submarines were designed to take station along a patrol line in the western Pacific between the Bonins and Marianas and make repeated attacks on the enemy fleet in order to wear it down prior to its meeting with the Japanese battle force.[54] By 1936 they were building 64,000-ton super-battleships armed with nine 18-inch guns designed to outrange any foreign dreadnought.

"The Washington Treaty places no limit on training and drill, does it?" Admiral Togo reminded disappointed naval officers in 1922. By the mid-1920s, acting on this theme, the Japanese navy was engaged in rigorous, even hazardous drills and exercises that tested sailors' skills to the limit. The Japanese fleet's yearly training cycle began in December and continued with few pauses until the end of October. Japanese sailors quipped that the navy's calendar consisted entirely of weekdays. Foreign observers noted that even when Japanese ships were in dock, sailors not on duty were kept constantly busy with calisthenics.[55] "We never dared to question orders, to doubt authority, to do anything but carry out all the demands of our superiors," recalled one former seaman. "We were automatons who obeyed without thinking."[56]

Exercises were frequently held in the stormy northern waters near the Kuril Islands to toughen the men and preserve secrecy. Special emphasis was placed upon training for night fighting, and for this purpose the Imperial Japanese Navy had developed special range finders, binoculars, and illumination devices. Maneuvers and exercises were carried out at high speed at night, by ships lacking radar or other electronic devices, and disastrous collisions were far from rare. Yet the navy persisted in its efforts to bring commanders and crews to a high state of proficiency for night fighting. The irrepressible Kato Kanji, appointed commander in chief of the Combined Fleet in the late 1920s, declared after a collision between a cruiser and a destroyer that cost 120 lives, "We must devote ourselves more and more to this kind of drill." Japan had to pit its "spiritual power" against America's material superiority, thus "turning an impossibility into a possibility."[57] Untroubled by the logical contradiction between their obsession with the importance of numbers and tonnage and their faith in the superiority of intangible "spiritual power," Japanese naval leaders continued their relentless training regimen while at the same time demanding superweapons as the only hope for victory.

If the Japanese navy indeed possessed unusual resources of vigor, will, dedication, and bravery, they resided primarily in its splendid enlisted force, which had so impressed Russian prisoners after the Battle of Tsushima. "It would be a poor compliment to Japanese naval men to call them brave," wrote British naval expert Fred T. Jane. "That they certainly are; but to great personal courage they add a fierce tenacity which

is no less impressive."⁵⁸ An American naval officer was "greatly impressed by the physical setup of the Japanese enlisted man. Most were
short and stocky but gave the impression of great physical strength. . . .
Their physical standards were so high it appeared to me they must have
been selected for their military character."⁵⁹

The Imperial Japanese Navy did indeed select its sailors for their military aptitude. The navy was a relatively high-status occupation in pre–
World War II Japan and was certainly a more popular choice with young
men than the army. Youths from poverty-stricken rural districts of Japan
also knew that they would eat better and more regularly in the navy
than as members of large impoverished farming families.⁶⁰ Kobayashi
Takahiro, the third son in a poor rural family, "decided to join the navy
to survive."⁶¹ Among the general public as well, the navy enjoyed a better reputation than the army. The latter was associated with harsh discipline and militarism while the navy was associated with adventure and
modern technology.⁶²

Although the navy could certainly have filled its manpower needs by
accepting only volunteers, it always accepted a significant percentage of
conscripts as well. The reason for this policy remains unclear. The
British naval expert Hector C. Bywater reported that the navy wished to
ensure that it received recruits from every area of the country, for by so
doing it would be able to balance the army's political influence in inland
towns and farming districts somewhat.⁶³ Another reason may have been
the army's unwillingness to allow the navy to siphon off all of the most
capable recruits through voluntary enlistment.

Whether conscript or volunteer, the entry of a young man into the
navy was an important ceremonial occasion both for his family and his
neighbors. Formal farewell parties attended by neighbors, relatives, and
other well-wishers marked a youth's departure for military service. The
day before his departure, Fujita Nobuhara, who entered the navy as a
"special boy sailor" at age fourteen, took part in such a celebration with
relatives and acquaintances. "But Mother could not sleep at all. And
the members of the Women's Association said, 'What a pity. He's so
small.'"⁶⁴

Fourteen-year-olds were by no means rare in the Japanese navy. The
service preferred to identify talented youths at an early age and train
them in academic and technical subjects within the navy. Thus, signalmen, weathermen, cryptographers, telegraphists, and hydrographers could
be enlisted as early as age fourteen. Aviators were accepted at fifteen and
bandsmen, medics, and pay clerks at sixteen. If successful, many of these

boy specialists received accelerated promotion to the rank of leading seaman or petty officer.[65]

At the training center many young recruits found that they were too short to sling their hammocks, while the "hammock ropes were so stiff our fingers became bloody from trying to hang them."[66] Mitsutani Tatsuo, who came from an isolated rural region of northern Honshu "cried every night after I joined the navy. Because of my strong dialect I could hardly have conversations with fellow sailors. In the morning my hammock ropes were wet from tears."[67]

Training was rigorous and exhausting, "very much like being a slave on a pirate ship."[68] Boy trainees arose at 5:00 A.M. in the summer, 6:00 A.M. in the winter. Mornings were devoted to ordinary academic subjects, while the afternoons were allocated to drill, military training, and "spiritual education." Drill instructors enthusiastically punched and slapped recruits or beat them with wooden bats called "spiritual bars." These beatings were administered for all types of offenses, including: failure to salute, sloppy appearance, and poor performance at drill. Some drill instructors were reputed to use metal instead of wooden bats, contrary to regulations. One recruit reported developing tooth problems later in life "due to the beatings."[69] Many instructors appeared to have regarded these frequent beatings as a sort of fatherly gesture. Following a beating one trainee was instructed to "look at the moon. Your father and mother will be looking at that moon and hoping you will become a sailor for the good of the emperor."[70] Fujita Nobuhara was punched in the face for a mistake in drill by an instructor, who then observed in a kindly voice, "You know, son, I've got a boy at home as old as you."[71]

Recalling these experiences many years later, former sailors remained bitter about what they saw as excessive brutality, but many also said they were glad they had such an experience. After training, one sailor recalled that "we no longer had any fear of death; life was so hard as it was."[72]

Life improved somewhat when the new sailors joined their ships. But the improvement was only relative. Japanese warships were designed to carry the maximum guns and armor on a given displacement, and to attain this, the accommodation space for the crews was readily sacrificed. At the same time the heavy armament of these ships required larger than normal crews, aggravating the already crowded conditions.

New sailors joining the ship were traditionally hazed by the sailors who had come in the previous year's draft. These "old ones" harassed the newcomers by constantly criticizing their work, their appearance, and their military bearing and administering frequent punches to the face and other parts of the body.[73] Watanabe Kiyoshi, a sailor in the super-battleship *Musashi*, found it "not a very comfortable place to live. [I was] smacked in the face and humiliated and chased every day."[74] It gives some indication of the state of living conditions aboard Japanese men-of-war that Japanese sailors regarded the cramped, uncomfortable, and poorly ventilated mess deck of a visiting British cruiser as that of "a luxury ship."[75]

A popular escape from the demands and discomforts of shipboard life was alcohol. Some sailors proved adept at improvising a kind of home brew by combining the industrial-type ethyl alcohol used in machinery with large quantities of water. Because ethyl alcohol has a strong smell, sailors would burn the excess alcohol in order to prevent any passing petty officer or officer from noticing the telltale odor. If the fumes had permeated the closed-in spaces, however, a sudden explosion could result. A number of Japanese warships sunk or damaged by accidental explosions, including Togo's flagship *Mikasa* and the battleship *Mutsu* in 1942, were widely believed to have been lost from such causes.[76]

As in the British and American navies, petty officers controlled most of the day-to-day routine of the ship. One former junior officer recalled that petty officers could "do pretty much what they wanted." Officers, as in other navies, had only limited day-to-day contact with enlisted sailors. Since Japanese ships, like their American counterparts, experienced very frequent turnovers of personnel, the petty officers provided an element of continuity and stability in the ship's administration.[77] The petty officers' power and authority was backed by ferocious corporal punishment. Watanabe Kiyoshi found "the beating by petty officers excruciating."[78]

In contrast to sailors, most petty officers and officers seem to have been relatively happy in the navy. Almost 90 percent of former petty officers contacted by one writer in the late 1980s said they enjoyed life in the navy. One recalled "the warm relations in the service and the respect and affection of the sailors toward the petty officers."[79]

Like the sailors they would later command, officer candidates entering Etajima were routinely beaten "to remove them from civilian habits." As at Annapolis, discipline of the entering class was entrusted to upperclassmen. Admiral Takagi Sokichi later recalled that those who were most enthusiastic about inflicting corporal punishment were usually the academically weakest students.[80]

Austere and demanding as it had been in Togo's day, the Naval Academy had by the 1920s grown even more regimented. Students were not allowed to read books not approved by the school, and rote memorization was the normal mode of learning. Sports and physical training proved so tiring that many students found it difficult to fight off sleep during their academic classes.

Class rank at Etajima was key to determining a naval officer's future. All cadets were ranked from the highest to the lowest, and a man's record in his three to four years at Etajima "had equal influence on his promotion prospects as his entire service record for the next 25 years." Cadets who ranked in the top four or five in their class were considered the future elite of the navy, potential chiefs of the Naval General Staff, fleet commanders, Navy Ministers, and their careers were closely monitored. Even the worst students, however, were expected to reach the rank of commander, the step just below captain, at the same time that the top graduates became captains.[81]

For those who survived the rigors of Etajima, the navy proved a relatively comfortable place. With assignments efficiently managed by the Navy Ministry upon the basis of seniority and class rank, there was little room for cutthroat competition or career anxiety. As in the Royal Navy, efficient, steady, and unimaginative men were greatly preferred.[82] In the stately progress through the ranks orchestrated by the Navy Ministry the age of officers in the various grades gradually increased until, by 1941, the average age of an admiral was about ten years older than in the Russo-Japanese War.[83] As in the Royal Navy, those officers thought to have the best brains tended to be assigned to specialize in gunnery. Unlike top officers in the British and U.S. navies, however, top Japanese naval officers tended to spend much of their time ashore filling key billets in the Naval General Staff and Navy Ministry. In 1942, for example, more than half of the top graduates of the Naval War College were assigned to bureaucracies ashore rather than to operational forces.[84]

Aviation appeared, to the Japanese, another effective means of reducing the superiority of an enemy fleet. Aerial attacks on London and other cities in World War I had suggested that in a future conflict Japan's cities might be vulnerable to bombing attacks from sea-based planes. Like the Americans, the Japanese had been impressed by the achievements of British naval aviation in the Great War and in 1920 had requested that a British naval aviation advisory mission be sent to Japan to assist the navy in organizing and modernizing its aviation elements. The British mission, called the Semphill Mission, remained in Japan for four years and enabled Japanese naval aviation to "leap from 1914 to 1918 in a single bound."[85] By 1927, the Japanese navy had almost four times as many aircraft as the Royal Navy.

During the 1930s under the leadership of Rear Admiral Yamamoto Isoroku, who headed successively the technical division of the Naval Aviation Department and then the entire department, the Japanese navy encouraged Japanese manufacturers to design and produce their own aircraft. Materials and equipment continued to be imported from abroad, but by the late 1930s, Japan's aircraft industry could produce planes that were equal or superior to the most advanced aircraft abroad.[86] At the end of the decade the navy had long-range bombers and torpedo planes in production. These aircraft were intended to deliver attacks against American ships as they crossed the Pacific.

In many ways developments in naval aviation in the United States and Japan appeared to parallel each other. Like the U.S. Navy, the Japanese navy had built a small experimental carrier, *Hosho*, completed in 1922, which was the first ship built from the keel up as a carrier. The Japanese had also converted two of their latest capital ships, *Akagi* and *Kaga*, to aircraft carriers under the Washington treaties. Like the U.S. Navy they had established a separate aviation bureau within the naval hierarchy with broad powers relating to the organization and development of aviation technology, personnel, and doctrine. Unlike the U.S. Navy, however, the Imperial Japanese Navy established no requirement that senior officers commanding air stations and carriers be qualified aviators.

Questions relating to aviation personnel proved as critically important in the Japanese navy as they had in the U.S. Navy. The Japanese navy was even less willing than the American to tolerate the entry of non–academy graduates into the line officer ranks. Indeed, the proportion of officers to enlisted personnel was smaller in the Japanese than in the U.S. Navy. In 1941, at the peak of its prewar buildup, a little under 8 percent of Japanese navy personnel were officers, while the U.S. Navy had more than 10 percent officers.[87] The number of officers was small both because of Japanese faith in the value of "quality over quantity" and because the navy sought to limit the size of classes at Etajima to the point where every graduate could have a likely chance of reaching high rank.[88] Between 1936 and 1941 the shortfall in numbers of officers to fill existing billets in the fleet was never less than 700 and sometimes as high as 1,150.[89]

Given this situation, there were few officers to spare for aviation assignments. Consequently, the Japanese turned to enlisted men to fill the majority of its pilot billets not out of egalitarianism, but as a result of an elitism even more pervasive than in the U.S. Navy. The Japanese navy drew its enlisted pilots directly from sailors in the fleet who qualified for aviation and from boys fifteen to seventeen years old who met the demanding physical standards of the navy. These boys required several years of general education and naval training before they could begin their aviation instruction. A second version of this program, introduced in 1937, was restricted to middle school graduates, who spent less time in training and were promoted more rapidly.[90] Competition for the small number of places in these programs was keen and standards very high. In 1937 only seventy enlisted men were selected for aviation training out of fifteen hundred applicants.[91]

To American aviation cadets at Pensacola, who spent a good part of their leisure time at the officers' club or on the golf course and attended dances each weekend, the regimen at the Imperial Navy Fliers School at Tsuchiura near Tokyo would have seemed fantastic.[92] At Tsuchiura student pilots were frequently required to climb a high iron pole. "At the top of the pole we were to suspend ourselves by one hand only. Any cadet who failed to support his weight for less than ten minutes received a swift kick and was sent scurrying up the pole again."[93] Candidates were also required to swim fifty meters in under forty seconds, to remain underwater for at least ninety seconds, and to somersault off a high wooden tower landing on their feet on the ground. To develop balance, students were required to walk on their hands and to stand on their heads for at least ten minutes. Students improved their reaction time by practicing snatching flies on the wing with their fists.

After graduation from Tsuchiura, pilots were sent to specialized training bases where they learned to fly fighters, bombers, torpedo planes, or seaplanes. Much of the operational training was carried out by the squadrons and groups themselves, a system that worked well as long as the squadrons were not heavily committed to combat. No advanced operational training units existed, and veteran pilots were not routinely rotated to training duties as they were in the U.S. Navy. This organizational arrangement was to prove a vital weakness once war began.

Both Japanese and American aviators operated in an extreme environment that made severe demands on their minds, senses, and vital organs. An aviator's vision had to be at least 25 percent better than normal, with perfect depth and peripheral vision and no color blindness. His body had to able to withstand the effects of dives and sharp turns at high speeds. These could increase the effective weight of a 150-pound man to over 750 pounds and cause blackouts.[94] Pilots flying in open cockpits suffered from the effects of high wind and cold, while the thinness of the air at altitudes above 8,000 feet could cause oxygen deprivation, which resulted in reduced concentration and physical coordination, sometimes with fatal results. Oxygen masks were available by the late 1930s but often had a limited supply of oxygen and were usually reserved for emergencies.[95] Another hazard was carbon monoxide, which could enter cockpits or cabins through ventilators or heaters or directly from the engines mounted on the nose. At altitudes above 10,000 feet even a minute amount of CO_2 leakage was enough to cause fatal carbon monoxide poisoning.[96]

In 1925, 3.5 percent of all U.S. naval fliers were killed in crashes or other accidents, about thirty-six times the number of deaths per thousand of all other sailors. Although planes became steadily more reliable during the next decade, flight operations also became more difficult and demanding. Flights were longer and there were more night operations and carrier landings. During the period 1923 to 1933, more than thirty-nine times as many aviators as nonaviators in the Navy died in accidents.[97] Dive-bomber pilot Boone T. Guyton considered his squadron's 1936–40 death rate of about one in ten as "just about average."[98]

Japanese aviators would probably have considered one in ten deaths very tame indeed. During the late 1930s accidents to naval aircraft in Japan were so frequent that newspapers sardonically observed that the army and navy must be competing for the distinction of having the most crashes. Rear Admiral Yamamoto, when commanding Carrier Division 1, referred his pilots to a plaque listing officers killed in action and declared, "The Naval Air Corps will probably never be really strong until the whole wardroom is plastered with names like these. I want you to be resigned to that idea in your work."[99]

If aviation was a generally hazardous occupation, carrier operations were the most hazardous type of aviation. "I believe that a carrier landing is the most thrilling action in peacetime," wrote Ensign Frederick Mears. "To take a fast plane heavy with armor plate, machine guns, gas and sometimes bombs and set it down on a short narrow deck requires all the attention and skill of the most experienced pilot. When pilots have never done it before and are nervous, to say the least, it is that much more spectacular."[100]

Pilots landed their planes in a kind of controlled stall onto a moving flight deck that might be rising and falling in the open sea. If the maneuver was performed successfully the plane would catch on an arresting wire, bringing it to a sudden, jolting halt. Any small error or momentary inattention could send the plane crashing onto the deck or careening across it. "Your wheels are over water then over the narrow, pitching deck and then you find yourself holding the throttle just a bit breathless as you wait for the arresting gear to stop all forward motion suddenly."[101] During routine carrier qualification training aboard the *Hornet* in early 1942, three of eighteen pilots crashed while attempting their first landings.

All three of the major navies tended to view naval airpower in a similar way. Aviation was essential for scouting and naval gunfire spotting. In addition, aviation could directly effect the outcome of a naval encounter through the destruction of the enemy's carriers and direct attacks on the enemy battle line. Unlike the battleship, however, the carriers were seen as having little staying power.[102] "Carriers combine great power with extreme vulnerability," one naval aviator observed.[103]

A battleship or a cruiser could fire dozens of rounds of shells, but a carrier had only one powerful round of firepower. A carrier would launch its planes in a single mass attack. It was unlikely that an opposing carrier, lacking armor protection and crammed with volatile fuel and ammunition, could survive such a mass attack. If the opposing carriers launched their strikes at approximately the same time they might well annihilate each other. Even if an aircraft carrier survived the enemy's counter air strike, it would probably have too few planes remaining to do much additional damage.[104] "The vulnerability of our own carriers constitutes the Achilles heel of our Fleet strength," declared the head of the U.S. Navy's war plans division in 1939.[105]

Nevertheless, by the late 1930s a few senior officers in the United States and Japan had come over to the view that airpower, not gun power, might be the decisive element in future battles. Some, like Vice Admiral William F. Halsey, argued that aircraft carriers could defend themselves with their own fighter aircraft if these were supported by radar and suitable communications arrangements. They agreed with the younger naval aviators, who were eager to cut the carriers loose from the slow, ponderous battle line and have them operate independently, perhaps in groups ranging from two to four ships. Others in the U.S. and Japanese navies argued that long-range land-based aircraft such as the two-engine Type 1 attack bomber, which was developed by the Japanese in 1939, and large long-range flying boats, such as the American Consolidated Catalina and the Japanese Kawanishi Type 2, could strike and destroy fleets hundreds of miles from land.[106]

Yet the superiority of airpower remained the minority view in the Japanese and American, as well as the British, navy—and not just for reasons of naval conservatism. Treaty limits and tight budgets had limited the sea powers to only a handful of carriers and a relatively small number of aircraft, making extensive experimentation and experience during the interwar years difficult or impossible. One reason the British Admiralty was not particularly worried about the threat of Japanese air attacks on the battle fleet was that until 1939 the Imperial Japanese Navy had only four large carriers and about three hundred aircraft.[107] And while naval aircraft improved rapidly in the 1930s, performing impressively in maneuvers, they still had limited range and bomb capacity. They could not remain aloft for extended periods and were dependent on daylight and good weather. Bombing ships from high altitude had generally proved ineffective, and the low-level attack techniques of torpedo planes and dive-bombers were still under development. The most advanced aircraft looked highly promising in 1939, but so did other devices such as radar and improved antiaircraft guns.[108] In sum, "there was just not enough evidence [before 1941] that aircraft carriers had become the dominant ship type."[109]

While the Japanese and U.S. navies moved steadily, if somewhat uncertainly, down the road toward new modes of warfare, the Royal Navy's leaders worried that it might well be losing its ability to prevail even in the traditional modes of naval operations. That the Royal Navy had, by the mid-1930s, been equaled or surpassed by the two great non-European navies would have seemed far from apparent to anyone observing the majestic spectacle of the Mediterranean Fleet gathered at Malta or the sight of the Coronation Naval Review of 1937. "With the end of World War I, the Royal Navy had gradually returned to pre-war standards of spit and polish, cutthroat competition for promotion and social striving as exemplified by life ashore in the Mediterranean Fleet."[110]

Malta was the center of the British naval world, its harbor often filled with warships immaculate in their fresh light-gray paint, brasswork gleaming in the Mediterranean sun. One officer calculated that in an average year a sailor spent 39 percent of his on-duty time on scrubbing decks, cleaning guns, polishing brightwork, and painting ship, 46 percent on "maintenance and upkeep of equipment," and less than 15 percent on drills and training.[111] "From colors to sunset the officer of the watch wore a frock coat and sword belt and carried a telescope. Our rig on Sundays was frock coats with, at divisions, swords and white kid gloves. In Malta, when attending the opera, we had to wear mess dress, which was also the rig for dances on board." Sailors working in overalls "had to keep out of sight and were never allowed on the upperdeck."[112]

Yet beneath the impressive pomp and majestic appearance the situation was dramatically changing. By the end of the 1930s both Italy and Germany had expanded their navies and had completed or were building more than a dozen modern battleships. The Italian fleet alone was almost a match for the French, Britain's only likely ally. With most of the British fleet already committed to sail for the Far East in the event of war with Japan, Great Britain faced a maddening strategic dilemma, in the event of war with even two of the three Axis powers.

The Royal Navy's leaders were acutely aware of this. Although they retained their supreme confidence, they knew that in the next war they would be fighting against odds.[113] They were also aware that the navy's record in the Great War left much to be desired, and that many of the shortcomings in its performance could be blamed on lack of initiative. Hence the major difference between the Royal Navy officers of 1914 and 1939: the latter were prepared to take risks and to innovate to a certain extent. Instead of being left solely to flag officers, tactics was now intensively taught to and studied by officers as junior as lieutenants. Command and control arrangements were revamped to give the captain of a ship as clear a picture as possible of the tactical situation. Fire control systems based on the more advanced Pollen system were also belatedly adopted.

Where Jellicoe had seen night fighting as ill-advised and risky, the Royal Navy, by the mid-1930s, "was investigating situations in which the battle fleet purposely sought out night action."[114] By the end of the 1930s the Mediterranean Fleet saw night fighting as its normal choice of action.[115]

The years of tight budgets and technical backwardness would cost the Royal Navy many defeats in World War II; but these would seldom be due to poor leadership or tactics. In World War I the Royal Navy had enjoyed overwhelming material superiority but had usually been unable to achieve decisive results. In World War II, British material was often quantitatively and sometimes qualitatively inferior, but bolder, better-trained leaders were able to use it to the best advantage.

NINE

"THE ZENITH OF EFFORT AND THE NADIR OF HOPE"

November 1940. France had fallen to the Germans. Italy had entered the war on the Axis side. England had survived the German air onslaught in the Battle of Britain and was now at war alone against Italy and Germany. The British Mediterranean Fleet under Sir Andrew Cunningham was preparing to carry out a surprise air attack against the Italian naval base at Taranto with his newly arrived carrier HMS *Illustrious*. The First Sea Lord, Admiral Sir Dudley Pound, had approved the idea but only as a kind of last-ditch suicide attack.[1]

On November 11, British reconnaissance planes confirmed that the entire Italian fleet of six battleships was in Taranto Harbor. At dusk the *Illustrious* left the Mediterranean fleet and steamed to a position 170 miles southeast of Taranto. "Good luck then to your lads in their enterprise," Cunningham signaled to the carrier.[2] In the bright moonlight the *Illustrious* turned into the wind and began to launch the first of her Swordfish torpedo bombers, primitive-looking two-seater biplanes with a top speed of less than 120 miles an hour. The first wave of twelve planes was on the flight deck, engines roaring. At a green-light signal, chocks were swept out from under the wheels, the folded wings were slammed into place, and the aircraft taxied to their launch position. Then at another signal the ungainly Swordfish rolled down the deck and rose slowly into the air.

Each plane carried extra fuel tanks, including a sixty-gallon gas tank that shared the rear cockpit with the observer. At 6,000 feet the open cockpits were bitter cold, "the sort of cold that fills you until all else is drowned save perhaps fear and loneliness."³ Although the Swordfish were themselves obsolescent, they carried the latest British torpedoes, 18-inch weapons that could dive under torpedo nets and explode either when they hit their targets or when they were close enough to be set off by a ship's magnetic field. Half of the Swordfish were armed with these torpedoes, the others with flares and six 250-pound bombs.

As Taranto's three hundred antiaircraft guns greeted the unexpected raiders, the torpedo planes swooped down to altitudes of less than fifty feet to launch their fish. The lead plane scored a fatal hit on the battleship *Conte de Cavour*. Other planes put two torpedoes into the new battleship *Littorio*. The second wave of eight Swordfish hit the *Littorio* again and torpedoed the battleship *Caio Duilio*. In all, two battleships had been crippled and one sunk, while only two airplanes were lost. "It was as if we had lost a great naval battle and could not foresee being able to recover from the consequences," wrote an Italian naval officer.⁴ The stunning success at Taranto has often been interpreted as marking the clear ascendance of naval aviation over the battle line, a portent and a prelude to Pearl Harbor. Yet a review of the war at sea during the first twenty-eight months after the fall of Poland might suggest that Taranto was more an exception than the beginning of a trend.

Until Taranto the naval war had proceeded pretty much as the Admiralty planners had anticipated. There were more than a dozen naval actions decided mainly or entirely by gunfire and torpedoes. Before Taranto, British carrier aircraft had sunk only one ship larger than a destroyer, while the British carrier *Glorious* had been sunk by German battleships during the Norwegian campaign in the spring of 1940. And two of the largest battle fleet actions of the European war took place *after* Taranto. At the end of March 1941, while pursuing the Italian fleet, Admiral Cunningham's battleships sank the heavy cruisers *Zara*, *Pola*, and *Fiume*. In May 1941 the new German battleship *Bismarck*, on a raid into the Atlantic, sank the British battle cruiser *Hood* and damaged the battleship *Prince of Wales* in a gun action and was herself sunk four days later by British battleships.

In both of these actions, carrier aircraft had played the role envisioned for them by prewar tacticians, delivering air strikes against the enemy ships to slow or cripple them so that they could be dispatched by the battle line. Swordfish from the carrier *Formidable* had crippled the Italian cruiser *Pola*, which led to the loss of that ship and her two sisters to the British battle line when they caught up with them after dark. The *Bismarck* was on the verge of eluding pursuing British capital ships and steaming safely into Brest when a twilight attack by Swordfish from the carrier *Ark Royal* wrecked her steering gear and left her easy prey for the British battleships *Rodney* and *King George V*. Given these experiences it was easy to conclude that the carrier was an important adjunct to the battleship but had not displaced it.

Land-based aircraft were a more serious threat. The German battleships *Scharnhorst* and *Gneisenau* were damaged by British planes at Brest, and Italian and German aircraft constantly harried the British Mediterranean fleet. Yet until the spring of 1941 it could not be said that aircraft had driven warships from the seas. In May 1941, however, the contest between ships and airplanes entered a new phase.

Three days after the British success at Taranto, Greek armies began a general offensive against the Italians, who had invaded Greece one month before. The Greeks easily pushed Mussolini's forces out of Greece and pursued them into Albania. Barely able to hold in Albania, Mussolini formally requested German help in December 1940. Hitler ordered German air force units to Italy and prepared to invade Bulgaria and Greece in the spring. Aware of German intentions, the Greek government accepted British offers of assistance, and in March, British forces arrived in Greece.

The German invasion of Greece on April 6 easily sliced through the Allied defenses, isolating large portions of the Greek army and forcing the British back to the west coast of Attica. The Greek and British governments agreed to evacuate their forces from Greece but to hold the island of Crete, which became the new headquarters of the Greek government. In the face of heavy German air attacks, Royal Navy warships and Greek merchantmen evacuated more than 50,000 troops from Greece at the end of April.

The British were aware, from decrypted German messages, that Hitler was next planning to attack Crete. He feared that Crete might be used by the British as an air base to attack Rumania's oil fields, a key source of supply for German forces preparing to invade Russia. The Germans planned a combined air and sea invasion spearheaded by General Kurt Student's Airborne Corps of parachute and glider troops. British, Australian, Greek, and New Zealand troops defending the island under General Bernard C. Freyberg outnumbered the invaders more than two to one. But the Germans would have almost complete control of the air, and the Commonwealth troops were short of equipment and exhausted after the Greek campaign. The Royal Navy's role was to prevent seaborne forces from reaching the island, a task they would have to carry out within easy range of German air bases. The struggle for Crete would thus mark the beginning of a significant new stage in the contest between ships and airplanes. For the men of the Royal Navy it was to be the most trying episode of the entire naval war, "the zenith of effort and the nadir of hope," in the words of a young destroyer officer.[5]

On May 20, German paratroopers supported by heavy air attacks began dropping on Crete. The Mediterranean Fleet, already at sea, moved into position to block any interference by the Italian battle fleet and cut off any attempt to reinforce Crete by sea. Crete was 440 miles from the British naval base at Alexandria, Egypt, while Axis air bases in southeastern Greece and on the island of Scarpanto dominated the approaches to the Aegean Sea and the Italian navy menaced the rear. The British had only one aircraft carrier, *Formidable*, with less than two dozen low-performance aircraft. The Royal Air Force in the Middle East had only a few dozen bombers and fighters, not all of which had the range to reach Crete from Egypt. Air bases on Crete itself were unfinished and were soon rendered unusable by German air attacks. Fliegerkorps VIII, the main German covering force for the invasion, had 280 two-engine bombers, 90 fighters, and 150 Ju-87 "Stuka" dive-bombers. The situation of the British "was like a fleet based on Lisbon trying to prevent invasion barges getting across from France to England, assuming that England had no Air Force and that the enemy had a large navy at Amsterdam," wrote Lieutenant Hugh Hodgkinson, who was aboard the destroyer *Hotspur*.[6]

Crete was a narrow mountainous island about 160 miles long. All the bays and harbors were located on the north coast, as were the major airfields. To reinforce, support, or evacuate Allied troops the Mediterranean Fleet would have to enter the German-controlled Aegean. "From the point of view of defense," observed Admiral Cunningham, "it would have suited us much better if the island could have been turned upside down."[7]

The sailors of the Mediterranean Fleet were already tired and worn from the effort of the Greek evacuation and fighting convoys through to the beleaguered island of Malta. Captain Lord Louis Mountbatten, commanding the destroyer *Kelly* at Malta, reported that "on average we have four daylight air raids and night raids. About 60 aircraft come over Grand Harbor together, bombs whistle down. . . . I won't pretend its fun."[8] Early in May, Cunningham had told the First Sea Lord that he and his senior officers "had noticed signs of strain among the officers and ratings particularly in the anti-aircraft cruisers and destroyers. The former have had a grueling time ever since the move of the Army to Greece. . . . Never a trip to sea without being bombed."[9]

Cunningham's fleet comprised four surface action groups or "forces" that he directed from Alexandria: Force A, the battleships *Warspite* and *Valiant*, and five destroyers under Rear Admiral H. B. Rawlings; Force B, cruisers *Gloucester* and *Fiji* with two destroyers under Captain H. A. Rowley; Force C, with the cruiser *Perth*, antiaircraft cruiser *Naiad*, and four destroyers, commanded by Rear Admiral E. L. S. King; and Force D, cruisers *Orion* and *Ajax*, four destroyers, and antiaircraft cruiser *Dido*, under Rear Admiral I. G. Glennie. In the course of the battle these groups would be reinforced and sometimes combined, but their ships generally operated together. All of these ships were beginning to run short on antiaircraft ammunition, and most entered the battle with only three quarters of their normal allotment.[10]

On the day after the Germans began their assault on Crete, Cunningham ordered King's Force C to pass through the Kaso Strait at the east end of Crete and patrol the north coast to look for seaborne invaders and Admiral Glennie's Force D to do the same from the Antikithera Channel. King, reinforced by the antiaircraft cruisers *Carlisle* and *Calcutta*, passed through the strait on the evening of the 20th but found no invaders and left the Aegean just before dawn. Glennie likewise found nothing. The following morning both King and Glennie were attacked by German and Italian aircraft. "A little after 6:00 A.M. the imperturbable A. B. Morgan, our best lookout, saw the first lot. He had a maddeningly deliberate way of reporting: 'six, eight, ten, sixteen, no, make that twenty aircraft, bearing green 140 sir. Look like Junkers 87's.' He sounded as though this were a fleet exercise. The Stukas kept coming our way, climbing and eventually circling like hawks on a thermal. Then down in groups of three; one after the other."[11]

The Ju-87 Stuka dive-bomber was a slow, hard-to-maneuver gull-winged aircraft with a fixed undercarriage. In any type of aerial combat its chances of survival were poor. But to the men aboard a ship with inadequate antiaircraft defense the Stuka seemed "a very frightening weapon."[12] "The scream of the aircraft as it made its dive and the infernal whistle of the bomb itself were quite terrifying," recalled Adrian Holloway, a midshipman in the destroyer *Nizam*. "Coupled with the horrendous din of our own guns you have a pretty fair picture of hell."[13]

Around 1:00 P.M. the destroyer *Juno* was hit with three bombs by an Italian high-level bomber. "The ship just split in half from stem to stern. She took about 90 seconds to sink. Round the spot where she sank all that remained were bits of wood, life belts and the water was one mass of oil."[14] Only about 60 of her crew of 183 survived. Petty Officer George Wheeler found himself in the water with half a dozen of his messmates.

"Looking in front of me I saw [destroyer] *Kandahar* stopping and lowering her whaler and that's where I swam for. Someone yelled, 'Wheeler! Jock can't swim!' Turning my head to the right, there was Jock going through the water like a torpedo. For one who couldn't swim he beat me to *Kandahar*'s whaler."[15]

While Axis aircraft were attacking Cunningham's ships, a German assault force sailed from Greece aboard commandeered motorized Greek fishing vessels called caiques. British signals intelligence soon learned of the invasion convoys and sent Forces C and D back into the Aegean to intercept. Admiral Glennie's Force D passed through Antikithera Channel and located an Axis convoy of about two dozen caiques and coasters north of Cannae late on the night of the 21st. The slow-moving caiques, loaded with heavily armed German and Italian troops and artillery, were blown to bits by the fire of the British cruisers and destroyers. Short of ammunition, Glennie's forces then retired to the southwest. When news of the destruction of the convoy reached German headquarters, the main invasion force of about forty caiques escorted by an Italian torpedo boat was ordered back to Greece. The convoy was still about twenty miles from the Greek mainland at 10:00 A.M. the next morning when it was spotted by Admiral King's Force C.

At that time, King himself was under heavy attack by German bombers and running low on ammunition. He decided not to spread his ships farther to attack the scattered convoy or go on but to keep his force concentrated for mutual protection against air attack and withdraw toward the Kithera Strait. Over the next three and a half hours, King's ships were bombed almost continuously. Sailors aboard the light cruiser *Naiad* counted 181 bombs dropped on the ship during two hours. In one ten-minute period there were more than thirty-six near misses.[16]

During these attacks the *Naiad*'s engine and boiler rooms "resembled the inside of a giant's kettle against which a sledge hammer is being beaten with uncertain aim," wrote Commander Louis Le Bailly. "Sometimes there was an almighty clang; sometimes the giant in his frustration seemed to pick up the kettle and shake or even kick it. The officer detailed to broadcast a running commentary suffered a breakdown during the battle so we heard little below but . . . came to understand something of what was happening on deck. Suddenly more speed would be called for, then we would hear our 5.25-inch turrets opening fire which told us that aircraft were attacking. Next the bridge telegraph might move to emergency full speed and we would see the rudder indicator go to hard-a-port or starboard at the moment of bomb release. This would be followed by the sound of *Naiad*'s short range weapons as the bomber pulled out of its . . . dive. . . . "[17] The *Naiad* had two turrets put out of action, and her speed was reduced to about eighteen knots. The cruisers *Carlisle* and *Perth* also received minor damage.

Admiral Rawlings with the *Warspite* and *Valiant* steamed north toward the Kithera Channel to support King. As the two forces joined, German bombers attacked the battleship *Warspite*. "We sighted 4 JU87s," wrote Midshipman T. Ruck-Keene. "As each in turn reached the designated spot he leisurely peeled off into a steep dive. . . . The first dropped his bomb without result and made off, the second was blown up halfway through his dive. The third I followed down with my glasses, watching with amazement his dive get steeper and steeper. Then I realized something was wrong. He was coming down absolutely vertically and began to spin. . . . When only a very few thousand feet up his tail broke off. . . . It was a sight I had never seen before; that of watching an enemy plane crashing into the sea and the sweetness of that moment would be hard to equal."[18]

Around 1:30 P.M. a 500-pound bomb from an Me-109 fighter-bomber hit the ship near the starboard 4-inch gun mounting and penetrated to the mess deck, killing many there and wrecking the 6-inch gun mountings.[19] The destroyer *Greyhound*, which had been detached to sink a caique, was attacked by eight dive-bombers and sunk by two bomb hits.

King, who was senior to Rawlings, assumed command of the combined force and ordered the destroyers *Kandahar* and *Kingston* to pick up the *Greyhound*'s survivors and the cruisers *Gloucester* and *Fiji* to support them. This proved a disastrous decision. The *Gloucester* had only 18 percent of her antiaircraft ammunition remaining and the *Fiji* 30 percent.[20] Moreover, the four-ship rescue party would be separated from the supporting fires of the rest of the fleet. One of the *Fiji*'s petty officers later paraphrased King's message as "equivalent of saying 'go back, shoot 100 of your men, drown 120 and sink your ship.'"[21]

Under heavy air attack the four ships managed to pick up a number of *Greyhound* survivors and shot off most of the cruisers' remaining ammunition. King, belatedly learning of the ammunition situation, had already ordered the ships to return when, around 3:30 P.M., the *Gloucester* was hit by two bombs that damaged a boiler room and set off her 2-pounder ammunition. Three more bombs completed the destruction of the ship, which sank about 5:15. Aboard the *Fiji*, Stoker Petty Officer Sid Manders "went down to the mess, got my money and photos of my dear wife knowing that our turn must come under such conditions."[22]

After surviving more than thirteen hours of air attacks including twenty bombing attacks in the last four hours, *Fiji* was crippled by a single bomb from an Me-109 fighter. The bomb hit the forward boiler room, blew in the ship's bottom, and caused the ship to keel over to port. Sid Manders directed his men to leave the rapidly flooding stokehold and engine room. However, in the undamaged after boiler room men remained at their posts, "keeping steam in the system and all the pumps going, knowing that their end was very near and meantime holding onto anything handy to keep themselves upright."[23]

A half hour later a second Me-109 scored a direct hit with three bombs, which brought down the foremast and wrecked the galley. The *Fiji*'s list increased, and her commander, Captain P.B.R.W. William-Pawlett, ordered her men to abandon ship. "By about 6:50 P.M., I should think, about 50 of us were left aboard and we thought it was time to go," recalled Petty Officer Manders.

> Some of us men were beginning to look down in the mouth knowing that we had to leave the ship that had put up such a brilliant fight and also to leave some men behind.... We could almost walk down the ship's side now.... I had my eyes on a Carley float that was sliding down the ship ahead of us. I said "Here goes" and got halfway down the ship's side and hung onto the rope, then as the float drifted down jumped into the water.... About 30 got to this float.... One seaman injured in the back with shrapnel looked a pitiful sight and we gave him as much room as possible. The sea was inclined to be swelly which made things awkward.[24]

At dark the destroyers *Kandahar* and *Kingston* returned to the scene and rescued about five hundred of the *Fiji*'s crew of eight hundred. "Those that needed attention were taken to the sick bay, others to the bathroom where a hot shower was more than welcome.... Then came a tot of rum and cigarettes were served out of the destroyer's canteen fund.... I was in overalls and a pair of sandals made from cardboard and string. Some of the lads had decent clothes on, some only a blanket, but the thing that counted was the high spirits of the men."[25]

While the *Kandahar* and *Kingston* were returning to Alexandria, six more destroyers from Malta under Lord Louis Mountbatten had joined Rawlings and had been sent through the Antikithera Channel to intercept any forces attempting to land on the north shore of Crete. Two of these destroyers, *Kelly* and *Kashmir*, bombarded the airfield at Maleme, which had fallen into German hands, and sank a troop-carrying caique on its way back through the channel in the early hours of May 23.

Admiral Rawlings, with his battleships *Warspite* and *Valiant*, was moving into position to support Mountbatten's destroyers after they passed through the channel. At 4:30 A.M. he suddenly received an order from Cunningham directing him to return to Alexandria. These orders were a result of serious mix-ups in communications. Late on the previous evening, Rawlings had sent Cunningham a summary of the day's actions and reported on the state of his ships and ammunition supply. A part of the message was garbled and indicated that Rawlings battleships were "empty of short-range ammunition." Aware that the destroyers and cruisers were very low on ammunition, Cunningham decided to recall Rawlings's fleet to Alexandria. It was only later that the commander in chief learned that the word "empty" should have read "plenty."[26]

The destroyers *Kelly* and *Kashmir*, joined later by the *Kipling*, had to make their withdrawal from Crete alone, and at first light they were attacked by German high-level bombers. The bombers were followed by twenty-four Stukas. "The Stukas did not come in from high up in a vertical dive as I had always understood," wrote Signalman John Knight. "They were about 3,000 feet up, went into a shallow dive and soon parted from the one bomb which they carried and whose trajectory was easy to predict. It was like knowing where to be to catch a cricket ball."[27] The *Kashmir* was hit and sank in only two minutes. As the water rose over the main deck, Ian Rhodes, a young Australian seaman, fired his 20mm antiaircraft gun at a nearby Stuka and brought it down even as the *Kashmir* disappeared beneath the waves.[28]

The *Kelly* was hit while the ship was making a turn at thirty knots and almost immediately capsized and sank. In the engine room, the stokers and technicians found themselves tossed onto the ceiling bulkhead as the ship turned. The overhead hatch was now underwater, but sunlight shone through in a "kind of Blue Grotto effect."[29] "'There you are,' said Commander [Mike Evans] the flotilla engineer. . . . 'You see that round hole? That's the way out. Take a deep breath and make sure you are clear of the ship before you surface.'"[30]

The *Kipling* was now the only ship still afloat in an oil-stained sea full of wreckage and desperate survivors clinging to a few rafts and debris. The Stukas, rearmed and refueled at nearby Greek bases, concentrated on the destroyer. For one hour the *Kipling*'s captain, Commander St. Claire-Ford, dodged six waves of attacks by Stukas and medium bombers and took aboard 128 men from the *Kelly* and 153 from *Kashmir*. Finally, "The Captain decided he could not wait any longer and set course for Alexandria unable to retrieve the motor boats which had been lowered to help in picking up survivors. The last we saw of the boat the leading seaman coxswain was standing up saluting."[31] The *Kipling* reached

Alexandria on the morning of May 24 to be greeted by thousands of sailors on shore and lining the rails of the ships to cheer the battered destroyer and her crew.

"And so ended the most costly operation since the war began," concluded Midshipman Ruck-Keene, writing of the events of May 22 and 23. In three days the Mediterranean Fleet had lost two cruisers, four destroyers, and one battleship, while two cruisers and four destroyers had been seriously damaged. Cunningham advised the Chiefs of Staff Committee in London that he believed it was no longer possible for the fleet to operate in the Aegean during daylight hours and that further losses like those of the past three days might "cripple the fleet without any commensurate advantage. . . . Sea control in the eastern Mediterranean could not be retained after another such experience."[32]

As if to prove the accuracy of Cunningham's observation, the *Formidable*, the fleet's only carrier, was damaged by German aircraft after carrying out a surprise raid on German and Italian air bases on Scarpanto on May 25. The incident appeared to be just another addition to the list of disasters, but it had several characteristics that presaged the next phase of the unfolding revolution in naval weaponry and operations. Most significant was that the *Formidable* had been able to strike and surprise an enemy air base out of range of British land-based aircraft. Her handful of obsolescent fighters had also managed to intercept twenty incoming planes and shot down three. And despite serious damage the ship had continued to steam and to operate fighters for the rest of the day.[33]

The Germans' domination of the air and their early capture of the principal airfield on Crete soon spelled defeat for the Greek and Commonwealth defenders of the island. As early as May 22, General Freyburg had reported that "in my opinion the limit of endurance has been reached by the troops under my command. . . . No matter what decision is taken by the Commanders-in-Chief, from the military view the situation is hopeless."[34] The next day the War Cabinet in London reluctantly approved the evacuation of Allied troops from Crete. "Cretan news terrible," wrote the permanent undersecretary at the Foreign Office in his private diary. "It's another disaster."[35]

Heraklion, on the north coast of Crete, and Sphakia, on the south, were chosen as the points of evacuation. Twenty-two thousand troops would have to be evacuated by a much-reduced Mediterranean Fleet. The remaining warships "had been driven hard for more than two months. . . . Their machinery had become unreliable and many were struggling on as best they could after damage by enemy bombing."[36] The

Royal Air Force promised maximum air cover but there were few fighters that could reach Crete and remain for very long.

"On the morning of the 28 May 1941 we slipped our buoys and
steamed out of Alexandria," recalled Stoker Petty Officer H. Speakman
of the cruiser *Orion*. "Having worked non-stop since our last fracas,
tiredness and taut nerves were taking their toll. Over the loudspeakers
came the pipe 'This is your Captain speaking. . . . Once again we have
another crisis on our hands. We, and the ships in company, are on our
way to evacuate those same troops we recently landed on Crete. . . . The
operation will be exactly as in Greece so you all know what is expected
of you. Good luck, that is all.' . . . So this was it. Everyone nursed their
own thoughts, but the tension was so real it could almost be cut."[37]

The *Orion* and the cruiser *Dido* with four destroyers arrived off Heraklion about 11:30 in the evening. Guided by small flashing lights, the
destroyers made their way to the piers and tied up two abreast. The larger
cruisers anchored in the harbor. The destroyers loaded about 500 troops
each, keeping 200 and transferring the rest to the cruisers.[38] By 3:20
A.M., having loaded almost 4,000 men, Rawlings's force set off at high
speed to clear the Kasos Strait by daylight. After only a few minutes the
steering gear aboard the destroyer *Imperial* jammed, and she steamed
wildly in circles, narrowly missing the cruisers.

If Rawlings stopped to repair the rudder or tow the *Imperial*, his whole
squadron would face annihilation when dawn came. Without slowing,
the *Orion* signaled the destroyer *Hotspur*, "Take off crew and sink *Imperial*. Make for Alex." Lieutenant Hodgkinson, aboard *Hotspur*, recalled
that, "reading into it then, we thought he had decided to get on as fast
as possible and leave us to try to get back as best we could, alone and at
least 30 miles astern of the rest. In my own mind this meant about 100
to 6 chance of ever getting back. . . . We had about 900 on board, instead of the normal complement of about 150."[39] Hodgkinson was helping the soldiers set up improvised antiaircraft positions on the deck with
their automatic weapons when the *Hotspur* sighted Rawlings's squadron,
which had slowed to allow her to catch up. To the sailors aboard *Hotspur*, the sight of Rawlings's ships was a welcome relief.[40] But the
squadron was now two hours behind schedule and would be in range of
German dive-bombers for almost six hours after daylight.

"Almost precisely at 6:00 the red warning went up in the *Orion* and it
stayed up, I think, for seven hours. . . . From now on . . . there were few
moments when there were not Stukas in sight. You could see them sailing off to the east after an attack and dropping down out of sight onto

Scarpanto Air Drome, knowing they would be back again in half an hour with other bombs."[41]

The destroyer *Hereward* was the first victim of the Stukas. A bomb that struck amidships caused her to lose speed and she had to be left behind. A short time later, she was sunk by repeated air attacks, but many of her crew and soldier passengers were rescued by Italian seaplanes and torpedo boats.

A few minutes after the *Hereward*, the destroyer *Decoy* was damaged by a near miss, but after that the Stukas concentrated their attacks on the *Dido* and *Orion*, which successfully fought off all attacks for over an hour. At 8:15, however, the *Dido* was hit by a bomb that penetrated B turret. One of the 5.25-inch guns of the turret was blown into the air and dropped smoking into the sea. The resulting explosion wrecked the marines' mess deck, which was crowded with soldiers evacuated from Crete, and started serious fires that took a long time to bring under control. Yet the ship could still steam and fight.

About an hour later, a bomb scored a direct hit on one of the *Orion's* forward turrets. It was blown to bits, and the gun barrels of the turret directly above were bent upward by the force of the explosion. An earlier near miss had flooded the after 6-inch magazine, so that now the ship had no 6-inch guns in action and her 4-inch antiaircraft guns were running low on ammunition. The blast injured the ship's captain, G.R.B. Back, who was taken below to the sick bay. A few minutes later, Chaplain Gerald Ellison was with him in the sick bay when a near miss rocked the ship. "Some of the men on cots began to get out and the Captain sat up and told them to be steady and still as it was only a near miss." Shortly after, he died and the executive officer, Commander T. C. Wynne, assumed command.[42] A lull followed as the Stukas withdrew to rearm. "Whilst the weary gun crews rested, the casualties were carried aft in an endless stream," recalled one sailor. "The dead were laid out on stretchers on the quarter deck. Instead of the usual burial service, a few short prayers had to suffice because we were still at first degree readiness."[43]

At 10:00 A.M., a second bomb dropped by a lone Stuka penetrated the bridge, passed through every deck below, and exploded in a 4-inch magazine. Ironically, the *Orion's* shortage of ammunition probably saved the ship, since by this time the 4-inch magazine was empty. The bomb exploded just below the stokers' mess deck, which was crowded with soldiers and wounded sailors. Many suffered burns, and the entire space was immediately filled with choking cordite fumes. Surgeon Lieutenant R. I. Bence was blown from the sick bay deck up against the ceiling bulkhead and landed on his hands and knees in the sick bay consulting room four-teen feet away in the adjoining compartment.[44] A gaping hole appeared in the center of the ship. "Side fuel and fresh water tanks had been breached and their contents, plus some of the main refrigerated and ship's stores, were all swilling about below. The occasional sight of a body amongst all this made looking down in the glare from the raging fire like a bird's eye view of Hades."[45]

Surgeon Lieutenant Bence directed the movement of the wounded to the after dressing station and began operating there. Between 11:30 A.M. and 5:00 P.M., Bence, the army medical officer, and a handful of sick berth attendants treated 300 cases. The doctors were handicapped by an acute shortage of fresh water for preparing solutions, since oil fuel from the ruptured tanks had contaminated most of the ships water supply. Despite this, more than 250 of Bence's 300 patients survived.[46]

Through desperate efforts, the Orion's engines were kept in operation and her steering gear repaired. Two more air attacks by high-level bombers during the afternoon did no damage, and at 8:00 P.M. the Orion steamed into Alexandria with only ten tons of fuel remaining and only two rounds of 6-inch shells.[47] "The Orion anchored outside the harbor," wrote a sailor. "She smelled of death from a great distance."[48] The carnage aboard the cruiser had been so great that no completely accurate estimate of casualties could be made, but more than 250 sailors and soldiers are believed to have lost their lives and about 300 were wounded.[49]

While Rawlings's force had waged its long battle against the Luftwaffe, four destroyers had reached the small village of Sphakia on the south coast of Crete and evacuated 750 troops with only sporadic interference from German bombers.

The following morning another cruiser-destroyer force under Admiral King set off for Sphakia together with the assault landing ship Glengyle. Cunningham's state of mind can be judged by his message to the admiralty warning that "tomorrow we must expect further casualties to ships accompanied with extremely heavy casualties to men" and reminding them that the Glengyle would be carrying 3,000 troops.[50]

King's force reached Sphakia near midnight and embarked 6,000 troops. German aircraft caught up with them at 9:30 and scored one hit, which caused minor damage to a cruiser. This time, however, RAF fighter aircraft finally made their appearance over the fleet and kept the Germans at a distance. No more hits were made, and King's ships arrived safely in Alexandria that night. Two destroyers that made the run into Sphakia the next night received fighter cover from early morning and returned to Alexandria with 1,500 troops.

Still, more troops remained on Crete. Cunningham met in the morning of May 31 with General Sir Archibald Wavell, the British Middle East commander, and the top British, Australian, and New Zealand army commanders. Wavell later recalled: "We gave ABC our decision and absolution from further effort on behalf of the Army. I saw the faces of his staff light up with relief. . . . Then Andrew C spoke briefly. He thanked us for our effort to relieve him of responsibility but said that the Navy had never failed the Army in such a situation and was not going to do so now; he was going in again that night with everything he had which would float."[51]

"We were all pretty glum at the prospect of another party," recalled Lieutenant Hodgkinson. "Most of the men reckoned we would be damned lucky if we could get away twice with a Crete evacuation."[52] By this time, however, many German aircraft had been withdrawn from the area to more urgent tasks. The final evacuation force, a cruiser, a minelayer, and three destroyers, commanded by Admiral King, reached Crete without incident, thanks to air cover from the RAF, and returned safely to Alexandria with about 3,700 troops. "It seemed to us a sort of miracle," wrote Hodgkinson.[53]

In two weeks, the Mediterranean Fleet had lost three cruisers to the Luftwaffe. Five more cruisers, eight destroyers, two battleships, and the fleet's only carrier were out of action. Only two battleships, three cruisers, a fast minelayer, and nine destroyers remained operational. The First Sea Lord, Admiral Dudley Pound, considered assigning any more carriers to the Mediterranean "a sheer waste," because any such ship was "bound to be knocked out within a very short time." Cunningham was more insightful. "The hasty conclusion that ships are impotent in the face of air attack should not be drawn from the battle of Crete."[54]

Dubious as such a statement may have seemed in the spring of 1941, it proved wholly accurate. Crete marked not the climax but simply another stage in the still evolving interaction of air and sea power. At this stage both ships and aircraft had proved relatively ineffective at their jobs. The German aircraft had scored a relatively small proportion of hits despite their overwhelming numbers and the availability of nearby bases. HMS Kipling, for example, had survived at least eighty-three air attacks in a few hours. Moreover, the German attack aircraft had been kept at bay by even small numbers of fairly low-performance RAF and naval fighters.

Similarly, the ships of the Mediterranean Fleet, despite the large volume of ammunition expended, had managed to shoot down only a few aircraft. Effective fire control for antiaircraft guns was virtually nonexistent, and many ships lacked sufficient antiaircraft pieces and could not elevate their main armament sufficiently to fire at high angles. "Our 5-inch machine guns did their best," reported one destroyer officer, "but little bullets like that weren't much use unless they hit the pilot in a painful place."[55] Close-range guns were aimed individually by a gunner using a spiderweb-shaped sight. Accuracy depended entirely on the talent and judgment of the gunner and "called for much the same skill as shooting grouse or pheasant."[56] Through fear or inexperience, many machine gunners opened fire too soon, when the attacking plane was still far out, and were often out of ammunition by the time the target was at optimum range.[57] Coupled with the apparently unbeatable German air superiority, the relative ineffectiveness of the ship's antiaircraft defense "was a great disappointment and naturally exerted a strong effect on sailors morale."[58] For many ships the most important antiaircraft defense was the captain's ability to maneuver the vessel at high speed.

The men had more of an adjustment to make than their machines. For forty years, naval combat had meant attacks by gunfire or torpedoes on ships of the opposing fleet. Although these encounters could result in horrifying carnage, they were relatively infrequent and lasted only a few hours. Tsushima and Jutland, the greatest naval engagements prior to World War II, had lasted only an afternoon and a night. At Jutland, the majority of British and German sailors were actually under fire for less than an hour. In the Mediterranean, ships could be under fire almost continuously during the daylight hours. The *Orion* was under continuous air attack for seven hours, the *Kipling* for five hours. "I cannot possibly begin to say where an attack began and another ended," noted a midshipmen in HMS *Warspite*. "Someone was always firing."[59] Lieutenant Hodgkinson remembered "four hours on and four hours off. Perhaps one day a week in harbor. . . . We were tired and jaded."[60]

For men aboard smaller ships like destroyers there was always "the certain knowledge that one—just one—of the aerial bombs that were aimed at us could probably sink the ship."[61] Adrian Holloway observed that "one knew that if the ship receives a direct hit, one will either be killed or thrown into the water to struggle gasping for breath and probably drowning. The bomb comes down, you try to find cover and cannot, the ship heels over trying to dodge the path, [the bomb] misses and a great spout of water is thrown up only yards from the ship. . . . If anyone tells you that in those circumstances he was not frightened I would say he was either a monumental liar or a very very brave man. You couldn't, of course, show that you were frightened. Like Charles I at his execution if you shivered it was due to the cold and nothing else."[62]

"I am not surprised that the sailors were shaken," wrote one British admiral. "On land, you don't feel that *you* are the target. At sea it's just too bloody obvious and has its effect accordingly."[63] In the brilliant Mediterranean sunlight with almost unlimited visibility and no air cover, most sailors felt terribly vulnerable. "On land there is usually some cover from aircraft, a tree, a house, a trench, but at sea there is absolutely nothing to hide you."[64]

Seaman Michael Milburn of the cruiser *Ajax* referred to the reaction of sailors to prolonged air attack as "stukaritis." Others compared it to the shell shock produced by long periods of trench warfare in which the nerves of even "well disciplined, intelligent and courageous officers and men give way because the strain of fighting has been too much for them."[65] Engine Room Artificer Clifford Simkin recalled that after one trip to Crete "one of my messmates could not take it any more. When we were in Greece he was white as a sheet and would not eat and now this breakdown. He came from a naval family and had been in the Navy since he was fifteen."[66]

Aboard the *Ajax* there were a reported thirty breakdowns among 800 men.[67] The crew of that ship had been under greater strain than most because the *Ajax* was denied even the short stays at Alexandria that provided the only respite for sailors between periods of combat. Instead, since the beginning of the campaigns in Greece and Crete, the ship had usually been refueled or resupplied at Suda Bay on the coast of Crete. Suda Bay was a sparsely protected anchorage with no recreational facilities ashore. The bay's exposed location and its scanty antiaircraft defenses meant that the crew, instead of resting ashore, had to be constantly on alert for air attacks.[68] "One of the best men on the ship . . . a leading seaman who was on the bridge with me as we got into Alexandria . . . turned round and said to me, 'If the old man tells us we are going back . . . we bloody well aren't going. . . .' These people were treated as sick and they went back to fight later on."[69] At one point Cunningham instructed his flag secretary to "bring me some warrants for hanging" in case any crew were to refuse to sail.[70]

"It is perhaps even now not realized how nearly the breaking point was reached," wrote Admiral Cunningham in his official report.[71] A substantial number reached that point, but most managed to adapt to the new demands and horrors of this new style of combat. This is all the more notable given the fact that not only was the operational situation in the Mediterranean grim, but Britain's prospects in the war as a whole appeared bleak indeed. "The psychological impact of the world picture," recalled I. R. Johnston, a lieutenant in the *Orion*, "varied with the strategic imagination of the individual. The more one knew the more this had a depressing effect."[72]

Many years later, survivors of the Battle for Crete gave varying answers to the question of what kept them going in the face of this seemingly hopeless situation. Some mentioned routine and self-preservation as important factors. "As for keeping going during combat, well, there wasn't much option," reflected Commander J.A.J. Dennis. "Unlike the infantry the only man who could 'run away' was the Captain. . . ."[73] Almost all former officers emphasized the traditions of the Royal Navy and their own training as important factors. "Deeply ingrained ideas of discipline, patriotism and tradition were immensely strong."[74] The Royal Navy's "tradition and 'maritime heritage' tells the recruit that he has joined an elite force and that when trained he is capable of being 'the best' and that the ship he serves in will always be well found."[75]

A key factor was leadership. As in all small ships, the character and ability of the destroyer captains in the Crete campaign, each of them an officer in his thirties, often spelled the difference between success and failure. On the captain's shoulders lay the entire burden of conning the ship and arriving at split-second decisions under air attack. "There is no doubt at all that he [was] the principal factor in keeping morale reasonably high in my ship," recalled an officer who served in HMS *Hero*. He was "a man of immense capacity and self-confidence who had already experienced all the tensions of maritime command in a hostile environment off Norway in 1940. . . . He communicated the impression that he was the master of our situation and that if anybody could contrive to dodge the bombing runs of a series of Ju-87s, he could."[76]

Above the level of the ship's captain, however, the role of leadership becomes more problematical. Although many officers expressed admiration for Admiral Cunningham, lower-ranking officers and enlisted men often voiced the familiar complaint that the higher levels of command had little understanding of their situation. There was generalized and widespread anger at the lack of fighter cover. Sailors blamed "anybody and everybody" ashore.[77] "I feel that Admiral Cunningham never understood how vulnerable his ships were without air cover," reflected Adrian Holloway. "It felt desperately naked and we also felt that the higher-ups did not understand this. They had been brought up as gunnery officers to believe that AA fire would protect the ships. Rubbish!"[78] Returning to Alexandria from their runs to Crete, crews were tired and jumpy. "Sick they were mate," recalled one bluejacket, "never air cover to speak of. . . . Bullshit talks from the CINC down, 'your courage and tenacity . . .' we'd nudge each other and say 'here comes the courage and tenacity bit.'"[79]

Cunningham's visits to ships damaged in the fighting off Crete, although intended to raise morale, also tended to engender "a certain amount of resentment. He came aboard [*Warspite*]," recalled one sailor, "and gave a fiery speech saying 'you're only slightly hurt, if I want you to go out tomorrow, you'll go out tomorrow.' And there were mutterings . . . they would have gone out . . . there would be no question of that but they were shaken."[80]

Aboard the cruiser *Ajax*, which had been damaged by a 1,000-pound bomb, Cunningham "cleared lower deck and he said 'Oh, I see you've been a little peppered but this is no time for men and ships to be loafing around the harbor. You will be ammunitioned and [receive] new guns and you'll be back to sea tomorrow.' And that was when it broke the camel's back, that's when those people all went off with anxiety neurosis. . . . There's no doubt about it, he was a very good man but his rapport and his understanding of the sailor's mentality was so different, all wrong. If he'd come in and said 'look I know you've had a bad time, but we've got to keep at it . . . or whatever . . .' people would have accepted it. But to come in there as if you're swinging the lead was wrong I've always felt."[81]

Many of these observations were probably unfair to Cunningham. He repeatedly reminded the Admiralty that the fleet was "facing an air concentration beside which, I am assured, that in Norway was child's play."[82] He knew that "no AA fire will deal with the simultaneous attacks of 10-20 aircraft" and that after more than a week of bombing, "in some ships, sailors began to crack a little."[83] At the same time he understood that "it was impossible to abandon the troops in Crete. Our naval tradition would never survive such an action."[84] Whatever his shortcomings as a group therapist, it was Cunningham's steely determination that he communicated to every man in the fleet that made possible the evacuation of almost 17,000 troops from Crete in less than five days.

At Crete, for the first time, sailors had seen the new face of war at sea. From this time on aerial attack and defense would become the most common combat experience of Navy men. Yet, even fifty years later many survivors of the Battle for Crete considered this first encounter the most intensely terrifying and trying experience they ever had in their years at sea. But in the end, it was a test of endurance that most passed credibly. "So now we are all happy again eagerly looking forward to seeing those we love, then ready to fight again for freedom, a thing that the

Germans do not understand," wrote Petty Officer Manders, survivor of the sunken *Fiji*. "We may not have made much progress yet, but the lads in blue are doing their stuff, the soldiers will be doing theirs soon and then the Germans will be like the Italians. But to accomplish this the effort must be shared by everyone and the sooner we realize it the sooner it will be over. So give us the tools and let's act quickly. That's all."[85]

TEN

"NEVER IN ALL MY YEARS HAD I IMAGINED A BATTLE LIKE THAT"

In the Pacific, the Americans and Japanese were rapidly developing sea-air warfare to levels of precision and lethality far beyond anything seen in the European conflict. Both the Japanese and Americans had long expected that at the outbreak of war, Japan would attack the Philippines and the U.S. Navy would launch a drive across the Pacific from Pearl Harbor as outlined in the various Orange Plans for war with Japan, developed by the General Board of the Navy and the Naval War College in the 1920s and 1930s. The Japanese had always planned to attack the American fleet with submarines and aircraft as it came within range of their island bases in the Central Pacific. After the American fleet had been worn down by these attrition attacks, the main battle would be fought at a location and time most favorable to Japan.

In the last weeks of peace, Admiral Husband E. Kimmel, commander of the U.S. Pacific Fleet, was preparing to put the Orange Plan concept into effect by launching an attack on the Marshall Islands. This was intended to provoke the Japanese into a fleet action, pitting the slightly superior American battle line against the battleships of the Imperial Japanese Navy. In this scheme the American carriers would provide air reconnaissance and act as bait.[1]

Yet by this time, the Japanese, under the prodding of the commander in chief of the Combined Fleet, Admiral Yamamoto Isoroku, had modified their strategy of waylaying the U.S. fleet as it sailed into the Central Pacific. Instead, the war began with a massive carrier air raid on Pearl Harbor in December 1941. Achieving complete surprise, Japanese planes sank five battleships and damaged three others as well as three cruisers and three destroyers. More than 2,100 sailors and marines lost their lives, more men than the U.S. Navy had lost in all of World War I and about as many as the Germans had lost at Jutland. Japanese losses were minimal.

In the weeks after Pearl Harbor, the Japanese moved swiftly to secure their objectives in Southeast Asia. Hong Kong, Malaya, Thailand, Burma, and the Dutch East Indies all fell to the Japanese within three months. Two days after the war began, the British battleship *Prince of Wales* and the battle cruiser *Repulse* were sunk by Japanese bombers and torpedo planes while attempting to defend Malaya. A mixed British, Dutch, American, and Australian cruiser-destroyer force was wiped out by the Japanese in the East Indies a few months later. The Philippines held out the longest, its American and Filipino defenders finally surrendering early in May after a long battle with hunger and disease as well as the Japanese.

Now only the Pacific Fleet remained to oppose the Japanese advance. All three of the fleet's carriers, *Lexington*, *Saratoga*, and *Enterprise*, had escaped the Pearl Harbor raid, and two additional carriers, *Yorktown* and *Hornet*, had arrived from the Atlantic. In the next twelve months these aircraft carriers would become the dominant weapons.

Even after Pearl Harbor neither the Japanese nor the American admirals had completely lost faith in the battleship. American battleships with light or moderate damage in the Japanese air attack were sent to California for repair and overhaul, while other battleships were summoned from the Atlantic. By the end of March 1942 the Pacific Fleet had seven operational battleships, six of which were more modern than the ships lost at Pearl Harbor.[2] Yet the battleships consumed more fuel than all the carrier task forces combined, and there were only a few tankers available to service the entire Pacific Fleet.

Kimmel's successor, Admiral Chester Nimitz, was loath to risk the psychological impact that would result from the loss of any additional battleships. He, and most of his principal commanders, preferred to save the old ships for the Orange Plan advance across the Central Pacific that they still hoped to put into effect eventually. The Japanese, too, preferred to hold back their battle line for a decisive battle at some future point.

So the field was left to the carriers, which could not, and did not, operate like a battle fleet. Both sides used their carriers for raiding and to support and oppose seaborne invasions. The six largest Japanese carriers, *Akagi*, *Kaga*, *Soryu*, *Hiryu*, *Shokaku*, and *Zuikaku*, which carried out the attack on Pearl Harbor, composed the First Air Fleet under Admiral Nagumo Chuichi, which operated in carrier divisions of two ships each. The planes of the two carriers in each division formed a single air group under a senior air group commander. Americans operated in "task forces" built around a single carrier screened by cruisers and destroyers.

In the weeks following Pearl Harbor, the Japanese carrier striking force supported the invasion of the U.S. Central Pacific outpost at Wake Island and the seizure of Rabaul on New Britain Island from the Australians. In mid-February, four Japanese carriers attacked the northern Australian town of Darwin. They sank more than a dozen ships in the harbor, destroyed eighteen aircraft, and sent the civilian population of the town streaming away in panic.

Many naval experts still believed that to send carriers against heavily defended land bases was too risky, except where surprise could be achieved as at Pearl Harbor. That view was emphatically not shared by the new commander of the Pacific Fleet, Admiral Chester Nimitz, nor by his boss, Admiral Ernest J. King, Chief of Naval Operations and Commander in Chief, U.S. Fleet, nor by the fiery senior carrier commander, Vice Admiral William F. Halsey. Consequently, the American carriers were even more active than the Japanese, although the two forces would not meet for more than five months. At the end of January 1942, after escorting reinforcements to Samoa, Halsey's Task Force 8, built around the carrier *Enterprise,* penetrated the northern Marshall Islands and raided Kwajalein, Wotje, and Taroa. At the same time, Task Force 17, with Rear Admiral Frank Jack Fletcher in the carrier *Yorktown,* struck targets in the southern Marshalls.

The raids did little damage, but they served to raise morale at a moment when the Allied cause in Asia seemed to be suffering nothing but defeat. "Entering Pearl Harbor after the Marshall raid was the most moving moment of the war for me," recalled a sailor in the *Enterprise.* "As we came down the channel the sunken and burned battleships along Ford Island in plain sight, the crews of the anchored ships at quarters, their white uniforms showing up against their gray ships, cheered us one after another again and again."[3]

More American raids followed. A task force under Vice Admiral Wilson Brown in the carrier *Lexington* was sent far to the southwest to strike the newly acquired Japanese base at Rabaul, while Halsey's task force carried out a raid on Wake Island, then went on to strike Marcus Island nine days later. Brown's force was spotted by Japanese search planes as it neared its launch point two hundred miles from Rabaul. Seventeen bombers from Rabaul struck the American task force in the late afternoon. They were intercepted by the *Lexington*'s fighters almost directly over the task force.

At least thirteen Japanese bombers were shot down and two more crash-landed. Lieutenant Edward ("Butch") O'Hare became the first U.S. naval fighter ace of the Pacific War, destroying at least three, and possibly five, planes. Aboard the ships of the American task force the crews whooped, cheered, and yelled encouragement to the fighters. As planes taxied to their spots on the *Lexington*'s flight deck, pilots were mobbed by cheering sailors.[4] Admiral Brown reported, "I often had to remind some members of my staff that this was not a football game."[5]

Although Americans focused on the aerial victories and quickly made a hero of O'Hare, the tactical significance of this brief air battle was far more important. The *Lexington* had demonstrated that a carrier's fighters could successfully defend the ship against attacks by land-based aircraft—something the British had never been able to manage in the Mediterranean. Whether they could defend against attacks by other carriers remained to be seen.

Reinforced by Rear Admiral Frank Jack Fletcher in the *Yorktown*, the *Lexington* headed back for another attempt at Rabaul. But by this time, word had come of more attractive targets. Japanese forces had landed at the villages of Lae and Salamau at Huon Gulf on the Papuan Peninsula of eastern New Guinea on March 8. Learning of this development, Admiral Brown set course for New Guinea. Steaming into the Gulf of Papua on the opposite shore of the peninsula, Brown sent more than a hundred aircraft from the *Yorktown* and *Lexington* to strike the surprised Japanese invasion forces. A gunboat, two transports, and a minesweeper were sunk and three warships damaged. It was the most important American naval success to date and an unexpected shock to the Japanese. The Huon Gulf raid was also the first coordinated American air strike mounted from two different carriers.[6]

The Pacific war of raids and counterraids was fought over a vast and empty region of ocean and sky, which filled the enormous watery triangle between Japan, Australia, and Hawaii. This was a strange and remote area of the world full of names like Kwajalein, Truk, Tonga, the Solomon Sea, New Britain, New Caledonia, and the Bismarck Archipelago, which sounded exotic, strange, remote, or simply incomprehensible to both Japanese and American sailors. "Hawaii would be the first strange place," recalled marine aviator Samuel Haynes, "the edge of a world that was not like anything back home. No one I knew had ever been there . . . and it existed in my imagination as a mixture of myths."[7]

Japanese sailors spoke of the "lands of eternal summer" in the romantic "Nanyo" or south seas.[8]

While the British and German battle fleets in the North Sea had gone to sea for a few days at a time, Japanese and American ships operated for weeks, crossing and recrossing the equator and the international date line, ranging from Hawaii to Japan, Australia to the Aleutians. The Americans refueled at sea from huge tankers named for rivers. The tanker would steam at the same speed and on a parallel course, twenty-five to fifty feet from the vessel it was fueling. Line handlers in life jackets passed lines and fuel hoses across the gap as the two ships rolled in the open ocean. "The waves between the ships in this operation were huge, and standing on the flight deck on the carrier you could watch the great bulk of the tanker rise up above you and then crash down."[9] The slightest brush between the two ships tore and mangled their steel superstructures "as though a head on collision had occurred. A parting manila hawser could snap back and kill a man."[10] Underway refueling enabled American fleets to remain at sea for long periods without having to reduce speed to conserve fuel.

Operating near the equator for extended periods, sailors often worked in conditions of stifling heat. "The bright sun sent out blazing rays and it was steaming hot inside the ship," wrote seaman Kuramoto Iki. "This completely dissipated my cherished illusions about the tropics."[11] Aviation Ordnanceman Alvin Kernan, who served in the *Enterprise* and *Hornet*, recalled that "heat rash tormented everyone particularly around the waist where several layers of wet clothes twisted and pulled inside the belt. A story circulated that when the heat rash . . . girdled your waist you died."[12]

Fresh water for bathing, washing, or laundering clothes was a constant concern. Aboard the *Hornet*, sailors used a single bucket of soapy water to wash both their clothes and themselves, then another bucket for rinsing, finishing up with a luxurious "five or ten seconds under the shower spray (with no time allowed to adjust the water temperature)."[13]

"The food on carriers is generally quite good for the first month," one naval aviator recalled. "Thereafter it begins to deteriorate. Fresh milk disappears almost immediately and the next to go are fresh eggs, greens, fresh vegetables and finally fresh meat. Officers and crew alike begin to live on powdered milk, powdered eggs and canned fruit and vegetables and meat."[14] A few more weeks and even the powdered milk and eggs would disappear. On one *Hornet* deployment, "beans were being ground up and called potatoes and there were beetles in the flour." Smaller ships in the task force served Spam and "a kind of artificial potato."[15] The *Saratoga*, which lacked adequate food storage space to accommodate her large wartime crew, went to sea with food stacked in the passageways.[16]

Heat, boredom, and fatigue were the staples of naval life in the Pacific. At sea, most sailors worked fourteen to sixteen hours a day. The day began for most seamen two hours before sunrise when a bugle sounded reveille followed by flight quarters and general quarters as sailors manned their battle stations and flight deck crews prepared to launch the first planes. From first light until dark, the flight deck was the scene of constant noise and activity. Although an aircraft carrier's crew of 2,000 to 3,000 men might include little more than a hundred pilots, carrier operations were a labor-intensive activity. A 1942 fighter squadron, for example, included only nineteen pilots, but 120 enlisted men.[17] Flight deck operations required a small army of mechanics, technicians, and plane handlers. Because the flight deck was invariably used to park aircraft, planes had to be pushed forward to allow room at the rear of the flight deck for landing. For takeoffs the evolution was reversed. The entire process of shifting and spotting aircraft had to be accomplished by hand with teams of plane handlers pushing aircraft back and forth at a dead run. Each team of specialists wore different-colored helmets and jerseys to aid in quick identification: "Chockmen," who handled the wooden chocks placed under a plane's wheels, wore purple. "Hookmen," who had the dangerous job of releasing the airplane's arrestor hook just before takeoff, wore green, fueling crews wore red, communications personnel wore brown, and so forth. The success of a carrier depended in large measure on how efficiently it could launch, recover, and reposition its aircraft. Aboard the *Hornet* about thirty airplanes could be shifted from forward to aft in less than six minutes.[18]

Departing planes were formed up aft as close together as possible. At the command "Start engines," dozens of engines roared to life, emitting small red and blue flames. The carrier was turned into the wind to provide maximum lift for the aircraft. The flight deck officer, the maestro conductor of the noisy concert of rumbling, thundering aircraft, held up his black-and-white-checkered flag. Following a signal from the flight deck officer, a pilot taxied his plane onto the "spot" for takeoff. With brakes set, the throttle was pushed far forward, bringing the engine to full power. When the flight deck officer waved down his flag, the brakes were released and the plane rolled down the deck and into the air.

Despite the minute precision of air operations, a carrier's flight deck remained a dangerous place even in the absence of the enemy. Accidents were far from rare. Guns in the plane's wings could go off accidentally, spraying the deck with .50-caliber bullets; lines could snap and whip across the deck, maiming or decapitating anyone in their path; busy crewmen occasionally walked into the whirring propellers of an air-craft. A plane crash on the flight deck almost always resulted in death or injuries to flight deck hands as well as to the aircrew.

Though the flight deck crews, mechanics, and ordnancemen were a critical element and hundreds of other ratings performed essential tasks, attention focused almost exclusively on the aviators, the sharp edge of the carrier's power. Mostly young men in their early twenties, with a sprinkling of older Annapolis graduates, enlisted pilots, and early gradu-ates of the aviation cadet programs, they were members of the navy's most select caste, and they knew it.

Aviation was still romantic, dangerous, and exciting in 1942. "None of the kids I knew had ever been in a plane or expected to be in one," re-called pilot Samuel Haynes.[19] The naval aviator, in particular, con-stantly performed his most essential and difficult function—landing on a narrow moving deck—before a large, sometimes admiring, sometimes critical, but always attentive audience. Even in his day-to-day functions, he was a kind of star soloist.

Japanese aviators also saw themselves as the superstars of the new air-sea warfare. Survivors of the almost inhuman rigors of the Japanese flight schools, many had been flying combat missions since the beginning of the Sino-Japanese War in 1937 and had accumulated hundreds of flying hours. In the carriers *Zuikaku* and *Shokaku* nearly all fighter pilots had more than two years of flight experience.[20]

Japanese naval aircraft were technically superior to most American land-based and carrier-based planes. Fighter pilots flew the Mitsubishi A6M2 Type 00 carrier fighter, the famous "Zero." Fast, light, and excep-tionally maneuverable, with a superior rate of climb and relatively long range, the Zero was the first carrier-based fighter to equal or surpass the performance of the best land-based fighters. It had dominated the skies in the China war, and several Japanese pilots had become aces. Only a few hundred Zeroes had been sufficient to maintain complete air superi-ority for the Japanese during their lightning conquest of Southeast Asia and the South Pacific. Losses had been very low. Fighter pilots compared their Zeroes "to master craftsmen's Japanese swords."[21] Other carrier air-craft, the Nakajima B5N2 Type 97 "Kate" torpedo plane and the Aichi D3A1 Type 99 "Val," were less spectacular but still equal or superior to their American counterparts.

Japanese aerial torpedoes were also far more reliable than similar Amer-ican weapons. The Japanese Type 91 aerial torpedo could be dropped from several hundred feet by a plane traveling at more than 200 hundred miles an hour. The American Mark 13, however, suffered from numerous technical defects. It had to be dropped at the height of no more than 200 feet by an airplane traveling less than 130 miles per hour. Once in the water, the Mark 13's speed was little greater than that of a destroyer.[22] In Admiral Brown's air raid on the Japanese forces at Huon Gulf, American torpedo planes scored several hits on ships but their torpedoes failed to explode. "You could see the streaks of torpedoes going right to the side of the cruisers and nothing happened," reported one aviator. "I saw one or two go right on underneath, come out the other side, and bury itself in the bank on the other shore."[23]

American fighter pilots flew the Grumman F4F Wildcat, a rugged well-armed aircraft with pilot armor, bulletproof windscreens, and self-sealing fuel tanks, but inferior to the Zero in speed, range, maneuverability, and rate of climb. A Zero could reach 20,000 feet in just under seven and a half minutes. A Wildcat required more than ten minutes. Americans also flew the Douglas Devastator torpedo bomber, which had been a very advanced design when it was introduced in 1937. It had been the fleet's first low-wing, all metal monoplane and could carry a 22-inch torpedo. So pleased had the navy been with the Devastator that it deferred procuring a new torpedo plane, the Grumman Avenger, until 1940; the result was that no Avengers reached the carrier squadrons until months after Pearl Harbor.[24] The Devastator's low speed and lack of maneuverability made it extremely vulnerable to enemy fighters and antiaircraft guns. That slowness also made it difficult for the short-range Wildcats to provide escorts for the torpedo planes on longer missions. Of U.S. carrier aircraft, only the rugged Douglas Dauntless dive-bomber was to prove a completely effective weapon, and it remained in service aboard carriers until late 1944.

At the end of March 1942, Admiral Nagumo, with five carriers, four fast battleships, three cruisers, and nine destroyers, left the Celebes Straits near Borneo and passed through the Strait of Malacca into the Indian Ocean. Around the same time, another force under Vice Admiral Ozawa, consisting of a small aircraft carrier, six cruisers, and eight destroyers, sailed from Malaya to attack shipping in the Bay of Bengal.

For a week, Nagumo's task force roamed the Indian Ocean virtually unchallenged by the British, whose Royal Navy had held undisputed sway there for 150 years. The main British bases at Colombo and Trincomalee in Ceylon were bombed by Nagumo's carrier planes, while

Ozawa's force sank almost 100,000 tons of shipping in the Bay of Bengal in just five days. The British Eastern Fleet under Admiral Sir James Somerville, which had only two modern carriers with less than a hundred aircraft, avoided a confrontation with the Japanese, but the heavy cruisers *Dorsetshire* and *Cornwall* and the small carrier *Hermes,* which were at Ceylon at the time of the air raids, were sunk by Nagumo's planes. The rest of the Eastern Fleet eventually withdrew to East Africa.

On April 18, while Nagumo's fleet was returning from its victorious foray into the Indian Ocean, the Americans pulled off a spectacular raid of their own. Sixteen Army Air Forces B-25 bombers flying from the carrier *Hornet* bombed Tokyo and a handful of other cities. The damage done was slight, but the psychological impact was enormous. "Our homeland has been air raided and we missed the enemy without firing a shot at him. This is exceedingly regrettable," reported Combined Fleet Chief of Staff Ugaki Matomi in his diary.[25]

The Tokyo raid helped resolve a long debate among the Japanese high command in favor of an offensive into the Central Pacific with the object of capturing the island of Midway and luring the American carriers into a decisive battle. Already scheduled operations in the Southwest Pacific to isolate Australia were moved forward.

The Japanese objective in the Southwest Pacific was the Australian town of Port Moresby on the south coast of the Papuan Peninsula. Once in Japanese hands, Port Moresby could serve as a base for the capture of Fiji, New Caledonia, and other points along the tenuous six-thousand-mile line of communications from the United States to Australia and New Zealand.[26] Two large carriers of Admiral Nagumo's striking force, *Shokaku* and *Zuikaku,* under Vice Admiral Takagi Takeo, were assigned to cover the invasion operations aimed at Port Moresby and the small island of Tulagi in the Solomons, which the Japanese wanted as a seaplane base. The Japanese planned to seize Tulagi first on May 3, 1942, to guard the left flank of the invasion. After that, the Port Moresby invasion force, protected by the small carrier *Shoho* and four cruisers, would sail from Rabaul.

American code breakers in Pearl Harbor, Melbourne, and Washington were by now reading large portions of the Japanese code and ciphers and alerted Nimitz to an impending Japanese offensive in the Southwest Pacific. Nimitz sent the carrier *Lexington* to join the *Yorktown,* under Admiral Fletcher, already cruising in the south Pacific. The *Lexington* task force, under Rear Admiral Aubrey Fitch, reached Fletcher on May 1 in the blue-green waters of the Coral Sea, the body of water separating Australia, the Solomons, and eastern New Guinea. *Yorktown* had been in the South Pacific for more than two months and her crew were "living on hard tack and beans."[27] Both task forces began refueling from their accompanying oilers, an extremely slow process that consumed most of the next two days.

On May 3, word reached Fletcher of Japanese landings at Tulagi and the admiral raced north with the *Yorktown* and other ships that had completed fueling to attack the invasion forces. Admiral Takagi's carrier striking force, which should have provided cover for the operations at Tulagi, was far away, having been delayed ferrying aircraft to Rabaul. Consequently, the *Yorktown*'s planes were unopposed when they roared down on the Japanese destroyers' transports and landing craft off Rabaul.

The pilots returned to their carriers in a jubilant mood to report destroyers, cruisers, and transports sunk. In fact, Japanese losses were confined to three small minesweepers and minor damage to other ships. This was a small success indeed for the number of bombs and torpedoes expended, but enough to send the remnants of the Tulagi force steaming hurriedly back to Rabaul.

Fletcher's air attacks alerted the Japanese to the presence of American carriers in the region, and now U.S. Navy code breakers confirmed the presence of the *Shokaku* and *Zuikaku* in the Coral Sea area. In response, Fletcher combined his two carriers into a single task force and headed for the Jomard Passage in the Loisiade Archipelago, through which he expected the Port Moresby invasion force to pass as it rounded the eastern tip of New Guinea. While he lacked precise information about the enemy carriers, he assumed they would be covering the flanks of the invasion force. In fact, only the small carrier *Shoho* was with the invasion force. Takagi's big carriers were actually behind—that is, to the northeast of—Fletcher's force, having rounded the Solomons and entered the Coral Sea on the 6th.

The Battle of the Coral Sea was to be the first between opposing fleets of carriers, and both sides made plenty of mistakes. At one point on the 6th, the Japanese and American fleets were less than seventy miles from each other, but failed to make contact. The following day the skies over the Coral Sea were filled with search planes as the opposing forces looked for each other. Searching to the south, Takagi's planes found the American oiler *Neosho* and the destroyer *Sims* stationed by Fletcher in what he believed was a safe location. They reported them as a carrier task force. Takagi flung his entire striking force, some eighty planes, at the two hapless ships, sinking the *Sims* and crippling the *Neosho*, which sank some time later. Fletcher's carriers, however, were left unmolested.

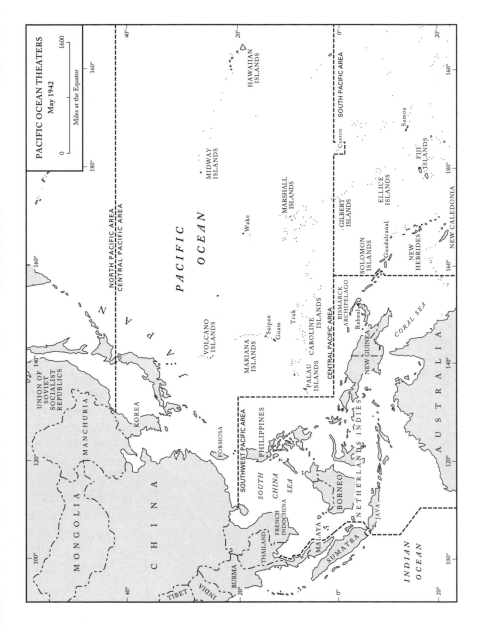

PACIFIC OCEAN THEATERS
May 1942

0   Miles at the Equator   1600

Still expecting the Japanese to come south through the Jomard Passage, Fletcher sent search planes to the north and west, and one of these happened upon the *Shoho* and her escorting cruisers. Convinced that they had found the *Shokaku* and *Zuikaku*, Fletcher and Fitch dispatched almost a hundred planes against the *Shoho*, which was soon reduced to a flaming wreck by successive waves of American bombers and torpedo planes. Thirty minutes after the *Shoho* disappeared beneath the sea, Lieutenant Commander Robert E. Dixon, leader of *Lexington's* Scouting Two, sent an electrifying message to the task force. "Scratch one flattop! signed Bob."[28]

Careful questioning of the jubilant aviators soon convinced the *Yorktown's* air staff that the carrier had not been either the *Shokoku* or *Zuikaku*, which were, therefore, still at large. Takagi had already learned that he had likewise missed the American carriers. The two opposing admirals now reached opposite decisions. Fletcher decided to keep his force concentrated and prepare for a battle the following morning. Tukagi decided to launch a late-afternoon strike even though the planes would have to make night landings on return.

Tukagi's twenty-seven bombers and torpedo planes had a harrowing ordeal. Picked up by the *Lexington's* radar, they were ambushed by American fighters, suffering eight losses. In the darkness and bad weather, several groups of Japanese planes mistook the American carriers for their own. As they approached the task force, the American cruisers and destroyers opened fire. They failed to hit any Japanese planes but came close to downing several American Wildcats preparing to land on the *Yorktown*. Ensign L. Wright, a *Yorktown* fighter pilot, was astounded to see the ship's entire starboard battery open up on him. Diving under the tracer bullets, Wright radioed the ship, "Why are you shooting at me for? What have I done now?"[29] Of Takagi's strike force, only two thirds returned safely to their carriers.

The following morning, search planes from the two fleets found the opposing carriers at almost the same time. The Americans attacked first, scoring three bomb hits on the *Shokaku*, which wrecked her flight deck but did no fatal damage. All of the torpedoes launched by the lumbering Devastators missed their targets or failed to explode. The torpedoes were so slow at long range that the Japanese ships could actually outrun them.[30]

A short time after the American attack on the *Shokaku*, Japanese bombers and torpedo planes sighted the *Lexington* and *Yorktown*. The American carriers, equipped with radar, located the attackers about seventy miles away, but this early radar could not distinguish the altitude of approaching planes and there was no way to determine which planes on the screen were friendly or hostile. Using this scanty information, the *Lexington's* fighter direction officer, an aviator, was supposed to direct her defending fighters, called the combat air patrol, to locations where they could intercept the attackers.

The *Lexington* and *Yorktown* had about twenty fighters aloft, but the fighter director had vectored them at too low an altitude and too close in to catch most of the attackers. As the Japanese planes closed on the carriers, the ships of the task force opened an intense antiaircraft fire at the attackers. "Never in all my years had I imagined a battle like that," observed Lieutenant Commander Shimazaki Shigekazu, a torpedo plane pilot. "We ran into a virtual wall of antiaircraft fire; the carriers and their supporting ships blackened the sky with exploding shells and tracers. . . . I had to fly directly above the waves to escape the enemy shells and tracers. In fact, when I turned away from the carrier I almost struck the bow of the ship for I was flying below the level of the flight deck."[31] Although it may have impressed Shimazaki, the task force's antiaircraft fire was erratic and inaccurate. The gunnery officer in the *Yorktown* claimed that the task force "started and ended our engagement by shooting at our own planes."[32]

As in the campaign off Crete, a ship's survival in the absence of other defenses depended on the captain's ability to execute violent evasive maneuvers at just the right moment. The *Yorktown*'s short turning radius enabled Captain Elliott Buckmaster to dodge all the aerial torpedoes. But several bombs barely missed the ship, and one bomb penetrated the flight deck and exploded just above a fire room.

The *Lexington*, far less handy than the *Yorktown*, was hit by three bombs and at least two torpedoes. Built as a battle cruiser, the *Lexington* had special antitorpedo protection called "bulges" so that despite the damage she was still able to steam at thirty knots. The *Yorktown*, with relatively minor damage, could make twenty-five knots. An hour after the Japanese attack ended, most of the damage aboard the *Lexington* had been temporarily repaired and fires put out, but at 12:47, gasoline released by one of the torpedo hits ignited and a violent explosion rocked the ship. Two hours later, a second internal explosion caused the fires already burning in the ship to rage out of control. Late that afternoon, the *Lexington* was abandoned; one of the escorting destroyers sank her.

The loss of the *Lexington* drastically changed the odds in the Coral Sea. Admiral Fletcher now had only a single carrier and about forty aircraft. He knew that at least one of the Japanese carriers remained in the fight, and he had received reports that an additional carrier might have joined the Japanese task force since the start of the battle.[33] Fletcher decided to withdraw, a decision confirmed by orders from Nimitz the next day. The Japanese were in no position to take advantage of Fletcher's retirement. The *Shokaku* had been damaged so badly that she had to head back to Truk and then to Japan for repairs. The *Zuikaku* was undamaged but was low on fuel and had fewer than forty operational aircraft, and there were still many Allied land-based aircraft, within range of Port Moresby. The Japanese consequently postponed the invasion of Port Moresby—as it turned out, forever.

As the first carrier battle, the encounter in the Coral Sea understandably attracted great attention. The tactics of the two sides and the quality and effectiveness of the opposing aircraft were much discussed. Yet the most serious losses on both sides were, in the end, due to defects in organization and training rather than weapons or tactics. The *Lexington* was ultimately lost because her crew were not as well trained in damage control and not as well equipped as they might have been. Firefighters lacked fog nozzles, asbestos suits, portable fire pumps, and modern breathing apparatus. The gas vapor explosion, which finally doomed the ship, was probably triggered by small fires that had not been quenched completely.[34] The presence of gas vapors was itself an indication of the lack of adequate control of aviation fuel. Over the next year, the U.S. Navy would institute enormous improvements in its damage control practices, making American ships the most survivable in history.

The Japanese carriers suffered no critical damage, but they were unable to operate for weeks after the Coral Sea because of weaknesses in the Japanese system of organization and training for naval aviation. Unlike the Americans, the Japanese had no system for advance training of replacement air groups for carriers. Thus, the pilots lost at the Coral Sea battle could not simply be replaced by another experienced air group. New aviators assigned to the *Zuikaku* and *Shokaku* had to be trained before the carriers could again be ready for combat.

By the time the damaged *Yorktown* arrived at Pearl Harbor for repairs, the rest of the Pacific Fleet was already preparing to meet the next Japanese onslaught. Since early May, intercepted Japanese messages being read by code breakers at Pearl Harbor and Melbourne pointed to a big Japanese offensive in the Central Pacific. On May 27, the day the *Yorktown* reached Pearl Harbor, code breakers definitively identified Midway as the target of the new Japanese thrust.[35] Halsey's carriers, *Enterprise* and *Hornet*, had arrived the day before the *Yorktown*, and Halsey, ill with dermatitis, turned over command of his task force to Rear Admiral Raymond Spruance.

By May 30 all three carriers were on their way to Midway. "The rumor mill began to whisper a fantastic story. The Japanese fleet, it was said, was about to attack Midway . . . and we, having broken their code, were going to lie off Midway and surprise them. . . . That deepest Navy secret—that we had broken the Japanese code and were reading their messages—was widely known among the enlisted men and the proposed strategy and tactics for the coming battle learnedly and gravely discussed by the admirals of the lower deck, who were on the whole, as always, of the opinion that the officers' plan would not work."[36]

The Midway operation involved practically the entire Japanese navy, minus the *Zuikaku* and *Shokaku*, and was intended by Yamamoto to create an opportunity for a decisive battle with the remaining American fleet. Japanese naval officers were so confident of success that they brought back aboard ship many personal belongings such as cameras, pictures, and games, which they had put ashore for safekeeping at the time of Pearl Harbor.[37]

Unaware of the American carriers lying in ambush for him northeast of Midway, Nagumo sent a strike force to attack the island on the morning of June 4. Shortly after the Japanese attack wave had been launched, Midway search planes sighted Nagumo's carriers and alerted Fletcher, who signaled Spruance, "Attack enemy carriers as soon as definitely located."[38] *Yorktown* would follow as soon as she had recovered her morning search planes. The two American carriers turned southwest toward the Japanese and Midway planes headed for the same target.

Spruance's optimum point for launching an attack was about a hundred miles from the enemy. At that distance his short-legged planes would have ample time to find the Japanese, maneuver for attack, and return. At 7:00 A.M., however, while still more than 150 miles from the reported Japanese position, Spruance decided to launch his attack, hoping to catch Nagumo while he was recovering his Midway strike. Admiral Fletcher received word of Spruance's launch, but held off for a time. Code breakers had predicted four Japanese carriers in the area and scouts had reported only two. He probably remembered how a faulty scouting report at the Battle of the Coral Sea had led him to waste his striking force on the small carrier *Shoho* while the big carriers went unmolested. Finally at 8:30 Fletcher decided to launch his dive-bombers and all of his torpedo planes, along with a few fighters, while holding back the rest of the aircraft to deal with whatever might develop.

Nagumo, already under attack by Midway-based planes, was in the midst of arming planes for a second attack on the island when, at 7:28, he received a report from one of his cruiser scout planes of enemy ships to his north. It took the scout almost an hour to determine that one of the American ships was a carrier. In the interim, more Midway-based planes attacked the Japanese fleet, but scored no hits and suffered heavy losses against the Zeroes of the carrier's combat air patrol.

Receiving word of the sighting of the American carrier, Rear Admiral Yamaguchi Tamon, commanding the *Soryu* and *Hiryu* of Carrier Division 2, signaled Nagumo, "Consider it advisable to launch attack force immediately."[39] At that point many of the Japanese strike planes lacked proper ship-killing bombs and torpedoes, having been rearmed for a second Midway strike. They would also have to make their attack without fighter escort, since almost all of the available fighters were already committed to combat air patrol or with the returning Midway strike force. Nagumo decided to wait. He would first recover the Midway attack force, then rearm and reorganize his forces for a balanced attack on the Americans.

Spruance had intended to launch a coordinated strike against the Japanese, but plane handlers aboard the *Enterprise* proved much slower than those aboard the *Hornet* in launching and respotting planes, so an impatient Spruance ordered the *Hornet*'s planes to depart together with whatever *Enterprise* aircraft had already been launched. The *Enterprise*'s fighters and torpedo planes followed fifteen minutes later.

Flying at various speeds and altitudes, and lacking information on the precise location of the enemy, Spruance's planes arrived at the estimated Japanese position to find it empty. After recovering his Midway strike, Nagumo had retired to the northeast in order to open the range between himself and the Americans while he rearmed and refueled. The *Hornet*'s fighters and dive-bombers never did find the carriers, and they had to return empty-handed when their fuel ran low. *Hornet*'s Torpedo Squadron Eight, led by Commander John C. Waldron, managed to locate the Japanese, however; it attacked alone and was destroyed. Not a single plane survived the relentless attacks of the Japanese Zeroes and the carriers' antiaircraft fire. A similar fate befell the *Enterprise*'s torpedo squadron under Lieutenant Commander Eugene E. Lindsey; it lost ten of its fourteen planes. Neither squadron scored any hits.

The *Yorktown*'s planes managed to stay together reasonably well and had less trouble finding the Japanese. Although starting later, they reached the target at about the same time as the *Enterprise*'s planes, which had had to search longer for it. Six *Yorktown* fighters led by Lieutenant Commander John S. Thach had to contend with at least thirty-five Zeroes attempting to protect the torpedo planes. "Zeroes were coming in on us on a stream from astern," Thach recalled. "Then I saw a second large group streaming right past us onto the torpedo planes. The air was like a beehive."[40] Surprisingly, the canny Thach, an expert on fighter tactics, and his five companions managed to shoot down at least six enemy fighters while losing only one of their own.[41] Yet they could not protect the *Yorktown's* torpedo squadron, which lost twelve of its fourteen planes and scored no hits.

The battle with the torpedo planes and Thach's fighters had absorbed the attention of the Japanese fighter pilots and drawn them to a fairly low altitude. The result was that they failed to notice the arrival of a new menace: the dive-bombers of the *Yorktown* as well as those of the *Enterprise* approaching at high altitude from the east. Thach "saw this glint in the sun and it just looked like a beautiful silver waterfall; the dive bombers coming down. I could see them very well because that was the direction of the Zeroes too. They weren't anywhere near the height the dive bombers were. I'd never seen such superb dive bombing."[42]

With little or no interference from the Zeroes, the dive-bombers unleashed a devastating rain of bombs on the Japanese carriers. Within minutes the *Akagi, Kaga,* and *Soryu* were enveloped in flames as bombs, torpedoes, and fuel on their crowded flight decks detonated in massive explosions. Only the *Hiryu,* which had become separated from the other carriers in the wild maneuvering to avoid the successive American air attacks, escaped unscathed.

For the thousands of sailors aboard the *Yorktown, Enterprise,* and *Hornet,* news of the battle was confused and fragmentary. Alvin Kernan, an ordnanceman with Torpedo Squadron Six, recalled:

> We waited for them on the deck of the *Enterprise.* Our fighters came back first intact, which seemed odd and then one, two, three, and four torpedo planes straggled in separately and that was it. The last of the planes was so badly shot up that it was deep sixed immediately after it landed. . . . The size of the loss was unimaginable and even when the crews, in a condition of shock, told us what a slaughter it had been, it was unbelievable. . . . Within a few minutes . . . the dive-bombers . . . began arriving in small clusters and singly. Shot up, some landing in the water out of gas, some crashing on deck with failing landing gear or no tailhooks and being pushed over the side instantly to make room for others coming in. But now the mood was triumphant. The bomber pilots could hardly contain

themselves. They were shouting and laughing as they jumped out of the cockpit, and the ship which had been so somber a moment before when the torpedo planes returned became now hysterically excited.[43]

Lieutenant Frederick Mears watched as "the returning pilots crowded into their ready room or the pantry gulping lemonade out of paper cups, mechanically stuffing sandwiches into their mouths and at the same time yammering and gesticulating to each other about their individual adventures. . . . Their hair when they took off their helmets was matted with perspiration. Their faces were often dirty and their light cotton flying suits were streaked with sweat. They were having one hell of a good time."[44]

Before noon, the *Hiryu* launched her surviving bombers and torpedo planes in two separate waves against the Americans. Only a few survived the fighters of the *Yorktown*'s combat air patrol, but they managed to heavily damage the carrier with three bomb and two torpedo hits. The *Yorktown* was later sunk by a Japanese submarine while being towed to Pearl Harbor for repairs. By that time the *Hiryu* had also been sunk, hit by dive-bombers from the *Yorktown* and *Enterprise* late on June 4.

It has become commonplace to say that the Coral Sea and Midway established the supremacy of the aircraft carrier in naval warfare. The gunpower of the opposing fleets had proved largely irrelevant to naval battles in which the opposing ships never sighted each other. Yet if airpower advocates had been proved correct about the power of carrier-based attack, the doubters had also been right about the carrier's vulnerability and lack of staying power. Carrier admirals still had to rely on finding the enemy first in order to launch as many of their aircraft as possible in one overwhelming blow. At Coral Sea the Americans lost half of their fleet and the surviving carriers of both sides were in no condition to continue operations. At Midway the Japanese lost their entire fleet, three quarters to the single massive first blow by the opposing fleet. The aircraft carrier might be "the new queen of the seas" as journalists proclaimed, but her reign would not be secure until she could defend herself effectively.

For the Japanese, the Battle of Midway was a devastating psychological as well as tactical defeat. Accurate news of the battle was rigorously suppressed, and the surviving crews were not allowed shore leave. "All in all we can't help concluding that the main cause of the defeat was that we had become conceited because of past successes," wrote Admiral Ugaki. "This is a matter for the utmost regret. . . . This is not a natural calamity, but a result of human deeds. . . . How to rehabilitate the fleet air force is imperative at this moment."[45]

The reorganization of the Japanese fleet's airpower began almost at once. In July, a new Third Fleet, built around the surviving carriers with their supporting cruisers and destroyers, came into existence. New carriers were laid down and large commercial and support ships were taken in hand for conversion.

While some two thirds of Japanese aviators—although not their planes—were reported to have survived the Battle of Midway, many had been injured and had to return to Japan for convalescence.[46] The loss of trained mechanics, armorers, and machinists was even more serious. Unlike American air groups and squadrons, which had their own maintenance personnel, all support personnel for a Japanese air group came from the crew of a carrier. Even if replacement pilots and airplanes became available, they might still be without ground support staff. Uninjured aviators were sent to the new Third Fleet at Kyushu to rebuild their air groups and train replacements, a task that was estimated to require two or three months.[47]

The Americans also faced the problem of rebuilding the squadrons and air groups that had fought at the Coral Sea and Midway. Nimitz reported that "new aircraft deliveries and new flight school graduates have done little more than balance operational and battle losses. . . ." Many aviators were suffering "operational fatigue due to long continued intensive operations at sea and heavy battle attrition without relief."[48]

King and Nimitz's solution to this problem was radical. The most experienced pilots, primarily those from the *Yorktown* and *Enterprise* squadrons, were sent back to the United States to train new pilots. Famous ace Butch O'Hare, for example, spent the remainder of 1942 and much of 1943 at Naval Air Station Maui training new pilots and squadrons. "Jimmy" Thach went to the United States to impart to others the secrets of the tactics that had enabled him to survive and win his encounter with three dozen enemy fighters.

To expand the pool of combat-ready pilots, King and Nimitz established "carrier replacement air groups." The nucleus of these groups was veteran pilots from the fleet who trained replacement squadrons in the latest combat aircraft. This expedient, made possible by increasing U.S. aircraft production and the personnel expansion measures introduced in 1939 and 1940, meant that squadrons could be rotated out of combat for rest and refitting and that new carriers would receive fully trained air groups.

The Japanese, too, intended to train new pilots to replace losses at Midway, but veteran aviators were not rotated away from combat duties, remaining with their air groups, which continued to provide their own advanced operational training for new pilots. Within four months, almost all of these veteran pilots would be dead.

ELEVEN

"SCARED AS HELL, HAVING A WONDERFUL TIME"

Writing in his diary on July 30, 1942, Admiral Ugaki noted, "The army . . . requests a traffic-raiding operation west of Australia. Shame on them! We can't do anything for the time being but take a nap."[1] Similarly, many in the United States believed that after Midway it was time for a breather. Admiral King emphatically disagreed. Only two weeks after Midway he persuaded the Joint Chiefs of Staff and the president to agree to a new offensive in the South Pacific aimed at the Solomon Islands and the major Japanese base at Rabaul on New Britain Island. U.S. Marines landed on the islands of Guadalcanal and Tulagi on August 7.

The campaign began disastrously when Japanese cruisers surprised an American-Australian cruiser force on the night of August 8–9 near Savo Island northwest of Guadalcanal. They sank four cruisers and damaged another. Vice Admiral Frank Jack Fletcher's carrier task force, which had supported the landings, had already withdrawn to the south, and the remaining transports, now exposed to attack, departed the next day.[2]

Although the isolated marines were in a perilous position, the Japanese high command was slow to react to the American invasion. The first Japanese attempt to recapture the island did not come until ten days later and ended in failure when the force of 1,000 troops was annihilated in an ill-conceived assault on the marines' perimeter along the Ilu River. In the interval the Americans had completed work on an airfield begun by the Japanese, and the first marine planes landed on the island less than two weeks after the Savo Island battle.

At the time of the Japanese defeat on the Ilu River, additional troops for Guadalcanal were already at sea supported by ships of the Combined Fleet, including the carriers *Shokoku,* and *Zuikaku* and the light carrier *Ryujo.* Fletcher's carrier task force was cruising southwest of Guadalcanal when American search planes found part of the Japanese fleet on August 23.

Unfortunately, Fletcher had already detached the carrier *Wasp* to refuel, so the odds, which might have favored the Americans, now slightly favored the Japanese, who had two large and one small carrier to oppose the American *Saratoga* and *Enterprise.* In the ensuing Battle of the Eastern Solomons, American planes found and attacked the *Ryujo,* which was supporting the reinforcement attempt. The *Shokoku* and *Zuikaku* were left unmolested and directed their entire complement of planes at Fletcher's carriers. One of the attack groups failed to find the Americans, however, and the other scored three hits on the carrier *Enterprise* but failed to sink her.

Both carrier forces withdrew, but the reinforcement transports and their supporting warships steamed grimly on for Guadalcanal. Shortly after daylight the next morning, marine dive-bombers from Henderson Field and B-17 heavy bombers from Espiritu Santo, an island south of Guadalcanal, found the Japanese convoy, damaged a light cruiser, sank a destroyer and a transport, and sent the surviving ships in a hasty retreat back toward Truk.

Over the next three months, both sides attempted to supply and reinforce their forces on Guadalcanal. American control of Henderson Field enabled the Americans to dominate the sea around the island during the day, but the Japanese, despite occasional painful losses, managed to run in troops and supplies by ship under cover of darkness, a practice the Americans called "the Tokyo Express." After delivering their reinforcements, Japanese warships often bombarded Henderson Field, making life miserable for the marines and sometimes forcing the curtailment of air operations by damaging aircraft or ground facilities. Japanese attempts to interfere with American reinforcements and American attempts to derail the Tokyo Express often resulted in major air and naval battles.

By mid-October the Japanese judged they had built up sufficient strength on Guadalcanal for an all-out offensive against Henderson Field. A powerful Japanese fleet stood by to engage any American warships that might appear. Once the airfield was captured, Combined Fleet carriers would fly in planes to operate against the remnants of the American forces. "The victory is already in our hands. Please rest your minds," reported the Japanese army commander on Guadalcanal.[3] In fact, the

Japanese assault on the airfield ended in failure after bloody battles on the nights of October 23 through 26.

At sea, Vice Admiral Kondo Nobutake impatiently awaited word of the capture of Henderson Field. With Kondo were two battleships, five cruisers, a dozen destroyers, and the carrier *Junyo*. About one hundred miles to the east were three more carriers, *Shokaku*, *Zuikaku*, and *Zuiho*, with a heavy cruiser and eight destroyers under Admiral Nagumo. A second battleship and cruiser force under Rear Admiral Abe Hiroaki and an additional cruiser-destroyer force under Vice Admiral Mikawa Gunichi, who had won the Battle of Savo Island, were deployed closer to Guadalcanal.[4] Early on the morning of October 26, Kondo received a message from his liaison officer on Guadalcanal confirming the fact that Henderson Field was still in American hands. By that point, Kondo had received word that an American fleet was in the area.

Out of the four with which Fletcher had begun the Guadalcanal campaign, only two carriers, *Hornet* and *Enterprise*, remained in the South Pacific. *Wasp* had been sunk and *Saratoga* damaged by submarine attack. Fletcher had also departed, replaced by Rear Admiral Thomas C. Kinkaid, and Halsey had replaced Vice Admiral Robert L. Ghormley as commander of the South Pacific Area and overall director of the Guadalcanal campaign. Both Halsey and the *Enterprise* had only recently arrived in the theater. Kinkaid's force, designated Task Force 61, comprised the *Hornet*, the *Enterprise*, the new fast battleship *South Dakota*, three heavy cruisers, and three new light cruisers with a special antiaircraft armament of sixteen 5-inch and many smaller guns. The *Enterprise* had a brand-new air group that had never been in combat as a unit. While Halsey and Kinkaid already knew of Kondo's activities, thanks to American code-breaking efforts and long-range reconnaissance, Kinkaid had only two carriers to four for the Japanese and 136 planes to 199 for Admiral Kondo.[5] Nonetheless, Halsey ordered Kinkaid north to attack, instructing him, "Strike, Repeat Strike."

Around noon on the 25th, Kinkaid received word from a patrolling seaplane of the sighting of two Japanese carriers 351 miles from his force. A midafternoon strike failed to find the enemy carriers, which had turned north. Looking for the Japanese fleet, the strike group leader went beyond his assigned search range and his planes did not return until after dark.

"The saddest sight I ever hope to see was the night when our planes were returning from the assault [sic] on the Japanese," wrote Gunner's Mate James O'Neil in his diary. "It was pitch dark and the [search] had lasted longer than expected and it was a difficult task to land on the car-

riers at night. . . . We had to risk a few lights for them to see."[6] Most of
the pilots were making their first night landings. The process was slow
and time-consuming, with many "wave-offs" by the landing signal officer. In the darkness, "planes cut each other out of the landing circle."
One bomber pilot disregarded a wave-off, hit the Enterprise and burst
into flame, then crashed into the tail of a second bomber. In the meantime, other planes, still waiting to land, were forced to ditch. Altogether
eight planes were lost through crashes or ditching, though all but one of
the crewmen survived.[7]

That night sailors made the "usual preparations for battle. Fire control
equipment was tested and ready ammunition was verified at each gunmount. All fire fighting equipment was double checked, fire buckets
filled with water or sand. . . . Officers were issued morphine to ease the
pain of the wounded. Food was assembled for the day of battle; donuts,
canned pineapple, mince pie and coffee. Last letters were written."[8] Sail-
makers made large numbers of body bags.[9] In the Hornet, a rash of high-
stakes gambling swept the ship, reminding Lieutenant Commander
Francis Foley, the air operations officer, of Bob Hope's quip that a carrier
was simply a floating crap game with a flight deck.[10] Aboard the battleship South Dakota the chaplain preached his Sunday sermon on the text
"Let your loins be girded and your lamps lit."[11]

Before dawn on the 26th, both fleets launched their first search planes
and combat air patrols. At 6:50 A.M. a pair of dive-bombers from the Enterprise sighted Admiral Nagumo's three carriers. As Zeroes swarmed
around the two planes, two other scout bombers dived through the cloud
cover and put a 500-pound bomb into the light carrier Zuiho, wrecking
her flight deck. Around the same time, one of Nagumo's search planes finally sighted an American carrier. Mindful of his experience at Midway,
Nagumo wasted no time in launching a sixty-plane strike. As the damaged Zuiho withdrew, Nagumo launched two additional smaller strikes,
so that by 9:10 there were 110 planes headed for the American carriers.

The Hornet began launching her attack group of twenty-one bombers
and torpedo planes and eight Wildcats at 7:30. The Enterprise's smaller
group of eight Wildcats, nine torpedo planes, and three dive-bombers
departed separately a few minutes later. As the Hornet began launching
her second strike, Life magazine artist Tom Lea watched the air group
commander's "specially marked, fully manned plane appear suddenly on
the empty deck, brought up from the hangar deck on an incredibly fast
elevator. It is like Toscanini being magically lifted to the podium by unseen angel hands—a winged roaring Toscanini about to lead a chorus of
war hawks."[12]

All ships went to general quarters in anticipation of the coming Japanese air attack. Aboard the carriers, aviation fuel lines were drained, then filled with CO_2 to prevent fire. Bombs and torpedoes were secured in the magazine. Men put on flashproof "denim clothing that was hot and smelled of moth balls."[13] The *South Dakota's* gun crews "looked like men from another planet. Grey-steel helmets protected the heads of those who were to operate in exposed stations; when you speak with one of these helmets on it sounds as if you are talking into a bucket. Bluish anti-flash hoods hugged their necks and ears underneath the helmets. . . . What little of the face escaped the hood was further masked by a nose filter so the men could breath through the stink of fire and by huge non-shatterable goggles."[14]

For the destroyer *Smith*, the coming engagement "was to be our first bona fide clash with the Japanese. . . . I think we all wanted to get into a battle and lose our inferiority complex."[15] More experienced sailors had other thoughts. Only six weeks before, the *Hornet's* crew had seen the *Wasp* hit and abandoned in less than an hour. A common belief was that an aircraft carrier was going to be sunk in every naval battle.[16] At Coral Sea it had been the *Lexington*, at Midway the *Yorktown*, at the Eastern Solomons the *Enterprise* had been nearly lost. "Aircraft carriers were always the prime target," recalled Aviation Machinist's Mate Bernard Peterson, who had been in the *Yorktown* when she was sunk. When he joined the *Enterprise* "we nineteen year olds found ourselves consciously seeking out the best possible protective shelter as we strolled around. . . . We would seek out the strongest bulkhead, the heaviest reinforced beams, the area the furthest away from aviation gasoline and the high explosives. The search was futile because there was no place that really met this test."[17]

Just before 9:00 A.M., American radar detected the first Japanese planes about forty-five miles away. The *Hornet* and *Enterprise* formed the nucleus of two separate task forces steaming five to ten miles apart, a formation that impressed the British liaison officer, Lieutenant Commander H.A.I. Luard, as "retaining all the disadvantages of concentration with none of its advantages."[18] Each task force operated its own combat air patrol, but the *Enterprise* fighter control officer controlled all fighters.

Although there were almost forty fighters protecting the task forces, only a few were able to engage the Japanese attackers. Most of the planes were too low or out of position. Altitudes were seldom provided and directions were given in reference to the position of ships that were frequently out of sight of the fighter pilots. Stationed only ten miles from the task force, the sluggish, heavily loaded Wildcats "could not climb or zip around from place to place and up and down."[19] Its slow rate of climb made it a poor interceptor of any plane flying above or ahead. "The VF [fighters] would start a climb only to see the dive-bombers and torpedo planes passing over them or possibly below them. They would attempt to attack and frequently followed their targets into their own [anti-aircraft fire], which was very heavy, in an effort to get a kill."[20] Communications were poor because pilots clogged the few available frequencies with chat and inessential messages. Lieutenant Albert D. Pollock, the leader of the *Enterprise* combat air patrol, noted sixty-four recorded transmissions plus others that were not recorded in the space of about thirty-five minutes.[21]

Evading most of the American fighters, the Japanese attack group was met by a wall of antiaircraft fire from the task force. The largest antiaircraft guns, 5-inch dual-purpose, were installed in double mounts, each with a crew of eight men. They could be elevated a full 90 degrees and could be fired "automatically" as fast as the guns could be loaded and the breeches closed. The elevation and train of the guns could also be centrally controlled. The "mounts could swivel from port to starboard so quick that it was sometimes hard to get your footing as the mounts jerked and jumped from side to side," recalled George O'Connor, who served in the antiaircraft cruiser *San Juan*. "To have all these guns banging away just as fast as the crews could load them, with decks heaving and jumping with recoil, the high speed turns and evasive tactics, the thumps of near misses of bombs, the jerking and spinning of the mounts is an experience never to be forgotten."[22]

About 9:10, a Japanese dive-bomber fell or crashed into the *Hornet*'s stack, causing its 500-pound bomb to explode. The plane glanced off the signal bridge, showering it with burning gasoline, then plunged on through the flight deck to the gallery deck ready rooms below. "There was a huge explosion. A bright red flame came like an express train down the passage knocking everything and everybody flat."[23] On the signal bridge, communications officer Oscar Dodson was shielded from the flames by one of the steel legs of the tripod signal mast. Most of the other signalmen were not as fortunate. Dodson attempted to beat out the flames or rip off the clothes of those who had been doused with burning gasoline, but his own gloves soon caught fire. "After removing my gloves I was helpless, could only watch in horror as the flames on burning sailors brought a swift and merciful death. . . . Medical personnel and fire fighters quickly arrived. . . . One signalman, still bleeding, signaled to nearby ships by semaphore: 'we are ready to receive messages.'"[24]

At almost the same time that the plane struck the stack, the *Hornet* was also hit by two torpedoes that ripped holes in her starboard side. Torrents of oil and seawater quickly flooded the fire rooms and the forward engine rooms. Three more bombs hit the ship in the next few minutes, but the *Hornet* was already gliding to a halt, having lost all power after the torpedo hits had wrecked her forward engines. A second Japanese dive-bomber crashed into the ship a few minutes later after being damaged by antiaircraft fire. The plane struck the port forward gun gallery, ripped through the ship, and exploded near the forward elevator. The fuselage with the bodies of the two crewmen hurtled down the elevator shaft while the plane's engine crashed through to the junior officers' quarters on the second deck.

While more than fifty Japanese aircraft were attacking the *Hornet*, fewer than twenty of Kinkaid's pilots managed to find and attack the Japanese carriers. The *Enterprise* had most of her bombers already out on scouting missions at the time the Japanese were located, so only nine fighters, three dive-bombers, and eight torpedo planes could be launched against the enemy carriers. When the *Enterprise* strike planes were only sixty miles from their carriers and before many of them had even armed their guns or turned on their radios, they were suddenly attacked by Zeroes. These were from the Japanese strike group that had been launched much earlier and was now approaching the American fleet. The *Enterprise* planes were at only 5,000 feet and had just begun a leisurely climb when they were surprised by nine Zeroes, which quickly shot down two torpedo planes and three fighters and forced three others to turn back because of damage.[25]

As at Midway, the various American strike groups soon became separated on the way to their target. Groups attacked independently, although all had at least minimal fighter escort. Fifteen *Hornet* dive-bombers under Lieutenant Commander William J. Widhelm attacked the *Shokaku*, wrecked her flight deck, and put half of her antiaircraft guns out of action. The ship was not fatally damaged, however.

Now occurred what Admiral Kinkaid would later call "a shocking failure in our communications."[26] Neither the *Enterprise* planes nor those of the *Hornet*'s second strike group ever received Widhelm's reports on the location of the Japanese carriers that he was about to attack. The complicated radio equipment carried by the American aircraft required that sets be tuned to exactly identical frequencies in order to send or receive messages, something that could seldom be achieved in actual combat flying.[27]

Unable to locate the carriers, the scattered groups attacked ships of Admiral Abe's battleship-cruiser force about sixty miles from the Japanese carriers. Six torpedo planes from the *Hornet* attacked the cruiser

Tone but scored no hits. The surviving planes of the *Enterprise* strike force attacked cruiser *Suzuya* but were likewise unsuccessful. The *Hornet's* second-wave attack group, nine torpedo planes and nine dive-bombers, heavily damaged the cruiser *Chikuma* but failed to sink her.

Unlike the Americans, Nagumo's second wave of attackers had little trouble finding their targets. Most of the second wave headed for the *Enterprise* task force, leaving the burning and crippled *Hornet* relatively unmolested. The *Enterprise* was in the center of a ring formation composed of a heavy cruiser, a light antiaircraft cruiser, the *San Juan*, and the battleship *South Dakota*. The *South Dakota* and the *Enterprise* had recently been fitted with new 40mm BOFORS antiaircraft guns. In range and stopping power they were a major improvement over the old-style 1.1-inch machine guns that had been the standard antiaircraft armament at the beginning of the war.[28]

These antiaircraft guns, including almost one hundred aboard the *South Dakota*, opened a heavy fire at the Japanese. "The whole scene was one of complete anarchy," recalled one gunnery officer. "Ships racing along, explosions, guns firing, the sky full of planes, shell bursts, shots, hollering." Gunner's Mate O'Connor "could never understand why more topside men were not hit by fire from other ships. A plane might come down between ships and everything would be banging away at it and they would keep firing until the plane hit the sea. This meant that they were shooting right across at one another."[29]

Only seven of the nineteen dive-bombers survived their assault on the *Enterprise*, but one plane scored a hit that exploded on the hangar deck, killing about forty men and destroying half a dozen parked planes. Two others scored near misses. The concussion from one of these sent a parked dive-bomber careening across the flight deck and into the 20mm gun gallery. After unsuccessful attempts to put the plane over the side, "someone asked what we should do with it; some wise seaman piped up, 'paint it war color and leave it there.'"[30] Using a rammer from a 5-inch gun, the landing signal officer, Lieutenant Robin Lindsey, took advantage of a sharp turn to port to finally lever the plane over the side.

Twenty minutes later, just before 11:00 A.M., sixteen torpedo planes from the *Zuikaku* appeared. As they maneuvered for attack, one group of torpedo planes encountered a flight of four Wildcats led by Lieutenant Stanley W. Vejtasa. In a few minutes "Swede" Vejtasa and his wingman shot down three of the attackers and damaged at least three of the others.

One of the damaged planes, already on fire and flying only fifty feet above the water, turned sharply and crashed into the bow of the destroyer *Smith*. "There was a large burst of flame as ruptured gasoline tanks enveloped the forward part of the ship and then the explosion of the warhead of the torpedo that had not been launched," recalled the *Smith*'s assistant gunnery officer. "All of a sudden I was sort of by myself still with my headset on. . . . Instead of calmly removing the headset, I tried to yank it off and break the cord; unable to do this I tore it off, threw it away angered beyond belief, cursing God, the human race, the people who perpetrated such barbarism, all airplanes, screaming with anger all the time."[31]

Lieutenant Commander Wood, the *Smith*'s captain, had to abandon the bridge for the after control station while the ship's quartermaster, Frank Riduka, took up position in the engine steering room from which he conned the ship. Firefighters battled flames while Wood maneuvered the ship directly astern of the *South Dakota*, whose mountainous wake helped to douse the fires.[32] The *Smith* remained on station, but at least fifty-seven men were dead and others wounded. "The sight and smell of the burnt corpses around the base of the bridge and along the ladders was dreadful. The fire had not only killed many, but burnt off much of their flesh leaving only bones or legs, hands, and arms. The mind sort of blanks out here but I still remember dogtags being removed and corpses being thrown into the ocean."[33]

Still another wave of Japanese planes, the first from the carrier *Junyo*, which had accompanied Admiral Kondo's battleship-cruiser force operating a hundred miles west of Nagumo's carriers, arrived over the American task force at about 11:15 in the morning, twenty minutes after the previous attack. The *Enterprise*'s radar had been knocked out during the earlier attacks, and the ship's radar officer, Lieutenant Dwight M. B. Williams, climbed the large flat latticework radar antenna to make repairs. He was still lashed to the antenna when the *Junyo*'s planes arrived. Williams continued working steadily in the midst of heavy antiaircraft fire, bombs, and the high-speed maneuvers of the ship. Thinking the radar had been repaired, someone switched on the power, sending Williams rotating majestically merry-go-round fashion on the now moving antenna.[34]

The weather, which had been clear and cloudless in the early morning, was now squally and overcast with thick clouds as low as 1,000 feet. This forced the Japanese bombers into shallow dives, which made them prime targets for the 40mm guns of the *Enterprise*. Other planes fell victim to patrolling American fighters. Only six of the seventeen *Junyo* bombers survived to return to their carriers. One bomb hit the *Enterprise*, causing minor damage and jamming her forward flight deck elevator in the up position. The *South Dakota* was hit by a 550-pound bomb on her forward 16-inch turret. The bomb broke up against her heavy armor but killed two men and injured forty-eight in exposed positions, including the captain. The *San Juan* was also hit by a bomb, which passed completely through her lightly built superstructure and exploded under the ship, causing minor flooding.

Despite her damage, *Enterprise* was able to land all but fourteen of the seventy-three returning aircraft from the *Hornet* as well as her own air group, respot her planes, and launch a new combat air patrol in a little over ninety minutes. At one point, her flight deck crews and her talented landing signal officers, Lieutenant Robin M. Lindsey and Lieutenant James G. Daniels III, landed forty-seven planes in forty-three minutes. "The flight deck rapidly congested. Soon aircraft spread abreast of the island and finally plane handlers had rolled them over the three folded wire barriers. . . . As the deck filled, Lindsey brought planes in farther aft with fewer arresting wires available." In a short time only number one and two wires remained. As each plane approached, Lindsey bet Daniels a dime he could bring it in on the number one wire. Five more dive-bombers and five more fighters came aboard. Finally lowering his signal paddles, Lindsey walked over to Daniels and collected ten dimes.[35]

While the *Enterprise* was landing her planes, the sailors in the *Hornet* were laboring to save their badly damaged ship. Destroyers came alongside to pass fire hoses to fire-fighting teams. Buckets were lowered sixty feet over the side, then passed down long chains of men to be hurled at the many small fires belowdecks. Fire parties worked among buckled and ruptured decks and twisted bulkheads, some still red-hot, with dead and wounded lying all around.[36] Pails of melting ice cream were passed up from the galley refrigerator to sailors, who eagerly scooped it up by hand.[37]

The ship's survival depended on her engineering personnel, who labored in ten-minute shifts in the darkened, suffocating fire rooms and engineering spaces, guided only by hand lanterns.[38] After five hours the engineering division had located an uncontaminated fuel tank and completed a complex arrangement for raising steam and pumping it through to the after generator room. Once the generator was operating and the ship's power restored, her electric pumps and other power-driven equipment could be brought on line.[39]

At 4:00 P.M., as the generator was being warmed up, the engineer officer heard the *Hornet*'s antiaircraft guns suddenly open fire. Seven torpedo planes from the *Junyo* attacked the American carrier, which now had no covering fighter planes. Only one plane scored a hit, but that was enough. A torpedo struck the starboard side near the site of the earlier hits. "A sickly green flash momentarily lighted the scullery compartment and seemed to run both forward toward Repair Station IV and aft into the scullery compartment for a distance of about fifty feet," reported the *Hornet's* engineering officer. "Immediately following the flash a hissing sound as of escaping air was heard followed by a dull rumbling noise."[40] The deck appeared to crack open, releasing a rush of fuel oil which immediately swept those in Repair Station V off their feet. Slipping and sliding in the pool of fuel oil, which soon rose to two feet, sailors formed a hand chain to a ladder leading to the only escape scuttle. The torpedo explosion had wrecked all but about ten inches of this ladder, but all those in Repair Station V managed to escape up the oil-covered rungs and through the scuttle.[41]

Several attempts to tow the *Hornet* had already been unsuccessful because of her jammed rudder, and this third torpedo spelled the end of any chance of saving her. The *Hornet's* skipper, Captain Charles P. Mason, decided to order abandon ship. He had already transferred all of the wounded and most of the aviation personnel to escorting destroyers, and in the late afternoon all of the remaining men followed. About three hundred of the *Hornet's* crew ended up aboard the destroyer *Anderson*. One *Hornet* evacuee, searching for the head, found it just behind one of the 5-inch guns. *Anderson* was periodically in action and ammunition was being passed through the head, but the sailor was undeterred. "I had had to take a crap all day, so I figured, 'what the hell.' I slept in that head all night."[42] The evacuation was completed by 5:15, leaving only the bodies of 111 men still aboard.

The *Enterprise* task force was already withdrawing, a decision confirmed a few minutes later by a signal from Admiral Halsey. *Hornet's* task force also headed south, leaving the destroyers *Mustin* and *Anderson* to finish off the crippled carrier. Despite eight torpedoes from the American warships, *Hornet* was still afloat when Japanese destroyers found her near midnight and finally sank her with four more torpedoes. After that the Japanese, pleased with their success and low on fuel, also retired.

Santa Cruz, as the October 26 engagement has become known, was the last of the great carrier battles of 1942 and the only one in which the Japanese won a clear-cut tactical victory. As at Midway, the Americans still experienced difficulties in coordinating their air strikes while the Japanese delivered two of the most effective combined dive-bomber and torpedo attacks of the war against the *Hornet*. The fighter defense of the

American carriers had also proved ineffective. "Radar detection and fighter direction seemed for a time to be the salvation of the aircraft carrier," observed one aviator. "It has not turned out that way."[43]

As in the case of long-range gunnery in World War I, it was not technical but human problems that were most critical. "In the opinion of the VF pilots it is not the entire fault of the equipment but rather the disorganized use of it that renders the radar machinery ineffective," wrote one squadron commander.[44] A radar expert reported that "officers aboard the Hornet in general did not understand what could be done with radar, particularly the radar aboard the Hornet."[45] Many aviators were critical of Kinkaid's decision to centralize all fighter control in the Enterprise when the Hornet's fighter direction center was far more experienced. "What is urgently needed," concluded the captain of the Enterprise, "is a sound doctrine for the fighter defense of carriers, something that can only be developed through extensive experiment and training."[46]

If the Americans were unhappy with the performance of the fighter direction system, they were even more unhappy with the fighters themselves. "The Wildcat was too heavy," declared Captain Donald MacAteer, a surgeon in the Hornet. "Those planes could hardly get off the deck. Our pilots knew the Zero could outfly them, outturn them, and outclimb them. Our pilots were good, but they had lousy planes."[47] Even before the Battle of Midway, there had been strong and persistent complaints about the inferior performance of American planes as compared to their Japanese counterparts. Criticism centered on the F4F Wildcat. The captain of the Yorktown noted that his pilots were "very disappointed with the performance of their Wildcats."[48] The leader of the Enterprise's fighter squadron, Lieutenant Commander James S. Gray, believed it "urgent a better performing model of this series be produced at once if U.S. Navy pilots are to be given anything approaching an even chance in combat."[49] Lieutenant Commander Jimmy Thach added that the inferiority of the F4F "not only prevents our fighters from properly carrying out an assigned mission but it has a definite and alarming effect on the morale of most of our carrier based VF pilots."[50]

The Bureau of Aeronautics, to which most of these complaints were ultimately directed, reacted defensively by arguing, on the one hand, that the Wildcat was the best that could be produced under the rush of 1940–41 rearmament and, on the other, that it would soon be replaced by two far more capable fighters, the Vought F4U Corsair and the Grumman F6F Hellcat. These would "be a tremendous advance in performance over the F4F-4."[51]

It is significant that these discussions of the F4F in the spring and summer of 1942 were carried on in terms of technical characteristics. All sides in the debate appeared to tacitly assume that the only conceivable solution to the technical inferiority of the Wildcat was to produce a technically superior fighter on the American side. There was relatively little thought given to adopting new doctrine, training, or tactics that would enable Americans to win even with technically inferior planes. The answer to advanced technology, all seemed to agree, could only be better technology. Unfortunately, the new superfighters, the Corsair and the Hellcat, were not due to join the fleet until mid-1943.

The Navy would have to learn how to use intelligence, tactics, training, and doctrine to neutralize the Zero. And, since the spring of 1941, Lieutenant Commander Thach, one of the loudest critics of the Wildcat, had been working on aerial tactics to defeat the Zero. Thach's solution was to deploy his squadron in two plane sections, each abreast of the other, at a distance equal to or greater than the turning radius of the F4F. Each section acted as lookouts for the other, particularly above and to the rear of the opposite section. If one section sighted enemy planes attacking from above and behind (the most favored method), the section observing would immediately turn toward the other section, thus bringing the attackers under fire. This would also be the signal for the threatened section to itself turn toward the other section, thus spoiling the attacker's aim and setting up a scissors or "weave."[52]

During the battle of Midway, Thach's six fighters had had to contend with at least thirty-five Zeroes during the *Yorktown* torpedo planes' attack on the Japanese carriers. Yet Thach and his five companions managed to shoot down at least six enemy fighters while losing only one of their own. Over all, the Japanese air raid on Midway had resulted in the usual one-sided victory for the Zeroes against the inexperienced pilots and largely obsolescent planes defending the island, but the carrier air battles had ended with eleven Zeroes lost in air combat as opposed to only six Wildcats.[53] At Santa Cruz, Lieutenant Commander James Flatley's fighters lost three planes to the deadly Japanese ambush of the *Enterprise* strike force, but the others survived by adopting the Thach weave and shot down three enemy aircraft. "The Japanese repeatedly reacted in surprise when erstwhile victims inexplicably evaded just at the right moment and received support from another Grumman countering from head on or to the side."[54] Later, while returning to their carrier short of fuel, Flatley's fighters fell in with some Zeroes attacking the American fleet. As Flatley reported, "low on gas and ammunition we avoided their attacks without employing more than fifty percent power and if the attacks had persisted we would have shot down the enemy VF.

As it was, they became discouraged after three or four attempts and pulled off." Flatley described the Thach weave as "undoubtedly the greatest contribution to air combat tactics that has been made to date."[55]

American naval aviators could successfully employ the Thach weave because, almost alone among prewar pilots, they had received training in "deflection shooting." This was a difficult and demanding skill involving long hours of training and practice. Once mastered, however, it enabled a pilot to hit a target from a variety of angles up to 90 degrees. Not only were U.S. Navy and Marine Corps pilots exceptional in having been trained in deflection shooting, but the much-maligned F4F with its downsloping cowling and cockpit high over the center of the fuselage was ideally configured for such tactics. In land-based fighters, pilots were often positioned so low and far back along the fuselage that visibility for deflection shooting was poor.[56]

Like Thach, Flatley had also given thought to making the best of second-best technology. In a report prepared for carrier fighter pilots, Flatley conceded that "no individual fighter pilot likes the thought of not being able to compete individually with the enemy fighter pilot. This condition exists when one F4F is compared to one enemy Zero fighter."[57] Fighters were no longer fighting individual combats as they had in World War I. The way to defeat the Zero was through the development of appropriate formation tactics and intensive training in these tactics. Fighters had to operate in sections of two planes each and fly in groups comprised of several sections. These sections should train together in gunnery using high-speed targets and practicing coordinated attacks. "Stop worrying about your plane's climb and maneuverability and learn how to get along without those features."[58]

Flatley emphasized the positive qualities of the F4F, especially its survivability. "If any fighter pilot is willing to give up the armor and protected fuel tanks or the strength of the F4F in favor of climb and maneuverability he ought to have his head examined." He also pointed out that the new folding-wing F4F-4s meant that more planes could be accommodated aboard a carrier and thus Americans were likely to outnumber their opponents in future carrier battles. "Let us not condemn our equipment," concluded Flatley. "Let's take that equipment and learn to use it more effectively."[59]

Although training and tactics were important, the greatest gain for American aviators was probably the disappearance of most of Japan's experienced pilots. In the Battle of the Santa Cruz Islands, Japanese and American losses in aircraft were roughly equal, eighty-one for the Americans and ninety-seven for the Japanese. Aircrew losses were wildly disproportionate, however. Only twenty-four American aviators were lost while the Japanese lost 148. Included among them were five squadron leaders and most of the experienced section leaders. Overall, 50 percent of Japanese dive-bomber pilots and 30 percent of the torpedo plane pilots were lost.[60] These were the last of the veteran pilots whose experience stretched back to the China war. Since the Imperial Japanese Navy had not followed Nimitz's practice of regularly rotating the veteran pilots back to the homeland, there were no comparable fliers to take their place. The Zero and other Japanese models remained excellent planes in the hands of an experienced pilot. The problem was that by the end of 1942 the Japanese had few experienced pilots left.

The final Japanese effort to gain control of Guadalcanal came in mid-November and resulted in a three-day series of night surface actions known as the Naval Battle of Guadalcanal. Both sides suffered heavy losses, and the Japanese were, in the end, forced to withdraw. This ended their last real chance to recapture the island, although fierce fighting continued mainly on land. For sailors, the campaign for Guadalcanal, which continued until the final Japanese evacuation of the island in February 1943, was one of the grimmest and most terrifying of the war. The Solomons themselves were "kind of spooky" with periods of overcast and squall alternating rapidly with bright tropical sunshine and towering cloud formations. There were soft tropical breezes but also smells of jungle and decaying vegetation from the shores. The struggle for Guadalcanal was "much more powerful and intense" than the raiding that had preceded Midway, recalled Alvin Kernan.[61] Air attacks now became a frequent experience for all seaman, whether in a cruiser, a minesweeper, or a transport. Aboard the *Hornet*, sailors had seen two others carriers sunk and two others damaged within two months. Some ships were lost with virtually their entire crew. The destroyer *Jarvis* disappeared without a trace and was not accounted for until after the war. Destroyer *Barton* sank in two minutes, and light cruiser *Juneau* blew up after being hit by a torpedo, instantly taking with her more than 600 of her 700-man crew.

Although sailors aboard battleships or carriers might have felt some sense of security from the sheer size of their ship, most sailors felt an extreme sense of vulnerability. "The Atlanta-class ships were not safe ships to be on," recalled one sailor. "They could put it out but could not take it. . . . They had a tendency to blow up easily."[62] Destroyer men knew that "crippled destroyers were generally considered expendable."[63]

Aboard a carrier the "thing you feared most was fire. You are surrounded by aviation gas. The Big E [*Enterprise*] carried more than 200,000 gallons."[64]

Adding to the sense of vulnerability was the fact that air attacks were visible to everyone on the weather decks and other exposed spaces. In World War I, enemy warships had appeared mainly as distant smudges and flashes on the horizon. In a World War II air attack, the attackers were close up and easily visible. "The 5-inch directors at the time were completely open to the sky . . . so as the dive bombers screamed downward toward us, I could clearly see the bright flashes as the pilots fired their machine guns at us . . . and of course the bombs as they left the plane and hurtled toward us."[65] I.R.V. Cole, a marine aboard the *Enterprise*, saw a "dive bomber coming right at our guns. He released his bomb and it had my name on it flashing like a neon light."[66]

There were a few instances of panic. After the *Smith* was hit by the plane that demolished her superstructure, "a sort of feeling was around that the *Smith* was about to blow up in a violent explosion of the ammunition magazines. Some of the sailors were preparing to abandon ship. . . . I tried to dissuade [them] . . . yelling at them that they were fools and idiots to do so, but some sadly did leave the ship not to be seen again."[67] In the *Enterprise* there were a few "here and there that had gone hysterical as their nerves gave under the din, destruction and death," but most carried on as best they could.[68] One young ensign in the *South Dakota* was observed at his post in main control babbling to himself, "I'm scared as hell, scared as hell, having a wonderful time."[69] A medical officer in the *Enterprise* considered that "about 90% of us were mentally unbalanced temporarily after the battle."[70] Shipfitter John Kielty, a survivor of the *Hornet,* was referred to a psychiatrist upon his return from the Battle of Santa Cruz Islands. The interview was quite short: "He asked, 'Were you afraid for your life while your ship was being torpedoed and bombed?' I answered, 'Yes, scared shitless.' 'You will do fine,' he said, 'when you understand fear and can admit to your fears, you have already conquered them.' I said 'really' which is how one says 'bullshit' to an officer, as he dismissed me."[71]

Since the days of sail, battles at sea had been bloody but infrequent affairs separated by weeks or often by months or years. With the introduction of aircraft, combat at sea could become a daily event with some of the same dynamics as prolonged combat on land.

Santa Cruz was fought only sixteen months after the sea battles off Crete, yet the contest between sea and air had reached a state of deadly precision that far eclipsed those earlier battles. Aircraft could now attack ships with much greater effectiveness, as the fate of more than a score of battleships, carriers, and cruisers could attest. What the German Stukas and Heinkels had taken hours of repeated attacks to achieve, even against weakly defended ships, could now be accomplished by coordinated attacks of fighters, dive-bombers, and torpedo planes in a few minutes. Yet the more significant development was the increased survivability of men-of-war. There was still much to be done, especially in regard to the integration of radar, fighters, and antiaircraft guns. Nevertheless, the combination of carrier-borne fighter interceptors, more and more effective antiaircraft guns, and steadily improving damage control had achieved a kind of rough balance between airborne attackers and their targets.

"There are few if any experienced naval officers who do not realize that air power is the dominant factor in this war," Captain M. B. Gardiner had observed a few weeks before the Santa Cruz battle. "That the aircraft carrier has replaced the battleship as the unit around which the Fleet is centered is evident to all. There is, however, a natural reluctance on the part of many to admit these facts and to support an organizational setup which takes cognizance of them."[72] For many months after Santa Cruz, aviators found the "organizational setup" highly unsatisfactory. Task forces built primarily around aircraft carriers were still commanded by admirals with little or no experience in aviation. Aviators were underrepresented and occupied relatively junior positions on important fleet staffs and headquarters. By October 1943, fliers composed 28 percent of flag officers in the U.S. Army but only 17 percent of flag officers in the U.S. Navy. This despite the fact that aviation was the fastest-growing segment of the officer corps, with 50 percent of new ensigns and 29 percent of the lieutenants junior grade being assigned to the navy's air arm.[73] "Naval aviators, as officers trained and experienced in naval aviation should have the dominant voice in all naval policy and not just aviation policy," declared Rear Admiral Frederick "Fightin' Freddie" Sherman, who had been captain of the carrier *Lexington*. He recommended that in the future all top positions in the navy, including Chief of Naval Operations, Chief of Naval Personnel, commanders in chief of all major fleets, and half of the General Board be filled by "active aviators."[74]

Few in the Navy Department were prepared to go so far as that, but no one could ignore the growing complaints from the airmen or the fact of aviation's emergence as a dominant arm of the fleet. Beginning in the spring of 1943, one of the three key positions on Admiral King's staff, assistant chief of staff for operations, was headed by Rear Admiral Arthur

C. Davis, former captain of the *Enterprise*. In July 1943 the president and the Secretary of the Navy approved King's proposal to create a new Deputy Chief of Naval Operations (Air), to be filled by an aviator with the rank of vice-admiral. Although the new deputy chief's job was mostly concerned with logistics and administration rather than strategy and operations, it was another important step for naval aviation. Final recognition of aviation's new preeminence came in the spring of 1944 when King issued an order that a nonaviator commanding a force that included carriers should have an aviator as his chief of staff. Similarly, a fleet commander who was an aviator was required to have a surface warfare officer as chief of staff.

Although senior aviators could draw satisfaction from airpower's growing preeminence in the navy, many of them were uncomfortably aware that Annapolis graduates, indeed career officers of any type, were a decided minority in the ranks of younger naval aviators. In October 1943 only 226 of more than 11,000 aviators in the grade of ensign were regulars. Of junior grade lieutenants less than 600 of about 7,000 were career men. Even in the grade of lieutenant commander, the rank at which officers became squadron commanders, almost 25 percent were reservists, while among lieutenants who could command divisions, one in three was a nonregular.[75]

Many career officers were concerned that these newcomers were being promoted "too rapidly and lack respect for their new rank." Lieutenant Commander Thomas F. Connolly, an Annapolis graduate, complained that even with more than ten years of service he was only one rank above many reservists who had been promoted from ensign to lieutenant junior grade to lieutenant in ten years. "Their appreciation of what they now have," Connolly contended, is "not commensurate with what they should feel."[76]

Annapolis men wondered to what extent these rapidly promoted reservists even thought of themselves as naval officers. "In the past the naval aviator, both regular and reserve, considered himself an integral part of the Navy," wrote one admiral. "We now have thousands of young naval aviators, who while competent along restricted lines, have not been able to obtain desirable and necessary Navy experience."[77] With few personal or professional ties to the navy as an institution, these reserve aviators might prove highly susceptible to appeals from the Army Air Forces, whose leaders continued to promote the argument for an independent air service that would include all types of aviation. "These young reserves came into the Navy to fly not to be naval officers," observed Captain H. B. Miller, a well-known prewar aviator. "It is not beyond belief that these youngsters may easily visualize their future as being more progressive if they were to become members of a separate air force."[78]

Admiral John H. Towers, Commander, Air Force, Pacific Fleet, argued that the navy's refusal to grant aviation the place it desired in policy and strategy reinforced the appeal of the idea of a separate air force.[79] That may have been the case, but the air force possessed another more concrete appeal: promotion in naval aviation, rapid as it may have seemed to the career officers, was still slower than in the Army Air Forces. "Joe Doaks and Bill Smith graduate from high school in Bingville together and go off to war, one joining the Army Air Forces and the other naval aviation. Later, Joe Doaks comes home a captain and when Bill finally gets home an ensign, he hears about it plenty."[80] By the spring of 1944, aviation's preeminence in the navy seemed assured not merely through new organizational structures but through sheer force of numbers, yet many career aviators, having won the battle for airpower within the navy, wondered whether the navy could long retain it.

TWELVE

"FROM NEWFY TO DERRY'S A BLOODY LONG WAY"

While the air-sea battles raged in the South Pacific, the greatest and most prolonged naval campaign in history was approaching a climax in the Atlantic. Along the great circle route from Europe to North America, sailors of half a dozen nations waged a continuous bloody struggle for control of the ocean lines of communication, which connected Britain with its overseas empire and with its most powerful allies in North America. At its most elemental level, the six-year battle pitted German submarines against Allied merchantmen and their defending warships and aircraft. Yet these bloody encounters at sea were sustained, directed, and sometimes decided by enormous and complicated efforts in industrial mobilization, scientific and technical research, intelligence collection, and training. The Battle of the Atlantic, as it came to be called, brought the interface between men and machines at sea to new levels of sophistication and complexity; it also called forth an unprecedented degree of integration and coordination between navies and the supporting political, social, and economic structures of their societies.

While the broad outlines of war in the Pacific had been foreseen and discussed for many years, the Battle of the Atlantic came as a surprise, at least to the Allied navies. The U-boat campaign of 1917–18 was remembered, but there was a widespread view that no country would again risk the hostility of the world's maritime powers by resorting to unrestricted submarine warfare. In any case, the combination of convoy, together with a newly invented underwater sound-locating device called "sonar" or "ASDIC" by the British, seemed to suggest that the days of submarine warfare were past. "The problem of dealing with the submarine is more than simplified by the invention of ASDIC," concluded the Royal Navy's Defense of Trade Committee in 1936. "This instrument . . . removes from the submarine that cloak of invisibility which was its principal source of strength in the late war."[1] In the U.S. Navy, exercises in the clear calm seas of the fleet practice areas appeared to suggest that submarines that rose to periscope depth to make an attack would be very easy to detect. U.S. submarine commanders were advised to remain at depths of at least 100 feet and use their own sonar rather than their periscope to locate their target. (Wartime experience soon showed such "sound attacks" to be completely ineffective.)[2] Issues of gunnery and fire control preoccupied interwar navies. In 1935, only eleven of 1,029 lieutenants and sixteen of 972 lieutenant commanders in the Royal Navy were specialists in anti-submarine warfare, and "it was perfectly possible for a junior officer to go through training up to the rank of lieutenant without any training in anti-submarine warfare at all."[3]

The German navy, once it had begun its rearmament under Hitler, was similarly concerned with big ships and big guns. Two 32,000-ton battle cruisers, *Scharnhorst* and *Gneisenau*, and two giant battleships, *Bismarck* and *Tirpitz*, were completed or almost complete by 1940. Hitler also had approved a program devised by Admiral Erich Raeder, commander in chief of the navy, called the Z Plan, which provided for the construction of more than a dozen battleships and battle cruisers by 1948. Like their British counterparts, most German naval planners viewed the failure of the U-boat offensive in 1917–18 as an indication that submarines could not, by themselves, be decisive. Yet the High Seas Fleet's policy of watchful waiting for a favorable opportunity had proved still more ineffective. In the next war German admirals expected to use the Z battle fleet not to fight a second Jutland but to attack the British trade routes and lines of communication. They planned to use submarines, fast cruisers, and aircraft as supplements to the fleet.[4]

One German officer who did not share this vision was Commodore Karl Dönitz, a World War I U-boat captain, now chief of the navy's submarine command. Notwithstanding the obstacles posed by convoy, sonar, and probably by aircraft, Dönitz believed that U-boats could still help win a war. Based on war games held in the winter of 1938–39, Dönitz believed that a force of 300 oceangoing submarines could prevail in a naval war against England. These boats, he argued, would attack convoys in large groups coached into position by radio messages from a central command. Neither Raeder nor Hitler found Dönitz's arguments persuasive. Raeder continued to plan for a balanced fleet for action in distant oceans. Hitler was unwilling to risk antagonizing the British, with whom he had concluded a naval arms treaty, by building large numbers of U-boats. He repeatedly assured Raeder and Dönitz that they need not be concerned about war with Britain before 1944. At the outbreak of war in September 1939, Dönitz had only fifty-seven submarines in commission, only two dozen of which were oceangoing.

During the first nine months of war, U-boats enjoyed only indifferent success against British shipping. The small number of oceangoing U-boats in commission meant that only about a half-dozen or so could be at sea on patrol at any given time. Moreover, many German torpedoes were found to be defective. Some failed to explode on impact; others exploded prematurely or passed harmlessly under the target. An investigation resulted in the court-martial and reported execution of some of the officers of the Torpedo Directorate, but all of the defects in German torpedoes were not corrected until late 1942.[5]

Though losses of British shipping were not serious during the early months of World War II, the organization of the convoy system nevertheless resulted in less frequent sailings and caused a drop of about 25 percent in British imports. Overall, however, the opening phase of the war at sea had unfolded roughly as the admirals in Germany and Britain had anticipated. Indeed, in 1939, surface raiders and mines accounted for almost twice as many Allied ships sunk as did U-boats. The most dramatic U-boat successes came against warships. In September, Kapitanleutnant Otto Schuhart in U-29 sank the British aircraft carrier *Courageous*, and the following month Kapitanleutnant Gunther Prien penetrated the defenses of Scapa Flow and sank the battleship *Royal Oak*. While the Germans hailed the feats of Schuhart and Prien, the British pointed with satisfaction to their success in maintaining the flow of shipping and to the fact that there was a greater tonnage of shipping available in the spring of 1940 than before the war began, thanks to new construction and purchases.

The defeat of France by Germany in June 1940 completely altered the strategic situation at sea as well as on land by giving the Germans unimpeded access to the Atlantic. Faced with the threat of invasion, the British were obliged to keep large numbers of destroyers and escort vessels in home waters to counter any attempted landing. Other destroyers were in need of repairs and refitting after the campaign in Norway and the evacuation of British troops from France at Dunkirk. As a result, during June and July, transatlantic convoys seldom had more than one or two escorts.

Dönitz still had no more oceangoing U-boats than he had had at the outbreak of war, but his submarines now had the enormous advantage of new bases on the Bay of Biscay in occupied France at Brest, Lorient, St. Nazaire, La Pallice, and Bordeaux. Possession of these bases enabled the U-boats to avoid the dangerous 450-mile voyage from Wilhelmshaven or Kiel to the open Atlantic. In addition, the German Signals Intelligence Service, called B-Dienst, was reading large parts of the British naval code as well as the "merchant navy code" used for radio messages to and between merchant ships.[6] Utilizing these intercepted messages, Dönitz had begun group or "wolf pack" attacks on convoys, although most sinkings in 1940 were still by individual submarines. Under these circumstances the small number of German U-boats—never more than sixteen at a time—commanded by experienced and daring captains enjoyed remarkable success. Tonnage of Allied and neutral ships lost to U-boats rose from an average of less than 80,000 a month to 375,000 in June and an average of more than 230,000 tons during July, August, September, and October.[7] In operations against convoys, German submarines generally attacked at night on the surface, rendering ASDIC of little use. The low silhouette and dark colors of the U-boats made them extremely hard to spot, and the primitive radar carried by some warships was generally ineffective against low-lying U-boats because the "clutter" from the sea distorted the radar signal. A submarine on the surface was also faster than most escort vessels, except destroyers, and could often outrun or outmaneuver its pursuers.

Faced with the new submarine menace, Prime Minister Winston Churchill sought assistance from the United States, which, though still neutral, transferred fifty World War I destroyers to Britain and Canada in return for the right to use British bases in North America and the West Indies. Following Roosevelt's reelection in November 1940, secret military contact between British and American military staffs, technical experts, and intelligence analysts began. The president also succeeded in pushing through Congress a broad-based economic and military assistance plan to aid Britain called Lend-Lease. Although technically still neutral, the United States was now committed to giving Britain "all aid short of war." British and American military contacts culminated in a series of secret staff conversations in Washington in February and March 1941 known as ABC-1, which laid the foundation for cooperation between the two countries in a common strategy to defeat the Axis. Acting on ABC-1, the U.S. Navy also began plans and preparations to convoy merchant shipping across the Atlantic.[8]

The other major British ally in North America, Canada, had entered the war in September 1939. In the Great War, Canada had sent large numbers of troops to fight on the Western Front, where they had won famous victories and suffered heavy casualties at Vimy Ridge and Passchendael. William Lyon Mackenzie King, the eccentric, canny Canadian prime minister, was determined not to repeat the Canadian experience in that war. A supporter of the Royal Canadian Navy, Mackenzie King intended that this time Canada's contribution to the Allied war effort would take the form of naval and air force operations. A large Canadian army in Europe could well mean high casualties and a renewal of conscription, which would be highly dangerous politically given the tensions between the French- and English-speaking population of the country. Development of a large air force and navy would also provide excellent opportunities for Canada's industrial expansion. In addition, Mackenzie King intended that so far as possible, Canadian naval forces would have an independent identity and mission and not simply act as an auxiliary of the Royal Navy.[9]

Though there were big plans for the Royal Canadian Navy, the force itself was tiny. During the height of the Great Depression the chief of the Canadian General Staff had actually proposed that the navy be abolished to provide sufficient money to keep the army and air force going.[10] At the outbreak of war, the Royal Canadian Navy consisted of six destroyers and a handful of minesweepers and patrol boats. The officers of this small fleet considered themselves almost a part of the British Royal Navy. They had been trained in RN schools, served aboard British ships, and routinely carried out maneuvers with British men-of-war.[11] Most had British accents, and indeed 28 percent had been born in the British Isles (compared to less than 8 percent in the general Canadian population).[12] Ordinary seamen, after basic new entry training, received all of their seagoing training and specialized schooling from the Royal Navy.[13]

During the 1930s all of the RCN's most important exercises had been carried out with the Royal Navy. Jellicoe and Beatty would have felt at home with these maneuvers, which included having Canadian destroyers practice screening the battle line and delivering coordinated torpedo attacks against the enemy's battle fleet.[14] The primary mission of Canadian warships, during the interwar period, aside from acting as a division of the British fleet, was believed to be combat against enemy cruisers and armed merchant raiders in the western Atlantic.

At the outbreak of war, the Royal Canadian Navy's senior officers were most interested in acquiring large well-armed destroyers like the British Tribal class for their own fleet. These were the types of ships that could give a good account of themselves in a fleet action or against a large raider. Yet Canadian yards were incapable of building any type of warship, let alone the large and complex Tribal-class destroyers, and the King government was unwilling to see lucrative shipbuilding contracts go overseas. What Canadian yards could produce was a modification of a commercial whaler, soon labeled a "corvette," which could be built in large numbers and employed as a patrol or escort vessel. The Canadian Naval Staff, therefore, proposed to build some of these corvettes for Canadian use and to "barter" the others for Tribal-class destroyers to be built in Britain. Although the barter scheme soon began to unravel, by the time France fell, Canada had more than sixty of these small escort vessels under construction or on order. Also by that time, all six of Canada's destroyers had sailed for England in response to urgent requests from Churchill and the British Admiralty. There they acted as convoy escorts in the waters around the United Kingdom and in the waters of the eastern Atlantic. The destroyers took most of Canada's most experienced officers and ratings with them. The remaining handful of experienced sailors had to be rounded up to man the first of the Canadian-built corvettes delivered to the Royal Navy in the fall and winter of 1940–41. The British, short of men themselves, insisted that the Canadian crews remain aboard the new corvettes even after they had been delivered to Britain instead of returning to Canada as planned.[15] Thus, as the war entered its second winter the Royal Canadian Navy found itself committed to commissioning and manning a fleet of more than fifty corvettes, six American destroyers acquired in the destroyer-bases deal, and two dozen minesweepers—with virtually all of its experienced personnel on the far side of the Atlantic.

It was a mind-boggling task. During the course of wartime mobilization the British Royal Navy had seen an eightfold increase in its strength. The U.S. Navy expanded by a factor of twenty. The Royal Canadian Navy would require a fiftyfold increase in manpower, from 1,800 men in August 1939 to 90,000 men and 6,000 women by 1944. And while the British and American navies could count on a cadre of highly experienced seamen, petty officers, and junior officers to form the nucleus around which a much larger force could be built, the Canadian equivalent of this small experienced nucleus of officers and men was already serving on the far side of the ocean. The result, as the official Canadian history bluntly states, was that "the first RCN corvettes were commissioned with scratch crews."[16]

In the great majority of corvettes and minesweepers commissioned from Canadian yards in 1941 and 1942, only a handful of officers and seamen had ever been to sea before. In HMCS *Chambly*, a corvette commissioned at the end of 1940, for example, only four of fifty-one ratings had served in the regular navy. Fourteen had been in the prewar Naval Reserve and the remaining thirty-three had no prior seagoing experience.[17] "If you were fortunate enough . . . to serve in a new ship commanded by an experienced merchant seaman . . . you were one of a lucky minority," recalled one Canadian officer. "Most of the new ships in the early months of the war were a shambles. . . . There was incompetence of every sort at every level; some of the ships were barely able to get to sea and once there were fortunate to find their way back without mishap."[18] One Canadian admiral noted that in the fall of 1941 a typical Canadian corvette had a "Sublieutenant, RCNVR (temp) of two months sea experience as senior watchkeeper, backed up by a Sublieutenant, RCNVR (temp) with no sea experience and a mate, RCNR (temp) who has lately risen from apprentice in a merchant ship and has never before been to sea in charge of a watch on the bridge."[19] "WHAT ARE YOU DOING!" an irate senior officer signaled to a new corvette captain after a particularly inept maneuver by the latter. "LEARNING A LOT," came the reply.[20]

The manning crisis quickly outpaced the capacity of naval training schools to properly prepare either officers or men for their duties. In the first few officer training courses at Halifax, "standards were set aside on the basis that someone who had failed a course was better trained than someone who had not had it at all."[21] One corvette captain recalled a representative conversation with one of his newly arrived officers.

"Your name May?"
"Yes sir."
"Been to sea before?"
"No sir."
"Do you know anything about gunnery?"
"No sir."
"Well you better learn in a hurry because we're off to sea in a fortnight and you'll be gunnery officer."[22]

The policies of the naval manning staff in Halifax actually helped to worsen the problem of inexperience by routinely "raiding key personnel from existing ship's companies to man new construction."[23]

The great majority of Canada's new naval officers came directly from schools and colleges or from white-collar occupations. More than 40 percent were engineers, accountants, lawyers, teachers, and doctors; the remainder were clerks, bank tellers, college students, and recent graduates. Sailors came from all parts of Canada, with the exception of the French-speaking parts of Quebec. Most had been in blue-collar or farm occupations or were former students.[24] While there were some real social and educational differences between officers and ratings, Canadian sailors were no more inclined than U.S. sailors to accept class differences as the natural order of things. A former corvette captain observed, "Canadians had not grown up 'knowing their place' like their British counterparts. . . . Saluting some fellow who had grown up just across the street came hard to the free spirits of raw new entries."[25] An officer of the Royal Navy was astounded to see a Canadian corvette with a large sign reading WE WANT LEAVE, painted on her superstructure as she came into harbor.[26] The obvious lack of experience and professional knowledge on the part of many new officers simply exacerbated the situation. "The combination of recalcitrant, inexperienced seamen and inadequate officers plagued the early days of the corvette navy and was chiefly responsible for the indifferent performance of so many Canadian ships."[27]

The ships in which these novice sailors went to war would have tried the skill and patience of far more experienced hands. Designed primarily for coastal patrol and escort work, the corvette was soon committed to convoy duty on the open ocean. A corvette was a short, squat, ungainly-looking vessel of about 900 tons and just under 200 feet in length. "In her nakedness her fat belly seemed to bulge over the floor of the dry dock. . . . Her rounded stern was inclined to turn up like a duck's tail."[28] The corvette's main armament, aside from her depth charges, consisted of a single 4-inch gun carried high on the forecastle, a pair of .50-caliber machine guns or Oerlikon 20mm guns on the bridge wings, and a 2-pounder antiaircraft gun in the after superstructure. Her top speed of sixteen knots—only rarely attained—was slower than that of a surfaced U-boat. She was equipped with Canadian Type 123A sonar, which was out of date even by 1940 standards. Canadian corvettes also lacked gyrocompasses, and their single magnetic compass was almost useless in plotting an accurate depth charge attack.[29] One ship, after trying to plot its position using the magnetic compass, signaled to another, "WHAT DO YOU MAKE OUR POSITION OTHER THAN PRECARIOUS."[30]

A ship's propensity to pitch and heave is governed mainly by its length, and in the rough cold waters and towering waves of the North Atlantic the corvettes tended to buck and roll dramatically, causing frequent motion sickness particularly among men unaccustomed to the sea.[31] The crew's quarters were in the forecastle, where the heaving and pitching were the worst. "Plunging into a head sea the noise and motion in the focsle must be experienced to be believed," recalled Lieutenant James Lamb. "A constant roar of turbulence, wind and water punctuated by a crashing thud as the bow bites into another great sea, while the whole little world is uplifted—up, up, up—only to come crashing down as the ship plunges her bows over and downward to land with an impact which hurls anyone and anything not firmly secured down to the forward bulkhead."[32]

Between the forecastle and the bridge was a large open gap in the main deck, "which insured that crew members going off watch and food being brought forward could be sure of a drenching in any head sea."[33] One naval veteran advised that to appreciate life in a corvette "you ought to go into the bathroom on the coldest night of the year, open the window, fill the tub with water then get in with your clothes on."[34] Lieutenant William H. Pugsley recalled that after a few days of heavy weather, "no one of us had any dry clothing left for the water had gotten into our lockers. The radiators were loaded with things we were trying to dry. Hammocks stayed slung. When you climbed in you put your oilskin on top to keep out the water dripping through from above. When you went on watch you lashed your mack tight or it would fill like a trough."[35] Wet weather and cold encouraged pneumonia, while poor ventilation resulted in more than a few cases of tuberculosis. The quality of life aboard these ships was probably captured most succinctly in the verses of a popular RCN song:

> Bless 'em all, bless 'em all
> These bloody corvettes are too small,
> In a rough sea they'll heave and they'll pitch,
> They'll make you as sick as a son of a bitch,
> And it's up to the railing you'll sprawl,
> And spew up that good alcohol.
> You'll finish the war on this one funneled whore,
> So cheer up my lads bless 'em all.

With all their faults, however, the corvettes had three sterling qualities: extreme ruggedness; good fuel capacity, which gave them relatively
long range; and a very small turning radius, less than half that of a destroyer. A tight turning circle was important because a warship would
normally need to make repeated passes over the position of a submerged
submarine in order to launch depth charges from her stern and side
throwers.[36]

Whatever its strengths and weaknesses, the corvette would be the
premier convoy escort on the North Atlantic through 1943. These
squat, gray, sea-stained ships, bearing the names of faraway Canadian
towns like Red Deer, Kamloops, Moose Jaw, and Regina, would become
the best-known icon of the Royal Canadian Navy and one of the most
famous symbols of Canada's war effort.

For Britain the breakneck expansion of the Canadian fleet came just
in time. With the extension of U-boat operations farther and farther
into the Atlantic, the Royal Navy began a plan to escort convoys across
the entire breadth of the ocean. Many RN destroyers actually lacked the
range to cross the Atlantic without refueling, and so, in spring of 1941,
the Admiralty requested that Canadian warships assume responsibility
for escort of convoys from Newfoundland to a point near Iceland called
the Mid-Ocean Meeting Point, where they would be picked up by Royal
Navy warships. On May 20, the first seven corvettes left Halifax for
Newfoundland, and on June 2, the first convoy under escort of the new
corvettes sailed from North America.

When the RCN entered the Battle of the Atlantic in early summer
1941, the balance in the submarine war had swung to some extent
toward the Allies. With the threat of Germany invading Britain waning
and the loan of the U.S. destroyers to the Royal Navy, more ships were
available to escort convoys. Royal Air Force bombers were now patrolling the Bay of Biscay, forcing submarines to submerge and thus
lengthening their time of passage. The British had begun to organize
their destroyers, frigates, and corvettes into permanent "escort groups"
that underwent rigorous training in anti-submarine tactics and procedures. Smaller ships—corvettes and later frigates—"worked up" at HMS
Western Isles, a base on the west coast of Scotland under the command
of Vice Admiral Gilbert Stephenson, a peppery hyperactive veteran
of World War I who had been recalled from retirement. According to
an oft-repeated story, Stephenson boarded a newly arrived corvette,

"snatched the gold-braided cap off his head, hurled it on the deck and yelled at the party of sailors drawn up to receive him: 'That's a live bomb! What are you going to do about it?' After a second's hesitation a quick-witted sailor kicked the cap into the sea. Glancing at the hat afloat in the water the Admiral yelled, 'That's a survivor! He's drowning! Jump over the side and rescue him.'"[37] Once individual ship training at Western Isles was complete, the smaller ships joined the rest of the escort group, which underwent training before proceeding on operations together. In this way some escort groups began to match the German wolf packs in skill and deadly results. During a fifteen-day period in March 1941, the three top German submarine "aces," Joachim Shepke, Otto Kretschmer, and Gunther Prien, the hero of Scapa Flow, were all sunk by British escort groups. (Kretschmer was the only one of the three to survive. He was picked up by the destroyer *Walker*, which had sunk his boat, U-99. The *Walker's* engineer, a bridge enthusiast, organized a foursome that included Kretschmer and two officers of the freighter *J.B. White*, sunk by U-99 the day before. The engineer later recalled that it was "the only time in the war that he managed to get a decent game.")[38]

These victories had relatively little impact on overall merchant ship losses, but they served to boost British morale and caused gloom and consternation in Germany where, as in World War I, submarine commanders were popular heroes. Other developments had a greater impact. A new type of "ten-centimeter" radar, which gave a much-improved target definition, made it easier for ships and aircraft to detect surfaced U-boats at night or in bad weather. Radio direction finding sometimes made it possible to pinpoint the location of wolf packs and route convoys around them. The greatest single advance, however, was Britain's growing ability to intercept and read German naval codes. The British code-breaking effort was consolidated at the euphemistically named Government Code and Cipher School at an estate called Bletchley Park in Buckinghamshire. At its peak, Bletchley Park employed some 10,000 people, including some of the brightest civilian scientists and intellectuals. In March 1941, several months before the RNC joined the Battle of the Atlantic, the British captured important cipher materials from the German patrol vessel *Krebs*, enabling Bletchley Park to make inroads into the German naval ciphers. Two months later, two RN destroyers and the RN corvette *Aubretia*, defending a westbound convoy, depth-charged and damaged U-110, forcing it to the surface. As the crew abandoned the sinking submarine, a whaler from the destroyer *Bulldog* closed on the U-110. The boarding party recovered not only all the confidential papers but also an entire German cipher machine—called "enigma"—and brought it back to England. This windfall, together with other code and cipher material captured from two German weather ships, made it possible for Bletchley Park to decipher German messages quickly enough to make the material of value in the ongoing Atlantic battle. From late May until December 1941, intelligence gleaned from these messages made it possible to reroute convoys around known U-boat locations.[39]

As the United States inched closer to involvement in the war, during the summer of 1941, American marines relieved British troops occupying Iceland and U.S. destroyers began escorting convoys in the western Atlantic. By the end of 1941 the Newfoundland Escort Force, a Canadian fleet of nearly seventy corvettes and a dozen destroyers, was operating between St. John's and Iceland. A division of labor was soon agreed upon between the two North American allies. The United States Atlantic Fleet, which included large numbers of destroyers, assumed responsibility for "fast convoys," those that included ships with a top speed of at least nine knots. The Canadians, with their much slower corvettes, would escort "slow convoys," composed of ships steaming at 7.5–8.9 knots. The slow convoys often included more than a few rusting tramp steamers with ancient unreliable engines. "These ships were prone to belching smoke, breaking down, straggling . . . or even romping ahead. . . . Slow convoys more often resembled an organized mob than an orderly assemblage of ships and their slow pace of advance made evasive action in the face of the enemy useless if not altogether impossible."[40] Because they took longer to cross the ocean, ships in a slow convoy also had a 30 percent greater chance of being sunk than those in fast convoys.

If the U-boats managed to find them, the combination of unruly slow convoys and the RCN's small, inexperienced escorts usually spelled trouble. In early September, convoy SC42 sailed for Iceland escorted by HMCS *Skeena*, a destroyer, and three Canadian corvettes. After intelligence reports indicated the presence of U-boats, HMCS *Chambly* and *Moose Jaw*, originally assigned to training duties, joined the escort force as reinforcements. Shortly after 9:00 P.M. on the 8th, the freighter SS *Muneric* was struck by a torpedo and sank with all hands. Six more ships in the convoy were torpedoed before daylight the next morning. Around noon an eighth ship, *Thistleglen*, was sunk by a U-boat. *Skeena* and two corvettes got solid sonar contacts, but their depth charge attacks were rewarded by nothing more than a large air bubble, and the ships had to break off their attack to rejoin the convoy. After dark the U-boats resumed their attacks and hit the freighters *Ulysses* and *Gypsum Queen*.

During this attack, *Chambly* and *Moose Jaw* had been approaching across the convoy's line of advance, hoping to catch any surfaced U-boats in the rear as they lay in wait for the convoy. Their lookouts saw no surfaced submarines, but *Chambly*'s sonar operator got a firm contact. Now the corvette's quick turning radius came into play. A 15-degree turn brought *Chambly* onto a converging path with her target. As the ship steadied on her new course, *Chambly*'s captain ordered, "Fire!" One of the men at the port depth charge rails was "a relief man on his first trip to sea [and] missed his cue. As a result there was a slight delay in firing the first and second depth charges and when they did go they went rather together."[41]

Seldom has ineptitude been more richly rewarded. The first depth charge hit just abaft of the submarine U-501's conning tower and the second, having been fired almost at the same time, hit nearby, causing a double explosion. U-501 was blown to the surface close by *Moose Jaw*, which drew alongside. As she did so, the U-boat's captain leaped aboard, much to the astonishment of the Canadians and his own crew. As U-501 drifted across the corvette's bow, *Moose Jaw* rammed the submarine, keeping her under fire to prevent the crew from manning her deck gun. *Chambly* then came alongside, and a boarding party under Lieutenant Edward Simmons, armed only with pistols, attempted to salvage the submarine. U-501 was too far gone, however, and Simmons was fortunate to escape with only one casualty.[42]

During the night of September 9, SC42 lost five more ships for a total of fourteen, making it one of the worst convoy disasters of the war. More were to follow as inexperienced and often outnumbered Canadian escort groups tried vainly to protect their unruly slow convoys against attacks by the wolf packs. In mid-September, SC44 lost four ships along with one of the escorting corvettes in a single night. Inexperience led to other problems as well. For example, the corvette *Shediac* became separated from her convoy when the latter made an emergency turn and spent the ensuing five days trying to find it. This time-consuming and potentially lethal error occurred because *Shediac*'s crew had no telescopes or binoculars to read the flag signals directing the turn and her wireless was not functioning properly.[43]

These setbacks were, of course, kept secret by the Allied governments. Canadians knew only that their navy, almost nonexistent before the war, was now playing an important role in the struggle at sea. The Royal Canadian Navy came to symbolize the nation's war effort, manned by "Canada's splendid young bluejackets whose hardworking mothers and fathers have taught them to live well and honestly and to face the world and its troubles with a grin."[44] Canadian papers were delighted to learn that Lieutenant Commander J. G. "Chummy" Prentice, who had commanded *Chambly* and *Moose Jaw* in their dramatic fight with U-501, had, before the war, been a rancher in the Caribou country of British Columbia. Prentice was now "on the job rounding up U-boats and applying the depth charge brand."[45] Actually Prentice was a Canadian graduate of the Royal Naval College, Dartmouth, who, after more than twenty years in the Royal Navy, had retired to become financial secretary of the Western Canada Ranching Company.[46]

In 1941 none of that mattered. The bold and dramatic fight with U-501 was seen as the symbol of the young navy's adventuresome, swashbuckling style. The *Toronto Daily Star* ran a photograph of HMCS *Moose Jaw*'s crest, which portrayed a "startled Hitler on the run from a fierce-eyed fire breathing moose that had skewered a U-boat on its horns and was now biting the seat of Adolf's pants."[47] The *Ottawa Journal* expressed the views of many Canadians when it proclaimed in November 1941 that the RCN was "living up to the traditions of the British Fleet."[48] A popular song saluted "the lads of Maple Leaf Squadron":

At hunting the U-boat it's seldom they fail,
Though they've come from the mine and the farm and the workshop,
The bank and the college and maybe from jail.[49]

The entry of the United States into the war in December 1941 resulted in a temporary cessation of the convoy battles in the North Atlantic as Admiral Dönitz shifted his U-boat offensive to an all-out attack on American shipping along the eastern seaboard. Between mid-January and early August, German U-boats sank more than 600 ships totaling more than 3.1 million tons off the East Coast and in the Gulf of Mexico during "Operation Roll of Drums." In April alone, thirty-three Allied tankers were sunk and six others damaged.

Most of the lost ships were sailing independently within a hundred miles of the coast. The British, committed to transatlantic convoys, and the Americans, whose first priority was the protection of troopships carrying American soldiers to Europe and the Pacific, had few escorts to spare for the Atlantic coast. Admiral King was mistakenly convinced that weakly escorted convoys were worse than none at all and did not begin convoying until April 1942. The fate of the weakly protected convoys escorted by the Royal Canadian Navy during the previous summer

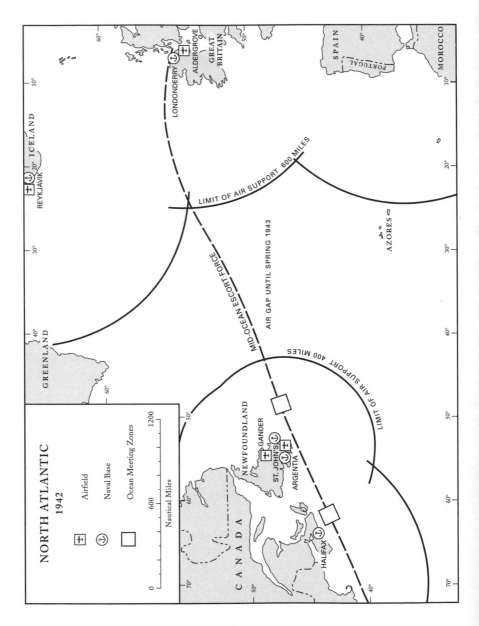

NORTH ATLANTIC
1942

⊞ Airfield

Ⓛ Naval Base

☐ Ocean Meeting Zones

Nautical Miles

0   600   1200

GREENLAND

ICELAND

REYKJAVIK ⊞ Ⓛ

LONDONDERRY Ⓛ

ALDERGROVE ⊞

GREAT BRITAIN

SPAIN

PORTUGAL

MOROCCO

AZORES

LIMIT OF AIR SUPPORT 600 MILES

MID-OCEAN ESCORT FORCE

AIR GAP UNTIL SPRING 1943

LIMIT OF AIR SUPPORT 400 MILES

NEWFOUNDLAND

GANDER ⊞ Ⓛ

ST. JOHN'S Ⓛ

ARGENTIA Ⓛ ⊞

CANADA

HALIFAX Ⓛ

and fall may have influenced American thinking on this question, but
ironically, after the RCN assumed responsibility for escorting all coastal
convoys north of Boston, there was not a single loss.[50] As convoys finally
began operating off the East Coast in May 1942, Dönitz shifted his sub-

marines south to the Gulf of Mexico until the convoy was extended to that area. In July 1942 he finally recalled most of his U-boats from American waters, having sunk more tonnage during the previous six months than at any time since the beginning of the war.

Nevertheless, the results of Roll of Drums, one-sided as they at first appeared, demonstrated clearly the long-term implications of adding the United States to the ranks of Germany's enemies. During the spring of 1942, while burning ships could still be seen from East Coast cities, German naval intelligence informed Dönitz that American shipbuilding output during the balance of the year would be about three times what had at first been estimated and that during 1943 it would be higher still.[51] By July 1941, the number of new vessels entering the Allied shipping pool was already slightly larger than the total of those lost to all causes. By early 1943, American shipyards were completing about 140 of the new mass-produced "Liberty ships" a month.[52]

Despite his knowledge of these grim statistics and public acknowledgment that "even more difficult times lie ahead of us," Dönitz was determined to attempt to wrest a victory in the Atlantic. He now had more than 350 U-boats available, and by renewing his attacks in the mid-Atlantic his submarines would be hundreds of miles closer to their bases. During the ten-month period between August 1942 and May 1943, the Germans averaged more than a hundred U-boats at sea, more than at any time during World War I.[53] In addition the B-Dienst was again reading the British naval cipher that encrypted messages to and from convoys. At the same time, Bletchley Park suffered a long blackout in its ability to read the Germans' codes after they introduced a new cipher machine wheel in February 1942.

"The German nation has long felt that our arm is the sharpest and most decisive," wrote Admiral Dönitz. In the years since World War I the U-boat service had lost little of its glamour and prestige in Germany. Since the Nazis' rise to power the gallant, tightly knit U-boat crews, selflessly facing death for the fatherland, had been extolled as a patriotic model for the nation's youth. As in World War I, U-boat aces became popular heroes and patriotic icons. (For decades following the death of Gunther Prien, "the Bull of Scapa Flow," periodic sightings of this hero similar to the Elvis Presley sightings in the United States were reported in Germany.)[54] A submarine novel by Ludwig Freiwald explained the ways in which U-boat men epitomized "the breakthrough of the racial ideal." In the concluding scene, Freiwald portrayed German sailors marching alongside Nazi storm troopers through the Brandenburg Gate in Berlin.[55] "The Führer gave us back our honor and weapon," declared a former U-boat captain in the Great War, now an SS officer. "German U-boats again stand guard in order to protect the peaceful work of the people."[56]

So many former members of the right-wing paramilitary *Freikorps* of 1918 were accepted into the navy that the submarine branch was sometimes referred to as Freikorps Dönitz. Several prominent officers of the Kaiser's navy, including three U-boat aces, joined the Nazi party prior to Hitler's installation as chancellor.[57]

Naval officers on active duty, unlike their retired brethren, were not Nazi Party members. Yet they shared the latter's affinity for the spirit and ideology of the Third Reich. An anonymous poem by a U-boat man, widely circulated in 1941, commemorated lost submariners killed in action.

> *Two hundred thousand tons at least,*
> *Now from the enemy we've torn.*
> *We take them with us as we die,*
> *As to our Führer we have sworn,*
> *A final Heil to the Reich we gave.*
> *Give us when we die on honor's field,*
> *In honor also one last wave.*[58]

And in a widely distributed speech on leadership, celebrated U-boat commander Wolfgang Lüth described how on some Sundays he would assemble the crew and "tell them about racial and population problems, all from the viewpoint of the struggle for the realization of the Reich."[59] A leading historian of the U-boat arm concluded, "Under Dönitz and the demands of total war, the navy completed its evolution from earlier affiliations and accommodation to an amalgam with National Socialism."[60] This transformation was so complete that in 1945, as Germany was about to surrender to the Allies, SS officers including Rudolf Höss, the commandant of Auschwitz, were issued papers and uniforms by the navy to enable them to pass as naval petty officers or enlisted men.[61]

The men who furnished the officers and commanders of the U-boat force differed relatively little in social background and outlook from those who had served in the High Seas Fleet.[62] About 25 percent were the sons of career officers, and most of the remainder were sons of higher civil servants, doctors, lawyers, architects, clergymen, and owners of large landed estates. Sons of industrialists and businessmen were admit-

Japanese naval cadets in their classroom at Etajima, the naval college. Class rank was key to determining an officer's future. The top four or five cadets in each class were considered the future elite of the navy. [U.S. Navy]

Gunnery drill at Etajima. Between 1900 and 1904, an average of 1,800 young men took the entrance examination for the naval college. Approximately half failed the rigorous medical examination. In 1904, of the 1,175 men who survived to take the academic examination only 349 passed. Only 183 of them were eventually admitted to Etajima. [U.S. Navy]

Japanese battleships opening fire at long range in the Battle of the Yellow Sea, August 10, 1904. The first of the two great naval battles of the Russo-Japanese War, it was a tactical defeat for the Russians, who lost several ships. The Russian squadron in Port Arthur, however, remained intact, forcing the Japanese into a costly and prolonged battle to capture the city from the land side. [U.S. Navy]

Your nearest and dearest in the Home-land await you.

God speed the Warrior grim and grey
For foreign stations bound
Bearing our dear ones far away
From home and friends around

I'll heartily welcome you. —

Rule, Britannia, Britannia rule the waves.

By the end of the nineteenth century, navies and sailors had come to be seen as epitomizing the best qualities of a nation. These postcards from Germany, Great Britain, Japan, and the United States express the association in the popular mind between sailors and adventure, manliness, patriotism, and technology. [*Author's Collection*]

Entry into the Imperial Navy was an important event for a young man and was usually marked by a formal gathering of his relatives and neighbors. [*Courtesy of Rear Admiral Hiramn Yoichi*]

Japanese signalman of the 1930s. The navy was a relatively high-status occupation in Japan and certainly a more popular choice with young men than the army. The army was associated with drill and harsh discipline while the navy was associated with adventure and modern technology. [*U.S. Navy*]

Sailors on the mess deck of the Japanese battleship *Mutsu*. As in contemporary British ships, the mess spaces are so crowded that a sailor at one table could have easily leaned against the back of the sailor at the next. [*U.S. Navy*]

"The cat's whiskers": officers, midshipmen, bluejackets, and marines of the Royal Navy in a rare informal group portrait. The photo commemorates the men's achievement in loading more than four hundred tons of coal in less than three hours. Note that the stokers in the front row are still in their coal-blackened overalls. [U.S. Navy]

HMS *Dreadnought*, designed and built under the direction of Admiral Fisher, First Sea Lord. The first "all-big-gun" battleship, the *Dreadnought* gave its name to an entire new generation of warship and helped to fuel the Anglo-German naval arms race. Fisher himself, however, favored replacing conventional battleships and cruisers with a fleet built around fast super-battle cruisers and submarines. [U.S. Navy]

Royal Navy bluejackets on a "coal ship." Parties of sailors with shovels boarded a collier and began shoveling coal into two-hundred-pound bags that were hoisted aboard ship by derricks and dumped into wheelbarrows to be tipped into bunkers. "Within minutes the ship was enveloped in a fog of coal dust. A thick layer formed around the eyelids. . . . All food from the galley carried a fine film of it." [U.S. Navy]

The super-dreadnought *Iron Duke*, Admiral Sir John Jellicoe's flagship, at the Battle of Jutland. Battleships like the *Iron Duke* could be built in about three years, but it took six years to train the large number of specialists necessary to man them. [U.S. Navy]

SMS *Seydlitz* opening fire at Jutland. Like the other German battle cruisers at Jutland, the *Seydlitz* suffered heavy damage; but only one, the *Lutzow*, sank. [U.S. Navy]

Two divisions of German S-class torpedo boats form up for maneuvers with the battle fleet. German destroyers were generally outgunned by their British counterparts and accomplished relatively little, although the threat of torpedo attack caused Jellicoe and other admirals great anxiety. [U.S. Navy]

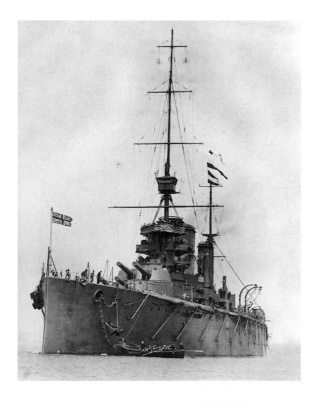

HMS *Lion*, Admiral Beatty's flagship at the Battle of Jutland. The British lost three battle cruisers at Jutland, but the *Lion* survived serious damage, thanks to the new methods of ammunition handling introduced by her chief gunner, Alexander Grant. These prevented the fatal explosions that destroyed the other ships. [U.S. Navy]

A German U-boat stops a suspected British merchant ship flying false colors during World War I. Such searches, in compliance with traditional prize rules, rendered the submarine vulnerable to ramming or attacks by gunfire if the freighter was armed. After 1915, those searches were practiced far less frequently than subsurface attacks without warning. [Author's Collection]

A World War I convoy at sea. Instead of making ships more vulnerable, as the Admiralty feared, the convoy system actually made them more difficult to locate. By July 1917, transatlantic convoys were in operation from Hampton Roads, New York, and Halifax. The convoy system resulted in an almost immediate reduction in shipping losses. However, not all ships sailed in convoy, and convoys were not available from every port. [U.S. Navy]

While the Allies denounced the U-boat sailors as pirates and murderers, the German public saw them as heroes enduring great danger and hardship to defend the fatherland against the British "hunger blockade." Romantic postcards such as this were very popular. [Author's Collection]

U.S. Navy ace David Ingalls, flying a British aircraft, destroys a German barrage balloon. Ingalls was a member of the First Yale Unit, a group of volunteer naval aviators mostly from Ivy League colleges who served with Admiral Sims's forces in European waters. In the closing days of World War I, a Royal Navy fighter launched from the sea attacked and destroyed a German zeppelin, demonstrating the potential of airplanes as interceptors in fleet air defense. [From a painting by Bruce Ungerland, U.S. Navy]

The first class of enlisted U.S. Navy aviators at Pensacola, Florida, March 1917. After the close of World War I, the navy did its best to avoid accepting enlisted men as pilots. However, chronic manpower shortages and congressional legislation obliged the navy to train outstanding first class or chief petty officers as "Naval Aviation Pilots." [National Archives]

Admiral Sir Andrew Cunningham commanded the British Mediterranean Fleet in the Battle of Crete, the first protracted contest between ships and aircraft. (Shown here as First Sea Lord with Admiral H. Kent Hewitt USN.) [*U.S. Navy*]

With a full load of soldiers evacuated from Crete, HMS *Orion* survived two bomb hits and arrived back at Alexandria with more than 500 casualties and only two rounds of 6-inch shell remaining. Surgeon Lieutenant Bence and an army doctor treated more than 300 casualties without benefit of access to running water. More than 250 survived. [*U.S. Navy*]

Off Crete, HMS *Fiji* survived more than thirteen hours of air attacks before finally being crippled by a bomb in the forward boiler room, which blew in the ship's bottom. Stokers in the undamaged boiler room remained at their posts, "keeping steam in the system and all pumps going, knowing that their end was very near and meantime holding on to anything handy to keep themselves upright" as the ship developed a steep list. [*U.S. Navy*]

A German Type VII U-boat equipped with a snorkel—a long tube that could be extended like a periscope to suck in enough air to allow a submarine to start its diesel engines underwater and expel the exhaust. With diesels running, the batteries could be recharged without forcing the submarine to surface. [*U.S. Navy*]

HMC Corvette *Chambly* in Conception Bay, Newfoundland, in May 1941. *Chambly* and HMCS *Moose Jaw* sank U-501 in September 1941. [*Library of J. Marc Milner*]

A boarding party from HMCS *Chilliwack* goes aboard U-744 in March 1944. Note the shell holes in the conning tower. Canadian ships sank or captured forty-seven U-boats in the course of the war. [*National Archives of Canada*]

The Grumman F4F-3A fighter was generally outclassed by the Japanese Zero; however, clever tacticians like Thach and Flatley soon devised ways to exploit the Wildcat's strengths against the Zero's weaknesses. In this photo, Thach is in F-1 while fighter ace E. H. "Butch" O'Hare is in F-13. [*U.S. Navy*]

Right: James Flatley, one of the U.S. Navy's leading fighter tacticians, shown here in 1945 as commander of Air Group 5, USS *Yorktown*. [U.S. Navy]

Below: Sailors man a 40mm gun mount aboard the battleship *South Dakota* during the Battle of the Santa Cruz Islands. "The mounts could swivel from port to starboard so quick it was sometimes hard to get your footing, as the mounts jerked and jumped from side to side." The 40mm proved highly effective against conventional air attacks, but less so against Kamikazes. [U.S. Navy]

Right: View of the damage to the USS *Smith* in the Battle of the Santa Cruz Islands after a torpedo plane crashed into her bow. "The sight and smell of the burnt corpses around the base of the bridge and along the ladders was dreadful. The fire had not only killed many but burnt off most of their flesh leaving only bones or legs, hands, and arms." [U.S. Navy]

Left: A destroyer comes alongside the crippled *Hornet* to help take off the crew. *Hornet* sailor John F. Kielty found himself aboard the destroyer *Anderson* and fell asleep in her head, despite the fact that ammunition was being passed through the hatches when the ship was in action. [U.S. Navy]

Left: Lieutenant Ronald Gift takes a much-needed drink after his night landing aboard the USS *Monterey* at the conclusion of the Battle of the Philippine Sea, June 1944. More than one third of the planes dispatched on the final long-range strike against Admiral Ozawa's carriers were lost, but more than 160 aviators were rescued from the water and only 49 were lost. *[National Archives]*

Right: Pilots in the ready room of an *Essex*-class carrier pass the time playing cards. Though technically illegal, gambling flourished in the U.S. and British navies, causing comedian Bob Hope to observe that an aircraft carrier was simply a floating crap game with a flight deck on it. *[Lieutenant Commander Charles Kerlee USNR, National Archives]*

Left: Aboard the escort carrier *Tulagi*, Steward's Mate Miles David King hoists a loaded 20mm gun magazine. African-American cooks, waiters, and orderlies of the steward's branch often manned part of the gun battery when the ship went to general quarters. It was not until the close of World War II that the U.S. Navy permitted black sailors to serve at sea in jobs outside the steward's branch. *[National Archives]*

Right: A sailor operating a forklift truck at a navy supply depot on Guam. The great majority of African-American sailors served ashore in supply and labor jobs such as this. Tensions between black sailors and white sailors and marines on Guam led to a serious outbreak of violence in December 1944. *[National Archives]*

Large numbers of Waves were employed in aviation training and support. The group photo (*below*) shows the first class of Waves to complete training in the operation of the low-pressure chamber at Pensacola in June 1944. The photo to the left shows a Wave receiving instruction on the operation of the Link trainer. After 1943 every aviator deploying to the Pacific had received at least a part of his training from a Wave. [*Mrs. Elizabeth G. Coombs*]

A Kamikaze pilot receives his *hachi-make*, a samurai headband, prior to leaving on his one-way mission. Many Kamikaze pilots were not career military men but former high school and college students. At Okinawa, about 1,900 suicide planes sank or seriously damaged more than 150 allied ships. [*U.S. Navy*]

Left: Along with the Swift boats, the fiberglass-hulled PBRs were the workhorses of the river war in Vietnam. Their new water–jet-propulsion system gave them a relatively high speed and enabled them to turn around in their own length. *[U.S. Navy]*

Right: A PCF Swift boat plows through a narrow river. The Swift's aluminum hull tended to corrode, and its engines operated poorly in the intense heat. It was so noisy it could be heard by the Vietcong "a mile away." This boat is partly manned by Vietnamese sailors being prepared to take over the river patrol program as part of the "Vietnamization" process. *[U.S. Navy]*

A U.S. Navy PBR stops a small Vietnamese craft in the Mekong Delta. Between 1966 and mid-1969, U.S. river patrol craft stopped and boarded more than 400,000 vessels, yet still failed to halt the flow of Communist supplies from Cambodia along the rivers, streams, and canals of the delta. *[U.S. Navy]*

Gunner's Mate 3rd Class Earnest McGowan in the .50-caliber machine gun tub of a PBR. Boat captains and patrol officers in the river war were often relatively junior enlisted men. *[U.S. Navy]*

Pilots aboard USS *Enterprise* crossing the flight deck during operations off North Vietnam in 1967. In the foreground is the arresting cable. During 1967, *Enterprise* pilots averaged sixteen to twenty-two combat missions a month. [U.S. Navy]

Commander Paul Engle, executive officer of VA-164, climbs into his A-4 Skyhawk aboard USS *Oriskany* during operations against North Vietnam. At the height of the air war, aviators sometimes were returned to Vietnam for second or third tours after intervals of only fourteen months. [U.S. Navy]

ted with some reluctance, as were sons of midlevel public servants. Only a small minority came from petty-bourgeois white-collar families.[63] The social appeal of a navy career with its fancy uniforms, prestige, impressive titles, and lifetime job security remained strong. While only a small number of officers came from families who were active Nazi supporters, naval officers were strongly attracted to the most reactionary political parties and had little love for the Weimar Republic. A study of one officer "crew" (roughly equivalent to a Naval Academy class) concludes that its members "welcomed Hitler's rise to power almost to a man."[64] While few joined the Nazi Party, they applauded Hitler's bellicose nationalism, his commitment to rapid expansion of the armed forces, and his promises of middle-class prosperity.[65] Some officers found the rowdyism of the storm troopers a little vulgar, but they readily accepted their racism and nationalist paranoia, which, indeed, was a basic staple of their parents' reactionary worldview.

Nor did the navy, an organization that from its inception had deliberately excluded all Jews, find much difficulty accepting Hitler's radical anti-Semitism. In his book *Submariners of Today*, the famous U-boat captain Joachim Schepke explained that, in the navy, the youngest member of the crew was traditionally labeled "Moses." But he hastened to assure his readers that this "doesn't mean that we have a Jew on board. . . . In the first place you don't find any Jews at sea at all; and secondly, the seamen would hardly share their space with such an aberration of nature."[66] Admiral Dönitz praised Hitler's leadership in saving the homeland from "the disintegrating poison of Jewry."[67]

At the outset of the war, U-boat commanders were products of the German navy's rigorous and lengthy officer training process, which included a cruise under sail, six months of classroom training at the Marine Schule, and a foreign cruise. Until the outbreak of war, all were volunteers chosen by Dönitz from the most promising younger officers of the navy. All had more than eighteen months of U-boat training. By 1941, as the U-boat fleet expanded, new submarine officers went directly to sea as midshipmen aboard a U-boat. At this point, about 80 percent of Marine Schule graduates were being assigned to submarines regardless of their own preferences.[68] Nevertheless, Dönitz's pre-1939 training programs provided a solid foundation for the growth of the U-boat force. Unlike the Royal Canadian Navy, the German navy was able to expand around a corps of experienced commanders, engineers, and senior petty officers who kept standards reasonably high until the final year of the war.

As the U-boat arm expanded and losses mounted, the German navy refused to abandon its practice of systematic, thorough, and patient training of U-boat crews. Although training periods were shorter than in the prewar period, they were still lengthy, especially in comparison with the Luftwaffe, the other "high tech" service, which progressively shortened its training time as the war went on.[69] Historian Timothy Mulligan examined the records of nine U-boats commissioned between the fall of 1943 and the summer of 1944 and found they spent an average of nine months on trials, tests, and exercises before departing on their first operational cruise.[70]

To compensate for a crew's relative inexperience, U-boat valves, levers, and other devices inside the submarine were clearly labeled with Bakelite nameplates that could be read even in the dark. In addition, valves and handles related to a single system such as water or pressurized air were given unique identifying shapes, so that they could be recognized by feel. Detailed instructional manuals were provided for the maintenance and repair of machinery.[71]

Unlike Canadian seamen, who often became acquainted with their ships only after they were at sea in a war zone, German submarine crews joined their U-boats weeks or months before, in the shipyard, for an intensive period of training called *Baubelehrung*. While the boat was still under construction, sailors worked with dockyard technicians to familiarize themselves with every piece of equipment in the boat and to see parts of the boat they would not be able to see once it was completed. This unique "training from the keel up" was to continue throughout the war. Although thorough, German submarine training after 1942 increasingly lacked realism. The older German torpedo boats that were assigned to play the role of Allied convoy escort vessels in training exercises could in no way duplicate the practices and tactics of British and American warships with their radar, high-frequency direction-finding gear, and sophisticated sonar.[72] Nor could the handful of Italian aircraft available for training in any way mimic the coordinated and deadly operations of Allied land-based and carrier-based planes.[73]

The U-boat crewmen were generally between twenty and twenty-four years of age, and most were drawn from the great industrial regions of the Ruhr and central Germany, with technical or mechanical backgrounds, particularly in the metalworking industries. This technical background gave U-boat sailors a special affinity for their complicated machines and enabled them to make emergency repairs and deal with unexpected mechanical difficulties while at sea.[74]

A U-boat crew was both a tightly knit team and a kind of authoritarian club whose members knew each other intimately. "You have to know not only the activities of your neighbor but his character, his way of thinking, and his strong and weak points," wrote former U-boat commander Erich Topp. "In such a group human relations can be strong; they go beyond natural instinct for self-preservation."[75] Fifty men or more occupied a space little larger than three railroad passenger cars filled with weapons and machinery. "The word 'hygiene' is greeted by U-boat crews like a comedy routine," wrote German photographer and propagandist Lothar Günther Buchheim. "Fresh water is precious, to be saved for brushing one's teeth and an occasional bath. . . . Hardly anyone thinks of shaving. Beards are tended with loving care. . . . No matter how long the period at sea, no one is encouraged to change his underwear."[76] One submarine commander recalled that "the very food tasted of U-boat, that is, diesel oil, with a flavor of mold. . . . The bulkheads sweated, every single thing turned moldy. Leather outfits and shoes went green in a fortnight if we didn't use them."[77]

Adding to the unique discomforts of U-boat life was the fact that conventional toilets could not be flushed at depths greater than thirty meters because of external water pressure. Later in the war, boats were fitted with specially designed high-pressure toilets that could be evacuated at lower depths. However, these were complicated to operate, and a single mistake in procedure could result in the toilet's occupant being drenched with waste and seawater. At least one U-boat is known to have been lost because of a toilet accident that allowed seawater to reach the electrical batteries. Those who demonstrated competence in operating the mechanism were called "toilet graduates" and assigned by commanders to supervise and assist those less expert in the art.[78]

Like small unit leaders in ground combat, U-boat skippers led by example and by force of personality. "As a submarine commander you were ultimately on your own," wrote one U-boat officer, Wolfgang Lüth. "Peering through the periscope you made the decisions all on your own. During an attack . . . you held the sole responsibility for the entire crew that was stuck with you inside that iron coffin. And so every hit you scored was a kind of vindication of yourself to the crew." These conditions of submarine combat put special stress on the captain as solo performer. "If a man is a success, his men will follow him even if he is a fool."[79]

By August 1942 the most decisive round in the long Battle of the Atlantic had begun. The German assault on the Allied convoy routes continued almost unabated for the next ten months. The U-boats were concentrated in the so-called "air gap," the area in mid-Atlantic out of range of most Allied land-based aircraft. They now operated in wolf packs of up to forty boats, forming patrol lines covering hundreds of miles. When a U-boat in the patrol line sighted a convoy, it would shadow the enemy while transmitting contact reports to other boats of the pack to allow them to converge on the area. B-Dienst intercepts also helped to guide the packs to convoy routes.

Nevertheless, even at the height of the German U-boat effort less than 40 percent of 174 Atlantic convoys were ever even sighted by a U-boat. Of those that were located by patrolling U-boats an additional one third escaped with no losses. Most of the remaining 30 percent suffered only minor losses. Of the 174 convoys, only sixteen lost more than four ships.[80] Whether a successful interception actually took place and Allied ships were sunk depended on a number of factors: the weather and visibility, the success of Allied countermeasures, the availability of airpower, and the composition and skill of the escort.

A significant number of escort ships were now equipped with high-frequency direction-finding gear, which enabled them to fix the position of a shadowing submarine by its radio transmissions. Aircraft, when available, could hunt submarines using airborne radar. Air attacks on submarines were rarely successful, but by forcing them to dive the aircraft could gain valuable time for a convoy to outdistance a U-boat traveling at low submerged speed.

A U-boat attack usually began at night. "A colossal flash leaped from the convoy. In a moment it resolved itself into a tremendous flame which shot upwards from the water accompanied by a roar like the passing of an express train. A great column of fire whose diameter might have been equal to the length of the ship from whose tanks it sprang seemed almost to reach the cloud base. The whole convoy was lit up by its brilliance. . . . Then with equal suddenness the light went out . . . leaving utter blackness . . ."[81]

Other attacks began less dramatically. Ships on the far side of a large convoy might hear only a dull thud. "At first you'd think it was an escort dropping depth charges," recalled Lieutenant Roy Dykes, "then you'd start receiving signals from the senior officer or another corvette where they were reporting that a ship had been attacked."[82]

Sailors in ships struck by a torpedo often had only a few minutes' chance for survival. "We had copper ore in every hold," recalled a merchant seaman, "all heavy stuff, and, as a rule once you got hit, that's it, you're down like a stone wallop. They've got no chance. Down in about a minute. Gone."[83] About 70 percent of merchant ships lost between 1940 and 1944 sank in fifteen minutes or less. Only 11 percent stayed afloat for more than an hour.[84]

Escorts were seldom the primary target of U-boats, but when they were hit, their small size and lack of compartmentalization gave them far less chance of survival than larger warships had. Of the twenty-three Royal Navy corvettes lost in the North Atlantic, just over half sank in under ten minutes. Only seven lasted as long as thirty minutes. Forty of the forty-four destroyers sunk went in under twenty minutes.[85] Corvette sailors were aware of the odds. "The men frequently joked about the matter, often deeming that they were better off if they were unable to swim, for in that case they would be spared the agony of swimming in bitter seas hour after hour," wrote one junior officer. "I still preferred the hope of dying in a comfortable bed . . . and it is certain that most sailors would agree with this hope, for the legend that sailors prefer the idea of drowning as a manner of leaving this world is a creation in the minds of romantic novelists."[86]

If he survived the sinking, a sailor's chances of survival depended on the extent of his injuries, the sea state, and the temperature of the water. A British Medical Research Council study found that the most dangerous time for sailors who survived the initial torpedo hit was in the interval between the time the ship was struck and the time they were able to reach boats, rafts, or other floating wreckage.[87] An officer of the Dutch freighter *Zaanland* described his experience in trying to launch one of the ship's lifeboats. "One moment there was slack in the boat falls, the next moment they were dangerously tight; we were buck jumping all the time. . . . When we got the afterblock free it started to swing dangerously over our heads. . . . Disengaging the forwardblock was impossible and in the end we cut the falls. We saw the other lifeboats also waiting for what was going to happen to our ship. We did not have long to wait, she sank very rapidly. . . . We heard a rumble like thunder."[88]

The sea near a sunken ship would often be covered by blazing oil, and survivors were often covered in oil or had swallowed large quantities of it along with seawater. "We used to have scrambling nets [over the side] but when they're covered in oil it's very difficult to get to grips with them," recalled Frank Richmond, an RNVR lieutenant in corvette *Clematis*. "Just to clean them up was a problem. But to try to expel this oil that was inside them was awful because it went into their lungs and everywhere. . . . Some, of course, would be very badly burned by the explosion or by the petrol catching alight. That often happened."[89]

After an attack the escorts fired parachute flares and began a sweep of the area, listening on their sonar for the telltale "ping-pong" that would indicate the presence of a submarine. Expert sonarmen could easily distinguish the ping of a U-boat from that of a school of fish, a whale, or the bottom of the sea. Once sonar had detected a submarine, the escort would steam in the direction of the contact. "You cannot see the submarine, you only have a mental picture of her," recalled Engine Room Artificer Clifford Simkin. "My reaction was always the same. When the attack started I would become aware of my heartbeat. When the attack started it was a heavy but normal rate; when we increased speed, the prelude dropping depth changes, my heart would increase speed until it raced with mad excitement."[90] When the pings became almost instantaneous, the ship would fire a barrage of depth charges, usually four in number.[91] "The first depth charge . . . would go off at about fifty feet," recalled Leading Seaman Cyril J. Stephens of HMS *Orchis*, "and it was almost as though you were lifted up in the air in the boat and dropped down again. A colossal volume of water would come up and as the depth charges [that] were deeper [exploded] it was almost like lightning going across the water."[92]

Below the surface, moving at low speed, the U-boat could only wait for the escort to lose contact or depart to rejoin their convoy. One U-boat sailor recalled an attack by three destroyers that continued for several hours. "We just had to last it out, though it was almost more than we could stand. . . . There was a frightful crack, just as if the boat had been struck by a giant hammer. Electric bulbs and glasses fly about leaving fragments everywhere. The motors have stopped. . . . We are now using special breathing apparatus to guard against carbon monoxide which may be in the boat."[93]

While some convoys were savaged by U-boats, a more constant enemy was the sea. "Most of the time it was very boring, some of the time it was fairly frightening. And all the time it was very wet,"[94] one sailor succinctly noted. "The world outside was perpetually gray. Sea, horizon, clouds, even the light itself had a dingy look."[95] The constant battle with wind, seas breaking across the deck, and the violent rolling and pitching motion of the ship made even the simplest duties difficult and left sailors in a constant state of fatigue.[96] Although most corvette sailors were young men in their late teens or early twenties, they soon "looked older."[97] The intense convoy battles of late 1942 and 1943 were especially difficult for the Royal Canadian Navy, which by mid-1942 was escorting convoys from Newfoundland as far as Londonderry, in Northern Ireland. As a verse in a popular RCN song succinctly observed, "From Newfy to Derry's a bloody long way."

Derry, in prewar years an economic backwater, hard hit by the depression and divided by age-old sectarian animosities, was by 1942 a major naval base; 149 ships regularly operated from Derry, and another ten or more from other bases were usually in port on any given day. About 11,000 American, British, Canadian, French, Dutch, and Norwegian sailors each month spent their shore leaves in Derry, a city whose prewar population had been less than 50,000.[98]

"Those sailors' lives were at risk every time they sailed out of Derry Quay," recalled longtime Derry resident Billy Gallagher. "None wanted to die for King or country or any other reason and they definitely did not want to go down with money in their pockets."[99] Derry offered plenty of opportunities for thirsty men to part with their money, and the restaurants offered steaks, real butter, and other foods that wartime rationing had made increasingly scarce and sought-after.

American and Canadian sailors were impressed with the beauty of the intense green hillsides surrounding the seaward approach to the city, but they found the frequent rain less appealing. American sailors quipped that the barrage balloons protecting the harbor were actually there "to keep this damned place from sinking."[100]

The impact of these maritime visitors on the town was dramatic. Many years later, wartime residents remembered how the comparatively well-paid American and Canadian sailors would round up gangs of small children and march them to the movie houses after buying each one a large bag of sweets.[101] They also recalled the story of two middle-aged spinsters, devout Catholics, who forgot to pull the blackout curtain over their front window. Late in the evening the ladies were astounded to see the front door open and a group of drunken Canadian sailors burst in. The sailors had noticed the red glow of the lamp in front of the sisters' image of the Sacred Heart and mistaken it for the characteristic red light of a brothel.[102]

Yet the most vivid memories were of the seemingly nonstop fights, between sailors of different ships, different nationalities, entire crews against other crews as well as full-scale riots. "Each successive American, British or Canadian escort group to arrive would take up the fights of the one just departed."[103]

Billy Gallagher believed the largest fight of the war was one that began with two hundred sailors of various nationalities fighting it out in front of a dance hall. Growing larger, the crowd of battling sailors "dispersed into Waterloo Street nearly a solid wedge of sailors fighting, wrecking, cruising down Harvey Street into Chamberlain. . . . The Yankee Shore Patrol arrived. They were charged by the sailors who chased them down the street." Eventually a large detachment of the Royal Ulster Constabulary supported by armored cars was required to break up the riot.[104]

All too soon the sailors' days in the bars, dance halls, restaurants, and brawls of Derry came to an end. Early in the morning, usually in the rain, ships would drop down past the hills of Lough Foyle toward the sea. "As one slipped down the narrow river, peaceful, shuttered cottages passed within biscuit toss. Blue peat smoke rose lazily into the air. . . . A corner of the river would be rounded, the wind would start keening through the rigging and we knew that by nightfall water would be sloshing about between decks and we would be lashing ourselves into our bunks."[105]

While the battle raged in the Atlantic, the government in Ottawa was still intent on using the war to promote the growth of Canada's industries and technology. The armed forces were therefore expected to utilize Canadian-built equipment whenever possible. For the RCN this meant forgoing the opportunity to utilize the excellent new British 271 shipboard radar, which could detect a periscope as far away as half a mile, in favor of Canadian-built SW1C radar, which some sailors claimed could not even detect a large iceberg.[106]

Almost 40 percent of convoys crossing the Atlantic from mid-1942 to January 1943 were escorted by RCN ships. These convoys, escorted by Canadian corvettes and destroyers that lacked modern radar—particularly the new ten-centimeter sets—and direction-finding equipment, suffered a disproportionate share of Allied shipping losses. Between June and December 1942, 80 percent of all sinkings on the transatlantic convoy route came in Canadian-escorted convoys.[107] One of the worst disasters occurred in December 1942 when a westbound slow convoy, ONS154, escorted by a Canadian destroyer and five Canadian corvettes, lost nine ships within two hours and fourteen ships within three days.[108]

The British attributed the poor Canadian performance to lack of training and leadership. "Their communications were bad, their radar was less efficient . . . and they lacked the excellent intensive training facilities which were available in the UK," wrote one British escort commander. "With such material it was folly to assume responsibility for valuable convoys. It would have been wiser if the Canadians had pocketed their pride and sailed their ships with experienced escort groups. . . ."[109]

That was precisely what the Canadian government and naval headquarters were determined to avoid. The RCN had responded to every Allied request, but Ottawa was determined that it should remain a *Canadian* force. There was more than a little irony in British complaints about the ineptness of Canadian escorts, since it was the Royal Navy that had importuned and pressured the Canadians to get as many ships as possible to sea quickly regardless of their state of training. In addition, the high loss rate of Canadian-escorted convoys could be partially accounted for by the fact that they fought more often. About 20 percent of convoys from the British Isles to North America were intercepted by U-boats, but 47 percent of Canadian-escorted convoys had U-boat contacts. The RCN, which provided a little more than 35 percent of Atlantic escorts, fought just over half of all German submarines that were able to make contact with a convoy.[110]

By early December 1942, the British Admiralty was urging that Canadian escort groups be temporarily withdrawn from the mid-Atlantic convoy routes for intensive training or to the less dangerous Gibraltar–United Kingdom route. British escorts from that route would replace the Canadians in the North Atlantic. The Canadian government was surprised and offended at the suggestion that their forces be withdrawn from the major theater of the Battle of the Atlantic. Mackenzie King wrote to Prime Minister Churchill, "It has been our policy to build up Canadian escort forces for the specific purpose of protecting North Atlantic trade convoys. . . . Public interest in the Canadian Navy is centered on the part it has taken in this task, which is without questions one of the highest and most enduring and priority [sic] upon which the outcome of the war depends."[111] It took a personal appeal from Churchill together with assurances from the Admiralty that Canadian groups were only being withdrawn temporarily for training and would be returned to the North Atlantic in three or four months before Ottawa reluctantly agreed to the transfer early in January 1943.

As the Canadian ships redeployed, the British and German navies prepared for what both sides believed would be the climax of the Atlantic campaign. The German Navy now had nearly 240 U-boats available for employment against the convoy routes, and Great Britain was suffering from an acute shortage of oil products. With the Canadian ships largely withdrawn and U.S. ships committed to the escort of troop convoys and deployments around the world, the burden of this campaign fell largely on the Royal Navy. Between the end of January and May a series of protracted battles erupted between the wolf packs and Allied escort groups.

The turning point came with remarkable suddenness. During March, four large Allied convoys were attacked by wolf packs; SC121 from New York to Great Britain lost thirteen of its fifty-two ships in five days of attacks by U-boats. At the same time, HX228 from New York was sighted by a pack of thirteen submarines, but its experienced escort group kept the attackers at bay, sinking two submarines while losing four cargo ships and a destroyer. A few days later a lengthy north-south patrol line of U-boats made contact with two convoys at opposite ends of the line. In the ensuing battle the two convoys were attacked by thirty-eight submarines, which overwhelmed the weak escorts and sank twenty-two out of ninety cargo ships and a destroyer. Only one submarine was lost.

Dismayed by these losses, the British began to think of giving up convoy altogether. Then, at the end of April, a wolf pack composed of more than forty U-boats made contact with ONS5, a slow convoy westbound from England, off the southern tip of Greenland. The number of submarines almost equaled the number of merchant ships in the convoy, yet their attacks proved costly to the Germans. Six submarines were sunk by the escorting ships, and two more were lost in a collision during a night attack. Several other submarines were damaged. Twelve merchantmen had been sunk.

One week later, an eastbound slow convoy, SC130, was intercepted by a large wolf pack. In addition to an experienced escort group commanded by Commander (later Admiral) Peter Gretton, a "hunter-killer group," which stayed with the convoy during its entire passage, protected the convoy. These hunter-killer groups, which included modern fast destroyers and small escort aircraft carriers, had been formed after the disasters of March and April to provide air cover and relieve the ships in the regular convoy escort of the need to leave their stations for extended periods of time to follow up U-boat contacts.

"Water splashed, steel shrieked, ribs moaned, valves blew, deck plates jumped and the boat was thrown into darkness," recalled Herbert Werner, an officer in U-230, whose submarine was attacked in what had been the "air gap" and was forced to crash-dive. "As the light flickered on, I saw astonishment in the round eyes of the men. . . . The idea of a convoy with its own air defenses smashed our basic concept of U-boat warfare." During the next few hours Werner's journal recorded:

11:10: I detected a glint of metal between the clouds. It was a small aircraft diving in to attack.

11:25: U230 surfaced.

11:42: Aircraft-alarm. U230 plunged into the depths.

12:04: We surfaced.

12:08: A call from below reached us on the bridge: Message for Captain. Signal just received, ATTACKED BY AIRCRAFT. SINKING. U89.

12:17: Aircraft dead astern alarm. U230 dived once more.

12:30: We surface again.

13:15: A twin engine plane suddenly dropped out of a low cloud only 800 meters overhead.

13:23: Urgent message to the Captain. ATTACKED BY AIRCRAFT, UNABLE TO DIVE, SINKING. U456.

13:50: Spotted a plane circling four miles ahead.

14:22: Aircraft astern.[112]

U-230 survived, but five other U-boats were sunk by SC130's air and sea escort, and not a single ship of the convoy was sunk or damaged. In attacks on four other convoys during May, the Germans lost six more submarines while failing to sink a single merchant ship.

"In the last two months the Battle of the Atlantic has undergone a decisive change in our favor," wrote Admiral Sir Max Horton, the ex-submariner commanding the convoy war in the Atlantic.[113] All the decisive elements in the Allied anti-submarine campaign had finally converged. The German codes were being read again. More and better-trained escorts were available, improved radar and direction finding was in use, and, as Werner and other submariners were dismayed to discover, the "air gap" had disappeared with the appearance of American B-24 super-long-range bombers and small escort carriers. By the end of May, having lost forty-three submarines in one month, Dönitz ordered his U-boats out of the North Atlantic.

In the immediate tactical sense, it was largely a victory for the Royal Navy, whose ships fought most of the important convoy battles—the last great naval campaign that the British would win alone. In a larger sense the victory was a result of the British and American ability to mobilize, integrate, and direct their enormous scientific and industrial resources to reinforce and supplement their fighting forces.

Few Canadian warships were directly involved in the climactic bat-

tles of April and May 1943, a fact that still causes more than a little ran-
cor among Canadian veterans of the era. Yet had it not been for the
brave and tenacious efforts of Canada's largely amateur sailors, who at
times were providing nearly 40 percent of all North Atlantic escorts,
there would have been no time or opportunity to assemble the decisive
components of the Allied victory in 1943.

Although the Battle of the Atlantic witnessed many dramatic combats, the Allied victory was primarily achieved by *not* fighting. As in
World War I, the best defense of shipping proved to be avoidance of the
enemy through the use of the convoy system. Yet for convoys to be possible, escorts were necessary. It was the success of the system and not the
outcome of individual encounters that determined the course of the battle. In that sense all of the Allied ships that sailed the gray waters of the
North Atlantic between 1939 and 1943 contributed to the final victory.

The Royal Canadian Navy, reinforced by larger and faster anti-
submarine escorts called "frigates," and a new type of corvette, the Castle class, ended the war having escorted more than 25,000 merchantmen
across the North Atlantic and sunk or captured forty-seven U-boats. Although it was a far different force from the enthusiastic novices of 1940,
Canadians retained their distinctive cockiness and individualism. A
Canadian corvette, steaming past Gibraltar in 1945, received the signal
"WHAT SHIP?" She replied, "WHAT ROCK?"

It was some time before the U-boat crews began to realize that the war
had turned against them. Even after the withdrawal from the North Atlantic, U-boat losses continued to be heavy. As the crisis in the Pacific
eased and American war production surged ahead, the United States
Navy reentered the battle in the Central and South Atlantic with more
hunter-killer groups of escort carriers and destroyers. Allied aircraft,
equipped with the new ten-centimeter radar, now ranged the Bay of Biscay, which the U-boats had to cross to reach their French Atlantic bases.
U-boats on the surface, previously shielded by the night or fog, were now
subject to sudden deadly attack from the air. Merchant shipping became
harder to find, while Allied aerial reconnaissance and communications
intelligence made U-boats easier to locate. During August 1943, forty-
one U-boats were lost in the Bay of Biscay. U-boat losses from all causes
reached 237 by the end of the year. Returning to duty in the fall of that
year, Herbert Werner "noticed many empty berths in the bunkers."
Many boats now failed to return. "We all knew that and had to reconcile
ourselves to it. We always saw off the crews of sea-going U-boats and
watched 'til they disappeared from sight. No more parties were given to

celebrate the start of an operation now—we just drank a glass of champagne in silence and shook hands, trying not to look each other in the eyes."[114]

Dönitz was nevertheless determined to continue the submarine war regardless of losses and "even if the goal of achieving greater success is no longer possible because the enemy forces tied up by U-boats are extraordinary."[115] U-boat production continued at a high level, and Dönitz encouraged his officers with promises of new weapons and devices that would restore the advantage to Germany in the undersea war. Among these was an acoustic torpedo, "Zaunkonig," which homed in on the sound of a target ship's propeller. These enjoyed a brief success but proved unreliable and were often defeated by decoy sound devices towed behind surface ships. At the same time, Allied aircraft began employing their own airborne acoustic torpedo, "Fido," against the U-boats.[116]

A more promising device was the "snorkel," a long tube that could be extended like a periscope and sucked in enough air to allow a submarine to start its diesel engines underwater and expel the exhaust. With diesels running, the battery could be recharged without the boat having to expose itself on the surface for long periods. But the production of snorkels and their installation on operational boats proceeded slowly. "The snorkels were a kind of orthopedic contraption—the symbol of the defensive role to which our boats were now reduced," wrote Lothar Günther Buchheim. "It was impossible to make use of the snorkel during daylight hours because the tip, with its valve, produced a rippling wake that was clearly visible from the air and because the exhaust fumes acted like a signal to passing aircraft. . . . Whenever a wave made the valve at the top of the snorkel shut off the air supply to the diesels, the engines satisfied their considerable need for oxygen by draining the air from the boat's interior. At times the men were writhing on the floor in torment as their eardrums burst."[117]

Dönitz's real hope was pinned on the acquisition of an entirely new type of U-boat, the Type XXI, a large deep-diving submarine, the first true submersible, with submerged speed of more than sixteen knots and a very large battery that enabled it to remain submerged for days if necessary. Technical problems and extensive Allied bombing slowed production of the Type XXI, and none were available until the last weeks of the war.

While they waited for Dönitz's miracle weapons, the U-boats continued their increasingly futile patrols. Losses were heavy. During the first half of 1944 almost 130 U-boats were lost, while they succeeded in destroying only about 120 merchantmen. In some months the number of submarines lost exceeded the number of Allied surface ships sunk.[118] British radio intercepts suggested that the younger generation of U-boat commanders were becoming less daring and aggressive and made "repeated and bitter complaints about the ubiquity and efficiency of Allied air patrols."[119] The inexperience of these younger U-boat commanders was itself a source of morale problems. Experienced petty officers divided U-boat captains into two categories: *Draufgangar*—dare devils—and those suffering from *Halsschmerz*—throat pain, that is, the desire to have a Knight's Cross to wear around their neck. The other class, more experienced commanders, were referred to as *Lebensversicherrung*—life insurance.[120]

By the end of the war, 28,000 of the 42,000 men who served in the U-boat arm were dead, a casualty rate of more than 65 percent, and 5,000 were prisoners.[121] Despite these fearful odds and despite the fact that after 1941, men were drafted for U-boat service rather than recruited from volunteers, most U-boat crews continued to carry out their missions as best they could. More than twenty-five U-boats were still at sea at the time of Germany's final surrender on May 8, 1945.

The submariners' devotion to duty, their willingness to serve their country to the last, became a popular theme in many writings about the U-boat war. "The steadfast courage of Dönitz's U-boat men had won the admiration of their bitterest enemies," concluded the author of a popular work on the submarine war in the Time-Life series of maritime histories. "No compulsion was needed to force them to sail out in their iron coffins. . . . Some quiet inward stratum compounded of resignation and adamantine dutifulness was the bedrock of the U-boat arm." A more recent repetition of this theme appeared in Philip Kaplan and Jack Curry's *Wolf Pack: U-Boats at War*, whose dust jacket declared that "the men of the Ubootwaffe were bound together by an intense camaraderie, by ever present dangers, by unity of purpose more powerful than any known to other sailors."[122]

The intense comradeship, common to all submariners, was certainly present, and the quality of leadership always remained high. Yet there were other important inducements both positive and negative. By 1944 all U-boat crewmen under the age of twenty-five had spent their entire adolescence in schools and youth groups oriented to Nazi ideology.[123] It was a relatively easy transition from the Hitler Youth, with its emphasis on adventure, discipline, and devotion to the leader, to the camaraderie and teamwork of a U-boat. By the time they entered the navy, most young men had already internalized the values and ideology of the Nazi state.[124] "My goal in this war is the formation of the Volk, the end of all previous history," wrote a twenty-year-old torpedo boat commander. "I believe in its holy destination and goals, in its reality as a decree of providence. It fights for its existence against a world."[125] Historian Omer Bartov, who examined dozens of German servicemen's letters and diaries for his study *Hitler's Army*, noted "the remarkable extent to which soldiers saw the war through the distorting lens of the regime's ideology. . . . They perceived reality at the front just as he [Hitler] did in the safety of his bunker, sharing his fantasies of conquest and grandeur of racial genocide and Germanic world rule."[126]

Like most younger members of the armed forces, U-boat men had a strong faith in the infallibility of the Führer, a faith encouraged by Admiral Dönitz, who admired Hitler intensely and shared the values of the Nazi leadership. In January 1944, Dönitz declared that "the battle for our people's freedom and justice continues. . . . The Führer shows us the way and the goal. We follow him with body and soul to a great German future."[127] Every three months, Admiral Dönitz came around to encourage his U-boat crews. "He always left me with the same impression of a reliable and energetic man perfectly confident that final victory would be achieved," recalled a U-boat commander. "He met all criticisms by short clipped references to ultra modern U-boats that could do quite fabulous things. . . . He argued that if he couldn't judge the situation then nobody could. He was continually seeing Hitler and the feeling at headquarters was one of complete confidence and rightly so. The Luftwaffe was trying out new prototypes and very soon we should see a complete turn of the tide in our favor, but we must hold on for the moment."[128] Even if he failed to share Dönitz's unshakable confidence in victory, the U-boat sailor had no trouble imagining the consequences of defeat. Like many citizens of the Third Reich, he feared that Germany's enemies and victims might well do unto the Germans what the Germans had done unto them.[129] A sailor captured from a U-boat at the end of 1942 told interrogators that the Germans "had shot and sterilized so many Poles he believed if Germany lost the war a huge number of his countrymen would be sterilized in return. He understood that 20,000 British doctors had already been mobilized for this purpose."[130]

Beyond ideology and propaganda, a complex system of rewards and punishments kept submariners at their duties. The rewards were ample. Despite the hazards and hardships of their calling, U-boat men were, in many ways, the pampered elite of the German armed forces. Their pay was almost twice as high as that of other sailors, and "they never lacked for specially prepared food for long patrols, nor for coffee, tea or chocolate. Surface crews received such things only in small rations, while the civilian population, of course, never received any of these items at all."[131]

Submarines returning to French Atlantic ports were greeted by bands and young nurses bearing fruit and flowers. Then followed extended leaves. Special trains transported U-boat men back to their homes in Germany, while other crewmembers vacationed at seaside resorts or commandeered French chateaux. Herbert Werner recalled "a 17th century castle nestling among rolling hills. . . . The food and wine were French and of excellent quality. The eating started early and continued late. The dancing ended after midnight as the lucky couples disappeared one by one into upstairs rooms where the drapery was velvet and bedding pure silk."[132]

At the opposite end of the spectrum lay grim punishments for sailors who appeared to lack loyalty, reliability, or commitment. SS operatives ashore and special "National Socialist Leadership officers" aboard U-boats kept a close eye on submariners for signs of disloyalty or defeatism. Ever present was the possibility of transfer to a penal battalion on the eastern front . . . or worse. One U-boat commander, Kapitanleutnant Oskar Kusch, one of the few to openly criticize the conduct of the war, was reported for sedition by his first officer, an ardent Nazi, and tried and shot.[133] The much-touted loyalty of Dönitz to his officers and of the officers to each other apparently had its limits.

In the course of almost six years of war, the U-boat men had managed to kill 30,000 merchant seamen, and sink 2,700 merchant ships and 175 men-of-war but never came near to winning the war. The entry of the two great North American powers had doomed Germany at sea as surely as her war on Russia had doomed her on land. The Battle of the Atlantic had brought the interface between industry, science, technology, and human beings in war at sea to a new level of complexity. To an unprecedented extent, navies were now dependent on shore installations, not only for supply and maintenance, as traditionally had been the case, but also for communications, intelligence, and command and control. Both the German submarine assault and the defense of convoys were directed from ashore. Industrial and scientific triumphs played a large role in their success or failure. Especially important was the Allies' ability to mobilize unprecedented levels of manpower to provide the sailors for the labor-intensive battle against the submarine. It was a contest between a small highly trained elite and a large scratch force of novice sailors, aging reservists, college students, and half-trained officers and civilians. In the end the scratch team won.

THIRTEEN

"THE HAVES AND THE HAVE-NOTS"

I t was June 6, 1944. As the sun rose over Majuro Atoll in the Marshall Islands, the fifteen American aircraft carriers, seven battleships, ten cruisers, and sixty destroyers anchored in the spacious blue-green waters of the lagoon were getting under way. While Allied troops in England—where it was still June 5—completed their final preparations for landing in Normandy, the massive American fleet steamed out of the lagoon. Almost all of the carriers and more than half of the battleships, cruisers, and destroyers had joined the fleet after the Battle of the Santa Cruz Islands. So vast was the assemblage of ships that it was almost five hours before the last vessel cleared the anchorage. Their destination was Saipan in the Marianas, only twelve hundred miles southeast of Japan.[1]

Only sixteen months had passed since the end of the Guadalcanal campaign. In that time the Americans had advanced more than three thousand miles through the tiny island chains of the Central Pacific, captured or destroyed the Japanese outposts in the Solomons, neutralized the Combined Fleet's major bases at Rabaul and Truk, and driven the Japanese back to the westernmost edge of New Guinea. In late 1943 the slow advance through the South Pacific toward Rabaul had been matched by an entirely new drive across the Central Pacific toward the Marshalls, Carolines, and Marianas along the lines anticipated in the old Orange Plan. Beginning haltingly with costly assaults on Tarawa and Makin in the Gilberts, the Central Pacific advance picked up speed in early 1944 with Nimitz's decision to strike boldly into the heart of the Marshalls at Kwajalein. A quick success there prompted the Pacific commanders and the Joint Chiefs of Staff to shorten their original timetable and seize the rest of the Marshalls during February rather than in May. Meanwhile, MacArthur and Halsey had isolated Rabaul and MacArthur had pushed on to the western end of New Guinea with a daring landing at Hollandia, bypassing an entire Japanese army.

Like their ships, most of the sailors were new to the Pacific and to the navy. The battles of 1942 and 1943 had been fought by men who had entered the service before Pearl Harbor. The officers mainly had been Annapolis men, reinforced by the reservists of the various aviation training programs. The sailors were volunteers who had joined the service to escape poverty and unemployment, to travel and see the world. Now, these men were reinforced by thousands of newcomers who had joined only to fight the war. "We had ex-farmers and policemen and horse trainers and salesmen, clerks and municipal employees, school teachers and deacons," one destroyer captain recalled.[2] The number of officers and enlisted men had expanded twentyfold by 1944. There had been 21,000 line officers in 1941, and by 1944 there were more than 206,000; the 3,400 aviators of 1941 had swelled to 37,000. Compared to about 250,000 enlisted men in 1941, there were now almost 3 million, including about 90,000 women.[3] The Marine Corps grew from 50,000 men in 1941 to more than 300,000 men and women in 1944.[4] While most navy recruits prior to Pearl Harbor had been youths in search of jobs and adventure, many of the wartime sailors were men with more substantial backgrounds. "We got a lot of older men from the States in their forties and fifties with big families about 3 weeks ago," wrote Seaman First Class James Fahey of the cruiser *Montpelier*. "It is a tough blow to send a man with children overseas. The new men who just came aboard would give anything to be back with their families."[5]

Every month, thousands of recruits passed through the navy's Great Lakes Naval Training Center near Chicago, where they learned basic seamanship, infantry drill, and military discipline under the attentive ministrations of perpetually angry chief petty officers. After a long train ride to the Midwest, most recruits' initial introduction to the navy was a hurried, rather rudimentary medical examination followed by a haircut "shorter than short." Recruits slept in hammocks lashed to steel rods, an experience one sailor compared to "sleeping on a tight clothesline." "When you manage to get into [a hammock] you lay there rigid like the filling of a cigar because if you moved at all you rolled out and found yourself stunned on the deck. Often at night petty officers would come around to test the tightness of the hammocks or merely to have their own kind of fun by dumping sleeping boots onto the deck. If anyone murmured the slightest protest he carried his full seabag lashed into his hammock for hours."[6] The training companies were under the command of experienced chief petty officers, usually fresh from sea duty, who sub-jected the "boots" to a steady barrage of verbal and sometimes physical abuse. One chief, a southerner, professed to be appalled to find himself in charge of a company of "Yankees" from the Midwest. "If I ever see a ship sailing upside down, I'll know you knuckle-headed Yankees will be on it."[7] By late 1942, however, most of the chiefs with sea experience had been recalled to the fleet and replaced by physical education teachers and other athletes co-opted by the navy from civilian life. Few recruits found them an improvement.

Boots spent long hours cleaning their barracks to standards far beyond any conventional measure of cleanliness and long hours on "the grinder," the training center's two-block concrete drill ground, baking in the summer sun or shivering in the freezing lake winds of winter. The unrelenting former phys ed teachers "ran us in formation miles wherever we had to go . . . on occasions when we merely marched, we had to sing 'Anchors Away' or 'Everybody Loves the Navy of the U.S.A.'—a very dubious proposition."[8]

A few men found the life intolerable and adopted various expedients to escape from the navy. Frank Albert encountered such a man in boot camp. "The day before graduation, our barracks was slated for a major in-spection by the commanding officer. My buddy, the one that has been trying to figure a way out of the Navy, was named Captain of the Head. I was on his detail. We had those toilets shining. . . . As the captain walked in, the bugler sounded attention. That captain went through the head with a fine tooth comb . . . not a speck of dust. We passed with fly-ing colors. Just as he turned his back to address his Marine orderly, my buddy . . . broke a Baby Ruth candy bar in half and threw it into one of the toilets. When the Captain heard the splash he yelled, 'What the hell is that?' My buddy retrieved it, took a bite and threw it back, yelling (with a snappy salute), 'That's shit sir.' He was out of the Navy the very next day with a Section 8."[9] The great majority of less imaginative sailors left boot camp after four weeks for specialized training schools or went directly to sea. After 1942, the ship in which most sailors went to sea for the first time was the one in which they went to war.

Although the navy was expanding at an exponential rate it was able to provide a cadre of experienced leaders for almost all of its new units, largely due to the slow promotion rates in the navy of the 1930s, which had created a large backlog of experienced seamen. Battleship sailors in the pre–Pearl Harbor Navy, for example, had to sit for the same competitive examinations a dozen times or more before advancing in rate. "There were so many men and so few advancements."[10] Once war began, however, these men could be rapidly promoted to higher rank and train others in their field of expertise. Aboard the destroyer *Saufley*, commissioned in 1942, "Only 30 percent had ever been to sea before. The rest of the crew were civilians who had joined after Pearl Harbor. . . .Our regular navy crew included good officers and chiefs. The enlisted men included Asiatic Fleet survivors, men from the brigs and hard-to-control men from almost any other area in the navy. They all liked whiskey, girls and liberty. The new volunteers were ours to mold and we molded them in the same fashion we had been molded."[11] These sailors of the old navy were to provide the crucial component of leadership and experience to the fast-growing ranks of inexperienced enlisted men—as well as to thousands of inexperienced officers, for by 1944 the navy's officer corps was a far different entity from what it had been four years earlier.

While prewar navy leaders must have recognized that additional officers would be needed to man the expanded fleet, already under construction by 1940, "the Bureau of Navigation made no plans for officer procurement which did not crumble before the realities of the Second World War." As late as January 1941, the bureau's plans were based on the assumption that an additional 10,000 officers would meet the needs of a wartime navy.[12] The number of peacetime reserve officers had been kept to a bare minimum, perhaps because of fears that reserve officers on active duty might "hold up promotion for naval academy graduates."[13] In actuality more than 286,000 naval officers were added to the fleet between December 1941 and the end of 1944. Less than 1 percent were graduates of Annapolis. Unlike the army and Marine Corps, which drew the great majority of their wartime officers from experienced noncommissioned officers and enlisted men who successfully completed officer candidate school, the navy drew only 2 percent of its officer trainees from the ranks and less than 19 percent of its new officers from experienced sailors. Instead, almost 130,000 new wartime officers received direct commissions from civil life and another 84,000 were commissioned through officer training programs that they entered without having served any time as enlisted men.[14]

In both cases the key requirement was a college degree. Until 1943 almost no man or woman who failed to meet this requirement could be considered for a commission in the navy.[15] After 1943 the Bureau of Naval Personnel reluctantly agreed to consider men with only two years of college "plus 5 years of good business experience," and some men over thirty were accepted on the basis of "an outstanding business record alone."[16]

So thorough was the navy's preoccupation with obtaining only college graduates for its officer corps that undergraduates still in their first or second year of college were provided the opportunity to be commissioned as officers though the so-called "V programs," which allowed them to complete college and enter the navy upon graduation. Whether either a college education or "an outstanding business record" was superior to seagoing experience or the rigors of an officer candidate school as criteria for the selection of naval officers was a question that scarcely occurred to navy leaders. The official history refers to the college-graduates-only standard as a "scantly debated decision." The rationale most frequently offered was that "the technical equipment of a naval officer justified the insistence on a good college education as a fundamental criterion."[17]

In a service so dependent on science and technology, this policy seemed eminently logical. Yet in reality, many hastily commissioned officers found little direct relationship between their academic training and their navy assignments. "The job didn't really require much knowledge," recalled one officer of his first seagoing assignment. "It turned out to be a real small ship and the guys, the most important guys on the ship, were the few enlisted men and one petty officer who knew mechanics and electricity. And we had several of those guys and they were the ones who were critical to the running of the ship."[18] Louis R. Harlan "added science courses including an entire year of physics in the expectation that its abstractions would somehow be transmogrified into useful knowledge when I became a naval officer. In fact, I never found any use whatever for physics in the Navy."[19]

An unstated but more compelling reason for the navy's insistence on college education for its officers may have been the social preferences of the career officers. If they were now compelled by necessity to share the bridge and the wardroom with non-Annapolis graduates they could at least ensure that these came from acceptable segments of society. "Officers and crew were set apart into the haves and the have-nots in different uniforms as though in the service of separate nations," recalled Louis Harlan. "Officers came from college—that was the crucial difference—and enlisted men straight out of high school or from blue-collar work. . . . In the 1940s college was only for the favored few, for those whose parents could afford to send them or help them through. To graduate from college or even to have been there, put one immediately on a higher status plateau. The Navy's hierarchical structure, its ranks and orders, challenged the democratic political credo of American society, but also reflected in high relief America's hierarchical social reality."[20]

College students and graduates who successfully passed a written test, a physical examination, and a series of interviews were assigned to midshipman's school for 90 to 120 days of training. Promptly labeled "90-Day Wonders," the graduates of the midshipman's schools often saw the ocean for the first time after they graduated and had been ordered to duty. Alfred Nisonoff, who served as an officer aboard an amphibious ship at Okinawa, trained at Plattsburgh, New York. "The only thing they used Lake Champlain for was passing the swimming test. . . . It was really a farce because we were learning gunnery and there were no guns. Learning about these parts in a gun and we didn't have a gun to play with."[21] Louis Harlan recalled that aside from a morning spent aboard a training ship his most extended seagoing experience had been aboard the Statue of Liberty ferry.[22]

With such training behind them most 90-Day Wonders felt less than total confidence when they joined their ships. "We suffered most (and this fact has been too generally ignored) from lack of confidence in ourselves and in those above and below us in rank and responsibility," recalled a sailor who served in an LST (Landing Ship Tank).[23] This problem of inexperience was exacerbated by the navy's practice of manning less imposing warships—destroyer escorts, minesweepers, subchasers, and amphibious craft—almost exclusively with reservists. When Lieutenant Commander Charles Chester took command of a new destroyer escort in 1944, he discovered that "the only officer aboard qualified to stand deck watches was the chief engineer who was not required to stand them."[24]

Many of these new types of officers went to new types of ships. As the Orange Plan had anticipated, the American advance across the Pacific soon became an island war featuring amphibious assault by heavily armed marine units backed by the guns and aircraft of the fleet. In the Southwest Pacific, MacArthur and Halsey's forces also moved mainly by sea to attack key points along the north New Guinea coast and up the chain of the central and northern Solomon islands.

By 1943 the Allies had developed a whole family of amphibious ships. The largest of the new vessels was the diesel-powered Landing Ship Tank, universally called the LST, a three-hundred-foot seagoing vessel that could carry more than two thousand tons of cargo in its cavernous interior. Its shallow draft enabled it to run right up onto or very close to a coral, sand, or mud beach, then discharge its cargo through the large doors and ramp in its bow. Its low speed and lack of maneuverability caused many sailors to declare that LST stood for "Large Stationary Target." Pacific commanders were soon busy adding extra antiaircraft guns to its original scanty armament.[25] Another seagoing amphibian was the LCI, Landing Craft Infantry, considerably smaller and faster than the LST, which discharged its troops and equipment down gangways hinged to a platform on the bow, "and lucky were the troops who got ashore in water less than shoulder high."[26] The smallest of the new beaching craft was the LCT, Landing Craft Tank, a bargelike vessel about 120 feet long, with a bow ramp that could be lowered to discharge its cargo of medium tanks or heavy vehicles. LCTs were normally transported overseas in sections and reassembled at their destination.

Leon Cannick had been out of midshipman's school less than two months when he was assigned command of an LCT. "We were supposed to have six weeks of training. When I got there . . . they told me right off there's no three [sic] weeks of training at all. Forget that. The next day they gave me my crew who were far more up on LCTs than I was. . . . I went out one day with another skipper and his crew. Then I went out the second day with my crew and another skipper on my boat. Then the third day they said 'there you are.'"[27] One of Cannick's fellow LCT skippers astounded an admiral by explaining that he could keep his ship out of the rays of the moon by zigzagging.[28]

Yet the navy's instincts in officer selection proved not wholly mistaken. The hordes of half-trained wholly inexperienced college students, professionals, and men with "an outstanding business record" quickly transformed themselves into a highly effective body of leaders and specialists. Wall Street bankers became combat intelligence officers. English majors became navigators, advertising men and lawyers became fighter director officers, mathematicians and musicians became code breakers. Overall, the ROTC graduates and 90-Day Wonders brought a breadth of experience and outlook to their jobs that was to prove invaluable in the rapidly changing arena of war. Captain Slade Cutter, a leading submarine commander, considered reservists in some ways superior to regulars. "The navy system promotes a hesitancy to do something without proper authority. . . . Academy graduates when they first got out there . . . would always say 'Captain to the bridge,' they didn't want to make a decision 'til the captain got up there. Your reserve—you never had to worry about him—he would do something. It might be wrong, but he would do it. And they didn't make too many mistakes."[29] Despite this, the navy "steadfastly denied" command of a submarine to even the most experienced and competent reservists until 1945.[30]

The navy's determination to keep the officer corps a social elite was matched by its tenacity in preserving the navy as an organization only open to white men. "Our taxes help keep up the Naval Academy where our boys may not attend," declared the NAACP magazine, *Crisis*, in 1940. "They help to maintain the numerous naval bases, navy yards and naval air bases from which we are excluded. . . . The training in numerous trades and skills which thousands of whites receive and use later in civilian life is not for us. . . . This is the price we pay for being classified as a race of mess attendants only! At the same time we are supposed to be able to appreciate what our white fellow citizens declare to be the 'vast difference' between American democracy and Hitlerism."[31]

In response to such arguments, the navy's senior officers generally took the position, as they had since the turn of the century, that crowded shipboard living conditions made it impossible to have African-Americans in rates other than messman.[32] "It is no kindness to the Negroes to thrust them upon men of the white race," declared Navy Secretary Frank Knox.[33] If integration was undesirable, segregation was impractical. The navy had neither the desire nor the resources to commission a fleet of ships crewed only by black sailors. Besides, many naval officers doubted that a sufficient number of African-Americans with the proper skills and aptitude for sea duty could ever be found, "even if you had the entire Negro population of the United States to choose from."[34] The Bureau of Naval Personnel believed that "the Negroes' relative unfamiliarity with the sea" gave them a "consequent fear of water."[35]

With the outbreak of war, the navy soon found that it was unable to maintain its traditional racial policies. Pressure from politicians, journalists, black community leaders, and the White House eventually had forced the navy and Marine Corps to begin accepting African-Americans for general service. The navy had continued to insist that only whites could serve on seagoing men-of-war. As a result, thousands of African-Americans were enlisted and later drafted into the navy to serve in harbor craft, in a few technical specialties, in the newly formed Naval Construction Battalions, or Seabees, and at naval supply and ammunition depots.

In June 1942, the navy opened a new, but segregated, boot camp for black recruits in an isolated section of Great Lakes Naval Training Center near Chicago. Named Camp Robert Smalls, after a black naval hero of the Civil War, this establishment was commanded by Lieutenant Commander Daniel Armstrong, an Annapolis graduate and son of the founder of Hampton Institute. Armstrong was a capable administrator who considered himself a genuine friend of African-Americans. But his peculiar administrative style and paternalistic philosophy caused problems for both white and black sailors at Camp Robert Smalls. White of-

ficers and petty officers complained that he was inclined to give black recruits special treatment and more lenient punishments. Aware of this
reputation, company commanders were inclined to handle their disciplinary problems by "taking a recalcitrant into a closed room, where there
were no witnesses and beating him."[36] For their part, black recruits resented what they considered Armstrong's patronizing attitude expressed
in such policies as having recruits "learn and recite a creed . . . dealing
with the advancement of the Negro race and having them sing spirituals
en masse on Sunday evenings."[37]

Leaving Camp Smalls for duty, many black sailors soon discovered
that navy service held many more unpleasant surprises besides compul-
sory singing. A small number of African-Americans did serve aboard
harbor and coastal patrol vessels or in technical specialties ashore, but
the majority served in less rewarding jobs. More than half of all African-
American sailors worked as unskilled laborers at supply bases, air stations, and ammunition depots in the United States. Another 7,000
served overseas with the Naval Construction Battalions. Some 38,000
served in the messman branch, now grown to enormous size to accommodate the large number of new ships and additional officers in the
wartime navy.[38]

In the segregated navy only the members of the steward branch could
fulfill the classic sailor's role, to fight at sea. When the ship was in action,
the cooks, stewards, and messmen often served as gun crews for one or
more of the numerous antiaircraft guns that were rapidly installed in
men-of-war after the first sea-air battles. And even before these installations had begun, Doris Miller, a steward's mate aboard the battleship
West Virginia, had become the first African-American hero of the war
when he manned a machine gun during the Pearl Harbor attack and
brought down two Japanese planes.

To many whites the presence of African-Americans as fighters and
not merely servants at sea must have proved disconcerting. After all,
part of the argument for the exclusion of blacks from the naval service
was precisely that they could not perform satisfactorily in these roles. Tra-
ditionalists reacted in two ways. Navy leaders praised the bravery of a
handful of "boys" like Miller who had been commended or decorated
for their bravery and recounted their achievements in language which
was often simultaneously laudatory and condescending. One African-
American hero was described in a magazine story entitled "The Messboy
of Squadron X." The subject of the story was "a favorite with the whole
squadron . . . as he scurried from table to table . . . his ebony face shining." His handwriting and spelling were so bad, however, that the ship's

censor told him that "less'n I could write better I couldn't write mor'n two pages to my wife. . . . He said he couldn't pass my last one nohow cause he couldn't read no part of it." After the messboy, acting as ammunition passer, replaces a wounded gunner and shoots down two enemy planes, a yeoman volunteers to type his letters for him. He was reported to have written his wife that he was "mighty glad that a little colored boy from down in Texas got a chance to do his bit."[39]

Not publicized, but far more widespread in larger ships, were persistent rumors that black gun crews panicked or froze in action. How any individual behaved during the confusion and terror of naval action is difficult if not impossible to document. Officers almost invariably reported that all hands performed well, since to do otherwise might reflect poorly on their own leadership. Yet it is significant that only stories about black sailors behaving timidly were widely reported. Among white sailors such stories may have provided a means of displacing their own anxieties and fears of displaying cowardice, while reassuring themselves that those they considered unworthy to be warriors really were different.[40]

Working long hours in menial, unpleasant, monotonous, and tiring jobs, with little prospect of promotion and commanded by inexperienced, sometimes incompetent white officers, black sailors ashore felt angry and frustrated. In June 1943 a riot occurred at a naval ammunition depot in Virginia. The following month more than seven hundred African-Americans of the 80th Construction Battalion staged a protest over segregation aboard the transport that was carrying them to their duty station in the Caribbean.

These signs compelled the navy to reexamine its racial policies. Top civilians in the Navy Department, such as Under Secretary James V. Forrestal and his special assistant Adlai Stevenson, who held far more progressive views than Secretary Knox, began pressing for new initiatives to eliminate discrimination and create additional opportunities for African-Americans. They were joined by Lieutenant Commander Christopher Sargent, who, in peacetime, was a member of the powerful law firm of Covington and Burling. Sargent, whose influence in Washington far exceeded his naval rank, worked tirelessly to break down racial barriers in the navy. Yet, the admirals still refused to consider assigning African-Americans to seagoing warships except as messmen. "You couldn't dump two hundred colored boys on a crew in a battle," declared the chief of the Bureau of Naval Personnel.[41] Nevertheless, he did agree to assign all-black crews to serve under white officers and petty officers aboard a newly commissioned destroyer escort and a subchaser as a test of the ability of black sailors to serve at sea. The destroyer escort *Mason* was commissioned in March 1944 and served on convoy duty in the Atlantic until the end of the war. As time passed her white petty officers and some of her junior officers were gradually replaced by African-Americans.

Although the U-boat threat had largely abated by the time the *Mason* went to sea, her sailors found the sea itself as formidable an opponent as ever. "In the North Atlantic when the water hits the steel deck it turns to ice," recalled Radioman Benjamin Garrison. "If a line was two inches thick, by the time it hit it got four times as big, and difficult to handle. . . . You can't walk upright. . . . The ship is rolling and pitching. . . . The handrails were only waist high. If the deck was slanting and you lost your grip you were gone. . . . It's rough, it's dark, total darkness. It's slippery. The ship is bucking up and down, right and left."[42]

In the end the North Atlantic weather provided the men of the *Mason* with their greatest challenge. In October 1944, NY119, a slow convoy that included tugs towing barges and car floats, escorted by *Mason* and four other destroyer escorts, encountered a massive Atlantic gale with forty-foot seas and wind gusts of ninety miles an hour. In the heavy weather the unwieldy barges quickly became unmanageable. Two tugs capsized as the barges to which they were attached plunged beneath the towering sea. The *Mason* was sent ahead with the faster ships of the convoy to make for Falmouth and then return with additional ships to bring in the tugs and barges, now almost stationary in the face of the winds and mountainous seas.[43]

At 6:00 P.M. that same day the *Mason* brought all twenty of her charges safely into Falmouth Harbor. Two hours later she was again under way headed back toward the slower elements of the convoy, still scattered about in the storm. Two Royal Navy sloops, ordered to accompany *Mason*, reported that they could make no headway in the forty-foot seas and turned back. The *Mason*, although damaged by the storm, continued on alone, making four knots while her engines made revolutions for twelve. Over the next two days, as the storm gradually abated, the *Mason* rejoined the remainder of the convoy and shepherded the surviving small craft to safety. It was an outstanding display of seamanship and determination that earned the ship special praise in the convoy commodore's report. After the *Mason* no one could doubt how blacks would perform at sea.[44]

Although blacks and whites served aboard the *Mason* with little friction, ashore and in port black sailors were constantly reminded that they still belonged to a segregated navy. "We had four ships tied up together and we were on the outer most side. To get back to the pier we had to cross every one of those ships," recalled Radioman James W. Graham. "There would be off-duty sailors on the ships and they would say some derogatory remarks as we passed. 'He's from the nigger ship' or 'Here come the coons.'"[45] In Charleston, a crowd of white shipyard workers, angered by the sight of white USO girls performing aboard the *Mason*, attempted to board the ship. "The Captain had us man our battle stations and we trained the guns on them. That stopped it. Really though we didn't need the guns. We could have taken them on one by one."[46]

A month after the *Mason* was commissioned, Navy Secretary Frank Knox died and was succeeded by Forrestal. A former naval aviator and Wall Street investment banker, the new secretary had been a member of the Urban League, a moderate civil rights organization. Forrestal believed that a segregated fleet, along the lines of the *Mason* experiment, was both impractical and undesirable. Instead, Forrestal began to take the first steps toward dismantling the whites-only navy. A handful of black officers, "the golden thirteen," had already been commissioned, and Forrestal pressed for more. With the support of Admiral King, he began the assignment of black sailors to "general service" (non-messman) duties at sea aboard fleet oilers, repair ships, and other auxiliaries. Black women were also admitted to the Waves, the navy's female branch. Specialized training schools were desegregated, and Lester Granger, a former head of the Urban League, joined the Navy Department as the secretary's special adviser on racial policy in 1944.[47]

All of this came too late to make much difference in the lives of most African-American sailors. The great majority of black sailors never went to sea except as waiters, cooks, or bakers. The rest continued as construction workers, warehousemen, and stevedores. In 1944 there were more racial incidents. At Port Chicago, at Mare Island Navy Yard, California, two ammunition ships exploded, killing more than three hundred people including about two hundred African-Americans serving in cargo-handling battalions at the ammunition depot. Those who survived, not surprisingly, concluded that the conditions were too hazardous to continue working. Refusing to return to work, they were charged with mutiny, and fifty sailors were convicted on this charge and sent to prison, although they were later granted clemency after strenuous efforts by Lester Granger and the NAACP, represented by future Supreme Court justice Thurgood Marshall.

A few months later, racial tensions exploded on the newly captured island of Guam in the Marianas, which was being rapidly converted into a major headquarters and supply base. The trouble grew out of fights between white marines and black sailors of the naval supply depot over relations with local women in the town of Agana. While fights between marines and sailors were far from rare, the trouble on Guam soon took on racial overtones. Marines in trucks or jeeps roared by the supply company camps, yelling racial insults and threats; they were met with showers of rocks from the sailors.[48] The situation was made worse by a lack of experienced leaders and effective discipline. All of the supply depot company's officers were inexperienced young white ensigns and lieutenants junior grade, some of the men with "an outstanding business record" to whom the navy had given direct commissions. The units also lacked experienced petty officers of either race.[49] The military police and shore patrol on the island was exclusively white.

In the face of repeated threats from white marines, the sailors began to arm themselves illicitly with rifles and knives. The marines, of course, had ready access to weapons. The spark that touched off the final explosion was the shooting of a black sailor by a white sailor in Agana on the night of December 24. That same night, shots were fired into one of the supply camps. Groups of black sailors commandeered trucks and attempted to drive to Agana but were stopped by military police. A riot and more shootings followed.

A navy court of inquiry was appointed to investigate the incident. The president of the court was an amiable officer, chiefly noted for his ability to ingest 190-proof torpedo alcohol. "He was just a nice guy with a little too much rank for his capability," recalled one sailor. "He wasn't the kind of officer to put in charge of an inquiry if you were really trying to find out anything, so he was probably perfect for the job."[50] Most of the African-Americans involved in the riot refused to testify before the all-white court of inquiry. Even a visit by the executive secretary of the NAACP, Walter White, failed to persuade them to come forward.[51]

The court found that while there was "an unfortunate tendency on the part of comparatively very few white service personnel to indulge in the use of slighting and insulting terms and acts of personal aggression applied to individuals of the Negro race on the Island . . . there is no organized or concerted racial prejudice or discrimination existing in the armed forces on the island of Guam." The court also deplored what it believed to be "a comparatively much more widespread tendency among a high percentage of Negro troops to magnify and accentuate the racial prejudice of a few white service individuals, to seek personal and unlawful redress, to foster groundless rumors of racial discrimination."[52] Given the navy's racial attitudes and assumptions, the court's conclusions were hardly surprising.

While the court thus found the status quo satisfactory, Admiral Nimitz, who had just moved his headquarters to Guam, was infuriated and, with King and Forrestal, was determined to move toward a deliberate policy of integration in the navy. This was finally achieved in February 1946 when the Bureau of Naval Personnel issued a circular letter notifying commanders that "effective immediately all restrictions governing types of assignments for which Negro personnel are eligible are hereby lifted. Henceforth they shall be eligible for all types of assignments in all ratings in all activities in all ships of the Naval Service." By the close of the war, the U.S. Navy had become, in policy, the most racially integrated of all the services. In practice it remained the least. Following V-J Day, the regular Navy had 7,000 black officers and sailors, just more than 2 percent of the total naval force, and nine out of ten of these black sailors were in the steward branch.[53]

While the idea of black sailors was unwelcome to many naval professionals, even more agreed with Senator David Walsh, the Naval Affairs Committee chairman, that women sailors would lead "to the decline of civilization." Rear Admiral John Towers, the chief of the Bureau of Aeronautics, saw it differently. Since the days of Admiral Moffett, aviation had been the most dynamic element in the navy, and Towers and his associates were long accustomed to looking outside the traditional navy organization for ideas and talented people. Just as aviation had been the first to welcome large numbers of reservists, so it now took the lead in incorporating women.

Towers had learned from Captain Ralph Ofstie, an aviator who had served as naval attaché in London, about the work of women in the Royal Navy, which had begun to recruit them even before the outbreak of World War II.[54] Originally assigned to replace male sailors as secretaries, cooks, telegraphists, code clerks, telephone operators, and drivers, the Women's Royal Naval Service, universally called the WRENS, quickly expanded into other occupations and specialties. "This is in praise of the WRENS," wrote an unknown bard in *Punch:*

> Boat WRENS, coder WRENS, steward WRENS.
> Quarters WRENS, general duties WRENS
> WRENS ashore and afloat
> Rolling off signals—"TOP SECRET" "IMPORTANT"
> WRENS in the dock yard
> WRENS on an MTV's deck

> With greasy small wrists and a spanner
> Plotting WRENS, messengers, sparkers
> Torpedo WRENS, ordnance WRENS, cooks
> Trim bright staunch overworked
> And, let it be gladly proclaimed,
> Utterly indispensable.[55]

Wrens also composed part of the crew of HMS *Philante*, the anti-submarine school training ship at Derry.[56] By 1944 there were more than 90,000 Wrens in the Royal Navy. Joy Hancock, the civilian head of public relations in the Bureau of Aeronautics (BUAER) returned from Canada with similar reports of women in the Royal Canadian Navy and Air Force.[57] At the same time, Captain Arthur Radford, head of the training section of the BUAER, was aware that dozens of new schools and airfields would soon be commissioned for the large-scale pilot training programs then getting under way. Radford began planning to employ women as instructors, technicians, machinists, and metalsmiths and in other essential duties in the training effort.[58]

Women's advocates, led by Eleanor Roosevelt and Congresswoman Edith Nourse Rogers, had succeeded in pressing the army into establishing a Women's Army Auxiliary Corps in late 1941, but the navy had remained unresponsive. When the chief of the Bureau of Naval Personnel queried navy bureaus and headquarters on positions that women could fill, most replied that they had few or none. Even while the Bureau of Naval Personnel was concluding that women were not needed, Towers and BUAER were working behind the scenes to push legislation through the House and Senate allowing women to serve in the navy. Congressman Melvin Maas, a Marine Corps Reserve aviator, was persuaded by a woman friend to introduce a bill, an amendment to the Naval Reserve Act of 1938, providing for a women's reserve. At the same time, Lieutenant Commander George Anderson of BUAER, who was related to Senator Walsh's legislative assistant, plied the senator with food and drink until Walsh, after several scotches, agreed to withdraw his opposition on condition "that the morals of these girls will be protected and never will anybody propose that they be sent to ships."[59] Legislation creating a women's division of the Naval Reserve, soon labeled "the Waves," passed Congress at the end of July 1942. Mildred McAfee, president of Wellesley College, was appointed director of the Waves with the rank of lieutenant commander. BUAER immediately requested 23,000 Wave officers and sailors.

McAfee's first challenge was to squelch a proposal that the Waves be fitted with a comic-opera red-white-and-blue-striped uniform.[60] Instead, Mrs. James B. Forrestal, wife of the Navy Under Secretary, arranged for a well-known fashion designer, Mainbocher of New York, to design a dignified but stylish set of uniforms that proved so successful they remained standard for more than twenty years.[61]

Before the new uniforms had even been issued, the first classes of Waves had already reported for training at Hunter College in New York, which the recruits immediately dubbed USS Hunter. Here they were subjected to much the same regimen of physical training, compulsive cleaning, and drill as boots at Great Lakes. In the early days, marine drill instructors were employed to teach close-order drill to the 6,000 women who passed through Hunter every few weeks. "We have two drill masters," wrote one young woman to her parents. "One has red hair and the other is handsome. . . . The one with red hair swears at us although we're not really sure what he is saying. . . ."[62] Another Wave recalled a dress parade at Hunter for a group of visiting VIPs:

> The morning of the review dawned dark and sleeting. The parade ground bordered a huge frozen reservoir and the chilly wind caused instant freezing as the sleet hit the paving. Our platoon, dressed smartly in havelocks, raincoats, gloves and rubbers, stood shivering at parade rest for over an hour. At last the reviewing party came into view. . . . The sergeant called "Attention!" whereupon we dutifully snapped our feet together leaving our rubbers solidly frozen to the paving. Instant reflex action sent us all stooping to retrieve our errant rubbers and dissolved the formation into chaos. With a wretched cry of agony the Marine [drill sergeant] snatched off his hat, threw it on the ground and stalked off the field.[63]

Entering the navy with hopes of adventure, travel, and new experiences, many Waves found themselves serving alongside other women in traditional "female" occupations: secretaries, stenographers, receptionists, waitresses, dispersing clerks, mail sorters, and performers of various auxiliary medical services. "Women would join expecting that they would get to the Pacific and they would see sights they had never seen," recalled Captain Jean Palmer, "and they ended up doing mess duty or something in Bainbridge, Maryland."[64] So many Waves were employed at headquarters and installations in the Washington, D.C., area that a popular Wave song proclaimed

> We joined the Navy to see the sea
> And what did we see?
> We saw D.C.

Among those in the most critical and most demanding occupations were the several hundred Waves assigned to the Office of the Chief of Naval Operations. By 1944, 70 percent of all decoders and 80 percent of all communicators in the Washington area were women.[65] Captain Wyman H. Packard, a veteran intelligence officer, who was in charge of a watch in the Navy Department code room, recalled, "The typing pool had the toughest task. They had to type up the ditto masters for all incoming messages and make additions to some outgoing messages. By the end of the watch they would have the blue ditto coloring all over their hands and sometimes on their faces. After eight hours of pressure trying to catch up with the backlog they would be exhausted."[66]

Not all Waves found the navy a happy experience. "Many of the patients we got at Bethesda [Hospital] were from communications," recalled a navy psychologist. "They had come into the navy expecting to work with men. They found the swarms of women at boot camp, then in their quarters, disillusioning and wanted out at any cost. The strain of secrecy at work was also a major problem."[67] Captain Jean Palmer agreed: "There were those who really cracked up. By far the majority just looked around their little cell, hung up their curtains and made themselves at home and had a wonderful time. We had a wonderful time. I've never worked such hours, never felt so much frustration, but you felt part of something."[68]

During the course of the war, Waves were never "sent to ships," but airplanes were another matter. As naval aviation expanded, women moved into more and more nontraditional occupations. By late 1942, women gunnery instructors were learning to fire service pistols, shotguns, and machine guns, to disassemble and repair all types of ordnance, and to qualify in aerial gunnery. By May 1943, Waves were being trained as aviation machinist's mates, aviation metalsmiths, parachute riggers, aerographers, aircraft gunnery instructors, and air traffic controllers.[69] Instruction in the new Link navigation trainer, introduced by Captain Luis de Flores, a brilliant engineer whose imagination and inventiveness gave birth to a family of realistic training devices that revolutionized flight instruction, was largely in the hands of Waves.[70] After 1943, no aviator was sent to the Pacific who had not received part of his training from a Wave.[71]

By the spring of 1944 this new wartime navy, built around the slender framework of the old, trained and supported on an unprecedented scale by outsiders—women, African-Americans, and civilians—and manned in large part by determined but inexperienced amateurs, was on its way to the two last and greatest naval battles of the twentieth century.

One thousand miles from Majuro lay the island of Saipan, one of three large islands in the Marianas that the Americans intended to use as advance naval and air bases. From airfields on Saipan and the nearby island of Tinian a new Army Air Forces superbomber, the B-29, could attack cities in the heart of Japan. The assault on the Marianas was entrusted to Admiral Raymond A. Spruance, as commander of the Fifth Fleet. Under him were more than 127,000 troops in the transports and landing craft of Vice Admiral Richmond Kelly Turner's Joint Expeditionary Force. They were divided into two segments. The Northern Attack Force, made up of two marine divisions with an army division in reserve, was to assault Saipan and after that Tinian. The Southern Attack Force comprised the 3rd Marine Division and the 1st Provisional Marine Brigade, the latter earmarked for Guam after the assault on Saipan.[72]

The fast carriers of Task Force 58 under Vice Admiral Mark Mitscher supported the landings. The fast carrier task forces had demonstrated their power and effectiveness already with attacks against Rabaul and Kwajalein in the fall of 1943. To support the invasion of the western Marshalls, Mitscher's carriers had attacked and crippled the major Japanese Central Pacific base at Truk, delivering thirty air strikes in two days, each of them more powerful than either of the two Japanese attack waves at Pearl Harbor. This was a vast improvement over the Guadalcanal campaign, when the Americans had never had more than three operational carriers. In the Marianas invasion, Mitscher would have fifteen fast carriers. Only the Enterprise remained from 1942, but there were six new Essex-class carriers. Large fast ships of 27,000 tons, they carried a crew of more than 3,000 men and could accommodate about ninety planes: thirty-six fighters, thirty-six dive-bombers, and eighteen torpedo planes. The first Essex-class carrier was commissioned on the last day of 1942, fifteen months ahead of schedule. The next ship of the class, Yorktown, was completed seventeen months early, a testimony to the extraordinary capabilities of American industry, labor, and technology, which, by late 1943, was to provide the United States with an enormous edge in the tools of war. [73]

Mitscher also had eight light fleet carriers of the *Independence* class, constructed on cruiser hulls. They were considerably smaller than the Essex class and embarked twenty-four fighters and nine torpedo planes. In all, Task Force 58 embarked more than 900 airplanes in its fast carriers. The "battle line," Task Group 58.7 under Rear Admiral Willis A. Lee, included four new fast battleships of the *North Carolina* and *South Dakota* classes, which had fought at Guadalcanal, and three new even larger and faster 45,000-ton *Iowa*-class battleships.

The carriers now operated in groups of three or four, a concentration made possible by much-improved radar, fighter direction, and communications developed after the bitter lessons of Santa Cruz. The *Essex*- and *Independence*-class carriers carried more than a hundred of the new deadly 40mm Bofors and 20mm Oerlikon cannons that had proved so effective against aircraft. Cruisers and destroyers carried so many of these new weapons in sponsons and gun tubs protruding from their sides and deck that one admiral declared that "they looked like the hanging gardens of Babylon."

The heaviest guns in the carriers, the 5-inch, .38-caliber, fired a new type of projectile, a shell equipped with a variable time or proximity fuse. Because even a near miss by a 5-inch projectile was usually enough to destroy a plane, a tiny radio transmitter and receiver built into the warhead detonated the shell when it came close to an aircraft. The *Essex*-class carriers were armed with eight 5-inch guns, the cruisers and battleships with as many as twenty. The new high-performance aircraft that the Bureau of Aeronautics had promised the frustrated fighter jocks in 1942 had arrived in the form of the F6F Hellcat, a single-seat plane that could outclimb and outdive the Zero. It was also thirty miles per hour faster, more heavily armed, and much better protected.[74]

Supporting the fast carriers was a mobile logistical fleet composed of supply ships, oil tankers, ammunition ships, hospital ships, tugs, floating dry docks, lighters, and cranes. "Every three to four days the carriers would steam away from the battle zone during the night and meet the tankers in the morning. After each carrier had taken on oil and aviation gas it would move on to the ammunition ships for bombs and shells and the provision ships for food. Battle ships and cruisers, waiting their turn with the tankers, would refuel the task force's destroyers, and escort carriers, with the logistics squadron, would fly replacement planes and pilots to the fast carriers. In this fashion the fast carrier task force could and did keep operating at sea for three months without respite . . . 4,000 miles from Pearl Harbor."[75] For maintenance and repairs the ships of the fast carrier force put into a protected lagoon where the floating docks,

cranes, repair ships, tenders, and tugs would be safe from submarine attacks and usually were out of range of air strikes. This mobile logistical
force, which followed the fast carriers through the Central Pacific, made
it possible for Task Force 58 to range the seas for far longer periods than
had ever been possible since the age of sail.

On June 15, after three days of air strikes by Mitscher's carriers and
bombardments by the older battleships of Admiral Turner's invasion
force, marines of the 2nd and 4th Marine Divisions landed on Saipan.
By nightfall almost 20,000 men were dug in on a beachhead a thousand
yards deep. Casualties were heavy, but the marines succeeded in repuls-
ing three large Japanese counterattacks against the 2nd Marine Division
during the night.

As the marines were digging in on Saipan, Lieutenant Commander
Robert Risser, captain of the submarine *Flying Fish*, was peering through
his periscope at a parade of Japanese battleships and carriers silhouetted
against the coastline of San Bernardino Strait in the central Philippines
about nine hundred miles from Saipan. It was the biggest group of targets
Risser had ever seen, but he knew that his first priority was to get word
of this fleet to Spruance and Nimitz. When darkness fell the *Flying Fish*
surfaced and sent out her message: "The Japanese fleet is headed for the
Marianas."[76]

The Japanese fleet, about to challenge the American invasion of the
Marianas, was more than twice as strong as the fleets that had fought at
Midway and Guadalcanal. Like the Americans, the Japanese carriers operated in task forces or "divisions" of three ships each. The most formidable ships were in Carrier Division 1, comprising the veteran *Zuikaku*
and *Shokaku* and the brand-new 29,000-ton carrier *Taiho* under the command of Vice Admiral Ozawa Jisaburo. Ozawa was also overall commander of the new First Mobile Fleet, organized that March. Beside
Carrier Division 1, the mobile carrier fleet included six more aircraft carriers that had been converted from fleet auxiliaries or fast passenger lin-
ers, seven battleships, and ten heavy cruisers. The mobile fleet's carriers
embarked just over 400 planes, compared to more than 900 in Task
Force 58. Yet the greatest disparity between the two fleets was not in
ships or planes but in pilots. By the end of the Guadalcanal campaign,
the Japanese were already beginning to suffer from critical shortages of
experienced aviators. "Veteran pilots were killed leaving us like a comb
with missing teeth. The development of planes fell behind and the training of pilots lagged."[77]

For many months after Guadalcanal, the Japanese navy's carrier-based
air units had been dispersed to defend scattered island bases and had suf-

fered heavy losses in the air battles over Rabaul and the central Solomons. "Not for a moment did the Americans ease their relentless pressure," recalled one Japanese aviator. "Day and night the bombers came to pound Rabaul, to smash at the airfields and shipping in the harbor while the fighters screamed low on daring strafing passes shooting up anything they considered a worthwhile target. . . . As the months went by we watched the qualitative superiority of the Zero fade before the increased performance of new American fighter planes which by now not only outfought but also outnumbered the Zeros. There existed a growing feeling of helplessness before this rising tide of American might. Our men felt keenly the great difference between American industrial and military strength and the limited resources of their own country."[78]

Yet it was not entirely American industrial superiority that underlay the dangerous manpower situation of the Japanese in late 1943. For one thing, the Japanese navy took very poor care of its pilots. Men flying from island bases in the Pacific, like those aboard carriers, were rarely rotated home except in the case of severe illness or injury. Moreover, the navy made little attempt to locate and recover downed pilots. "Any man who was shot down and managed to survive by inflating his life raft realized that his chance for continued survival lay entirely within his own hands." In contrast, "the Americans sent out flying boats to the areas in which their planes had fought, searching for and rescuing air crews. . . . Our pilots could not fail to be impressed with these daring search missions."[79]

Food and medical care at the advanced air bases was also poor, often inadequate. The noncommissioned officers, who made up the great majority of aircrews, resented the special privileges afforded to the small minority of commissioned officers. "If they had the gold stripe or two stars of a lieutenant, well, they were 'honorable lieutenant, honorable officer.' [The rest of us] were billeted out in the drafty common room while the nation put them into their own individual rooms. . . . They were young kids . . . fresh from the homeland who'd never be able to get themselves or their Zeros back if they went into action. . . . Meals were completely different too. Veteran aces were fed with food and provisions best fit for horses, while those who hadn't done anything were given restaurant meals. . . . When we were at the airfield our ready room and the officers' ready rooms were separate. When were we going to consult? When were the leaders, the officers and the non-coms in the 2nd and 3rd planes to get to know each other . . . to develop the unspoken understanding needed for combat?"[80]

In Ozawa's fleet steaming toward the Marianas, most of the pilots had less than six months of experience. Some had as little as two months. By contrast, even the newest American aviator assigned to a carrier had at least 525 hours of flying time. Senior Japanese air group commanders with Ozawa were on the average ten years younger and ten years less experienced than those who had sailed with Admiral Nagumo at Midway. In practice bombing operations against an old battleship moving at sixteen knots (half the speed of a modern warship), some of the Japanese dive-bomber squadrons had failed to score a single hit.[81]

The Imperial Japanese Navy's plan for meeting the American advance across the Pacific, Operation A-Go, anticipated that a decisive sea battle would be fought in the area of the Palaus or the western Carolines. In those regions the Japanese counted upon using their land-based airpower to compensate for their inferiority in carriers. Despite the plan, the invasion of the Marianas was too serious to be ignored. By stretching their fuel supplies and using unprocessed Borneo petroleum (good but highly flammable), the fleet could give battle near the Marianas. On June 15, Ozawa received orders to activate Operation A-Go.[82]

Although outnumbered almost two to one in aircraft, Ozawa was confident he could handle the Americans. His planes, owing to lack of armor and self-sealing fuel tanks, had a greater range than those of his opponents. Japanese planes could search as far out as 560 miles and attack at 300 miles, whereas Mitscher's could search only to about 350 miles and attack at 200. Ozawa was counting heavily on land-based planes at Guam, Rota, and Yap to whittle down the American fleet; in actuality these forces had done no damage to Task Force 58 but had instead already been well worked over by Mitscher's planes. Vice Admiral Kakuta Kakuji, who commanded the land-based planes, had so misled Ozawa about his strength that Ozawa steamed into battle expecting substantial help from Guam and Tinian.[83] Ozawa also expected to use Guam to rearm and refuel his own aircraft after striking the Americans.

When he learned of the approach of the Japanese, Spruance sailed from Saipan in his flagship, the cruiser *Indianapolis*, accompanied by seven other cruisers and twenty-one destroyers to join Task Force 58. He left behind the older battleships and a few cruisers and destroyers to support the beachhead.

Around midnight on the 17th, the U.S. submarine *Cavalla* reported a Japanese task force eight hundred miles west southwest of Saipan and closing. In the morning the *Cavalla* radioed again that the Japanese fleet was still on course and a hundred miles closer to Saipan. Mitscher wanted to steam southwest at high speed to close on the *Cavalla*'s contact, but Spruance wanted to keep Task Force 58 in position to cover Saipan against all eventualities. He feared that the Japanese might divide their forces, using one portion as a decoy and the other to make an end run around Task Force 58 to get at the transports. Additional intelligence from high-frequency direction finders, which pinpointed Ozawa's position during the night of the 18th, failed to dissuade him. Mitscher again asked to head for the area of contact so as to be in position to launch an attack in the morning, but Spruance actually ordered the fleet to double back toward Saipan to prevent any Japanese force from passing them in the darkness.[84]

Thanks to the greater range of his search planes, Ozawa had already located the American fleet late on the afternoon of the 18th, and on the morning of the 19th he launched four massive strikes against Mitscher's carriers. Spruance and Mitscher were still in ignorance of Ozawa's exact whereabouts when the first Japanese raid of about seventy planes showed up on American radar screens about a hundred miles distant.[85] "Over the ship's bull horn every few minutes came announcements of the bearing and distance of incoming raids. 'Raid I now 232.86 miles. Raid II now, 238.78 miles.' These announcements were punctuated by the air officers' exhortations to flight deck crews . . . who were engaged in pushing the planes aft."[86]

The key role in defense of the task forces now fell to a handful of reserve officers and enlisted men, the fighter directors in each of the task groups. They had the responsibility for detecting and identifying enemy raids, for allocating the right number of fighters to intercept them, and for directing the fighters to the best possible position and altitude for an interception. The fighter director officers were young reservists in their twenties, most of whom had been in the navy less than two years. Aboard the carrier *Langley* the fighter direction team included an advertising executive, a lawyer, a college instructor, and "an Atlanta architect who specialized in the design of Methodist Churches."[87] The fighter director and his team worked in a small dimly lit compartment surrounded by radar screens, plotting boards, and radios. "CIC was not a happy place to be," recalled one fighter direction officer. "Here you sat around these radar screens and watched these things happen with young seamen who were 18 or 19 years old, just off the farm or out of the shoestore or what have you, and their reactions were, for the most part, wonderful. . . . We had a few who lost control of themselves and started weeping, crying, praying and things like that. Nobody minds people praying but it's not a happy circumstance for men at their battlestations."[88]

This was the system that had been attempted with indifferent results at Santa Cruz, but on this occasion it worked superbly. And all four Japanese raids were intercepted at fifty or sixty miles from the task force. The veteran American pilots, flying superior aircraft, made it a very uneven contest. Only one U.S. plane was lost to this first wave of attackers. Those Japanese who survived the onslaught of the Hellcats ran into a blizzard of fire from the fast battleships accompanying Mitscher's carriers. Using proximity fuses, the battleships and their escorts downed a dozen more Japanese planes. Only one enemy plane scored a hit, which did minor damage to the battleship *South Dakota*. The second raid, more than 125 aircraft, suffered even heavier losses. Only a handful survived the gauntlet of fighters and fire from the battle line to attack Mitscher's carrier; none did any damage. The third group of attackers eluded the battle line by circling around to the north; it attacked one of the carrier task groups after fighting its way through intercepting Hellcats. Again no carriers were hit. The final wave of attackers became separated and attacked piecemeal during the early afternoon. Many failed to find the American task force at all and were intercepted and shot down while trying to land on Guam. In all fewer than a hundred of the 373 planes which had attacked Task Force 58 in the four mass attacks managed to return to their carriers. The Americans lost only twenty-nine planes in the one-sided action, which one of Mitscher's pilots in *Lexington* labeled "the Great Marianas Turkey Shoot."

Some of the returning Japanese fliers found no carrier to land on. U.S. submarines *Albacore* and *Cavalla* made contact with Ozawa's fleet and sank the carriers *Shokoku* and *Taiho*, obliging Admiral Ozawa to transfer his flag to a destroyer and then to the carrier *Zuikaku*.

In Task Force 58 there was elation at the day's results, combined with frustration over inability to find the Japanese. As darkness fell the Americans knew no more about the whereabouts of Ozawa's fleet than they had known that morning—and because the U.S. carriers had been obliged to steam east into the wind to launch and recover their planes they were still no closer to the enemy. It was not until 8:00 P.M. on the 19th that Mitscher completed recovering all his planes and detached one carrier group under Rear Admiral W. K. Harrill to fuel and keep Japanese air bases on Guam and Roda under attack. There were a handful of night-fighting Hellcats and Avengers that could have conducted night searches, but, as in the case of radar, most admirals were uninformed and skeptical about night fighters. In addition, most night fighter pilots had been trained for short-range interceptions, not long-range searches. There were no searches that night.[89]

The next day the sky was filled with American search planes, flying boats from Saipan, heavy bombers from Manus and the Admiralties, bombers and torpedo planes from the carriers. One group of Hellcats from the *Lexington,* with belly tanks, flew out as far as 475 miles but found nothing. Afternoon came; nerves were on edge and tempers grew short aboard the carriers. Then around 4:00 P.M. a plane from the *Enterprise* sighted Ozawa's fleet about 275 miles from Task Force 58.

That was a very long range. But with only three hours of daylight remaining, Mitscher could delay no longer in launching his warplanes. Attacking at that distance, some planes would probably have insufficient fuel to return. The rest would have to land on their carriers after dark, something for which they had not been trained. Mitscher consulted his operations officer, Commander W. J. Widhelm. "It's going to be tight," was Widhelm's reply.[90] At 4:10, pilots and crews who had been on alert all afternoon received the order: "Man aircraft." Boldly chalked on the ready rooms' blackboards were Mitscher's final instructions: "Get the Carriers."[91]

Working at a frenzied pace, deck crews launched more than 200 planes in under twelve minutes. As the planes left their carriers, additional reports and calculations by Mitscher's staff revealed that the Japanese were sixty miles farther west than had been first anticipated. This unhappy news was relayed to the pilots and crews already headed for Ozawa's fleet. Aviators made quick worried calculations. It was clear that even under the best circumstances the chances of having sufficient fuel to return from this longer trip were slim indeed. "The intercom chatter, today quite subdued, died away to almost nothing as the pilots realized the import of the new position report."[92]

Only twenty minutes before dark, Mitscher's tired pilots finally found the Japanese fleet. The attackers sank the carrier *Hiyo,* badly damaged three other carriers, and sank two of the accompanying oilers. Three other Japanese carriers escaped unhurt, and the damaged ships returned to Japan for repairs.

It was pitch dark, with no moon and only occasional flashes of lightning from an approaching thunderstorm, by the time the first American planes finally returned to their carriers. "I turned on my lights dim," recalled Lieutenant James D. Ramage, "ate an apple which I brought along and then readjusted my oxygen mask as I was feeling tired and my eyes were seeing things that weren't there. . . . Apparently there were many of our pilots that day who hadn't used their fuel economically. The results began to show. . . . I heard one pilot tell his rear seat man to get ready for a water landing. . . . I saw a group of lights to my right getting lower and lower, then there weren't any more. Apparently a whole section of planes had been low on gas and decided to go in together, thus giving a greater chance of being picked up. I heard some pilot, apparently lost, calling desperately for a carrier. His base was too far away to pick him up. Finally he called again, he was out of gas, bailing out, then silence."[93]

Mitscher's carriers sighted the first returning planes at 8:30. As the carriers reversed course from west to east to come into the wind, Mitscher ordered the task groups to turn on their lights. Standard flight operating procedure provided for carriers to display their deck landing and ramp lights for night landings even though this might reveal the ship to lurking submarines.[94] Mitscher went much further, ordering the carriers to flash their signal lights and point a searchlight beam straight into the sky. Cruisers and destroyers illuminated the area with star shells and turned on all of their navigating lights. To one night fighter pilot sent aloft to guide the planes home, the scene seemed like "a Hollywood premier, Chinese New Year and the Fourth of July all rolled into one."[95]

Chaos reigned as groups of planes, almost out of fuel, attempted to land on the closest visible carrier deck. "By the time we arrived there was bedlam," reported one *Enterprise* pilot. "It was too pitiful to be disgusting. Planes made passes at everything afloat."[96] Carrier decks periodically "closed" as crews cleared away the wreckage of planes that had ignored wave-offs and crash-landed aboard. The carrier *Bunker Hill* experienced a double disaster when a dive-bomber disregarded frantic warnings and hit the crash barrier, toppling onto its nose. While flight deck crews struggled to dislodge the bomber an Avenger torpedo plane, likewise ignoring wave-offs, crashed on the deck and careened into the wrecked dive-bomber, killing four men and wounding others.[97]

As the planes were forced down in the water, cruisers and destroyers left formation to search for crews. Radios crackled with reports, orders, and questions as dozens of ships maneuvered at over twenty knots in the darkness.

LZT MESSAGE   20 June 1944

2045 TG 58.3 V CTG 58.3.	Execute to follow. Turn 090. ComDes Ron 50 acknowledge, over.
(Ack'd for).	
TG 58.3 V CTG 58.3.	Standby . . . Execute, Turn 090.
2103 CTG 58.3 V KNAPP.	Am dropping out to pick up plane, over.
KNAPP V COMDESRON 50.	After completion your recovery, trail approximately 3000 yards astern, over.

COMDESRON 50 V KNAPP.   Wilco, out.

2105 CTG 58.3 V KNAPP.   We are going after one on our port side. How about the flare, over.

(Ack'd for).

2106 HEALY V COMDESRON 50.   Drop astern and find that man in area astern then trail 2000 yards astern, acknowledge, over.

(Ack'd for).

2107 CTG 58.3 V KNAPP.   Request permission to turn off searchlight, over.

V CTG 58.3. Affirmative.   COMDESRON 50 assign another of your boys to searchlight duty, over.

2108 BRAINE V CTG 58.3.   Did you see plane just outside screen to port about abreast of LEXINGTON, over.

2109 BRAINE V COMDESRON 50.   Leave screen abeam of LEXINGTON for man in water acknowledge, over.

2110 COMDESRON 50 V CTG 58.3.   Where do you have ANTHONY now, over.

CTG 58.3 V COMDESRON 50.   ANTHONY is astern of LEXINGTON as plane guard. COGSWELL is on other side. Have directed HEALY to drop back and pick up pilot on starboard side of KNAPP.

2113 CTG 58.3 V PRINCETON.   Am ready to pancake two or three if desired, over.

CTG 58.3 V SAN JACINTO.   Our two planes are trying to come aboard, may we take them, over.

TG 58.1 V CTG 58.1.	My course 110, speed 28, out.
CTG 58.3 V SAN JACINTO.	Answer please my last request, over.
CTG 58.3 V PRINCETON.	Did you receive my last transmission, over.
V CTG 58.3.	Negative, Say again, over.
V PRINCETON.	I can take 2 or 3 if desired, over.
V CTG 58.3.	Roger, out.
2117 PRINCETON V CTG 58.3.	If any come around you and wanting to come aboard take them aboard, over.
(Acknowledged for).	
TG 58.3 V CTG 58.3.	One in water on port bow of ENTERPRISE.
COMDESRON 50	Acknowledge, over.
V COMDESRON 50.	Wilco.[98]

Well over a third of the planes that had begun the return flight from Ozawa's fleet were lost in ditching or deck crashes. More than 160 pilots and crewmen were pulled from the water during the night of the 21st and over the next few days, however. Only forty-nine aviators were lost.

"The enemy had escaped," concluded Mitscher's chief of staff, Captain Arleigh Burke, in the action report he drafted for Mitscher. It was a succinct expression of the feeling of frustration and disappointment among many of Spruance's commanders. "We could have gotten the whole outfit!" declared Burke many years later. "Nobody could have gotten away if we had done what we wanted."[99] Spruance's decision on the night of the 18th-19th to turn back toward Saipan rather than continue west to place Mitscher's search planes within range of the Japanese fleet by morning immediately became the subject of controversy and has remained so until the present. Spruance's defenders argue that his decision—although based on the faulty premise that the Japanese had divided their forces—in the end worked out for the best. The last of

Japan's carrier-based planes and pilots were virtually annihilated at small cost to the United States. Spruance's critics, on the other hand, have gone so far as to suggest that he and his battleship-oriented staff, trained at the Naval War College to refight the Battle of Jutland, did just that, allowing the Japanese to slip away exactly as Admiral Jellicoe had allowed the Germans to rush by him in 1916.[100]

While the strategy of the Japanese and Americans has remained a subject of debate, the operational results were clear and striking. The aircraft carrier, when organized in task forces and equipped with radar, high-performance aircraft, and powerful antiaircraft guns firing proximity-fused shells, was more than capable of holding its own against any size surface or air attack. The extreme vulnerability of warships to mass air attack, so graphically demonstrated at Crete, had been almost completely reversed. Warships were now not only highly survivable, they were capable of destroying large land-based air forces, as the Pacific carriers demonstrated at Rabaul and Kwajalein in the fall of 1943 and at Truk in 1944. Warships once again ruled the waves, but the contest between ships and planes had not ended. The final round would not begin until some nine months after Saipan.

Whatever Japan's losses in the Marianas, the foundation of her defeat had already been laid. The root of this defeat lay in Japan's inability to protect the shipping upon which her war economy depended. By the end of 1944, U.S. submarines operating from bases in Australia, New Guinea, and Hawaii had sunk more than half of Japan's merchant fleet, including about two thirds of her tankers. Japanese industries, almost totally dependent on imported oil and raw materials, had been dealt a devastating blow.[101] This defeat came as a complete surprise to both the Japanese and U.S. navies. Before Pearl Harbor neither navy had expected to imitate the German submarine war against merchant shipping. Instead Japanese and American submarines were expected to play a role in the fleet actions that both sides had confidently expected.

The Japanese navy, obsessed with the need to reduce the odds in an encounter with the superior U.S. battle fleet, gave its submarines the mission of observing and blockading enemy ports and bases. Once the enemy fleet put to sea, the submarines would keep it under surveillance and make repeated attacks to sink or cripple the American battleships and carriers.[102] In U.S. Navy thinking, the submarines were to act as an advance scouting line for the battle fleet, attacking the enemy's battleships and carriers in a coordinated underwater attack. Of thirty-six submarine exercises conducted by the Pacific Fleet during 1940–41, twenty-one were directed against battleships and aircraft carriers, eight were against cruisers and destroyers, and only one was against a convoy of cargo ships.[103] One submarine tactical publication noted that, "in battle the primary objectives of submarines are enemy heavy ships. A heavy ship is defined as a battleship, a battlecruiser or an aircraft carrier. Attacks on secondary objectives while an opportunity for attack on primary objectives remains possible or which would in any manner prejudice the success of the main attack should not be made."[104]

The personnel of both the Japanese and American submarine service were a specially selected elite comparable to naval aviators. American candidates for submarine duty, all volunteers, were carefully screened through tests and personal interviews to determine whether they held "any unfounded objections to undersea service, probably instilled by their mothers. To belong [a submariner] *must be a man* regardless of age or background."[105] Since the 1920s, both officers and enlisted men assigned to U.S. Navy submarines had been required to "qualify" by demonstrating that they had mastered the skills and knowledge required to perform the duties in their area of responsibility. This knowledge could only be acquired through service in an operational submarine. An officer, besides mastering the technical knowledge about the submarine and its weapons, had to direct ten practice dives and mock attacks successfully before being permitted to wear the distinctive dolphin badge of a qualified submariner.

Far more completely than the captain of a surface ship, the captain of a submarine and his key subordinates could, in effect, set their own rules and standards for their crew and reject any individual who failed to measure up. Like the German U-boat men, American and Japanese submariners lived in a claustrophobic world of machinery, stale air, and unpleasant smells. Japanese I-class long-range submarines carried provisions for more than three months so that "the entire deck space except for the diesel engine room was covered with bags of rice, boxes of dried food and tins of provisions to a depth of two feet. It looked like our crewmen were living in a circular food warehouse." In the torpedo room men had to squeeze between "the two foot floor of food and the 'steel fish' in order to get needed rest."[106] An American submariner described the unique odor of a submarine as a by-product of diesel fumes plus the "three Fs—feet, farts and fannies—of eighty-one souls living in close quarters with limited bathing and laundry facilities."[107] American submariners did have one great advantage over their counterparts in the Japanese, German, and British navies. U.S. submarines built since the mid-1930s were air-conditioned—more for the welfare of the machinery than of the sailors. Though air-conditioning equipment took up additional space inside the cramped hull, it made submarines far more livable, especially in tropical waters. Condensate from the air-conditioning units also provided an additional supply of water, which could be used for a kind of primitive laundering.[108]

Both the Japanese and U.S. navies held a high opinion of their own submariners and a correspondingly low opinion of their likely opponents. Japanese submariners were popularly believed to possess "almost supernatural skill" while Americans were considered too soft and luxury-loving to cope with the austerity of submarine duty.[109] Ikezaki Chuko, a popular writer on naval affairs, assured readers of his book, *Nippon Sensuikan* ("Japanese Submarines"), that Japan's inferiority in capital ships would be more than compensated for by the superior design of Japanese submarines and the high quality, morale, and offensive spirit of their crews.[110] The Americans disagreed. An intelligence report, endorsed by the commander in chief of the Pacific Fleet as "a shrewd analysis," observed that though the Japanese had "quick lively minds" they were woefully lacking in initiative. "This mental sluggishness in reacting to new situations appears to be the basic reason for indifferent results the Japanese have attained in submarine and air operations."[111] German technical experts working with submarines in Japan told an American diplomat that "the Japanese make poor submarine personnel. . . . They do not react quickly enough in emergencies. They react only per instruction not by instinct." Japanese submarines reportedly "rarely dive to depths greater than 70 feet." The Germans believed "they are afraid to dive to greater depths. . . ."[112]

Yet World War II had opened with resounding failures by both the U.S. and Japanese submarine forces. Americans were shocked by the failure of their submarines to interfere seriously with the Japanese invasion of the Philippines. "We had the greatest concentration of submarines in the world there," recalled correspondent Hansen W. Baldwin, "but we didn't do a thing."[113] Japanese submarines did almost as poorly at Pearl Harbor. Specially designed midget submarines, attacking shortly before the carrier planes, failed to do any damage, and their activities almost alerted the base. Larger Japanese submarines lurking in Hawaiian waters failed to sink or even sight an American warship, while I-70 was sunk by planes from USS *Enterprise*.

During 1942, U.S. submarines sank 180 Japanese ships, for a total of about 725,000 tons. Japan was able to replace all but 90,000 tons by new construction, and she actually increased her tonnage in tankers. Imports of raw materials from Southeast Asia remained unimpaired. U.S. submarine operations were handicapped by faulty torpedoes, which suffered from defects in their depth mechanisms and their warhead exploders. The last of these imperfections was not corrected until well into 1943.[114]

During 1942, almost 30 percent of all U.S. submarine commanders were relieved for unfitness or lack of results. About 14 percent were removed for these reasons during 1943 and 1944.[115] Prewar submarine commands had generally gone "principally on the basis of seniority, to men who had not tried to force new ideas on their seniors, who had behaved themselves ashore, had kept their submarines clean and their sailors out of trouble," recalled a wartime submarine officer. What was required was "a good man with a tough mind—one who did not have an oversupply of imagination. There were enough real problems . . . to leave no place for a man who saw shadows. A sort of dogged, imperturbable stolidity was preferable to brilliance and imagination. But there had to be at least some of the latter, combined sometimes with an almost reckless aggressiveness, to get the best results."[116]

Prewar submarine doctrine had not emphasized reckless aggressiveness. Experience in prewar maneuvers and exercises also had given naval officers an exaggerated idea of the effectiveness of aircraft and destroyers in locating and sinking submarines. Submarine commanders had been cautioned against making attacks from periscope depth if the sea was calm or the target was screened by destroyers. In prewar years, it was generally believed that a depth charge exploding anywhere closer than a half mile from a submarine would prove fatal, while actual war experience demonstrated that boats could survive explosions as close as fifteen or twenty feet. Given the supposed vulnerability of the submarines, attacks by periscope had been considered generally too dangerous. Commanders had been encouraged to attack from one hundred feet or more, using sonar to locate the target. Such a "sound attack was considered far safer than one utilizing the periscope. It was also, as war experience would demonstrate, completely impractical."[117]

By mid-1943 a number of favorable developments vastly increased the effectiveness of the U.S. submarine war. Reliable torpedoes were finally available and more aggressive skippers had replaced many of the overly cautious commanders of the early war. Code breakers at Pearl Harbor were reading the Japanese code and transmitted the schedule and routing of convoys so that American submarines could be sent directly into the path of slow-moving Japanese shipping, eliminating the need for long, fuel-consuming searches in the vast Pacific. Beginning in late 1943, submarine admirals at Pearl Harbor and Australia began to direct coordinated attacks against enemy convoys. In addition, substantial numbers of new submarines began to arrive in the Pacific. By July 1944 there were about one hundred U.S. submarines operating from Pearl Harbor and forty more from Australia.[118]

The Japanese were singularly unprepared to deal with the deadly onslaught. Prewar Japanese plans had concluded that transport of petroleum and food supplies to the home islands would not be much of a problem.[119] Japanese strategists expected to lose about 800,000 tons of shipping the first year of the war but then expected a sharp drop in the rate of losses.[120] The indifferent success of the U.S. submarine effort during the early months of the war, together with evidence of American torpedo failures, served to reinforce this false sense of security.[121]

Japanese complacency rapidly dissipated as sinkings by U.S. submarines mounted. By the end of 1943, these losses were already twice the expected total, and by the end of 1944 more than four times the prewar estimate. For every ton of shipping Japan could build, she lost three tons to submarines.[122] In addition, many Japanese submarines also fell victim to American men-of-war coached on to their locations by code intercepts. The Japanese were slow to react to this growing crisis. At the beginning of the war the Imperial Japanese Navy had no units assigned exclusively to antisubmarine warfare. Combined Fleet admirals demanded the best destroyers for duty with the combat forces. The first two escort groups, formed in April 1942 to protect communications to Singapore and Truk, had only a handful of old destroyers. In November 1943 a Grand Escort Command Headquarters was established to coordinate and direct protection of all overseas shipping, but the Combined Fleet continued to get the best escort vessels while the Grand Escort Command received only older ships.[123]

Japanese submarines might have mounted a counteroffensive but failed to do so. They had been trained in the same supercautious mode of "sound attacks" and self-preservation as the prewar U.S. sailors, and unlike the Americans they seem never to have entirely abandoned it.[124] Japanese strategists reasoned that a submarine blockade of the entire United States West Coast was impractical and also unnecessary since the Pacific war was expected to be short. In addition, they decided to divert more and more submarines to carry supplies to beleaguered Japanese garrisons in the Pacific. Japanese submarine commanders protested this dangerous and unrewarding assignment, but the navy high command, unimpressed by the I-boats' performance in the first year of the war, were more willing to assign subs than the more highly valued destroyers to supply and reinforcement duties. The navy even laid down a new type of cargo-carrying submarine.

The U.S. submarine offensive against Japan was one of the decisive elements in ensuring the empire's defeat. A force comprising less than 2 percent of U.S. Navy personnel accounted for 55 percent of Japan's losses at sea. U.S. submarines sank more than 1,300 Japanese ships, including a battleship, eight aircraft carriers, and eleven cruisers, in the course of the war.[125] Yet, the cost was high. About 22 percent of U.S. submariners who made war patrols in World War II failed to return—the highest casualty rate for any branch of service. For the Japanese, the cost in lives was higher still. About 16,000 merchant seamen were killed as a result of submarine attacks and some 53,000 were wounded. The number of civilians, including women and children, who lost their lives in merchant and passenger ship sinkings has not been calculated.

FOURTEEN

"MY GRAVE SHALL BE THE SEA"

The American seizure of the Marianas had coincided with the final stages of General MacArthur's advance west along the northern coast of New Guinea. In the fall of 1944, the combined forces of Nimitz and MacArthur descended upon the Philippines. MacArthur's troops, supported by the fast carrier forces, now under the command of Admiral Halsey, landed on the island of Leyte on October 20. In response to this new threat the Japanese fleet sortied from its bases in the East Indies. Having lost almost all of their remaining planes and pilots in futile attacks on Halsey's fleet during the previous two months, the Japanese devised a bold plan. They would use their nearly planeless carriers to decoy the American fleet north, away from the landing beaches, while two powerful task forces of battleships and cruisers would strike the transports and amphibious forces in the Leyte Gulf. The battle plan was designed to allow the Imperial Japanese Navy to make optimum use of its single remaining asset: the largely undiminished power of its battle line and heavy cruisers. The Combined Fleet's aircraft carriers were virtually helpless, with few planes and fewer pilots, but of the ten battleships with which Japan had entered the war, seven were still undamaged, and two of the gigantic Yamato-type battleships had since joined the fleet.

The details of the plan, called Sho-1, were very complicated, but its essential aim was to lure Halsey's Third Fleet north away from the invasion beaches while the two task forces would steam north from Linga Roads near Singapore. After threading their way through the central

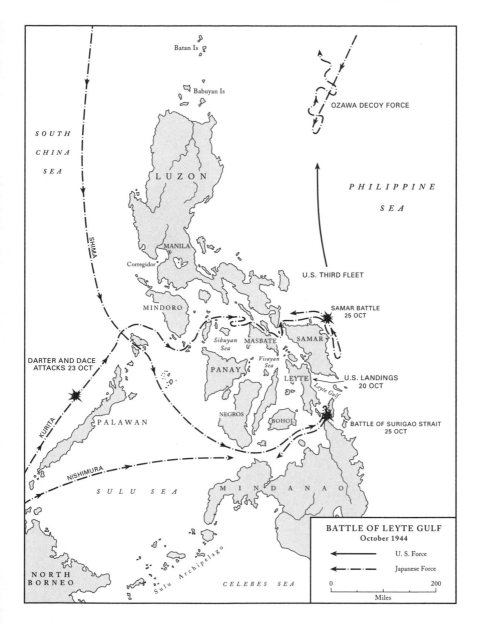

Batan Is

Babuyan Is

OZAWA DECOY FORCE

SOUTH
CHINA
SEA

LUZON

PHILIPPINE

SEA

SHIMA

MANILA

Corregidor

MINDORO

U.S. THIRD FLEET

SAMAR BATTLE
25 OCT

Sibuyan
Sea MASBATE SAMAR

DARTER AND DACE
ATTACKS 23 OCT

PANAY

Visayan
Sea

LEYTE

Leyte Gulf

U.S. LANDINGS
20 OCT

KURITA

PALAWAN

NEGROS

BOHOL

BATTLE OF SURIGAO STRAIT
25 OCT

NISHIMURA

SULU SEA

M I N D A N A O

NORTH
BORNEO

Sulu Archipelago

CELEBES SEA

BATTLE OF LEYTE GULF
October 1944

⟵————— U. S. Force

⟵—·—·—· Japanese Force

0   200

Miles

Philippines—one by Surigao Strait, the other by San Bernardino to
Leyte Gulf—the two striking forces were to emerge into Leyte waters at
roughly the same time—a difficult feat of coordination indeed.[1]

The Surigao Strait force included the battleships *Fuso* and *Yamashiro*,
a heavy cruiser, and four destroyers under Vice Admiral Nishimura

Shoji. Nishimura's fleet was supposed to be reinforced by a second cruiser force from the Inland Sea under Vice Admiral Shima Kiyohide. The two never made contact, however, and entered the strait separately. A far more powerful force, under Vice Admiral Kurita Takeo, was assigned to the San Bernardino Strait approach. Kurita's formation included the super-battleships *Yamato* and *Musashi*, three older battleships, ten heavy cruisers, two light cruisers, and more than a dozen destroyers.

Kurita's luck was bad almost from the first. American submarines, alerted by code breakers, ambushed his fleet as it steamed through the Palawan Passage northwest of Borneo early on the morning of October 23. After radioing word of the Japanese approach to MacArthur's forces, the U.S. submarines *Darter* and *Dace* attacked Kurita's force, which was moving at a speed of only sixteen knots to conserve fuel. The heavy cruiser *Atago*, Kurita's flagship, was torn apart by four torpedoes from the *Darter* and sank in eighteen minutes. Admiral Kurita and his staff had to swim to a nearby destroyer, which transferred them to the battleship *Yamato*. The *Darter* also hit the heavy cruiser *Takao*, sending her limping back to Borneo, and *Dace* hit the heavy cruiser *Maya*, which blew up and sank in four minutes. A badly shaken Admiral Kurita continued north with the *Yamato* and his remaining battleships and cruisers.

Off the Philippines, both MacArthur's Seventh Fleet, commanded by Vice Admiral Thomas Kinkaid, and Admiral William F. Halsey's Third Fleet prepared for battle. Halsey's fleet, which included all the fast carriers, was not under MacArthur or Kinkaid but reported to the Commander in Chief, Pacific Fleet, Admiral Nimitz. Halsey's mission was to act in "strategic support" of the Leyte operations by keeping Japanese naval and air forces from interfering with the landings.[2] Halsey's carriers prepared to attack Kurita's force, while Kinkaid prepared to take on Admiral Nishimura's Surigao Strait force.

On the bridge of the *Yamato*, now in the brilliant blue waters of the Sibuyan Sea, Admiral Kurita anxiously scanned the horizon. He knew that American carrier planes would find him soon. Where was the land-based fighter cover allocated to his force in the Sho-1 plan? After a time, a handful of planes arrived and took station over his fleet, but most of the land-based Japanese aircraft had been sent to attack the American carrier forces. While they sank the light carrier *Princeton*, they suffered severe losses.

At 10:30 A.M. a swarm of black spots appeared out of the east, the first strike from Halsey's carriers. "We are reconciled to impending death," wrote Watanabe Kiyoshi, a seaman in the great battleship *Musashi*. "We have no hope nor expectation, nor anything to believe in; and in the end we shall be burned to death and disappear into the ocean."[3] All that day American carrier planes worked over Kurita's task force, concentrating on the giant Musashi, the biggest target any of the pilots had ever seen. The augmented antiaircraft batteries on the Japanese men-of-war put up an impressive display but failed to do much damage to the attackers. By evening the Musashi was a wreck, hit by nineteen torpedoes and almost as many bombs, all her power gone, badly flooded forward, her bow nearly underwater.

When the Musashi's list had increased to about 30 degrees, her captain ordered her abandoned. Watanabe Kiyoshi was preparing to leave the ship when he suddenly heard a shout, "'The Emperor's portrait! Move aside!' I saw two petty officers carrying the portrait covered in a white cloth. . . . I thought the portrait ought to be left where it was. After all, the Musashi is the emperor's ship. It would be better to concentrate on getting the sailors off the ship. I reflected that because of that one picture, I might lose my life."[4] A few minutes later Watanabe was blown overboard by an explosion. He landed in the water, where he was rescued by destroyers along with about 1,100 of the Musashi's 2,400-man crew.[5]

Rather than face further air attacks, Admiral Kurita reversed course in the late afternoon to get out of range of Halsey's strike planes. Although Kurita could not have known it, his order came at the moment when the Sho-1 plan was on the verge of success.

Far to the north, Admiral Ozawa, his four carriers, Zuikaku, Chitose, Chiyoda, and Zuiho, left with only about 110 planes after the slaughter of earlier air battles, was doing his best to act as bait for the Third Fleet. That morning he had flung his few remaining planes at an American task group, but the expected massive counterblow from the American carriers never came. In desperation, Ozawa ordered the Ise and Hyuga, two peculiar battleships that had been fitted with flight decks aft, to run south with some destroyers and engage the enemy. It was this force that was finally sighted by American search planes at about 4:00 in the afternoon. An hour later, other searchers finally spotted Ozawa's carriers.

Halsey and Kinkaid now knew the location of all three Japanese striking forces. Kurita's retreat had been reported. Nishimura's task force had been attacked by planes from Vice Admiral Ralph E. Davison's Carrier Task Group 4 that morning. But these strikes had little effect. Nishimura was still coming on, and ever since noon, Kinkaid's Seventh Fleet had been preparing to give him a hot reception.

Halsey decided to steam north to attack Ozawa's carriers, which he assumed must be the main enemy striking force, as they had been in all the earlier battles. Halsey's decision was based partly on reports by Mitscher's carrier pilots, who claimed far more damage to Kurita's fleet than they had actually inflicted, but he had other reasons as well. The Third Fleet commander and his staff were well aware of the criticism that had been leveled at Admiral Spruance for allowing the Japanese fleet to "escape" at the Battle of the Philippine Sea.[6] Mitscher's chief of staff, the outspoken Arleigh Burke, had even sent a copy of his critique of Spruance's operations to his friend Rear Admiral Robert B. Carney, Halsey's chief of staff. As Burke observed, Halsey "didn't want any damn super-cautious business tied to him. . . ."[7] In addition, Nimitz's orders to Halsey included the sentence "In case opportunity for destruction of major portion of the enemy fleet is offered, or can be created, such destruction becomes the primary task."[8] Halsey saw an attack on Ozawa's force as just such an opportunity.

Earlier, when Halsey had been preparing for a fight with Kurita, he had transmitted a battle plan to his task group commanders. The plan called for four battleships, two heavy and three light cruisers, and fourteen destroyers to be pulled out of the carrier formations to form a new Task Force 34, which would be commanded by Vice Admiral Willis A. Lee. The new unit's mission would be to take on any heavy surface forces that might be encountered. A later dispatch advised that the task force would not be formed until Halsey so directed.

Halsey's message was intended for his own commanders, but copies were sent for the information of Admiral Nimitz in Hawaii and of Admiral King in Washington. Admiral Kinkaid was not an addressee, but his communicators intercepted the plan and showed it to him. Kinkaid was pleased with the news; it was "exactly what I would do."[9] And it would allow his Seventh Fleet to concentrate on Surigao Strait, confident that Halsey's Task Force 34 was guarding San Bernardino. Not having received the later dispatch, Kinkaid, Nimitz, and King all assumed that Task Force 34 had actually been formed. This conclusion seemed to be confirmed by a message Kinkaid received from Halsey around 8:00 that night. The message read: "Central Force [Kurita] heavily damaged according to strike reports. Am proceeding north with three groups to attack carrier forces at dawn."[10] Since the Third Fleet had three carrier task groups, Admiral Kinkaid interpreted this message to mean that Halsey was going north with his three carrier groups, but leaving Task Force 34—the *fourth* group—behind to watch San Bernardino Strait.[11]

But Task Force 34 was not at San Bernardino Strait. In fact, it had never been formed. Its battleships and cruisers were with Halsey's carriers, proceeding north at a leisurely sixteen knots. Meanwhile Kurita, spurred on by urgings from the Combined Fleet, had turned his force around, passed through San Bernardino Strait around midnight, and turned south for Leyte Gulf.

Far to the south, Admiral Kinkaid's battleships and destroyers under Rear Admiral Jesse B. Oldendorf virtually annihilated Nishimura's force in an engagement known as the Battle of Surigao Strait. Admiral Shima's smaller force arrived too late for the battle and withdrew without fighting after Shima's flagship collided with one of Nishimura's crippled survivors.

Well satisfied with the night's work, Kinkaid held a final meeting of his staff early on the morning of October 25. As the meeting broke up, Kinkaid turned to his chief of staff, Captain Richard H. Cruzen.

"Now Dick, is there anything we haven't done?"

"Admiral, I can think of only one thing," Cruzen answered. "We have never directly asked Halsey if TF34 is guarding San Bernardino Strait."

"Well, let's ask him," Kinkaid replied.

At 4:12 he radioed Halsey: "Is TF34 Guarding San Bernardino Strait?"

Because of unaccountable delays, the message was not received by the *New Jersey* until 7:00 A.M. It was then that Kinkaid received the disquieting reply: "Negative. TF34 is with me pursuing enemy carrier force."[12] Twenty minutes later came another message, this time from the small escort carriers and destroyers supporting the landing forces in Leyte Gulf. They were under attack by Kurita's battleships and cruisers.

After his pounding on the 24th, Kurita had been amazed and relieved to find his passage through San Bernardino Strait unimpeded. Expecting to fight their way out, his men had been even more elated to find only open water awaiting them as they emerged into the Philippine Sea and swept down the east coast of Samar toward Leyte Gulf. About half an hour after sunrise, lookouts aboard the flagship *Yamato* sighted two masts to the southeast.[13]

The masts belonged to ships of Rear Admiral Clifton T. Sprague's "Taffy 3," one of three groups of escort carriers under Rear Admiral T. L. Sprague (no relation) supporting the operations of MacArthur's troops ashore. Sprague's escort carriers, which were actually converted merchant ships to which a flight deck had been added, were built to provide anti-submarine protection to convoys in the Atlantic. In the Pacific they also had been employed to beef up the close-in air support for amphibious operations. Sprague's five carriers were too slow to outrun even a battleship; they had no armor and only a single 5-inch gun.

Shortly after 6:30 in the morning the pilot of an Avenger, on anti-submarine patrol, radioed Sprague's flagship, *Fanshaw Bay*, that he had sighted an enemy force of four battleships, seven cruisers, and eleven destroyers closing on Taffy 3 at thirty knots. "Air Plot, tell him to check his identification," yelled Sprague, annoyed at what he took to be the young reserve aviator's mistake in misreporting friendly ships of Halsey's fleet. "Identification confirmed," came the reply. "Ships have pagoda masts."[14]

Although utterly surprised, Admiral Clifton Sprague reacted as if he had been rehearsing the situation for weeks. He changed course so as to open the range but still keep near enough to the wind to launch planes, ordered all ships to make smoke, and rapidly flew all his remaining planes to attack the enemy. A fantastic running battle now ensued between Sprague's fleeing carriers and Kurita's fleet. The Japanese commander, believing he was engaging Halsey's big fleet carriers and other heavy ships, excitedly ordered "General attack!" This sent his battleships, cruisers, and destroyers racing in pell-mell to attack the American carriers. It was almost as if, having finally achieved their objective, the Japanese had gone to pieces.

Even at that, the slow "baby flattops" could not have escaped annihilation for long, had it not been for good luck and the courageous improvisation of Sprague's sailors and aviators. Planes from the carriers made repeated vicious, slashing attacks on the Japanese battleships and cruisers. Many of the planes were armed only with small, general-purpose bombs that could not penetrate warship armor. Others had no bombs at all, but made repeated "dry runs" to distract the attacking warships and cause them to change course. Fortunately, bombers from Rear Admiral Felix Stump's Taffy 2, just south of Sprague's group, had been properly armed with torpedoes. These planes soon entered the battle, inflicting heavy damage on Kurita's cruisers and helping to sink three of them.

Now chasing salvos, now dodging into a friendly rain squall, Sprague's carriers fought to delay the inevitable. As the pursuers closed in, Sprague ordered his destroyers and destroyer escorts to deliver a torpedo attack. Three times, the handful of destroyers and destroyer escorts dashed out of the smoke screen to engage whole columns of battleships and cruisers. Two of the destroyers and one destroyer escort were sunk, but their attacks distracted and disorganized the Japanese pursuit. Battleship *Yamato* steamed so far north to avoid torpedo tracks that she took herself completely out of the battle. A Japanese destroyer squadron was so badgered by the damaged destroyer *Johnston* that it fired torpedoes prematurely at long range. An Avenger torpedo plane from carrier *St. Louis* actually managed to explode one of the torpedoes in the water by strafing; another was picked off by a 5-inch gun from the same ship.[15]

Even after frantic messages for help from Sprague and Kinkaid had begun to come in, Halsey long refused to turn back south to engage Kurita. Only after receiving a garbled query from Admiral Nimitz, which he took as a rebuke, did Halsey form Task Force 34 and send it south with one of the carrier task groups to rescue Sprague. Kinkaid had long since ordered his old battleships, which had fought at Surigao Strait, to head north for Leyte Gulf, but they were more than three hours away, and many were short of ammunition.

"The situation is getting a little tense, isn't it?" remarked a sailor in the carrier *White Plains* to an officer.[16] Sprague's carriers were being steadily herded in toward Leyte Gulf to the southwest. The carrier *Gambier Bay* was on fire and sinking. Kurita's ships were now coming within range of Admiral Stump's middle group of escort carriers. The situation was rapidly going from very bad to desperate. Then, around 9:30 that morning, the incredible happened: the enemy cruisers and destroyers flanking Sprague's carriers abruptly turned northward and retired. "G-dammit, boys, they're getting away!" yelled a signalman on Admiral Clifton Sprague's flagship, *Fanshaw Bay*. The admiral, who had expected "at best to be swimming by this time," could not believe it.[17]

Rattled and thoroughly tired, Kurita had all along believed he was engaging Halsey's carriers. The improvised air strikes from the escort carriers, though piecemeal and uncoordinated, had still confronted the Japanese, at times, with more than a hundred very aggressive planes in the air. At least two planes are known to have strafed the bridge of Kurita's flagship. His first flagship had been sunk by air attack the day before. The Japanese had also intercepted Kinkaid and Sprague's calls for help, which were broadcast in plain English, making Kurita wonder what additional forces might be closing in on him.[18] The Japanese commander therefore decided to break off action and at least give his scattered force a chance to reform. After milling about for more than two hours, rounding up stragglers and cripples and fighting off more air attacks, he signaled Tokyo at 12:30 that he was heading north for San Bernardino Strait. Halsey, delayed by the need to fuel his escorting destroyers, arrived too late to stop him.

The Battle of Leyte Gulf cost the Japanese four aircraft carriers, three

battleships, ten cruisers, and eleven destroyers and left the Combined
Fleet crippled as a unified striking force. Yet even as the Americans appeared at last to be in uncontested control of the seas, the next and final
phase of the contest between ships and planes had already begun.

As Admiral Kurita's battered warships were withdrawing from their
confused duel with the escort carriers off Samar, six Japanese fighters
from Davao attacked another group of escort carriers about one hundred
miles farther south, damaging the escort carriers *Santee* and *Suwanee*.
What made this encounter unusual was that the attacking planes deliberately crashed into their targets.

These new aerial tactics, soon dubbed Kamikaze attacks, were the
brainchild of Vice Admiral Onishi Takijiro, a leading Japanese aviator.
By late 1944, Onishi had concluded that American superiority at sea
and in the air was now so great that the only effective means to counter
the relentless American advance was to organize "special attack units"
for the purpose of carrying out suicide attacks in bomb-laden planes
against enemy warships. First organized in the Philippines from regular
pilots of the naval air force, the Kamikaze units made their initial appearance on the last day of the Leyte Gulf battle. On October 28, three
hours after the attacks on the *Suwanee* and *Santee*, Lieutenant Seki
Yukio, who had graduated from the Naval Academy one month before
Pearl Harbor, led five aircraft from Luzon against Taffy 3, Rear Admiral
Clifton Sprague's escort carrier group, which had earlier fought off Kurita's surface attacks.

Evading radar detection by flying at very low altitude, a Zero fighter
crashed into the escort carrier *Kitkun Bay*. The plane careened off the
carrier into the sea, but its bomb exploded, causing considerable damage. Lieutenant Seki crashed through the flight deck of the escort carrier
St. Lo. His plane exploded, setting off explosions of torpedoes and
bombs on the hangar deck. The *St. Lo* blew up and sank in twenty minutes.[19]

As MacArthur's forces, supported by the navy, advanced through the
Philippines, the Kamikaze attacks increased. In the invasion of the island of Mindoro, just south of Luzon, the cruiser *Nashville* was hit by a
suicide dive-bomber that killed thirteen men and wounded 190 others.
Two LSTs were also fatally damaged and other ships disabled. "Aircraft
flew over masthead straight for director, just missed, glanced off bow into
water—whew! Soaked with gas, scared to death, pieces of plane everywhere—living on borrowed time," wrote Lieutenant Pete Hamner of the
destroyer *Haworth* in his journal.[20]

Kamikazes usually operated in formations of five planes, three suicide planes and two escorts to provide some protection against intercepting aircraft and to report results of the attack. The attackers attempted to approach at high or very low altitudes to evade U.S. radar, which had difficulty tracking targets near the surface or at altitudes over 20,000 feet. A plane making a low-altitude approach would climb sharply as it closed in on the target, then execute a steep dive aiming at some vital part of the target vessel.[21]

MacArthur's invasion of Luzon proper in December 1944 and January 1945 brought on Kamikaze attacks of such fury they "made the Kamikaze raids of the past two and a half months seem just a warming-up period."[22] On the long voyage north from Leyte to Luzon, Rear Admiral Jessie B. Oldendorf's bombardment and support force of escort carriers, battleships, cruisers, and destroyers were repeatedly attacked by Japanese planes from nearby Philippine airfields. The escort carrier *Ommaney Bay* was sunk by a lone bomber that crashed the flight deck and started fires in the engine room and bunkers. The following day Kamikazes damaged a second escort carrier, a destroyer, and two heavy cruisers.

Yet the worst attacks were still to come. As the ships entered the Lingayen Gulf off the east coast of Luzon and began their preliminary bombardment and minesweeping off the landing beaches, Kamikazes appeared in successive waves. Many were intercepted by the fleet's combat air patrol of screening fighters; others were destroyed by antiaircraft fire—but some got through. The battleships *New Mexico* and *California*, cruisers *Louisville*, *Columbia*, and *Australia*, and a number of smaller ships were damaged and the destroyer escort *Long* was sunk.[23] A diary kept by a seaman aboard the destroyer *Mustin* gives some idea of the intensity of the attacks on the ships supporting the invasion.

January 8   About 9 A.M. we went to general quarters; a lone Jap plane came over the whole formation then crashed the transport.

January 9   We are still at general quarters. Arrived in Lingayan Gulf about 2 A.M.; at 6:30 a Jap plane strafed our ship and crash-dived a nearby destroyer escort. Jap planes have been around us all night and we had some close calls. . . . One plane suicided into a Limey cruiser. About 7:30 P.M. some Jap planes came over our group of ships and made things hot. One was shot down and no damage was done.

January 10   We are still at general quarters. . . . About 7 A.M. a few Jap planes came over the formation and a couple were shot down. One crashed into one of our ships. Jap planes were all around us keeping us alert and ready for action.

January 11   We are still at general quarters. . . . About 7 P.M. two groups of Jap planes came over and made things hot again. No damage was done. About 8:30 a lone Jap plane gave us more trouble and almost crash-dived our ship.

January 12   We are still at general quarters. It is pretty foggy and a couple of Jap planes are flying low over our formation. This almost drives a man batty, waiting for something you don't want and don't know when you are going to get it.[24]

In all, some twenty-five ships were hit during the Lingayan operation. Oldendorff's fleet had suffered a rate of damage reminiscent of that of Cunningham's fleet at Crete. Slightly more than a quarter of the Kamikazes managed to hit a ship and one in thirty-three to sink a ship.[25] To defend against attacking Kamikaze planes, American antiaircraft fire had to completely destroy, not simply damage them, since even fragments of a plane could cause casualties or start fires. Unlike the Germans at Crete, however, the Japanese in the Philippines were rapidly running out of serviceable planes, and Lingayan proved their last major attempt to stop MacArthur's seaborne advance. Yet the Japanese were pleased with the success of their new methods. Plans were already under way to organize much-expanded Kamikaze air groups for the defense of the home islands and their inner defenses.

"The men who can save the country are not the military or political leaders," declared Admiral Onishi. "The salvation of Japan lies in the young people of 25 to 35—or even younger—in their body-hitting spirit."[26] "Kamikaze" means "divine wind" and refers to the typhoon that shattered the great invasion fleet of Emperor Kublai Khan in the thirteenth century. The original Japanese name for the suicide units was "Shimpu," a more dignified reading of the characters for "divine wind," and throughout the war the Japanese called them "Shimpu units," although they are remembered by the more daredevil connotation, "Kamikaze."[27] The first Shimpu units had been composed mainly of regular navy pilots, but most of the suicide pilots who followed were recent university graduates or students, many of whom had been in the service only a short time. Their flying skills were rudimentary. Captain Rikihei Inoguchi, a naval air staff officer in the Philippines, told of one pilot who returned to base having flown more than two hundred miles off course because of his lack of training in navigation and the fact that the navy had not bothered to issue him a map or chart.[28] In the last months of the war, Kamikaze volunteers were taught only basic pilot skills. Training in landing was considered unnecessary.

Although they were represented to the public as godlike heroes whose souls would soon rest in the warriors' shrine at Yasukuni, these ex-students were viewed with some distaste by the career officers and NCOs. "When in uniform they were roughly treated as belonging to the intelligentsia," wrote a university instructor who had known many pilots. These feelings were warmly reciprocated. "We are all going to die [but] I will never fight for the navy," wrote Hayashi Norimasa, a twenty-five-year-old university graduate. "I will fight for my country for my personal honor, but never for the navy which I hate. . . . it is dominated by a clique of officers from the Naval Academy."[29]

The main motivation of most Shimpu pilots, as expressed in their last letters, was not military glory but rather feelings of obligation and gratitude toward their family and their country. "On learning that my time had come I closed my eyes and saw visions of your face, mother's, grandmother's, and the faces of my close friends," wrote Ensign Teruo Yamaguchi to his father. "It leaves a bad taste in my mouth when I think of the deceits being played on innocent citizens by some of our wily politicians but I am willing to take orders from the high command and even from the politicians because I believe in the nation of Japan. . . . I must smite the foe who violates our homeland. My grave shall be the sea around Okinawa and I will see my mother and grandmother again."[30]

Many pilots took with them a *senniburi*, a ceremonial sash sewn with individual stitches by well-wishers. Others took with them dolls, pictures, bibles, or flags. "I think I will also take along the charm and the dried bonito from Mr. Tateishi," wrote Ensign Hayashi Ichizo. "The bonito will help me rise from the ocean, mother, and swim back to you."[31]

Not all Kamikazes accepted their fate as serenely as these letters suggest. As the war situation grew more desperate, more and more young men were pressured to "volunteer." "It was cowardly to say no," a student at the Imperial University recalled. "You couldn't refuse when your friends went one by one."[32] Even Captain Inoguchi, a disciple of Admiral Onishi, conceded that "many of the new arrivals [at Kamikaze bases] seemed at first not only to lack enthusiasm but indeed to be disturbed by their situation." The captain hastened to add that this "passed with time and eventually gave way to a spiritual awakening."[33] At least a few pilots, however, appeared to have been denied this spiritual awakening. There is at least one recorded instance of a pilot strafing the squadron command post on his way to his fatal encounter with the American fleet.[34]

As MacArthur's troops on Luzon fought to recapture the Philippine capital of Manila in bloody house-to-house fighting, other forces were gathering for the final assault on Japan's inner defenses. The objective was the sixty-mile long banana-shaped island of Okinawa, only 350 miles southwest of Japan. Okinawa, the largest of the Ryukyu Islands, would be the jumping-off point for the projected invasion of Japan itself, planned for late 1945. It would also serve as an important air and naval base. Medium bombers flying from Okinawa could add their weight to the devastating air attacks on Japan already being carried out by the new B-29 superbombers, which had operated from Saipan since late 1944.

More than 180,000 assault troops were put ashore from a huge armada of transports and amphibious craft in the first days of April 1945 without serious opposition. Lieutenant General Ushijima, who commanded the 32nd Army, charged with the defense of Okinawa, had learned well the lessons of earlier island battles. His forces would defend neither the beaches nor even the airfields in the northern portions of the island. Instead the 32nd Army had constructed a system of strong concentric defensive positions centered on the old castle town of Shuri, utilizing the natural caves that dotted the mountainous region of southern Okinawa.

Fanning out across the northern section of the island, American troops easily captured the airfields at Kadena and Yontan with few losses. "There is every indication that American casualties may be a record low for Pacific operations," wrote one reporter.[35] On April 4, however, soldiers of the 96th Division came up against the first of Ushijima's defensive lines on the Kaakazu Ridge, near the town of Machinato, north of Naha. It took three American divisions two weeks to clear the interlocking network of concealed firing positions, caves, artillery positions, machine guns, and antitank guns and cost them heavy casualties. And that was only the first line of Ushijima's defenses; for the next ten weeks American soldiers and marines would fight one of the bloodiest campaigns of the war through the deadly gorges, draws, and ridges of southern Okinawa. The navy would fight the longest-sustained battle in naval history.

In the Central Pacific campaigns, American carrier task forces had usually neutralized all Japanese air bases within striking distance of the objectives before D-Day. Okinawa, however, was out of range of American air bases, but well within range of Japanese airstrips on Japan and

Formosa. These were too numerous to knock out, and their aircraft were well dispersed and concealed. As a result, American warships would have to remain off Okinawa as long as necessary to shield the landing forces and to provide air and gunfire support. Until the airfields on Okinawa could be put into operation, carriers would also have to supply all aerial protection for the fleet and the troops ashore. The carriers, battleships, and other craft off Okinawa became "the fleet that came to stay."

The Japanese hoped to cripple or drive off this fleet utilizing their new weapon, the Kamikaze. By the eve of the Okinawa campaign the skill and experience of the suicide pilots had declined even further, but there were more of them. The Japanese planned to use them in coordinated mass attacks called Kikusui or "floating chrysanthemums" to saturate American defenses.

The Americans, fresh from the battles off the Philippines, had taken measures to meet the new threat. Carriers off-loaded some of their dive-bombers and torpedo planes to accommodate additional fighters. A big Essex-class carrier now embarked about seventy-three fighters in her air group of some one hundred planes. To provide additional early warning, the navy established sixteen "radar picket" stations. These were composed of pairs of radar-equipped destroyers and destroyer escorts stationed around Okinawa at distances of up to seventy-five miles along the most probable approach routes of attacking aircraft. The patrols were supported by small landing craft, which the sailors referred to as "meat wagons" and which provided additional firepower as well as often taking aboard dead and wounded from sunk or damaged ships. Embarked in the destroyers were fighter direction teams who directly controlled a combat air patrol of six to eight fighters and who could call on additional planes from the task force. The stations were spaced so that contacts detected by one ship could be passed to another while still maintaining the original contact.[36]

The first and largest of the Kikusui attacks, which were to continue until late June, began on April 6. All those who survived remembered it as a beautiful day, sunny, clear, with a warm breeze blowing from the East China Sea. In midafternoon the destroyer *Colhoun*, patrolling radar picket station number two, north of Okinawa, picked up several large groups of planes on her radar. They were a part of a 700-plane attack force, half of them Kamikazes, which struck the American fleet in successive waves that day. Large numbers were shot down by the combat air patrol, but those planes that got through did a lot of damage. Three destroyer-type ships, an LST, and two ammunition ships were sunk and ten other ships, mostly destroyers, were severely damaged.[37]

Among them was the destroyer *Mullaney*, which had been patrolling off the east coast of Okinawa late in the afternoon when she was attacked by a lone fighter. It crashed into the after deckhouse, between two 5-inch gun mounts, and exploded, destroying the gun mounts and the after directors, disabling the steering control, and spraying the ship with burning gasoline. As the ship glided to a halt, five more planes approached, but the remaining guns shot down three of them and drove the others away. By this time, however, fires were raging out of control and beginning to "cook off" the depth chargers and shells in the handling rooms. Her captain, Commander Albert O. Monn, ordered the ship abandoned.[38]

The destroyer *Purdy* and the destroyer-minesweeper *Gherardi* were ordered to assist *Mullaney*. They arrived to find the ship on fire and small amphibious craft picking up survivors in the water. "I was shocked at the scene I beheld," recalled a sailor in the *Gherardi*.

> There in the oily waters were survivors in their life jackets, some not moving, others yelling for help, while others were moaning and groaning. . . . Men who could climbed aboard. Others were hoisted aboard and we prepared to highlight it out of the area. . . . We moved off quickly and battened down all hatches once again. . . . We were some distance away from the *Mullaney* when I was told to go to the galley to pick up our gun crew's portion of rations. . . . When I opened the hatch to the galley I was shocked once again. There on one of the mess tables sat a sailor from the *Mullaney*. He had his arms outstretched and was wrapped from head to toe in bandages. The only open spot on his whole body was where his eyes and nostrils were located. . . . Other survivors were in the compartment and their burns and wounds were being attended to. . . . By the time I got back to the 5-inch gun I felt sick and couldn't eat anything. It was difficult even to tell the gun crew what I had seen. . . . I entered the navy at the age of 17 and the month before, in March, I had just turned 18. I wondered if I would make it to age 19.[39]

After fighting the fires from the *Purdy*, Captain Monn, with a salvage crew, reboarded the *Mullaney* and got the ship under way to Kerama Retto, the fleet anchorage and support base about fifteen miles west of Okinawa that the Americans had seized toward the end of March. Over the next weeks the roadstead at Kerama Retto would fill up with burned and twisted ships. "Scorched, scarred and half-wrecked destroyer *Leutze* was alongside repair ship *Egeria* with part of a Kamikaze still resting on her fan tail; [destroyer] *Newcombe* with number two stack gone, number one leaning crazily starboard, her entire deck abaft the superstructure buckled into the contour of a roller coaster and her fan tail six inches above the water. . . . Both ships had to be beached or drydocked and there was some question whether they were worth repairing," wrote Navy historian Samuel Eliot Morison, describing the interior of the roadstead after the first Kikusui attacks of April 6–7.[40]

American sailors regarded the Kamikazes with a mixture of disbelief, dread, and disdain. A frequent observation was that this Japanese innovation was outside all normal human experience.[41] "Every time one country gets something all the others have it," observed Jimmy Thach. "One country gets radar but soon all have it. One gets a new type of engine or plane, then another gets it. But the Japs have got the Kamikaze boys and nobody else is going to get that because no one else is built that way."[42] Rear Admiral F. Julian Becton, a destroyer skipper, recalled that for many men the Kamikaze was a phenomenon "for which [they] had no frame of reference."[43] Lieutenant Tom Parkerson talked with an American-educated Kamikaze pilot captured off Okinawa who explained that he would never be able to return to Japan because he had allowed himself to be taken prisoner. "The idea of this great humiliation of being taken alive was not really comprehensible to me."[44] Machinist's mate Arthur Hogan, a survivor of Pearl Harbor, believed that the Kamikazes at Ormoc had been much worse than anything on December 7, 1941, "not in losses, but in the way the Japanese had executed their [suicide] attacks. . . . [He] just couldn't make any sense out of them."[45]

In a war in which the enemy was frequently defined in racial terms, many observers explained the Kamikaze in terms of the Japanese inhuman lust for death and killing. "Americans who fight to live find it difficult to realize that another people will fight to die," wrote Admiral Halsey.[46] "We had taken the measure of the skilled professionals and knew how to handle them," recalled Admiral Becton, "but these Kamikazes were fanatics, religious fanatics and that was beginning to worry me."[47]

Though many other sailors were "worried" as well, they were not, as the Japanese hoped, disheartened and intimidated by the new weapon. Indeed, it is possible to see a strange parallel in the attitudes of American sailors and their Japanese protagonists in this final stage of the war. Both conceived themselves to be trapped in a nightmarish battle to the death. "I didn't have nothing for them but some 20 millimeter cannon bullets. . . . I didn't have any sobering second thoughts," declared a sailor aboard an Okinawa destroyer. "For sure if somebody's got to die, if you don't make the other guy die first than you are going to die."[48] A sailor in the destroyer *Saufley* recalled, "We wanted to send him, creepy and crawly to Hell any way we could. We learned that no quarter in battle can work both ways. Time and distance plus loneliness make a tasteless soup, hard to stomach for long periods of time and ours was a long, long time. . . . We had sharp deadly fights at sea while the marines and army landed. . . . It was kill or be killed."[49]

Although they had no inclination toward suicide, many sailors developed a strong fatalism, a recognition that the odds were not in their favor. "Somebody's got to get it and we may be lucky or unlucky," wrote Yeoman Orville Raines, in the destroyer *Howorth*.[50] "Up until [1945] I felt like I might have a chance to get home," recalled one sailor. "But after the Philippines, when they started the suicide tactics, then I never expected that I would be home ever. I thought I would die in the Pacific. I never had any feeling that I would ever return."[51] As a sailor in the USS *Luce* put it, "I thought to myself, well, it's just a matter of time. It's not if you're going to get it, it's when."[52]

On the second day of the Kikusui offensive the super-battleship *Yamato*, the largest warship in the world, sortied from Japan. It had been designed to confront the American fleet in what both sides had expected, in the 1930s, would be the great mid-Pacific battle. With only enough fuel for a one-way trip and accompanied only by a light cruiser and a few destroyers, she was little more than a Kamikaze herself. Still far from Okinawa, she was set upon by successive waves of American planes from twelve different carriers. The *Yamato*'s toughness bore out all her builders' expectations: it took five bombs and ten torpedoes to sink her. Yet she sank in less than two hours. Her enormous power, far exceeding the giants of Jutland, was now almost irrelevant to the deadly battles raging in the seas and skies around Okinawa.

Day after day, week after week, the Japanese onslaught continued. There were nine more massed Kamikaze attacks, three in April, four in May, and two in June. The main targets were the destroyers and smaller supporting vessels on radar picket duty. At one station, during early May, four out of six vessels—including two destroyers—were sunk in a single day. Major attacks had a terrifying sameness. A large number of planes, sometimes forty or more, would approach a patrolling destroyer to begin the onslaught. Destroyers *Hugh W. Hadley* and *Evans* were attacked by five successive waves of planes in less than two hours. The largest of these waves had fifty planes, the next-largest thirty-six.[53]

Most attacks occurred at dawn or twilight when the attacking planes were harder to see. The attacker came in low to evade radar detection; a large percentage fell victim to the American combat air patrol or to the ships' antiaircraft fire, but inevitably some planes would get through. Hits or damage sometimes were not enough to deflect a suicide plane. "If you kill the pilot and he turns the controls loose normally the plane would come in on a glide pattern," observed one sailor in USS *Luce*. "You had to get the wings or the engines."[54]

"I don't believe I'll ever forget the noise a plane made as it came racing in," recalled an officer aboard the carrier *Bennington*. "Something like when a plane flat hats a field or a house. But instead of trailing away in the distance, it ends with a sudden startling splat!"[55] Machinist's Mate Emory Jernigan's battle station was in the after steering room of a destroyer. "These stations were as close to Hell as a man could get in this world. . . . The number five gunmount would start to fire, dumping several hundred shell-cases a minute on the quarter-inch deck plate. When the ship's propellers would speed up the vibrations would shake everything. The propeller shafts would start making a warping sound as if they wanted to leave the mounts. The rudders and hydraulic lines would moan in their labors and underwater explosions would hit the hull just outside. . . . Your skivvies would be just a little damp where you almost wet yourself. Later when battle stations were secured, stinking salty sweat would cover your body like a warm wet rag."[56]

Even a glancing hit could cause damage, while a direct hit by a Kamikaze almost always resulted in an explosion of flaming gasoline and showers of jagged metal. If the fire occurred in the vicinity of depth charges, ammunition, or torpedoes, there would be further explosions. Some ships were sunk by a single hit. A Kamikaze crashed the *Luce* in the vicinity of the number three gun, killing everyone near the mount and causing extensive underwater damage. Machinist's Mate Michael Heron noticed that the crew of the gun mount appeared to have vanished. He "saw no one except a guy on the gun with no body—just shoulders—no head, no nothing."[57] The *Luce* sank with the loss of more than 150 of her 335 men. Other ships, tougher or luckier, survived many hits. The destroyer *Laffey* was attacked in mid-April by more than twenty planes. Her gunners shot down nine of them, but six others crashed into the ship, and she was hit by four bombs and near misses. With the rudder jammed, fires blazing, three compartments flooded, mainmast and yardarm shot away, the *Laffey* continued to steam and fire back at her attackers. In the ship's wardroom surgeon Matthew Driscoll was wounded in the hand by bomb fragments but continued to treat the sixty wounded men, working with his remaining good hand while verbally directing his assistants in aiding the other wounded.[58]

The destroyer *Hugh W. Hadley* was attacked by ten planes simultaneously. Her gunners claimed to have shot down all ten but two suicide planes hit the ship as well as a *baka* or piloted bomb flown by a Kamikaze; a conventional bomb also exploded within the ship. Large gashes were opened in the hull, and both engine rooms and one fire room were flooded. A large fire raged in the rear of the ship. As the fire reached the ammunition, there were explosions, and the entire ship, now listing badly, was engulfed in choking black smoke. Fearing that the *Hadley* would explode, the captain, Commander Baron J. Mullaney, ordered most of the crew to abandon ship. A party of fifty men remained aboard to make a last effort to save the stricken destroyer. One group fought fires while a second jettisoned torpedoes and other excess weight to bring the list under control. Within fifteen minutes the fires were extinguished and the ship was under tow to Kerama Retto. The crew later found the remains of two Kamikaze pilots in the bilges.[59]

Ships like *Laffey* and *Hadley* survived because of the courage and skill of their crews but also because of the tremendous strides the U.S. Navy had made in damage control since 1942. Like radar, damage control was a subject to which few career line officers or the navy had paid much heed until well after Pearl Harbor. Before the war a man-of-war could have been considered a "smart ship," with excellent ratings in operational efficiency, without ever being called upon to demonstrate its proficiency in damage control. Midshipmen at the Naval Academy received a theoretical course in damage control and were expected to train their men when opportunities arose. Prewar shipboard training, when it took place, consisted of "problems" in which the crew were required to decide what measures would be taken in dealing with hits by different types of weapons on various parts of the ship.[60] Because the navy had expected to fight a battle line duel with the Japanese fleet, the emphasis was on keeping damaged ships afloat and in the line of battle by controlled flooding, as the German battle cruisers had successfully done at Jutland. The Naval Academy's textbook in damage control devoted half its pages to flooding control and only a single page to fire fighting.[61]

All of this rapidly changed as war experience demonstrated that fire as well as water could be a menace to a ship. By late 1942 the navy had begun an intensive program of training in fire fighting techniques for all sailors. By 1943 there were twelve specialized fire fighting schools that could train ninety sailors a week and four more under construction. At these schools damage control parties were trained and sailors familiar-

ized with the fundamentals of fire fighting. What marksmanship training was to the army, fire fighting and damage control drills became to
the navy. Navy warships received new damage control equipment: mobile gasoline-operated pumps, portable steel-cutting outfits, rescue and
breathing gear, and foam-generating fire mains that could operate even
when the ship's power was knocked out.[62] The equipment and training
were extremely effective. Destroyer *Purdy* was hit by a Kamikaze in the
April 12 attacks off Okinawa, for example. The hit caused a large explosion. Despite the fact that half of her fire fighting equipment was
knocked out, sailors had high-pressure hoses on the fire within three to
five minutes.[63]

As the Kamikaze battles continued, the nerves of sailors with the
Fifth Fleet began to wear thin. Endless alerts, lack of sleep, the possibility of sudden fiery death at any hour—all began to take their toll. In
some cases crews were so keyed up that they learned to listen for the telltale click and static of the ship's loudspeakers being activated and were
already running for their battle stations by the time general quarters was
sounded.[64]

American communications intelligence enabled the American commanders to anticipate the larger air attacks. At first crews were alerted
accordingly, "but this practice," recalled one correspondent, "had to be
stopped. The strain of waiting, the anticipated terror, made vivid from
past experience sent some men into hysteria, insanity, breakdown."[65]
Aboard the *Enterprise*, Frank Albert recalled his friend who had feigned
insanity in boot camp. Albert believed he had discovered a navy regulation that provided that men who were bed-wetters be sent home with a
medical discharge. "The next day I must have drank over a quart of water. In fact I drank so much water it was coming out of my nose. That
night I climbed up into the top bunk of my sack, and in the still of the
night I let it go. . . . [Then] I jumped up screaming! The Master at Arms
came running in. When he found out what happened, I was thrown in
the brig. Two days later the sailor I wet came down with pneumonia. He
was discharged with a medical instead of me."[66]

The navy, in conjunction with the reluctant Army Air Forces, responded to the Kamikaze onslaught with heavy raids on known and suspected Kamikaze bases. Bases in the southern Ryukus and parts of
Formosa were the special target of Task Force 57, the striking force of the
newly formed British Pacific fleet. Task Force 57 included four fast carriers, two modern battle ships, five cruisers, fifteen destroyers, and its own
supply and service squadron. Its mission brought the British their share
of attention from Kamikazes, but the British carriers, whose design sacri-

ficed plane-carrying capacity for armored hangars and flight decks, proved far better able to stand up to suicide crashes than the thin-skinned American carriers. By a supreme irony, Task Force 57 was commanded by Vice Admiral Sir Bernard Rawlings, who had led portions of the Mediterranean Fleet off Crete in 1941, thus making him probably the only flag officer in any navy to have commanded in the two bloodiest sea-air battles of World War II.

Despite the combined efforts of the two navies and the bombers of the Army Air Forces it was only the heavy attrition of Japanese planes in successive Kikusui attacks that finally caused the Kamikaze onslaught to slacken. By the time of the final collapse of Japanese forces on Okinawa on June 21, fewer than fifty planes, including obsolete trainers, were still available for attacks. Yet the Japanese were highly pleased with the performance of their secret weapon and were energetically preparing hundreds more planes along with human torpedoes, *baka* bombs, midget submarines, and suicide motorboats for the anticipated Allied invasion of Japan proper when the atomic bomb and the Russian declaration of belligerency finally put an end to the war.

The Japanese had expended about 1,900 suicide planes at Okinawa. Fifty-seven Allied warships were sunk by Kamikazes in the Philippines and at Okinawa, and more than 100 were so extensively damaged as to be out of the war for extended periods; a few were subsequently scrapped. Another 300 ships suffered some degree of damage.[67] The navy had almost 5,000 killed and another 5,000 wounded in the Okinawa campaign, the heaviest losses of any naval campaign of World War II, and about 30 percent greater than those at Pearl Harbor.

Compared to a conventional air attack, a Kamikaze attack had a far greater chance of causing damage. A postwar analysis showed that at Okinawa, 32 percent of all Kamikazes that were able to leave their bases succeeded in hitting a ship. That was seven to ten times the success rate of conventional sorties.[68] Most Kamikaze attacks were nevertheless far less effective than they might have been, because the inexperienced pilots, often under heavy attack by combat air patrol, tended to aim for the first ships they saw rather than endeavoring to hit the more valuable carriers and shipping. Indeed, the predilection for the Kamikazes to focus all their attention on the outlying ships of the radar picket stations was so marked that one hard-pressed destroyer crew erected a huge arrow-shaped sign pointing rearward and reading "Carriers This Way."[69] However ineffective the choice of targets, postwar analysts viewed the increased lethality of the suicide plane with concern, seeing in it a direct precursor of the guided missile.

Though the Kamikaze seemed to presage a further round of more sophisticated and lethal naval warfare, it was also a return to a much older form of combat at sea, one not seen since the early nineteenth century. Since the beginning of the twentieth century, war at sea had become increasingly impersonal, with gunnery duels at steadily increasing ranges. Submarines and surface ships attacked by submarines often never saw their assailants. Carriers sent their waves of planes off to strike hundreds of miles away. Yet in the air-sea battles off Okinawa, men saw their opponents in an intimate, almost one-on-one manner reminiscent of the days of boarding parties. As one sailor put it, "When a target approached my ship and I was his target then it was between me and the other man. One of us had to die, that was on my mind."[70]

It is ironic that the last and greatest naval encounter of World War II should have become not a contest of technology but a contest of wills. Admiral Onishi and other Japanese leaders believed that Allied fighting men would be shocked and disheartened by the Kamikazes' determination and disdain for death. Americans were shocked and fearful of the new weapon, but they were not discouraged. One ship followed another on the radar picket stations. The Allies never considered abandoning their conquest of Okinawa or their plans for the subsequent invasion of Japan. Thus, the net result of the Kamikaze attacks was to add still another level of fatalism and bloodshed to what was already a grim and merciless war.

FIFTEEN

"THE REALLY BATTLE-WORTHY CAPITAL SHIP"

On the morning of July 3, 1950, exactly seven days after 100,000 North Korean soldiers, equipped and trained by the Soviet Union, had invaded South Korea, a U.S.–British task force of two aircraft carriers, two cruisers, and ten destroyers steamed north through the Yellow Sea toward the west coast of the Korean Peninsula. The South Korean capital of Seoul had been captured easily by the Communists four days before. The United Nations Security Council had condemned the attack and called upon UN members to assist South Korea. In Washington, President Truman had ordered American air and naval forces to aid in resisting the invasion. In London, the Cabinet Defense Committee had voted to place all British naval forces in Japanese waters at the disposal of the U.S. Far East Command.[1]

Just before dawn on July 3, the British carrier *Triumph* began launching her Seafire fighters and Firefly attack aircraft to carry out strikes against North Korean airfields near the town of Haeju. An hour later the American carrier *Valley Forge* launched sixteen Corsair fighters and twelve AD Skyraiders for an attack on Pyongyang, the North Korean capital.

The Corsairs and Skyraiders, like the British planes, were World War II–style aircraft. But now, as the last of these disappeared over the horizon, the *Valley Forge*'s elevators began to deliver a different type of aircraft to the flight deck, the F9-F2 Panther jet fighter. In a pattern that would be employed throughout the next three years, the fast but fuel-thirsty jets would depart later than the propeller planes to save fuel.

They would then use their superior speed to catch up with the strike group.[2]

In this first American carrier raid of the Korean War, Valley Forge's eight Panthers streaked across the Pyongyang airfield catching the North Koreans completely by surprise. In their haste to clear the single runway some North Korean fighters actually took off toward each other.[3] The few propeller-driven Yak-9 fighters that got into the air were no match for the much swifter Panthers, which shot down two fighters and destroyed two more on the ground. The Corsairs and Skyraiders then attacked the airfield with bombs and rockets, destroying hangars and fuel storage areas. Additional attacks during the afternoon damaged the Pyongyang rail yard and railroad bridge across the Taedong River.[4] No American or British aircraft were lost to enemy action, but in a landing accident aboard the Valley Forge a damaged Skyraider bounced over a crash barrier and destroyed two aircraft as well as damaging six others.

The Pyongyang raids had no discernible influence on the Communist advance into South Korea, but they did mark the beginning of a new pattern of naval operations and the employment of navies that would persist until the last decade of the twentieth century.

Not long after the Korean conflict, former naval officer Eugene Burdick wrote a widely read article in Holiday magazine in which he concluded, "In all probability fighting ships will never again come together in the classic form of battle." In 1958, a dozen years after the close of World War II, few readers found Burdick's observation much more than a truism or disputed his conclusion that the navy "will have a role in our future strategy but it will not the kind of Navy we knew in the 19th and much of the 20th century."[5]

Thirty years after the publication of Burdick's article, monster warships, more powerful than anything seen in the era of the super-dreadnoughts, still roamed the seas. One-hundred-thousand-ton aircraft carriers that could steam for months without refueling, "battle cruisers" as large as any that fought with Beatty and Hipper, "destroyers" the size of World War II cruisers, and dozens of nuclear-powered submarines able to cruise underwater at speeds five times greater than a World War II U-boat ranged the sea from the Arctic Circle to the Indian Ocean. Yet Burdick's prediction was largely vindicated; the era of "war at sea" in the sense it had been understood in the first half of the twentieth century had ended. The clash of great fleets above, below, or on the sea, was never to be seen again in the twentieth century.

With the surrender of Japan and the dawn of the nuclear age, the U.S. Navy had entered a strange new world. It was a world in which new types of sailors, some of whom never went to sea, would play a role as important as those in more traditional occupations. The great American armada created to fight Japan and Germany simultaneously now found itself without an enemy. The Axis fleets had been destroyed, and the Royal Navy was facing crippling financial problems. Relations with the Soviets were strained and getting worse, but that country was not a maritime power.

The horrific introduction of the atomic bomb at the close of the war suggested to many that future wars would be swift and destructive affairs, dominated by atomic bombs delivered by fleets of giant bombers. "All military issues will be settled by relative strength in the skies," explained airpower advocate Alexander P. de Vsebersky.[6] This scenario left little room for traditional naval operations. Yet after the war, most navy leaders had assumed that the country would want a sizable peacetime fleet as "peace insurance" and to support the newly established United Nations.

The reality had been different: the navy was rapidly demobilized. Scores of ships under construction were canceled, 2,000 were put in mothballs and 7,000 were sold for scrap.[7] Drastic as they were, the cuts in the fleet were less serious than the shrinkage in naval personnel. At the close of the war the navy had had more than 3,380,000 men on active duty. By June 1946 there were less than a million, and by the beginning of 1950 there were only about 380,000 sailors still on active duty. "Most of the old timers who were trained got out at the end of the war," recalled one officer.[8] Secretary of the Navy James Forrestal noted that there were "a very large number of vessels in the active fleet which cannot go to sea because of the lack of competent personnel."[9]

In these straitened circumstances the navy had been obliged to define a role for itself in the strange twilight world of the Cold War. Since late 1946, Washington leaders had become increasingly less hopeful of reaching a satisfactory resolution of their differences with the Soviet Union and increasingly concerned with what they saw as Soviet expansionism. If war with the USSR came, it might begin with atomic attacks, but there were too few bombs in the late 1940s to decide a war. Any nuclear exchange would probably be followed by a prolonged conventional war. In that case the navy leadership believed that the Red Army could easily overrun Europe. The navy's role would then be to attack the periphery of Europe and maintain sea control so as to make it possible for an invasion force to retake the continent as it had done in World War II.[10]

The Soviet surface navy was relatively small and obsolete. The principal threat came from the Soviet fleet of more than 250 submarines. At the conclusion of the war the Soviets had acquired four complete Type XXI U-boats, the new and very advanced model submarine completed by the Germans too late to take part in the fighting. With its high submerged speed, large battery capacity, and quieter operation, the Type XXI seemed to pose a great threat to Allied shipping in a future war. Moreover, the Soviets had obtained a number of German submarine designs and technical personnel in addition to blueprints, construction records, and equipment. The Soviets were widely believed to be hard at work building a large fleet of Type XXIs. In 1946, the Office of Naval Intelligence predicted that the Soviets would have 300 of the new submarines by 1950, and Navy Secretary John L. Sullivan told the Navy League in 1948 that the Russians were completing about twenty to thirty Type XXIs a month.[11] In fact, the Soviets were incapable of producing hordes of submarines during the late 1940s and early 1950s. Soviet shipyards had been wrecked by the war, and the Soviet shipbuilding industry simply lacked the technology and manufacturing capabilities to turn out large numbers of state-of-the-art warships.

U.S. intelligence analysts had little detailed knowledge of Soviet naval matters. They did know that the Russians had the Type XXIs, that Stalin was interested in a big navy, and that Fleet Admiral N. G. Kutznetsov, the Soviet commander in chief, had declared in 1948 that the Russian navy aimed at having 1,200 submarines.[12] That was enough for the U.S. Navy. Under the leadership of Vice Admiral Forrest B. Sherman, Deputy Chief of Naval Operations, the navy developed a plan to deal with the Soviet threat, which brilliantly combined its traditional role of control of the seas with its new capability to project power from the sea.

Sherman argued that the enormous numbers of advanced submarines could not be countered simply by the traditional methods of convoy and anti-submarine warfare; the Soviet submarine threat must be attacked "at the source," using naval air to attack submarines in their bases and destroy their support facilities. To do that, aircraft carriers would have to approach close to the Soviet Union within range of land-based Russian aircraft. These planes would have to be destroyed on the airfields as Sherman had seen the Pacific Fleet do at Truk and other Japanese bases during World War II. Thus Sherman, an aviator, justified the continued existence and growth of the navy's air arm by linking it inextricably with the solution to the Soviet sea control threat. The carriers, with their powerful strike forces of fighters and bombers able to strike precision targets, could also be used to support a land campaign ashore, especially from the Mediterranean.[13] By the end of 1946 the United States had established a permanent naval presence in the Mediterranean in the form of a powerful force of cruisers, destroyers, and aircraft carriers that would, in a few years, be designated the Sixth Fleet.

The creation of the Sixth Fleet together with the retention of sizable forces in the Far East marked a departure from patterns of naval operations over the past fifty years. Since Fisher's redeployment of the British fleet and the expansion of the German navy in the 1900s, the Great Powers had tended to keep their most powerful and modern naval forces close to home. Older cruisers and gunboats looked after their interests overseas while the really battle-worthy ships conducted fleet maneuvers and exercises relatively close to their home bases. This had been the pattern of the U.S. and Japanese fleets between the wars as well as for the British, German, and Italian navies. (The Royal Navy's Mediterranean Fleet appeared to be an exception to this practice, but the British had considered the control of the Mediterranean a direct part of the defense of Britain.) Now the pattern had been broken, with the permanent stationing of the most advanced and powerful warships of the U.S. Navy far from home in positions close to the likely scene of future threat or hostilities. This practice, termed "forward deployment," was to continue until the end of the century and have a strong impact on all other naval issues.

While the U.S. Navy planned for beating the Soviet threat, a more immediate danger seemed to be posed by the U.S. Army and U.S. Air Force. The National Security Act of 1947, among many other measures, had created three separate though equal services: The navy, army, and a new independent air force. It also had established a Secretary of Defense to coordinate the three service departments and had given legal authority to the Joint Chiefs of Staff created during World War II. In 1949, amendments to the act gave the Secretary of Defense additional authority as head of a unified Department of Defense. The service secretaries were given access to the president only through the Secretary of Defense.

The navy had long had grave misgivings about unification, suspecting, not without reason, that the other two services would gang up on the sea service. They also suspected that the air force coveted the navy's air assets and the army wished to reduce the Marine Corps to a token force. The navy was now increasingly dominated by aviators, and the air force's plans and intentions appeared particularly threatening to them. Admiral Towers and Admiral Arthur Radford told Forrestal that "for 25 years naval air had been trying to protect itself both within and outside the Navy." Admiral Towers said "the Army airforce was already raiding the Navy for able young fliers," and Forrestal had received a report "that a Lieutenant Commander, one of our best pilots with a splendid war record in the Pacific, had been approached by the Army airforces with an offer to make him a Lieutenant Colonel in that organization if he would transfer."[14]

After much bickering and compromise the 1947 National Security Act had allowed the navy to maintain its air arm and provided for the continued existence of a sizable Marine Corps, which by that time had become, in effect, a separate service within the Navy Department. Yet mutual suspicions and disagreements among the services continued over their roles and missions as well as over their share of the steadily shrinking defense budgets of the late 1940s. These quarrels and suspicions reached a climax with the so-called "revolt of the admirals" in late 1949.

On April 23, 1949, the newly appointed Defense Secretary, Louis Johnson, suddenly canceled construction of the navy's supercarrier United States. By this point both the military services and the public had become preoccupied with the vision of "air-atomic war." The navy's sea-control, power-projection plan was based on the assumption of a long war and had never been adequately explained to lawmakers and the public. And by 1949 many navy aviators had moved away from this complex concept to the more easily understandable and dramatic role of delivering atomic attacks against the Soviet Union. The giant United States was designed to accommodate a new type of aircraft that could carry an atomic bomb. Since air force bombers could not reach the Soviet Union from the United States, some naval aviators believed that the aircraft carrier could be a strong contender to carry out the "air-atomic" mission. In any case, carrier aircraft armed with tactical atomic weapons would be necessary to attack Soviet naval and air bases that threatened U.S. sea-control operations.

The administration and Congress found the air force's new intercontinental bomber, the B-36, more appealing, however. At the same time that he canceled construction of the supercarrier, Secretary Johnson had approved procurement of three dozen additional B-36s. The squalid controversy that ensued provided the military services a rare opportunity to publicly display their narrow-mindedness, paranoia, and parochialism— and they rose to the occasion. There were leaks to the press by the navy describing the B-36 as "a billion-dollar blunder." There were congressional hearings. The chairman of the Joint Chiefs of Staff, General Omar Bradley, called the admirals a "bunch of fancy Dans." Several naval officers skated on the edge of court-martial. The Chief of Naval Operations was fired, and other admirals were prematurely retired.[15]

When the smoke cleared, the air force's B-36 program remained unthreatened, but some naval officers consoled themselves with the thought that they had at least made the case for naval aviation. They had not made it to Secretary Johnson, who openly declared to associates that the navy ought to be reduced to one carrier, "for the old Admirals to ride around on." But the new Chief of Naval Operations, the canny Forrest Sherman, had been able to halt the decline in the size of the active fleet and to begin a program of carrier modernization. Taking advantage of the Truman administration's developing reevaluation of its security needs and astutely cultivating support on the Hill, Sherman also had succeeded in securing funds for development of a nuclear-powered submarine and congressional approval for construction of a supercarrier of the type canceled only a year before.[16] Yet the navy was still shrinking. The defense budget for the 1951 fiscal year provided for only 239 major combat ships and only 40,000 men. The number of active carriers would be reduced to seven.[17]

Then, on June 25, 1950, North Korean troops and tanks crossed the 48th parallel into South Korea. The following day, President Truman ordered air and naval operations in defense of South Korea, and three days later he approved the deployment of U.S. ground forces to the peninsula. The Korean War strongly reinforced American leaders' fears and expectations of Communist military aggression and laid the foundation of a new Cold War navy.

At the time the British and American carriers made their first strikes against Pyongyang, the North Korean army was well on its way toward overrunning all of South Korea. During the next two weeks the Communist forces brushed aside the poorly armed, poorly trained U.S. Army troops sent to oppose them, routed the South Korean army, and, by late July, had pushed the defending forces into a small redoubt near the last remaining port of Pusan in southeastern Korea.

At the outbreak of war, the U.S. Seventh Fleet, under Admiral Arthur D. Struble, responsible for the western Pacific, had only one aircraft carrier, one cruiser, and a handful of smaller ships. Admiral Forrest Sherman summoned ships from as far away as the Mediterranean to rapidly reinforce Struble's fleet, however. By early August there were three fleet carriers and two escort carriers assigned to the Seventh Fleet. A marine division and large numbers of amphibious ships were also on the way.

The carriers were urgently needed, since by the end of July, the North Koreans had captured all of the U.S. air bases on the peninsula. Most U.S. Air Force fighters lacked the range to operate over Korea from bases in Japan. On July 23, General Walton Walker, who commanded U.S., Korean, and other UN forces in the perimeter, sent an urgent request for direct support of his troops by carrier aircraft. When the escort carrier *Sicily* docked in Kobe, Japan, her captain was immediately summoned to a meeting with the admiral commanding U.S. Naval Forces, Far East. "How soon can you get under way?" asked the admiral. The captain replied that he expected to be ready by the following morning. "You don't understand," replied the admiral. "I mean how soon can you get under way right now? Because if you don't, there won't be any use in getting under way. It'll be too late." One hour later the *Sicily* was steaming down the Kobe channel toward the open sea. The following day she launched her first air strikes against North Koreans attacking the Pusan perimeter.[18]

Navy and marine Corsairs and Douglas AD Skyraiders, the latter a single-engine plane that could carry as much ordnance as a World War II heavy bomber, provided continuous air support to the embattled soldiers and marines in the perimeter. Journalist Max Miller observed that marine planes, operating from the *Sicily*, "frequently would return with mud on them as a result of their own explosions. This is how closely they worked to the ground. . . ."[19] In World War II, carrier aircraft had delivered about one seventh of a ton of ordnance per flight. During the summer of 1950, the average was just over half a ton.[20] During August alone, navy and marine Corsairs and Skyraiders logged almost 7,200 combat flight hours.[21]

As the North Korean advance, blunted by air attacks and the continuous arrival of additional United Nations troops, ground to a halt, General Douglas MacArthur, the U.S./UN commander, staged a surprise amphibious attack against the port of Inchon on the west coast not far from the Korean capital of Seoul. The 1st Marine Division, withdrawn from the Pusan perimeter, and a newly arrived army division landed at Inchon on September 15 to find the North Korean defenders ill-prepared and confused.

While the Inchon landing force advanced toward Seoul, General Walker's forces began an attack out of the Pusan perimeter. With enemy forces now to their rear, the North Koreans began a rapid retreat. Truman and his advisers, delighted by this remarkable battlefield reversal, authorized MacArthur's forces to pursue the Communist forces into North Korea and bring about the reunification of the country.

To support his drive to the north, MacArthur ordered another amphibious landing, this time at Wonsan on the east coast of North Korea. Communist mining of the harbor delayed the landings for more than a week and demonstrated how rapidly the navy's minesweeping capabilities had ossified since the close of World War II. The North Korean collapse was so complete, however, that MacArthur's troops had already captured the city from the landward side by the time the landing force came ashore.

The UN advance continued through October against increasingly ineffective North Korean resistance. On October 21, the commander of the Seventh Fleet's carriers reported that he was actually running out of enemy targets.[22] This situation changed dramatically on November 25 when Chinese armies intervened with general offensives against UN forces that had been advancing up the east and west coast of the peninsula. It was, General MacArthur declared, "an entirely new war."

The rapid buildup of naval power necessitated by the outbreak of the Korean War immediately created a need for large numbers of officers and enlisted men. The overall strength of the fleet grew by 50 percent as ships in mothballs were recommissioned. Personnel requirements increased by 60 percent.[23] The navy met this need by extending the enlistment of all personnel already serving, by acquiring sailors through the Selective Service System, and by calling up large numbers of reserve officers and enlisted men.[24]

A substantial number of World War II sailors had opted to join the Naval Reserve, which offered two weeks of paid training a year. Other younger men had joined to avoid the draft. Neither group expected to be called for active service in a major war less than five years after V-J Day. By the autumn of 1950, about 120,000 reservists "had been extracted without mercy from home and families."[25]

It "was tougher for married men," recalled aircrewman Jack Sauter. "But I guess the biggest loss was one of freedom. For most of the next eight months, none of us could take a walk longer than the distance of a flight deck. . . . We were locked in just as if we were in a penitentiary. . . . Our youth only made it more painful when it came to putting the length of our deployment in context. When you're in your teens or twenties, eight months can seem like eight years. So the time stretched interminably."[26]

Many of these unhappy reservists were veterans of World War II with more professional knowledge and combat experience than the regulars they were supplementing. Other reservists were "young men who'd joined the Naval Reserve to avoid the draft. These were the so-called 'weekend warriors.' . . . College graduates for the most part, they drifted into jobs where they were altogether over-qualified. Not desiring to be commissioned or extend their two-year tour of duty, they spent much of their time shuffling papers and keeping out of everyone's way. None even tried to make 'seaman,' the grade above apprentice, and they wore their two lowly white stripes with a sort of reverse pride."[27]

Reserve aviators faced a special problem. Many fighter squadrons had recently made the transition from propeller to jet aircraft. "Pity the unfortunate recalled reservist," observed Captain E. T. Woolridge, "a multiengine or seaplane pilot during the war, a family man suddenly thrust into flying situations that were totally foreign to him. . . ."[28] Most received relatively little time to become familiar with their fast, more unforgiving airplanes before they were on their way to the western Pacific.[29] Jet squadrons were "sometimes led by pilots who did not understand what jets could do, and often through ignorance or stubbornness, placed their pilots in situations from which there was no safe way out."[30]

Among the most basic problems of jet aircraft was that the carriers deployed to Korea had never been designed to handle planes whose approach speed and weight were far greater than those of World War II carrier planes. To launch a jet, a carrier had to attain a speed of at least thirty knots to produce enough wind over the deck. Planes had to be catapulted into the air using old World War II–style hydraulic catapults. "Our catapult run was only about 300 feet long and we had to attain a speed of 120 knots in this distance. That will give any pilot a pretty good jolt on take-off," recalled one Korean War aviator.[31]

Landing at high speed, a jet had only one chance to snag an arresting line. When the plane's tailhook caught the arresting wire the plane underwent "a fierce, violent deceleration of about 100 knots of relative speed in less than three seconds. . . . An enormous amount of energy is dissipated into the innards of the ship in a screeching of wires over cables, hydraulic fluid screaming past tiny valve orifices and air grunting under the compression of monstrous pistons."[32] If a pilot missed his "trap," he crashed into a nylon barrier. If, as sometimes happened, the barrier failed to stop the jet, there was no place to go except into a parked aircraft at the far end of the flight deck.[33]

When jets were being landed, flight deck personnel completely cleared the deck and took cover in the narrow catwalks. "Hung rockets (misfires) would come off the plane and hurtle into our work zone," recalled William Crouse, an electronics technician who served in Air Group 2 aboard the carriers *Valley Forge* and *Philippine Sea.* "The ship's Airboss would give us ample warning, 'hung rocket,' 'crippled aircraft,' or 'no wheels,' etc."[34]

In bad weather the marginal capability of the World War II carrier to handle jets could spell disaster. In the spring of 1951, the *Valley Forge* attempted to exchange its F9F Panther squadrons with those of *Philippine Sea* as part of a redeployment. "We ran into one of those unfortunate conditions when the wind was from one direction and the sea from another," recalled Vice Admiral Gerald E. Miller. "[There was] quite a swell and the decks started to pitch. . . . We had a lot of those fighters in the air. Then we tried to bring them down and it was a tough job getting them aboard. They were running out of fuel and there was no base on the beach to send them to. . . . We broke up those planes in some numbers." Altogether twenty-three of 130 aircraft were wrecked or damaged in landings, though no lives were lost. "It was a horrible mess. . . . Because of the size of the ship, the nature of the airplanes and straight deck operations."[35]

As the Chinese offensives broke over MacArthur's forces in North Korea, the Seventh Fleet was once again called upon to support land operations. The carrier *Valley Forge* was recalled from her return voyage to the United States, and the British carrier *Theseus* was dispatched from Hong Kong. An additional carrier, *Princeton*, was on its way from the West Coast.

Neither Rear Admiral James H. Doyle, who commanded the Seventh Fleet's amphibious forces, nor Major General Oliver P. Smith, who commanded the 1st Marine Division and army troops in the northeast portion of North Korea, had ever shared Washington's and MacArthur's confidence that the war was all but won. Doyle had already begun to plan for a large-scale evacuation of X Corps, the marine and army units in the east, through the port of Hungnam on the east coast of Korea north of Wonsan. General Smith had insisted on keeping his command in relatively close contact and on rapidly building an airstrip at the town of Hagaru, a little south of the Chosin Reservoir.

These prudent steps made possible the skillful withdrawal of the 1st Marine Division and other UN forces through the icy mountains and defiles from the vicinity of the reservoir to Hagaru and then southeast to Hungnam. Chinese troops greatly outnumbered the marines and controlled many of the mountain ridges and narrow passes, blocking the American route of withdrawal. Yet all Chinese attempts to stop the marines' "attack in another direction" or to annihilate isolated portions of the division met with defeat. Navy fighter-bombers supported and protected the withdrawal and inflicted heavy casualties on the Chinese forces each time they massed for an attack. "At dawn I had a chance to admire the magnificent Corsairs again," recalled Dr. Henry Litvin, battalion surgeon, 2nd Battalion, 5th Marines. "They were like dark guardian angels. God bless those valiant young pilots who shepherded us to Hagaru. In later years I bought a Revell model kit of a Corsair and assembled the parts with Testor's glue. . . . It's still on a shelf beside my desk at home and I must have looked at it a thousand times over the years."[36]

Navy leaders were determined that the evacuation from Hungnam would bear no resemblance to the hasty, desperate operations at Dunkirk and Crete in World War II. Because the U.S. Navy had almost undisputed control of the seas and skies around Hungnam, the Seventh Fleet was able to hurl enormous destructive power at the advancing Chinese armies. Three carriers, a battleship, two heavy cruisers, and eight destroyers covered the loading of almost eighty amphibious craft, transports, and cargo ships. The 1st Marine Division, which had brought out most of its equipment, was loaded first, followed by U.S. Army and South Korean forces. Along with these came 17,500 vehicles and 350,000 tons of cargo. One hundred thousand Korean civilians were also evacuated, although many others had to be left behind.[37] On Christmas Eve, as the last ships cleared the harbor, navy demolition teams went ashore and destroyed the last remaining munitions and installations in a final fiery cataclysm.

In western Korea, the U.S. Eighth Army and other UN forces continued to fall back before the advancing Chinese. Seoul changed hands again shortly after the New Year, and Washington began to consider the evacuation of the entire peninsula. The fighting fronts in Korea had already begun to stabilize, however. In late January, General Matthew Ridgway, who had assumed command of all UN forces in Korea, launched a series of offensives that led to the recapture of Seoul on February 15, 1951, and pushed the Chinese back to the 38th parallel, the prewar boundary of the two Koreas, by early April.

In July 1951, armistice talks began between representatives of North Korea, the People's Republic of China, and the United Nations Command. Although the fighting fronts remained stabilized along the old 38th parallel, the two sides remained far from agreement for the next two years. Truman refused to allow Ridgway to continue his offensives into North Korea, and the last significant Communist offensives in the fall and winter of 1951 ended in failure.

For the next year, the navy's carrier aircraft were employed, along with those of the air force, in "interdiction" campaigns designed to cut Communist supply routes to their front-line forces by bombing bridges, tunnels, road junctions, and railroads. Battleships, cruisers, and destroyers on the two coasts joined in the effort, attacking railroads, bridges, and highways within range of their guns and providing fire support for UN troops involved in local battles along the 38th parallel.

After the summer of 1952, the interdiction operations were succeeded by a series of "air pressure" attacks against North Korea's dams, power plants, factories, and oil refineries and against the North Korean capital, Pyongyang. Although the interdiction attacks destroyed hundreds of bridges—some several times over—and the air pressure campaign left North Korea almost without electric power, neither had a decisive impact on the war, which remained stalemated until the summer of 1953.

For aviators, the new types of air war meant increasing casualties and increasing frustration. North Korean bridges and rail lines were now protected by heavy concentrations of antiaircraft artillery supplied by China and the Soviet Union. "Korean antiaircraft fire had improved dramatically by late 1951," wrote a former attack plane (AD) pilot. "A direct hit from high altitude flak blew one of our ADs out of the air in our squadron's very first flight. This occurred even though we came onto target at 13,000 and rolled in for only one steep dive. Such tactics were totally different from the low level race-track patterns that were routine during the earlier part of the war."[38] Even without antiaircraft fire, flying the rugged mountains and deep ravines of northeast Korea could prove hazardous in fog or bad weather.

Targets were harder to find. Much of North Korea's supplies moved at night by truck or porters. Repeated successful attacks on bridges and rail junctions failed to yield any decisive results. Bridges and rail lines were frequently reported as "out for good. But always a few days later locomotives pulling trains were operating at these very locations."[39] "This was a time when the North Koreans had really dug into the mountainsides," observed Vice Admiral Gerald Miller. "They were in deep ravines and hard to hit. . . . It was a period of searching, trying to find targets. We'd sit up there, arc around for awhile . . . then we'd go lower and take a look. We'd come down with a stream of four or eight aircraft and couldn't see anything. All of a sudden, Bang! The shells would start popping around."[40] During the final year of war, aviator casualties averaged around 10 percent.

Another enemy was the weather. High winds and fog were common in the Yellow Sea, making carrier recoveries especially difficult.[41] In winter it could become "so cold that the salt-water spray would freeze, and when salt water freezes you get icicles hanging all over the ship . . . and on the flight deck, but the flight deck crew did a magnificent job in keeping the catapults and arresting gear free and keeping the deck from being too slippery with ice. They'd go out there with shovels and hoes and break it up and rake it off."[42]

During World War II, many carrier operations had involved sudden raids against enemy targets followed by rapid withdrawals before land-based aircraft could react by attacking the carriers. In the Korean War, with no threats from the air, carriers were able to remain on station off the coasts of the peninsula for weeks at a time. As many as four carriers steamed together about four miles apart. The outer circle of the formation was composed of as many as eighteen destroyers. Cruisers were stationed in between the carriers and destroyers to provide antiaircraft protection. Although helicopters had begun to be widely used for rescue operations, carriers still depended on a "plane guard" destroyer stationed off one quarter to provide for the recovery of pilots and planes lost during takeoffs and landings.[43]

Normally an aircraft carrier would be "on the line," that is, operating its aircraft over the peninsula, for three days at a time. On the fourth day, the carrier would leave station to meet its replenishment ships at sea, then return the following day.[44] While the carrier was on the line, the day usually began with the launching of some of the carriers' F4U Corsairs to serve as combat air patrol, CAP. Then the first strike of the day, usually AD Skyraiders and Corsairs escorted by F9F jet fighters, would be launched. An AD pilot usually flew one or two missions a day while Corsair pilots alternated between strike and CAP missions.[45] CAP missions were the less popular. They were boring, and patrolling at high altitude in a Corsair, which lacked a pressurized cabin, was extremely tiring.[46]

Flight operations continued all day. Strike aircraft were recovered and launched, CAP fighters were launched, relieved, and recovered. In addition to these routine operations, the ship had to be prepared to take aboard planes returning earlier than scheduled because of battle damage, mechanical difficulties, or shortage of fuel. Sometimes the scheduling of landings became so tight that damaged planes had to be pushed over the side to clear the flight deck for incoming aircraft.[47]

For flight deck crews, the day began at 5:00 A.M. After a quick shave and shower, they joined two or three hundred other hungry men in a chow line for breakfast. If the ship went to general quarters, breakfast was dispensed with. Sailors frequently were obliged to miss meals, and many became adept at cadging food. "I still will not eat fruit cocktail to this day," declared Aviation Electronics Technician William Crouse. "It was one of our favorite off-duty foods. Let's also add baked beans to that list."[48] The sailors' regular diet was equally uninspiring, with little fresh milk, fruits, or vegetables.

Most men lived in a noisy, crowded environment that was hot in summer and bone-chillingly cold in winter. Twenty-eight men slept in a compartment fifteen feet wide, eight feet tall, and twenty-five feet long. The beds were canvas racks stretched on a steel frame and covered with a two-inch mattress. The racks were arranged in stacks of three from deck to ceiling with about twenty inches between each rack. "If the man above was in the two-hundred-pound range, he would often sag down into your 'air space.' Rolling over was then a cooperative measure. Pipes and electrical cables ran close to the overhead and one learned early on not to sit up too quickly. Stories abounded of sailors knocking themselves senseless while responding to General Quarters in darkened berthing spaces."[49]

Berthing spaces had few or no portholes, and air was supplied by blowers. These were frequently very noisy but seldom contributed much toward lowering the heat and humidity. Most ships followed a regimen of "water hours" with fresh water available only at certain times of the day.[50] Sailors who came off duty covered in grease, soot, or dirt from their jobs were nevertheless obliged to await the propitious time for a shower or even sometimes to wash their hands.

A carrier normally spent about thirty days on the line, then went into a Japanese port for a week to ten days. Whether in search of a bar, a brothel, a golf course, a souvenir, or a quiet inn, sailors generally had their pick of the best facilities in Japan. The Japanese economy had barely begun to recover from the ravages of World War II, and the lowest-ranking bluejacket suddenly found himself a relatively wealthy man. The contrast between the idyllic conditions in Japan and the grim, exhausting regimen in the icy seas off Korea was a memory sailors retained long after the war.

Sailors were even more struck by the widespread lack of interest in the war in the United States. "The influx of news tended to make us feel, if anything, more isolated," recalled one sailor. "Here we were steaming off Korea in a sea no one had heard of. . . . Roberts had just received *Life* magazine and it was passed around. To read the magazine, you'd never know there was a war on."[51] The Korean War did not transform American life as had World War II. There were no patriotic demonstrations, no mass mobilization of citizen's efforts. "Subconsciously, I had expected to return to coffee and gasoline rationing and windows with blue-star flags," wrote a young destroyer officer. "Not this time. In April–May 1951, people had other things to do and unless your son was there, nobody seemed to care much about Korea. . . . There seemed neither a need nor the will and I wasn't much interested in describing what we had done. . . . So silence seemed the message. Korea just didn't seem to exist."[52] AD pilot Tex Atkinson was "well aware that most of our country, at the time of Korea was thinking only of settling down. Trying to forget World War II was a national project."[53]

Korean War sailors drew on other motivations than public support or patriotic exhortations from home. "Where do we get such men?" wonders the admiral in the movie The Bridges at Toko-Ri, released in 1954. "They leave this tiny ship and fly against the enemy. Then they must seek the ship, lost somewhere on the sea. And when they find it they have to land on the pitching deck."[54] Aircrewman Jack Sauter was asked, "'Where do you find the guts to take off and land on this thing day after day?' I mumbled something stupid, like 'You get used to it.' A truer reply would have been, 'I didn't have the guts not to.' The fear of looking bad in the eyes of your fellow crewmen is far worse than the fear of flying."[55]

Many other sailors recalled being so busy and so absorbed in their own work they had little time for thoughts of anything else. "We were just sort of in our little world, very, very busy," recalled Vice Admiral Charles L. Melson, who served in the battleship Iowa during the last months of the war. "News was scarce. In a war of this nature your days are full. The crew were at battle stations a good percentage of the time. . . . When we were on the bomb line, all the gun stations were manned almost twelve hours a day, while it was daylight."[56] "Most of us wanted to be where we were," recalled Tex Atkinson. "We just wanted to fly. We were not bitter because of the lack of attention back home."[57]

Korea gave the navy far greater stature in the defense structure. Interdiction by carrier aircraft, close air support, maintenance of maritime communications in a war in which almost all Allied forces and equipment came by sea, amphibious landings and withdrawals, naval gunfire support, and blockade all proved to be surprisingly important concerns even in the "air-atomic era." Yet the Korean War did not distract the navy, or indeed the other services, from their primary preoccupation: a general war with the Soviet Union.

For the navy, the Soviet threat meant, first of all, the maintenance and expansion of its carrier striking forces. In the event of war with Russia, carriers operating from the Mediterranean, Norwegian, Barents, and Bering seas would strike Soviet military targets up to six hundred miles inland. By the mid-1950s, the navy had jet-powered carrier attack aircraft capable of delivering nuclear strikes, and six new Forrestal-class supercarriers were in commission or under construction. When President Dwight D. Eisenhower's New Look defense policies shifted emphasis to reliance on strategic nuclear weapons, the navy was prepared to play a role in this mission as well, by emphasizing the ability of its carriers to deliver strategic as well as tactical strikes.

The principal Soviet naval threat still appeared to be the large subsurface fleet, which now numbered more than 400 submarines. Keeping the sea-lanes open would be vital to the success of any attempt by the United States and its allies in the North Atlantic Treaty Organization, formed in 1949, to halt a Soviet attack on Western Europe. If the war was a long one, instead of the lightning strike envisioned by the air force, defeat of a Soviet submarine offensive would become the navy's primary mission.

The U.S. Navy intended to meet the Soviet submarine threat in three ways. The first was through air strikes against Soviet submarine bases and shipyards in the manner envisioned a decade earlier by Admiral Forrest Sherman. The second was to intercept and destroy Soviet submarines as they sortied from their bases. To provide data on the comings and goings of these submarines, an extensive system of submerged hydrophones called SOSUS (Sound Surveillance System) were anchored to the ocean floor at points leading from the Soviet bases to the Barents and Baltic seas and the Sea of Japan. Waiting at longer range would be American submarines ready to trail or sink any Soviet vessels exiting the straits. In the open ocean, hunter-killer groups equipped with sophisticated electronic and acoustic devices would detect and sink any Soviet submarine that managed to reach the Atlantic.

Submariners argued that in the future, the best tracker and killer of submarines would be another submarine, and the U.S. sub fleet now began to acquire a revolutionary type of submersible propelled by a nuclear power plant. The first ship of this type, the *Nautilus*, went to sea at the beginning of 1955.

While the navy prepared for a long war against the Soviets, many American leaders continued to believe that any future clash between the two superpowers would probably take the form of a lightning exchange of nuclear bombs and missiles. In this role, the delivery of strategic nuclear weapons, the navy seemed destined to lose out to the air force. At the end of 1956, however, Chief of Naval Operations Admiral

Arleigh Burke decided to press ahead with a program for a solid-fuel long-range missile that could be launched from a submerged submarine. The Soviets had already deployed World War II–style cruise missiles aboard a few of their submarines, but Burke's Polaris, as the new strategic weapon system was called, was a quantum leap beyond such primitive experiments. Polaris was a ballistic missile able to carry an atomic warhead more than 1,500 nautical miles. Its base aboard a high-speed nuclear submarine gave it exceptional flexibility and concealment, making it almost invulnerable to surprise attack. With Polaris, the navy became a player in the game of strategic nuclear deterrence that preoccupied defense planners in the 1950s and 1960s.

As the first *Polaris* submarines went to sea in the early 1960s, the nature and objectives of undersea warfare underwent radical change. In the two world wars, submarines had proven most effective against enemy shipping and highly successful against enemy warships as well. By the end of the 1950s, however, submarine planners and tacticians began to focus almost entirely on submarine versus submarine operations.[58] Not only did this appear to be the best method for meeting the threat of Soviet attack submarines but, with the appearance of the submarine-launched ballistic missile, the survival of one's own submarines and the ability to find and destroy those of one's opponent became of critical importance to the strategic balance between the superpowers.

The first American nuclear-powered submarines had top speeds of just over twenty knots and were the fastest undersea boats in the world. The Soviets commissioned their first nuclear submarine in 1958, and by the mid-1970s the Soviets had made considerable progress in submarine design and construction. Before the end of the decade they had commissioned twenty-three "second-generation" nuclear attack submarines and thirty-four nuclear ballistic missile submarines. These submarines were thought to have a top speed of more than thirty knots.[59]

"Today and for many years to come, the really battle-worthy capital ship is the nuclear-powered submarine," wrote Vice Admiral George P. Steele in the *Washington Post*. "It has the unique ability to get close enough to destroy the enemy surface ship . . . regardless of how much air power is ranged against it. The only adversary that it really need fear is another and better submarine."[60] Symbolic of this change in the order of sea power was the naming of the first British nuclear-propelled submarine HMS *Dreadnought,* and *Jane's Fighting Ships,* the standard naval reference book, soon came to list submarines ahead of carriers, battleships, and cruisers in its pages—an exact reversal of the order of the 1940s.

The new era of submarine warfare produced its own human demands and requirements just as had the dreadnought, the conventional submarine, and the aircraft carrier. Submarine operations had always been among the most elemental forms of naval warfare, concerned almost entirely with killing. Submarines did not provide "presence," support land campaigns, escort shipping, or signal political intentions. They sought to attack suddenly and lethally and, if effectively attacked themselves, had little chance of survival.

American submariners emerged from World War II a proud and self-confident society. They were well-aware that their small group, representing less than 2 percent of all naval personnel, had accounted for 55 percent of all Japanese ships sunk, while their own casualty rate had been higher than that of any other group in the navy.[61] "What did an officer do during the war?" was the question most frequently asked in assignments and promotions.[62] "[A] submarine war record meant a tremendous lot," recalled Admiral Charles K. Duncan, "because the subs were on their own."[63]

Before he could enter the submarine service, an officer or sailor had to have served at sea aboard a surface ship. If he survived the six months of submarine school, an officer reported to a boat for almost a year of on-the-job education and practice, performing the most onerous tasks. During this time he was referred to by the experienced officers as "George," a label "which equates to something between a billy goat and a fool."[64] At the end of the probationary year, if he passed a stiff oral and written examination, "George" would find his submariner's insignia, a pair of gold dolphins, at the bottom of a ten-ounce glass of whiskey.

The advent of nuclear technology and missiles brought drastic changes. The submarine of the first half of the century had been based on the principles of the diesel engine, the wet-cell battery, and the steam torpedo; to these various electronic devices, sonar, target computers, and radar had been added gradually. The new submarines were based on complex new principles and technologies, derived from the outer edge of scientific knowledge.

The high priest and presiding genius of this transition to the new technologies was Admiral Hyman Rickover. Rickover's hard-driving style and irascibility were legendary.[65] The nuclear navy, declared Rickover, did not want family-oriented "builders of nests and hatchers of eggs." Submarine officers quipped that the designation SSN did not stand for nuclear-attack submarine but rather "Saturdays, Sundays and Nights."[66]

A key figure in the development of the nuclear submarine and surface ship, Admiral Rickover derived much of his power from his unique dual status as both a naval officer and a civilian official. He was Deputy Commander for Nuclear Propulsion, Naval Ship Systems Command, a navy billet ultimately under the control of the Chief of Naval Operations, charged with the design, production, and maintenance of the engineering plants of nuclear-powered ships. As the Director, Division of Naval Reactors, in the Atomic Energy Commission, he was responsible for the development, manufacture, and safety of the ship's nuclear reactors. In that role he reported to the civilian chairman of the Atomic Energy Commission. "He was a master at blurring the line, pretty fuzzy to begin with, between the two jobs."[67] Special statutory authority provided that "training of officers of nuclear ships must continue to emphasize knowledge of reactors and reactor safety," and for that purpose, "the experience and technical judgment of the Naval Reactors Branch [of the Atomic Energy Commission] must be utilized to the maximum extent. . . ." Armed with this authority, Admiral Rickover soon came to preside over almost a second navy within the U.S. Navy. A great favorite of the media with many powerful admirers in the House and Senate, he presided over the nuclear empire for more than a quarter century.

All officers to receive nuclear training were personally selected by Rickover. The selection process included a personal interview with the admiral that soon became the stuff of legend. Officers and Naval Academy first classmen, considered by the navy to be the best and the brightest, were subjected to blistering, sarcastic, insulting, and demeaning interrogations. No subject was off-limits, and the candidate was never credited with a satisfactory answer.

Commander Elmo Zumwalt, later Chief of Naval Operations, wrote an account of his interview soon afterward. A portion of the conversation included the following:

Adm. R.: Where did you go to high school?
Cdr. Z.: Tulare Union High School.
Adm. R.: Where did you stand in high school?
Cdr. Z: I was the valedictorian.
Adm. R.: I said where did you stand?
Cdr. Z: Number one.
Adm. R.: How many in the school?
Cdr. Z: (Pause) About . . .
Adm. R.: Answer the question, approximately.
Cdr. Z: 300.

Adm. R.: Aside from the summers, did you work or did your family support you? (Grimacing)

Cdr. Z: (Having in mind the answer, "I worked in the summers, during the school year, and my family supported me.") I worked in the summers . . .

Adm. R.: Listen to my questions, God damn it. You've been an aide too long. You're too used to asking the questions. You are trying to conduct this interview again. I said aside from the summers. Now do you think you can answer the question or do you want to stop the interview right now?

Cdr. Z: My family supported me.

Adm. R.: What did you do after high school?

Cdr. Z: I went to prep school for a year.

Adm. R.: Why? To learn what you should have learned in high school?

Cdr. Z: I didn't have an appointment to the Naval Academy yet.

Adm. R.: Why didn't you go to college?

Cdr. Z: I had a great awe of the Academy and wanted to have a better background.

Adm. R.: In other words, you did go to prep school to learn what you should have learned in high school? Where did you stand at the Naval Academy?

Cdr. Z: In the top 3 percent.

Adm. R.: Did you study as hard as you could?

Cdr. Z: Yes, sir.

Adm. R.: Do you say that without any mental reservations.

Cdr. Z: Yes, sir.

Adm. R.: Did you do anything besides study?

Cdr. Z: Yes, sir.

Adm. R.: In other words, you didn't study as hard as you could?[68]

Many submariners would probably have agreed with Zumwalt, who considered the interview "a part of the hazing considered necessary to put me through the plebe year in nuclear college."[69] Rickover himself claimed that the interviews were intended to test the coolness, presence of mind, and quick-wittedness of the candidate.[70] Many others in the navy saw the interviews as unnecessarily harsh at best, arbitrary or downright zany at worst. "I had numerous instances of officers coming to me after their interview with Rickover and stating that they didn't want to stay in a Navy which had an officer like Admiral Rickover," recalled a former chief of the Bureau of Naval Personnel. "He made fun of this boy's father, said he was one of those dumb football players at the Naval Academy who didn't have sense to come in out of the rain. . . . He made that young man so mad he said he'd never go into that nuclear program."[71]

Officers and enlisted men destined for nuclear-powered ships spent six months at a nuclear power school, where they received more than seven hundred hours of instruction in mathematics, physics, reactor theory, engineering, chemistry, and other subjects. This was followed by six months at a reactor prototype site located in a remote part of Idaho hundreds of miles from the sea. The students were closely and relentlessly monitored. About 12 percent of the officer students and 20 percent of enlisted men failed to complete the program.[72]

Rickover's approach to selection and training marked a drastic break with the traditional approach to officer development and, indeed with the entire concept of what a naval officer ought to be. "I can say without hesitation that, in my opinion, success or failure in battle with the fleet is in no way dependent on knowledge of biology, geology, ethics, literature or foreign languages or fine arts," declared a Naval Academy superintendent in the 1930s.[73] Now Rickover had reversed the priorities. Academic and scientific ability were among the core qualities of the new Rickover-style officers, generally referred to as "nucs." Where navies had traditionally stressed character and boldness, Rickover stressed expertise and reliability. Navies had stressed practical training at sea, Rickover stressed lengthy classroom instruction ashore. Where traditional navies had stressed combat experience and seamanship, the nucs stressed safety and good technical judgment.

There was more than a little irony in this. Since the turn of the century, navies had wrestled with the question of the extent to which engineering specialists should be integrated into the line and given the prerogatives of command. In less than a decade, the nucs had reversed this state of affairs. Now only nuclear-qualified officers, that is, highly trained engineering specialists, could hope to command a nuclear submarine. This reversal of traditional standards was not accepted warmly by the nonnuclear components of the navy, least of all by the World War II–era submariners. "This to the submarine community was revolutionary, to have an 'engineering duty-only' officer sitting over there saying who could and could not command a submarine," recalled Admiral Duncan. "I just can't describe how deeply they felt . . . to have a man who'd never been in combat or in command saying who could have command of these submarines."[74]

The nucs would have been the last to deny that they required a new type of officer and enlisted man. An accident aboard a conventional warship could well result in many fatalities and even loss of the ship, but except in extraordinary circumstances it was unlikely to bring physical harm to other ships, shore installations, or towns. An accident aboard a nuclear ship, however, could result in a release of fission isotopes, and spread deadly radiation well beyond a ship in harbor. Even one such incident would mean the end of public confidence in a nuclear navy. "To the degree that one believes that we need a nuclear component of the navy, one must accept that reactor safety is paramount," wrote one nuc. Consequently the nuclear navy could "accept only proven achievers . . . insist on compliance with proven procedures; demand the highest quality material and teach our subordinates the simple rule—never gamble."[75]

Few disputed that the operation of a nuclear reactor justified special procedures and elaborate precautions. Yet some wondered whether a group of naval officers whose motto was "never gamble" might be the proper individuals to command a submarine in the essentially ambiguous and unpredictable environment of war at sea. A persistent complaint was that the nuc was so preoccupied with the flawless operation of the engineering plant that he scarcely had time to think of his ship as a weapons system.[76] The Nuclear Reactor Branch's endless round of examinations and inspections in which failure could end an officers' career "brought intense pressure to concentrate on one end of the boat. . . . Most officers, perhaps unconsciously, decided that qualification as a submarine officer simply would have to take second place . . . with technical qualification requirements."[77] A weapons officer in a Polaris submarine reported that even the ship's fearsome nuclear missiles received scant attention compared to the power plant. "This almost total devotion to nuclear power seems to be to the exclusion of anything else on board. . . . One of the benefits is that we are quite independent since the command is so wrapped up in the care and feeding of the reactor."[78]

Critics also charged that nucs neglected seamanship and navigation. A report by Commander, Submarines, Atlantic Fleet in 1979 cited fourteen major submarine accidents that were, in whole or in part, due to "less than sufficient performance with respect to seamanship." A retired nuclear submarine skipper declared that "an American submarine might run aground due to total incompetence in navigation and ship handling, but the reactor-control division records would be perfect as it hit."[79]

By 1960, there were thirteen nuclear submarines in the U.S. Navy with thirty-five more planned or under construction. In addition, the navy expected to commission a nuclear carrier and a nuclear cruiser. As the number of nuclear attack and ballistic missile submarines increased and as nuclear-powered cruisers and aircraft carriers joined the fleet, the requirements for nuclear power officers and enlisted men soon outstripped the supply of volunteers. "They [the Polaris submarines] were coming off the ways," recalled Admiral Duncan. "The President said it was the nation's highest priority. So we put orders out on people who had not volunteered. The first time in modern history that a non-volunteer had been sent to submarines. . . . We got some right from destroyer school. . . . people in class were called and told 'you're going into nuclear power.'"[80] But while the navy could order men to serve in nuclear-powered ships, it could not order them to stay. As early as 1971, an article in the *Naval Institute Proceedings* referred to the personnel situation in the nuclear navy as a "crisis."[81] During the 1960s and 1970s almost two thirds of nuclear-qualified officers left the service at their earliest opportunity.[82]

Those who remained, however, came to play an increasingly greater role in the leadership of the navy. Seven of the officers who had commanded the first ten nuclear submarines became admirals, and by 1972, almost a quarter of the navy's three-star vice admirals were nuclear-qualified. By 1975 both the Chief of Naval Operations, Admiral James L. Holloway, and the superintendent of the Naval Academy were nucs.[83] In addition, when the Deputy Chief of Naval Operations for Submarines and Deputy Chief of Naval Operations for Surface Warfare were established in 1971, submariners and surface warfare officers achieved equal bureaucratic status with aviators—at least in principle.

While submariners, along with other nucs, had come to play a significantly greater role in the navy, submarines had come to play new and increasingly critical roles in the navy's competition with the Soviets at sea. These new roles and missions would test not only the technical competence of submariners but their imagination, nerve, and leadership, subjects not particularly emphasized in the year-long nuclear power training courses.

American and German submarines of World War II had been most effective when employed against shipping. The Soviets were far from being dependent on shipping, however. It was U.S. and NATO shipping that would be vulnerable to attack by the large Soviet undersea fleet. Therefore the new target for U.S. and British submarines could only be their counterparts in the Soviet fleet. This was a tall order. There had been only one recorded instance in World War II in which a submerged submarine had sunk a submerged enemy submarine.[84]

In order to practice this new type of warfare, submarines would require high speeds to reach patrol areas near Soviet bases and excellent
sonar to find their underwater targets. Unfortunately, the sonar of a submarine of the late 1940s had an effective range of only 4,000 to 7,000
yards. If the attacking sub took elaborate precautions to achieve "ultra-
quiet," shutting down air-conditioning, ventilation, blowers, and fresh-
water stills, avoiding loud talk or other sounds from within the boat,
then the attacker might achieve a contact at 12,000 yards.

While efforts to meet these technical requirements were under way,
American and British submarines conducted reconnaissance and surveillance of Soviet bases and operating areas in order to study Soviet operational methods, tactics, communications, and electronic emissions.
Some of the earliest patrols were carried out in the Norwegian and Barents Sea and in La Perouse Strait in the Pacific.[85] In one of these early
surveillance missions, the USS Cochino was lost on her return voyage because of a battery explosion and fire.[86] Cochino thus became one of the
earliest victims of the long undersea war between the United States and
the Soviets that continued over the next four decades. A war in which,
as Captain Ramius observed in the novel The Hunt for Red October,
"there were no battles, no victories, no defeats, only casualties."[87]

By the early 1950s, an effective submarine-versus-submarine war in
waters near the Soviet Union had begun to look far more probable with
the success of the nuclear submarine, a true submersible that could remain underwater indefinitely without having to surface or use a snorkel
to recharge its batteries. The high speed of the atomic submarine made
it possible for it to deploy to distant waters quickly and to maneuver for
a favorable tactical position once an enemy submarine was detected.
The navy also had adopted a new sonar—the BQR-4—that could detect
another submarine at a distance of thirty miles.[88]

From this point on, Soviet and U.S. submarines began their own
"silent war," a war made more intense by the appearance of the ballistic
missile submarine. The Russians opted for fast and deep-diving boats,
the Americans for extreme quietness and superior detection devices.[89]
U.S. submarines off Soviet ports attempted to silently acquire and trail
Soviet submarines as they departed on their patrols. The shadow war was
played out beneath the Arctic ice, in the North Pacific, in the shallow
waters of the Mediterranean, and under the broad seas of the Atlantic.[90]

Ballistic missile submarines were considered especially important targets for surveillance.[91] The USS Lapon under Commander Chester M.
Mack trailed a Soviet "Yankee" ballistic missile submarine for six weeks,
at times getting so close to the Soviet submarine that the Lapon's sonar-

men could hear everything from the rattling of tools to the dropping of toilet lids.[92] According to newspaper accounts, U.S. submarines passed as close as fifty feet to Soviet boats they were shadowing. Lieutenant Commander Kinnaird R. McKee, who would one day succeed Admiral Rickover as head of the nuclear navy, gained fame—at least in the supersecret submarine world—for his two daring patrols in the Barents and Kara seas, where he had taken close-up photographs of two of the latest types of Soviet submarines, then escaped pursuit by Soviet surface forces by diving under the Arctic ice.[93]

These tactics had their price. There are at least eight known instances in which American submarines collided with Soviet vessels under surveillance. Altogether the United States lost four submarines during the Cold War, all from operational causes or accidents. About 140 U.S. submariners lost their lives. The Soviets lost at least six submarines. In addition, one expert asserted that by 1988, the Soviet navy had had about two hundred serious submarine accidents, including some in which sailors were killed by radiation poisoning.[94]

During the 1960s the U.S. Navy began to install TV monitors inside its submarines. This made it possible for sailors to see the same view that was visible to the captain through the periscope. According to one reporter, this development "made it easier for everyone from cooks to mechanics to second-guess the captain. Some sailors derisively referred to skippers who were reluctant to go in close to Soviet vessels as 'Chicken of the Sea' or 'Charlie Tuna.'"[95] How many of Admiral Rickover's meticulously trained nucs received such a rating or how many instead resembled Mack and McKee cannot be known. However, there can be little doubt of the ability, dedication, and nerve of the sailors and petty officers who rode the nuclear submarines.

Life aboard a nuclear submarine resembled life aboard submarines of earlier eras—except more so. "Being intelligent, competitive and aggressive by nature, submariners create an atmosphere of stress around themselves that translates into constant teasing and ribbing," observed Dr. Duncan MacIvor, a submarine medical officer. "New crewmembers and old alike are constantly probed for chinks in their armor and if weaknesses are found they may be exploited without mercy." Newcomers in particular were constantly teased and made the object of elaborate practical jokes.[96]

Sailors younger than college seniors were expected to flawlessly maintain and operate complex, even revolutionary technologies under conditions of constant fatigue and professional pressure. Above all, there was the intense pressure to "qualify." Newcomers to the submarine service were subject to verbal abuse, made to feel like outsiders, and denied privileges such as watching movies until they passed their initial qualification.[97] Once he achieved this, the newcomer was "in," a life member of the fraternity of submariners. The round of qualifications did not end there, however. "In addition to the initial submarine qualifications, the submariner is required to requalify on each new boat he goes to. He also has to qualify at his watch station and subsequent more senior watch stations as he advances."[98] Between watches, maintenance periods, paperwork, and the endless study of reactor mysteries, sailors were fortunate to have five to six hours of sleep in twenty four. Many submariners reported that they worked in a perpetual state of near exhaustion. The situation was exacerbated by a chronic shortage of qualified sailors throughout the 1960s and 1970s. Many submarines went to sea lacking a full complement of petty officers and enlisted ratings.[99]

It was not unusual for an attack submarine to spend close to two months at sea, most of it submerged. Missile subs regularly spent sixty days at sea followed by about a month of training. Each ballistic missile submarine had two complete crews—"blue" and "gold"—so that the boats could spend the maximum amount of time underwater. When a sub returned to base there would be a fifteen-day turnover period involving both crews. Then the crew staying ashore would train for two months, some part of which theoretically included leave.

Dr. MacIvor observed that a man who had made fifteen or more patrols "has spent the equivalent of several years confined in submarines away from home. . . . Submariners routinely miss important family events such as birthdays, anniversaries, graduations, childbirths, hospitalizations and major surgery on loved ones. Sometimes they arrive home to find they have missed a broken engagement, a legal separation or a divorce."[100]

Once a nuclear submarine had departed on its long mission a well-developed family support system fell into place. Wives and children of the crew kept in close contact with one another through wives' clubs, coffees, weekly get-togethers, movies, and other activities. All wives' clubs had "telephone trees" for quickly contacting members, and many published newsletters.[101] During the submarine's deployment a family's only contact with those aboard, except in emergencies, was through "family grams," blank sheets of paper containing forty lines. Each line could contain only one word and families were limited to eight family grams for a patrol. Though these terse messages could be transmitted, they could not be replied to.

The only other opportunity to communicate with husbands at sea occurred if a submarine was obliged to put into port to drop or pick up "riders," dignitaries, contractors, or engineers, or to remove an ill or injured crew member. On these rare occasions, all the resources of the wives' club swung into action. Messages were faxed to and from parents, wives, girlfriends, sisters, and brothers all over the world. These were collected by the wives' club and rushed down to the boat's expected arrival point, where mail from sailors aboard would also be picked up. Sometimes this entire operation had to be accomplished in less than a day.

The eventual return of a boat from patrol was always a joyous and memorable occasion for all family members, but nuclear sailors, even in port, generally carried a workload that left them relatively little time to spend with their families. On one occasion a chief petty officer aboard a ballistic missile submarine was unable to be with his wife during an operation even though his boat was in port. "His leave was canceled at the last minute because he was needed on board during a weapons handling evolution." On another occasion a submarine's loading of its Mark 48 torpedoes was delayed by problems and had to be continued late into the night before departure. "One of the torpedo men missed the birthday party his family had prepared for him at home and left the next day without seeing them."[102] Some psychologists and physicians compared the reaction of wives and families to the prolonged absences at sea to the "grief response" experienced after the death of a loved one or close friend, except in this case the reaction would be experienced again and again.

Compared to World War II submarines, the nuclear-era boats were spacious. The enlisted mess area of the Los Angeles–class attack submarines, which entered service in the late 1970s and 1980s, were large enough to hold soft drink machines, an ice cream maker, and a dispenser for "bug juice," a kind of powdered drink that was used both as a beverage and as a scouring powder for cleaning decks and bathrooms. Almost half the crew could be accommodated at the six mess tables with bench seats. Yet spaciousness was relative. As in World War II, the number of sailors exceeded the number of available bunks, so more than a third of the enlisted men had to share one of the narrow bunks, stacked three high, that lined the bulkhead. Only the captain slept in a bunk that had no other bunk above or below it.[103]

With the introduction of nuclear power the chief limiting factor on the duration of submarine patrols became the quantity of food that could be accommodated aboard ship. Cold War–era submarines had relatively larger galleys and refrigerators, but, as in World War II, every available space was used to store tightly packed containers of extra food and other consumables. Another factor was habitability. Despite a sophisticated array of air purifiers and filters, the interior of a nuclear submarine during the 1950s and 1960s resembled a "closed sewer pipe" after a few weeks at sea. The contaminated air was made still more foul by the frequent use of cigarettes by many members of the crew. (The first "no smoking" submarine was commissioned in 1990.) The high carbon monoxide levels could lead to headaches, nausea, and lethargy. Very high levels of contaminants produced by a malfunction of the ship's machinery could cause serious illness and death. In 1964, most of the crew of the ballistic missile submarine USS *Tecumseh* were almost disabled by an anesthetic gas caused by accidental heating of the glue in the ship's paneling.[104]

Admiral Rickover insisted that his nuclear reactors were safe and reliable and posed little if any radiation risk to the crew. Many experts agreed with him. But this did not mean that submarines were now free of hazards. A small error in maintenance, a small leak in a valve, a minor computer malfunction, or a mistake in navigation could all spell disaster. As in the past, a mistake or an instance of carelessness on the part of a single sailor could result in the loss of the ship. Men considered weak, unreliable, or incompetent were ruthlessly weeded out. It was not unusual for a skipper to put up to half a dozen men ashore for such reasons at the conclusion of a patrol.

By the early 1960s, the navy was a far different force from that of 1945. Polaris submarines could destroy entire cities and carriers could intervene in any land battle, but the navy's ability to fight at sea against enemy warships, the classic naval role, had become more questionable than ever. Surface ship vulnerability to attacks by aircraft and missiles seemed to have reached an all-time high. The captain of one of the newest type of destroyers, commissioned during the late 1950s, called her "obsolescent when she was designed." Another called her "a great ship for shore bombardment and surface gunfire, [but] in the face of jet air attack she was almost hopeless. CIC was still operated by grease pencil and elastic band routes. There was no height finder in her air search radar."[105] The navy had developed a family of antiaircraft missiles to provide improved fleet air defense, but the "Three T's, Terrier, Talos, and Tartar," were not wholly reliable and only Tartar could be used aboard ships smaller than a cruiser.

To make matters worse, the Soviets had developed a practical ship-to-ship missile with a maximum range of almost 150 miles. By 1958, American intelligence sources had confirmed a new class of Soviet destroyers configured to carry the new missile.[106] The Soviets had also developed a class of fast coastal patrol boats armed with a smaller, shorter-range, but equally lethal missile. The U.S. Navy of the 1950s had little to match these new Soviet capabilities or to defend against them. Its principal cruise missile program, the Regulus, had become a budgetary casualty in 1958.

While navy leaders in the Pentagon planned for and argued about nuclear deterrence, sea control, and the defense of Europe, in practice the U.S. Navy had returned to a sort of gunboat diplomacy reminiscent of the nineteenth century. Yet in the Cold War, the gunboats had been replaced by fleets of the navy's most powerful warships ready, if necessary, to fight a war on the spot. Carrier task forces and amphibious task forces carrying combat-ready marines ranged the oceans ready to provide a show of support for friendly governments, intimidate unfriendly ones, protect American citizens, or simply display American power. In all the Cold War crises of the 1950s—Dien Bien Phu, Suez, the Taiwan Strait, and Berlin—the navy played a prominent, often a leading, role. Unlike the army and air force the navy was not solely dependent on forward bases, airfields, or lengthy supply lines. The navy's ability to transport men and planes to critical areas rapidly and, if necessary, withdraw them equally rapidly was greatly valued by politicians and diplomats in the Cold War. The Chief of Naval Operations, Admiral David L. McDonald, pointed out that between 1950 and 1960, carrier task forces had been deployed to the scene of crises on at least fourteen different occasions.[107] In the Cuban Missile Crisis of 1962, more than 150 Navy ships and 250 planes enforced the American-proclaimed "quarantine" of Cuba, tracked Soviet submarines, and evacuated American dependents from Guantanamo Bay. Facing more powerful nuclear weapons, the Russians had no realistic hope of challenging the American naval armada in the Caribbean, or in any other distant ocean, with their own naval forces. The Cuban Missile Crisis was the high-watermark of American naval superiority in the Cold War.

Within the navy, the Cold War continued and accelerated the social and institutional transformations begun during World War II. The shore-based administrative, logistical, and technical "tail" of the navy was now larger and even more expensive than the fleet itself. In 1940, 89,000 out of a total of 116,000 enlisted sailors were serving at sea. In 1960 the number of officers in "staff corps"—doctors, supply corps personnel, civil engineers, dentists and others—had grown to over 28 percent of the total officer force.[108] By the mid-1960s the navy had more than a third of its men serving ashore. In addition the navy employed between 360,000 and 400,000 civilians and funded a vast research and development empire. By 1954, the navy was spending more than fifty times what it had spent for scientific and technical research in 1940.[109]

In the officer corps, as Admiral Towers had hoped and others had feared, naval aviators had become the predominant element within the navy. As early as 1949, ten of twenty-two vice admirals on active duty were aviators.[110] By early 1953, only two of the five four-star admirals on active duty came from the traditional "surface navy." Between 1945 and 1955, aviators at the rank of captain had double the chances of making admiral as nonaviators of the same rank.[111] *Every* Chief of Naval Operations appointed during the 1960s was an aviator.[112]

The officers of the prewar navy had formed a homogeneous group led by specialists in gunnery and torpedo warfare. The Cold War navy was divided into three separate but unequal "platform communities" or "unions": aviation, submarines, and surface warfare, with the surface warfare officers now at the bottom of the pecking order. A handful of others, officers serving in amphibious craft or mine warfare, though nominally part of the surface warfare "union," in fact ranked even lower in status and promotion prospects.

Although the Cold War navy was considerably smaller than that of World War II, the service's dependence on non–Naval Academy graduates and reservists to fill its officer ranks continued to be high. In 1956, only 55 percent of naval officers on active duty were regulars.[113] Of the regulars, the majority came from a greatly expanded Naval Reserve Officers Training Corps program established at more than fifty civilian colleges and universities under the leadership of Vice Admiral James Holloway, Jr. Often referred to as "the Holloway Plan," the program provided a four-year college scholarship and other financial support to selected young men, who received a regular commission upon graduation. Additional officers came from the navy's Officer Candidate School at Newport, Rhode Island. As in the war years, the navy's officer candidate program was overwhelmingly oriented toward college men, with only a small percentage of OCS students coming from the enlisted ranks of the regular navy.

Whether in ROTC or OCS, many of these new types of officers did not want to make the navy a career. By the mid-1960s, about 80 percent of Annapolis graduates had remained on active duty after their initial four years of obligated service, while 57 percent of NROTC graduates and 67 percent of OCS men took the earliest possible opportunity to leave the service.[114] Many had never intended to stay in the first place. They looked upon a commission in the navy as a greatly superior alternative to the military draft. One destroyer commander reported that "it was a popular thing to knock the navy" in Officer Candidate School, and that "away from Navy activities, the young officer finds the first question he is usually asked is 'How long do you have to do?'"[115] In the robust economic conditions of the 1950s and 1960s, young officers had no incentive to remain in the service for reasons of economic security. Most of those who left, however, declared that they were not dissatisfied with the pay but rather with the bureaucracy, paperwork, and mindless regulations of the peacetime navy. Many also felt that the navy lacked a really competitive system for advancement and promotion.[116]

If the navy suffered from retention problems in its officer corps, problems in finding and keeping high-quality enlisted men were even more severe. Although the existence of the peacetime draft provided the navy with plenty of "volunteers," few of these men were inclined to spend more than the absolute minimum of time in the sea service. Their junior officers, mostly one-term reservists, were not inclined to dissuade them. Like these officers, but with far greater conviction, enlisted men saw the navy as a low-status occupation characterized by red tape and petty harassment.[117] Gone were the golden days of the 1930s when the navy was seen as a coveted haven from the economic upheaval of the depression. The buoyant economic atmosphere of the Eisenhower and Kennedy years seemed to promise unlimited opportunities, especially for men with advanced technical training.

While dislike of navy life and the lure of civilian jobs had long served to dampen the chances of reenlistment, the navy now encountered still another obstacle: marriage. Where the navy of the 1930s had been overwhelmingly a bachelor society, the navy of the 1950s included record numbers of married sailors. Though the navy provided numerous "fringe benefits" such as free housing and medical care to service families, few wives saw the navy, with its long periods of separation and frequent relocations, as a desirable way of life.[118]

By the mid-1950s the navy faced problems of retention equal to those of the worst years of the early twentieth century. The reenlistment rate for sailors completing their first term of service usually was less than 20 percent.[119] The total number of deserters in any single year in the decade would have been enough to man twelve guided missile cruisers.[120] Nonjudicial punishment rates in 1950–60 were more than double what they had been in 1940, and the number of sailors in navy brigs equaled the number in the entire submarine service.[121]

Further complicating matters was the gradual disappearance of the social structure of the prewar navy. Until the end of World War II, only petty officers in the ratings of boatswain's mates, gunners' mates, torpedomen, turrett captains, singalmen, fire control men, quartermasters, and minemen, who wore their badges on the right sleeve of their uniforms, were responsible for general military authority aboard ship. They took precedence over sailors and petty officers in other ratings who were viewed primarily as technical specialists. The precedence afforded to the "right-arm ratings" reflected their connection to what had traditionally been the key missions in a man-of-war: seamanship, gunnery, and visual signaling with flag and lights.

The emergence of aviation and electronics as the foundation of naval warfare in the 1950s led to a loss of prestige and authority for the older ratings and the growth in importance of sailors skilled in mechanical maintenance, electronics, and radio communications. In the postwar navy, petty officers were viewed to a large extent as technical supervisors rather than as military leaders and disciplinarians, a change symbolized by the 1948 uniform regulation which directed that all badges be worn on the left arm only. In addition, the introduction of the Uniform Code of Military Justice introduced procedural safeguards and administrative requirements that made it far more difficult for petty officers and junior officers to rely on the old system of informal persuasion, intimidation, and summary justice.[122]

In addition to the constant turnover of new sailors, the service was also experiencing the loss of many of its most experienced petty officers, those who had enlisted during the 1930s and were now reaching retirement age. When those men had entered the navy, sailors spent years at sea, often in the same ship. Officers served a much shorter time in any particular ship, but spent the majority of their time with the fleet, sometimes in back-to-back commands.[123] In the 1950s both enlisted men and officers were caught up in a complex revolving-door system of personnel changes designed to ensure that no one stayed at sea or on shore longer than merited. Although every sailor now had the opportunity to serve ashore, often with his family close by, some categories of sailors served ashore far more frequently than others. Those in occupations critically needed at sea and for which few billets existed ashore tended to serve much longer tours afloat. "Thank you and the members of the U.S. Navy who are responsible for keeping my husband away from his family for the second year in succession," wrote one navy wife to the Secretary of the Navy. "I hope you all have a Merry Christmas."[124] One sailor told a reporter that he had "been spending ten months away from home every year for the past three years. My wife and I are pretty tired of second honeymoons."[125]

For those who did serve at sea, the routine was far different than that of the 1930s, when the battle fleet would normally return to its home ports every Friday for the weekend. Most of the navy's large ships were now "forward deployed" in the Mediterranean, the western Pacific, and the North Atlantic, close to areas likely to be flash points in the Cold War. Individual ships sailed from the United States to join these far-flung fleets and relieve other ships due to return home. Some ships were permanently based abroad and only their sailors returned, after long intervals, to the United States. These cruises in distant waters or "deployments" lasted not weeks but months. The old distinction between peacetime and wartime cruises had become blurred. Warships remained, most of the time, in a high state of readiness and were often called upon to intervene in local crises that lay in the twilight area between war and peace.

Some sailors in the Cold War navy enjoyed luxuries undreamed of by their predecessors. Newer ships were air-conditioned and featured laundries, soft drink machines, and libraries. The new supercarriers of the Forrestal class had three barbershops, three soda fountains, and four ship's stores.[126] Most sailors, however, served aboard World War II–era ships, more or less updated for the new era. Admiral Charles K. Duncan, who commanded the Atlantic Fleet Cruiser-Destroyer Force in the early 1960s, recalled that "the World War II destroyers were the bulk of my force." Their enlisted men berthed in "compartments with 60-70 men, bunks three high. . . . A big man couldn't even walk between the bunks without bumping them. . . . The access to the compartment came down the hatch from the weather deck. No interior covered access. There were three doors leading out of this after compartment. One to the steering engine room which was very noisy and boiling, and the watch had to be relieved every four hours with the watertight doors banging. Another door led to a carpenter shop . . . the third to an electricians shop." Admiral Duncan estimated that the sailor could expect to spend thirteen or fourteen years of a twenty-year career in this type of environment. "If . . . you were a First Class Petty Officer you were still living in this type compartment. You might get a bunk near the ventilator or away from the hatch . . . but you lived in this environment."[127] The captain of an Essex-class carrier reported on "the totally unsatisfactory conditions for berthing and messing" aboard the big ship. Berthing space had been converted to offices for the larger staffs and larger air groups of the 1950s, and newer and larger pieces of equipment had claimed additional space. Many sailors were forced to occupy cots or hammocks in the passageways or even sleep on the deck.[128] Aboard a large aircraft carrier crew members might spend much of their mealtime waiting in lengthy chow lines to be served their meals cafeteria style on metal trays. In the *Essex*-class ships, the ammunition hoists that carried bombs and other ordnance to the flight or hangar deck ran through the messing spaces. In the postwar era of almost continual flight operations ordnancemen would, in effect, be constantly moving ammunition through the sailors' dining room, adding considerably to the noise and crowding.[129]

While the enlisted force included too few older men, the fleet contained too many older ships. Eighty percent of the ships in the navy dated from World War II. Naval leaders began to talk of "block obsolescence," a time in the near future when many of these ships would have reached the end of their useful life. Ships in commission had been worked hard, and the Board of Inspection and Survey pronounced more than 70 percent of them to be "in unsatisfactory material condition."[130]

Under Eisenhower's New Look policy, relatively little money had been available for new construction, and much of that was spent on the increasingly expensive Polaris program. Admiral Burke and others in the navy were aware that Polaris was a serious drain on the navy's budget, but the program was critical to keeping the service in the big league of strategic deterrence and nuclear warfare.[131] Yet the price was high. In his last posture statement in March 1961, Admiral Burke reported that the navy had been "squeezed down to the bare minimum which will do the jobs the navy must do."[132] Yet whatever problems the navy faced in 1961 were to pale into insignificance in comparison to those it would face in the coming decade of Vietnam.

SIXTEEN

"STRICTLY A SECONDARY AND COLLATERAL TASK"

It was one of the many ironies of the Vietnam War that a conflict that would be decided almost entirely by combat on and over the land should begin with an old-fashioned naval engagement. During the spring and summer of 1964 the United States, anxious to shore up the tottering government of South Vietnam, began to organize and support a series of commando-type raids by the South Vietnamese navy on military installations in North Vietnam. On the last day of July 1965, four Vietnamese navy patrol boats bombarded Hon Me in the Hon Nie Islands off the coast of North Vietnam. The U.S. destroyer *Maddox* was on patrol in the Gulf of Tonkin that day conducting electronic surveillance of North Vietnam and southern China. Two days later the *Maddox* was intercepted by three North Vietnamese motor torpedo boats.

The *Maddox* managed to evade the North Vietnamese torpedoes and hit one torpedo boat with a 5-inch round. All three boats were further damaged by carrier aircraft that soon arrived on the scene. Two nights later the *Maddox* and another destroyer, the *Turner Joy*, reported that they were again under attack by torpedo boats. Neither ship was hit, and many experts, including the *Maddox's* skipper, soon developed suspicions that reports of the second attack were the result of freak weather effects on radar and imagined sighting by excited crewmen.[1]

Whatever the doubts, President Lyndon Johnson and his advisers, who for several months had been considering stronger action against North Vietnam, including possible air strikes, seized on the two incidents to secure passage of a congressional resolution authorizing the

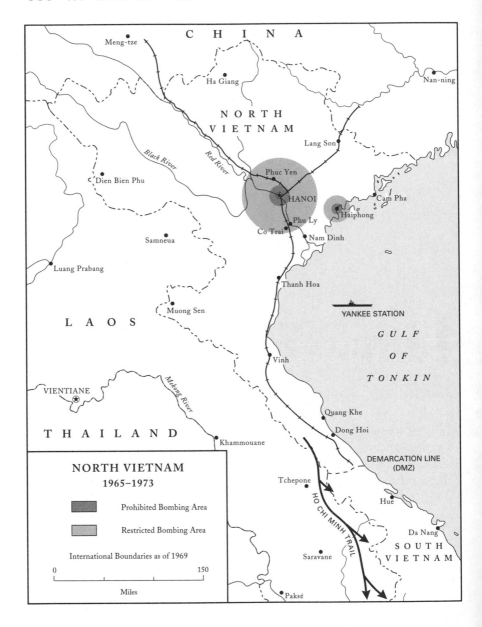

president to adopt "all necessary measures to repel any armed attack against the forces of the United States," and "to take all necessary steps, including the use of armed force to assist American allies in Southeast Asia." Johnson had already ordered air strikes by navy carriers against

North Vietnamese naval bases. Over the next seven years the navy would be caught up in the war in Southeast Asia. The navy's sustained combat operations began more than six months after the Tonkin Gulf Incident when President Johnson, who had won reelection in November 1964, ordered continuous air attacks on North Vietnam in an attempt to stave off the impending defeat of South Vietnam at the hands of Communist insurgents supported by the North. The South Vietnamese setbacks continued unabated. The president and his advisers took the fateful decision to order U.S. Army and Marine Corps combat units to Vietnam in July 1965. For the navy, "America's longest war" was to prove operationally inconclusive, professionally frustrating, and institutionally disastrous.

The navy fought several distinct, almost separate, wars in Vietnam. Only one of them, an elaborate patrol and surveillance operation along the twelve-hundred-mile South Vietnamese coast called "Market Time," much resembled the traditional naval role of securing and protecting maritime lines of communication through combat on the high seas. Market Time was intended to interdict the seaborne flow of supplies by junk and trawler from North Vietnam to Communist forces in the South. While Market Time appeared successful in this effort, the North Vietnamese responded by simply rerouting most of their supplies through supposedly neutral Cambodia and thence into South Vietnam by river.[2]

None of the Communist powers attempted to challenge the U.S. free use of the sea. Consequently, most of the navy's other efforts were almost exclusively devoted to attempting to influence events ashore. Ships of the Seventh Fleet also provided naval gunfire and carrier air strikes against targets ashore in support of army and Marine Corps force combat operations in South Vietnam.

The most visible and ambitious of the navy's Vietnam operations was the sustained bombing of North Vietnam between 1965 and early 1968. Generally two to four attack carriers operated in the South China Sea, sending their reconnaissance and strike missions against military installations, railroads, bridges, roads, and supply facilities in North Vietnam and against the long Communist supply routes from North Vietnam through the mountains of Laos into South Vietnam. Other carriers provided direct air support for ground operations inside South Vietnam, but it was the air war in the North that received most attention. At first, air force and naval aircraft carried out their attacks on the north in separate three-hour periods, but the services soon adopted a system of zones or "route packages" with the two services responsible for a varying number of "route packages" each week.[3]

The carriers' air wings usually included F-8 Crusader Fighters, A-4 Skyhawk attack planes, and F-4 fighter bombers. Beginning in 1966, a new attack aircraft, the A-6 Intruder, an all-weather plane able to carry the heaviest bombload of any carrier-based aircraft, began to join the carrier air wings. The propeller-driven Douglas A-1 Skyraider, nicknamed "the SPAD," designed at the end of World War II and able to carry the bomb load of a B-17, proved invaluable in providing close air support to troops in South Vietnam and for protecting search and rescue helicopters.[4]

Hopes that the air attacks on North Vietnam might persuade Hanoi to cease or scale back its war for the South soon faded, but the bombing continued. Washington's hope was that if the air attacks could not intimidate the North they could at least destroy its ability to supply and reinforce its forces in South Vietnam. By the end of 1966, air force, navy, and Marine Corps aircraft had flown 148,000 sorties against North Vietnam and dropped 128,000 tons of bombs aimed at barracks, ammunition depots, railroads, bridges, airfields, and radar installations. By the conclusion of 1967 the United States had dropped a greater tonnage of bombs on North Vietnam than it had used to attack Japan in World War II.[5] Yet destructive as it seemed, the bombing campaign was in fact carefully controlled and limited by Washington. Many of President Johnson's key advisers had painful memories of the Chinese intervention in the Korean War, and all had experienced the superpowers' close brush with nuclear war during the Cuban Missile Crisis.

The president's advisers had solid reasons for their concern. Following the Tonkin Gulf Incident, Chinese Premier Mao Zedong moved four air divisions and an antiaircraft division to Kunming and Guangzhou provinces adjacent to Vietnam and dispatched more than a dozen MiG-15 and MiG-17s, with their pilots, to Hanoi to train North Vietnamese pilots. By 1966 there were more than 50,000 Chinese serving in military engineer, technical, antiaircraft, and logistical units in Vietnam.[6] "If the American madmen bombard China without constraints," Chinese leader Zhou Enlai told the president of Pakistan, "China will not sit there waiting to die. . . . Bombing means war. The war cannot have boundaries. It is impossible for the United States to finish the war simply by a policy of bombing."[7]

With these real and imagined dangers in mind, U.S. Secretary of Defense Robert McNamara and the State Department exercised minute control over the manner, timing, and strength of the air attacks against the North. Each list of targets to be attacked had to be submitted one (later two) days in advance through a long chain of officials: Commander in Chief, Pacific, the Joint Chiefs of Staff, McNamara's civilian deputies, and the secretary himself. At each level comments, additions, and deletions might be added. The final decision on targets was made by the president himself at a Tuesday lunch at the White House attended by the Secretary of Defense, the national security adviser, the Secretary of State, and the president's press secretary.

As the war continued the list of targets was gradually increased, but important areas of North Vietnam remained off-limits. These included the cities of Hanoi and Haiphong and surrounding areas and any target within twenty-five miles of the Chinese border. Communist aircraft could be attacked in the air but not on the ground. The North Vietnamese were well aware of these self-imposed American restraints and missed no opportunity to exploit them for their own purpose. In July 1966, the Soviet Ministry of Shipping complained that port authorities at Haiphong were intentionally delaying the unloading of Soviet ships "evidently believing that the longer they held the large tonnage vessels the less risk they would run of U.S. bombing raids. Moreover, they usually placed those Soviet vessels in close proximity to the most dangerous areas (e.g. near antiaircraft guns) in hopes of ensuring their safety. . . ."[8]

Once the "Tuesday Cabinet" in Washington had agreed on targets, strike orders were dispatched to the carriers in the South China Sea. The orders, which would send the carrier's 3,000–4,000-man crew into action, were most often received between 1:00 and 3:00 A.M. Over the next few hours, planes were fueled and armed, breakfast was served to hundreds of men, intelligence officers collected the latest target intelligence, and pilots assembled in their ready rooms. As the sky grew brighter, hundreds of ordnancemen, plane handlers, firefighters, and catapult operators, all wearing distinctly colored shirts, swarmed over the flight deck and around departing aircraft, loading weapons, disengaging chocks and chains, and making last-minute checks.

Around dawn the air would fill with the loud hiss and whine of jet engines as flight deck directors guided the first planes onto the catapult tracks. The pilot pushed his throttle to full power and signaled the catapult officer by saluting him. Standing to the side and front of the plane, the catapult officer would suddenly raise his arm and bring it sharply down. The catapult would engage, hurtling the plane along the deck and into the air.

Sometimes more than a hundred aircraft would be launched in large multicarrier "alpha strikes." Sometimes smaller groups of aircraft struck roads, bridges, truck convoys, trains, and ferries in North Vietnam. Flight deck crews aboard aircraft carriers "on the line" worked sixteen-to-eighteen-hour days. "Frequently they would be so tired they would simply flop down on the deck or crawl into a corner to catch some much needed sleep," recalled Commander John D. Nichols. "Carriers are noisy crowded places to work at the best of times. In war with strikes launching and recovering and ordnance being handled and loaded constantly, the pressure of the place is enormous."[9]

As the bombing continued the North Vietnamese gradually acquired a formidable air defense system. China and the Soviet Union supplied them with sophisticated antiaircraft guns, radars, and missiles as well as MiG-17 and MiG-21 fighter aircraft. By 1967, North Vietnam had one of the most modern and capable antiaircraft systems in the world. Even before then, by August 1965, the navy had suffered its first losses to ground-to-air missiles, and the fleet now added the frustrating and costly mission of destroying antiair missile sites to its operations.

In these missions, one or two A-4 or A-6 attack planes, escorted by a larger number of F-8s, attempted to locate and destroy missile sites.[10] The A-4 was armed with a Shrike antiradar missile that would home in on the missile battery's radar emissions. The Shrike "had a Willy-Peter [white phosphorous] warhead so it made a real big flash," recalled one F-8 pilot, "and since the way the SAM [surface-to-air missile] sites were set up with radar in the center and the missiles and all storage areas around it, if you got there with [the F-8's] 20mm and just hosed it down you could start secondaries. A lot of time we would do that and you'd see missiles squirting across the ground like great big Roman candles. You'd get into a whole shed full of those 35 foot long things and set fires and you'd see them scurry across the ground, go into the air and blow up. I mean it was really spectacular."[11]

By the end of 1965, the North Vietnamese had added the new delta-wing MiG-21 armed with heat-seeking missiles to its arsenal. U.S. fighters and other planes, built with an eye toward a nuclear conflict with Russia, were not as maneuverable as the smaller, lighter MiG. The U.S. Navy version of the F-4 Phantom did not even carry guns. It had been designed to intercept high-flying Russian bombers, not to dogfight with high-performance fighters. The Sparrow missile carried by the F-4 was mechanically delicate, frequently unreliable, and useless at short range. The rocket motor failed to ignite in at least 25 percent of all Sparrows fired in one year. During the spring of 1968, F-4s from the carriers *Amer-*

ica and *Enterprise* fired a total of twenty-seven of these $150,000 missiles without obtaining a hit.[12] Although U.S. pilots managed to shoot down two MiGs for every American plane lost in air-to-air combat, this record could not compare with the 8:1 ratio in Korea or the 5:1 ratio in World War II.[13]

While the technical faults in the Sparrow could be dealt with, the problem of poor pilot flight skills could not be so easily solved. Having been fixated on the New Look and war with the Soviets, navy leaders had paid little attention to preparing pilots for air-to-air combat. The Fleet Air Gunnery Unit, the only U.S. Navy institution concerned with fighter tactics and doctrine, had closed its doors in 1960. As one senior officer observed, "The point is, we sent our people out there not trained for dog fighting. We sent aircraft out there not equipped for dog fighting . . . and occasionally (I probably should use the word frequently) we got into a nose-to-nose combat situation where neither the guy flying the airplane nor the airplane had ever before fired a missile."[14]

Responding slowly to the service's air-to-air deficiencies, the navy established a Fighter Weapons School at Mirimar, California, to teach advanced air combat methods and techniques. Soon dubbed the Top Gun School, Mirimar enrolled its first class in March 1969. Students practiced flying against aircraft that mimicked the characteristics and tactics of Soviet-type aircraft and eventually against actual MiGs captured by the Israelis in the Six-Day War. When the air war over North Vietnam resumed in earnest in 1972 the navy ratio of planes destroyed to planes lost was 12:1.[15]

Despite the embarrassment they caused the navy's leadership, losses to MiGs counted for only a small proportion of naval aircraft losses in Vietnam. Most airplanes were lost neither to other airplanes nor to the sophisticated surface-to-air missiles but to antiaircraft guns. The missile threat forced airplanes to fly at very low altitudes, thus making them easier targets for the guns. The combined losses were heavy. More than 400 naval aircraft were lost in attacks on North Vietnam between 1965 and 1968.[16] Between July and October 1967 the carrier *Oriskany* lost nearly 40 percent of her combat aircraft. One squadron "went out with 14 brand new A-4s and something like 12 were shot down. Of course we picked up replacements, but really only one or two of the original planes were with us when we came home."[17] Four hundred fifty-eight of the aircrews whose planes were lost through combat or accident were rescued by Task Force 77's efficient search and rescue organization, which comprised plane guard destroyers, armed helicopters, rescue helicopters, and attack aircraft to provide cover for rescues over land.[18] Of the 800 not recovered, an undetermined number, at least 174, became prisoners of war. The 138 who eventually returned at the conclusion of the war in 1973 had been subjected to systematic torture, isolation, beatings, deprivation, and near starvation in primitive prisons in North Vietnam.

"The difference between going home, becoming a POW and getting killed was primarily bad luck," observed Lieutenant D. D. Smith, an A-4 pilot. "Denial is a necessary trait for survival in the business."[19] A pilot aboard USS *Oriskany* reflected, "Death couldn't help but get to you, but naval aviation is a pretty close club. . . . Nobody expects it's going to happen, nobody broods when it happens. Yes, it's very emotional, a traumatic situation. But the next morning you just shut it out and continue to do the job at hand."[20] Vice Admiral Kent Lee recalled, "I think most naval aviators come to terms with death, it's not that they become hardened. It's the fact that they have to carry on. . . ."[21]

Although losses among aircrews were heavy, the navy's worst casualties among enlisted sailors came as a result not of enemy action but of disastrous accidents aboard the ships. The first occurred in the carrier *Oriskany* during the night of October 26, 1966, when a magnesium flare dropped by a crew member accidentally ignited. Before the flare could be hosed down, it ignited the ship's flare locker, sending eight hundred flares into a huge ball of fire. Deck spaces and passages soon filled with flame and smoke. By the time the fire had been brought under control, forty-four men were dead and another thirty-eight injured.

Less than a year later a Zuni rocket carried by an F-4 aboard the USS *Forrestal* was accidentally fired. The flight deck was crowded with heavily armed planes preparing to launch, and the rocket triggered an immense series of explosions among the closely parked aircraft. The entire after flight deck was quickly reduced to charred wreckage. Fires burned for twelve hours, killing 134 men and injuring sixty others. More than sixty aircraft were damaged or destroyed. Damage to the *Forrestal* was so extensive that the ship was obliged to return to the United States for repairs.[22]

An explosion aboard the *Enterprise* in 1969 was the third and last of these costly accidents. With the after flight deck in flames, Captain Kent Lee turned the ship into the wind and ordered general quarters. There was no way of fighting the fires on the after flight deck, but it was essential to prevent the spread of fires to the anchor deck. "Burning fuel was pouring off all sides of the flight deck, so we had to keep water sprayed on those sides and on the fantail," recalled Captain Lee. "Our people had just finished underway training and we'd had hundreds of drills. That training paid off; we were able to confine the fire to the after part of the flight deck. After about three hours the fire had burned itself out."[23] Twenty-eight men died in this conflagration, but the *Enterprise* was quickly repaired at Pearl Harbor and returned to the western Pacific.

Unlike air force pilots, who generally served a single tour of one hundred missions or one year, naval aviators could find themselves serving repeated tours of duty each time their carriers deployed to Vietnam. Pilot shortages and the reluctance of the navy to shuttle pilots between the Pacific and Atlantic air wings meant that aviators sometimes returned to Vietnam at intervals as short as fourteen months. In the case of fighter pilots, "constant shortages of carrier F-8 pilots throughout the war meant that the same pilots flew mission after mission over Vietnam with very little prospect of relief."[24] One Department of Defense study reportedly found that pilots were averaging sixteen to twenty-two combat missions per month, while some were flying as many as twenty-eight per month.[25] A naval aviator in the carrier *Enterprise* observed that "if you'd have collectively looked at the air wing crews in those days there wasn't any happiness. It was dog shit hard work and we were losing [men] every day."[26] Many naval aviators later reported suffering extreme fatigue, anxiety, nervousness, depression, and other symptoms usually associated with post-traumatic stress syndrome.[27]

Most pilots also bitterly resented the micromanagement of the air war from Washington, which many blamed on Defense Secretary McNamara and his civilian assistants. "Of course our people in our airplanes were just pawns in this game that these men in Washington found so fascinating," reflected Admiral John J. Hyland.[28] "There were a lot of concerns about what we were doing from both the younger and older group," recalled Commander Wes MacDonald, a carrier air wing commander. "I think we dumped most of the blame on the politicians."[29] A small number of aviators took a broader view. Captain Glen Giuliani, an A-4 squadron commander, observed that "the theory of just tightening the screw a little at a time to accomplish your diplomatic aim was, I think a valid one, when the big bomb is what's lying at the end of the road."[30]

A far greater number of pilots believed that Washington's close supervision was unnecessary, capricious, and a danger to pilots' lives. "It was really very taxing in that many times we thought we had the North Vietnamese down where they could not function properly but our government would let them go," recalled an aviator in USS *Constellation*. "The idea that they had to keep the peace feelers going all the time . . . that was the worst part. . . . We'd bomb them . . . to where we finally could win this damn thing and they wouldn't let us."[31] Whether a primarily agricultural country with few industries whose military equipment came almost entirely from China and the Soviet Union could ever be truly defeated by bombing was a question seldom asked in the air wings. In the summer of 1966, American planes had destroyed 80 percent of North Vietnam's petroleum, oil, and lubricant storage capacity without visible effect on the progress of the war.[32] Most aviators nonetheless continued to agree emphatically with the Commander in Chief, Pacific, Admiral Ulysses S. Grant Sharp, who declared that "the armed forces of the United States should not be required to fight this war with one arm tied behind their backs."[33]

Unlike soldiers and marines ashore, naval aviators could terminate their tour of duty in Vietnam at any point simply by "turning in their wings," i.e., requesting nonflying duties. Yet relatively few chose this option. Some were deterred by reluctance to desert their close friends and comrades or to be thought a "quitter" or worse. Most stayed on for other reasons, however. Flying off a carrier was the most challenging, exciting, and adventurous life any of them could conceive. Naval aviation was their world and the air wing and the squadron their family. Competition and the urge to prove oneself remained strong even in the frustrating environment of the air war over Vietnam.[34] "My guys, with very few exceptions, enjoyed the act of flying off carriers," recalled Commander Ed McKellar, who commanded an attack squadron aboard the carrier *Ticonderoga*, "and they reveled in the camaraderie, being with others who enjoyed this profession."[35] As one aviator reflected many years later, "Now I realize we had no business over there. God damn it, it wasn't all that fun but it was fun being part of it."[36]

A relief from the routine of the South China Sea was provided by periodic visits to Olongapo on Subic Bay in the Philippines. Liberty in the towns surrounding Subic Bay offered cheap beer, cheap whiskey, and thousands of prostitutes. The officers' club at Cubi Point, a favorite of aviators, was periodically wrecked by drunken parties and fistfights. According to one widely repeated story, the carrier *Kitty Hawk*, returning to station off Vietnam, received a message from the Philippines demanding $1,500 for damage done to the Cubi Point club during the carrier's visit. The ship replied with a check for $3,000 and a note that explained that $1,500 was for the previous visit, while the other $1,500 was intended to cover the next one.

In contrast to carrier operations, which involved the very core of the navy's self-image, its most prestigious weapons, and its most influential officers, the navy's two other main activities in Vietnam received relatively little attention from the admirals. They were the navy's patrol operations designed to interdict North Vietnamese seaborne supplies to the South and the navy's "brown-water" operations on the rivers of South Vietnam. These involved small patrol craft, "Swift boats," PBR river patrol boats, and amphibious craft, commanded by relatively junior officers, often reservists or ROTC graduates. The most outstanding aviators served in the carriers deployed off North and South Vietnam, but few served "in-country" in South Vietnam. As for the "nucs," Vietnam had little impact on their operations and missions. "We sent some wonderful people and we sent some people we wanted to get rid of," recalled Admiral Duncan. "Of course, we had many other things going on. We had nuclear subs, new aircraft. . . . We did not send our best people to this war."[37] The Chief of Naval Operations "paid little attention to what was going on in-country," recalled one naval officer, viewing the protracted war being waged in the mountains, jungles, and rice paddies of South Vietnam as "an adjunct to what the major war was."[38]

Surface warfare officers were assigned to the "brown-water war" in the South, but few welcomed the opportunity. "Why would you want some duty that has nothing to do with your career?" recalled one former officer.[39] A navy surface warfare officer's career involved service aboard cruisers or destroyers, not time spent in odd, shallow watercraft that offered little but danger and discomfort. "The [commanding officer], a regular officer, is in many ways ignorant of this river patrol business," wrote one junior officer who commanded a section of PBRs. "He has no confidence in my ability, probably because I'm a brand spanking new Lt. (J. G.) with no fleet experience. Still, he doesn't have half the experience I have. . . . Success in fighting this war doesn't come from years of naval service or age or intelligence. It comes from a sense of survival and the ability to profit from one's experience."[40] Admiral Elmo Zumwalt, upon assuming command of the U.S. naval forces deployed in South Vietnam, concluded that Vietnam was "a dumping ground for weak officers at the commander and captain level."[41]

The high-tech navy of the 1950s and 1960s designed to confront the Soviets had scant room for or interest in the shallow-water operations in Vietnam. Indeed, the "Swifts" and PBRs that provided the backbone of the brown-water force were in reality based on civilian commercial and pleasure craft. The navy, preoccupied with supercarriers and Polaris submarines, had no desire to design and build really effective small combatants for its unwelcome brown-water war in South Vietnam.

Swift boats, designated PCFs, were fifty feet long, had a top speed of twenty-eight knots, and carried a crew of one officer and five enlisted men. They were armed with a pair of ring-mounted .50-caliber machine guns over the pilothouse and a single .50-caliber machine gun and 81mm mortar mounted aft. They operated in the coastal waters of South Vietnam and, after 1968, on the rivers of the Mekong Delta.[42] Originally designed as tenders to offshore oil rigs, the Swifts proved indifferent combatants. At sea they could not operate well in rough water. "Some of us . . . still visit chiropractors for the crashes we endured" in the thirty-foot waves of the South China Sea, recalled Senator John F. Kerry, a former Swift boat commander. "We soon learned to deal with them by lying prone on a bunk and leaving one guy at the helm."[43] On the rivers, the Swifts' aluminum hulls tended to corrode. Their engines operated poorly in the intense heat and were so noisy that "once Charlie [the Vietcong] got the idea of what we were doing he was pretty much able to avoid us, because the Swift boats, you can hear them a mile off."[44] As time passed, the Swifts' propeller shafts and blades bent from frequent grounding of the boats in the shallow rivers and streams.[45]

A more successful design was the PBR (Patrol Boat River), a thirty-foot fiberglass shallow-water patrol boat that carried a crew of four and was armed with three .50-caliber machine guns. The PBRs had a new water-jet propulsion system that gave them a speed of up to twenty-five knots and enabled the craft to turn around in its own length. When struck by bullets, the fiberglass hull did not shatter into deadly fragments, as metal hulls frequently did, and many heavier armor-piercing rounds tended to pass right through it without exploding.[46] The Swifts and PBRs were the workhorses of the river forces, engaging in firefights, setting ambushes, transporting troops, providing fire support, and carrying out medical evacuations.

Their most important function was to interdict the suspected flow of riverborne supplies and ammunition to the Vietcong. To accomplish that mission, PBRs and Swifts stopped and searched thousands of sampans and other watercraft. Between mid-1966, and mid-1969, U.S. patrols boarded some 400,000 craft and engaged in 2,000 firefights.[47] "We expected to get ambushed every time we stopped a boat," recalled one officer. "Hell, we couldn't speak Vietnamese. We got some Vietnamese policemen to start riding the boats and this helped, [but] we caught a few pressuring the people we stopped for money."[48] Despite all this activity, "not once" during 1968 did the brown-water "force seize an important shipment of Vietcong munitions or supplies although such shipments were necessary for the enemy to keep active in the Delta."[49]

Along the narrow rivers and streams, the Vietcong and North Vietnamese established numerous ambush sites. Low-lying mud bunkers, well concealed in the foliage lining the riverbank, could not be destroyed by any weapon carried by the Swifts and PBRs.[50] On the other hand, all American rivercraft were vulnerable to fire from 57mm recoilless rifles and armor-piercing rocket-powered grenade rounds.[51] "You really feel like a sitting duck when you're riding those boats going down the small canals," observed Boatswain's Mate 2nd Class William M. Harris. "You know that the VC are in the area and you know that if he wants to he's going to hit you. . . . The only trouble is he always gets the first punch, so to speak. . . . When he does, all you can do is hope that you can get him worse than he does you."[52]

The common Vietcong practice was to use sampans, which appeared to be fleeing American surveillance, to lure a PBR or Swift boat into an area where it could be ambushed by forces concealed on the riverbank. Lieutenant (Junior Grade) Robert Moir described one such ambush against a PBR near My Tho in 1968. "When [PBR] 153 was about 75 meters from the south bank the VC opened up from the treeline. [The boat] took two rockets almost simultaneously. The first hit the radar dome and blew shrapnel all over the boat. The second hit . . . in front of the coxswain stand and set the boat afire. [The boat] commander was thrown to the deck, jerking the throttle into reverse as the blast knocked him." The other three crew members were also wounded, but the after gunner "got off a good blast of return fire with the after gun. Then he saw the boat was backing into the south bank—so he left his mount and jumped into the coxswain flat which was burning pretty hot by then. He pushed the throttle ahead and drove the boat into the middle of the river. If it hadn't been for Mac we might have lost everyone and the boat too."[53] To deal with Communist bunkers a few amphibious craft were converted to fire flame throwers or 105mm howitzers. However, Swift boats could only completely destroy a bunker by landing and throwing explosives onto its roof or walls.

For sailors the river war was not only hazardous but uncomfortable and debilitating. "We carried huge cans of insect repellent and spread it on like shaving cream when we went on patrol," recalled one Swift boat commander, "but those damn mosquitoes would still be at us like bees on a hive. . . . Most of the time we lived in our own sweat. Even at night the temperature would hover around 80 degrees with high humidity. Daytime temperature soared to 110 degrees. You couldn't stand your own smell after a while. The only way to clean up was to jump in the river. But the rivers were as dirty as we were."[54] A PBR patrol might last up to a week or more. All available space aboard the tiny vessel would usually be utilized to store ammunition and supplies, allowing little sleeping room for the six-man crew even had they been inclined to try to sleep in the airless 100-degree heat. "It's hot in Viet Nam," observed one boat commander. "Guys sweat, get bored and become grouchy, which is [to be] expected, but the majority seem to keep a cool head and perform efficiently."[55]

Yet the discomforts and dangers of the riverine force gave it a special élan. "They were ordinary sailors," observed Lieutenant Commander Don Sheppard, who commanded a river division of PBRs, "who for a short period in their lives were somebody. They controlled a slick powerful fighting machine that let them play out the fantasy of the American hero."[56] Consequently the navy never lacked for bold and independent-minded young petty officers and junior grade lieutenants to captain the boats. And morale remained high. "Aboard a ship, [when] you're a first class petty officer, somebody tells you whether to start the job, somebody else comes up and tells you how it's going to be done," observed Engineman First Class Emil Cates. "As patrol officer if you're out on [river] patrol, you made the decision and decided whether those people were going to be alive or dead in the next two minutes."[57]

Many younger enlisted sailors welcomed the increased prestige and responsibility of the jobs in the brown-water war. "There's no officer, no chief, no first and no second," declared Gunner's Mate Second Class William Armstrong. "No matter what your rate is or what your grade is when you're a boat captain you have to make the decision and that's the difference between the brown water and the blue water."[58] Unlike the thousands of sailors deployed aboard ships in the Tonkin Gulf, who seldom saw the coast of Vietnam, riverine sailors had little doubt they were in a real war. As one group of PBR sailors chanted as they passed a destroyer:

> PBRs get all the pay,
> Get the tin cans out the way,
> PBRs roll through the muck.
> While the tin can sailors suck.[59]

In addition to its patrol craft, the brown-water navy converted some World War II–era landing craft into a river assault force called the Joint Army–Navy Mobile Riverine Force. The U.S. Army provided an infantry brigade, which was housed aboard floating barracks converted from ships. The soldiers sortied from their river base aboard armored landing craft supported by other landing craft converted to heavily gunned "monitors." These converted LCMs could make little more than six knots on bodies of water where the currents sometimes exceeded five knots.[60]

In the swamps, mud flats, streams, and flooded rice fields of the Mekong Delta the riverine force provided a practical means of penetrating Vietcong bases and strongholds. Yet the low speed of the rivercraft and the narrowness of many delta rivers often made the river force a large floating target for Vietcong armor-piercing rockets, machine guns, and recoilless rifles. Bloody ambushes were far from rare.

Ironically, it was the ugly plodding boats of the mobile riverine force that came closest of all naval forces in Southeast Asia to exercising a decisive influence on the course of the Vietnam War. When the Communist Tet attacks burst on South Vietnam at the end of January 1968, the towns in the delta suddenly found themselves under siege. The boats of the riverine force, with their infantry embarked, were the only forces in position to reinforce the South Vietnamese forces in the embattled delta towns. "It was sort of like the cavalry coming to the rescue of the fort besieged by Indians, or rather with the Indians already in it," observed Captain Robert Salzer, who commanded the naval component of the river assault force.[61]

In bitter and destructive fighting over the next two weeks, the river assault force forced the Communist troops out of the large delta towns of My Tho, Binh Long, Can Tho, and Chau Doc, although the towns themselves were reduced to ruins. The commander of the U.S. forces in Vietnam, General William Westmoreland, credited the mobile riverine force with having "saved the Delta." Unfortunately it could not save the doomed American effort to ensure the survival of South Vietnam. Nor could it stop the waterborne infiltrations of Communist supplies into South Vietnam through the Cambodian ports of Kampot and Sihanoukville to outfit depots along the Cambodian border and in Vietnam along the vast and intricate waterways of the delta. Even when the new commander of naval forces in Vietnam, Vice Admiral Elmo Zumwalt, pulled all Swifts off blockade duty in the fall of 1968 and sent them up the treacherous rivers and canals of the delta in search of Communist supply junks and sampans, they were not able to stop the flow of materials into the country.

Though Zumwalt liked to refer to the Swifts as his "cruisers," the PBRs as his "destroyers," and the monitors as his "battleships," the river war was fought not on the empty ocean but in the midst of one of the most heavily populated regions of Southeast Asia. The sheer destructiveness of the incessant combat between the riverine force and the Communists meant the frequent destruction of houses, fishing facilities, boats, and other property of the Vietnamese in the Mekong provinces and often the loss of life as well. General Westmoreland had established "Rules of Engagement" governing when and under what circumstances U.S. forces could employ artillery air strikes or naval gunfire and even when they could reply to enemy fire. The Rules of Engagement, based on generally recognized principles of the law of land warfare and frequently updated, were legally "impeccable."[62] Yet few officers even at the highest levels were thoroughly familiar with these Rules of Engagement, which, in any case, were open to conflicting interpretations and left much to the judgment of the officer on the scene.[63] "You'd get a couple of rockets shot from the center of the town. Well, it's very easy for me to say they will not be responded to by fire," observed Captain Arthur Salzer. "But it's very hard for the boat crew that's been hit and perhaps lost its captain, had one or two men seriously wounded to remember that when they have guns in their hands and see their friends bloody and dead."[64] Any hamlet could be viewed as a Vietcong hamlet if it happened to be occupied by Communist forces, if Americans took fire from the hamlet, or even if tunnels or bunkers were found there. In the delta, American helicopter pilots routinely strafed and sank junks loaded with rice simply because they had been sighted traveling a portion of a canal in a free-fire zone. The crews of the junks, well aware of this practice, abandoned their craft and jumped into the water at the first sight of choppers. Such unusual behavior confirmed to the pilots that the crews were Vietcong, and they proceeded to attack them in the water.[65]

Sailors who had been told they were in Southeast Asia to protect the Vietnamese quickly joined American soldiers in their suspicion and contempt for the people of the delta. "The majority of these people are very simple and to me very primitive," declared one sailor. "They live in grass houses or [houses] made out of tin, old beer cans, boxes . . . eating fish heads and rice . . . no clothing or what clothing they can scrounge up, and very happy with just living off the land. . . . It doesn't really feel like the people around us care."[66] Like GIs, sailors suspected that most Vietnamese were passively or actively aiding the Communists. Boatswain's Mate William Harris believed that there were a few Vietnamese "who really want to keep the VC and the Communists out of this country but . . . overall people either are VC sympathizers or they just don't care. . . ."[67] By the end of 1968, many Americans had come to agree with the GIs that South Vietnam might not be worth saving. Following the Tet Offensive, President Johnson halted the bombing of much of North Vietnam and entered into protracted peace negotiations with the North Vietnamese. Richard Nixon, elected president in the fall of 1968, while insisting that he would achieve "peace with honor," soon found himself obliged to take further steps to "wind down the war" by announcing periodic withdrawals of American troops and accelerating the process of turning over most of the responsibility of fighting the war to the Vietnamese, a policy dubbed "Vietnamization."

Brown-water sailors had a perspective on Vietnamization different from that of Washington. Boat commanders and patrol officers who had been instructed to prepare Vietnamese sailors to take over the river war reported that Vietnamese sailors would frequently desert before a patrol. Those who did go frequently "refused to fire, would jump down into the well deck areas of the boats or down into a place where they could get protection and stay away from the open areas where the guns were."[68] Boatswain's Mate Harris observed that he had had four Vietnamese aboard his boat as trainees. One "refused to do anything at all except go on liberty and eat chow." One was "too scared and refused to fire the guns," and a third "tried to kill me."[69] Gunner's Mate Young observed that "we're trying to turn this war over to the Vietnamese whose war it really is. My boat is due to turn over February 7, 1970. We've got more Vietnamese coming aboard now than we've had at the start. Teaching them and having them take over. Myself, I don't really think it's going to work."[70]

"Vietnamization" and winding down the war did little to make life easier for the thousands of sailors deployed in Vietnam and the western Pacific. Obsolescence and shrinking defense budgets had reduced the total size of the navy from 926 ships to 597 between 1968 and 1972, yet the navy was still obliged to deploy more ships overseas than at any time since 1965.[71] This resulted in ever longer deployments and a larger proportion of time on deployments spent in active intense combat or combat-training operations, what the navy called "high operating tempos." For many younger sailors, their first experience away from home might be a nine-month deployment to the South China Sea. During such a deployment the ship would be under way almost 85 percent of the time, with only a few brief visits to foreign ports for upkeep and liberty. The aircraft carrier *Kitty Hawk* spent fifty-four consecutive days conducting flight operations from the South China Sea during 1971.[72] At the height of the 1968 Tet crisis, cruisers and destroyers of the Seventh Fleet, operating off the coast of Vietnam, spent 85 percent of their time at sea.[73]

Many career officers and senior petty officers had experienced almost seven years of such deployments. By the middle of 1973 the carrier *Con-*

stellation had made six combat tours to the Gulf of Tonkin in the past eight years.[74] A sailor serving in a ship based in San Diego, California, could expect to spend fewer than seventy nights—not days—a year at home with his family.[75] As the ship readied for sea, younger sailors would be urged by antiwar activists, sometimes acquaintances or friends, to miss the sailing.

In the Korean War, aviators and other sailors had frequently complained about the indifference of the public back home to the fact that the armed forces were engaged in a large, costly war. This time it was different. The public, or at least an articulate minority of the public, actively opposed the war. Military and naval bases in the United States often felt themselves under virtual siege by antiwar demonstrators. Writing of his experience in World War II, Alvin Kernan recalled the departure of escort carrier *Suwanee* from San Francisco for the western Pacific in February 1945: "Sailing under the Golden Gate Bridge . . . everyone went to quarters in undress blue uniforms lining the flight deck as we went under the bridge and the ship's horn sounded a salute to the country left behind and got in return blasts from all the other ships in the harbor. It was a valedictory; a moving, powerful, sensory image of a country united in war."[76] More than a quarter of a century later, in January 1972, the carrier *Hancock* left the same harbor for the same destination: "Demonstrators surrounded the ship in little boats and some of the women stripped off their clothing and began to throw their blood soaked tampons at the *Hancock*. As the ship passed under the Golden Gate Bridge, the skipper put the ship on general quarters, fearing that a protester might drop a Molotov cocktail on the flight deck."[77]

Few of these sailors of the early 1970s were inclined to look upon naval service as either an adventure or a patriotic duty. The sense of urgency, danger, and exhilaration, which crews in combatant ships had experienced during the two world wars, was almost wholly absent in most of the ships operating off Vietnam. Aviators felt the keen emotions of combat, but the ground crews who kept them in action did not, though they endured all the stress and fatigue of working at a combat base.

By the early 1970s the Vietnam War had become the most unpopular in American history and the prestige of the American military was at an all-time low. "It was not a good time," recalled Vice Admiral Gerald Miller, a former commander of the Sixth Fleet. "I was getting needled by our own Army and Air Force people about the appearance of our sailors on the beach. I was getting some static from the Greek authorities about the appearance of our sailors. . . . The Greeks resented the blacks coming ashore in loud costumes. The whites were going ashore in dungarees, cutoff dungarees, muscle shirts and that kind of thing."[78] An American living in Venice complained that "the crews coming ashore offer the spectacle of an unrelieved panorama of untidiness and odd costumes. . . . While many of the crew members are well-behaved, a larger number appear not to be, there is a lack of the tight discipline which seems to be apparent in other navies."[79]

Even at the U.S. Naval Academy, the shrine of naval professional wisdom, 25 percent of officers on the faculty planned to leave the navy at the end of their current term of service. "I called them the MDH people," recalled a former Naval Academy superintendent, "because they could, and did constantly tell the midshipmen exactly how many months, days and hours were left before they could finally get out."[80] The reenlistment rate in the navy during fiscal year 1970 was less than 10 percent.[81]

Some sailors expressed their discontent with the navy and the war in more dramatic ways. *Time* magazine reported that "the anti-war sentiment that has so bedeviled the Army in recent years seems to be finding a home in the navy now. . . . Acts of sabotage have surfaced in recent months."[82] The carrier *Ranger* was forced to undergo extensive repairs after metal parts were thrown into her gears. A fire aboard the *Enterprise* was attributed by some to sabotage, as was a fire that did extensive damage to the carrier *Forrestal* at Norfolk.[83] A congressional subcommittee reported "literally hundreds of instances of damage to naval property wherein sabotage is suspected. . . . The magnitude of the problem both in the frequency of suspicious incidents and in total damage to government property is alarming."[84]

Recreational drugs, which had become widely popular among youth of the early 1970s, was a frequent choice of sailors who wished to "tune out" of their uncomfortable shipboard environment. Cheap and plentiful supplies of drugs were available to sailors when their ships visited Subic Bay and in many Mediterranean ports.[85] Aboard many ships there was an elaborate substructure for the acquisition, concealment, sale, and distribution of drugs. At the top of the underground structure was "the boss or head pusher," most likely "a petty officer of E-4 to E-6 level. He is in business for money. . . . He is intelligent and is expert at avoiding the attention of 'straight' seniors and officers. He therefore works hard but no so hard as to become a key individual likely to occasion extraordinary notice."[86]

The head pusher presided over a network of drug runners, addicts, and habitual and casual users. Most casual and moderate drug users were not marginal or troublesome young men but "often . . . a hardworking productive sailor with traits of considerable potential."[87] Among such sailors drug abuse was difficult to detect. One senior officer noted that at least "a few of the more stable and intelligent experimenters and moderate users [may] have become senior petty officers" and that abuse among commissioned officers was far from unknown.[88]

Since the early years of the Cold War, navy recruiting had benefited from the existence of the peacetime military draft in the United States. With the "winding down" of the war, fewer men were needed each year, and President Nixon and his advisers were making plans to replace conscription entirely with an "all-volunteer" armed force. For most of the twentieth century the navy had, in fact, been an all-, or nearly all-, volunteer service but without the spur of the draft and with the shrinking number of men who would come of military age during the 1970s the prospects for recruitment looked particularly dire.[89]

If the navy was to meet its manpower needs in the future, it would have to place greater reliance on finding recruits among people it had previously marginalized. Although the navy had ended World War II with the most progressive racial policies, it had continued to retain the most reactionary practices. In 1949, African-Americans had constituted 4.0 percent of total personnel of the navy. By 1969 the figure was only 4.8 percent. In contrast, the Marine Corps, which had been 1.9 percent black in 1949, was almost 11 percent black in 1969.[90] Changes in the racial composition of the army and air force had been equally dramatic. In March 1971 close to 14 percent of army enlisted personnel and about 12 percent of air force enlisted personnel were black, compared to only 5.3 percent in the navy. Black officers constituted only a small proportion of the total in any service, but the army's proportion of black officers was five times that of the navy's.[91] Admiral Zumwalt, upon becoming Chief of Naval Operations in July 1970, was acutely aware of the navy's manpower problems and of the navy's need to attract high-quality recruits of all races to the service. Zumwalt immediately took steps to increase the attractiveness of navy life. His famous personnel directives known as "Z-Grams" were squarely aimed at reducing burdensome and demeaning petty regulations and excessive bureaucracy variously described by sailors as "Mickey Mouse," "chickenshit," or "bullshit." Such rules, minutely regulating the sailors' appearance, dress, and deportment, had existed in all navies since the turn of the century. They tended to grow in complexity and comprehensiveness in time of peace and to languish in time of war, but no one had made such a head-on assault on them since Lionel Yexley and the reformers of the Edwardian period.

At one stroke Zumwalt decreed that sailors could, within limits, decide on their own hairstyles, including mustaches, beards, sideburns, and Afros, all of which were extremely popular among young people of the time, and that they might wear any sort of civilian clothing on liberty. Even uniforms were redesigned to make sailor and chief petty officer dress more similar.

Zumwalt encouraged active recruiting of African-Americans. He increased the number of black midshipmen at the Naval Academy and encouraged the establishment of Reserve Officer Training Corps programs at historically black colleges.[92] In compliance with Defense Department policies, the navy also took steps to make African-Americans and their families feel more welcome in the navy. Base commanders were instructed to crack down on discrimination in local housing, PXs began stocking items of food and clothing frequently requested by blacks, and major barbershops were directed to hire barbers qualified to give Afro haircuts. Every ship, station, squadron, and base was required to have a minority affairs council, and commanding officers were expected to appoint a minority officer or petty officer as his special assistant for minority affairs.[93]

Unfortunately the navy's belated move toward racial equality came at a most inauspicious time. American society had been shaken by major racial upheavals throughout the late 1960s, beginning with major urban race riots in Los Angeles in the summer of 1965 and in Cleveland, Newark, Milwaukee, and Chicago in 1966. A new group of black leaders began to espouse "Black Power," a doctrine calling for both black separation and militant confrontation with what they viewed as white racism and oppression. The assassination of Dr. Martin Luther King, Jr., in the spring of 1968 sparked further rioting and greater racial polarization.

By the end of the 1960s the armed forces had also felt the impact of the growing racial antagonisms in the civilian community. Aboard ship, whites and blacks were forced to work and live together; ashore they tended to go their separate ways. What were euphemistically called the recreation areas of Subic Bay were, by 1970, rigidly divided between "the strip," which contained the bars and brothels frequented by white sailors, and "the jungle," which contained similar establishments patronized by blacks.[94] Black sailors told navy investigators that they chose to avoid visiting clubs or bars frequented by whites "because they have found that even whites who normally appear to be devoid of prejudice display symptoms of deep seated prejudice after having a few drinks. Numerous blacks related that under these circumstances they felt degraded, or insulted when their white drinking companion begins to relate that he 'is not prejudiced' 'understands color people,' etc. A great many blacks clearly conveyed the impression that they felt a mixing of alcohol and integration. . . . frequently spells trouble."

For their part, white sailors considered their black shipmates exclusionists. "Many whites offered that they found offensive the Afro haircut, Afro costuming and the 'Black Power' salute. They found the dialect with which blacks communicate among themselves difficult to comprehend. . . . Almost all whites interviewed regarded the 'Black Power' salute as a symbol of militancy, whereas the blacks profess to see it to be a symbol of unity."[95]

Many African-Americans entering the service at the end of the 1960s had been recruited at the time that the navy had been obliged to accept men who scored relatively low on its standardized test of education and academic aptitude, called the Armed Forces Qualification Test. Test-takers were grouped according to their scores, with Group 1 being the highest and Group 5 the lowest. In the heyday of the draft, the navy was able to obtain many of its new entrants from Groups 1 and 2 and almost all the remainder from Group 3, but in fiscal year 1971, 14 percent of new recruits were classified as in Group 4, while in fiscal year 1972, 20 percent fell in this group. More than half of minority recruits were classified as Group 4, being thus ineligible to attend any of the of the navy's special schools for electronics technicians, mechanics, administrators, electricians, communicators, and other highly prized specialties. It was precisely to acquire such skilled training that most blacks, like most whites, joined the navy. Instead of learning marketable technical skills, many black recruits, lacking a high school diploma and scoring poorly on standardized tests, found themselves assigned to menial low-skill jobs such as laundry man, mess cook, ammunition handler, etc.[96]

Even more annoying to African-Americans was their perception that the navy was still a racially biased organization that discriminated against blacks in matters of efficiency ratings, promotion, awards, and access to training. Whether or not young African-Americans "enlisted with a chip on their shoulder,"[97] as one congressional panel argued, there was substantial evidence to show that at least in the matter of naval discipline, discrimination did exist. Statistics from 1972 show that blacks in the navy were more than two and a half times as likely as whites to be confined in brigs or prisons. Even when facts such as age and grade and education were taken into account, the incarceration rate for black sailors was significantly higher than for whites.[98] Either blacks in the military committed more crimes than whites, a proposition few social scientists and even fewer blacks were prepared to accept, or the navy justice system was indeed skewed in some way in favor of whites.

During 1972 all of these factors—racial polarization, suspicion of the white power structure, disappointment with job opportunities, and the general stress and irritation of the high tempo of operations—came together to produce the most serious manifestation of unrest in the navy's history. In October 1972, while the carrier Kitty Hawk was in Subic Bay for a short upkeep period, a number of black and white sailors on liberty became involved in a series of fights and brawls in clubs ashore. The Kitty Hawk departed Subic Bay next morning, and her officers began an investigation of the incident.

When one young black sailor was summoned to make a statement, he arrived with nine others, refused to make a statement, stormed out of the meeting, and proceeded with his friends to the after mess deck, assaulting a white sailor on the way. Disorderly groups of black sailors roamed the ship, assaulting white sailors. When order was restored, forty-six people had been injured, forty of them whites. Twenty-six sailors were charged with various offenses.[99]

Four days later at Subic Bay a group of black sailors aboard the fleet oiler Hassayampa assaulted several white sailors who they believed had stolen their money. Marines boarded the Hassayampa and arrested eleven black sailors, six of whom were subsequently tried for assault and rioting.[100]

The most serious incident occurred aboard the carrier Constellation in November 1972. For several weeks a group of black sailors had been meeting after hours in one of the ships three barbershops to discuss common concerns and grievances. In accordance with Navy Department directives, the Constellation had a "human relations council" that included a black chief petty officer, but the council held no meetings between its organization in April and the following October. African-American sailors had little confidence in the organization. The relative importance that the commanding officer attached to the council could be judged by the fact that its most senior member was the ship's dental officer.

In addition to some of the common grievances of perceived discrimination in jobs, promotion, and punishments the black crewmen aboard the Constellation believed that the captain unjustly suspected them of sabotage. During September and October, racial tensions steadily escalated. The final spark was provided by reports that six

African-American sailors nearing the end of their term of enlistment would be separated from the service with general, rather than honorable, discharges. On November 3, while the ship was conducting exercises off San Diego, six black sailors, soon joined by others, staged a tumultuous sit-down strike on the after mess deck. Negotiations with members of the human relations council proved futile, and the sit-down continued for the entire night, with some protestors threatening to "tear up the ship." The captain sealed off the mess deck and returned the ship to San Diego.[101]

At San Diego, Captain J. D. Ward, the Constellation's captain, formed a beach party of 130 seamen including most of the dissidents and sent them to the North Island Air Station. The Constellation then returned to sea while the navy vacillated between disciplining and negotiating with the dissidents. By this time word of the uprising had reached the media and the militant black sailors had become the focus of considerable press interest. By the time the Constellation returned to San Diego the incident had become the focus of attention for Commander in Chief, Pacific Fleet, the Chief of Naval Operations, and the Secretary of the Navy. After protracted negotiations, Captain Ward, under intense pressure, agreed to a review of nonjudicial punishments and administrative discharges and to receive back all the militants aboard the ship without disciplinary action. The dissidents were bused to the Constellation's wharf the following morning, but instead of boarding the ship they engaged in a second eight-hour demonstration, fists raised in Black Power salutes for the television cameras and microphones.[102]

Although the Kitty Hawk and Constellation incidents received the most publicity, racial unrest in the navy was worldwide in nature. Serious but little-noticed flare-ups occurred in ships of the Sixth Fleet in the Mediterranean. Aboard the carrier Intrepid, a night-time confrontation between blacks and whites was only ended by the captain ordering the ship to general quarters. Three amphibious ships also experienced serious incidents. "One ship particularly had a series of incidents that were pretty bad on the beach, to the extent that the CO ordered all the crew back aboard one night and got them under way."[103]

Admiral Zumwalt and much of the media blamed the unrest on the navy's residual racism and the slowness of naval officers in implementing Zumwalt's aggressive social programs.[104] Flag officers and conservative congressman blamed the incidents on Zumwalt's "People Programs," which, they argued, undermined the authority of officers and senior petty officers and encouraged an atmosphere of permissiveness in the fleet.[105] Retired captain Paul V. Ryan probably spoke for many senior officers when he concluded that "the Navy had been too hasty in diluting its traditional doctrine and time-tested discipline."[106]

In this sour and contentious mood the U.S. Navy greeted the end of the Vietnam War.

SEVENTEEN

"THE HITHERTO UNLIKELY SCENARIO"

W riting in the *Naval Institute Proceedings* in 1972, Vice Admiral Malcolm W. Cagle observed that in both the Vietnam and Korean Wars, "aircraft carriers had been deployed as floating airfields. . . . Attack carriers can indeed be so deployed—as Korea and Vietnam amply proved. This deployment notwithstanding, the main mission for attack carriers is to assist in carrying out the navy's prime mission, control of the sea. Supporting the land battle is strictly a secondary and collateral task."

In the aftermath of the long Vietnam conflict it appeared that for the first time since World War II the navy might indeed be called upon to carry out its "main mission." For a credible challenge to control of the seas had now appeared in the form of the Soviet navy. Hopelessly outclassed at the time of the Cuban Missile Crisis, the Soviet navy had, by the mid-1970s, grown into the largest fleet in the world. In terms of numbers, though not tonnage, the Soviet Navy was two and a half times as large as the U.S. Navy.[1] More than 90 percent of ships and submarines in the Soviet navy were less than twenty years old.[2]

In contrast, the U.S. Navy had continued to shrink. To pay for the Vietnam War the Johnson and Nixon administrations had canceled or postponed construction of new navy ships. Between 1966 and 1970, the U.S. Navy had added 88 new ships, the Soviets 209.[3] "The navy's resources were gobbled up by the war," recalled Admiral Zumwalt. After the end of fighting in Southeast Asia, tight budgets, imposed by the Ford and Carter administrations, meant continued shrinkage in the navy. Between 1975 and 1980, the Soviets acquired another 200 warships, the United States 68.[4]

The Soviets had no huge aircraft carriers, but their surface ships and submarines carried powerful batteries of antiship cruise missiles. At the Baltic shipyard in Leningrad, which had once built battleships for the tsars, the Soviets were constructing the 24,000-ton Kirov-class battle cruisers. Except for aircraft carriers and large amphibious ships the Kirovs were the largest warships built by any navy since World War II. They carried a battery of almost three hundred antiship and antiaircraft missiles in fifty launchers.[5] Even small fast patrol boats like the Osa and Manuchka classes were armed with these ship-killing missiles. In October 1967, three Soviet-made Styx missiles fired by the Egyptian navy from inside Port Said harbor sank an Israeli World War II–type destroyer fifteen miles away. Six years later the Israeli navy, using its own short-range Gabriel missile, sank nine Egyptian and Syrian warships in four separate engagements during the 1973 Yom Kippur War.[6] The threat Soviet surface ships armed with cruise missiles posed to aircraft carriers was a frequent subject of discussion and debate in the Pentagon and on Capitol Hill.

By the late 1970s, the American edge offered by the nuclear submarine and the Polaris missile had largely disappeared. In 1978, the Soviets had 142 nuclear-powered submarines compared to 109 for the United States.[7] The Soviets had developed their own fleet of ballistic missile submarines, called by the U.S. analysts the Yankee class. These cruised the Atlantic sometimes within a hundred miles of the United States. More advanced Soviet ballistic missile submarines developed during the mid-1970s were armed with multiwarhead missiles with a range of more than 5,000 nautical miles.[8] These submarines had no need to make the hazardous voyage to the Atlantic but could remain in Soviet coastal waters and still target North America with their missiles. Worst of all, in early 1979, U.S. satellite photos revealed that the Soviets were assembling large quantities of steel and enlarging the graving dock at the Nikolayev shipyard complex on the Black Sea. Together with other intelligence and reports that the Soviets were experimenting with catapults and arresting gear, the photos suggested that the Soviets intended to build large attack aircraft carriers.[9]

The Soviets had not been slow to flex their new muscles at sea. Soviet naval squadrons frequently cruised the Mediterranean, the Caribbean, and the Indian Ocean and were stationed permanently in the Mediterranean, where they used Egyptian and Syrian ports. In two worldwide exercises in 1970 and 1975 the Soviets simultaneously conducted maneuvers in the Baltic Sea, Black Sea, and Mediterranean, Atlantic, Arctic, and Indian oceans involving more than two hundred ships all coordinated by Soviet naval headquarters in Moscow.

Soviet warships and land-based aircraft routinely shadowed American task forces in the Mediterranean. During a U.S.-Soviet crisis in the Middle East during the 1973 October War, the Soviets ships deployed to the Mediterranean outnumbered the U.S. Sixth Fleet. In addition to their missile-armed warships the Soviets were able to count on air support from land-based aircraft flying from Egypt and Syria. Each of the Sixth Fleet's three carrier task groups was shadowed by a Soviet surface action group that included at least one missile cruiser and destroyer. "The U.S. Sixth Fleet and the Soviet Mediterranean Fleet were in effect sitting in a pond in close proximity and the stage for the hitherto unlikely 'war at sea' scenario was set," wrote the Sixth Fleet commander, Vice Admiral Daniel Murphy.[10] Tensions eased after a few days, but for years afterward politicians and pundits pointed to the 1973 confrontation as evidence of the Soviet navy's readiness to confront the United States in any contingency.

Under the direction of its head, Admiral Sergei Gorschkov, the Soviet navy had added several hundred ships to its fleet in the twenty years since 1960. Gorshkov, a sort of Cold War Tirpitz, wrote two books on naval history and strategy whose turgid, convoluted prose seemed to many observers to point to a bid for Soviet ascendancy on the high seas.

Here indeed was a serious challenge to U.S. maritime supremacy, one that resembled in magnitude the German challenge to Great Britain at the turn of the century. American naval officers were not slow to point with alarm to the Soviet threat. Admiral Zumwalt told a Senate committee in 1971 that in the event of a bilateral conventional naval war with the Soviets, "we would lose,"[11] while Admiral Hyman G. Rickover told another committee that in case of a confrontation he would rather be in command of the Soviet submarine fleet.[12] Yet Congress and the public were unimpressed. In the aftermath of the Vietnam War, few Americans were inclined to call for a new naval race. Defense budgets during the Ford and Carter administrations continued to shrink. In fiscal year 1964, the navy had received more than 12 percent of the total federal budget. In 1975, the navy's share had declined to 8.5 percent.[13]

Moreover, the cost of ships and planes, fueled by the 1970s inflation, had increased enormously. The Forrestal-class carriers, constructed between 1955 and 1961, had each cost about $250 million; the Nimitz-class supercarriers, the first of which was laid down at the end of the 1960s, cost $2 to $2.5 billion each. The F-4 fighter-attack plane cost about $3 million, while the price of its replacement, the F-14 Tomcat, was around $25 million.[14] Sailors had also become far more costly now that young men had to be enticed into the service by good wages rather than intimidated into enlisting by the draft. Though the number of sailors in 1977 was 20 percent fewer than in 1964, the navy was spending more than double the amount on personnel it had expended in 1964.[15]

Toward the end of the 1970s, a series of menacing developments in foreign affairs, particularly the overthrow of the shah of Iran and the Soviet invasion of Afghanistan, led the Carter administration, under pressure from Congress, to agree to a significant increase in the navy's shipbuilding program. What the Carter administration had undertaken with reluctance the incoming Reagan administration took up with enthusiasm. Reagan came to office committed to an assertive foreign policy and a renewed policy of political and military containment of the Soviet Union. His Secretary of the Navy, John Lehman, called for a program of naval expansion "to recapture maritime superiority for the United States."[16]

Drawing on the work of the brightest of the navy's strategists over the past five years, Lehman offered a coherent, integrated framework for naval planning and procurement which he called the Maritime Strategy. An astute politician and bureaucratic infighter, Lehman forced Rickover, the navy's long-reigning nuclear czar, into retirement. The new secretary forged his own connections with key congressmen and senators. He took personal control of the selection process for the navy's top flag officers, rewarding supporters and ensuring that his naval allies would fill key posts. Taking full advantage of President Reagan's commitment to a massive defense buildup, Lehman secured congressional approval to build ten additional nuclear-powered attack submarines. The secretary's oft-repeated goal was a "600 ship navy," which would include 100 attack submarines, four reconditioned battleships, and fifteen carrier battle groups. That goal was never achieved, but the navy did grow from 479 to 580 warships in less than eight years.

Several technologies that had been under development for decades finally reached maturity in the 1980s, making the warships of those years far more capable fighting machines than those of the preceding two decades. Surface ships, which had been vulnerable to air attack and almost defenseless against cruise missiles, now embarked close-in point defense weapons and improved electronic countermeasures as well as a potent offensive punch in the form of the Harpoon ship-to-ship missile and the long-range Tomahawk cruise missile, which could be precision-targeted against both sea and land opponents. The new *Aegis* antiaircraft cruiser, whose radar, computers, and missiles could track and engage dozens of aircraft simultaneously at a range of 200 miles, gave the fleet the most potent antiaircraft weapon it had had since the days of the proximity fuse.

By the mid-1980s, Pentagon strategists were debating and testing operational scenarios involving early offensive action against the Soviet Union by forward deployed battle groups and amphibious forces positioned in the Norwegian Sea and the North Pacific. In a general war, the plans called for navy forces to attack the Soviet fleet in its home waters, including the remote Barents Sea. Marines would land in Norway, the Kamchatka Peninsula, and other points along the Soviet periphery.

While naval officers, defense analysts, and lawmakers speculated and debated relative Soviet and U.S. naval roles and capabilities, pored over Admiral Gorshkov's books, and argued about tactics, operational scenarios, and technological development, relatively little attention was paid to the quality of personnel on the two sides of the U.S. and Soviet naval race. As in earlier naval arms races, both sides, after declaring their sailors to be superior, proceeded to devote almost all of their attention to strategy, tactics, and above all technical capabilities. A few perceptive individuals, however, did suggest from time to time that there were striking differences between the sailors of the two superpower navies.

The end of the Vietnam War had provided no solution to the U.S. Navy's manpower problems. Racial tensions eased considerably as more enlightened racial and equal opportunity policies took hold and the most intransigent sailors, black and white, left the service—voluntarily or otherwise. The "all-volunteer force" proved a major headache, however. Although the new organization was intended to attract volunteers through generous pay and benefits, little was done to adjust pay raises to keep up with the galloping inflation of the 1970s. Many sailors with families found themselves obliged to rely on food stamps. "During the late 1970s we experienced the lowest sustained retention in the history of the navy," asserted John Lehman. "Recruiting was so bad we almost had to resort to press gangs. We were taking in convicted felons, drug addicts and illiterates."[17] Many ships experienced problems related to undermanning.

By 1978, defense analysts and administration officials were seriously discussing the possibility of reconstituting the draft. But a substantial increase in pay and benefits in 1980 followed by an even larger boost, as part of the Reagan defense buildup, in 1981 helped to close the gap with civilian pay. At the same time, improving service conditions and waning memories of Vietnam helped to attract better-quality recruits. By the mid-1980s the personnel of the "all-volunteer" navy compared well with the draft-induced sailors of the 1960s.

The Soviet navy, although in principle a military arm of a radically egalitarian, socialist state, in fact had more in common with the old Imperial Russian Navy. Like its predecessor it was characterized by unhappy conscript sailors, a shortage of expert senior enlisted men, and a privileged officer corps in which influence and connections counted as much as talent and ability. As in pre-Communist Russia, the navy had access to many of the best educated men in the conscript pool, only ranking behind the Strategic Rocket Forces in priority.[18] Draftees were called for military service twice a year and served for a period of three years, one year longer than the Soviet land forces. New recruits were assigned to basic training camps ashore for four or five weeks. Men in technical specialties received additional training in specialist schools before joining the fleet.[19]

Russians dominated the leadership of the navy as they did other segments of the Soviet state, and Russians, Belorussians, and Ukrainians from urban areas were the favored recruitment source for sailors. Yet with the proportion of Russians in the Soviet Union steadily declining, the navy was obliged to accept a larger and larger proportion of racial and cultural minorities. During the 1970s about 28 percent of navy conscripts were drawn from the peoples of Central Asia and the Transcaucasia regions. By the late 1980s, the proportion had risen to about 37 percent.[20]

Most of these young men had had little exposure to modern technology. Many of them spoke Russian poorly or not at all and required additional training for even the most rudimentary jobs. The Soviet navy's predominantly Russian officers lacked both the background and the inclination to deal effectively with multiethnic sailors. Distinctive customs and religious practices were treated with impatience and contempt. "One Muslim conscript had refused to take off a religious charm until an officer tore it off of the seamen's neck, after which the conscript committed suicide."[21] While life in the navy was especially difficult for non-Slavic minorities and Jews, few sailors of any ethnic group greatly enjoyed their navy experience. High rates of unauthorized absence and desertion were openly acknowledged in Soviet publications.[22]

Living conditions aboard Soviet warships resembled those in British and American ships of the 1930s. Older ships lacked a general mess, and food was still carried from the galley to the berthing spaces as had been the case in the pre–World War II Royal Navy. Visitors to the helicopter carrier/missile cruiser *Moskva*, completed in the late 1960s, spoke of "limited space, Spartan living conditions, [and] rudimentary equipment." Destroyers of the numerically large Kotlin class, completed in the late 1950s and early 1960s, lacked water fountains in the crew spaces. Water was available only "from a portable metal barrel with a community drinking cup."[23]

In principle, the Soviet sailor was fed very well. Indeed, his official caloric intake per day exceeded that of U.S. sailors. In practice his food was poorly prepared and monotonous. An American serviceman's daily allowance included two and a half times more meat and meat products, twice as much fruit and vegetables, and six times more eggs. On the other hand, the Soviet sailor consumed three times as much bread as his U.S. counterpart. Widespread theft of food by civilians and minor officials and shortage of refrigerator space meant frequent shortages of more desirable items.[24] A sailor who served in a cruiser based at Murmansk declared that he had never seen fresh fruit served during the entire time of his tour of duty.[25] Whatever the quantity or quality of his food, the Soviet sailor ate far better than the Soviet soldier and better than most civilians. Sailors were served some type of meat almost every day and were the only servicemen to regularly receive rations of coffee.[26]

Though Soviet warships were sometimes dispatched to distant destinations for exercises or to show the flag, most spent a good deal of time in waters close to the Soviet Union or in port. Even the Soviet Mediterranean squadrons were in port or at anchor a high percentage of the time. Much time at sea and in port was devoted to the maintenance of equipment and frequent, repetitive drill. In theory, sailors were entitled to two hours of rest and relaxation a day. However, much of this time was taken up by lectures and cultural activities devoted to political consciousness-raising. Leave was infrequent and subject to very restrictive conditions. Only men who had not been found wanting in their conduct and job performance and were not in trouble with the political officer could hope to go ashore at all.[27] Even when they did go ashore, the bases were located in some of the remotest regions in the world. Towns such as Murmansk, on the barren windswept Kola Peninsula near the Arctic Circle, and Petropavlovsk, on the Kamchatka Peninsula of Siberia, had few bars and almost no restaurants, dance halls, or cinemas.

Except for a few weeks in high summer, Murmansk was perpetually covered by a layer of snow.[28]

As in other navies, the lower deck of a Soviet warship was a separate society with rules and customs of its own. The most prominent feature of enlisted life was a system of hazing. Third-year enlisted sailors, called *stariki* ("old men"), lorded it over new conscripts in their first year, called *molovye* ("young ones"), with the passive acquiescence of the senior petty and warrant officers. All of the most unpleasant and menial tasks were assigned to the *molovye*. In addition they were expected to perform personal chores and errands for one or more *stariki*, who, in turn would protect them from harassment by the other "old men." Among the first chores required of the new men was to exchange their brand-new uniforms for the older uniforms of *stariki* who were nearing the end of their service and wished to return home smartly dressed.[29]

Given the conditions of service it is unsurprising that less than 10 percent of the enlisted force opted to remain in the navy. Most of those who did were encouraged to enter the *michman* (warrant officer) program to receive advanced technical training for one or two years, followed by three or four years of sea duty. The *michman* was viewed as a career specialist and served aboard ship as a deputy to division officers and a direct supervisor of enlisted men.[30]

Officers in the Soviet navy suffered none of the petty indignities of enlisted men but shared the problems of isolation and prolonged absence from home. Though a representative of a nation committed to world revolution and a classless society, the Soviet naval officer was, like his foreign contemporaries, an essentially bourgeois product. He was "most often an urban, possibly well educated, essentially middle-class youth."[31] Many were the sons of naval officers and Communist Party officials.

Especially well-connected youths had the opportunity of attending the Nakhimov Naval Preparatory School at Leningrad, which they entered at age fifteen.[32] By that age the aspiring officer would have already demonstrated his political reliability by participating in various Communist youth organizations. At fifteen he was eligible to join the "All Union Lenin Communist Youth League," the Komsomol. Membership in Komsomol qualified one for party membership at age 28.[33] Whether or not they had attended Nakhimov, officer candidates were trained at one of eleven different naval colleges. Five schools trained line officers for duty aboard surface ships, two trained engineer officers, and the others trained submariners, political officers, civil engineers, and radioelectronics specialists.

Reporting to his first ship, a newly commissioned officer would be assigned to a department or division appropriate to his school specialty and would remain in that same assignment for up to six years. Where a novice American officer would probably begin his duty at sea as a division officer or assistant and as an apprentice officer of the deck, a new Soviet officer was required first to qualify as a master technician before moving on to other duties.[34] Lacking large numbers of experienced, technically qualified NCOs, Soviet officers were obliged to directly supervise and often personally perform many of the more complex technical functions of their departments.[35]

Political reliability was an essential requirement for any officer, and 95 percent were party members or candidates. Officers carried the burden of political indoctrination of their sailors and of leading them in competitive intraship or intership tests and drills referred to as "socialist competition." In addition, each ship or shore command had a "political officer," a career naval officer who devoted all his time to the morale, welfare, propagandizing, and ideological training of the crew. To further monitor political reliability, the Committee for State Security, or KGB, secretly recruited sailors and officers to act as informants reporting directly to it.

The knowledge that he was being closely, and often secretly, monitored combined with the pattern of naval training that stressed strict adherence to rules and regulations led many American analysts to conclude that "as a group, Soviet naval officers suffered from an inability to innovate or handle unusual situations. They appear, at times, to be inflexible and almost afraid or unable to take the initiative to deviate from pre-planned routines."[36] On the other hand, Soviet naval officers spent far more time in each assignment than their American counterparts and often remained in the same ship for four or more years. Many exceptionally able or perhaps well-connected officers benefited from a rapid promotion system that enabled them to achieve command of a frigate or destroyer as young as thirty years of age.[37]

Unlike the U.S. Navy, with its frequent turnover of reservists and ROTC graduates, the Soviet navy retained an estimated 90 percent of its officers for twenty years or more.[38] Officers were a privileged class in the classless Soviet Union. The pay was ample compared to most civilian occupations, and officers received access to well-stocked special stores and resorts. They received priority for housing and enjoyed a relatively high status in Soviet life.[39] One young woman told an American, "A Soviet officer is a hell of a catch."[40]

One bond that did serve to unite privileged officers and conscript sailors was a proclivity toward alcoholism. In a society in which alcohol purchases accounted for one third of all consumer food expenditures, it was unsurprising that reports and stories of drunkenness and neglect of duty appeared almost continually in accounts by Soviet veterans who defected to the West. Because alcoholic beverages were tightly controlled aboard ship, Soviet sailors often resorted to producing their own beverages from the industrial alcohol used in cleaning and maintenance products. A sort of home brew produced in farm stills was also easily available through the black market.[41]

How the Soviet navy, with its formidable warships, uncertain technology, and unhappy sailors, would have fared in the great encounters at sea envisioned by Gorshkov and the American authors of the maritime strategy would, in the end, never be known. The collapse of the Soviet empire and the end of the Cold War in 1989 meant the end of any possibilities that the great battles on the seas, such as those during the first half of the twentieth century, might be fought in the second. The "hitherto unlikely scenario" remained only a scenario.

While the Soviet and American navies conducted their shadow wars of simulations, maneuvers, surveillance, and intimidation, less powerful navies were fighting the first real wars of the missile era.

On October 6, 1973, the Jewish holiday of Yom Kippur, the Egyptian army crossed the Suez Canal, beginning the longest and bloodiest of the Arab wars with Israel since 1948. Syria simultaneously attacked the Golan Heights. Other Arab nations soon joined the war, and Israel found itself in a precarious situation. After hard fighting and with the assurance of American military supplies, the Israelis regained the Golan Heights and advanced to within artillery range of Damascus. In the west the Israelis established a bridgehead across the canal and had encircled two Egyptian armies by the time a U.S.–Soviet sponsored cease-fire was imposed in late October.

While desperate struggles unfolded in the Sinai and the Golan Heights, the Arab and Israeli navies experienced the first real test of missiles at sea. The forces involved were tiny compared to the NATO and Eastern Bloc navies. The Israeli navy had fourteen fast-attack missile boats, of which the largest was less than five hundred tons. Two had not yet been fitted with their missiles.[42] The Egyptian navy had ten submarines, three destroyers, two frigates, and about two dozen minesweepers and patrol craft. There were also twelve Osa-class and Komar-class Soviet-made missile boats. These were even smaller than the Israeli boats, but their Styx missiles far outranged the Israeli Gabriel missiles. The Syrians had about eight Osa and Komar missile attack boats and about a dozen torpedo boats and minesweepers.[43]

On the night of October 6, a force of five Israeli missile boats made a sweep of the Syrian coast, hoping to draw out the Syrian missile boats based at Latakia. The Syrians obliged and were able to lure the Israeli boats into range of three of their own missile boats. Despite their advantage in range, however, the Syrian Styx missiles failed to score a single hit. Even as the last of the Syrian missiles were still in flight, the Israeli boats launched their Gabriels, destroying two Syrian boats and damaging a third, which was later finished off by gunfire.

The overwhelming Israeli success was attributed by many to the excellence of Israeli electronic countermeasures, by others to Syrian errors in handling or firing the Styx missile.[44] Whatever the reason, the Israeli success was repeated two nights later when four Israeli boats engaged four Egyptian missile boats off the coast of Egypt near the Nile Delta. The Egyptians fired their missiles with no success, then turned and ran for port, but the superior speed of the Israeli boats brought them into range in about twenty minutes. Three Osas were hit and sunk by Gabriel missiles.[45]

In all, Israeli missile boats sank at least nine warships without loss or damage to themselves. By the last days of the war the two Arab navies had retreated to their harbors, where they occasionally attempted to fire their missiles while still protected by their own coastal artillery. In the meantime the Israelis freely ranged the seas carrying out raids and bombardments along the Mediterranean coast and in the Gulf of Suez.[46]

As in the Battle of the Yalu in 1894, fought between the then minor powers of China and Japan, in which "the elaborate contrivances [of the ironclad age] had at last been tested at sea in a general action,"[47] so the engagements off the Egyptian and Syrian coasts provided the first example of war at sea between ships armed primarily with missiles. Whether, as some analysts insisted, the new style of warfare had banished large warships only to the broad oceans, leaving narrow seas like the Mediterranean to submarines and missile attack boats, remained to be seen, but there could be little doubt that the requirements of naval war had changed. While missiles were not wholly unlike shells or torpedoes they were, in principle, far more accurate, putting a premium on the ability to get off the first shots. In the past a ship's ability to survive an attack had been dependent on the strength of its armor and its defensive armament, and to a lesser extent on the captain's ability to maneuver advantageously. Now the chief hope of defeating a missile attack depended on the possession of various devices to provide electronic countermeasures and the ability of her crew to operate them in a precisely orchestrated manner.

A decade later, the conditions of the new warfare were again graphically demonstrated when Argentina and Great Britain fought the largest naval campaign of the 1980s over control of the remote Falkland Islands, scene of the World War I battle between the Royal Navy and Admiral von Spee's squadron. After Argentine forces seized control of the islands in March 1982 a British task force of fifty-one ships was dispatched on an eight-thousand-mile voyage to regain control of the islands which few Britons had ever heard of.

During the four decades since the end of World War II the Royal Navy had undergone a gradual but steady process of diminution that by 1982 had reduced it from a major fleet with global responsibilities to a fairly large anti-submarine force in the NATO naval forces. The last true aircraft carrier had been scrapped in 1979, and the largest ships of the task force were two anti-submarine carriers, HMS *Hermes* and *Invincible*, which between them could carry fewer than two dozen Sea Harrier short-takeoff fighter-bombers.

The quality of the sailors, however, remained remarkably high. Long-overdue reforms had ended the castelike separation between engineering and line officers and opened the possibility of a commission to young men of all social backgrounds. By the mid-1960s, 70 percent of new officer entrants came from "state-aided," that is, public, schools.[48] Training for enlisted sailors was modernized, and skills of all ranks were kept sharp by the navy's involvement in various overseas operations "east and west of Suez" and by continuous participation in NATO exercises. The net result was that the sailors heading for the South Atlantic in 1982 were no less confident and aggressive and probably more skilled and educated than those that had left Scapa Flow to fight von Spee in 1914.

The slight air of unreality about this implausible war was abruptly dispelled on May 2 when the nuclear submarine *Conqueror* torpedoed and sank the old Argentine cruiser *General Belgrano* with heavy loss of life. *Conqueror* was the first nuclear submarine to sink an enemy warship. Her presence in the remote South Atlantic was possible only because her nuclear engines had provided the high speed that enabled her to arrive in the operations area as quickly as the surface ships.

Two days later the destroyer *Sheffield* was hit by a sea-skimming Exocet missile fired by an Argentine fighter bomber. The missile hit the ship's starboard side amidships. Although it failed to explode, the burning of its unspent fuel quickly started fires in the fuel tanks of the ship's gas turbines. Paintwork, plastics, and other flammable materials ignited and spread clouds of black acrid smoke throughout the ship. At the same time, both generators failed, plunging the interior spaces into darkness. Several men were killed instantly, and others died of asphyxiation. All of the surviving crew including twenty-four injured were taken off by the frigate *Arrow* and by helicopter.[49]

Aboard the other ships of the task force, "people started to sleep above the waterline. There were camp beds and mattresses ranged along the passageways. . . . This sort of self-protection was really only applicable in the Second World War when a torpedo could come in below the waterline, but it made people feel safer. . . . Nor after *Sheffield* was there any further need to exhort people to wear their anti-flash gear. . . ."[50]

Supporting British amphibious operations from the confined waters of Falkland Sound, the task force suffered additional losses to Argentine air attacks. Two frigates, a second destroyer, an amphibious ship, and a supply ship were sunk and others damaged before British troops completed their operations to regain the Falklands. The "advanced materials" such as graphite, plastics, and adhesives used by shipbuilders in the 1960s and 1970s not only proved to be highly flammable but tended to generate toxic by-products once they had begun to burn.[51] "I was aware of a flash, heat and the crackling of the radar set in front of my face as it disintegrated," wrote Captain David Hart-Dyke of the destroyer *Coventry*, which capsized and sank in less than half an hour. "As I came to my senses nothing could be seen, except for people on fire through the dense black smoke."[52]

No one believed that it was possible to give contemporary warships strong passive defenses such as the armor or antitorpedo bulges of battleships and cruisers of an earlier era. Instead attention was focused on electronic devices to detect and defeat attacks by enemy planes and missiles. One of the factors most often cited for the relatively heavy losses to the Royal Navy in the Falklands was the task force's lack of airborne early warning radars. The best of these could be provided only by aircraft requiring a large deck carrier—like the one scrapped in 1979.

The dependence on electronic devices had altered many of the traditional practices aboard a warship in action. The captain no longer commanded from the bridge but from a windowless combat operations center filled with radar and sonar consoles, listening devices, and communications equipment. The strain on the officers and sailors operating the sensors, collating information, and making split-second inferences and predictions was enormous. "It was like a fast-moving computer game, full of tensions, all eyes strained and almost impossible to win. We knew we would lose if we could not keep up with the quickening pace."[53] In the operations center of an Israeli missile boat, "faces would pale and sweat break out as the instrumentation indicated a missile headed directly toward them. Sometimes the men sitting at the consoles could not control their bowels in their fear but kept doing their job without faltering."[54]

In earlier naval battles, survival had depended on the gunners and fire directors, on the engine room staff to keep up speed, and on the captain's ability to maneuver the ship. In the electronic age it chiefly depended upon the ability of a dozen or more twenty-year-old technicians to manipulate, orchestrate, and instantly interpret information contained on lighted screens. When information did appear on the screens or over the communications net, "there are vital seconds in which to act." The officer in command "must immediately say and do the things which deal with the worst possible interpretation of the limited facts."[55] In war, commanders had for centuries been obliged to deal with the related conditions of limited time and incomplete knowledge. In the electronic age the time factor had drastically shortened while leaving the relative degree of uncertainty more or less unchanged.

This was demonstrated in dramatic fashion on July 3, 1988, when the U.S. Aegis cruiser *Vincennes* accidentally shot down an Iranian airliner over the Persian Gulf. The American naval war in the Persian Gulf was even more implausible than the British operations in the South Atlantic. In the midst of a long war between Iran and Iraq, the gulf state of Kuwait requested the U.S. Navy to provide protection for her tankers from the threat of air attacks and mines by the Iranians. Iraqi aircraft had long been attacking Iranian and neutral shipping in the northern gulf. As a supporter of Iraq, the Kuwaitis feared Iranian retaliatory attacks on their shipping. Washington reluctantly agreed, after the Kuwaitis made clear that they would turn to the Soviet navy if their requests were denied. Eleven Kuwaiti oil tankers were hastily reregistered as American-flag vessels and the U.S. Navy began convoy operations in July 1987. One of the first two tankers to be escorted by the United States struck an Iranian mine and was forced into a nearby port. It was soon discovered that the Iranians had recently laid a large minefield along the route of the tankers.

For the next several months the Iranians harassed the Kuwaiti convoys with mines, Silkworm long-range missiles, and attempted air strikes. The U.S. Navy was even less prepared to deal with the threat of mines than at the time of the Wonsan debacle during the Korean War. Nevertheless, by scraping together a handful of available minecraft, working with mine countermeasure helicopters, the navy appeared to have the mine threat under control. In addition an Iranian minelaying craft was captured and an Iranian oil platform being used as a communications and missile guidance center was destroyed by naval gunfire and demolitions.

By the fall of 1987 the situation in the gulf appeared stable. More than two dozen convoys made the passage safely, and Washington began to reduce the number of warships assigned to the mission. Then, on April 14, 1988, the frigate *Samuel B. Roberts* struck a mine recently laid by the Iranians. Only new fire-fighting devices and a well-trained crew prevented the loss of the ship.

U.S. retaliation was swift. On April 18, American warships destroyed two Iranian oil platforms in Operation Praying Mantis. Three Iranian warships that attempted to intervene were sunk by aircraft from the carrier *Enterprise* and by missiles and surface ships.[56] There was no damage to U.S. ships or aircraft. As in the Yom Kippur War, it was the success of electronic countermeasures that produced the one-sided victory against an opponent who possessed some of the best available weaponry—including American-made Harpoon antiship missiles and F-14 fighters.

There was more than a little irony in the fact that the largest American sea battle in forty years should be fought not against the Soviets on the high seas but in the narrow waters of the Persian Gulf against a country that until ten years before had been a staunch American ally. Still, naval officers could take satisfaction in the fact that the navy's sophisticated technology had performed well against an opponent who also possessed advanced weapons. A few months later, however, the limits of even the best technology would be graphically demonstrated.

In the weeks after Praying Mantis, Iran appeared to try to avoid major confrontations with the United States. The captain of a gulf frigate found that the conduct of Iranian military forces "was pointedly non-threatening. They were direct and professional in their communications and in each instance left no doubt concerning their intentions."[57] During late June, however, intelligence reports seemed to indicate that Iran was planning some surprise move against American naval forces in the gulf, possibly to coincide with the Fourth of July.[58] There was "an undercurrent of tension and a sense of imminent danger," recalled one officer. "Crews of ships reporting to the Middle East Force in the summer months were noticeably on edge. Numerous 'mines' were reported that later proved to be bags of trash." At the same time many sailors felt "just a little cheated at having missed out on a chance to have been a part of Praying Mantis."[59] One ship, which appeared to some especially eager to prove itself, was the Aegis cruiser *Vincennes*. Her reputed aggressiveness had prompted sailors in other ships to refer to her jokingly as "Robo-Cruiser," after "Robo-Cop," a movie cyborg action hero.[60]

The Aegis cruiser is the most technically advanced of all the surface ships of the electronic age. Its sophisticated radars can detect and track numerous attacking aircraft at the same time, at ranges out to 200 miles. At the same time its computers automatically derive the correct targeting data for the ship's antiaircraft missiles. The Vincennes's combat operations center looked like something out of Star Wars with banks of consoles and huge bulkhead display screens in which small comet-shaped objects indicated the position of aircraft being tracked by the ship's Spy-1A radar.

On July 3, the Vincennes had just completed escorting a southbound convoy. On her return trip the cruiser became involved in an action with two Iranian Boghammer speedboats that had fired on her helicopter. These speedboats, armed with machine guns and antitank weapons, could not hope to sink a large warship, but could nevertheless hope to damage her electronic or communications equipment or propulsion machinery.

In the first half of the century such an attack on a cruiser would have been met with a wall of projectiles from the ship's quick-firers or, in the 1940s, her even more deadly 20mm and 40mm multiple cannons. The Vincennes main gun armament, however, consisted of only two 5-inch guns. One of these guns promptly jammed, forcing the Vincennes to maneuver radically at high speed to keep her remaining gun on target.[61]

While the ship was engaging the speedboats, the Vincennes's Spy radar detected an approaching aircraft forty-seven nautical miles from the ship. This was Iran Air passenger airliner Flight 655, which had just left Bandar Abbas airport for its regular flight across the gulf. Because Bandar Abbas was both a civilian and a military airport and a base for Iranian F-14 fighters, it was important for the Vincennes's combat information center to identify the oncoming aircraft as soon as possible. As in the South Atlantic, the Vincennes's sailors would have only a few minutes to take action if the plane was hostile. The Vincennes's missiles could intercept the plane only within a certain range. That left some six to seven minutes for a decision.

Almost from the first, word spread within the combat operations center that the contact was an F-14. Later, no one could remember who initiated this report, but within three minutes several officers and men were referring to the aircraft as an F-14.[62] The Vincennes's identification supervisor quickly reviewed the commercial air schedule for flights over the gulf. Because Flight 565 had departed twenty-seven minutes late, he incorrectly concluded that the contact could not be a civilian airliner. At that point, *Vincennes* reported the contact to higher headquarters as an F-14.[63] The *Vincennes* began broadcasting warning messages to the airliner (which probably never received them on its frequencies).

At this point the ship was still making tight turns at high speed. Sailors in the combat operations center could feel the vibration of the ship's 5-inch gun firing. Metal wall lockers flew open and their contents spilled onto the deck as the ship heeled over in its radical maneuvers. There was a good deal of noise and shouting as technicians and operators called out their increasingly anxious reports.[64]

The tactical information coordinator, new to his job, apparently read the decreasing range figures on his instruments as decreasing altitude and reported to the antiair warfare officer that the aircraft was descending at increasing speed toward the ship.[65] In fact the airliner was climbing away from the ship at a speed of 380 knots. Although several other individuals were involved in verifying altitude, no one contradicted this report.[66]

The *Vincennes's* captain, Captain Will Rogers, was informed that the approaching aircraft "had veered from its flight path into air attack profile." The contact was still classified as an F-14. The aircraft had not answered any of the repeated radio challenges. When the aircraft reached a range of 10 miles, Rogers made his decision. The antiair warfare officer turned his firing key. Seventeen seconds later the first of two missiles left the rail. In less than a minute both missiles struck the airliner, killing all aboard.

The tragedy of Flight 655 led to worldwide embarrassment and humiliation for the United States, furious protests and threats from Iran, and several investigations. All reached roughly the same conclusion: the technology had worked flawlessly but its operators had still made critical errors. Senator William Cohen of the Senate Committee on Armed Forces wondered aloud whether the operation of supersophisticated systems, in which even a small mistake could be fatal, might in fact *increase* the probability of human error because of the stress generated by the necessity to take action in a very short time span and in exactly the right sequence.[67] At the end of the twentieth century, as at the beginning, not technology but human interaction with technology had proved the critical element in naval warfare.

I n his classic account of the Spanish Armada campaign, Garrett Mattingly observed: "This was the beginning of a new era in naval warfare, of the long day in which the ship-of-the-line . . . was to be queen of battles, a day for which the armor-plated, steam-powered battleship with rifled cannon merely marked the evening. . . ."[1] The long twilight of seagoing warships, armed primarily with big guns, was already well advanced by the time Mattingly published his book in 1959. By that time the primary mission of fighting ships had long since become one of supporting or combating attacks from the air or beneath the sea. This continued well into the 1990s when, in a surprising reversal, new types of surface ships armed with ship-killing missiles and long-range land-attack missiles appeared not unlikely to succeed the increasingly expensive and manpower-intensive aircraft carrier. By the 1990s, in any case, navies had become as concerned with surveillance, communications and information processing, and with protecting these against penetration or interference by the enemy, as they were with ship types.

It may now be possible to reach some tentative conclusions about the issue of social and psychological factors in naval warfare that was first raised at the beginning of this book. The reader who has followed the development of naval warfare briefly described in these pages will probably have already concluded that questions about the precise relationship between the human factor and success and failure in naval warfare are indeed complex. Not only is the question of the exact relationship between technology, tactics, and personnel difficult and puzzling but it also becomes apparent that these three are in turn influenced by issues of politics, finance, and national policy. For example, British naval policy in the age of Admiral Fisher, Japanese naval policy in the 1920s, and U.S. naval policy in the 1960s and 1970s were all influenced and restrained by questions of finance. But in specific cases, policy may also be shaped by the fact that politicians and statesmen may be more willing to spend money on ships and weapons than on people. British leaders were willing to pay for dreadnoughts but never to provide sufficient money for adequate numbers of specialists to man them; Congress was willing to buy large numbers of planes for Admiral Moffet's naval aviation programs but not to expand the navy's manpower to provide crews and support personnel; Polaris submarines came off the ways on schedule, but the shortage of nuclear-qualified personnel to operate them caused the navy to have to change not only its manpower system but its entire philosophy of how sailors ought to be selected for duty.

Whatever the nature of naval policy and finance, it may be said, in general, that peacetime navies have usually been unsuccessful, except during dire economic conditions, in retaining their most valuable enlisted personnel. The officer corps had been more stable during the first half of the century, with most officers regarding their profession as a long-term career. Beginning in World War II, however, as the officer corps began to include large numbers of reservists and regulars who had not attended the service colleges, officer retention also became a problem. This was particularly true in the case of many officers who were aviators, engineers, or other highly trained technical specialists, for whom a lucrative market existed in the private sector.

A sailor of the 1990s had e-mail, satellite TV, air-conditioning, gyms, and salad bars, but ships now spent far longer at sea than in the years before World War II. Aboard many warships on long deployments, "fatigue was a way of life."[2] A chief petty officer of the U.S. Navy, writing in 1998, identified "monotony," "constant drill and seeming endless cleaning," as constants of sea service that had remained unchanged for more than 150 years.[3] If a sailor of the nineteenth-century Royal Navy would not have found shipboard conditions in the 1930s very different from his own, an American sailor of the Cold War navy would not have found living aboard a World War II warship—as indeed many did into the 1970s—entirely unfamiliar. In addition, sailors continued to live and work within a minutely regulated, tightly disciplined environment that many found oppressive, bureaucratic, and arbitrary. An anonymous e-mail message written by a sailor in 1998 succinctly captures one man's view of navy life at the end of the century:

Ah—the Navy—It's an adventure. . . . The suggestions below are made on behalf of those who think the navy is a "TOP GUN" existence. You know, those who watched one too many episodes of "JAG," and think that Navy life is glamorous. To experience Navy life, try a couple of these—right in the comfort of your own homes.

1. Buy a dumpster, paint it gray and live in it for 6 months straight.

2. Run all of the piping and wires inside your house on the outside of the walls.

3. Pump 10 inches of nasty, dirty water into your basement, then pump it out, clean up and paint the basement "deck gray."

4. Every couple of weeks, dress up in your best clothes and go to the scummiest part of town, find the most run down, trashy bar you can, pay $10 per beer until you're hammered, then walk home in the freezing cold.

5. Perform a weekly disassembly and inspection of your lawnmower.

6. On Mondays, Wednesdays and Fridays turn your water temperature up to 200 degrees, then on Tuesday and Thursday turn it down to 10 degrees. On Saturdays and Sundays declare to your entire family that they used too much water during the week, so all showering is secured.

7. Raise your bed to within 6 inches of the ceiling.

8. Have your next-door neighbor come over each day at 5 A.M., and blow a whistle so loud that Helen Keller could hear it and shout "Reveille, Reveille, all hands heave out and trice up."

9. Have your mother-in-law write down everything she's going to do the following day, then have her make you stand in the back yard at 6 A.M. and read it to her.

10. Eat the raunchiest Mexican food you can find for three days straight, then lock the bathroom door for 12 hours, and hang a sign on it that reads "Secured—contact OA DIV at X—3053."

11. Submit a request form to your father-in-law, asking if it's OK for you to leave your house before 3 P.M.

12. Invite 200 of your not-so-closest friends to come over, then board up all the windows and doors for 6 months. After the 6 months is up, take down the boards, and since you're on duty, wave at your friends and family through the front window of your home . . . you can't leave until the next day.

13. Shower with above-mentioned friends.
14. Make your family qualify to operate all the appliances in your home (i.e. dishwasher operator, blender technician, etc.).
15. Walk around your car for 4 hours checking the tire pressure every 15 minutes.
16. Sit in your car and let it run for 4 hours before going any-where. This is to ensure your engine is properly "lit off."
17. Empty all the garbage bins in your house, and sweep your driveway 3 times a day, whether they need it or not.
18. Repaint your entire house once a month.
19. Cook all of your food blindfolded, groping for any spice and seasoning you can get your hands on.
20. Have your neighbor collect all your mail for a month, ran-domly losing every 5th item.
21. Spend $20,000 on a satellite system for your TV, but only watch CNN and the Weather Channel.

One result of this chronic inability to attract and retain sufficient numbers of qualified personnel has been the pattern of extending re-cruiting to segments of society who, before the turn of the century, would have been considered inappropriate or undesirable for service at sea. At the beginning of the twentieth century, most navies still attempted to recruit their sailors from the same seafaring coastal communities that produced seamen for fisheries and merchantmen. Officers of all navies formed a more or less closed elite recruited primarily from the upper middle class but with many aristocratic pretensions and traditions. As navies became larger, more technically complex, and more manpower-intensive, larger and larger groups and races came to be reluctantly in-cluded. By the early 1990s, close to 18 percent of naval enlisted men and more than 4 percent of officers in the U.S. Navy were African-Americans.[4] The Naval Academy graduated it's first black midshipman in 1949. The first woman entered the Naval Academy in 1976.

As the twentieth century drew to a close, the U.S. Navy and other navies were wrestling with the opportunities and problems of introduc-ing women into many of their combat vessels and warplanes. In 1993, fe-male aviators in the U.S. Navy became eligible to fly the latest attack and fighter aircraft. By 1999, women composed 13 percent of the U.S. Navy. Of the 117 combatant ships in commission, fifty-seven were manned by integrated crews of male and female sailors. Five women had been selected to command combat and assault vessels, including a guided missile frigate that had no other females in its crew.[5]

Many of the social changes were due to the efforts of political leaders and advocacy groups, but they were also due to the navy's changing personnel needs and policies. Just as machine-age navies had earlier discovered that they would be obliged to recruit men from industrial areas without any maritime tradition, so the numerically large but "all-volunteer" U.S. Navy of the Cold War era could not rely solely upon recruiting white men. One flag officer bluntly observed, "We're not turning down any qualified men. . . . We've bottomed out in the demographics of the age group we're talking about. . . . We're not getting enough qualified recruits, plain and simple. We need to take these women."[6]

Like ships and weapons, the experience of war at sea had changed dramatically over the course of the century. While an infantryman of World War I would not have found ground combat in World War II or even Korea entirely unfamiliar, sailors engaged in combat aboard submarines or against submarines, in aircraft or against aircraft, underwent a fundamentally different experience from those who fought in battles between big-gun ships.

Sailors have not only had to perform under fire like their military counterparts ashore but, as the century progressed, have been obliged to undertake increasingly complex and intellectually challenging tasks. In addition, the increasing speed at which combat situations could develop has made for an ever shorter decision cycle. In the age of sail, with fleets at the mercy of changeable winds and seas, it was often many hours or even days between the time opposing fleets first sighted each other and the time they came within firing range. At the Battle of Trafalgar, the opposing fleets approached each other at less than three knots, and five hours passed between the time the enemy was first sighted and the time the first rounds were fired. By World War I, fleets of warships, moving at the speed of contemporary express trains, could come within gunnery range within ten to fifteen minutes after first sighting each other. In an air attack, a ship might have only thirty seconds, sometimes less, to open fire once an enemy plane was sighted. A 1950s-type jet bomber attacking at low altitude would be visible from a ship for only about twenty-five seconds. Even with the aid of radar, crews threatened by air attack could have as little as five to ten minutes of warning. In the age of missiles, warning time was sometimes reduced to seconds. At the same time the man behind the guns, around the engine, or in the cockpit or conning tower was increasingly dependent upon the help of large and sophisticated shore establishments for surveillance and early warning, communication and intelligence, and logistical and technical support.

Few would argue with the belief that throughout the century good leadership has remained essential to success in war at sea. Yet analyses of this element simply in terms of the personalities of the top commanders, as is often done, is frequently inadequate in explaining the outcome of naval battles and campaigns. More than Admiral Togo's fierce determination or his unorthodox tactics, it was the fact that his well-trained experienced gun crews could fire faster and perform coolly under fire that secured the victory at Tsushima. Similarly, neither the cautious methodical Jellicoe nor the aggressive, more unorthodox Beatty could achieve decisive results, on the few occasions when this was possible, because of the expectations, training, skills, experience, and initiative, of relatively low-level officers in their fleet.

Leadership indeed seems to be most critical at the lower levels. As in the days of sail, the captain's leadership appears most important. This is especially the case in smaller ships. In ground combat, troops will often be too busy, too confused, or too frightened to pay much attention to the actions and demeanor of their junior officers. Aboard ship the captain's actions and decisions, his skills and demeanor, are on display continually for large numbers to observe. Nevertheless, if leadership appears to be centralized in the role of the captain, it is in fact also decentralized into distinct fighting and technical teams often isolated and working independently under the supervision of very young officers or petty officers.

The relative rarity of mass panic and breakdowns in unit performance under fire compared to those in land warfare has been frequently noted by veterans and observers. Aside from the possibility that sailors are braver than anyone else there are a number of plausible explanations for these differences. Among the most apparent is that the sailor in combat has no place to escape to. As a veteran of Crete observed, the only man who could run away was the captain. While a terrified or demoralized man might wish to move to what he believed to be a safer part of the ship, he would know that this would be prevented by sealed hatches and the immediate presence of his petty officers. The French naval tactician Ambroise Baudry wrote, "A shaky body of troops ceases fire and breaks rank in a rout. . . . Battleships, on the contrary, may be full of panic, but it is a local and compartmentalized panic, and they continue to fire."[7] Military veterans frequently observe that their first experience of combat was utterly like anything they had trained for or expected. They also often remark on their feeling of isolation on the battlefield. In contrast, sailors often say that they found themselves doing virtually the same job in combat as in peacetime drills. They know that they are not alone and that their friends or superiors may see and remember any sign of panic or shaky performance. In addition, most naval actions, though often at least as lethal as land battles, have been short and infrequent. Where this has not been true, as in the battles of Crete and Okinawa, signs of combat fatigue, similar to those in land warfare, usually appear.[8]

Even highly capable leadership cannot always ensure success against an opponent with superior weaponry or a superior operational system, as was graphically demonstrated at Crete and again in the last two years of the U-boat war. Frequently, however, relatively minor changes in weapons, training, organization, or doctrine can make large differences, as was demonstrated in the Battle of the Atlantic. In the Pacific, aircraft carriers, which during the first years of war appeared highly vulnerable to coordinated air attacks, were by 1944 being successfully defended by virtually the same types of weapons as had been available in 1942. What appears most important is not the possession of the most advanced technology but skill in using the technology one has. The British were never able to properly exploit their superior fire control equipment in World War I, and the Americans took some time in the Pacific before they could fully exploit radar. On the other hand, American pilots were able to obtain the maximum results from their nominally inferior Wildcat fighters by exploiting their strong points and devising appropriate aerial tactics.

At first sight, navies appear to be highly conservative, even reactionary organizations. Throughout the century, officers from societies as diverse as the United States, Imperial Japan, Imperial Russia, Great Britain, and the Soviet Union exhibited, and continue to exhibit, a surprising number of common characteristics. Sailors entering the twenty-first century still retain uniforms, rank structure, a special language, and customs dating back some 150 years or longer. Political scientist Robert Jervis has observed that among social scientists, "it is a common-place that navies are even more hide-bound than most bureaucracies."[9] One theory, popular among many students of the military, holds that important innovations in military organizations occur only as a result of drastic changes in the political environment, defeat in war, revolution, or intervention by civilian authorities. That theory is increasingly under challenge and cannot be supported by the evidence presented in this book.

Indeed, a view from the last century would probably suggest that navies, beneath their rituals and regalia, are extremely adaptive, fast-changing organizations. Entirely new types of seagoing warfighters and specialists have been accommodated within the traditional structure of the service. The leading navies made the transition from sail to steam, from line-of-sight to long-range gunnery, from surface to air and undersea warfare, from steam to nuclear power, and from projectile weapons to missiles without fragmenting into separate arms or military organizations and without losing their ability to fight effectively.

Many of the most important innovations appear to have come wholly or in part from within the services. Long-range gunnery was popularized by the British media and encouraged by some civilian leaders, but most of the actual concepts and techniques were developed by individuals within the navy. Similarly, naval aviation, indeed all aviation, was strongly supported by the American public and their leaders, but all the significant developments from dive-bombing to the "Thach weave" to the fast carrier task force were developed within the navy. Other innovations, such as wolf pack operations, amphibious warfare, and the development of night-fighting techniques by the British and Japanese, were of little if any interest to political leaders until introduced by the navies. Indeed, a more accurate characterization of the social structure of navies, and one supported by this book, would be the proverbial old sailor's observation "The navy isn't what it used to be—and never was."[10]

NOTES

Chapter 1: Tsushima, May 1905

1. Where not otherwise noted, the description of naval operations of the Russo-Japanese War is based on Sir Julian Corbett, *Maritime Operations in the Russo-Japanese War, 1904–1905*, 2 vols. (Annapolis: Naval Institute Press, 1994).
2. Corbett, *Maritime Operations*, vol. 1, pp. 306–7.
3. V. P. Kostenko, *Na Orle v Tsusime*, cited in J. N. Westwood, *Witnesses of Tsushima* (Tokyo: Sophia Univ. Press, 1970), pp. 80–83.
4. Westwood, *Witnesses of Tsushima*, p. 117.
5. *Ibid.*, pp. 31–32.
6. R. M. Connaughton, *The War of the Rising Sun and the Tumbling Bear* (London: Routledge, 1988), p. 259.
7. Dennis and Peggy Warner, *The Tide at Sunrise* (New York: Charterhouse, 1974), p. 496.
8. Extracts from "Appointment, Education and Promotion of Japanese and Russian Naval Officers," *Marine-Rundschau*, August–September 1905, Office of Naval Intelligence, Register 79; January 23, 1906, Record Group 38, National Archives.
9. The discussion above is based primarily on David Evans's excellent study, "The Satsuma Faction and Professionalism in the Japanese Naval Officer Corps of the Meiji Period, 1868–1912," Stanford Univ. dissertation, 1978.
10. Evans, "Satsuma Faction," p. 75.
11. *Ibid.*
12. *Ibid.*, p. 79.
13. *Ibid.*, p. 105.
14. Office of Naval Intelligence, "Regulations Governing Education of Officers and Enlisted Men, Japanese Navy," May 24, 1907, Register 397, Record Group 38.
15. Office of Naval Intelligence, "Naval College at Etajima Japan," July 24, 1907, Register 569, Record Group 38.
16. Cecil Bullock, *Etajima: The Dartmouth of Japan* (London: Sampson Low Marston, 1942), p. 28.
17. *Ibid.*, pp. 31–32.
18. *Ibid.*, pp. 44–45.
19. *Ibid.*, p. 46.
20. Office of Naval Intelligence, "Recruiting and Training of Enlisted Men in Foreign Navies," ONI Register 1396 (1906), Record Group 38.
21. Comment by Commander Robert A. Theobald, 11 Feb 1927, encl. to USNA, Tokyo to ONI, Sept 9, 1927, ONI Register 18603, Record Group 38.

22. Hector C. Bywater, *Seapower in the Pacific: A Study of the American-Japanese Naval Problem* (Boston: Houghton Mifflin, 1921), pp. 189–91.
23. *Ibid.*
24. Office of Naval Intelligence, "Systems of Appointing and Educating Naval Cadets," May 9, 1903, Register 59, Record Group 38.
25. Westwood, *Witnesses of Tsushima*. p. 66.
26. *Ibid.*, p. 59.
27. *Ibid.*, p. 286.
28. *Ibid.*, p 22; Captain Seaton Schroeder, "Gleanings from the Sea of Japan," *Naval Institute Proceedings* 22, January 1906, pp. 53–54.
29. Admiralty Ordinance Department, "The Russian-Japanese War from the Point of View of Naval Gunnery," p. 13, copy in Ministry of Defense Library, London.
30. *Ibid.*
31. Westwood, *Witnesses of Tsushima*, p. 66.
32. W. C. Pakenham, May 6, 1905, in Admiralty Intelligence Department, "Reports from Naval Attachés," copy in Ministry of Defense Library, London.
33. Schroeder, "Gleanings from the Sea of Japan," p. 50.
34. Extracts in *The Fleet* from an article by Admiral A. T. Mahan in *Collier's Weekly*, June 1905, p. 71.
35. *Ibid.*
36. *Ibid.*
37. Westwood, *Witnesses of Tsushima*, p. 162.
38. "Reports from Naval Attachés," p. 359.
39. Westwood, *Witnesses of Tsushima*, p. 163.
40. David Evans and Mark S. Peattie, *Kaigun* (Annapolis: U.S. Naval Institute Press, 1997), p. 117–23. My explanation of Togo's actions is based on the above and on Corbett, *Maritime Operations*, vol. 2; pp. 244–46, and Westwood, *Witnesses of Tsushima*, pp. 177–78.
41. "Reports from Naval Attachés," p. 368.
42. Richard Hough, *The Fleet That Had to Die* (New York: Viking, 1958), p. 164.
43. "Reports from Naval Attachés," pp. 424–25.
44. Hough, *Fleet That Had to Die*, p. 168.
45. "Reports from Naval Attachés," p. 368.
46. *Ibid.*
47. Togo Kichitaro, *The Naval Battles of the Russo-Japanese War* (Tokyo: Gogakukyokwai, 1907), p. 51.
48. Evans and Peattie, *Japanese Navy*, p. 41.
49. R. D. White, "With the Baltic Fleet at Tsushima," *U.S. Naval Institute Proceedings* 22 (June 1906), p. 607.
50. Captain Vladimir Semeonov, *The Battle of Tsu-Shima*, trans. Captain A. B. Lindsay (New York: Dutton, 1913), pp. 60, 64–65.
51. White, "With the Baltic Fleet," p. 606.
52. Westwood, *Witnesses of Tsushima*, p. 184.
53. *Ibid.*, p. 187.
54. Semeonov, *Battle of Tsu-Shima*, pp. 70–71.
55. White, "With the Baltic Fleet," p. 607.
56. Westwood, *Witnesses of Tsushima*, pp. 296–97.
57. *Ibid.*, p. 233.
58. *Ibid.*, p 205.
59. Corbett, *Maritime Operations*, vol. 2, p. 333.

Chapter 2: "The Supreme Influence of the Human Factor"

1. For much fuller discussion of the innovations described above, see Arthur J. Marder, *The Anatomy of British Seapower* (New York: Alfred A. Knopf, 1940); Bernard Brodie, *Seapower in the Machine Age* (New York: Macmillan, 1940); Theodore Ropp, *The Development of a Modern Navy* (Annapolis: Naval Institute Press, 1978); and H.W. Wilson, *Ironclads in Action*, 2 vols. (London: Sampson Low Marston, 1896).

2. Evans and Peattie, *Japanese Navy*, p. 48.
3. "Mines and Torpedoes in the Late War," *Jane's Fighting Ships 1906* (London: Sampson Low Marston, 1906), p. 423.
4. See Peter Gay, *The Cultivation of Hatred: The Bourgeois Experience, Victoria to Freud* (New York: Norton, 1993), pp. 35–45, 514–37, and *passim*.
5. Quoted in Michael L. Hadley, *Count Not the Dead: The Popular Image of the German Submarine* (Annapolis: Naval Institute Press, 1995), p. 9.
6. Theodore Ropp, *The Development of a Modern Navy* (Annapolis: Naval Institute Press, 1978), pp. 181–202.
7. Marder, *Anatomy of British Seapower*, p. 162.
8. Hadley, *Count Not the Dead*, p. 13.
9. Paul Kennedy, *The Rise of Anglo-German Antagonism* (London: Allen & Unwin, 1979), pp. 87–102; Marder, *Anatomy of British Seapower*, p. 55.
10. Marder, *Anatomy of British Seapower*, p. 486.
11. Jon T. Sumida, *In Defense of Naval Supremacy: Finance, Technology and British Naval Policy, 1889–1914* (Boston: Unwin Hyman, 1989), pp. 23–24.
12. *Ibid.*, pp. 47–48.
13. Arthur J. Marder, *From the Dreadnought to Scapa Flow*, vol. 1, *The Road to War, 1904–1914* (London: Oxford University Press, 1961), p. 414.
14. Charles H. Fairbanks, "The Origins of the Dreadnought Revolution: A Historiographical Essay," *International History Review* 13 (May 1991), p. 249.
15. The most complete discussion of problems of long-range gunnery may be found in Sumida, *In Defense of Naval Supremacy*, pp. 71–158, 297–305; and his more recent "The Quest for Reach: The Development of Long-Range Gunnery in the Royal Navy."
16. Sumida, "Quest for Reach," p. 11.
17. Fairbanks, "Origins of the Dreadnought Revolution," p. 248.
18. *Ibid.*, pp. 256–59. See also Sumida, *Defense of Naval Supremacy*; Nicholas Lambert, "Admiral Sir John Fisher and the Concept of Flotilla Defense," *Journal of Military History*, October 1995.
19. Marder, *Road to War*, pp. 329–30.
20. Sumida, *In Defense of Naval Supremacy*, pp. 51–60; Fairbanks, "Origins of the Dreadnought Revolution," pp. 256–57, 263.
21. Marder, *Road to War*, p. 152.
22. "Men v. Material," *Fleet*, July 1905, p. 50.
23. Seaton Schroeder, "Gleanings from the Sea of Japan," *U.S. Naval Institute Proceedings* 22, January 1, 1906, p. 93.
24. F. T. Jane, *The Imperial Russian Navy*, (London: Cassell, 1904), p. 492.
25. White, "With the Baltic Fleet," p. 619.
26. Westwood, *Witnesses of Tsushima*, p. 187.
27. The sentence was later commuted to life imprisonment, and he was released after a few years.
28. P. K. Kemp, ed., *The Papers of Admiral Sir John Fisher*, vol. 2 (London: Naval Records Society, 1964), pp. 28–30.
29. Christopher McKee, *A Gentlemanly and Honorable Profession* (Annapolis: Naval Institute Press, 1987), p. 168.
30. Wilson, *Ironclads in Action*, vol 2, p. 106. The ratio could be much larger in one-on-one encounters.
31. Cited in Mary Conley, "Sentinels of Empire: Images of Naval Seamen in Popular Culture in Late Victorian and Edwardian Britain," paper presented at the New England Conference in British Studies, Fall 1998, p. 3.
32. *Ibid.*, pp. 173–74.
33. A. Trystan Edwards, *Three Rows of Tape: A Social Study of the Royal Navy* (London: Simpkin Marshall, 1940), p. 119.
34. Conley, "Sentinels of Empire," p. 4.
35. John Winton, *Hurrah for the Life of a Sailor* (London: Michael Joseph, 1977), p. 218.
36. David Marcombe, *The Victorian Sailor* (London: Shire, 1972), p. 7. The portrait was based on a painting of an actual sailor, Thomas Hintley Wood, who later shaved off his beard to avoid the unwelcome notoriety.
37. Conley, "Sentinels of Empire," p. 4.
38. Winton, *Hurrah*, p. 220.

39. Report of the Honorable Josephus Daniels, Secretary of the Navy, 64th Cong., 1st sess., March 30, 1916.
40. John Leyland, "The Reorganization of the Personnel," *Brassey's Naval Annual 1904*, p. 184.
41. *Ibid.*, pp. 181–82.
42. Norman E. Saul, *Sailors in Revolt: The Russian Baltic Fleet in 1917* (Lawrence: University Press of Kansas, 1976), p. 16.
43. Filson Young, *With the Battlecruisers* (London: Cassell, 1921), p. 65.
44. Chief Petty Officer Telegraphist William Halter interview, p. 26, Department of Sound Recordings, Imperial War Museum.
45. Leyland, "Reorganization of the Personnel," pp. 181–82.
46. J. L. Bashford, "The Imperial German Navy," *Brassey's Naval Annual 1905*, pp. 197–98.
47. Frederick S. Harrod, *Manning the New Navy* (Westport: Grunwood Press, 1978), pp. 188, 191–92.
48. Stanley Bonnet, *The Price of Admiralty: An Indictment of the Royal Navy, 1805–1966* (London: Robert Hale, 1968), p. 187.
49. N.A.M. Rodger, "British Naval Thought and Naval Policy: Strategic Thought in an Era of Technological Change," in Craig Symonds, ed., *New Aspects of Naval History: Papers Presented at the 4th Naval History Symposium* (Annapolis: Naval Institute Press, 1981), pp. 147–78.
50. Captain John Wells, *The Royal Navy: An Illustrated Social History, 1870–1982* (Gloustershire: Alan Sutton, 1994), p. 66.
51. Quoted in Marder, *Road to War*, p. 31. In addition to the memoirs and oral histories cited below, the account of the experiences of cadets and midshipmen is based on a collection of some two dozen oral histories with graduates of Osborne Royal Naval College in the Imperial War Museum, Office of Sound Recordings, and on my own correspondence with former cadets of the same era.
52. Fisher to Lionel Yexley, August 3, 1910, Fisher Papers, Churchill College, Cambridge.
53. William Butler interview, p. 12, Oral History Collections of the Royal Naval Museum.
54. D. Tighe with Commander Sheppard interview, 19/3/92, p. 10, Oral History Collections of the Royal Naval Museum.
55. Captain Robert Hale interview, p. 3, Department of Sound Recordings, Osborne Royal Naval College Series, 9895/2, Imperial War Museum.
56. Sheppard interview, p. 10.
57. "Report of the Committee Appointed to Enquire into the Education and Training of Cadets, Midshipmen and Junior Officers of His Majesty's Fleet, 1912," p. 31, copy in Ministry of Defence Library.
58. "The Royal Marines and the New Scheme of Naval Training," Kemp, ed. *Fisher Papers*, p. 248.
59. Jose Harris, *Private Lives, Public Spirit: Britain, 1870–1914* (New York: Penguin, 1993), p. 68.
60. Admiral Sir Charles Madden interview, p. 2, Osborne Royal Naval College Series, 9869/111.
61. Young, *With the Battlecruisers*, p. 256.
62. Commander H. L. Jenkins interview, p. 1, Osborne Royal Naval College Series, 9896/2.
63. C. Whayman with Commander A.F.C. Layard interview, 27/2/92, Oral History Collections of the Royal Naval Museum.
64. "Report of the Committee . . . Training of Cadets," p. 30.
65. *Ibid.*
66. Stephen W. Roskill, "A Sailor's Ditty Bag," p. 6, unpublished memoirs, Roskill Papers, Churchill College, Cambridge.
67. Captain Robert Hale interview, p. 4.
68. Commander W. O. Bradbury interview, p. 4, Osborne Royal Naval College Series, 9898/2/2.
69. Roskill, "A Sailor's Ditty Bag," p. 6.
70. Quoted in David Howarth, *The Dreadnoughts* (Alexandria, Va.: Time-Life, 1979), p. 30.
71. *Ibid.* Vice Admiral Sir Louis Le Bailly, *The Man Around the Engine: Life Below the Waterline* (Emsworth, Hampshire: Kenneth Mason, 1990), p. 15.
72. J. J. Bryan interview, p. 5, Osborne Royal Naval College Series, 9898/12.
73. Commander W. O. Bradbury interview, p. 13.
74. Midshipman H. W. Fisher (HMS *Indomitable*), unpublished memoirs, 1010 File, Imperial War Museum.
75. Roskill, "A Sailor's Ditty Bag," p. 8.
76. K.G.B. DeWar, *The Navy from Within* (London: Victor Gollancz, 1939), p. 43.
77. Roskill, "A Sailor's Ditty Bag" p. 8.

78. Rodger, "British Naval Thought and Naval Policy," p. 148.
79. *Ibid.*, p. 149.
80. "Dartmouth 1931–35," *Naval Review* 14 (July 1965), p. 91.
81. *Ibid.*
82. See Mark Girouard, *The Return to Camelot* (New Haven, Conn.: Yale University Press, 1981).
83. Andrew Gordon, *The Rules of the Game: Jutland and British Naval Command* (Annapolis: Naval Institute Press, 1996), p. 18.
84. Vice Admiral Sir Louis Le Bailly letter, December 3, 1998. Sir Louis added, "My experience of what happens/happened at Annapolis or VMI or Charleston or West Point is that the RN methods were preferable as 'hazing' can produce lifelong enmities which hard tough discipline, where all suffer, does not."
85. Le Bailly, *Man Around the Engine*, p. 18. Whether this reply expressed pride or irony is still a debated subject.
86. *Ibid.*, p. 21.
87. Rear Admiral G.W.G. Simpson, *Periscope View: A Professional Autobiography* (London: Macmillan, 1972), p. 25.
88. *Ibid.*, p. 26.
89. *Ibid.*
90. Stephen King-Hall, *My Naval Life, 1906–1929* (London: Faber & Faber, 1952), p. 25. "Gunroom evolutions" continued, at least in some ships, into the 1930s. (See letter, Mdm. Brian Jones to his parents, April 30, 1931, in Dudley Pound Papers, Churchill College, Cambridge.) A novel by former naval officer Charles Morgan that described some of the routine instances of gunroom hazing caused a minor sensation among civilian readers but was greeted with scorn by most Royal Navy officers. A representative comment was that what occurred in the gunroom was a "very reasonable, good and humane scheme of character building." Another officer declared that "Morgan's trouble was he did not like games [sports]. . . . It is hard to make a naval officer of a boy whose chief idea was to get his work done as quickly as he could so that he could get away in a corner and read his favorite author." *Naval Review,* Correspondence, vol. 9, Feb. 21, p. 165.
91. Young, *With the Battlecruisers*, pp. 255–56.
92. Lionel Yexley, *The Inner Life of the Navy* (London: Pitman, 1908), p. 6.
93. "Evidence to Committee of Enquiry into the Loss of the *Atalanta* by Second Naval Lord," in John B. Hattendorf et al., *British Naval Documents, 1204–1960* (London: Scolar Press, 1993), p. 731.
94. Henry Baynharn, *Men from the Dreadnoughts* (London: Hutchinson, 1976), p. 74.
95. Chief Telegraphist William Halter interview, p. 17, Department of Sound Recordings, Imperial War Museum.
96. Sir Richard Vesey Hamilton, "The New Admiralty Education Scheme," *Brassey's Naval Annual 1903*, p. 216.
97. Quoted in Marder, *Road to War*, p. 30.
98. Lord Brassey, "Prize Firings," *Brassey's Naval Annual 1904*, p. 28.
99. Gordon, *Rules of the Game*, p. 168.
100. Yexley, *Inner Life of the Navy*, p. 173.
101. "The Training of Officers," *Naval Review* 8 (1917), p. 42.
102. On Pollen and the Admiralty see the fine discussion by John Sumida, *In Defense of Naval Supremacy* (London: Unwin Hyman, 1989). The *Iowas*, like other battleships completed in World War II, had the very great additional advantage of radar.

Chapter 3: "The Cat's Whiskers"

1. Lord Brassey, "Naval Reserves," *Brassey's Naval Annual, 1902*, p. 66.
2. Sumida, *In Defense of Naval Supremacy*, p. 9.
3. Jon T. Sumida, "British Naval Administration and Policy in the Age of Fisher," *Journal of Military History* 54, (January 1990), p. 21.
4. *Ibid.*, pp. 11–12.
5. Lambert, *Revolution*. p. 113.
6. These themes are developed in depth in the works by Lambert and Sumida cited above.

7. Recruiting Committee, "Preliminary Report: Recruiting for the Royal Navy," 5 January 1898, pp. 2, 5, copy in Ministry of Defence Library.
8. Yexley, *Inner Life of the Navy*, p. 3.
9. Baynham, *Men from the Dreadnoughts*, p. 59.
10. Max Arthur, *The True Glory: The Royal Navy, 1914–1939* (London: Hodder & Stoughton, 1996), p. 35.
11. Yexley, *Inner Life of the Navy*, p. 32.
12. Quoted in Samuel Hynes, *The Edwardian Turn of Mind* (Princeton, N.J.: Princeton University Press, 1968), p. 24.
13. Alexander Grant, "Through the Hawse Pipe," unpublished memoirs, p. 41, Imperial War Museum, 66/28311.
14. Victor Hayward, *HMS "Tiger" at Bay: A Sailor's Memoire* (London: Kimber, 1977), p. 14.
15. Leading Seaman Arthur W. Ford interview, p. 45, Department of Sound Recordings, Imperial War Museum.
16. Chief Yeoman of Signals William F. Sweet interview, p. 45, Department of Sound Recordings, Imperial War Museum.
17. Paul Thompson, *The Edwardians: The Remaking of British Society* (Chicago: Academy Chicago, 1985), pp. 29, 31, 39, and *passim*.
18. Baynham, *Men from the Dreadnoughts*, p. 61.
19. *Ibid.*
20. Kenneth Poolman, *The British Sailor* (London: Arms & Armour, 1982), p. 9. Of the thirty-six former sailors who contributed information to Baynham's book, six explicitly mentioned lack of work as their motivation for joining.
21. Lieutenant William George Bruty MBE interview, p. 14, Department of Sound Recordings, Imperial War Museum.
22. "Preliminary Report: Recruting," p. 9.
23. John Chessman, "Under, Over and Through," unpublished memoir, ca. 1972, p. 34, Imperial War Museum, DS/MISC/39.
24. In addition to the unpublished memoirs and diaries cited below, this account of life in the Edwardian navy is based on twenty-two oral histories in the "Lower Deck" series of interviews in the Department of Sound Recordings, Imperial War Museum, and on the accounts presented in Baynham, *Men from the Dreadnoughts*.
25. William Sweet interview, p. 21.
26. Baynham, *Men from the Dreadnoughts*, p. 69.
27. "Reminiscences of Reverend T.W.L. Casperez, Chaplain, RN," Imperial War Museum.
28. Chief Petty Officer Telegraphist William Halter interview, p. 14, Department of Sound Recordings, Imperial War Museum.
29. G. C. Connell, *Jack's War* (London: Kimber, 1985), p. 20.
30. *Ibid.*, p. 22.
31. Chessman, "Under, Over and Through," p. 41.
32. I am grateful to Major General Julian Thompson, author of a forthcoming history of the Royal Marines, for providing the information above.
33. See James Leary interview, p. 3, and Albert Masters interview, p. 56, Department of Sound Recordings, Imperial War Museum.
34. Sidney Knock, *Clear Lower Deck* (London: Philip Alan, 1932), p. 47.
35. James Leary interview, p. 3.
36. John Marsden, "An Account of Wartime Service in the Royal Navy of John Marsden," unpublished memoirs, p. 1, Royal Naval Museum.
37. Alan Erara, *The Invergordon Mutiny* (London: Routledge, 1981), p. 18.
38. Commander G. von Schoultz, *With the British Battle Fleet: War Recollections of a Russian Naval Officer*, trans. Arthur Chambers (London: Hutchinsen, 1925), p. 22.
39. Chessman, "Over, Under and Through," p. 35.
40. Klinker Knocker, *Aye, Aye Sir!: The Autobiography of a Stoker* (London: Richard Cowan, 1938), p. 89.
41. Chief Carpenter G. M. Clarkson interview, p. 96, Department of Sound Recordings, Imperial War Museum.
42. William Sweet interview, pp. 77–78.
43. Hayward, *HMS "Tiger" at Bay*, pp. 49–50.
44. Carew, *Lower Deck*, p. 18.

45. Anonymous, *The Seaman of the Royal Navy: Their Advantages and Disadvantages as Viewed from the Lower Deck* (London, 1877), p. 35.
46. Eugene L. Rasor, *Reform in the Royal Navy* (Hamdon: Archer Books, 1976), p. 35.
47. Malcolm Brown and Patricia Meehan, *Scapa Flow: The Reminscences of Men and Women Who Served in Scapa Flow in Two World Wars* (London: Penguin Press, 1968), pp. 71, 73.
48. *Ibid.*, p. 72.
49. *Ibid.*, p. 74.
50. Brian de Courcy Ireland in Arthur, *The True Glory*, p. 62.
51. Anonymous letter to Arnold White, no date [1902], Arnold White Papers, National Maritime Museum.
52. *Ibid.* Admiral Le Bailly recalls spending most of his disposable income as a midshipman on Brasso to polish the brass funnel on his picket boat. *Man Around the Engine*, p. 21.
53. Quoted in Wells, *Royal Navy*, p. 47.
54. Baynham, *Men from the Dreadnoughts*, p. 169.
55. Letter, Vice Admiral Sir Louis Le Bailly to author, December 3, 1999.
56. Chief Carpenter G. M. Clarkson interview, pp. 102–3.
57. *Ibid.*, pp. 101–2.
58. Carew, *Road to Invergordon*, p. 39.
59. Arnold White, untitled speech to the Navy League, no date, Arnold White Papers, National Maritime Museum, Greenwich.
60. Carew, *Road to Invergordon*, p. 45.
61. Chief Carpenter G. M. Clarkson interview, p. 275.
62. Baynham, *Men from the Dreadnoughts*, pp. 88–89.
63. Carew, *Road to Invergordon*, p. 45.
64. Lieutenant William Parsons interview, p. 53, Department of Sound Recordings, Imperial War Museum.
65. Chessman, "Over, Under and Through," p. 107.
66. Clinker Knocker, *Aye, Aye Sir*, p. 202.
67. *Ibid.*
68. Carew, *Road to Invergordon*, pp. 63–64.
69. *Ibid.*
70. *Ibid.*, p. 63.
71. *Ibid.*, pp. 68–69. Among the thirty-six sailors in Baynham's *Men from the Dreadnoughts* none could recall any acquaintance with sailors' organizations or with Lionel Yexley's lower deck magazine, *The Fleet*. Baynham, p. 70.
72. *Ibid.*, p. 68.
73. *Ibid.*, p. 23.
74. Lieutenant J. K. McLeod to Lieutenant General Sir J. C. McLeod, February 12, 1913, in Albert Smith, "A Family at War, Part One," *Poppy and the Owl* 16 (June 1995), p. 5.
75. Arnold White, speech to Navy League of Newcastle.
76. Filson Young, *With the Battlecruisers* (London: Cassell, 1921), p. 19.
77. Edwards, *Three Rows of Tape*, p. 54.
78. Able Seaman Richard Rose interview, pp. 77–78, Department of Sound Recordings, Imperial War Museum.
79. Yexley, *Inner Life of the Navy*, p. 40.
80. Lieutenant William George Bruty interview, pp. 56–57.
81. Sidney Knock, *Clear Lower Deck* (London: Philip Allen, 1932), p. 39.
82. Bruty interview, pp. 57–58.
83. Knock, *Clear Lower Deck*, p. 39.
84. Quoted in Marder, *Road to War*, p. 406.
85. King-Hall, *My Naval Life*, pp. 93, 97–98.
86. This discussion is derived from the analysis in Modris Eckstein, *Rites of Spring: The Great War and the Birth of the Modern Age* (New York: Anchor Books, 1989), pp. 66–73.
87. Reinhard Scheer, *Germany's High Seas Fleet in the World War* (London: Cassell, 1919), pp. 66–73.
88. Theodore Pluvier, *The Kaiser's Coolies* (London: Cassell, 1924), p. 103.
89. Holger Herwig, *The German Naval Officer Corps: A Social and Political History, 1890–1918* (Oxford: Clarendon Press, 1973), pp. 30–33.
90. *Ibid.*, p 63.

91. *Ibid.*, p. 115.
92. Daniel Horn, *The German Naval Mutinies of World War I* (New Brunswick: Rutgers University Press, 1969), p. 11.
93. Daniel Horn, ed. and trans., *War, Mutiny and Revolution in the German Navy: The World War I Diary of Seaman Richard Stumpf* (New Brunswick: Rutgers University Press, 1970, p. 44).
94. Scheer, *Germany's High Seas Fleet*, p. 14.
95. Holweg, *German Naval Officer Corps*, p. 44.

Chapter 4: "The Biggest Sea Battle That Has Ever Been"

1. H. W. Fawcett and G.W.W. Hooper, *The Fighting at Jutland: The Personal Experiences of Sixty Officers and Men of the British Fleet* (Glasgow: MacLure, MacDonald, 1920), p. 9.
2. *Ibid.*, p. 8.
3. *Ibid.*, p. 93.
4. Horn, *War, Mutiny and Revolution*, p. 198.
5. Chief Steward Ernest G. Fox interview, p. 46, Department of Sound Recordings, Imperial War Museum.
6. Young, *With the Battlecruisers*, p. 49.
7. Chief Yeoman of Signals George Ernest Haigh interview, p. 88, Department of Sound Recordings, Imperial War Museum.
8. Wells, *Royal Navy*, p. 95.
9. Scheer, *Germany's High Seas Fleet*, p. 11.
10. Horn, *War, Mutiny and Revolution*, p. 27.
11. Smith, "Family at War," p. 6.
12. Paul G. Halpern, *A Naval History of World War I* (Annapolis: Naval Institute Press, 1994), p. 23.
13. Marder, *Road to War*, p. 420.
14. Hough, *Great War at Sea*, p. 196.
15. Stephen King-Hall, *A Naval Lieutenant, 1914–1918* (London: Methuen, 1919), pp. 18–19.
16. Rear Admiral W. S. Chalmers, *The Life and Letters of David Beatty, Admiral of the Fleet* (London: Hodder & Stoughton, 1951), p. 161.
17. Clinker Knocker, *Aye, Aye Sir*, pp. 168–69.
18. Horn, *War, Mutiny and Revolution*, p. 27.
19. Chief Petty Officer [later Captain] Karl Melms letter, no date [1974], 1010 File, Imperial War Museum.
20. Horn, *War, Mutiny and Revolution*, p. 31.
21. Alfred von Tirpitz, *My Memoirs* (New York: Dodd, Mead, 1919), vol. 1, pp. 95–96.
22. Horn, *War, Mutiny and Revolution*, pp. 82–83.
23. Tobias Philbin, *Admiral von Hipper: The Inconvenient Hero* (Amsterdam: B.R. Toruner, 1980), p. 12.
24. Horn, *War, Mutiny and Revolution* p. 125.
25. Philbin, *Admiral von Hipper*, pp. 65–67.
26. Halpern, *Naval History of World War I*, pp. 38–39.
27. The above account is based primarily on James Goldrick, *The King's Ships Were at Sea: The War in the North Sea, August 1914–February 1915* (Annapolis: Naval Institute Press, 1984).
28. Quoted in *ibid.*, p. 197.
29. *Ibid.*, pp. 204–8.
30. Stephen Roskill, *Earl Beatty: The Last Naval Hero: An Intimate Biography* (New York: Atheneum, 1981), p. 116.
31. Grant, "Through the Hawsepipe," p. 81.
32. Wilfred Ernest Davey interview, p. 44, Department of Sound Recordings, Imperial War Museum.
33. A.F.C. Layard interview, p. 16.
34. Lieutenant Heinrich Bassinge [SMS *Elbing*], 1010 file, Imperial War Museum.
35. King-Hall, *Naval Lieutenant*, p. 128.
36. Machinist Otto Frost [Torpedo Boat V-1], 1010 file, Imperial War Museum.

37. Commander Humphrey Walwyn, "Jutland Impressions," Admiral E. M. Philpott Papers, Imperial War Museum.
38. Petty Officer William Read [HMS *New Zealand*], 1010 file.
39. Von Hasse, *Kiel and Jutland*, p. 151.
40. "Narrative of a Midshipman Stationed in the Foretop of Neptune," in Fawcett and Hooper, *Fighting at Jutland*, p. 193.
41. The discussion below is based primarily on Commander Herbert S. Howard, "Details of Naval Design from Jutland," in *Transactions of the Society of Naval Architects and Marine Engineers*, 30 (1922), p. 67.
42. Walwyn, "Jutland Impressions."
43. "Reminiscences of Q. Turrett, HMS *Lion*," in Bryan Ranft, ed., *The Beatty Papers* (London: Navy Records Society, 1993), p. 355.
44. "Point of View of a Medical Officer," in Fawcett and Hooper, *Fighting at Jutland*, p. 421.
45. Clinker Knocker, *Aye, Aye Sir*, p. 150.
46. Horn, *War, Mutiny and Revolution*, p. 199.
47. John Sumida, "Capital Ship Gunnery at the Battle of Jutland," p. 1, unpublished paper presented to the 1988 Annual Meeting of the American Military Institute.
48. *Ibid.*, pp. 6–7.
49. Arthur J. Marder, *Jutland*, (London: Oxford, 1967), p. 196.
50. Admiral of the Fleet Lord Chatfield, *The Navy and Defence* (London: Heinemann, 1942), p. 151.
51. "Narrative of the Navigating Officer, HMS *New Zealand*," in Fawcett and Hooper, *Fighting at Jutland*, p. 29.
52. Stuart Legg, ed., *Jutland: An Eyewitness Account of the Great Battle* (New York: John Day, 1967), p. 48.
53. Anonymous letter by a survivor of HMS *Queen Mary*, Liddle Collection, The Library, University of Leeds.
54. Von Hase, *Kiel and Jutland*, p. 113.
55. "Letter from HMS *Moorson*," in Fawcett and Hooper, *Fighting at Jutland*, pp. 51–52.
56. Liddle, *Sailor's War*, p. 110.
57. "Narrative of HMS *Nicator*," in Fawcett and Hooper, *Fighting at Jutland*, p. 55.
58. Marder, *Jutland*, p. 72.
59. N.J.M. Campbell, *Jutland: An Analysis of the Fighting* (Annapolis: Naval Institute Press, 1986), pp. 134–35.
60. *Ibid.*, p. 113.
61. Engineer Commander Otto Looks, "The Engine Room Staff in the Battle of the Skaggerarck," trans. by Engineer Lieutenant Commander D. Hastie Smith, *Naval Review* 10 (1922), p. 315.
62. *Ibid.*, pp. 120–21; Marder, *Jutland*, p. 39.
63. Admiral Sir Frederick Dreyer, *The Sea Heritage* (London: Museum Press, 1955), pp. 146–47.
64. Admiral of the Fleet Earl Mountbatten, "The Battle of Jutland" [Summary of Madden's remarks at the Naval Tactical School, February 1934], *Mariner's Mirror* 66 (May 1980), p. 104.
65. *Ibid.*
66. Fawcett and Hooper, *Fighting at Jutland*, p. 151.
67. Walwyn, "Jutland Impressions."
68. Liddle, *Sailor's War*, p. 108.
69. Marder, *Jutland*, pp. 121–22.
70. Horn, *War, Mutiny and Revolution*, p. 209.
71. Langhorn Gibson and J.E.T. Harper, *The Riddle of Jutland* (London: Cassell, 1934), pp. 219–20.
72. King-Hall, *A Naval Lieutenant, 1914–1918* (London: Methuen, 1919), pp. 149–151.
73. Marder, *Jutland*, p. 178.
74. *Ibid.*
75. *Ibid.*, p. 180.
76. Telegraphist A. J. Bristoe letter, 1010 File, Imperial War Museum.
77. Engine Room Artificer Gordon Davis letter, 1010 File, Imperial War Museum.
78. Bristoe letter.
79. *Ibid.*
80. Ordinary Telegraphist Frederick J. Arnold, 1010 file, Imperial War Museum. See also Surgeon Probationer R. Smythe, same file.

81. K. L. Philips letter, June 8, 1916, 1010 file, Imperial War Museum.
82. Signalman Franz Motzler, 1010 file, Imperial War Museum.
83. Chief Petty Officer Karl Melms, 1010 file, Imperial War Museum.

Chapter 5: "Something Not Quite Right Within"

1. Quoted in Halpern, *Naval History of World War I*, p. 328.
2. Based on figures in Marder, *Jutland*, pp. 250–51 and *passim*; and Campbell, *Jutland*, pp. 347–51.
3. Campbell, *Jutland*, p. 355.
4. Correli Barnett, *The Swordbearers: Studies in Supreme Command* (New York: William Morrow, 1964), p. 101.
5. Campbell's figures are: Hipper, 3.89 percent; Fifth Battle Squadron, 1.43 percent; Grand Fleet battleships, 3.70 percent; German battleships, 2.37 percent.
6. Campbell, *Jutland* p. 400–01.
7. See Chief Yeoman of Signals A. J. Bristoe, 1010 file, Imperial War Museum.
8. Gordon, *Rules of the Game*, pp. 487–88.
9. *Ibid.*, p. 664.
10. Captain Alexander Grant, RN, "Through the Hawse Pipe," p. 109, unpublished autobiography, Imperial War Museum.
11. *Ibid.*
12. "Jutland," *Naval Review* 46 (April 1958), p. 240.
13. Engine Room Artificer C. B. Clarkson, "Impressions of Jutland from Inside HMS *Malaya*," unpublished memoir, Liddle Collection.
14. *Ibid.*
15. Admiral Viscount Jellicoe, *The Grand Fleet: Its Creation, Development and Work* (London: Cassell, 1919), pp. 62–65.
16. A.F.C. Layard in Arthur, *True Glory*, p. 76; Gordon, *Rules of the Game*, pp. 46–47.
17. Hough, *Great War at Sea*, p. 213.
18. Marder, *Jutland*, p. 170.
19. "Reminiscences of Sub-Lieutenant H. O. Owens, HMS *Moorson*," Liddle Collection.
20. Bristoe, 1010 file, Imperial War Museum.
21. Engine Room Artificer Arthur C. F. Crown diary, Imperial War Museum.
22. Torpedoman William A. Parson interview, p. 76. Department of Sound Recordings, Imperial War Museum.
23. "Narrative of an Officer in the Engine Room of HMS *Tiger*," in Fawcett and Hooper, *Fighting at Jutland*, p. 84.
24. Looks, "The Engine Room Staff in the Battle of Skaggerack," p. 309.
25. Engine Room Artificer Gordon Davis letter, 1010 file, Imperial War Museum.
26. Midshipman [later Rear Admiral] Royer M. Dick, "My Second Naval Battle," unpublished memoir, Liddle Collection.
27. Signalman John E. Atrill, HMS *Marlborough*, Imperial War Museum.
28. Walwyn, "Jutland Impressions."
29. Leading Stoker Samuel H. A. Roberts, 1010 file, Imperial War Museum.
30. Signalman Reuben Poole, 1010 file, Imperial War Museum.
31. Electrical Artificer Frank T. Hall, 1010 file, Imperial War Museum.
32. Boy Telegraphist Arthur R. Lewis, 1010 file, Imperial War Museum.
33. Clarkson, "Impressions of Jutland," Liddle Collection.
34. Captain G. P. Biggs-Withers letter to Mrs. Biggs-Withers, no date, Liddle Collection.
35. See, for example, "Narrative of an Officer in 'A' Turret, HMS *Conqueror*" in Fawcett and Hooper, *Fighting at Jutland*, p. 197.
36. "Propaganda on Board a Ship in Action," *Naval Review* 7 (1919), p. 226. See also Chaplain Thomas F. Bradley diary, 1010 file, Imperial War Museum.
37. Telegraphist Frederick J. Arnold, HMS *Malaya*, 1010 file, Imperial War Museum.
38. Bradley diary.
39. Franz Motzler, 1010 file, Imperial War Museum.
40. Commander W. M. Phipps-Hornby, 1010 file, Imperial War Museum.
41. Bradley diary.

42. Surgeon Lieutenant C. E. Leake, "Account of the Battle of Jutland," 31 May 1917, 1010 file, Imperial War Museum.
43. Anonymous account of the sinking of HMS *Queen Mary*, Liddle Collection.
44. Signalman J. J. Newman, "My Experience of the Sea Battle of May 31, 1916," unpublished manuscript, Liddle Collection.
45. R. M. Dick, "My Second Naval Battle."
46. Theodore Pluvier, *The Kaiser's Coolies*, trans. William F. Clarke (London, 1931), p. 132.
47. Shipwright Charles H. Petty, 1010 file, Imperial War Museum.
48. Young, *With the Battlecruisers*, p. 213.
49. Signalman John E. Atrill diary, 13 July 1916, 1010 File, Imperial War Museum.
50. Arthur, *True Glory*, p. 80.
51. Rear Admiral Frank Llewellyn Houghton, "A Sailor's Life for Me," unpublished memoir, p. 18, copy in Directorate of History, National Defense Headquarters, Ottawa.
52. Stephen King-Hall, *My Naval Life*, p. 106.
53. *Ibid.*
54. Brown and Meahan, *Scapa Flow*, p. 64.
55. Grant, "Through the Hawse Pipe," p. 111.
56. A. J. Bristoe, 1010 File, Imperial War Museum.
57. Brown and Meahan, *Scapa Flow*, p. 64.
58. Schoultz, *With the British Battlefleet*, p. 32.
59. Brown and Meahan, *Scapa Flow*, p. 115.
60. Simpson, *Periscope View*, p. 23.

Chapter 6: "The Most Formidable Thing"

1. Quoted in Arthur Marder, *1917: Year of Crisis* (London: Oxford, 1969), p. 40.
2. Halpern, *Naval History of World War I*, p. 328.
3. Scheer, *Germany's High Seas Fleet*, pp. 168–69.
4. Nicholas A. Lambert, "British Naval Policy, 1913–1914: Financial Limitation and Strategic Revolution," *Journal of Modern History* 67 (September 1996), p. 607.
5. "Some Early Submariners, Part III," *Naval Review* 51 (January 1963), p. 192.
6. Lambert, "British Naval Policy," pp. 609–15.
7. *Ibid.*, pp. 619–21.
8. *Ibid.*, p. 621.
9. Marder, *Road to War*, p. 364.
10 R. H. Gibson and Maurice Prendergast, *The Germans Submarine War, 1914–1918* (London: Constable, 1931), pp. 333–34.
11. Wesley Frost, *German Submarine Warfare: A Study of Its Methods and Spirit* (New York: D. Appleton, 1918), pp. 90–91.
12. Halpern, *Naval History of World War I*, p. 341; Gibson and Prendergast, *German Submarine War*, pp. 140–41.
13. Gibson and Prendergast, *German Submarines War*, p. 146.
14. Robert M. Grant, *U-Boat Intelligence, 1914–1918* (Hamden, Conn.: Archer, 1969), pp. 11–12 and *passim*.
15. Marder, *Year of Crisis*, pp. 75–76.
16. *Ibid.*, pp. 71–72.
17. *Ibid.*, pp. 112–13.
18. Elting Morison, *Admiral Sims and the Modern American Navy* (Boston: Houghton-Mifflin, 1942), p. 342.
19. Cited in John Terraine, *The U-Boat Wars, 1914–1918* (New York: Putnam, 1989), pp. 52–53.
20. Donald Macintyre, *The Battle of the Atlantic* (London: Batsford, 1961), p. 13.
21. Winston S. Churchill, *The World Crisis*, vol. 2 (New York: Scribner's, 1923), p. 1234.
22. "Our Submarines," *Berlin Lokalanzeiger*, May 7, 1917, Office of Naval Intelligence Translation, Office of Naval Intelligence Register, 6–17–23, E-6–A, Record Group 38, National Archives.
23. Michael L. Hadley, *Count Not the Dead* (Annapolis: Naval Institute Press, 1995), p. 41.
24. "Our Submarines," *op. cit.*

25. U.S. Naval Attaché, London, "German Submarine School," March 9, 1917, "Notes on Training of Crews of Submarines," October 26, 1916, both in Register 6-17-23, ONI Registers, Record Group 38, National Archives.
26. Rear Admiral William S. Chalmers, *Max Horton and the Western Approaches* (London: Hodder & Stoughton, 1954), pp. 5–6.
27. King-Hall, *Naval Lieutenant*, p. 209.
28. Karl Neureuther and Claus Bergen, *U-Boat Stories: Narratives of German U-Boat Sailors*, trans. Eric Sutton (London: Constable, 1931), p. 41.
29. Pluvier, *Kaiser's Coolies*, pp. 228–29.
30. Chief Petty Officer Telegraphist William Halter interview, p. 94, Department of Sound Recordings, Imperial War Museum.
31. Hadley, *Count Not the Dead*, p. 41.
32. *Ibid.*
33. Frost, *German Submarine Warfare*, p. 48.
34. Neureuther and Bergen, *U-Boat Stories*, p. 55.
35. U.S. Naval Attaché, February 18, 1918, Sub: Enrolling of submarine crews, ONI Register, No. 670 P, Record Group 38, National Archives.
36. Gibson and Prendergast, *German Submarine War*, p. 182.
37. Neureuther and Bergen, *U-Boat Stories*, p. 16.
38. Hadley, *Count Not the Dead*, p. 63.
39. Peter Padfield, *Dönitz: The Last Führer* (New York: Harper, 1984), p. 67.
40. Len Wincott, *Invergordon Mutineer* (London: Weidenfeld & Nicholson, 1953), pp. 31–32.
41. Lowell Thomas, *Raiders of the Deep* (Annapolis: Naval Institute Press, 1994), p. 271.
42. Hadley, *Count Not the Dead*, p. 27.
43. Herwig, *German Naval Officer Corps*, p. 191.
44. *Ibid.*
45. Wincott, *Invergordon Mutineer*, p. 32.
46. Marder, *Year of Crisis*, p. 264.
47. Quoted in Hadley, *Count Not the Dead*.
48. Frost, *German Submarine Warfare*.
49. *Ibid.*, pp. xi–xii.
50. Neureuther and Bergen, *U-Boat Stories*, p. 49.
51. Gibson and Prendergast, *German Submarine War*, p. 379.
52. Hadley, *Count Not the Dead*, p. 37.
53. Neureuther and Bergen, *U-Boat Stories*, p. 205.
54. Arthur Marder, *Victory and Aftermath, January 1918–June 1919* (London: Oxford Univ. Press, 1970), p. 169.
55. Herwig, *German Naval Officer Corps*, p. 247.
56. Halpern, *Naval History of World War I*, p. 445; Daniel Horn, *The German Naval Mutinies of World War I* (New Brunswick: Rutgers Univ. Press, 1969), pp. 203–6.
57. Herwig, *German Naval Officer Corps*, p. 247.
58. Horn, *War, Mutiny and Revolution*, p. 283.
59. *Ibid.*, p. 37.
60. Quoted in Marder, *Victory and Aftermath*, p. 175.
61. Herwig, *German Naval Officer Corps*, pp. 252–53.
62. Horn, *War, Mutiny and Revolution*, p. 283.
63. Horn, *German Naval Mutinies*, p. 42.
64. *Ibid.*
65. *Ibid.*, pp. 164–65.
66. Erich Eyck, *A History of the Weimar Republic*, vol. 1 (Cambridge: History Univ. Press, 1962), pp. 41–42.
67. Horn, *War, Mutiny and Revolution*, p. 306.
68. Quoted in Marder, *Victory and Aftermath*, p. 334.
69. Chatfield, *Navy and Defense*, p. 150.
70. Marder, *Victory and Aftermath*, p. 332.
71. Admiral Sir Reginald Bacon, *The Concise Story of the Dover Patrol* (London: Hutchinson, 1932), p. 298.
72. Quoted in Marder, *Victory and Aftermath*, p. 334.

73. Quoted in Douglas Bottin, *The U-Boats* (Alexandria, Va.: Time-Life, 1979), p. 75.
74. Horn, *War, Mutiny and Revolution*, p. 419.
75. Marder, *Victory and Aftermath*, p. 193.

Chapter 7: "Look Upward to the Skies"

1. H. A. Jones, *The War in the Air*, vol. 6 (Oxford 1937), pp. 365–67.
2. Cedric Outhwaite, "The Sea and the Air," *Blackwood's Magazine*, November 1927, p. 663.
3. *Ibid.*, p. 662.
4. Henry Newbolt, *Naval Operations*, vol. 5 (London: Longmans, 1931), pp. 345–46; Jones, *War in the Air*, p. 373.
5. Newbolt, *Naval Operations*, vol. 5, p. 347.
6. Outhwaite, "Sea and the Air," p. 665.
7. Jones, *War in the Air*, p. 373.
8. Marder, *1917: Year of Crisis*, p. 20.
9. *Ibid.*, pp. 236–38.
10. Halpern, *Naval History of World War I*, pp. 441–42.
11. Marder, *1917: Year of Crisis*, p. 18.
12. Jones, *War in the Air*, p. 375.
13. Halpern, *Naval History of World War I*, p. 444.
14. Stephen Roskill, *Naval Policy Between the Wars*, vol. 1, *The Period of Anglo-American Antagonism, 1919–1929* (New York: Walker, 1969), pp. 236–37.
15. Thomas C. Hohn and Mark D. Mandeles, "Interwar Innovation in Three Navies: U.S. Navy, Royal Navy and Imperial Japanese Navy," *Naval War College Review* 40 (Spring 1987), p. 65.
16. Norman Friedman, *Carrier Airpower* (New York: Rutledge Press, 1981), pp. 164–71 and *passim*.
17. Roskill, *Naval Policy*, vol. 1, p. 241.
18. Adrian Holloway, *From Dartmouth to War* (London: Buckland Publications, 1996), p. 61.
19. Roskill, "A Sailor's Ditty Bag," chap. 4, p. 1.
20. Geoffrey Till, *Air Power and the Royal Navy, 1914–1945* (London: Jane's, 1979), p. 45.
21. A pioneering and still useful account of the Washington Conference is Harold and Margaret Sprout, *Toward a New Order of Seapower* (Princeton, N.J.: Princeton University Press, 1940). See also Roskill, *Naval Policy Between the Wars*, vol. 1; Roger Dingman, *Power in the Pacific: The Origins of Naval Arms Limitation* (Chicago: University of Chicago Press, 1976); and the two indispensable articles by Asada Sadao, "The Japanese Navy and the United States," in Dorothy Borg et al., *Pearl Harbor as History: Japanese-American Relations* (New York: Columbia University Press, 1973); and "Japanese Admirals and the Politics of Naval Limitation," in Gerald Jordan, ed. *Naval Warfare in the Twentieth Century* (London: Crane Russak, 1977).
22. Frederick S. Harrod, *Manning the New Navy: The Development of a Modern Naval Enlisted Force, 1890–1940* (Westport, Conn.: Greenwood Press, 1978), pp. 173–75.
23. *Ibid.*, p. 17.
24. William F. Fullam, "The System of Naval Training and Discipline Required to Promote Efficiency and Attract Americans," *U.S. Naval Institute Proceedings* 16 (1890), p. 479.
25. Quoted in Harrod, *Manning the New Navy*, p. 18.
26. Unsigned memo to Sec. Navy, October 30, 1919, enclosing draft response to Honorable Rueben L. Haskell, M.C., Records of the Morale Division, Bureau of Naval Personnel Records. Record Group 24, National Archives.
27. Harrod, *Manning the New Navy*, pp. 181–82.
28. *Ibid.*, pp. 101–11.
29. *Ibid.*, pp. 183–84.
30. *Ibid.*, p. 59.
31. E. E. Wilson, "Gift of Foresight," pp. 69–70, unpublished oral history, copy in Navy Department Library. The fact that Wilson still found this incident amusing in the 1960s says a good deal about racial attitudes among naval officers in the 1920s and 1930s.
32. Letter, Dr. G. E. Hooper to NAACP, Encl. To Ltr Walter White to the Honorable Curtis D. Wilbur, December 28, 1928; attachment to BuNav to Commandant, Third Naval District, December 29, 1928, Record Group 24, National Archives.

33. Letter, Walter White to Honorable Curtis D. Wilburn, December 20, 1928, att. To BuNav to Commandant, Third Naval District, December 29, 1928, Record Group 24, National Archives.
34. Commanding Officer, USS *Arkansas*, to Commander Bat Div Two, January 6, 1929, Encl. To Commandant, Third Naval District, to BuNav, February 1, 1929, Record Group 24, National Archives.
35. Daniels to Edward Frensdorf, June 25, 1918, Daniels Papers, Library of Congress.
36. Daniels, handwritten draft of 1914 edition of *The Making of a Man-of-War's Man*, Daniels Papers.
37. *Report of the Secretary of the Navy, 1916*, 64th Cong., 1st Sess., March 30, 1916, pp. 3554–65.
38. "U.S. Navy Rejects Boy Sentenced to It to Reform Him," *New York American*, August 25, 1915; Harrod, *Manning the New Navy*, pp. 51, 55–56.
39. Harrod, *Manning the New Navy*, p. 68.
40. Midshipman J. R. Haile, "One View of Our Enlisted Problem," *Naval Institute Proceedings* 55 (April 1929), p. 285.
41. Lieutenant Commander J. R. Taussig, "The Enlisted Personnel of the Navy," *Naval Institute Proceedings* 41 (November–December 1915), p. 1797.
42. Harrod, *Manning the New Navy*, pp. 176–77.
43. Lieutenant Ridley R. McLean, "Permanency of the Enlisted Force of the Navy," *Naval Institute Proceedings* 32 (1906), p. 1261.
44. Harrod, *Manning the New Navy*, p. 198.
45. Quoted in McLean, "Permanency of the Enlisted Force of the Navy," p. 1262.
46. George P. Dyer, "The Modern General Mess," *Naval Institute Proceedings* 32 (1905), p. 636.
47. Harrod, *Manning the New Navy*, p. 198.
48. Lieutenant Commander J. C. Thom, "Rebuilding the Navy's Enlisted Personnel and Reestablishing its Morale," *Naval Institute Proceedings* 49, pp. 1627, 1631.
49. Jarvis Cartwright letter to author, April 30, 1997.
50. Harrod, *Manning the New Navy*, p. 177; Vice Admiral Gerald Miller conversation with author, March 19, 1998.
51. Alvin Kernan, *Crossing the Line: A Bluejacket's World War II Odyssey* (Annapolis: Naval Institute Press, 1994), p. 7.
52. Connell, *Jack's War*, p. 24.
53. *Report of the Secretary of the Navy, 1909*, p. 310.
54. Frederick Wigby, *Stoker, Royal Navy* (London: Blackwood, 1967), p. 121.
55. Alistair Reid conversation with author, August 12, 1994.
56. Captain John M. Kennedy USN (Ret.), "Shipboard Living Conditions in our Navy, 1919–1949," unpublished manuscript, pp. 3–4, Naval Historical Foundation, Washington, D.C.
57. *Ibid.*, p. 4.
58. *Ibid.*
59. Jonathon G. Utley, *An American Battleship at Peace and War* (Lawrence: Univ. Press of Kansas, 1991), pp. 55–56.
60. *Ibid.*, p. 59.
61. *Ibid.*, pp. 54–55.
62. Miller conversation with author.
63. Utley, *An American Battleship*, p. 52.
64. Miller conversation with author.
65. *Ibid.*; Paul Stillwell, *Battleship Arizona* (Annapolis: Naval Institute Press, 1991), p. 144.
66. Charles Minor Blackford, *Torpedoboat Sailor* (Annapolis: Naval Institute Press, 1968), p. 135.
67. Reid conversation with author.
68. Anonymous letter from "Sailor-USN" to Editor, *Ft. Smith Times-Record*, enclosure to J. F. Henry from Josephus Daniels, January 3, 1914, Daniels Papers.
69. Felix Shay, "Felicitations," *The Fra*, April 1914, p. 4.
70. J. Remsan Bishop letter to Josephus Daniels, November 19, 1913, Daniels Papers.
71. Kernan, *Crossing the Line*, pp. 152–53.
72. Peter Karsten, *The Naval Aristocracy: The Golden Age of Annapolis and the Emergence of Modern American Navalism* (New York: Free Press, 1972), p. 7, 9.
73. *Ibid.*, pp. 8–9, 73.

74. William Glover, "The RCN: Royal Colonial or Royal Canadian Navy?" in Michael L. Hadley, Rob Huebert, and Fred W. Crickard, eds., *A Nation's Navy: In Quest of Canadian Naval Identity* (Montreal and Kingston: McGill University Press, 1966) p. 72.
75. "Reminiscences of Admiral Draper L. Kauffman," p. 24, Naval Institute Oral History Collection; "Reminiscences of Admiral Gerald Miller," No. 1, p. 26, Naval Institute Oral History Collection.
76. David Rosenberg, "Arleigh Burke and Officer Development in the Inter-War Navy," *Pacific Historical Review* 44 (November 1975), p. 509; Karsten, *Naval Aristocracy*, p. 41.
77. Karsten, *Naval Aristocracy*, p. 41.
78. "Reminiscences of Admiral Kauffman," p. 23.
79. "Reminiscences of Vice Admiral Miller," Part 1, p. 26.
80. "Reminiscences of Admiral Thomas C. Hart," pp. 25–46, Naval Institute Oral History Collection.
81. Rosenberg, "Arleigh Burke," p. 507.
82. "Reminiscences of Admiral Kauffman," pp. 26–27.
83. Naval Air Systems Command, *United States Naval Aviation, 1910–1970* (Washington, D.C.: GPO, 1970), pp. 9–10, 35.
84. Quoted in Hone and Mandeles, "Interwar Innovation in Three Navies," p. 72.
85. Clark G. Reynolds, *Admiral John H. Towers: The Struggle for Naval Air Supremacy* (Annapolis: Naval Institute Press, 1991), pp. 109–16.
86. *Ibid.*, p. 109.
87. Ralph O. Paine, *The First Yale Unit: A Story of Naval Aviation, 1916–19* (Cambridge, Mass.: Riverside Press, 1925), vol. 1, pp. 79–80 and *passim*.
88. *Ibid.*, p. v.
89. Lieutenant F. W. Wead, "The Navy and Naval Aviation," *Naval Institute Proceedings* 52, May 1926, p. 8. F. W. ("Spig") Wead, a pioneer aviator, resigned following a disabling accident. He became a successful Hollywood screenwriter and was himself the subject of the 1957 John Ford movie, *Wings of Eagles*.

Chapter 8: "Essentially and Fundamentally a Different Profession"

1. CincUS, confidential Rpt. to CNO on Fleet Problem Nine, 18 March 1929, Record Group 80, National Archives; Eugene E. Wilson, *Slipstream: The Autobiography of an Air Craftsman*, 2nd ed. (New York: Whittlesey House, 1950), p. 148.
2. Charles M. Melhorn, *Two Block Fox: The Rise of the Aircraft Carrier, 1915–1929* (Annapolis: Naval Institute Press, 1974), p. 113.
3. Robert Love, *History of the U.S. Navy* (Harrisburg, Pa,; Stackpole Books, 1992), pp. 546–47.
4. Burke Davis, *The Billy Mitchell Affair* (New York: Random House, 1967), p. 118.
5. "Reminiscences of Captain Joy Bright Hancock," No. 1, p. 21, Naval Institute Oral History Collection.
6. Wilson, *Slipstream*, p. 71.
7. The best study of Moffett's years as chief of the Bureau of Aeronautics is William F. Trimble, *Admiral William A. Moffett: Architect of Naval Aviation* (Washington: Smithsonian, 1994). See also Edward Arpee, *From Frigates to Flat-Tops: The Story of the Life and Achievements of Rear Admiral William Adger Moffett* (Lake Forest, Ill.: privately printed, 1953).
8. See Wead, "Navy and Naval Aviation," pp. 881–82 and *passim*; Wilson, *Slipstream*, p. 59.
9. Davis, *Billy Mitchell Affair*, p. 217.
10. Clark G. Reynolds, *The Fast Carriers: The Forging of an Air Navy* (New York: McGraw-Hill, 1968), pp. 15–16.
11. Unless otherwise indicated the following discussion is based on Edward S. Miller, *War Plan Orange* (Annapolis: Naval Institute Press, 1991).
12. Melhorn, *Two Block Fox*, p. 106.
13. Archibald D. Turnbull and Clifford L. Lord, *History of U.S. Naval Aviation* (New Haven, Conn.: Yale University Press, 1949), p. 229.
14. Melhorn, *Two Block Fox*, p. 96.
15. CincUs Confidential Report to CNO on Fleet Problem Nine, 18 March 1929, p. 30, Record Group 80, National Archives.

16. Melhorn, *Two Block Fox*, p. 95.
17. Turnbull and Lord, *History of U.S. Naval Aviation*, p. 229.
18. Wead, "The Navy and Naval Aviation," pp. 884, 886.
19. "Background on Naval Aviation Pilots," unpublished monograph prepared by the Aviation History Section, *Naval Aviation News*, December 1986, pp. 2–3.
20. *Ibid.*
21. *Ibid.*, p 7.
22. King to AsstSecNav, 14 Dec 1934, File AER-GB, L1-1, Record Group 72, National Archives.
23. Moffett to CNO, 20 April 1925, AER-F-ANZ 803-0, Record Group 72, National Archives.
24. Historical Section, DCNO (Air), "First Draft Narratives, Vols. XXI–XXII: Aviation Personnel," p. 98, copy in Naval Historical Center.
25. *Ibid.*, p. 100.
26. William A. Riley, "The 'Chiefs' of Fighting Two," *American Aviation Historical Society Journal* 14 (Fall 1969), pp. 147–49.
27. "First Draft Narratives," p. 101.
28. Ralph M. Freeman, "Why Not Commission Them?," *Our Navy*, May 1, 1942.
29. Lieutenant Howell M. Sumrall letter to Eric Hammell, August 8, 1982, Eric Hammell Collection, Naval Historical Center.
30. Melhorn, *Two Block Fox*, p. 96.
31. Trimble, *Moffett*, p. 136.
32. "First Draft Narratives," pp. 14–15.
33. Captain Joe Hill USN (Ret.), *Some Early Birds: The Memoirs of a Naval Aviation Cadet, 1935–1945* (Manhattan, Kans.: Sunflower University Press, 1983), p. 2.
34. John Lundstrom, *The First Team: Pacific Air Combat from Pearl Harbor to Midway* (Annapolis: Naval Institute Press, 1984), Appendix 6, pp. 490–95. The first aviation cadet class, in 1936, had only one student who lacked a northern European surname. Hill, *Some Early Birds*, p. 38.
35. Hill, *Some Early Birds*, pp. 6–12.
36. *Ibid.*
37. "First Draft Narratives," Part 3, p. 53.
38. Lundstrom, *First Team*, p. 452.
39. Clark G. Reynolds, *Admiral John H. Towers: The Struggle for Naval Air Supremacy* (Annapolis: Naval Institute Press, 1991), p. 323.
40. Lieutenant Barrett Studley, "Flight Training of Student Aviatiors," *Naval Institute Proceedings* 53, July 1927, p. 767.
41. Lieutenant Spencer S. Warner, "A Naval Aviatior in the Making," *Naval Institute Proceedings* 54, June 1928, p. 471.
42. Asada Sadao, "From Mahan to Pearl Harbor: The Imperial Japanese Navy and the United States," chap. 4, p. 15. I am grateful to Prof. Asada for allowing me to use the draft English translation of this book, which is scheduled to be published by the U.S. Naval Institute Press.
43. An often-reproduced painting of the Battle of Tsushima by Tojo Shotaro shows Kato Tomosaburo immediately behind Admiral Togo atop the pilothouse of the *Mikasa*.
44. Asada, "From Mahan to Pearl Harbor," chap. 4, p. 15.
45. *Ibid.*, p. 9.
46. Ian T. M. Gow, "Political Involvement of the Japanese Naval General Staff," paper presented at the U.S. Naval Academy, October 1–2, 1981.
47. Asada, "The Japanese Navy and the United States," in Borg and Okamoto, *Pearl Harbor as History*, pp. 726–27.
48. Kumagaya Mitsuhisa, *Nihon no Jinteki Seido To Mondaiten no Kenkyu* (a study of personnel policy in the Japanese navy) (Tokyo: Toshihanko Kai, 1992), p. 145.
49. Asada, "From Mahan to Pearl Harbor," chap. 4, p. 82.
50. Takagi Sokichi, *Jidenteki Nihon Kaigun Shimatsuki* (Autobiographical account of the end of the Japanese navy) (Tokyo, 1971), p. 22.
51. Agawa Hiroyuki, *The Reluctant Admiral: Yamamoto and the Imperial Navy* (Tokyo: Kodansha, 1979), p. 149.
52. Stephen E. Pelz, *Race to Pearl Harbor: The Failure of the Second London Naval Conference and the Onset of World War II* (Cambridge: Harvard University Press, 1974), pp. 14–15.
53. Asada, "Japanese Navy and the United States," p. 230.
54. Asada, "From Mahan to Pearl Harbor," chap. 4, pp. 32–33.

55. "Comment by Commander R. A. Theobald," 11 Feb 1927, Enclosure to USNA Japan Rpt 7 Sept 1929, ONI serial 18603, E-7-C, Record Group 38, National Archives.
56. Sakai Subaru with Martin Caidin and Fred Saito, *Samurai* (New York: Dutton, 1957), p. 21.
57. Asada, "From Mahan to Pearl Harbor," chap. 5, p. 23.
58. Hector C. Bywater, *Seapower in the Pacific* (Boston: Houghton Mifflin, 1921), p. 188.
59. "Comment by Commander R. A. Theobald."
60. Ishizuka Koji, *Nihon no Guntai* (Armed forces in Japan) (Tokyo: Iwanami, 1991), p. 128.
61. Kobayashi Takahiro, *Yaro Yomoyama Monogatari* (Some stories of friends in the navy) (Tokyo: Koujinsha, 1980), p. 17.
62. *Ibid.*; Arthur Marder, *Old Friends, New Enemies: The Royal Navy and the Imperial Japanese Navy* (New York: Oxford University Press, 1981), p. 266.
63. Bywater, *Seapower in the Pacific*, p. 117.
64. Iwata Shioka, ed., *Kaigun Tokubetsu Nenshohei no Shuki* (Witnesses to history: Recollections of special boy sailors) (Tokyo: Kaigun Tokuniki, 1998), p. 106.
65. *Nihong Kaigun Shi* (History of the Japanese navy) (Society for the Preservation of Naval Records, Kaigun Rekishi Hozun-ka, Tokyo, 1996), vol. 5, pp. 111–14.
66. Shioka, *Kaigun Tokubetsu*, p. 36.
67. *Ibid.*, p. 141.
68. *Ibid.*, p. 15.
69. *Ibid.*, p. 21.
70. *Ibid.*, p. 16.
71. *Ibid.*
72. *Ibid.*, p. 63.
73. Kobayashi, *Yaro Yomoyama*, pp. 74–82.
74. Watanabe Kiyoshi, *Senkan Musashi no Saigo* (The last of battleship *Musashi*) (Tokyo: Asahi Shimbum, 1982), p. 257.
75. Bullock, *Etajima*, pp. 78–79.
76. Ishizuka, *Nihon no Guntai*, pp. 121–22.
77. Kobayashi, *Yaro Yomoyama*, p. 80.
78. Watanabe, *Senkan Musashi no Saigo*, p. 257.
79. Iizuka, *Nihon no Guntai*, p. 140.
80. Kageyama Noboru, *Kaigun Heigakko no Kyoiku* (Education at the Naval Academy) (Tokyo: Daichi Hoki Shuppan Kabashiki Kaisa, 1978), p. 96.
81. Ikeda Kiyoshi, *The Navy and Japan* (Tokyo: Chur Koron-sha, 1981), p. 37.
82. Yoshida Toshio, *Kaigun Sambo* (The naval staff officer) (Tokyo: Bungei Shiju, 1939), pp. 29, 54.
83. *Senshi Sosho Dai Houei Honei Kaigun Bu Dai Toa Senso Kaisan Kei* (War history series: "Circumstances leading to the opening of the great East Asian war.") (Tokyo: Asagumo Shinbum Sha, 1979), vol. 1, chap. 1.
84. Yoshida, *Kaigun Sambo*, p. 58.
85. John Ferris, "A British 'Unoffical' Aviation Mission and Japanese Naval Developments, 1919–1929" *Journal of Strategic Studies* Sept. 1982, p. 418.
86. Evans and Peattie, *Kaigun* (Annapolis, Md.: U.S. Naval Institute Press, 1997), pp. 304–5 and passim.
87. *Ibid.*, chap. 14, table 141. "Percent in Grade Based on Total Officers and Enlisted Personnel on Active Duty, 30 June 1935–1938," in Annual Report, Navy and Marine Corps Military Personnel Statistics, 30 June 1960, copy in Operational Archives, Naval Historical Center.
88. Evans and Peattie, *Kaigun*, chap. 14, p. 13.
89. *Ibid.*, chap. 14, table 14–2.
90. Lundstrom, *First Team*, pp. 454–55.
91. Sakai, *Samurai*, p. 24.
92. A description of the amenities at Pensacola is in Robert A. Winston, *Dive Bomber Pilot* (New York: Holiday House, 1939), pp. 26–27.
93. Sakai, *Samurai*, pp. 27–28.
94. Lieutenant Commander (MC) Eric Liljencrantz, "Aviation Medicine: Its Responsibilities and Problems," *Naval Institute Proceedings*, vol. 64, December 1938, pp. 1756–57.
95. Sakai, *Samurai*, p. 34.
96. Liljencrantz, "Aviation Medicine" pp. 1757–58.

97. Memo, Chief BuAir to Chief BuNav, sub: Flight Pay, 17 April 1925, Memo Board on Aviation Flight Pay to SecNav, 29 April 1933, both in Records of BuAir, Record Group 72, National Archives.
98. Boone T. Guyton, *Air Base* (New York: McGraw-Hill, 1941), p. 46.
99. Agawa, *Reluctant Admiral,* pp. 109–10.
100. Frederic Mears, *Carrier Combat* (New York: Doubleday, 1944), p. 24.
101. Guyton, *Air Base,* p. 77.
102. The discussion that follows is based primarily upon the analysis in Thomas Hone, Norman Friedman, and Mark Mandeles, *Carrier Aviation in the U.S. and Royal Navies* (Annapolis: U.S. Naval Institute Press, 1999). I am grateful to the authors for allowing me to see the manuscript in draft. All page references are to the draft.
103. Hone et al., *Carrier Aviation,* p. 78.
104. *Ibid.,* pp. 97–98; Peattie and Evans, *Kaigun,* pp. 332–33.
105. Hone et al., *Carrier Aviation,* p. 119.
106. Evans and Peattie, *Kaigun,* pp. 334–39.
107. Geoffrey Till, "Airpower and the Battleship in the 1920s" in Bryan Ranft, ed., *Technical Change and British Naval Policy, 1860–1939* (London: Brassey's, 1983), p. 41.
108. Captain Charles D. Allen, "Forecasting Future Forces," *Naval Institute Proceedings,* vol. 108, November 1982, p. 77.
109. Thomas C. Hone and Mark D. Mandeles, "Managerial Style in the Inter-War Navy," *Naval War College Review,* September–October 1980, pp. 90, 95–6.
110. Jon Tetsuro Sumida, "The Best Laid Plans: The Development of British Battlefleet Tactics, 1919–1942," *International History Review* 14, (November 1992), pp. 697–98.
111. "When Is a Sailor Not a Sailor?" *Naval Review* 20 (1937), pp. 687–88.
112. Layard in Arthur, *True Glory,* p. 209.
113. Marder, *Old Friends, New Enemies,* pp. 36–40, 50–55; Sumida, "Best Laid Plans," pp. 693–701.
114. Gordon, *Rules of the Game,* pp. 572–73.
115. Sumida, "Best Laid Plans," pp. 699–700.

Chapter 9: "The Zenith of Effort and the Nadir of Hope"

1. Viscount Cunningham of Hyndhope, *A Sailor's Odyssey* (London: Hutchinson, 1951), p. 273.
2. *Ibid.,* p. 285.
3. M. R. Maunds, "A Taranto Diary," *Blackwood's,* March 1942, p. 17.
4. Marc Antonio Bragadin, *The Italian Navy in World War II* (Annapolis: Naval Institute Press, 1957), p. 45.
5. Lieutenant Commander Hugh Hodgkinson DSC RN, *Before the Tide Turned: The Mediterranean Experience of A British Destroyer Officer* (London: George Harrap, 1944), p. 117.
6. *Ibid.*
7. Cunningham, *Sailor's Odyssey,* p. 358.
8. Philip Ziegler, *Mountbatten* (New York: Knopf, 1985), p. 141.
9. Cunningham, *Sailor's Odyssey,* p. 358.
10. *Ibid.,* p. 363.
11. Commander J.A.J. Dennis Papers, Imperial War Museum.
12. Admiral Sir Frank Twiss interview with Chris Howard Bailey, p. 14, Oral History Collections of the Royal Naval Museum.
13. Adrian Holloway, *From Dartmouth to War,* p. 85.
14. Able Seaman Jeffrey Burgess, "Main Events Since I Left England," unpublished manuscript, in G. Sear Papers, Imperial War Museum; "The Sinking of HMS *Juno,*" unsigned report, G. Sear Papers.
15. "Sinking of HMS *Juno.*"
16. S.W.C. Pack, *The Battle for Crete* (Annapolis: Naval Institute Press, 1973), p. 36.
17. Vice Admiral Sir Louis Le Bailly, *The Man Around the Engine* (London: Kenneth Mason, 1990), p. 82.
18. Midshipman T. Ruck-Keene journal, May 23, 1941, Imperial War Museum.
19. *Ibid.*
20. Pack, *Battle for Crete,* p. 37.

21. "An Adventure at Crete with HMS *Fiji*: An Account by the Late Stoker Petty Officer W. Manders Soon After the Battle," p. 2, unpublished manuscript, Imperial War Museum.
22. *Ibid.*, p. 7.
23. *Ibid.*, p. 8.
24. *Ibid.*, p 12.
25. *Ibid.*
26. Cunningham, *Sailor's Odyssey*, p. 374.
27. John Knight, "Memoirs of a Miscreant," p. 64, unpublished manuscript, Imperial War Museum.
28. David Thomas, *Crete 1941: The Battle at Sea* (London: New English Library, 1975), p. 179.
29. Knight, "Memoirs of a Miscreant," p. 66.
30. *Ibid.*
31. *Ibid.*
32. Cunningham, *Sailor's Odyssey*, p. 76.
33. Pack, *Battle for Crete*, p. 61.
34. MacDonald, *Lost Battle*, p. 268.
35. *Ibid.*, p 275.
36. Cunningham, *Sailor's Odyssey*, p. 380.
37. H. Speakman DSM, "The Evacuation of Crete (on Board HMS *Orion*)," unpublished manuscript, Imperial War Museum.
38. Hodgkinson, *Before the Tide Turned*, pp. 136–37.
39. *Ibid.*, pp. 138, 140.
40. *Ibid.*, pp 142–43.
41. Speakman, "Evacuation of Crete," p. 3.
42. Chaplain's Report, HMS *Orion*, appendix to "Letter of Proceedings, 28th to 30th May 1941," copy in T. C. Wynne Papers, Imperial War Museum.
43. Speakman, "Evacuation of Crete," p. 6.
44. Surgeon Lieutenant R. I. Bence, "A Narrative of Action During 29 May 1941," in T.C.T. Wynne Papers.
45. Speakman, "Evacuation of Crete."
46. Bence, "Narrative of Action During 29 May 1941."
47. Thomas, *Crete 1941*, p. 215.
48. *Ibid.*
49. *Ibid.*, p. 218.
50. John Winton, *Cunningham* (London: John Murray, 1998), p. 219.
51. *Ibid.*, p. 221.
52. Hodgkinson, *Before the Tide Turned*, p. 150.
53. *Ibid.*, p. 152.
54. Quoted in Michael Simpson, "Wings over the Sea: The Interaction of Air and Seapower in the Mediterranean 1940–42," in N.A.M. Rodger, ed., *Naval Power in the Twentieth Century* (Annapolis: Naval Institute Press, 1996), p. 141.
55. Commander J.A.J. Dennis Papers.
56. Admiral Sir Frank Twiss interview, pp. 14–16.
57. Holloway, *From Dartmouth to War*, p. 87.
58. Commander I. R. Johnston RN (Ret.) letter to author, January 30, 1998; Commander J.A.J. Dennis RN (Ret.) letter to author, October 21, 1997.
59. T. Ruck-Keene journal 23 April 1941.
60. Hodgkinson, *Before the Tide Turned*, p. 117.
61. Captain R.F.C. Ellsworth RN (Ret.) letter to author, October 8, 1997.
62. Adrian Holloway letter to author, February 27, 1998.
63. Simpson, *Wings Over the Sea*, p. 141.
64. Holloway, *From Dartmouth to War*, p. 132.
65. Quoted in MacDonald, *Lost Battle*, p. 285.
66. Engine Room Artificer Clifford Simkin, "The War from the Engine Room," unpublished manuscript, Imperial War Museum.
67. Cunningham to Admiral Sir Dudley Pound, 30 May 1941, in Michael Simpson, ed., *The Cunningham Papers* (London: Naval Records Society, 1999), pp. 410–11.
68. Commander I. R. Johnston letter to author, March 10, 1999.
69. MacDonald, *Lost Battle*, p. 234.

70. Winton, *Cunningham*, p. 215.
71. Cunningham, *A Sailor's Odyssey*, p. 390.
72. Commander I. R. Johnston letter to author, January 30, 1998.
73. Letter, Commander J.A.J. Dennis to author, October 21, 1997.
74. Commander I. R. Johnston letter to author, January 30, 1998.
75. Captain R.F.C. Ellsworth letter to author, October 8, 1997.
76. Captain J.A.F. Somerville RN (Ret.) letter to author, August 22, 1997.
77. D. Auffret interview, p. 23, Department of Sound Recordings, Imperial War Museum. 10681/4/2.
78. Adrian Holloway letter to author, February 27, 1998.
79. Connell, *Jack's War*, p. 89.
80. Auffret interview.
81. G. W. Deacon interview, p. 41, Imperial War Museum, Department of Sound Recordings, 9316/4/4.
82. Simpson, *Cunningham Papers*, p. 417.
83. *Ibid.*, pp. 416, 490.
84. Quoted in Winton, *Cunningham*, p. 211.
85. "Adventure at Crete with HMS *Fiji*," p. 4.

Chapter 10: "Never in All My Years Had I Imagined a Battle Like That"

1. Miller, *War Plan Orange*, pp. 297–308.
2. The discussion below is based on David C. Fuquea, "Task Force One: The Wasted Assets of the United States Pacific Battleship Fleet, 1942," *Journal of Military History* 61 (October 1997), pp. 707–34.
3. Kernan, *Crossing the Line*, p. 39.
4. Lundstrom, *First Team*, p. 106.
5. Samuel Eliot Morison, *History of U.S. Naval Operations in World War II*, vol. 3, *The Rising Sun in the Pacific* (Boston: Little, Brown, 1951), p. 267.
6. Where not otherwise indicated, the account of Pacific carrier operations is based on the author's more extensive discussion in *Eagle Against the Sun: The American War with Japan* (New York: Free Press, 1985).
7. Samuel Hynes. *Flights of Passage: Reflections of a World War II Aviator* (Annapolis: Naval Institute Press, 1988), p. 159.
8. John Prados, *Combined Fleet Decoded* (New York: Random House, 1995), p. 237.
9. Kernan, *Crossing the Line*, p. 35.
10. Edward P. Stafford, *The Big E: The Story of the USS Enterprise* (Annapolis: Naval Institute Press, 1992), p. 93.
11. Prados, *Combined Fleet Decoded*, p. 237.
12. Kernan, *Crossing the Line*, pp. 44–45.
13. Lisle A. Rose, *The Ship That Held the Line: The USS Hornet and the First Year of the Pacific War* (Annapolis: Naval Institute Press, 1992), p. 93.
14. Lundstrom, *First Team*, p. 159.
15. Rose, *The Ship That Held the Line*, p. 194.
16. E. T. Wooldridge, ed., *Carrier Warfare in the Pacific: An Oral History Collection* (Annapolis: Naval Institute Press, 1995), interview, p. 122.
17. Lundstrom, *First Team*, p. 6.
18. Report of Lt Comdr. H.A.I. Luard RN, attachment to PACFLT enclosure to CINCPAC serial 00421, January 8, 1943, Naval Historical Center.
19. Hynes, *Flights of Passage*, p. 13.
20. Lundstrom, *First Team*, p. 487.
21. Masatake Okumiya and Jiro Hirokoshi, *Zero!* (New York: Dutton, 1956), p. 62.
22. James H. Belote and Willim M. Belote, *Titans of the Sea: The Development and Operations of Japanese and American Carrier Task Forces During World War II* (New York: Harper, 1978).
23. "Reminiscences of Admiral James Thach," Part 2, p. 146, Naval Institute Oral History Collection.

24. Curtis A. Utz, "Carrier Aviation Policy and Procurement in the U.S. Navy, 1936–1940," M.A. thesis, University of Maryland, 1989, p. 34.
25. Prange, *Fading Victory*, p. 115.
26. The discussion of Coral Sea and Midway has been adapted from the author's more extensive account in *Eagle Against the Sun*.
27. Lundstrom, *First Team*, p. 205.
28. *Ibid.*, p. 206.
29. Lundstrom, *First Team*, p. 216.
30. Samuel Eliot Morison, *Coral Sea, Midway and Submarine Actions* (Boston: Little, Brown, 1950), p. 91.
31. Okumiya and Hirokoshi, *Zero!*, p. 93.
32. Quoted in Robert W. Love, *History of the U.S. Navy*, vol. 2, *1942–1991* (Harrisburg, Pa.: Stackpole, 1992), p. 27.
33. Naval War College, "The Battle of the Coral Sea: Strategical and Tactical Analysis," p. 101, copy in Naval Historical Center, Washington, D.C.
34. Action Report USS *Lexington*, 15 May 1942, Naval Historical Center. The discussion of damage control in Chapters 10 to 12 is based in part on a paper written for my World War II seminar (December 1996) by Mr. David Atkinson, graduate student, Elliot School of International Affairs, George Washington University.
35. Prados, *Combined Fleet Decoded*, pp. 315–16.
36. Kernan, *Crossing the Line*, pp. 47–48.
37. Walter Lord, *Incredible Victory* (New York: Harper & Row, 1967), p. 12.
38. ComCarPac War Diary, Operational Archives, Naval Historical Center.
39. Mitsuo Fuchida and Masatake Okumiya, *Midway: The Battle That Doomed Japan* (Annapolis: Naval Institute Press 1955), p. 150.
40. "Reminiscences of Admiral Thach," Part 2, pp. 245–52.
41. Lundstrom, *First Team*, pp. 352–60.
42. "Reminiscences of Admiral Thach," Part 2, p. 360.
43. Kernan, *Crossing the Line*, pp. 54–55.
44. Mears, *Carrier Combat*, p. 58.
45. Prange, *Fading Victory*, pp. 161–62.
46. Prados, *Combined Fleet Decoded*, p. 337. R.Adm. Takata Toshitana, a member of the Combined Fleet staff, put aviator losses at 30 percent killed and 40 percent injured. *U.S. Strategic Bombing Survey: Interrogations of Japanese Officials*, p. 262.
47. *Strategic Bombing Survey*, p. 262.
48. CINCPAC to COMINCH 1552201 June 42, CINCPAC War Diary, Record Group 216, National Archives.

Chapter 11: "Scared as Hell, Having a Wonderful Time"

1. Prange, *Fading Victory*, p. 174.
2. Portions of the foregoing account of the Guadalcanal campaign are adapted from the author's lengthier treatment in *Eagle Against the Sun*.
3. Richard Frank, *Guadalcanal* (New York: Random House, 1990), p. 341.
4. *Ibid.*, pp. 369–72.
5. These are Frank's figures for operational aircraft. Total aircraft with the carriers were Japanese 233, American 163. *Ibid.*, p. 373.
6. Gunner's Mate Second Class James E. O'Neil diary, in Eric Hammel Papers, Naval Historical Center.
7. Lundstrom, *First Team*, pp. 351–52.
8. Rear Admiral Oscar H. Dodson letter to Eric Hammel, July 23, 1982, enclosing copy of article in *Coinage* magazine, May 1966, Hammel Papers.
9. John F. Kielty interview with author, April 26, 1997.
10. Rose, *Ship That Held the Line*, p. 224.
11. Sidney Shalett, *Old Nameless: The Epic of a U.S. Battlewagon* (New York: Appleton-Century, 1943), p. 54.

12. Tom Lea, "Aboard the USS *Hornet*," *Life*, December 1942.
13. Ralph C. Morgan letter to author, January 12, 1997.
14. Shalett, *Old Nameless*, pp. 56–57.
15. Herbert S. Damom letter to Eric Hammel, Hammel Papers.
16. Dodson letter; Morgan letter.
17. Aviation Machinist's Mate 2d Class Bernard W. Peterson, unpublished memoirs, Hammel Papers.
18. Report of LtComdr. H.A.I. Luard, att. To PACFLT encl. To CINCPAC serial 00421 Jan 1, 1943, Naval Historical Center.
19. Narrative of Lt. Albert D. Pollock, encl. "C" to C.O. *Enterprise*, CINCPAC serial 00413, Jan 6, 1943, Naval Historical Center.
20. Comments on Fighter Direction from the *Enterprise*, by C.O. VF-10, encl. "I" to C.O. *Enterprise*, CINCPAC serial 00413, Jan 6, 1943.
21. Pollock narrative.
22. George O'Connor letter to Eric Hammel, no date [1982], Hammell Papers.
23. Alvin Kernan, *Crossing the Line*, p. 70.
24. Dodson letter.
25. Comments on action by Comdr James H. Flatley to C.O. *Enterprise*, CINCPAC serial 00413, Jan 6, 1943, Naval Historical Center.
26. COM, TF61, Rpt of Action of *Hornet* Air Group, Oct 26, 1942. CINCPAC serial 00413, Jan 6, 1943.
27. Action Rpt, C.O. VF-8, to C.O. *Hornet*, CINCPAC serial 00413, Jan 6, 1943.
28. Peter Hodges and Norman Hodges, *Destroyer Weapons of World War II* (Annapolis: Naval Institute Press, 1979), pp. 128–29.
29. O'Connor letter.
30. Lundstrom, *First Team*, p. 416.
31. Damon letter.
32. Frank, *Guadalcanal*, pp. 390–91.
33. Damon letter.
34. Lundstrom, *First Team*, p. 430.
35. *Ibid.*, pp. 442–43.
36. Peterson memoirs.
37. Rose, *The Ship That Held the Line*, p. 214.
38. Thomas W. Reese letter to Eric Hammel, Hammel Papers.
39. Memo, Engineer Officer to C.O. USS *Hornet*, Sub: Report of Action with the Enemy on Monday, Oct 26, 1942, CINCPAC serial 45530, Oct 30, 1942, Naval Historical Center.
40. *Ibid.*
41. "Reminiscences of Rear Admiral Francis D. Foley," p. 61, Naval Institute Oral History Collection.
42. John F. Kielty letter to author, May 4, 1997.
43. Com VF-72 to Com TF17, sub Action Rpt, encl., to CINCPAC serial 00413, Jan 6, 1943, Naval Historical letter.
44. *Ibid.*
45. Digest of Contents of Recorded Interview with Lt. C. O. Morrison, USMCR, April 29, 1944, Naval Historical Center.
46. C.O. *Enterprise* to CINC PACFLT, sub Battle of Santa Cruz, CINCPAC serial 034372, Naval Historical Center.
47. Dr. Donald MacAteer interview with author, May 21, 1997.
48. Lundstrom, *First Team*, p. 442.
49. *Ibid.*
50. *Ibid.*
51. *Ibid.*
52. "Reminiscences of Admiral Thach," Part 1, pp. 246–50.
53. Barrett Tillman, *Wildcat: The F4F in WWII*, 2d ed. (Annapolis: Naval Institute Press, 1982), p. 66.
54. Flatley comments.
55. *Ibid.*
56. Lundstrom, *First Team*, p. 462.

57. Memo, CO, Fighting Squadron Ten to Commander, Carriers PacFlt., Sub: The Navy Fighter, 25 June 1942, Cdr. C. H. Jorgenson Papers (Courtesy John Lundstrom).
58. *Ibid.*
59. *Ibid.*
60. Frank, *Guadalcanal,* pp. 400–1.
61. Professor Alvin Kernan conversation with author, February 27, 1997.
62. George O'Connell letter to Eric Hammel, Hammel Papers.
63. Herbert S. Damon letter to Eric Hammel, Hammel Papers.
64. Bernard W. Peterson memoirs.
65. Unsigned letter, June 8, 1982, Hammel Papers.
66. I.R.V. Cole letter to Eric Hammel, March 3, 1942.
67. Damon letter.
68. Dale Harrison, "The Old Lady of Mars," *Enterprise Bulletin,* Fall 1992, pp. 27–29, USS *Enterprise* Collection.
69. Shallot, *Old Nameless,* pp. 62–63.
70. Harrison, "Old Lady of Mars."
71. John F. Kielty letter to author, May 4, 1997.
72. Captain M. B. Gardiner letter to Rear Admiral Harry E. Yarnell, 25 August 1943, Harry E. Yarnell Papers, Box 7, Naval Historical Center, Washington, DC.
73. Rear Admiral Harry E. Yarnell to COMINCH, "Report on Naval Aviation," 6 November 1943, Yarnell Papers.
74. Reynolds, *Fast Carriers,* pp. 46–47.
75. Yarnell, "Report on Naval Aviation."
76. Lieutenant Commander Thomas F. Connolly letter to Yarnell, 8 November 1943, Yarnell Papers.
77. Yarnell, "Report on Naval Aviation."
78. H. B. Miller letter to Yarnell, 13 September 1943, Yarnell Papers, Box 7.
79. Reynolds, *Towers,* p. 432.
80. Captain M. B. Gardiner letter to Yarnell, 25 August 1943.

Chapter 12: "From Newfy to Derry's a Bloody Long Way"

1. David Zimmerman, *The Great Naval Battle of Ottawa* (Toronto: University of Toronto Press, 1989), p. 10.
2. "Employment of Submarines," Staff Presentation, U.S. Naval War College, 21 Aug 41, in Strategic Plans Division Records, Series 2, Naval Historical Center; Clay Blair, *Silent Victory: The U.S. Submarine War Against Japan* (Philadelphia: Lippincott, 1981), pp. 45–46; Wilfred J. Holmes, *Undersea Victory* (Garden City, N.Y.: Doubleday, 1966), pp. 47–48.
3. William Glover, "Manning and Training the Allied Navies," in Stephen Howarth and Derek Law, eds., *The Battle of the Atlantic, 1939–1945* (London: Greenhill Books, 1944), pp. 191–92.
4. Donald P. Steury, "The Character of the German Naval Offensive October 1940–June 1941" in Timothy Ryan and Jan M. Copes, eds., *To Die Gallantly: The Battle of the Atlantic* (Boulder, Colo.: Westview Press, 1994), pp. 79–80.
5. G. Hessler, *The U-Boat War in the Atlantic,1939–1945* (London: HMSO, 1989), p. 26.
6. Rohwer, "Codes and Ciphers" in Stephen Howarth and Derek Lawleds, *The Battle of the Atlantic 1939–45.* 50th Anniversary International Naval Conference (London: Greenhill, 1994) pp. 44–45.
7. V. E. Tarrant, *The U-Boat Offensive, 1914–1945* (Annapolis, Md.: Naval Institute Press, 1989), p. 149.
8. Samuel Eliot Morison, *The Battle of the Atlantic, 1939–1943* (Boston: Little, Brown, 1957), pp. 53–55.
9. Marc Milner, *North Atlantic Run: The Royal Canadian Navy and the Battle for the Convoys* (Toronto: University of Toronto Press, 1985), pp. 14–15.
10. *Ibid.,* p. 6.
11. William Glover, "The RCN: Royal Colonial or Royal Canadian Navy?" in Michael L. Hadley, Rob Hurbert and Fred W. Crickard, eds., *A Nation's Navy: In Quest of Canadian Naval Identity* (Montreal and Kingston: McGill University Press, 1996), p. 72.

12. David Zimmerman, "The Social Background of the Wartime Navy: Some Statistical Data," in *ibid.*, p. 259.

13. Michael Whitby, "In Defense of Home Waters: Doctrine and Training in the Canadian Navy During the 1930s," *Mariner's Mirror* 77 (May 1991), pp. 169–70.

14. *Ibid.*, p. 171.

15. Milner, *North Atlantic Run*, pp. 24–25.

16. Joseph Schull, *Far Distant Ships: An Official Account* (Annapolis: U.S. Press, Naval Institute, 1987), p. 76.

17. Glover, "Manning and Training," p. 195.

18. James B. Lamb, *The Corvette Navy* (Toronto: Macmillan of Canada, 1977), p. 15.

19. Quoted in Glover, "Manning and Training," p. 200. RCNVR (Royal Canadian Navy Volunteer Reserve) were officers who had been commissioned for war service from civilian life. RCNR (Royal Canadian Navy Reserve) were officers who had served in the merchant marine.

20. Lamb, *Corvette Navy*, p. 144.

21. Glover, "Manning and Training," p. 196.

22. Jeffrey V. Brock, *The Dark Broad Seas: Memoirs of a Sailor* (Toronto: Macmillan & Stuart, 1974), vol. 1, p. 46.

23. Glover, "Manning and Training," pp. 199–200.

24. Zimmerman, "Social Background," pp. 264–71.

25. Lamb, *Corvette Navy*, pp. 49–50.

26. Donald MacIntyre, *U-Boat Killer* (London: Weidenfeld & Nicholson, 1956), p. 87.

27. Lamb, *Corvette Navy*, pp. 49–50.

28. Alan Easton, *50 North: Canada's Atlantic Battleground* (Toronto: Ryerson, 1966), p. 13.

29. Milner, *North Atlantic Run*, pp. 36–37.

30. Lamb, *Corvette Navy*, p. 144.

31. David K. Brown, "Atlantic Escorts 1939–1945," in Howarth and Law, *Battle of the Atlantic*; Lieutenant William H. Pugsley RCNVR, *Saints, Devils and Ordinary Seamen: Life on the Royal Canadian Navy's Lower Deck* (Toronto: Collins, 1954), pp. 47–48.

32. Lamb, *Corvette Navy*, p. 24.

33. *Ibid.*, p. 52.

34. Private communication to the author, August 2, 1995.

35. Pugsley, *Saints, Devils and Ordinary Seamen*, p. 9.

36. Brown, "Atlantic Escorts," p. 468.

37. Dan Van Der Vat, *The Atlantic Campaigns: World War II's Great Struggle at Sea* (New York: Harper & Row, 1988), p. 153.

38. MacIntyre, *U-Boat Killer*, p. 52.

39. The literature on this subject is extensive. In addition to Rohwer, cited above, see Patrick Beesly, *Very Special Intelligence* (New York: Doubleday, 1978); David Kahn, *Seizing the Enigma* (Boston: Houghton Mifflin, 1991); and Ralph Bennett, *Ultra in the West* (New York: Scribners, 1979).

40. Milner, *North Atlantic Run*, p. 53.

41. *Ibid.*, p. 72.

42. Shull, *Far Distant Ships*, pp. 84–85.

43. Milner, *North Atlantic Run*, pp. 82–83.

44. Michael L. Hadley, "The Popular Image of the Canadian Navy," in Hadley, Hurbert, and Crickard, *A Nation's Navy*, p. 37.

45. *Ibid.*, p. 41.

46. Milner, *North Atlantic Run*, p. 45.

47. Hadley, "Popular Image," p. 39.

48. *Ibid.*

49. *Ibid.*, p. 35.

50. Marc Milner, "Squaring Some of the Corners: The Royal Canadian Navy and the Pattern of the Atlantic War," in Runyan and Copes, *To Die Gallantly*, pp. 128–31. The literature on Operation Roll of Drums is large. See Michael Gannon, *Operation Drumbeat* (New York: Harper & Row, 1990); and Eliot A. Cohen, "Failure to Learn: American Anti-Submarine Warfare in 1942," in Eliot Cohen and John Gooch, *Military Misfortunes* (New York: Free Press, 1990). These accounts are challenged by Dean G. Allard, "A United States Overview," in Howarth and Law, eds., *Battle of the Atlantic*, pp. 567–75; Robert G. Love, "The U.S. Navy and Opera-

tion *Roll-of-Drums*, 1942," in Runyan and Copes, *To Die Gallantly*, pp. 95–120; and Clay Blair, *Hitler's U-Boat War*, vol. 1, pp. 689–96 and *passim*.

51. Tarrant, *U-Boat Offensives*, p. 106.
52. *Ibid*.
53. *Ibid*., p. 108.
54. Jordan Vause, *Wolf: U-Boat Commanders in World War II* (Annapolis: Naval Institute Press, 1997), p. 230.
55. Hadley, *Count Not the Dead*, p. 68.
56. *Ibid*., p. 74.
57. Mulligan, *Neither Sharks Nor Wolves: The Men of Nazi Germany's U-Boat Arm, 1939–1945* (Annapolis: Naval Institute Press, 1999), p. 221.
58. Quoted in Vause, *Wolf*, p. 91.
59. *Ibid*., p. 157.
60. Mulligan, *Neither Sharks Nor Wolves*, p. 235. Mulligan argues that this did not mean that all naval officers embraced Nazi ideology. See p. 228–33 and *passim*.
61. Peter Padfield, *Dönitz: The Last Fuhrer* (London: Gollancz, 1984), p. 423.
62. Eric Rust, *Naval Officers Under Hitler: The Story of Crew 34* (Westport, Conn.: Praeger, 1991), pp. 21–24.
63. *Ibid*.
64. *Ibid*.
65. *Ibid*., p. 64.
66. Quoted in Hadley, *Count Not the Dead*, p. 85.
67. Padfield, *Dönitz*, p. 350. The author found Mulligan's argument that Dönitz's anti-Semitism was only rhetorical unconvincing. See Mulligan, *Neither Sharks Nor Wolves*, p. 229.
68. Vause, *Wolf*, pp. 164–65.
69. Williamson Murray, *Strategy for Defeat: The Luftwaffe, 1933–45* (Maxwell Airforce Base AC Air University Press, 1983), pp. 254, 278.
70. Mulligan, *Neither Sharks Nor Wolves*, p. 149.
71. U.S. Naval Technical Training Mission to Europe, Technical Report, 304–45, Series IV, "Training Aids for Submarine Operating Personnel," p. 4. For a more detailed discussion see Sarandis Papadopoulos, "Feeding the Sharks: The Logistics of Undersea Warfare 1935–45," pp. 250–65, Ph.D. dissertation, George Washington Univ., 1999.
72. Timothy P. Mulligan, "German U-Boat Crews in World War II: Sociology of an Elite," *Journal of Military History*, pp. 273–78.
73. Papadopoulos, "Feeding the Sharks," p. 273.
74. Mulligan, *Neither Sharks Nor Wolves*, p. 149.
75. Erich Topp, "Manning and Training of the U-Boat Fleet," in Howarth and Lau, *Battle of the Atlantic*, p. 215.
76. Lothar Günther Buchheim, *U-Boat War* (New York: Knopf, 1978), chap. 2, no pagination. Buchheim, a wartime illustrator and propagandist, later wrote *Das Boot*, the basis for the popular motion picture. See Hadley, *Count Not the Dead*, pp. 140–71 and *passim*.
77. Heinz Schaeffer, *U-Boat 977* (London: William Kimber, 1952), p. 76.
78. Timothy P. Mulligan, *Neither Sharks Nor Wolves*, pp. 12–13.
79. Vause, *Wolf*, p. 83.
80. Jürgen Rohwer, *The Critical Convoy Battles of March 1943* (London: Ian Allen, 1977), p. 36.
81. Easton, *50 North*, p. 80.
82. Chris Howard Bailey, *The Battle of the Atlantic: The Corvettes and Their Crews: An Oral History* (Annapolis: Naval Institute Press, 1994), p. 63.
83. Leslie Bevan, quoted in Edward Smithies and Colin John Bruce, eds., *War at Sea, 1939–1945* (London: Constable, 1992), p. 63.
84. R. A. McCance, C.C. Ungley, J.W.L. Crosfil, and E. M. Widdowson, *The Hazards to Men in Ships Lost at Sea, 1940–1944*, Medical Research Council Special Report No. 291 (London: HMSO, 1956), p. 7.
85. Brown, *Atlantic Escorts*, p. 468.
86. Robert Harling, *Amateur Sailor* (London: Chatto & Windus, 1947), p. 252.
87. McCance et al., *The Hazards to Men in Ships Lost at Sea*, p. 10.
88. Quoted in Martin Middlebrook, *Convoy* (London: Allen & Unwin, 1976), p. 175.
89. Bailey, *Battle of the Atlantic*, pp. 78–81.

90. Simkin, "War from the Engine Room."
91. Bailey, *Battle of the Atlantic*, p. 66.
92. *Ibid.*, p. 68.
93. Schaeffer, *U-Boat 977*, p. 85.
94. Bailey, *Battle of the Atlantic*, p. 69.
95. Lamb, *The Corvette Navy*, pp. 113–16.
96. Pugsley, *Saints, Devils and Ordinary Seamen*, p. 41.
97. *Ibid.*; James B. Lamb, *On the Triangle Run* (Toronto; Macmillan of Canada, 1986), pp. 29–30.
98. Richard Dougherty, *Key to Victory: The Maiden-City in the Second World War* (Antrim: Greystone Books, 1995), p. 19.
99. Paul Kingsley, *The War Years, Derry 1939–45* (Londonderry: Derry Guildhall Press, 1992), p. 40.
100. Dougherty, *Key to Victory*, p. 54.
101. Kingsley, *War Years*, pp. 38–39.
102. Dougherty, *Key to Victory*, pp. 50–51.
103. *Ibid.*, p. 56.
104. Kingsley, *War Years*, p. 40.
105. Captain Donald Macintyre RN, quoted in Doughtery, *Key to Victory*, pp. 56–57.
106. Lamb, *On the Triangle Run*, pp. 27–28. On radar see David Zimmerman, *The Great Naval Battle of Ottawa* (Toronto: Univ. of Toronto Press, 1989), chap. 9 and *passim*.
107. Milner, *North Atlantic Run*, p. 213.
108. *Ibid.*, pp. 205–21.
109. MacIntyre, *U-Boat Killer*, p. 88.
110. Milner, *North Atlantic Run*, pp. 190–91.
111. Milner, "Squaring Some of the Corners," p. 133–35.
112. Herbert Werner, *Iron Coffins* (New York: Holt, Rinehart & Winston, 1969), pp. 136–39.
113. Quoted in Milner, *North Atlantic Run*, p. 212.
114. Werner, *Iron Coffins*, p. 128.
115. Quoted in Van Der Vat, *Atlantic Campaigns*, p. 337.
116. Padfield, *Dönitz*, p. 306.
117. Buchheim, *U-Boat War*, chap. 24.
118. Van Der Vat, *Atlantic Campaigns*, pp. 366–67.
119. John Terraine, *The U-Boat Wars* (New York: Putnam, 1989), Appendix D, p. 768.
120. Padfield, *Dönitz*, p. 283.
121. Mulligan, "German U-Boat Crews" p. 261.
122. Douglas Botting, *The U-Boats* (Alexandria, Va.: Time-Life Books, 1979), p. 164. For the more recent repetition of this theme, Philip Kaplan and Jack Currin, *Wolfpack: U-Boats at War, 1939–1945* (Annapolis: Naval Institute Press, 1997), dust jacket.
123. Michael Burleigh and Wolfgang Wipperman, *The Racial State: Germany, 1933–45* (Cambridge: Cambridge Univ. Press, 1991), pp. 201–40 and *passim*; Omer Bartov, *Hitler's Army: Soldiers, Nazis and War in the Third Reich* (New York: Oxford Univ. Press, 1992), pp. 108–9.
124. On the Hitler Youth, see H.W. Koch, *The Hitler Youth* (New York: Stein & Day, 1976).
125. Bartov, *Hitler's Army*, p. 174.
126. *Ibid.*, pp. 147–48.
127. Padfield, *Dönitz*, p. 347. After his appointment as commander in chief of the navy at the beginning of 1943, Dönitz was privy to decisions at the highest levels and a close confidant of Hitler's. He was present at the conference of government and party leaders in the fall of 1943 at which SS Reichsfuhrer Heinrich Himmler outlined the plans and policies for the "Final Solution," or extermination of Jews under German control. See Padfield, pp. 323–25, and Adelbert Reif, *Albert Speer* (Munich: Bernard and Graefe, 1978), pp. 395, 404.
128. Schaeffer, *U-Boat 977*, p. 146.
129. Bartov, *Hitler's Army*, pp. 124–25.
130. Padfield, *Dönitz*, p. 247. For similar views among Germans on the home front see Ian Kershaw, *Popular Opinion and Political Dissent in the Third Reich* (New York: Oxford Univ. Press, 1983).
131. Topp, "Manning and Training the U-Boat Fleet," in Howarth and Law, eds., *Battle of the Atlantic*, p. 217; "Addendum to Germany Intelligence Report: The German Navy: Organization and Function, November 1944," Intel. Div., Naval Staff, Admiralty, CB01818 (N) Public Record Office, ADM 239/467.
132. Werner, *Iron Coffins*, p. 125.
133. For a discussion of the Kusch case, see Vause, *Wolf*, pp. 188–90.

Chapter 13: "The Haves and the Have-Nots"

1. William T. Y'Blood, *Red Sun Setting: The Battle of the Philippine Sea* (Annapolis: Naval Institute Press, 1981), p. 33.
2. Frederick J. Bell, *Condition Red: Destroyer Action in the South Pacific* (New York: Longmans, Green, 1943), p. 169.
3. NAVPERS Annual Report, Navy and Marine Corps Personnel Statistics, 30 June 1959, copy in Naval Historical Center.
4. Millett, *Semper Fidelis*, pp. 345, 372.
5. James J. Fahey, *Pacific War Diary, 1942–1945: The Secret Diary of an American Sailor* (Boston: Houghton Mifflin, 1992), p. 153.
6. Charles Allen Smart, *The Long Watch* (Cleveland and New York: World, 1968), p. 18.
7. Frank Albert reminiscences, USS *Enterprise* Collection, Patriots Point Museum, Charleston, S.C.
8. Smart, *Long Watch*, p. 18.
9. Albert remiscences.
10. Bell, *Condition Red*, p. 169.
11. Emery J. Jernigan, *Tin Can Man* (Arlington, Va.: Vandermere Press, 1993), p. 51.
12. History of U.S. Naval Administration, "The Bureau of Naval Personnel: Officer Personnel Procurement," p. 1, copy in Naval Department Library.
13. "Reminiscences of Captain Slade Cutter," vol. 1, pp. 84–85, Naval Institute Oral History Collection.
14. "Wartime Sources of Navy Officers," p. 28, Bureau of Naval Personnel Information Bulletin, February 1945, copy in Navy Department Library.
15. "Officer Personnel Procurement," p. 40.
16. *Ibid.*, p. 23.
17. *Ibid.*, p. 26.
18. "Interview with Alfred Nisonoff, August 1944," p. 17, Rutgers Oral History Archive of World War II, Rutgers University.
19. Louis R. Harlan, *All at Sea, Coming of Age in World War II* (Urbana, IL: University of Illinois Press, 1996), p. 4.
20. *Ibid.*, p. 35.
21. Nisonoff interview, p. 16. Dr. Nisonoff further observes, however, that "Plattsburgh . . . may have trained only one group (ours). I have assumed they were fulfilling a need for warm, not necessarily well-trained, bodies. Other schools may have been better equipped." Nisonoff to author, 14 April 2000.
22. Harlan, *All at Sea*, pp. 8–9.
23. Smart, *Long Watch*, p. 5.
24. Charles Chester, *A Sailor's Odyssey*, privately published, p. 187.
25. Frank O. Hough, *The Island War* (Philadelphia: Lippincott, 1947), pp. 101–2.
26. Vice Admiral George C. Dyer, *The Amphibians Came to Conquer* (Washington, D.C.: Department of the Navy, 1969), vol. 1, p. 500.
27. M. Leon Cannick interview, p. 14, Rutgers Oral History Archive of World War II.
28. Daniel E. Barbey, *MacArthur's Amphibious Navy* (Annapolis: Naval Institute Press, 1969), p. 51.
29. "Reminiscences of Captain Slade Cutter," vol. 1, p. 86.
30. Clay Blair, Jr., *Silent Victory: The U.S. Submarine War Against Japan* (Philadelphia: Lippincott, 1975), p. 793.
31. Quoted in Dennis D. Nelson, "The Integration of the Negro into the U.S. Navy," p. 13, copy in Navy Department Library.
32. Walter White, *A Man Called White* (New York: Viking, 1948), p. 191.
33. Quoted in Morris J. MacGregor, *Integration of the Armed Forces, 1940–1965* (Washington, D.C.: Center of Military History, 1981), p. 60.
34. *Ibid.*, p. 63.
35. "History of U.S. Naval Administration: The Bureau of Naval Personnel," p. 54. Copy in Navy Department Library.
36. Nelson, "Integration of the Negro," p. 30.
37. *Ibid.*, p. 32.
38. MacGregor, *Integration of the Armed Forces*, pp. 73–75.
39. Lieutenant F. T. Greene USNR, "Mess Boy of Squadron X," in William H. Fetridge, ed., *The Second Navy Reader* (Indianapolis: Bobbs-Merrill, 1944), pp. 259–62.

40. Veterans who corresponded with or were interviewed by the author sometimes mentioned these rumors in response to questions about behavior in combat. Instances of panic or irrational behavior by whites were also mentioned but always in terms of *individuals*, while black sailors as a group were frequently mentioned as prone to panic.
41. MacGregor, *Integration of the Armed Forces*, p. 84.
42. Mary Pat Kelly, *Proudly We Served: The Men of the USS "Mason"* (Annapolis: Naval Institute Press, 1995), p. 103.
43. *Ibid.*, p. 1.
44. *Ibid.*, pp. 114–15. Although the convoy commodore recommended a special letter of commendation for the *Mason*, none was awarded.
45. *Ibid.*, p. 151.
46. *Ibid.*
47. Townsend Hoopes and Douglas Brinkley, *Driven Patriot: The Life and Times of James Forrestal* (New York: Knopf, 1992), pp. 180–82.
48. Information on the Guam incident is taken from Record of Proceedings of a Court of Inquiry, Naval Supply Depot Guam to Enquire into the Unlawful Assembly and Riot . . . At Naval Supply Depot, 30 Dec 44, copy in Naval Historical Center.
49. Mr. Allan G. LeBaron letter to author, February 25, 1985.
50. *Ibid.*
51. Record of Proceedings. White's autobiography does not mention this incident.
52. *Ibid.*
53. MacGregor, *Integration of the Armed Forces*, p. 98.
54. "Reminiscences of Captain Hancock," No. 1, p. 49.
55. Quoted in Wells, *Royal Navy*, p. 216.
56. Doherty, *Key to Victory*, p. 30.
57. "Reminiscences of Captain Hancock," No. 1, p. 52.
58. Reynolds, *John H. Towers*, p. 380.
59. *Ibid.*, p. 381.
60. Joy Bright Hancock, *Lady in the Navy: Personal Reminiscences* (Annapolis: Naval Institute Press, 1972), p. 152.
61. Susan H. Godson, "The Waves in World War II," *Naval Institute Proceedings* 107, December 1981, p. 49.
62. Elizabeth Allen Butler, *Navy Waves* (Charlottesville, Va.: Wayside Press, 1988), p. 31.
63. Marie Bennett Alsmeyer, *Old Waves Tales: Navy Women: Memoirs of World War II* (Conway, Alaska: HAMBA Books, 1982), p. 8.
64. "Reminiscences of Captain Jean Palmer," No. 1 p. 37, Naval Institute Oral History Collection.
65. Butler, *Navy Waves*, p. 90.
66. *Ibid.*, p. 91.
67. *Ibid.*
68. "Reminiscences of Captain Palmer," No. 1, p. 37.
69. Hancock, *Lady in the Navy*, pp. 139–47.
70. *Ibid.*, p. 141.
71. "Reminiscences of Captain Hancock," No. 1, p. 54.
72. Portions of this account of the Battle of the Philippine Sea have been adapted from the author's lengthier discussion in *Eagle Against the Sun*.
73. Norman Friedman, *U.S. Aircraft Carriers: An Illustrated Design History* (Annapolis: Naval Institute Press, 1983), pp. 133–34; Reynolds, *Fast Carriers*, pp. 53–56.
74. The view of many writers—including this author in an earlier work—that the Hellcat's design was a result of secrets learned from a captured Zero is mainly myth. As noted earlier, the Hellcat was already in an advanced stage of development by the time of Pearl Harbor. See Lundstrom, *First Team*, pp. 533–36.
75. John Monsarrat, *Angel on the Yardarm: The Beginning of Fleet Air Defense and the Kamikaze Threat* (Annapolis: Naval Institute Press, 1991), pp. 45–46.
76. Blair, *Silent Victory*, p. 624.
77. Sakai Saburo interview in Haruko Taya Cook and Theodore F. Cook, *Japan at War: An Oral History* (New York: New Press, 1992), p. 138.
78. Okumiya and Hirokoshi, *Zero*, pp. 301, 306.
79. *Ibid.*, pp. 311–12.
80. Sakai interview, pp. 138–39.

81. Okumiya and Hirokoshi, *Zero*, pp. 236–38.
82. "The A-GO Operation 1944," Japanese Monograph No. 60, p. 18, copy in U.S. Army Center of Military History.
83. Okumiya and Hirokoshi, *Zero*, pp. 232–33; Paul Dull, *A Battle History of the Imperial Japanese Navy* (Annapolis: Naval Institute Press, 1978), pp. 317–19.
84. Y'Blood, *Red Sun Setting*, pp. 86–91.
85. *Ibid.*, pp. 95–99.
86. Lt. J. Periam Danton, "The Battle of the Philippine Sea," *Naval Institute Proceedings* 71, (September 1945), p. 1025.
87. "Reminiscences of Vice Admiral Fitzhugh Lee," Naval Institute Oral History Collection.
88. CTF 58 to CINCFLT, "Operations in Support of the Capture of the Marianas," TF58 serial 003858, 11 Sept 44, Naval Historical Center.
89. Reynolds, *Fast Carriers*, pp. 195–96.
90. *Ibid.*; Samuel Eliot Morison, *New Guinea and the Marianas* (Boston: Little, Brown, 1956), pp. 290–92; "Reminiscences of Admiral Arleigh Burke," Part 4, pp. 320–21, Naval Institute Oral History Collection.
91. Y'Blood, *Red Sun Setting*, p. 151.
92. "Reminiscences of Rear Admiral James D. Ramage," Part 2, p. 31, Naval Institute Oral History Collection.
93. *Ibid.*
94. Reynolds, *Fast Carriers*, pp. 197–98.
95. Morison, *New Guinea and the Marianas*, p. 299.
96. Y'Blood, *Red Sun Setting*, p. 191.
97. *Ibid.*
98. COM Task Force 58, "Operations in the Marianas."
99. "Reminiscences of Admiral Burke," Part 4, p. 326.
100. For a discussion of this controversy, see Morison, *New Guinea and the Marianas*, pp. 315–16; E. B. Potter, *Nimitz* (Annapolis: Naval Institute Press, 1976), pp. 302–5; Reynolds, *Fast Carriers*, pp. 165–66, 209–10; Thomas E. Buell, *The Quiet Warrior: Raymond E. Spruance* (Boston: Little, Brown, 1974), pp. 270–72 and *passim*; and Y'Blood, *Red Sun Setting*, pp. 204–11.
101. Blair, *Silent Victory*, p. 792.
102. Hashimoto Mochitsura, *Sunk* (New York: Holt, 1954), pp. 50, 156–57; Evans and Peattie, *Kaigun*, pp. 214–15. A general discussion of Japanese submarines and naval strategy can be found in Evans and Peattie, *Kaigun*, pp. 213–19, 428–34; and in Carl Boyd and Akimiko Yoshida, *The Japanese Submarine Force and World War II* (Annapolis: Naval Institute Press, 1995), pp. 3–7.
103. Sarandis Papadopoulos, "Feeding the Sharks: The Logistics of Undersea Warfare, 1935–1945," dissertation, pp. 293–98, George Washington Univ., 1999.
104. Quoted in *ibid.*, pp. 291, 294.
105. "Outline and Discussion of Methods Used in Selecting Enlisted Candidates for Submarine Training," Medical Research Report No. 34, 1943, cited in Papadopoulos, "Feeding the Sharks," p. 287.
106. Orita Zenji, *Japanese I-Boat Captain*, (Carroga Park, Calif.: Major Books, 1976), p. 21.
107. Paul R. Schratz, *Submarine Commander* (Lexington: University Press of Kentucky, 1988), p. 107.
108. *Ibid.*; Blair, *Silent Victory*, p. 44.
109. Hashimoto, *Sunk*, p. 157.
110. Mark R. Peattie, "Forecasting a Pacific War, 1912–1933," in James W. White, ed., *The Ambivalence of Nationalism: Modern Japan between East and West* (Lanham, Md.: University Press of America, 1990), pp. 124–25.
111. Captain C. S. Freeman to Office of Naval Intelligence, sub Japanese Morale, 31 Jan 27, File 18603, Records of the Office of Naval Intelligence, Record Group 38; Endorsement by CINC U.S. to ONI, 4 Feb 27, same file.
112. W. J. Sebald, Memo for Office of Naval Intelligence, sub Employment of German Experts in Japan, 4 Nov 28. File 11942, E-7-0, Records of the Office of Naval Intelligence.
113. "Reminiscences of Hanson W. Baldwin," p. 334, Naval Institute Oral History Collection.
114. Blair, *Silent Victory*, pp. 410–11.
115. *Ibid.*, pp. 87–89, 93, 176–78, 523.
116. James F. Calvert, *Silent Running: My Years in a World War II Attack Submarine* (New York: Wiley, 1995), pp. 53, 55.

117. Wilfred J. Holmes, *Undersea Victory* (New York: Doubleday, 1966), pp. 47–48; Blair, *Silent Victory*, pp. 45–46; Schratz, *Submarine Commander*, p. 72.
118. Blair, *Silent Victory*, p. 668.
119. Saburo Ienaga, *The Pacific War: World War II and the Japanese, 1931–45* (New York: Random House, 1978), p. 140.
120. Holmes, *Undersea Victory*, p. 192.
121. Hashimoto, *Sunk*, pp. 158–60.
122. Blair, *Silent Victory*, p. 792.
123. Absushi Oi, "Why Japan's Anti-Submarine Warfare Failed," *Naval Institute Proceedings* 78 (June 1952), pp. 588, 593–97.
124. On this point see Evans and Peattie, *Kaiguna*, pp. 432–33, 496–97.
125. Blair, *Silent Victory*, pp. 851–53.

Chapter 14: "My Grave Shall Be the Sea"

1. Portions of the discussion of the Battle of Leyte Gulf that follows have been adapted from the author's more comprehensive analysis in *Eagle Against the Sun*.
2. Samuel Eliot Morison, *Leyte: June 1944–January 1945* (Boston: Little, Brown, 1953), p. 57.
3. Watanabe, *Senkan Musashi no Saigo*, p. 205.
4. *Ibid.*, p. 249.
5. Morison, *Leyte*, p. 186.
6. "Reminiscences of Admiral Burke," Part 4, p. 330.
7. *Ibid.*, pp. 329–30.
8. Morison, *Leyte*, p. 58.
9. "Reminiscences of Admiral Thomas C. Kinkaid," Part 3, p. 317, Naval Institute Oral History Collection.
10. Morison, *Leyte*, p. 58.
11. "Special Notes by Admiral Thomas C. Kinkaid," in Hanson W. Baldwin, *Battles Lost and Won* (New York: Harper & Row, 1966), p. 476.
12. "Reminiscences of Admiral Kinkaid," Part 3, p. 318.
13. James A. Field, *The Japanese at Leyte Gulf* (Princeton, N.J.: Princeton University Press, 1947), pp. 98–100.
14. William T. Y'Blood, *The Little Giants: U.S. Escort Carriers Against Japan* (Annapolis: Naval Institute Press, 1987), p. 156.
15. Morison, *Leyte*, p. 273.
16. Y'Blood, *Little Giants*, p. 189.
17. Morison, *Leyte*, p. 288.
18. *Ibid.*, p. 298; Field, *Japanese at Leyte*, pp. 121–25.
19. Dennis Warner and Peggy Warner with Sadao Seno, *The Sacred Warriors: Japan's Suicide Legions* (New York: Van Nostrand, 1982), pp. 45–48, 106–8; Morison, *Leyte*, pp. 300–2.
20. William M. McBride, ed., *Good Night Officially: The Pacific War Letters of a Destroyer Sailor* (Boulder, Colo: Westview Press, 1994), p. 10.
21. Captain Rikihei Inoguchi and Commander Tadashi Nakajima, *The Divine Wind: Japan's Kamikaze Force in World War II* (Annapolis: Naval Institute Press, 1994), pp. 91–92; Center for Naval Analysis, "Defense Against Kamikaze Attacks in World War II and Its Relevance to Anti-Ship Missile Defense," Operations Evaluation Group Study 741, Vol. I Nov 1970, pp. 62–63.
22. Samuel Eliot Morison, *The Liberation of the Philippines* (Boston: Little, Brown, 1959), p. 98.
23. *Ibid.*, pp. 106–7, 132–52.
24. Bernard R. Yohe, "Life Aboard Ship: USS *Mustin* DD-413," unpublished diary lent by Mr. Al Tumlinson, Hornet-Mustin Assoc. (The "Limey cruiser" was HMS *Australia*.)
25. Morison, *Liberation of the Philippines*, p. 53.
26. Warner and Warner, *Sacred Warriors*, pp. 243–44.
27. Ivan Morris, *The Nobility of Failure: Tragic Heroes in the History of Japan* (New York: Holt-Rinehart, 1975), pp. 288–89.
28. Inoguchi and Tadashi, *Divine Wind*, p. 95.
29. Warner and Warner, *Sacred Warriors*, p. 217.

30. Quoted in Inoguchi and Tadashi, *Divine Wind*, pp. 198–99.
31. *Ibid.*, p. 204.
32. Warner and Warner, *Sacred Warriors*, p. 231.
33. Inoguchi and Tadashi, *Divine Wind*, p. 158.
34. Warner and Warner, *Sacred Warriors*, p. 217.
35. Quoted in James and William Belote, *Typhoon of Steel: The Battle for Okinawa* (New York: Harper & Row, 1970), p. 74.
36. CINCFLT Secret Information Bulletin No. 24, "Battle Experience: Radar Pickets and Methods of Combatting Suicide Attacks," pp. 81-1 to 81-3, copy in Navy Department Library; R. L. Wehrmeister, "Divine Wind over Okinawa," *Naval Institute Proceedings* 83, June 1957.
37. Samuel Eliot Morison, *Victory in the Pacific* (Boston: Little, Brown, 1975), pp. 182–97.
38. Belote and Belote, *Typhoon of Steel*, pp. 102–3; Morison, *Victory in the Pacific*, pp. 192–93.
39. Paul Thurman, *Picket Ships at Okinawa* (New York: Carlton Press, 1996), pp. 38–39.
40. Morison, *Victory in the Pacific*, p. 185.
41. On the racial rhetoric of both Japanese and Americans in World War II, see John Dower, *War Without Mercy* (New York: Random House, 1989).
42. Quoted in Warner and Warner, *Sacred Warriors*, p. 145.
43. Rear Admiral F. Julian Becton with Joseph Morsehauser III, *The Ship That Would Not Die* (Englewood Cliffs, N.J.: Prentice-Hall, 1980), p. 171.
44. Ron Surels, *DD 522: Diary of a Destroyer* (Plymouth, N.H.: Valley Graphics, 1996), p. 97.
45. Becton, *Ship That Would Not Die*, p. 72.
46. Quoted in Warner and Warner, *Sacred Warriors*, p. 145.
47. Becton, *Ship That Would Not Die*, p. 160.
48. Surels, *DD 522*, p. 82.
49. Jernigan, *Tin Can Man*, p. 93.
50. MacBride, *Good Night Officially*, p. 262.
51. Surels, *DD 522*, p. 83.
52. *Ibid.*, p. 101.
53. Morison, *Victory in the Pacific*, p. 256; "Battle Experience: Radar Pickets," pp. 81–86.
54. Surels, *DD 522*, p. 131.
55. Commander J. Davis Scott, "No Hiding Place—Off-Okinawa," *Naval Institute Proceedings* 83, November 1957, p. 1211.
56. Jernigan, *Tin Can Man*, pp. 121–22.
57. Surels, *DD 522*, p. 131.
58. Belote and Belote, *Typhoon of Steel*, pp. 233–36; Breton, *Ship That Would Not Die*, pp. 207–18.
59. "Battle Experience: Radar Pickets,"; Morison, *Victory in the Pacific*, p. 258.
60. This section is based in part upon David Atkinson, "And Strong Ships All: Damage Control in the Pacific War," paper prepared for my research seminar, December 1996.
61. *Ibid.*
62. Morison, *Victory in the Pacific*, pp. 98–99. A brief description of a short course at one of these schools is in Fahey, *Pacific War Diary*, p. 115.
63. "Battle Experience: Radar Pickets," p. 8-1-17.
64. Private communication to the author by an officer who served in USS *New Mexico*.
65. Hanson W. Baldwin, *Battles Lost and Won* (New York: Harper & Row, 1966), p. 377.
66. Frank Albert Reminiscences, USS *Enterprise* Collection.
67. Warner and Warner, *Sacred Warriors*, p. 320.
68. "Defense Against Kamikaze Attacks in World War II," vol. 1, pp. 60–64.
69. Belote and Belote, *Typhoon of Steel*, p. 147.
70. Surels, *DD 522*, p. 82.

Chapter 15: "The Really Battle-Worthy Capital Ship"

1. Eric J. Grove, *Vanguard to Trident: British Naval Policy Since World War Two* (Annapolis: Naval Institute Press, 1987), p. 137.
2. Richard P. Hallion, *The Naval Air War in Korea* (Baltimore: Nautical and Aviation Publishing, 1986), p. 35.

3. Malcolm W. Cagle and Frank A. Manson, *The Sea War in Korea* (Annapolis: Naval Institute Press, 1957), pp. 37–38.

4. Hallion, *Naval Air War in Korea*, p. 36.

5. Eugene Burdick, "The United States Navy," *Holiday* 24, (October 1958), p. 101.

6. A. P. de Seversky, *Victory Through Air Power* (New York: Simon & Schuster, 1947), p. 182.

7. Love, *History of the U.S. Navy*, vol. 2, p. 291.

8. "Reminiscences of Admiral Burke," Part 7, p. 43.

9. Walter Millis, ed., *The Forrestal Diaries* (New York: Viking, 1951), p. 196.

10. The foregoing summary is based on Michael Palmer, *Origins of the Maritime Strategy: American Naval Strategy in the First Post-War Decade* (Washington, D.C.: Naval Historical Center, 1988) and Steven T. Ross, *American War Plans, 1945–50* (New York: Garland, 1955).

11. Jan Breemer, *Soviet Submarines: Design Development and Tactics* (Coulsden, Surrey: Jane's, 1989), p. 78; Norman Polmar and Jurrin Noot, *Submarines of the Russian and Soviet Navies, 1718–1990* (Annapolis: Naval Institute Press, 1991), pp. 139–46.

12. Breemer, *Soviet Submarines*, p. 81.

13. On Sherman's concept see Palmer, *Origins of the Maritime Strategy*.

14. Millis, *Forrestal Diaries*, p. 226.

15. The literature on the "revolt of the admirals" is extensive. The discussion above is based upon Paul Y. Hammond, "Super Carriers and B-36 Bombers," in Harold Stein, ed., *American Civil-Military Decisions: A Casebook of Studies* (Birmingham: Univ. of Alabama Press, 1963); Jeffrey G. Barlow, *The Revolt of the Admirals: The Fight for Naval Aviation, 1945–50* (Washington, D.C.: Naval Historical Center, 1994); and Warren A. Trest, "View from the Gallery: Laying to Rest the Admirals' Revolt of 1949," *Air Power History* 42 (Spring 1995).

16. Michael T. Isenberg, *Shield of the Republic: The U.S. Navy in an Era of Cold War and Violent Peace*, vol. 1, *1945–1962* (New York: St. Martin's, 1993), p. 153.

17. Clark G. Reynolds, "Forrest Percival Sherman," in Robert W. Love, ed., *The Chiefs of Naval Operations* (Annapolis: Naval Institute Press, 1980), pp. 215–17.

18. "Reminiscences of Admiral Thach," Part 6, pp. 527–28.

19. Max Miller, *I'm Sure We've Met Before: The Navy in Korea* (New York: Dutton, 1951), p. 99.

20. CINCPACFLT, Korean War Interim Evaluation, No. 2, September 1951, vol. 2, p. 422, copy in Naval Historical Center.

21. Richard P. Hallion, *The Naval Air War in Korea* (Baltimore: Nautical and Aviation Press, 1986), p. 43 and *passim*.

22. *Ibid.*, p. 51.

23. Isenberg, *Shield of the Republic*, p. 224.

24. *Ibid.*, p. 70.

25. Charles F. Cole, *Korea Remembered: Enough of a War* (Las Cruces, N.M.: Yucca Tree Press, 1995), p. 22; Isenberg, *Shield of the Republic*, p. 234.

26. Jack Sauter, *Sailors in the Sky: Memoirs of a Navy Aircrewman in the Korean War* (Jefferson, N.C.: McFarland, 1975), p. 153.

27. *Ibid.*, p. 152.

28. Captain E. T. Wooldridge, USN (Ret.), ed., *Into the Jet Age: Conflict and Change in Naval Aviation, 1945–1975: An Oral History* (Annapolis: Naval Institute Press, 1995), p. xix.

29. "Reminiscences of Admiral Roy L. Johnson," Part 2, p. 117, Naval Institute History Collection.

30. Woolridge, *Into the Jet Age*, pp. xviii–xix.

31. Lieutenant Commander Bert G. Homan USN (Ret.), *A Twentieth Century Life Story* (privately published), p. 124.

32. Captain Gerald G. O'Rourke in Wooldridge, *Into the Jet Age*, p. 42.

33. Captain Theron B. Taylor USN (Ret.) letter to author, October 12, 1998.

34. William Crouse letter to author, September 30, 1998.

35. "Reminiscences of Vice Admiral Miller," Part 2, pp. 211–12. This incident is also described in William Crouse letter to author, September 30, 1998.

36. Quoted in Martin Russ, *Breakout: The Chosin Reservoir Campaign, Korea 1950* (New York: Fromm International, 1999), p. 327.

37. James A. Field, Jr., *History of United States Naval Operations: Korea* (Washington, D.C.: GPO, 1962), pp. 269–73.

38. Atkinson, "Navy Pilot Stories," p. 22, unpublished manuscript, courtesy Mr. Atkinson.

39. James A. Van Fleet, *Rail Transport and the Winning of Wars*, p. 35, cited in Hallion, *Naval Air War in Korea*, p. 98.

40. "Reminscences of Vice Admiral Miller," No. 2, p. 197.
41. "Reminiscences of Vice Admiral Johnson," Part 2, p. 129.
42. "Reminiscences of Admiral Thach," Part 7, p. 585.
43. Cole, *Korea Remembered*, p. 73; Allan G. Le Baron, *Black Shoe, Brown Shoe: A White Hat's Memories of Life Aboard an Aircraft Carrier, Korea, 1950–51* (Moulton, Ala.: privately published, 1996), p. 89.
44. Captain Theron B. Taylor letter to author, October 12, 1998.
45. *Ibid.*
46. Le Baron, *Black Shoe, Brown Shoe*, p. 88.
47. *Ibid.*
48. Crouse letter, September 30, 1998.
49. Sauter, *Sailors in the Sky*, p. 151.
50. Crouse letter, September 30, 1998; Owen W. Dykema, *Letters from the Bird Barge* (Roseburg, Or.: Dykema, 1997), pp. 88–89.
51. Sauter, *Sailors in the Sky*, p. 198.
52. Cole, *Korea Remembered*, p. 212.
53. Atkinson, "Navy Pilot Stories," p. 6.
54. Quoted in Lawrence Suid, *Sailing on the Silver Screen: Hollywood and the U.S. Navy* (Annapolis: Naval Institute Press, 1996), p. 104.
55. Sauter, *Sailors in the Sky*, p. 223.
56. "Reminiscences of Vice Admiral Charles L. Melson," Naval Institute Oral History Collection, Part 2, pp. 181–82.
57. Atkinson, "Navy Pilot Stories," p. 6.
58. Richard Compton-Hall, *Submarine Versus Submarine: The Tactics and Technology of Underwater Confrontation* (New York: Orion Books, 1988), p. 19; Command History, Sub Development Group TWELVE, 1949–1977, p. 1., copy in Naval Historical Center; "The Evolution of Sub-DevGroup Two," *Submarine Review*, Vol. I, No. 1, April 1983), pp. 4–7.
59. Jan Breemer, *Soviet Submarines: Design Development and Tactics* (London: Janis Information Group, 1989), pp. 101–14.
60. Vice Admiral George P. Steele, "A Fleet to Match Our Real Needs," *Washington Post*, May 16, 1976.
61. Blair, *Silent Victory*, vol 2, pp. 851–53.
62. "Reminiscences of Admiral Charles K. Duncan," Part 9, p. 787, Naval Institute Oral History Collection.
63. *Ibid.*
64. Captain Tom B. Thamm, "The Quiet Crisis in the Silent Service," *U.S. Naval Institute Proceedings*, August 1971, p. 52.
65. On Rickover, see Richard Hewlett and Francis Duncan, *Nuclear Navy, 1946–62* (Chicago: University of Chicago Press, 1974); Francis Duncan, *Rickover and the Nuclear Navy: The Discipline of Technology* (Annapolis: Naval Institute Press, 1990); Norman Polmar and Thomas B. Allen, *Rickover: Controversy and Genius* (New York: Touchstone, 1982); Harold C. Hamond, "The Flip Side of Rickover," *Naval Institute Proceedings* 115 (July 1989), pp. 42–47; and Harvey Sapolsky, "Technological Innovators: Raborn and Rickover," in Arnold R. Shapack, ed., *Naval History Symposium* (Annapolis: U.S. Naval Academy, 1973).
66. Polmar and Allen, *Rickover*, pp. 640–41.
67. Elmo R. Zumwalt, Jr., *On Watch: A Memoir* (New York: Quadrangle, 1976), p. 97.
68. *Ibid.*, p. 187.
69. "Reminiscences of Vice Admiral William R. Smedburg," Part 5, p. 406, Naval Institute Oral History Collection.
70. *Ibid.*
71. Polmar and Allen, *Rickover*, p. 304.
72. Quoted in Ensign Daniel N. Edelstein, "Worlds Apart?" *Naval Institute Proceedings*.
73. "Reminiscences of Admiral Duncan," Part 9, p. 788.
74. Lieutenant James D. Jones USN, "Some Thoughts from an Unrepentant Nuc," *Naval Institute Proceedings*, 103, November 1977, p. 87.
75. Lieutenant Ralph E. Chatham USN, "Leadership and Nuclear Power," *Naval Institute Proceedings*, 104 (July 1978), p. 78.
76. Thamm, "Quiet Crisis in the Silent Service," p. 52.
77. Quoted in Chatham, "Leadership and Nuclear Power," p. 81.

78. "Sub Danger: Too Much Work, Too Little Training," *Chicago Tribune*, January 8, 1991.
79. "Reminiscences of Vice Admiral Duncan," Part 9, pp. 810–11.
80. Thamm, "Quiet Crisis in the Silent Service," p. 50.
81. Chatham, "Leadership and Nuclear Power," p. 79.
82. Polmar and Allan, *Rickover*, pp. 336–37.
83. Frank A. Andrews, "Submarine Against Submarine," *Naval Review, 1966*, p. 43.
84. "Evolution of SubDevGroup Two," p. 7; Captain Wyman H. Packard USN (Ret.), *A Century of U.S. Naval Intelligence* (Washington, D.C.: Dept. of the Navy, 1996), p. 123; Reminiscences of Admiral Harry D. Train II, Part 1, p. 69, Naval Institute Oral History Collection.
85. "Evolution of SubDevGroup Two," p. 7. The sinking and rescue of most of the crew of *Cochino* is described in Sherry Sontag and Christopher Drew, *Blind Man's Bluff: The Untold Story of American Submarine Espionage* (New York: Public Affairs, 1998), pp. 13–24.
86. Tom Clancy, *The Hunt for Red October.*
87. "Evolution of SubDevGroup Two," p. 9.
88. Joel S. Wit, "Advances in Anti-Submarine Warfare," *Scientific American* 244 (February 1981), pp. 31–41.
89. On Arctic operations, see Waldo K. Lyon, "Submarine Combat in the Ice," *Naval Institute Proceedings*, 118, February 1992, pp. 35–39; William M. Leary, *Under Ice: Waldo J. Lyon and the Development of the Arctic Submarine* (College Station: Texas A&M Press, 1999).
90. "For U.S. and Soviets: An Intricate Undersea Minuet," *Chicago Tribune*, January 9, 1991, p. 1.
91. *Ibid.*, p. 8.
92. Sontag and Drew, *Blind Man's Bluff*, pp. 279–84; Compton-Hall, *Sub vs. Sub*, pp. 11–12.
93. "A Risky Game of Cloak and Dagger Under the Sea," *Chicago Tribune* January 7, 1991, p. 8.
94. "Sub Danger," *Chicago Tribune*, January 8, 1991, p. 8.
95. Lieutenant Commander Duncan MacIvor (MC) USN, "Trident Submarine Medicine: A Primer for Medical Officers and Corpsmen Bound for New Construction Submarines," rough draft of Naval Undersea Medical Institute thesis, 1983, p. 50, courtesy Dr. MacIvor.
96. Dr. Duncan MacIvor conversation with author, November 17, 1999.
97. MacIvor, "Trident Submarine Medicine," p. 53.
98. Tom Clancy, *Submarine: A Guided Tour inside a Nuclear Warship* (New York: Berkley Books, 1993), pp. 102, 105, 107; Thomas B. Allen and Norman Polmar, "Silent Chase," *New York Times Magazine*, January 1, 1984, p. 15.
99. MacIvor, "Trident Submarine Medicine," pp. 52–53.
100. The foregoing account is based on information in questionnaires completed by submarine wives for the Smithsonian Museum of American History exhibition "Fast Attacks and Boomers: Submarines in the Cold War." I am grateful to Dr. Bartin J. Hacker, Dr. Margaret J. Vining, and their colleagues at the Museum of American History for allowing me to examine this material.
101. MacIvor, "Trident Submarine Medicine," footnotes 20, 22.
102. Allen and Polmar, "Silent Chase," p. 15.
103. "Sub Danger," *Chicago Tribune*, January 8, 1991, p. 9; "Crew's Silent Menace: The Air They Breathe," *Chicago Tribune*, January 10, 1991, p. 20.
104. Quoted in Malcolm Muir, Jr., *Black Shoes and Blue Water: Surface Warfare in the U.S. Navy, 1945–1975* (Washington, D.C.: Naval Historical Center, 1996), p. 62.
105. *Ibid.*, p. 75.
106. Admiral David L. McDonald, "Carrier Employment Since 1950," *Naval Institute Proceedings* 90 (November 1960), pp. 31–33.
107. James F. Downs, "Naval Personnel Organization: A Cultural Historical Approach," p. 105, Development Research Associates, 1982, copy in Center for Naval Analysis Library.
108. Isenberg, *Shield of the Republic*, p. 294.
109. Muir, *Black Shoes*, p. 9.
110. *Ibid.*, p. 71.
111. *Ibid.*, p. 117.
112. Isenberg, *Shield of the Republic*, p. 459.
113. *Ibid.*, p. 465.
114. Commander Russell S. Crenshaw, "Why We are Losing Our Junior Officers," *Naval Institute Proceedings* 83 (February 1957), pp. 128–29.
115. *Ibid.*, pp. 129–30.

116. Milton Leitenberg, "Why Are They Quitting?" *Saturday Evening Post* v 228, p. 70.
117. *Ibid.*
118. Chief Quartermaster W. J. Miller, "Reenlistment: A Key Factor in A Strong Navy" *Naval Institute Proceedings* 80 (April 1954), p. 403.
119. Isenberg, *Shield of the Republic*, p. 493.
120. Downs, "Naval Personnel Organization," pp. 22, 85, 99, 116; Isenberg, *Shield of the Republic*, p. 493.
121. James F. Downs, "Environment, Communication and Status Change Aboard an American Aircraft Carrier," *Human Organization*, vol. 17, fall 1958, pp. 15–17.
122. Downs, "Naval Personnel Organization."
123. *Ibid.*, p. 164.
124. Leitenberg, "Why Are They Quitting?" p. 70.
125. *Ibid.*
126. Lieutenant (Junior Grade) W. J. Ashton, "Jet Age Carrier," *Naval Institute Proceedings* 82 (May 1956), p. 52.
127. "Reminiscences of Admiral Charles K. Duncan," Part 10, pp. 918–19.
128. CV-47 letter, serial 1108, 1 May 1951: COM Seventh Flt Records; CV-47/16–13 20/ EMS/ds, Naval Historical Center.
129. Downs, "Environment . . .," p. 16.
130. Commander R. L. Schreadley USN (Ret.), *From the Rivers to the Sea: The United States Navy in Vietnam* (Annapolis: Naval Institute Press, 1992), p. 47; Baer, *One Hundred Years of Seapower*, p. 360.
131. Harvey M. Sapolsky, *The Polaris System Development: Bureaucratic and Programmatic Success in Government* (Cambridge, Mass.: Harvard Univ. Press, 1972), p. 172 and *passim.*
132. David Alan Rosenberg, "Arleigh Albert Burke," in Love et al., *The Chiefs of Naval Operations*, p. 310.

Chapter 16: "Strictly a Secondary and Collateral Task"

1. The most thorough account of the Tonkin Gulf Incident is Edwin E. Moise, *Tonkin Gulf and the Escalation of the Vietnam War* (Chapel Hill: Univ. of North Carolina Press, 1996).
2. For an insightful analysis see Clarence Wunderlin, Jr., "Paradox of Power: Infiltration, Coastal Surveillance and the U.S. Navy in Vietnam, 1965–68," *Journal of Military History* 53 (July 1989), pp. 280–86.
3. Rene J. Francillon, *Tonkin Gulf Yacht Club: U.S. Carrier Operations Off Vietnam* (Annapolis: Naval Institute Press, 1988), p. 33; Schreadley, *From the Rivers to the Sea*, p. 122. The most complete accounts of carrier operations in the Vietnam War are Edward J. Marolda, *Carrier Operations* (New York: Bantam Books, 1987); and Francillon.
4. For a detailed discussion of naval aircraft employed in the Vietnam War see Francillon, *Tonkin Gulf Yacht Club*, appendix 2, pp. 172–208.
5. *The Senator Gravel Edition of the Pentagon Papers* (Boston: Beacon Press, 1972), vol. 4, pp. 1–232.
6. Qiang Zhai, "Beijing and the Vietnam Conflict, 1964–65: New Chinese Evidence," *Cold War International History Project Bulletin*, Winter 1995/96, pp. 234–35. See also Chen Jian, "China's Involvement in the Vietnam War 1964–69," *China Quarterly* 142 (June 1995), pp. 357–87.
7. Qiang Zhai, "Beijing and the Vietnam Conflict," p. 236.
8. Ilya V. Gaiduk, "The Vietnam War and Soviet-American Relations, 1964–73: New Russian Evidence," *Cold War International History Project Bulletin*, Winter 1995/96, p. 233.
9. Commander John B. Nichols and Barrett Tillman, *On Yankee Station: The Naval Air War over Vietnam* (Annapolis: Naval Institute Press, 1987), p. 45.
10. Marolda, *Carrier Operations*, pp. 63–65.
11. Quoted in John D. Sherwood, *Fast Movers* (New York: Free Press, 1999), p. 244. I am grateful to Dr. Sherwood for allowing me to see the manuscript version of this book. All page references are to the manuscript.
12. Robert K. Wilcox, *Scream of Eagles: The Creation of Top Gun and the U.S. Air Victory in Viet-

nam (New York: Wiley, 1990), pp. 100–6; "Report of the Air to Air Missile System Capability Review, July–November 1969, Naval Air Systems Command, January 1969, Part 4, pp. 28–29 and *passim*.

13. *Ibid.*; Wilcox, *Scream of Eagles*, pp. 96, 107.
14. Quoted in Wilcox, *Scream of Eagles*, p. 108.
15. *Ibid.*, p. 288–90.
16. Edward J. Marolda, *By Sea, Air and Land: An Illustrated History of the U.S. Navy and the War in Southeast Asia* (Washington, D.C.: Naval Historical Center, 1994), p. 82.
17. Grant, *Over the Beach*, p. 190.
18. Marolda, *By Sea, Air and Land*, pp. 79–80.
19. Jeffrey L. Levinson, *Alpha Strike Vietnam: The Navy's Air War, 1964–73* (Novato, Calif.: Presidio, 1989), p. 66.
20. Levinson, *Alpha Strike*, p. 74.
21. "Reminiscences of Vice Admiral Kent E. Lee," p. 136, Naval Institute Oral History Collection.
22. Marolda, *Carrier Operations*, pp. 88–89, 101–04.
23. "Reminiscences of Admiral Kent E. Lee," pp. 196–205.
24. Sherwood, *Fast Movers*, p. 66.
25. Levinson, *Alpha Strike*, p. 176; Malcolm W. Cagle, "Task Force 177 in Action off Vietnam," *Naval Institute Proceedings* 98 (May 1972), p. 79.
26. Wilcox, *Scream of Eagles*, p. 93.
27. Sherwood, *Fast Movers*, p. 268.
28. "Reminiscences of Admiral John J. Hyland," p. 187, Naval Institute Oral History Collection.
29. Levinson, *Alpha Strike*, p. 63.
30. *Ibid.*, p. 136.
31. Wilcox, *Scream of Eagles*, p. 92.
32. *Gravel Edition*, vol 4, p. 111; Mark Clodfelter, *The Limits of Air Power* (New York: Free Press, 1989), pp. 93–99.
33. *Gravel Edition*, vol. 4, p. 39.
34. Grant, *Over the Beach*, pp. 53, 64, 199; Sherwood, *Fast Movers*, p. 250.
35. Levinson, *Alpha Strike*, p. 152.
36. Sherwood, *Fast Movers*, p. 115.
37. "Reminiscences of Admiral Charles K. Duncan," Part 13, p. 1150.
38. Captain Howard Kerr interview, cited in Love, *History of the United States Navy*, vol. 2, pp. 545–46.
39. Captain Peter Swartz USN (Ret.), conversation with author, May 6, 1997.
40. Lieutenant (Junior Grade) Richard Strandberg, River Patrol Section 533, letter, 14 November 1967, in Bernard Edelman, ed., *Dear America: Letters Home from Vietnam* (New York: Norton, 1985), p. 122.
41. Elmo R. Zumwalt Jr. and Elmo R. Zumwalt III, *My Father, My Son* (New York: Macmillan, 1986), p. 82.
42. Norman Friedman, *U.S. Small Combatants: An Illustrated Design History* (Annapolis: Naval Institute Press, 1987), pp. 302–06.
43. John F. Kerry, "Swift Boats Remembered," *Pull Together*, Summer 1998, pp. 2–3.
44. Lieutenant Commander Forrest L. Edwards interview with Lieutenant (Junior Grade) Luther J. Ellingson, March 5, 1970, p. 30, Naval Historical Center, Accession No. 887105.
45. Friedman, *Small Combatants*, pp. 303–6.
46. *Ibid.*, pp. 312–14.
47. Love, *History of the U.S. Navy*, vol. 2, p. 544.
48. Don Sheppard, *Riverine: A Brown Water Sailor in the Delta* (Novato, Calif.: Presidio, 1992), p. 7.
49. Love, *History of the U.S. Navy*, vol. 2, p. 544.
50. Zumwalt and Zumwalt, *My Father*, p. 67.
51. Friedman, *Small Combatants*, p. 32.
52. Lieutenant Commander Forrest L. Edwards interview with Boatswain's Mate 2nd Class William McLoud Harris, January 6, 1970, pp. 12–13, Naval Historical Center, Accession No. 884105.
53. Lieutenant (Junior Grade) Robert Moir, River Patrol Section 533, letter, January 29, 1968, in Edelman, *Dear America*, p. 90.

54. Zumwalt and Zumwalt, *My Father*, pp. 82–83.
55. Harris interview, p. 8; Lieutenant Commander Forrest L. Edwards interview with Chief Gunner's Mate George Edward Allen, January 7, 1970, p. 10, Naval Historical Center, Accession No. 887103.
56. Sheppard, *Riverine*, p. 120.
57. Lieutenant (Junior Grade) Reed interview with Engineman First Class Emil Cates, no date [1970], p. 11, Naval Historical Center, Accession No. 887111.
58. *Ibid.*, pp. 10–12.
59. Peter A. Huchthausen & Nguyen Thi Lung, *Echoes of the Mekong*, (Baltimore: Naval and Aviation Publ. Co., 1996), p. 20.
60. Schreadley, *From the Rivers to the Sea*, p. 105.
61. Reminiscences of Vice Admiral Arthur Salzer, p. 274, Naval Institute Oral History Collection.
62. Guenther Lewy, *America in Vietnam* (London: Oxford Univ. Press, 1978), pp. 233, 235, 238–39.
63. *Ibid.*
64. Reminiscences of Vice Admiral Salzer, p. 361.
65. Memo, M.Gen G.S. Eckhardt to Dept CORDS, April 4, 1968, IV Corps Senior Advisor File, CORDS Records, U.S. Army Center of Military History.
66. Lieutenant Commander Forrest L. Edwards interview with Gunner's Mate Second Class Michael Raymond Young, no date [1970], pp. 16–17, Naval Historical Center, Accession No. 884105.
67. Harris interview, p. 5.
68. *Ibid.*, p. 10.
69. *Ibid.*, p. 5.
70. Young, interview, p. 14.
71. *Hearings Before the Special Subcommittee on Disciplinary Problems in the U.S. Navy of the Committee on Armed Services*, House, 92nd Cong., 2nd Sess., HASC 93–13 (1973), pp. 18–19.
72. *Ibid.*
73. Muir, *Black Shoes*, p. 160.
74. Henry P. Leiferman, "A Sort of Mutiny: The *Constellation* Incident," *New York Times Magazine*, February 18, 1973, p. 17.
75. *Subcommittee Report*, p. 19.
76. Kernan, *Crossing the Line*, p. 137.
77. Sherwood, *Fast Movers*, p. 92.
78. "Reminiscences of Vice Admiral Miller," No. 8, p. 696.
79. Yvon Antoine Milne, "The Navy's Unwelcome Visitors," *Naval Institute Proceedings*, July 1974, pp. 101–2.
80. Reminiscences of Rear Admiral Kauffman," No. 7, pp. 671–72.
81. Elmo R. Zumwalt, Jr., *On Watch* (New York: Quadrangle, 1976), p. 167.
82. "Keelhauling the United States Navy," *Time* 100 (November 27, 1972), p. 20.
83. *Ibid.*
84. *Subcommittee Report*, p. 17684.
85. *Ibid.*, p. 17686.
86. Captain Raymond E. Helms, Jr., "Shipboard Drug Abuse," *Naval Institute Proceedings* 101, December 1975, p. 42.
87. *Ibid.*, p. 43.
88. *Ibid.*, pp 43–44.
89. Zumwalt, *On Watch*, pp. 210–21.
90. Ronald W. Perry, "The American Dilemma at Sea: Race and Incarceration in the Naval Justice System," *Phylon* 41 (February 1980), p. 51.
91. Morris J. MacGregor and Bernard C. Nalty, *Blacks in the U.S. Armed Forces: Basic Documents* (Wilmington, Del: Scholarly Resources, 1977), vol. 13, p. 61.
92. Nalty, *Strength for the Fight*, p. 314.
93. Zumwalt, *On Watch*, pp. 202–3.
94. *Ibid.*, p. 207.
95. L. Howard Bennett, "Command Leadership and the Black Serviceman," *Naval Institute Proceedings* 97, April 1971, p. 45.
96. *Special Subcommittee Report*, p. 17671; Leiferman, "Sort of Mutiny," p. 27.

97. *Special Subcommittee Report*, p. 17685.
98. Perry, "American Dilemma at Sea," pp. 52–53, 55–56.
99. *Special Subcommittee Report*, p. 10.
100. *Ibid.*
101. Leiferman, "Sort of Mutiny," p. 21.
102. Captain Paul B. Ryan USN (Ret.), "USS *Constellation* Flare-up: Was it Mutiny?" *Naval Institute Proceedings* 102, January 1976, p. 50.
103. "Reminiscences of Vice Admiral Miller," No. 8, pp. 709, 712, 717–18.
104. "Keelhauling the United States Navy," *Time*, November 27, 1972, p. 20.
105. *Special Subcommittee Report*, pp. 17690–91.
106. Ryan, "*Constellation* Flare-up," p. 52.

Chapter 17: "The Hitherto Unlikely Scenario"

1. Unless otherwise indicated the discussion that follows is based upon Lawrence J. Korb, "The Erosion of American Naval Pre-Eminence," in Kenneth J. Hagan, ed., *In Peace and War: Interpretations of American Naval History* (Westport, Conn.: Greenwood Press, 1978), pp. 327–44.
2. Baer, *One Hundred Years of Seapower*, p. 397.
3. Korb, "Erosion," p. 337.
4. Muir, *Black Shoes*, pp. 170–71.
5. Norman Polmar, *Guide to the Soviet Navy*, 4th ed. (Annapolis: Naval Institute Press, 1986), pp. 102, 172–73.
6. Muir, *Black Shoes*, p. 200.
7. Korb, "Erosion," p. 332.
8. Breemer, *Soviet Submarines*, pp. 122–23, 130.
9. Polmar, *Guide to the Soviet Navy*, pp. 164–65.
10. Quoted in Zumwalt, *On Watch*, p. 447.
11. Muir, *Black Shoes*, p. 202.
12. John Finney, "Rickover Challenges Administration's Navy Plans," *New York Times*, May 5, 1976, p. 31.
13. Korb, "Erosion," p. 338.
14. *Ibid.*
15. *Ibid.*
16. John Lehman, "Where Do We Stand?" *Shipmate*, June 1983, p. 26.
17. John F. Lehman, Jr., *Command of the Seas* (New York: Scribner, 1988), p. 162.
18. Captain W.H.J. Manthorpe, Jr., USN, "The Influence of Being Russian on the Officers and Men of the Soviet Navy," *Naval Institute Proceedings*, March 1978, p. 134.
19. Polmar, *Guide to the Soviet Navy*, pp. 78–79.
20. Mikhail Tsypkin, "Men and Technology in Today's Soviet Navy," Naval Post Graduate School, AD-A227–072, NPS-56–70–007, April 1990, p. 2.
21. *Ibid.*, p. 14.
22. Gregory D. Young, "Mutiny on the *Storozhevoy*: A Case Study of Dissent in the Soviet Navy," Naval Post-Graduate School thesis, March 1982, AD A118196, p. 74.
23. *Ibid.*, p. 48.
24. Tsypkin, "Men and Technology," p. 12.
25. Young, "Mutiny," p. 55.
26. *Ibid.*, p. 54.
27. Robert Bathhurst, *Understanding the Soviet Navy: A Handbook* (Newport, R.I.: Naval War College Press, 1979), pp. 105, 108–9.
28. *Ibid.*, p. 105.
29. Young, "Mutiny," pp. 59–61.
30. Polmar, *Guide to the Soviet Navy*, pp. 82–83; Manthorpe, "Influence of Being Russian," p. 135.
31. Manthorpe, "Influence of Being Russian," p. 135.
32. Polmar, *Guide to the Soviet Navy*, p. 83.
33. Young, "Mutiny," p. 64.

34. Young, "Mutiny," p. 67; Captain James W. Kehoe USN, "Naval Officers: Ours and Theirs" *Naval Institute Proceedings*, vol. 104, February 1978, pp. 55–56.
35. Manthorpe, "Influence of Being Russian" p. 135.
36. Polmar, *Guide to the Soviet Navy*, p. 89.
37. Kehoe, "Naval Officers," p. 53.
38. *Ibid.*, p. 56.
39. *Ibid.*, p. 58.
40. Colonel Donald L. Clark USAF (Ret.), "Who Are Those Guys?" *Air University Review*, May–June 1979, p. 55.
41. Young, "Mutiny," p. 63.
42. Abraham Rabinovich, *The Boats of Cherbourg* (New York: Seaver Books, 1988), p. 201.
43. Major General Chaim Herzog, *The War of Atonement, October 1973,* (Boston: Little, Brown 1975), p. 264.
44. Muir, *Black Shoes*, p. 200.
45. Rabinovich, *Boats of Cherbourg*, pp. 258–61.
46. *Ibid.*, p. 257; Rear Admiral Shlomo Evell, "Israel's Saar FPB's Pass Combat Test in Yom Kippur War," *Naval Institute Proceedings* 100 (September 1974), p. 118.
47. Wilson, *Ironclads in Action*, vol. 2, p. 104.
48. Wells, *Royal Navy*, pp. 235–36.
49. Anthony Preston, *Sea Combat off the Falklands* (London: Willow Books, 1982), pp. 63–65; Admiral Sandy Woodward, *One Hundred Days: The Memoirs of the Falklands Battle Group Commander* (Annapolis: Naval Institute Press, 1997), pp. 15–19; Captain Arthur M. Smith MC USNR, "Can We Effectively Control Human Costs During War at Sea?" *Naval War College Review* 45, (Winter 1992), pp. 14–15.
50. Woodward, *One Hundred Days*, p. 177.
51. Smith, "Human Costs," p. 16.
52. Captain David Hart-Dyke, "War and Its Effects on People," *Naval Review*, April 1991, p. 117.
53. *Ibid.*
54. Rabinovich, *Boats of Cherbourg*, p. 279.
55. Woodward, *One Hundred Days*, p. 173.
56. Captain J. B. Perkins III USN, "Operation Praying Mantis: The Surface View," *Naval Institute Proceedings* 115, June 1989, pp. 66–71; Captain Bud Langston USN and Lieutenant Commander Don Bringle USN, "Operation Praying Mantis: The Air View," *Naval Institute Proceedings* 115, June 1989, pp. 54–60.
57. Captain David R. Carlson USN, "The *Vincennes* Incident," *Naval Institute Proceedings* 115 (September 1989), pp. 87–89.
58. Norman Friedman, "The *Vincennes* Incident," *Naval Institute Proceedings* 115 (September 1989), pp. 87–89.
59. Carlson, "*Vincennes* Incident," p. 87.
60. *Ibid.* The author, who was in the gulf at this time, was also aware of this nickname.
61. Norman Friedman, "The *Vincennes* Incident," *Naval Institute Proceedings* 115 (May 1989), p. 74.
62. *Hearings Before the Committee on Armed Services, U.S. Senate,* 100th Cong., 2nd sess., "Investigation into the Downing of an Iranian Airliner by the USS *Vincennes,*" September 8, 1988, pp. 10–11.
63. *Ibid.*
64. *Ibid.*, pp. 21, 28, 38–39.
65. *Ibid.*, p 38; Friedman, "*Vincennes* Incident," p. 76.
66. *Hearings on Downing* p. 29.
67. *Ibid.*, p. 28.

Epilogue

1. Garrett Mattingly, *The Armada* (Boston: Houghton Mifflin, 1962), p. 277.
2. Lieutenant Commander W. Boothe Higgins USNR, "Quality of Life at Sea," *Naval Institute Proceedings* 125 (January 1999), p. 55.

3. Chief Signalman Scott Baxter USNR, "'White Jacket' Revisited," *Naval Institute Proceedings* 124, February 1998, p. 41.
4. Paul Stillwell, ed., *The Golden Thirteen* (New York: Berkley Books, 1994), appendix C, p. 288.
5. Gunner's Mate First Class Terry L. Buckman USN, "Gender Integration: What's Next?" *Naval Institute Proceedings*, 125, February 1999, p. 31.
6. Mackubin Thomas Owens, "It's Time to Face the Gender Paradox," *Naval Institute Proceedings* 124 (July 1998), p. 46.
7. Amboise Baudry, *The Naval Battle: Studies of the Tactical Factor* (London: Hugh Rees, 1914), p. 37.
8. See S.L.A. Marshall, *Men Against Fire* (New York: Apollo, 1961), pp. 51–60, 72–79; Alexander L. George, "Primary Groups Organization and Military Performance" in Roger W. Little, ed., *Handbook of Military Institutions* (Beverly Hills, Calif.: Sage, 1971); and Samuel Stauffer et al., *Studies in Social Psychology in World War II*, vol. 2 (New York: Wiley, 1965).
9. Robert Jervis, "Navies, Politics and Political Science," in John B. Hattendorf, ed., *Doing Naval History* (Newport, R.I.: Naval War College Press, 1995), p. 47. See also Barry Posen, *The Sources of Military Doctrine: France, Britain and Germany Between the Wars* (Ithaca: Cornell Univ. Press, 1984).
10. See Stephen Peter Rosen, *Winning the Next War: Innovation and the Modern Military* (Ithaca: Cornell Univ. Press, 1991); and Deborah Avant, *Political Institutions and Military Change: Lessons: From Peripheral Wars* (Ithaca: Cornell Univ. Press, 1994) Avant concludes that "civilian intervention is neither a necessary nor a sufficient condition for military adaptation" (p. 133).

PRIMARY SOURCES

Significant secondary works have been briefly discussed in the endnotes. Only those primary sources actually cited or directly utilized in the text have been listed below. Those interested in further research in the collections cited are urged to consult the excellent guides available from repositories such as the Imperial War Museum, the National Archives, the U.S. Naval Institute, the Royal Naval Museum, and Churchill College, Cambridge. At least some of these are available online.

Unpublished Sources

I. GOVERNMENT DOCUMENTS
    A. Ministry of Defence Library, London
        "Preliminary Report: Recruiting for the Royal Navy," 5 January 1898.
        Admiralty Intelligence Department, "Reports from Naval Attaches," 1904–5.
        Admiralty Ordnance Department, "The Russian-Japanese War from the Point of View of Naval Gunnery."
        "Report of the Committee Appointed to Enquire into the Education and Training of Cadets, Midshipmen and Junior Officers of His Majesty's Fleet, 1912."
    B. National Archives, Washington, D.C.
        Record Group 38: Office of Naval Intelligence
        "Systems of Appointing and Educating Naval Cadets," May 9, 1903. Register 59.
        "Recruiting and Training of Enlisted Men in Foreign Navies." ONI Register 1396 (1906).

"Regulations Governing Education of Officers and Enlisted Men, Japanese Navy," May 24, 1907. Register 397.

"Naval College at Etajima Japan," July 24, 1907. Register 569.

"Notes on Training of Crews of Submarines," October 26, 1916. Registers 6-17-23.

U.S. Naval Attaché, London, "German Submarine School," March 9, 1917.

"Our Submarines," *Berlin Lokalanzeige*, May 7, 1917. Office of Naval Intelligence Translation. Registers 6-17-23, E-6-A.

U.S. Naval Attaché, London, Sub: Enrolling of submarine crews, February 18, 1918. Register 670 P.

"Japanese Morale," 31 Jan File 1803, Register E-7-0.

Record Group 24: Records of the Bureau of Navigation
Records of the Morale Division.
Third Naval District Correspondence 1927-29.

Record Group 72: Records of the Bureau of Aeronautics
Confidential Correspondence, 1922-1940.

Record Group 80: Records of the Office of the Secretary of the Navy
CincUS, confidential report to CNO on Fleet Problem Nine, 18 March 1929.

C.   Naval Historical Center, Washington, D.C.

1.   Aviation History Section, *Naval Aviation News* "Background on Naval Aviation Pilots."

2.   Naval Administrative Histories: Office of the Deputy Chief of Naval Operations (Air); Office of the Bureau of Naval Personnel.

3.   Commander in Chief Pacific (Cincpac) Files: Action Reports:
USS *Lexington* serial 00421
USS *Enterprise* serial 00413
USS *Hornet* serial 45530
CTF 58, "Operations in Support of the Capture of the Marianas," serial 003858
Korean War Interim Reports

4.   Miscellaneous Documents:
"Employment of Submarines," 21 Aug 41, Strategic Plans Division Records, Series 2.
General Board, "Enlistment of Men of the Colored Race," 23 January 1942.
"Proceedings of a Court of Inquiry, Naval Supply Depot, Guam, to Enquire Into the Unlawful Assembly and Riot . . . at Naval Supply Depot," 30 Dec 44.
CINCFLT Secret Information Bulletin No. 24, "Battle Experience: Radar Pickets and Methods of Combatting Suicide Attacks," pp. 81-1 to 81-3. (Navy Department Library)
U.S. Naval Technical Training Mission to Europe, Technical Report, 304-45, Series IV, "Training Aids for Submarine Operating Personnel."

D. Congressional Documents

Report of the Honorable Josephus Daniels, Secretary of the Navy, 64th Cong., 1st sess.

Hearings Before the Special Subcommittee on Disciplinary Problems in the U.S. Navy of the Committee on Armed Services House, 92nd Cong. 2nd sess. HASC 93-13 (1973) , pp. 18–19.

Hearings Before the Committee on Armed Services, U.S. Senate, 100th Cong., 2nd sess. "Investigation into the Downing of an Iranian Airliner by the USS *Vincennes.*" September 9, 1988, pp. 10–11.

II. UNPUBLISHED LETTERS, DIARIES, AND MEMOIRS

A. Imperial War Museum

"Reminiscences of Reverend T.W.L. Casperez"

John Chessman. "Under, Over and Through." Unpublished memoir, c. 1972. DS/MISC/39.

ERA Arthur C.F. Crown. Diary.

Commander J.A.J. Dennis. Papers.

Alexander Grant. "Through the Hawse Pipe." Unpublished memoirs. 66/28311.

John Knight. "Memoirs of a Miscreant." Unpublished manuscript.

"An Adventure at Crete with HMS *Fiji:* An Account by the Late Stoker Petty Officer W. Manders Soon After the Battle."

Admiral E. M. Philpott. Papers.

Midshipman T. Ruck-Keene. Journal.

G. Sear. Papers.

Engine Room Artificer Clifford Simkin. "The War from the Engine Room." Unpublished manuscript.

H. Speakman DSM. "The Evacuation of Crete (on Board HMS *Orion*)." Unpublished manuscript.

Captain T.C.T. Wynne. Papers.

File 1010: Battle of Jutland.

Ordinary Telegraphist Frederic J. Arnold. Letter.

Signalman John E. Atrill. Diary.

Lieutenant Heinrich Bassinge. Letter.

Thomas Bradley. Letter.

Telegraphist A. J. Bristoe. Letter.

Engine Room Artificer Gordon Davis. Letter.

Machinist Otto Frost [Torpedo Boat V-1]. Letter.

Midshipman H. W. Fisher. Unpublished Memoir.

Electrical Artificer Frank T. Hall. Letter.

Surgeon Lieutenant C.E. Leake. "Account of the Battle of Jutland," dated 31 May 1917.

Boy Telegraphist Arthur R. Lewis. Letter.

Chief Petty Officer Karl Melms. Letter.

Signalman Franz Motzler. Letter.

Shipwright Charles H. Petty. Letter.

K. L. Philips. June 8, 1916. Letter.

Signalman Reuben Poole. Letter.

Petty Officer William Read [HMS *New Zealand*]. Letter.

Leading Stoker Samuel H. A. Roberts. Letter.

Surgeon Probationer R. Smythe. Letter.

B. Liddle Collection, The Library, University of Leeds

Anonymous letter by a survivor of HMS *Queen Mary*.

Captain G. P. Biggs-Withers. Letters.

Engine Room Artificer C. B. Clarkson, "Impressions of Jutland from Inside HMS *Malaya*." Unpublished memoir.

Midshipman [later Rear-Admiral] Royer M. Dick. "My Second Naval Battle." Unpublished memoir.

Signalman J. J. Newman. "My Experience of the Sea Battle of May 31, 1916." Unpublished manuscript.

"Reminiscences of Sub-Lieutenant H. O. Owens, HMS *Moorson*."

C. Royal Naval Museum, Portsmouth.

John Marsden. "An Account of Wartime Service in the Royal Navy of John Marsden." Unpublished memoir.

D. National Maritime Museum, Greenwich

Admiral K.G.B. DeWar. Papers.

Admiral Sir W.W. Fisher. Papers.

Admiral Sir Herbert Richmond. Papers.

Arnold White. Papers.

E. The British Library

Admiral Sir Andrew Cunningham. Papers.

F. Churchill College, Cambridge

Sir John Fisher. Papers.

Stephen Roskill. Papers.

G. Directorate of History, National Defense Headquarters, Ottawa

Rear Admiral Frank Llewellyn Houghton. "A Sailor's Life for Me." Unpublished memoir.

H. U.S. Naval Historical Center, Washington, D.C.

Eric Hammel Collection. Battles of the Guadalcanal Campaign.

Rear Admiral Harry E. Yarnell. Papers.

I. Naval Historical Foundation, Washington, DC

Captain John M. Kennedy USN (Ret.). "Shipboard Living Conditions in Our Navy 1919–1949."

J. Other

Bernard A. Yohe. "Life Aboard Ship: USS *Mustin*." (Lent to the author.)

III. LETTERS TO THE AUTHOR

Tex Atkinson (Korea)

Robert G. Brown (Santa Cruz Islands)

R.V. Cole (Santa Cruz Islands)

William Crouse (Korea)

Jarvis Cartwright (Santa Cruz)

Vincent Davis (Korea, Naval Aviation)
Commander J.A.J. Dennis RN (Ret.) (Crete)
Captain R.F.C. Ellsworth RN (Ret.) (Crete)
Adrian Holoway (Dartmouth, Crete)
Lieutenant Commander I.R. Johnson RN (Ret.) (Crete)
Alvin Kernan (Naval Aviation)
John F. Kielty (Santa Cruz Islands)
Vice Admiral Sir Louis Le Bailly RN (Ret.) (Dartmouth, Crete)
Alan G. LeBaron (Guam)
Dr. Duncan MacIvor (Nuclear Submarines)
Ralph C. Morgan (Santa Cruz Islands)
Thomas W. Reese (Santa Cruz Islands)
Alistair Reed (Royal Navy)
Clifford Simkin (Royal Navy)
Captain J.A.F. Somerville RN (Ret.) (Crete)
Captain Theron B. Taylor USN (Ret.) (Korea)
Major General Sir Julian Thompson RN (Ret.) (Royal Marines)

IV. PUBLISHED LETTERS, DIARIES AND REMINISCENCES
A. Royal Navy

Brown, Malcolm, and Patricia Meehan.*Scapa Flow: The Reminiscences of Men and Women Who Served in Scapa Flow in Two World Wars*. London: Penguin, 1968.

Chalmers, Rear Admiral W.S. *The Life and Letters of David Beatty, Admiral of the Fleet*. London: Hodder & Stoughton, 1951.

Viscount Cunningham of Hyndhope. *A Sailor's Odyssey*. London: Hutchinson, 1951.

DeWar, K.G.B. *The Navy from Within*. London: Victor Gollancz, 1939.

Dreyer, Admiral Sir Frederick. *The Sea Heritage*. London: Victor Gollancz, 1955.

Fawcett, H.W. and Hooper, G.W.W. *The Fighting at Jutland: The Personal Experiences of Sixty Officers and Men of the British Fleet*. Glasgow: MacLure, MacDonald, 1920.

Hart-Dyke, Captain David. "War and Its Effects on People." *Naval Review*, April 1991.

Hayward, Victor. *HMS "Tiger" at Bay: A Sailor's Memoir*. London: Kimber, 1977.

Hodgkinson, Lieutenant Commander Hugh, DSC, RN. *Before the Tide Turned: Mediterranean Experience of a British Destroyer Officer*. London: George Harrap, 1944.

Holloway, Adrian. *From Dartmouth to War*. London: Buckham Publications, 1996.

King-Hall, Stephen. *A Naval Lieutenant, 1914–1918*. London: Methuen, 1919.

King-Hall, Stephen. *My Naval Life, 1906–1927*. London: Faber & Faber, 1952.

Klinker Knocker (pseud.). *Aye, Aye Sir!: The Autobiography of a Stoker*. London: Richard Crown, 1938.

Knock, Sidney. *Clear Lower Deck*. London: Phillip Allen, 1932.

Le Bailly, Vice Admiral Sir Louis. *The Man Around the Engine: Life Below the Waterline*. Emsworth, Hampshire: Kenneth Mason, 1990.

Le Bailly, Vice Admiral Sir Louis. *From Fisher to the Falklands*. London: Marine Management Holdings, 1991.

Liddle, Peter. *The Sailor's War, 1914–1918*. London: Blandford, 1985.

MacIntyre, Donald. *U-Boat Killer*. London: Weidenfeld & Nicholson, 1956.

Outhwaite, Cedric. "The Sea and the Air." *Blackwood's Magazine*, November 1927.

Von Schoultz, Commander G., *With the British Battle Fleet: War Recollections of a Russian Naval Officer*. Trans. Arthur Chambers. London: Hutchinson, 1925.

Simpson, Rear Admiral G.W.G. *Periscope View: A Professional Autobiography*. London: Macmillan, 1972.

Simpson, Michael, ed. *The Cunningham Papers*. London: Naval Records Society, 1999.

Smith, Albert. "A Family at War, Part One." *Poppy and the Owl* 16 (June 1995).

Wigby, Frederick. *Stoker, Royal Navy*. London: Blackwood, 1967.

Wincott, Len. *Invergordon Mutineer*. London: Weidenfeld & Nicholson, 1953.

Woodward, Admiral Sandy. *One Hundred Days: The Memoirs of the Falklands Battle Group Commander*. Annapolis: Naval Institute Press, 1997.

Yexley, Lionel. *The Inner Life of the Navy*. London: Pitman, 1908.

Young, Filson. *With the Battlecruisers*. London: Cassell, 1921.

B.   U.S. Navy

Alsmeyer, Marie Bennett, *Old Waves Tales: Navy Women, Memoirs of World War II*. Conway, Alaska: HAMBA Books, 1982.

Barbey, Daniel E. *MacArthur's Amphibious Navy*. Annapolis: Naval Institute Press, 1969.

Becton, Rear Admiral F. Julian, with Joseph Morsehause III. *The Ship that Would Not Die*. Englewood Cliffs, N.J.: Prentice-Hall, 1980.

Bell, Frederick J. *Condition Red: Destroyer Action in the South Pacific*. New York: Longmans, Green, 1943.

Calvert James F. *Silent Running: My Years in a World War II Attack Submarine*. New York: Wiley, 1995.

Carson, Captain David R. "The Vincennes Incident." *Naval Institute Proceedings* 115 (September, 1989).

Chester, Charles. *A Sailor's Odyssey*. Privately published.

Cole, Charles F. *Korea Remembered: Enough of a War* Las Cruces, N.M.: Yuca Tree Press, 1995.

Dykema, Owen W. *Letters from the Bird Barge*. Roseburg, Ore.: Dykema, 1997.

Edelman, Bernard, ed. *Dear America: Letters Home from Vietnam*. New York: Norton, 1985.

Fahey, James J. *Pacific War Diary, 1942–1945: The Secret Diary of an American Sailor*. Boston: Houghton Mifflin, 1992.

Guyton, Boone T. *Air Base*. New York: McGraw-Hill, 1941.

Hancock, Joy Bright. *Lady in the Navy: Personal Reminiscences*. Annapolis: Naval Institute Press, 1972.

Harlan, Louis R., *All at Sea: Coming of Age in World War II*. Urbana: University of Illinois Press, 1996.

Hill, Captain Joe, USN (Ret.). *Some Early Birds: The Memoirs of a Naval Aviation Cadet, 1935–1945*. Manhattan, Kans. Sunflower University Press, 1996.

Homan, Lieutenant Commander Bert G., USN (Ret.). *A Twentieth Century Life Story*. Privately published.

Huchthausen, Peter A. and Nguyen Thi Lung. *Echoes of the Mekong*. Baltimore: Naval & Aviation, 1996.

Hynes, Samuel. *Flights of Passage: Reflections of a World War II Aviator*. Annapolis: Naval Institute Press, 1988.

Jernigan, Emery J. *Tin Can Man*. Arlington, Va.: Vandermere Press, 1993.

Kerry, John F. "Swift Boats Remembered." *Pull Together*, Summer 1998.

Kernan, Alvin. *Crossing the Line: A Bluejacket's World War II Odyssey*. Annapolis: Naval Institute Press, 1994.

Lea, Tom. "Aboard the USS *Hornet*." *Life*, December 1942.

Le Baron, Allan G. *Black Shoe, Brown Shoe: A White Hat's Memories of Life Aboard an Aircraft Carrier, Korea, 1951–52*. Moulton, Ala. privately published, 1996.

Lehman, John F. Jr. *Command of the Seas*. New York: Scribner, 1988.

McBride, William M., ed. *Good Night Officially: The Pacific War Letters of a Destroyer Sailor*. Boulder, Colo. Westview, 1994.

Mears, Fredric. *Carrier Combat*. New York: Doubleday, 1944.

Miller, Max. *I'm Sure We've Met Before: The Navy in Korea*. New York: Dutton, 1951.

Millis, Walter, ed. *The Forrestal Diaries*. New York: Viking, 1951.

Monsarrat, John. *Angel on the Yardarm: The Beginning of Fleet Air Defense and the Kamikaze Threat*. Newport, R.I.: Naval War College Press, 1985.

Nichols, Commander John B., and Barrett Tillman. *On Yankee Station: The Naval Air War over Vietnam*. Annapolis: Naval Institute Press, 1984.

Sauter, Jack. *Sailors in the Sky: Memoirs of a Navy Aircreman in the Korean War*. Jefferson, N.C.: McFarland, 1975.

Schratz, Paul R. *Submarine Commander*. Lexington: University Press of Kentucky, 1988.

Shalett, Sidney. *Old Nameless: The Epic of a U.S. Battlewagon*. New York: Appleton-Century, 1943.

Sheppard, Don. *Riverine: A Brown Water Sailor in the Delta*. Novato, Calif.: Presidio Press, 1992.

Smart, Charles Allen. *The Long Watch*. Cleveland and New York: World, 1968.

Surels, Ron. *DD 522: Diary of a Destroyer*. Plymouth, N.H.: Valley Graphics, 1996.

Wilson, Eugene. *Slipstream*. New York: Whittlesey House, 1950.

Winston, Robert A. *Dive Bomber Pilot*. New York: Holiday House, 1939.

Zumwalt, Elmo R., Jr. *On Watch: A Memoir*. New York: Quadrangle, 1976.

Zumwalt, Elmo R., Jr., and Elmo R. Zumwalt III. *My Father, My Son*. New York: Macmillan, 1986.

C.   Japanese Navy

Bullock, Cecil. *Etajima: The Dartmouth of Japan*. London: Sampson Low Marston, 1942.

Hashimoto Mochitsura. *Sunk*. New York: Holt, 1954.

Kobayashi Takahiro. *Yaro Yomoyama Monugatari* (Some stories of friends in the navy). Tokyo: Koujinsha, 1980.

Inoguchi Rikihei, Captain, and Commander Tadashi Nakajima. *The Divine Wind: The Japanese Kamikaze Force in World War II*. Annapolis: Naval Institute Press, 1958, 1994.

Iwata Shioka, ed. *Kaigun Tokubbetsu Nenshohei no Shuki* (Witnesses to history: Recollections of special boy sailors.) Tokyo: Kaigun Tokuniki, 1998.

Okumiya Masatake and Hirokoshi Jiro. *Zero!* New York: Dutton, 1956.

Orita Zenji. *I-Boat Captain*. Canoga Park, Calif.: Major Books, 1976.

Prange, Gordon W., with Donald Goldstein and Katherine V. Dillon. *Fading Victory: The Diary of Admiral Ugaki Matomi*. Pittsburgh: University of Pittsburgh Press, 1992.

Sakai Subaru with Martin Caidin and Fred Saito. *Samurai*. New York: Dutton, 1957.

Takagi Sokichi. *Jidenteki Nihon Kaigun Shimatsuki* (Autobiographical account of the end of the Japanese navy). Tokyo: Koujinsha, 1971.

Togo Kichitaro. *The Naval Battles of the Russo-Japanese War*. Tokyo: Gogakukyokwai, 1907.

Watanabe Kiyoshi. *Senkan Musashi no Saigo* (The last of battleship *Musashi*). Tokyo: Asahi Shimbum, 1982.

D.   Canadian Navy

Brock, Jeffrey V. *The Dark Broad Seas: Memoirs of a Sailor*. Vol. 1. Toronto: Macmillan & Stuart, 1974.

Easton, Alan. *50 North: Canada's Atlantic Battleground*. Toronto: Ryerson, 1966.

Harling, Robert. *Amateur Sailor*. London: Chatto & Windus, 1947.

Lamb, James B. *The Corvette Navy*. Toronto: Macmillan of Canada, 1977.

Lamb, James B., *On the Triangle Run*. Toronto: Macmillan of Canada, 1986.

Pugsley, William H. *Saints, Devils and Ordinary Seamen*. Toronto: Macmillan, 1945.

Pugsley, William H. *Sailor Remember*. Toronto: Collins, 1948.

E.   German Navy

Bucheim, Lothar-Günther. *U-Boat War*. New York: Knopf, 1978.

Hase, Commander Georg von. *Kiel and Jutland*. London: Skeffington & Sons, 1921.

Horn, Daniel, ed. and trans. *War, Mutiny and Revolution in the German Navy: The World War I Diary of Seaman Richard Stumpf* (New Brunswick, N.J.: Rutgers Univ. Press, 1970.

Looks, Engineer Commander Otto. "The Engine Room Staff in the Battle of the Skaggerack." Trans. Engineer Lieutenant Commander D. Hastie Smith. *Naval Review* 10 (1922).

Neureuther, Karl, and Claus Bergen, eds. *U-Boat Stories*. New York: Richard R. Smith, 1931.

Plievier, Theodore. *The Kaiser's Coolies*. London: Cassell, 1924.

Schaeffer, Heinz. *U-Boat 977*. London: William Kimber, 1952.

Scheer, Reinhard. *Germany's High Seas Fleet in the World War*. London: Cassell, 1919.

Thomas, Lowell. *Raiders of the Deep*. Annapolis: Naval Institute Press, 1994.

Von Tirpitz, Alfred. *My Memoirs*. New York: Dodd, Mead, 1919.

Werner, Herbert" *Iron Coffins* (New York: Holt, Rinehart & Winston, 1969.

F.   Russian Navy

Nebogatoff, Rear Admiral Nicholas. "The Surrender at Tsushima." *Jane's Fighting Ships 1906–7*.

Semenov, Captain Vladimir. *The Battle of Tsu-Shima*. Trans. Captain A. B. Lindsay. New York: Dutton, 1913.

Westwood, J. N. *Witnesses of Tsushima*. Tokyo: Sophia Univ. Press, 1970.

White, R. D. "With the Baltic Fleet at Tsushima." *Naval Institute Proceedings* 22 (June 1906).

INDEX